Critical Perspectives in
Food Studies

Edited by **Mustafa Koç, Jennifer Sumner** and
Anthony Winson

OXFORD
UNIVERSITY PRESS

OXFORD

UNIVERSITY PRESS

Oxford University Press is a department of the University of Oxford. It furthers the University's objective of excellence in research, scholarship, and education by publishing worldwide. Oxford is a registered trade mark of Oxford University Press in the UK and in certain other countries.

Published in Canada by
Oxford University Press
8 Sampson Mews, Suite 204,
Don Mills, Ontario M3C 0H5 Canada
www.oupcanada.com
Copyright © Oxford University Press Canada 2012
The moral rights of the author have been asserted
Database right Oxford University Press (maker)

First Edition published in 2012

Library and Archives Canada Cataloguing in Publication

Critical perspectives in food studies / edited by Mustafa Koç, Jennifer Sumner and Tony Winson.

Includes bibliographical references and index.
ISBN 978-0-19-544641-8

1. Food. 2. Food—Canada. I. Koç, Mustafa, 1955-
II. Sumner, Jennifer, 1949- III. Winson, Anthony, 1952-

TX353.C75 2012   641.3   C2012-902504-6

Cover image: Sue Jackson/iStockphoto

Printed and bound in the United States of America
6 7 — 16 15 14

Contents

Part I   The Changing Meanings of Food and Food Studies

Part II   Analytical Perspectives in Food Studies

Part V   Food for the Future

Contributors

Elisabeth Abergel has been working on GM issues since the 1990s. She has written several articles on GM regulations and more specifically has been working on the interplay between science and politics in the development of regulatory principles to govern GMOs. More recently she has been researching the relationship between agricultural biotechnology and climate change as well as the cultural politics of the life industries. She is also working on various aspects of the bioeconomy. She is co-editor with Prof. Rod MacRae of a book on Canadian agro-environmental and health policy published by UBC Press, released in 2011. Prof. Abergel is currently teaching in the Sociology Department at the Université du Québec à Montréal (UQAM).

Robert Albritton is Professor Emeritus in the Department of Political Science, Social and Political Thought Program at York University, Toronto. His book publications include *Let Them Eat Junk: How Capitalism Creates Hunger and Obesity* (Pluto Press, 2009); *A Japanese Approach to Stages of Capitalist Development* (Macmillan, 1991); *Economics Transformed: Discovering the Brilliance of Marx* (Pluto Press, 2007); *Dialectics and Deconstruction in Political Economy* (Palgrave, 2001).

Deborah Barndt is a popular educator and community artist who teaches in the Faculty of Environmental Studies at York University in Toronto. For over 35 years, she has been involved in social justice movements in Latin America, the United States, and Canada and has published and exhibited widely. Over the past two decades, she coordinated collaborative transnational research on the food system (*Women Working the NAFTA Food Chain: Women, Food and Globalization* [ed.; Sumach Press, 1999] and *Tangled Routes: Women, Work and Globalization on the Tomato Trail* [Rowman and Littlefield, 2007]) and on popular education and community arts (*Wild Fire: Art as Activism* [ed.; Sumach Press, 2006; and ¡VIVA! *Community Arts and Popular Education in the Americas* [Between the Lines, 2011]). She is currently co-coordinator of the Community Arts Practice Program at York University (www.yorku.ca/cap) and co-coordinates The FoodShed Project with fellow contributor Harriet Friedmann.

Brenda Beagan is a sociologist specializing in social inequality and health and illness. She is associate professor at Dalhousie University School of Occupational Therapy, and currently holds a Tier II Canada Research Chair in Women's Health.

Alison Blay-Palmer is an associate professor at Wilfrid Laurier University where she does research in alternative food systems and sustainable economic development. Dr. Blay-Palmer has over 15 years of research experience related to sustainable food systems. Her more recent work uses the broader lens of food systems as a vehicle for building healthy communities. Her books, *Imagining Sustainable Food Systems: Theory and Practice* (Ashgate, 2010) and *Food Fears: From Industrial to Sustainable Food Systems* (Ashgate, 2008), explore pressures and opportunities related to food system sustainability. Her most recent SSHRC-funded project is to develop Food Counts, a report card for sustainable food systems in Canada. Alison is a former Social Sciences and Humanities Research Council Postdoctoral Fellow, and has received awards for teaching and faculty activism. She teaches courses in global food security, globalization, and research methods.

Jennifer Brady is a doctoral student at Queen's University as well as a writer, researcher, and registered dietitian. Her past writing and research endeavours have included critical perspectives of dietetic practice, nutrition communication, and food work, as well as online food and beverage marketing. She is currently exploring cooking as a method of embodied scholarly inquiry. Her doctoral research will provide a critical, historical perspective of the evolving relationships between dietetics, home economics, and feminism throughout the twentieth century.

Sarah Cappeliez is a doctoral student at the Department of Sociology at the University of Toronto. Her research interests focus on food, identity and cultural processes, and in particular, on how the concept of terroir legitimates foods and drinks and how this process of cultural legitimation functions in different national contexts. Her past work experience in food culture includes working for the Slow Food association in Italy and France and the *Université Européenne des Senteurs & Saveurs* in France. She also worked as a restaurant critic in the Ottawa area and currently volunteers at the Evergreen Brickworks farmers' market in Toronto.

Gwen Chapman is a professor in food, nutrition and health in the Faculty of Land and Food Systems at the University of British Columbia. Her research uses qualitative methods to study how people's everyday food practices and concerns are shaped by socially constructed notions about food, health, bodies, and social roles.

Jennifer Clapp is a CIGI Chair in Global Environmental Governance and a professor in the Balsillie School of International Affairs and in the Environment and Resource Studies Department at the University of Waterloo. Her research covers the themes of global food and agriculture governance, food aid, agricultural trade, and the global food crisis. Her most recent books include *Paths to a Green World: The Political Economy of the Global Environment* (2nd edn; co-authored with Peter Dauvergne; MIT Press, 2011), *Global Governance, Poverty and Inequality* (co-edited with Rorden Wilkinson; Routledge, 2010), *The Global Food Crisis: Governance Challenges and Opportunities* (co-edited with Marc J. Cohen; WLU Press, 2009), and *Corporate Power in Global Agrifood Governance* (co-edited with Doris Fuchs; MIT Press, 2009). She is co-editor of the journal *Global Environmental Politics* (MIT Press).

Nathalie Cooke is associate provost and professor at McGill University in Montreal. Her publications focus on moments of pivotal change and continuity in Canadian literature, culture, and foodways. She is editor of *What's to Eat? Entrées in Canadian Food Practice* (McGill–Queen's University Press, 2009), and founding editor of the ejournal *Cuizine* (see www.cuizine.mcgill.ca).

Annette Aurélie Desmarais was a farmer in Saskatchewan for 14 years and worked in technical support with La Vía Campesina for over a decade. She then obtained a PhD in geography at the University of Calgary and now is associate professor of International Studies at the University of Regina. She is the author of *La Vía Campesina: Globalization and the Power of Peasants* (Fernwood Books, 2007), which has been published in French, Spanish and Italian, and co-editor of *Food Sovereignty: Reconnecting Food, Nature and Community* (Fernwood Books, 2010) and *Food Sovereignty in Canada* (Fernwood Books, in press). Her research focuses on rural social movements, food sovereignty, gender, and rural development.

Harriet Friedmann is professor of sociology, geography and planning at the University of Toronto. She has published in international and interdisciplinary journals on many dimensions of agriculture and food, including family farms; international corporate strategies in the food sector; food policies at municipal, regional, national, and international scales; changing patterns of diet and consumption; and social movements to change the food system. She developed the food regimes approach (with Philip McMichael), and is currently preparing a book on the political ecology of food (with Tony Weis). Friedmann is a member and former community chair of the Toronto Food Policy Council, and a member of several editorial boards of journals related to food and agriculture. In 2011, she received the Canadian Association for Food Studies Lifetime Career Achievement Award.

Jacqui Gingras is a registered dietitian and assistant professor in the School of Nutrition at Ryerson University. Her teaching and research interests involve theoretical and experiential explorations of critical dietetics epistemology or what counts as dietetic knowledge. She has a particular interest in how dietitians' subjectivities are constituted by power and discourse. Her research engages narrative and arts-informed methods as a means for situated and particular understandings of dietetic theory, education, and practice. She is the managing editor of the *Journal of Critical Dietetics*.

Josée Johnston is associate professor of sociology at the University of Toronto. She focuses her research on the sociological study of food, investigating aspects of culture, consumerism, gender, and politics. Johnston co-authored (with Shyon Baumann) *Foodies: Democracy and Distinction in the Gourmet Foodscape* (Routledge, 2010). She has published articles in venues including *American Journal of Sociology*, *Theory and Society*, *Signs: Journal of Women in Culture and Society*, *Gender and Society*, and *Antipode: A Radical Journal of Geography*. Her current research projects investigate ethical food consumption, as well as the impact of class, place, and gender on food practices.

Irena Knezevic is currently completing her doctoral work on food policy in the Western Balkans and her home base is the Communication and Culture Program at York and Ryerson Universities. She previously studied at the University of Windsor in the Communication and Social Justice program. Knezevic has taught food studies courses at Ryerson University, Wilfrid Laurier University, and St Lawrence College, and is one of the founding members of the Canadian Association for Food Studies. She has researched and written about genetically modified food, geographical indications and terroir, hunting and the food system, public relations firms and agri-business, agricultural policy in the European Union, and more generally on economic globalization.

Mustafa Koç is a professor at the Department of Sociology at Ryerson University. He received his BA at Bogazici University in Istanbul, Turkey, his MA at University of Waterloo, and his PhD at the University of Toronto. His research and teaching interests involve food studies, food security and food policy, globalization, and sociology of migration. He was among the founders of the Centre for Studies in Food Security (coordinator 1995–2005), Food Secure Canada (chair 2005–6), and the Canadian Association for Food Studies (president 2005–8).

Shannon Kornelsen is a recent MA graduate of Wilfrid Laurier University. Her research interests include food citizenship, food democracy, food and agricultural education, sustainable food systems, and animal welfare. She is currently working as a project coordinator to develop a report on industrial animal agriculture in Canada.

Rod MacRae is an assistant professor in the Faculty of Environmental Studies at York University in Toronto. A political ecologist, his teaching and research focuses on the transition to sustainable and health promoting food systems, with particular emphasis on Canadian food policy development. With many colleagues, he has written extensively on this subject in the popular and academic literature, with recent publications appearing in *Agriculture and Human Values*, *Journal of Sustainable Agriculture*, *Renewable Agriculture and Food Systems*, *Sustainability*, and *Journal of Health and Environmental Nutrition*. Prior to joining York University, he worked as a food policy analyst and consultant to all levels of government and numerous Canadian NGOs. He was the first coordinator of the Toronto Food Policy Council.

Debbie Martin is of mixed Inuit and European descent and a member of NunatuKavut, the territory of the south and central Inuit in Labrador. She holds a Bachelor of Recreation from Memorial University, of Newfoundland and from Dalhousie University, a Master of Arts in health promotion and an Interdisciplinary PhD. Dr Martin is currently assistant professor of health promotion at Dalhousie University. Her research interests include the social determinants of Indigenous peoples' health; the relationships between Aboriginal culture, health, and food; and Indigenous methodologies. Dr Martin is a co-principal investigator of the Atlantic Aboriginal Health Research Program (AAHRP) and represents AAHRP on the national Aboriginal Health Research Networks Secretariat (AHRNetS). She is also a member of the Executive Committee of AHRNetS.

Wendy Mendes holds a PhD in urban geography from Simon Fraser University, Vancouver. Her research interests are local governance, sustainability, and participatory decision making with a specialization in urban food systems in Canada, the United States, and Latin America. Dr Mendes is currently adjunct professor at the School of Community & Regional Planning at the University of British Columbia (Vancouver); research associate at Ryerson University's Centre for Studies in Food Security (Toronto); and urban (food systems) planner for the City of Vancouver. From 2006 to 2008 she was Postdoctoral Research Fellow at the University of Toronto's Centre for Urban Health Initiatives (CUHI). Dr Mendes has published her research in *International Journal of Urban & Regional Research*; *Space & Polity*; and *Journal of the American Planning Association*.

Andrea Noack is assistant professor in the Department of Sociology at Ryerson University. She specializes in survey design and social statistics. Dr Noack is interested in understanding how practices of survey design work as a form of social governance and moral regulation. Her current research focuses on the Canadian Census, specifically the development of the first self-enumerated census in 1971 and the elimination of the long-form census in 2011.

Elaine Power is associate professor in the School of Kinesiology & Health Studies at Queen's University, where she teaches courses in the social determinants of health, health policy, food studies, and qualitative research methods. Her research interests lie at the intersection of food, health, and the body, with particular attention to issues of class and poverty. She is a founding member of the Canadian Association for Food Studies.

Jennifer Sumner is director of the Certificate Program in Adult Education for Sustainability in the Adult Education and Community Development Program in the Ontario Institute for Studies in Education at the University of Toronto. Her research and teaching interests include food studies, sustainable food systems and the political economy of food, as well as globalization, sustainability, and organic agriculture. She is the author of the book *Sustainability and the Civil Commons: Rural Communities in the Age of Globalization* (University of Toronto Press, 2005), plus numerous articles and chapters on food-related issues.

Aparna Sundar is assistant professor in the Department of Politics and Public Administration, Ryerson University, Toronto. Her doctoral research examined capitalist transformation and political mobilization in a south Indian fishery, and she has closely followed the Indian and global fishworkers' movements for several years. Relevant writing includes "Sea Changes:

Organizing Around the Fishery in a South Indian Community" in Jonathan Barker et al., *Street-Level Democracy: Political Settings at the Margins of Global Power* (Between the Lines Press, 1999); 'Review of "Conversations: A Trialogue on Power, Intervention and Organization in Fisheries"', *Samudra Report*, March 2003; and 'Marine Resources' in *Marketing the Earth: The World Bank and Sustainable Development* (Halifax Initiative, Canada and Friends of the Earth, USA, 2002).

Carole Suschnigg is an assistant professor in the Department of Sociology at Laurentian University. She teaches statistics, survey research, contemporary sociological theories, and global health issues at the undergraduate level, and community-based research at the graduate level. She has worked as a community developer in Vanuatu, New Zealand, and Canada. Her previous publications include a critique of efforts to reform Canada's primary health-care system and an analysis of midwives' resistance to being publicly managed within Ontario's publicly funded health care system. Her current research interests include housing co-operatives and food security policies in Uruguay, and the social historical phenomenon of 'blackbirding' in the South West Pacific during the late 1800s.

Jonathan Turner is a Masters of Environmental Studies candidate at Wilfrid Laurier University in Waterloo, Ontario. His research interests include, but are not limited to, food systems and food security issues at local and global scales. Currently, Jonathan is researching the use of indicators in measuring the sustainability of local food systems in Ontario. This research is part of the Food Counts project at the Department of Geography and Environmental Studies at Wilfrid Laurier University.

Özlem Güçlü Üstündağ is assistant professor at the Food Engineering Department at Yeditepe University in İstanbul, Turkey. After getting her PhD from University of Alberta in food and bioresource engineering she worked as a postdoctoral fellow at the University of Alberta, Agriculture and Agri-Food Canada, and the Centre for Studies in Food Security at Ryerson University. Her research interests include development of sustainable technologies in food and bioprocessing, and food policy.

Tony Weis is associate professor of geography at the University of Western Ontario. His research is broadly located in the field of political ecology and the intersection of agrarian political economy, environmental degradation, and small farmer livelihoods, with related interests in land reform and farmer co-operatives. He

is the author of *The Global Food Economy: The Battle for the Future of Farming* (Zed Books, 2007). Recent research has focused on the 'accelerating' contradictions of industrial capitalist agriculture and the causes of worsening global food insecurity.

Nettie Wiebe is an organic farmer and professor of ethics at St Andrew's College, University of Saskatchewan. She was women's president of the National Farmers Union (six years), president of the NFU (four years), and a leader in La Vía Campesina's International Coordinating Commission (ICC). Nettie's research interests focus on agrarian feminism; the intersection of environmental, agricultural, and women's issues in rural communities; and the role of family farms in the food system. She contributes regular columns in *The Western Producer* farm paper and has published chapters in edited books, popular magazines, and *Canadian Woman Studies/les cahiers de la femme*. Recent publications include: 'The Origins and Potential of Food Sovereignty' in *Food Sovereignty: Reconnecting Food, Nature and Community* (eds. Wittman, Desmarais & Wiebe; Fernwood, 2010) and. "Nurturing Food Sovereignty in Canada" in *Food Sovereignty in Canada: Creating Just and Sustainable Food Systems* (eds. Wittman, Desmarais & Wiebe; Fernwood Books, in press).

Anthony Winson is professor at the Department of Sociology and Anthropology at the University of Guelph. His research and publications have focused on agriculture, food, and rural development issues related to Canada and the Third World. He is the author of *Coffee and Democracy in Modern Costa Rica* (Macmillan, 1989), *The Intimate Commodity: Food and the Development of the Agro-Industrial Complex in Canada* (Garamond, 1993), and more recently, with Belinda Leach, *Contingent Work, Disrupted Lives: Labour and Community in the New Rural Economy* (University of Toronto, 2002). This last book won the John Porter book prize of the Canadian Sociology and Anthropology Association for 2003. He has published in such international and Canadian journals as *Rural Sociology*, *Comparative Studies in Society and History*, *Latin American Perspectives*, *Agriculture and Human Values*, *Economy and Society*, *Canadian Review of Sociology and Anthropology*, *Estudios del Trabajo*, *Ruralia*, *Canadian Journal of Sociology*, and *the Journal of Sustainable Tourism*. Recent publications include analyses of factors shaping contemporary North American food environments with empirical studies in supermarkets and high schools. He is presently completing a book on the degradation of food and the struggle for healthy eating.

Preface

This volume evolved out of our growing recognition that the emerging field of food studies needed a formal text to represent the depth and breadth of its diverse range of interests and to give it a critical orientation that would link the field to the larger problems humanity is facing. It began as an idea, germinated through a chance conversation, and blossomed through co-operation and love of learning.

Over recent years, the study of food has occupied increasing portions of our research, teaching, and writing. This preoccupation with food is in keeping with Marion Nestle's (2010) observation that within her academic lifetime, the use of food as a means to examine critical questions about the causes and consequences of production and consumption has grown dramatically. Her observation emphasizes what we have also realized—that food is not only a worthy object of study in itself, but also an entrée into larger issues that concern humankind: sustainability, development, globalization, governance, and power.

This volume addresses both emphases—the study of food itself and the exploration of larger issues surrounding food—from a critical perspective. In doing so, it aims to contribute to the development of the emerging field of food studies by presenting the work of leading Canadian scholars. Readers will learn about the changing meanings of food and food studies, the different theoretical lenses for looking at food, crises and challenges in the current food system, ways of challenging food governance, and visions of food for the future.

Reference:

Nestle, Marion. 2010. 'Writing the Food Studies Movement'. *Food, Culture and Society* 13(2): 160–8.

Acknowledgements

More people than we can name contributed to the genesis of this volume. In particular, we would like to thank the Canadian Association for Food Studies (CAFS) for the stimulation provided by its annual meetings and Oxford University Press for its leadership in supporting this project. Special thanks to our editors Mark Thompson and Sarah Carmichael, our copy editor Leslie Saffrey, three anonymous reviewers, and all the contributors to this volume. And we would also like to thank our readers—you are participating in an exciting new field of inquiry in Canada: food studies.

Introduction

The Significance of Food and Food Studies

Mustafa Koç, Jennifer Sumner, and Anthony Winson

To survive we need to eat. Yet food is more than a source of the energy and nutrients essential for human health and well-being. What we eat, if we eat, how we eat, when we eat, and with whom we eat reflect the complexity of our social, economic, political, cultural, and environmental arrangements around food. Eating is one of the most common human activities we engage in on a regular basis. Food is

> sustenance. . . . a symbol, a product, a ritual object, an identity badge, an object of guilt, a political tool, even a kind of money. Food determines how tall we are, how healthy, the extent of our civic peace, the sorts of jobs we hold, the amount of leisure we enjoy, the crowding of our cities and suburbs, what we look for in life, how long we look to live—all of that and much more. (Reardon 2000: 1)

Most human interactions involve producing, preparing, and consuming food. The English word *companion* is derived from the Latin for 'people sharing bread together'. From birth to death, almost all human rituals involve food. It is an important element that unites family members around the table. It denotes ethnic, regional, and national identity. It helps us to develop friendships, offer hospitality, and provide gifts. It is an important part of holidays, celebrations, and special occasions. It plays an important role in many religious rituals and taboos. It is a marker of status. It can control the behaviour of others when used as a reward, punishment, or political tool. It is the subject of creative expression by cooks and artists. It can make people feel secure. For all these reasons, and many more, food is worthy of study.

And yet, despite our everyday encounters with eating, studying food seems to be a real challenge, given its multi-significant and complex nature. This tension between familiarity and complexity most likely explains why, until recent years, food studies did not emerge as a coherent field of inquiry. Instead, most disciplinary attempts have focused on a cross-section of activities, processes, and sectors dealing with food. In a sense, we have had many food studies fields as separate and only selectively interrelated areas of research and scholarship. For example, the study of nutrition has focused on the role of different nutrients in human health and the causes and consequences of malnutrition, but left the relationship between malnutrition and poverty, or between obesity and the food industry, to social scientists. Agricultural economics has focused on optimal approaches to increase food production, but avoided the problem of simultaneous hunger and food surpluses or the role of the agri-food industry in the obesity epidemic or in the farm crisis. These examples can be multiplied. What is clear is that such a segmented focus leaves many questions unanswered and creates disciplinary silos, making difficult the cross-fertilization of ideas and insights from different disciplines.

For many years, various researchers in diverse areas of interest dealing with food practices, structures, institutions, and policies have recognized the need for a broader interdisciplinary perspective that would borrow analytical and methodological insights from various disciplines studying food. In response, New York University offered the first graduate program in food studies in 1996.

Food studies is a relatively new field of research and scholarship that focuses on the web of relations, processes, structures, and institutional arrangements that cover human interaction with nature and other humans involving the production, distribution, preparation, consumption, and disposal of food. As such, food studies can be considered to constitute a new movement, not only as an academic discipline but also as a means to change society (Berg et al. 2003).

Defining the boundaries of food studies is a challenging task because food is a topic of interest for diverse academic disciplines, such as food science and engineering, nutrition, chemistry, biology, agricultural sciences, environmental sciences, health sciences, business administration, the social sciences, and the humanities. Each body of scholarship has a unique, often discipline-focused approach to certain aspects of food. In contrast, food studies aims to create a space of scholarship for interdisciplinary inquiry. What distinguishes food studies from disciplinary or multidisciplinary studies of food is the awareness of a need for a synthetic approach that would use 'every conceivable method for studying the historical, cultural, behavioral, biological, and socioeconomic determinants and consequences of food production and consumption' (Berg et al. 2003).

Many influences over the years have contributed to the development of food studies. For example, anthropological approaches looking at continuity and change in different cultural traditions around the world have been one of the key influences. Among the anthropological contributions we can list French structuralists such as Claude Levi-Strauss looking at the material aspects of culture and seeking universal behavioural codes; Roland Barthes and Mary Douglas's examination of different food conventions and the communicative properties of food; the American foodways school's folkloric focus on shared cuisines, eating styles, structures, and behaviours; Arjun Appadurai's insights on the formation of national cuisines; Marvin Harris's cultural materialist approach looking at various taboos and cultural practices as forms of social adaptation to the material environment; and Sydney Mintz's examination of broader trends such as colonialism and industrialization in transforming tastes and cuisines.

A second major influence in food studies has been the political economy approach. Influenced by the Marxist critique of the transformative role of the capitalist economy in modern society, political economy became influential among a group of sociologists and geographers, such as Larry Busch, Fred Buttel, William Friedland, Harriet Friedmann, Phillip McMichael, and Anthony Winson. The political economy approach has examined the role of economic institutions and inequalities of power and property in explaining the relationship between processes such as industrialization, urbanization, colonialism, imperialism, globalization, and many changes in the agri-food system, food regimes, and commodity chains. While the political economy approach has mostly focused on production, some scholars from this tradition, including Pierre Bourdieu, David Goodman, and Ben Fine, pointed to the role of consumption.

A third major source of influence behind food studies has been the emergence of interdisciplinary perspectives such as cultural studies, women's studies, and environmental studies—areas often neglected by earlier approaches. With the rise of cultural studies and especially postmodern and poststructuralist criticism, many researchers looked at knowledge and traditions of food and eating as social constructs and came to question, and even reject, the effectiveness of 'objective' scientific or descriptive historical approaches to food.

While the postmodern and poststructuralist approach is very diverse in itself, we can identify George Ritzer's study of 'McDonaldization', Georgi Scrinis's critique of nutritionism,
and Alan Warde, Jonathan Murdoch, and David Goodman's work on consumption as some
of the major contributions reflecting this tradition. Discourses of food, popular culture,
analyses of identity and subjectivity, the role of the media, advertising, and institutional
practices of industry and governments in constructing reality and patterns of consumption
have been the focus of many studies sharing a postmodern viewpoint.

Like cultural studies, women's studies questioned the shortcomings of the mainstream
disciplinary approaches. Women's studies brought feminist criticism—lacking in the
major academic disciplines—to such subjects as the patterns of gender inequality and its
consequences, the ignorance of the contributions of women's labour at home and in the
workplace, and the relationship between food, the body, and eating disorders.

Another interdisciplinary influence in the development of food studies is environmental studies. Concern for the effects of factory farming and overfishing on the
environment in general, and particularly issues such as sustainability, climate change,
soil erosion, declining water quality, decreased biodiversity, and pollution from toxic
chemicals have brought natural and social scientists together to offer a more critical
perspective on the consequences of the modern industrial food system. The environmental perspective not only provided critique, but also offered insights on alternative
food systems that are sustainable and resilient. Notable pioneers in this area have been
Lester Brown and Rachel Carson. Mathis Wackernagel and William Rees's concept of
the ecological footprint and Stuart Hill's work on ecological agriculture also rank among
early influences with environmental sensitivity. More recently, diverse contributions
have emerged from scholars in a variety of disciplinary fields.

Influences on the development of food studies are not limited to academics. *The Land
of Milk and Money*, reporting the findings of the People's Food Commission, presented a
comprehensive profile of the agri-food system in Canada in the late 1970s. In addition,
numerous public intellectuals and community-based researchers have contributed to the
development of food studies from outside of academia, strengthening the links between
communities and institutions of higher education. This cross-fertilization of insights between
universities and community organizations—community–university partnerships—has
provided fertile ground for research and policy contributions in food studies.

Finally, we should note the critical contributions of those coming from major academic
disciplines who questioned some of the dominant professional practices and demanded
change. These dissenting voices have been crucial in the development of critical inquiry
and paradigm shifts not only within their own disciplinary frameworks but also in the
development of food studies.

The common element in all these different influences is a critical perspective in
perceiving existing problems as resulting from the normal operation of the food system
and everyday practices. This critical inquiry examines how patterns of social inequalities,
institutional arrangements, structures, and organizations such as the patriarchal family,
corporations, governmental bodies, international treaties, and the media contribute to the
farm crisis, hunger, the obesity epidemic, eating disorders, food insecurity, and environmental problems.

A critical perspective does not mean being negative, but rather developing a deeply
inquiring attitude, analytical capacity, and research skills. Being critical also means understanding how our current food system works and envisioning an alternative food system

that is more sustainable and just. Food studies in this sense offers both a critical and a constructive approach to issues pertaining to food.

In addition to a critical perspective, a few other commonalities can be identified within food studies:

- Interdisciplinarity
- Linkages among the social sciences, the humanities, and the natural sciences
- Holistic approach
- Historical specificity

In spite of these commonalities, food studies utilizes diverse analytical and methodological approaches developed by various disciplines. In this sense, food studies has much in common with other interdisciplinary areas. By synthesizing insights from broad bodies of knowledge, perspectives, methodologies, skills, interconnections, theories, and epistemologies, food studies aims to contribute to research, scholarship, education, and change.

The emergence of food studies has been paralleled by a growing interest in food in the wider society. Television programming devoted to food and publications such as Michael Pollan's *The Omnivore's Dilemma* (2006) and Eric Schlosser's *Fast Food Nation* (2001) have raised the profile of food in the public mind. Food policy has emerged as a field of specialization required by government programs and international agencies. Community-based food projects, food policy councils, food security programs, anti-hunger and sustainable food systems initiatives, and international relief agencies require expertise in analytical and research skills that could respond to their special needs. These demands have created new career opportunities for people with a holistic understanding of how the food system operates.

This book aims to capture the excitement, vitality, and promise of food studies by presenting the work of leading Canadian scholars in this emerging area of inquiry. Our overall objective is to develop an accessible text responding to the needs of both students and faculty. Our task is to inform readers about the breadth and depth of this new 'interdiscipline', and to introduce some of the key concepts and debates. We envision this volume as not only a book for those interested in food studies, but also as an invitation for critical inquiry in this dynamic field of human endeavour.

References:

Berg, J., M. Nestle, and A. Bentley. 2003. 'Food Studies'. In *The Scribner Encyclopedia of Food and Culture*, Vol. 2, ed. S.H. Katz and W.W. Weaver. New York: Charles Scribner's Sons, 16–18.

Pollan, Michael. 2006. *The Omnivore's Dilemma: A Natural History of Four Meals*. New York: Penguin.

Reardon, P.T. 2000. 'We Are What We Ate'. *Chicago Tribune*, 11 June. Available at http://articles.chicagotribune.com/2000-05-11/entertainment/0006170192_1_hunger-food-french-revolution.

Schlosser, Eric. 2001. *Fast Food Nation: The Dark Side of the All-American Meal*. Boston: Houghton-Mifflin.

PART I

The Changing Meanings of Food and Food Studies

From source to stomach, food involves complex relations among people and between people and nature. While different aspects of these relations have been the focus of various academic disciplines, in recent years researchers have recognized the need for a critical approach that would integrate insights from diverse disciplinary perspectives and situate food at the centre of its focus. This recognition has led to the emergence of a new field of inquiry: food studies.

Part I looks at the changing meanings of food and food studies. What is common among these chapters is an awareness of the complexity of the field and the need for an interdisciplinary approach to respond to this complexity. In Chapter 1, Koç, MacRae, Noack, and Üstündağ review some of the arguments for considering food studies to be an academic field. Based on the observations of researchers studying food systems, the authors identify three characteristics of food studies as a field: the use of a multi-level, holistic systems approach; a focus on applied and/or transformative work; and an approach that spans traditional academic disciplines.

Food plays a key role in all market economies. In Chapter 2, Friedmann explores the larger socio-economic context in which food is traded as a commodity. Interested in understanding how food systems operate and how they can change, she underlines the significance of different analytical models such as commodity studies, food regimes, and actor-network theory, as well as communities of food practice.

While some researchers look at how the food system reflects and re-creates patterns of socio-economic and political inequalities in society, others see these changes as reflections of multiple factors—cultural, economic, historical, and so on. By looking at the changes in cookbooks from a historical perspective in Chapter 3, Cooke identifies the multi-faceted significance of food and the diverse factors that have influenced food choices over time in Canada.

While food is essential for human survival, humans tend to be selective in choosing what they eat. In Chapter 4, Johnston and Cappeliez focus on the cultural aspects of food and eating, and the transformative power of food culture. They argue that by looking at culture as a tool kit, we can move beyond simplistic understandings of individual choice and willpower, and appreciate the complex and multi-dimensional ways individuals use culture in daily life.

The transformative aspect of food culture is further explored in the final chapter of this section, Chapter 5. Barndt looks at popular, holistic, and place-based education as well as multiple forms of collective cultural expression through community arts in various sustainable food initiatives. According to Barndt, popular education and community art are forms of resistance to the commodification of food, education, and art. By celebrating both biodiversity and cultural diversity, these resistance efforts not only become a means to achieve a sustainable food system but also reveal the ways that education and art catalyze creativity in the food justice movement, affirming that another world is possible.

What Is Food Studies?
Characterizing an Emerging Academic Field through the Eyes of Canadian Scholars

Mustafa Koç, Rod MacRae, Andrea M. Noack, Özlem Güçlü Üstündağ[1]

Learning Objectives

Through this chapter, you can:

1. Understand some of the analytical challenges in defining the disciplinary boundaries of food studies
2. Describe methodological triangulation by using multiple data gathering techniques
3. List key defining characteristics of food studies

Introduction

In recent decades, food-related issues have received increasing public attention worldwide. While ongoing social problems such as hunger and poverty maintain their significance (though with a shifting focus from food supply to access), the emergence of diet-related health and environmental problems further highlights the impact of the food system on human and environmental health.

In the academic arena, these developments have been paralleled by increased scholarly interest in food within social and environmental sciences and humanities, beyond the traditional food-related areas of agriculture and nutrition. The extent of this interest is evidenced by the increasing number of food-related presentations at mainstream academic conferences, articles in diverse scholarly periodicals and anthologies,

associations and societies focusing on the study of food, conferences devoted to food or food-related streams within traditionally non-food disciplines, new academic journals, culinary history societies, new books and book series, serious analyses of the food system, and food-related websites. There has also been a marked increase in food-related university courses and food studies concentrations and degrees (which are established separately or within conventional disciplines).

Food involves many aspects of human life and social relations: a source of nutrition; a symbol; a commodity; a basis for ritual acts; an object of pleasure, anxiety, or fear; an indicator of quality of life and health; a marker of class and ethnic identity; and a political tool. Food studies represents a new **interdisciplinary** perspective in social sciences and humanities, forming linkages and interconnections among food-related issues. Using a systems perspective that benefits from rich methodological and analytical insights offered by various disciplines, researchers in this field study the 'historically specific web of social relations, processes, structures, and institutional arrangements that cover human interactions with nature and with other humans involving production, distribution, preparation, and consumption of food' (Power and Koç 2008: 2).[2]

As an emerging field, however, the term *food studies* can be difficult to define. Academics have widely used it in recent years as an umbrella term to cover the study of food, cooking, and eating from a social sciences and humanities perspective. Despite this widespread usage, however, a rigorous analysis of food studies as a field or discipline has been lacking in the literature. In this chapter, we further define *food studies* by using a mixed-method approach to gather data from Canadian scholars working in areas generally deemed part of food studies (see Koç et al. 2010).

The Challenges of Defining a New Field

The relative historical neglect of food-related issues has been noted by many scholars. Warren Belasco attributes this neglect in academia to the 'classical dualism that prizes mind over body', the gendered nature of separate spheres of consumption (female) and production (male), technological utopianism, and the distancing from nature and tradition (through technology and industry). He notes that, while food production has received considerable attention in established disciplines (such as economics, chemistry, agronomy, engineering, marketing, and labour relations), analysis of food consumption has largely been limited to the study of 'negative pathologies of malnutrition, hunger, and adulteration' rather than its 'more intimate

and positive features' (2008: 2). The rather recent introduction of a gendered and feminist perspective into food studies has expanded the breadth of work on food and women from a limited focus on women's food pathologies (such as anorexia and bulimia) to include the richness and complexity of women's relationship to food practices (Avakian and Haber 2005).

Taking a closer look at food issues in sociology and explaining relative neglect of these matters in that field, Beardsworth and Keil (1997) note the very much taken-for-granted nature of eating and the perception of food issues as the intellectual property of other professions or academic disciplines (on the production side, agronomists, economists, and geographers, and on the consumption side, nutritionists and dieticians). They point, for example, to the shift in sociology's centre of gravity from production to consumption, and to the increasing salience of issues related to the experiences of women when explaining the recent sociological interest in food-related issues.

From Discipline-based Focus to Interdisciplinarity

The 1960s rise of cultural studies and postmodernism possibly offered one of the most consistent criticisms of the earlier structuralist and modernist approaches that prevailed for most of the twentieth century (Nestle and McIntosh 2010). Area and regional studies (such as African studies, Indigenous studies, women's studies, and environmental studies) emerged and created new spaces for scholarship, borrowing analytical and methodological insights from diverse disciplinary traditions to develop their own perspectives. Food studies was a late bloomer in this tradition. The first food studies graduate program as a legitimate field of study emerged in 1996 at New York University. Associations, such as the Association for the Study of Food and Society

(ASFS—since 1985); the Agriculture, Food, and Human Values Society (since 1987); the International Sociological Association's (ISA) Research Committee on Agriculture and Food (since 1988); and the Canadian Association for Food Studies (CAFS—since 2005), were the academic homes of interdisciplinary researchers interested in a more holistic understanding. New journals emerged that would emphasize the importance of interdisciplinary and **multidisciplinary** collaboration (see a selected list under Further Reading in this chapter). With various journals, lists of core readings, and various compendiums of syllabi of courses (see ASFS and CAFS websites) there now exists a respectable body of literature in food studies.

The interdisciplinary focus, even though it would not be identified as 'food studies', became the dominant trend in many food societies and journals by the 1990s. Fine et al. (1996) argue that an interdisciplinary focus was possibly easier for certain disciplines, such as sociology, anthropology, and history of food, that allowed a much greater space for human and social agency than those such as economics, nutrition, (agricultural) geography, and much of psychology. Instead of disciplinary divide, new focal points appeared around certain theoretical debates, historical processes, and trends in the food system. In the 1980s and 1990s, Atkins and Bowler (2001) classified contributions to this interdisciplinary field into categories such as historical, cultural and sociological, **post-modern** and **post-structuralist**, and food systems approaches. Avakian and Haber (2005) used the categories of colonialism, political economy, globalization, history, popular culture, and sociocultural analyses to capture the trends associated with research on food and women (while noting that they do not constitute an analytical framework nor are definitive) that spans diverse fields (such as philosophy, political economy, anthropology, sociology, history, and cultural studies) and topics (from minute studies of a single food item to close readings of

food and its representation as the basis for broad cultural analyses).

At first glance, interdisciplinarity emerges as one of the main defining characteristics of food studies. Of course, both disciplinary boundaries and patterns of interdisciplinary collaboration evolve over time and are contested both inside and outside the disciplines. Warren Belasco, while discussing the 'emerging' field of food studies, also notes that 'it may be premature to announce the birth of a new discipline'. He highlights the need to use interdisciplinary approaches in the study of food, 'which requires crossing of disciplinary boundaries' and 'a careful integration of themes or models on which to hang all these disparate ideas and insights' (2008: 5, 7). Avakian and Haber also stress the interdisciplinary nature of food studies:

> Like other interdisciplinary fields, food studies and women's studies cover a wide range of topics and use approaches and methodologies from more traditional disciplines or develop new interpretive modalities. (2005: 7)

While an interdisciplinary focus was hailed by some as a strength, a lack of clear analytical focus to connect many of these diverse debates and perspectives is seen as a shortcoming by others. Fine et al. note the disparate and fragmented nature of food studies and question its adequacy to meet the emergent challenges:

> Food studies has always been a disparate discipline or collection of disciplines. This proved more or less acceptable while each fragment could remain exclusively preoccupied with its own concerns in isolation from the concerns of the others. Developments over the past decade in the production of food, the composition of diet, the politics and content of policy-making, etc., have sorely revealed the inadequacies of food studies. (1996: 26)

Fine further asserts that 'certain themes are essential if food studies is to constitute an academic field that is coherent and integral but also distinctive from other areas, especially if food is to be set apart from other items of consumption' (1998: 13), and that it is investigations of this nature that have been neglected rather than the study of food itself.

A problem common to most of this earlier interdisciplinary food research is that it focused on food for reasons related to other research agendas, such as looking at the food industry to demonstrate a theoretical perspective on the 'new international division of labour', or the globalization of the economy. As Belasco and Scranton note, instead of being the end focus, food was 'a novel means to illuminate already accepted disciplinary concerns' (2002: 6). In this view, food studies as a new disciplinary field would emerge only when researchers came to see various aspects of food from production to consumption as 'important in themselves—and not just because they can illuminate some other dynamic or theory' (ibid).

While the domain of food studies has extended enormously, it has been equally diverse in its analytical methods in ways that do not specifically mark out food. As Fine complains, 'the various approaches to food have been fragmented and heterogeneous, defying an overall coherence. . . . the study of food tends to presume the existence of a general underlying framework of analysis or object of study even if this is essentially negated in practice through the cumulative scholarship around food' (1998: 15). The result is a field of food studies in name but not in analytical coherence.

The Integrating Capacity of Food Studies

Several analysts have argued that, rather than relocating the various sub-topics from their present fields, the objective of food studies is to gather knowledge from these diverse fields and unite them to discover their relationships and interconnections. Food studies is, thus, a fusion of the social sciences and humanities realm with the world of science and technology (Duran and MacDonald 2006; University of Michigan 2007).

Most observers agree that food studies covers a wide range of topics by using methodologies and approaches from traditional disciplines as well as through the development of new 'interpretive modalities'—perspectives unique to the field (Avakian and Haber 2005; Berg et al. 2003; Nestle and McIntosh 2010). From this viewpoint, food studies is described as the study of food and its representation through the lenses of diverse disciplinary traditions such as philosophy, political economy, anthropology, sociology, history, and cultural studies.

Others focus less on the fusion and more on seeing the interlinkages between various stages such as production, distribution, consumption, and even waste management—a systemic approach. As Fine argues, 'food studies can be defined as the analysis, conscious or otherwise, of (the components) of the food system. Contributions to the discipline are stronger the more they are integrated, or capable of integration, into an analysis of the food system whilst acknowledging its organic content' (1998: 17).

In being analyzed in terms of both its organic content and its distinct systems of provision, food is thus established as an object of study. As a result, the rationale for 'an integral discipline of food studies' lies in the analytical insights it involves. To achieve this

. . . the different factors influencing the consumption and significance of food need to be situated in relationship to one another, and attached to the systems of provision for particular foods. The point is that the separate elements that make up the world of food need to be related to one another in order that, even in isolation from one another, the significance of each can be fully and properly understood and situated. (Fine 1998: 17)

McGill University's new food journal, *Cuizine: The Journal of Canadian Food Cultures*, suggests that food 'acts as a window into multiple cultural publics and thus lends itself to various interrogations' through history, material culture, literary studies, sociology, anthropology, ethnography, art history, religious studies, communications, and environmental studies (*Cuizine* 2008). In addition, the study of food encompasses anything pertaining to food and eating, such as cooking and cuisine, dining and drinking, dieting, food quality, and food safety (Avakian and Haber 2005; Duran and MacDonald 2006). Food is a central element linking together many diverse academic disciplines and sources of knowledge that are otherwise unrelated.

In 'Canadian Food Studies', a special issue of the journal *Food, Culture and Society*, Power and Koç define food studies as examining a 'historically specific web of social relations, processes, structures and institutional arrangements that cover human interaction with nature and with other humans involving production, distribution, preparation and consumption of food' (2008: 2), and note that the interdisciplinary field of food studies offers scholars the ability to investigate the complex relationships and connections between various food-related issues. Clapp states that food studies comprises a broad and multi-faceted academic field of inquiry where food issues can be studied through various lenses. Hunger and **food security**, health and nutrition, culture, environment, workers' rights, and corporate control over the food system are a few examples of such lenses. She explains that even though the field of food studies may at times seem too broad, it is essential that all issues are considered in order to understand food in a holistic and complete sense (2008).

In Canada, food studies is an emerging field. The Canadian Association for Food Studies was founded in 2005. CAFS identifies its objectives as 'promoting critical, interdisciplinary scholarship in the broad area of food systems: food policy, production, distribution and consumption' (2007).

The association recognizes 'the need for coordinated interdisciplinary research efforts in response to societal needs for informing policy makers, assessing the outcomes of community-based work, and demonstrating the environmental and social impacts of changes affecting food systems and food policies', drawing a membership from a wide array of disciplinary backgrounds such as adult education, agriculture, anthropology, economics, environmental studies, health studies, home economics, nutrition, geography, philosophy, politics, public health, rural studies, sociology, social work, urban planning, women's studies, and more. 'CAFS encourages research that promotes local, regional, national, and global food security, but does not advocate or endorse specific policies or political platforms' (CAFS 2007).

While this book is the first extensive volume on Canadian food studies, earlier compilations by Koç, MacRae, and Bronson (2007/2008) and Power and Koç (2008) present some of the contributions of CAFS members in earlier conferences. We should, however, recognize that these contributions follow in the footsteps of earlier interdisciplinary food systems thinking and research in Canada, dating back to the mid 1970s. A unique aspect of Canadian contributions to food studies is the inclusion of both academic and non-academic works. Among these earlier studies, we can list Don Mitchell's *Politics of Food* (1975); John W. Warnock's *Profit Hungry: The Food Industry in Canada* (1978) and *The Politics of Hunger* (1987); the People's Food Commission report *The Land of Milk and Money* (1980); Jon Bennett's *The Hunger Machine* (1987); Brewster Kneen's *From Land to Mouth: Understanding the Food System* (1989); and Anthony Winson's *The Intimate Commodity* (1993). These earlier contributions reflect an orientation towards social justice, democratic citizenship, and critical inquiry and were not confined to universities.

Besides this engaged orientation, a parallel line of inquiry emerged in folklore and culinary history. Though the authors never claimed to be food studies experts, Pierre and Janet Berton's writings, especially *The Centennial Food Guide* (1966); Margaret Visser's *Much Depends on Dinner* (1986) and *The Rituals of Dinner* (1991); Carol Fergusson and Margaret Fraser's *A Century of Canadian Home Cooking: 1900 Through '90s* (1992); and Elizabeth Drivers's monumental work *Culinary Landmarks: A Bibliography of Canadian Cookbooks, 1825–1949* (2008), are examples of a different culinary, cultural, historical side of food studies that remains largely outside the critical tradition. (For a more detailed account on Canadian cookbook writing, see Chapter 3.)

Research Methodology and Participants

To further characterize the field of food studies, we solicited the views of food studies researchers, using the meanings they assign to the term to flesh out its characteristics. The status of food studies as an emerging field makes it necessary to use a mixed-methods approach. This use of multiple research methods and avenues of inquiry makes it possible to triangulate results in order to ensure increased **validity**. That is, if different research methods produce similar results,

those results are seen to be accurate. Data was collected from three different groups: members of CAFS, researchers funded by the Social Sciences and Humanities Research Council (SSHRC) whose projects were in the area of food studies, and experts in the field of food studies. In addition, data from SSHRC's online award database and Google Scholar's citations database were analyzed. In using these methods, we combined strategies that have been successfully used by other researchers.

The purpose of our study was to develop a more nuanced understanding of food studies as a field. A general overview of the type of work being done in the area of food studies can be gleaned by reviewing the most common research keywords for CAFS members, the most common research keywords for SSHRC-funded food studies researchers, and the most common terms among projects rated as food studies in SSHRC's awards database (see Table 1.1).

The prominence of keywords like *security, sustainability*, and *agriculture* suggests that there is a substantial body of work around ensuring people's continued access to food. Keywords like *health* and *nutrition* highlight the biomedical aspects of food studies research. As a group, these keywords imply a certain type of approach to food. From the feedback of experts,

Table 1.1 Keywords Associated with Food Studies

Research keywords of CAFS members	Research keywords of SSHRC-funded food studies researchers	Keywords used to predict projects rated as food studies[1]
food security	history	food
health	agriculture	sustain(able)
food system	development	urban
sustainable	community	global
urban agriculture	food security	agricultur(e)
gardening	health	securit(y)
nutrition	inequality	consum(ption)
		culture
		nutrit(ion)

1. These keywords were used to develop the automatic rating system discussed in section 2.1 of our study.

three characteristics emerged that seem to define food studies as a field: the use of a multi-level systems approach, a focus on applied and/or transformative work, and an approach that spans traditional academic disciplines.

A Multi-level Systems Approach

Goodman et al. (2000) describe the importance of a 'food system'—the institutions, inputs and outputs, activities, and cultural beliefs within a social group dealing with production, distribution, and consumption of food. Not surprisingly, when experts and CAFS members were asked about the defining features of food studies, their responses consistently addressed the need to understand food within a larger social and cultural context.

> Food studies has to do with the entire food system; while particular studies may focus on one or another element, the field is holistic, from seed to sewer. (CAFS member)

> [Food studies is the] exploration of the political, economic and cultural aspects of food and the food system, along with the health and sustainability of that system. (Expert panellist)

Other responses focused on the need to work at multiple scales (local, provincial, national, and global) and to understand how changes at one scale potentially affect the entire system. This systems approach has also been highlighted by Fine (1998).

Applied and/or Transformative Work

Many participants argued that another defining feature of food studies was that it must have 'real world' connections or applications. Expert panellists in particular argued that food studies must be connected with key problems and should be oriented toward creating some sort of public good.

> A common theme in food studies research in general, is that this work is intended to solve immediate problems (of hunger, food insecurity, unsustainable agriculture and fisheries, lack of access to clean water, etc.). (Expert panellist)

> [Food studies is] an applied field in which the global and local food system (or food systems) are described and analyzed from a political economy and human rights perspective with implications for developing national and international food policy. (Expert panellist)

The vast majority of SSHRC-funded food studies researchers reported using an approach that combines theoretical and empirical approaches to knowledge. Qualitative approaches seem to be preferred in food studies: half of these researchers (51 per cent) say that they use only or mainly qualitative methods, about a third of researchers say that they use qualitative and quantitative approaches equally, and only 13 per cent say that they use only or mainly quantitative methods. The preference for qualitative work in food studies may be typical of an approach which seeks to explain how people understand and negotiate the complexity of the social world.

The applied nature of food studies as a discipline means that research in it is particularly likely to have impacts and outcomes that go beyond academia. One feature of food studies research is its connection to community organizations. Among CAFS members who had successful SSHRC grants for food-related work, 42 per cent had both community and academic co-applicants. Among the SSHRC-funded food studies researchers, about a quarter had non-academic collaborators, such as members of Aboriginal and First Nations groups, farm and rural groups, and community organizations. This tendency to involve community members in research groups reflects the applied and potentially transformative approach of food studies.

An Approach that Spans Traditional Academic Disciplines

Food research is done by individuals across various disciplines ranging from psychology, sociology, and anthropology to history and geography, and taking in nutrition, medicine, public health, and epidemiology (Pelto and Freake 2003). Many participants noted that the crossing of traditional disciplinary boundaries is a central feature of food studies. Expert panellists were specifically asked about the defining features of food studies as a field, and replied:

> [I] believe that interdisciplinarity is critical, and not only across the social and natural sciences. Researchers in the humanities and fine arts also have important contributions to make, as a means of targeting and interrogating the food practices of everyday life. (Expert panellist)

> I see food studies as a convergence of disciplines, rather than as a discipline—and believe that this is the most important defining characteristic of the field. (Expert panellist)

In both the survey of CAFS members and that of SSHRC-funded food studies researchers, respondents were asked which definition of food studies best matched their own perceptions of the field. The results overwhelmingly favoured a field that spans research in the social sciences, humanities, health sciences, and natural sciences (see Table 1.2). Only one respondent doubted that food studies is a field, saying, 'Although I agree that "food studies" has been loosely approached by humanities, social, health and natural sciences, it is not yet an established field' (SSHRC-funded food studies researcher). Belasco (2008) has expressed similar reservations.

Although there seems to be agreement about food studies spanning multiple disciplines, there is some confusion and dispute around the use of the terms *interdisciplinary, multidisciplinary*, and **transdisciplinary**. An interdisciplinary approach typically integrates and unites perspectives from various disciplines. This contrasts with multidisciplinarity, which joins two or more disciplines, but lacks integration. Finally, a transdisciplinary approach typically falls between and beyond disciplines, and includes the integration of knowledge from outside academia.

> Food studies should be interdisciplinary and multidisciplinary. Food scholars might necessarily work within disciplines, but there is much to be gained from learning from other disciplines. (Expert panellist)

Table 1.2 Most Popular Definitions of Food Studies

Which of these definitions best matches your own idea of what "food studies" refers to?	% of SSHRC-funded researchers (n=35)	% of CAFS members (n=59)
A field that spans social science, humanities, health and natural sciences research	74.3	24.27
A field that primarily encompasses social science research	14.3	2.2
A field that primarily encompasses health and natural sciences research *or* A field that primarily encompasses humanities research	8.6	2.0
I don't think food studies is a field	2.9	0.0

Food studies, to my mind, uses food as a lens through which to identify, explore, and explain broad trends of change and continuity over time. As such, it is fundamentally interdisciplinary in nature. (SSHRC-funded food studies researcher)

For my part, I applaud inter- and multi-disciplinary initiatives, but become concerned with trans-disciplinary ones. While we all benefit from speaking across disciplines, I believe we do well to leverage the benefits of disciplinary methods of analysis that have evolved to ensure precision. This involves collaborative work and discussion over time. (Expert panellist)

For some researchers, the applied nature of food studies may tip the balance towards a transdisciplinary approach that can incorporate forms of knowledge that are not associated with typical disciplinary ways of knowing. For others, however, disciplinarity provides a strength to build on, not something to be surpassed.

Despite the common perception that food studies is a field that spans a broad range of disciplines, there is some clear disciplinary clustering. For instance, among the SSHRC projects identified as food studies, large proportions were in anthropology (15 per cent), geography (13 per cent), and sociology (13 per cent). Among SSHRC-funded food studies researchers, the most commonly reported disciplinary affiliations were sociology (21 per cent) and anthropology (21 per cent). CAFS faculty/researchers were commonly housed in departments of nutrition (27 per cent), geography (18 per cent), environmental studies (14 per cent), and sociology (14 per cent). These findings do not take away from the possibility of inter/multi/transdisciplinary work; rather, they suggest that there are likely some areas or departments where it is easier to do work that crosses disciplinary boundaries. Earlier research has identified some food-related disciplines, particularly agriculture and nutrition, that are tightly bound to traditional disciplinary paradigms, with a premium placed on conformity to those paradigms

for professional advancement (Busch and Lacy 1983). The findings also suggest that there is a tendency for food studies researchers to be affiliated with disciplines that emphasize the relationships among culture, society, and environment.

However, this confusion regarding disciplinarity may indicate a lack of analytical maturity in Canadian food studies. Long suggests that food acts as a focal point for the many different academic domains 'somewhat like the hub of a wheel with the spokes being the various avenues of study' (2002: 1). In this view, there are infinite perspectives and approaches one can take when considering the study of food, and here the field of food studies comes into play. The goal of food studies research is to provide an area where these various perspectives and disciplines can be integrated. Thus the field of food studies takes an interdisciplinary, rather than a multidisciplinary, approach to food. Hinrichs notes that interdisciplinary study and research require the articulation and integration of knowledge and theory from all of the participating disciplines. While multidisciplinary research does exchange information between two or more academic disciplines, the participants' research goals and outputs are generally framed in their own 'home' disciplines, rather than integrated as in interdisciplinary work (2008).

Conclusion

Food studies is a field of multi-level systems analysis that privileges applied work. Although there seems to be agreement about food studies spanning multiple disciplines, researchers need to find clarity and consensus on the use of the terms *interdisciplinary, multidisciplinary*, and *transdisciplinary*. This confusion regarding disciplinarity may indicate a need for further work in defining the analytical boundaries of food studies. Collective engagement among scholars, such as in this volume, will continue to contribute to the development of shared analytical insights and methodological tools.

Discussion Questions

1. How does food studies differ from earlier discipline-based approaches focusing on food?

2. What are the three key characteristics of food studies as identified by food studies researchers?

3. What are some of the advantages and challenges of an interdisciplinary approach to food research?

Further Reading

1. *Agriculture and Human Values*

   An interdisciplinary journal published since 1983. It covers a wide range of issues critically questioning the values that underlie and characterize conventional and alternative approaches to the agri-food system, encompassing production, processing, distribution, access, use, and waste management.

2. *Alternatives*

   Published since 1971, it is Canada's oldest environmental magazine. It focuses on issues of sustainability through a wide range of papers examining the impacts of the food system on the environment.

3. *Appetite*

   An international journal that focuses on normal and disordered eating and drinking, dietary attitudes and practices, and all aspects of the bases of human and animal behaviour toward food.

4. *Cuizine: The Journal of Canadian Food Cultures/ Revue des cultures culinaires au Canada*

   A relatively new entry (since 2008), *Cuizine* is an interdisciplinary journal looking at Canada's diverse culinary traditions from a multicultural perspective. It includes papers from diverse social science, humanities, and environmental studies perspectives.

5. *Food, Culture and Society*

   Published since 1997, this journal is dedicated to exploring the complex relationships among food, culture, and society from numerous disciplines in the humanities, social sciences, and sciences, as well as in the world of food beyond the academy. It is one of the few journals that specifically identify food studies as their focus.

6. *Food and Foodways*

   An interdisciplinary and international journal publishing articles on the history and culture of human nourishment. Since 1985, *Food and Foodways* has published work by anthropologists, biologists, economists, ethnobotanists, historians, literary critics, nutritionists, psychologists, sociologists, and others who use food as a lens of analysis.

7. *Food Policy*

   Dating back to 1975, *Food Policy* is a multidisciplinary journal publishing original research and critical reviews on issues on the formulation, implementation, and analysis of policies for the food sector, dealing with diverse issues dealing with production, trade, food safety, food security, and food aid.

8. *Gastronomica*

   Combining scholarship, humour, fiction, poetry, and visual imagery since 2001, this journal brings together diverse voices and an eclectic mix of articles. *Gastronomica* views food as an important source of knowledge about different cultures and societies, provoking discussion and encouraging reflection on the history, literature, representation, and cultural impact of food.

9. *International Journal of Sociology of Food and Agriculture (IJSAF)*

   An open-access journal published since 1991, IJSAF provides theoretical and empirical articles on the study of labour, production, market, policy, technology, and global and local change mostly from a political economy perspective. Past issues can be accessed online.

10. *Journal of Hunger and Environmental Nutrition (JHEN)*

Published since 2007, JHEN examines hunger and the interconnectedness among individual, political, and institutional factors that govern how people produce, procure, and consume food and the implications for nutrition and health. It focuses on hunger and environmental nutrition issues—specifically food access, food and water security, agriculture, food production, sustainable food systems, poverty, social justice, and human values.

Notes

1. We are grateful to the Social Sciences and Humanities Research Council of Canada for the support provided for this project. We also thank Sara Dilauro, Kasia Bulgarski, and Rebecca Merchant for their assistance in the project.

2. To explore the broad scope of food studies, see Hamelin et al. (2007), McIntyre (2003), Ostry (2006), Riches (2002), Tarasuk and Eakin (2005), CAFS (2007), Koç et al. (2007), Barndt (2002), Desjardins et al. (2002), Friedmann (2000), and Koç and Dahlberg (1999).

References

Atkins, Peter, and Ina Bowler. 2001. *Food in Society: Economy, Culture, Geography*. London: Arnold.

Avakian, Arlene Voski, and Barbara Haber (Eds). 2005. *From Betty Crocker to Feminist Food Studies: Critical Perspectives on Women and Food*. Boston: University of Massachusetts Press.

Barndt, Deborah. 2002. *Tangled Routes: Women, Work, and Globalization on the Tomato Trail*. Lanham, MD: Rowman & Littlefield.

Beardsworth, Alan and Teresa Keil. 1997. *Sociology on the Menu*. London: Routledge.

Belasco, Warren. 2008. *Food: The Key Concepts*. Oxford: Berg.

Belasco, Warren, and Philip Scranton. 2002. *Food Nations: Selling Taste in Consumer Societies*. London: Routledge.

Bennett, Jon. 1987. *The Hunger Machine: The Politics of Food*. Montreal: CBC Enterprises.

Berg, Jennifer, Amy Bentley, and Marion Nestle. 2003. 'Food Studies'. In *Encyclopedia of Food and Culture*, Vol. 2, ed. Solomon H. Katz and William Woys Weaver. New York: Charles Scribner's Sons, 16–18.

Berton, Pierre, and Janet Berton. 1966. *The Centennial Food Guides: A Century of Good Eating*. Toronto: McClelland and Stewart.

Busch, Larry, and Lacy, William B. 1983. *Science, Agriculture and the Politics of Research*. Boulder, CO: Westview Press.

CAFS. 2007. Canadian Association for Food Studies. Accessed May 2011 at www.foodstudies.ca/about.html.

Clapp, Jennifer. 2008. 'A Global Outlook on Food Studies'. *Food, Culture and Society* 11(3): 281–6.

Cuizine. 2008. *Cuizine: The Journal of Canadian Food Cultures / Revue des Cultures Culinaires au Canada*. Accessed July 2008 at http://cuizine.mcgill.ca/.

Desjardins, Ellen et al. 2002. 'A Systemic Approach to Community Food Security: A Role for Public Health, a position paper of the Ontario Public Health Association Food Security Workgroup'. Accessed 15 November 2007 at www.opha.on.ca/ppres/2002–01_pp.pdf.

Drivers, Elizabeth. 2008. *Culinary Landmarks: A Bibliography of Canadian Cookbooks, 1825–1949*. Toronto: University of Toronto Press.

Duran, Nancy, and Karen MacDonald. 2006. 'Information Sources for Food Studies Research'. *Food, Culture and Society* 9(2): 233–43.

Fergusson, Carol, and Margaret Fraser. 1992. *A Century of Canadian Home Cooking: 1900 Through '90s*. Toronto: Prentice-Hall.

Fine, Ben, Michael Heasman, and Judith Wright. 1996. *Consumption in the Age of Affluence: The World of Food.* New York: Routledge.

Fine, Ben. 1998. *The Political Economy of Diet, Health and Food Policy.* London: Routledge.

Friedmann, Harriet. 2000. 'What on Earth is the Modern World-system? Food-getting and Territory in the Modern Era and Beyond'. *Journal of World-System Research*, VI(2), 480–515.

Goodman, Alan, Darna Dufour, and Gretel Pelto. 2000. *Nutritional Anthropology: Biocultural Perspectives on Food and Nutrition.* Mountain View, CA: Mayfield.

Hamelin, Anne-Marie, Céline Mercier, and Annie Bédard. 2007. 'The Food Environment of Street Youth'. *Journal of Hunger and Environmental Nutrition* 1(3): 69–98.

Hinrichs, Clare. 2008. 'Interdisciplinarity and Boundary Work: Challenges and Opportunities for Agrifood Studies'. *Agriculture and Human Values* 25: 209–13.

Kneen, Brewster. 1989. *From Land to Mouth: Understanding the Food System.* Toronto: NC Press.

Koç, Mustafa et al. 2010. *Capturing the Outcomes and Impacts of SSHRC Funding in Food Studies. 1998–2000.* Report to Social Sciences and Humanities Research Council (SSHRC). Toronto: Department of Sociology, Ryerson University.

Koç, Mustafa, Rod MacRae, and Kelly Bronson (Eds). 2007/2008. *Interdisciplinary Perspectives in Food Studies.* Toronto: McGraw-Hill Ryerson.

Koç, Mustafa, and Kenneth A. Dahlberg. 1999. 'The Restructuring of Food Systems: Trends and Research and Policy Issues'. *Agriculture and Human Values* 16(2): 109–16.

Long, Lucy. 2002. 'Food Studies: Interdisciplinary Buffet and Main Course'. *Appetite* 38(1): 81–82.

McIntyre, Lynn. 2003. 'Food Security: More Than a Determinant of Health'. *Policy Options* (March): 46–51.

Mitchell, Don. 1975. *The Politics of Food.* Toronto: James Lorimer & Company.

Nestle, Marion, and W. Alex McIntosh. 2010. 'Writing the Food Studies Movement'. *Food, Culture and Society* 13(2): 159–79.

Ostry, Aleck. 2006. *Nutrition Policy in Canada, 1870–1939.* Vancouver: University of British Columbia Press.

Pelto, Gretel, and Hedley Freake. 2003. 'Social Research in an Integrated Science of Nutrition: Future Directions'. *Journal of Nutrition* 133: 1231–4.

People's Food Commission. 1980. *The Land of Milk and Money.* Kitchener, ON: Between the Lines.

Power, Elaine, and Mustafa Koç. 2008. 'A Double-Double and A Maple-Glazed Doughnut'. *Food, Culture and Society* 11(3): 263–7.

Riches, Graham. 2002. 'Food Banks and Food Security: Welfare Reform, Human Rights and Social Policy. Lessons from Canada?'. *Social Policy and Administration* 36(6): 648–63.

Tarasuk, Valerie, and J.M. Eakin. 2005. 'Food Assistance through "Surplus" Food: Insights from an Ethnographic Study of Food Bank Work'. *Agriculture and Human Values* 22: 177–86.

University of Michigan, Harlan Hatcher Graduate Library. 2007. Accessed July 2008 at www.lib.umich.edu/grad/collections/foodstudies/.

Visser, Margaret. 1991. *The Rituals of Dinner: The Origins, Evolution, Eccentricities, and Meaning of Table Manners.* Toronto: Harper Collins.

Visser, Margaret. 1986. *Much Depends on Dinner.* Toronto: Harper Collins.

Warnock, John. W. 1987. *The Politics of Hunger.* Toronto: Methuen.

Warnock, John. W. 1978. *Profit Hungry: The Food Industry in Canada.* Vancouver: New Star Books.

Winson, Anthony. 1993. *The Intimate Commodity: Food and the Development of the Agri-Industrial Complex in Canada.* Toronto: University of Toronto Press.

2

Changing Food Systems from Top to Bottom
Political Economy and Social Movements Perspectives
Harriet Friedmann

Learning Objectives

Through this chapter, you can:

1. Gain an appreciation of the social context surrounding the study of food systems
2. Understand the strengths and shortcomings of commodity studies
3. Explain global change through the food regimes approach
4. Understand how food regimes and actor-network theory can complement each other in the analysis of food system change

Introduction

The study of food systems takes a broad view of all dimensions of food from soil to stomach, and all scales of organization, from gardens, farms, and cooking pots to international organizations. The social and political context for the academic field was a series of 'food crises' beginning in 1973, which created a period of volatile prices after decades of stability, and which raised issues of hunger and food security. The same period saw an ongoing farm crisis and environmental critiques of industrial agriculture. Academically, national studies were proving too limited as trade grew, culminating in the 1990s in international agreements that changed food production and consumption in all countries. One transnational approach was commodity studies, in which researchers track patterns of production, trade, consumption, and ideas about a single commodity such as wheat, milk, or tomatoes. A larger approach called **food regimes** combines commodity studies with world-systems analysis to identify long periods of stability and change in agri-food systems. **Actor-network theory**, which tracks human and non-human 'actants' from below, is increasingly seen as complementary to food regimes theory. Together, the two approaches help to analyze food system change, which is an unusual combination of economic change and social movements.

This chapter first explores the social context of the study of food systems, followed by an overview of commodity studies. It then discusses food regimes as a way to understand global change, and briefly discusses actor-network theory. The chapter concludes by combining these two approaches to help us think about food system change, focusing on the concept of 'communities of food practice'.

Social Context for the Study of Food Systems

In the 1970s, big changes brought food to the forefront of world affairs for the first time in decades. The first 'world food crisis' was declared in 1972–3 when the prices of the most important traded food crops of the time—soy, maize, and especially wheat—doubled or tripled. This change interrupted a long period of low and declining prices, in which even poor people could afford to eat and Third World countries happily became dependent on food imports while they fostered the growth of cities and industries. High prices suddenly confronted those relying on cheap food and imports with the prospect of growing hunger; even middle-class people complained about the high cost of meat, which became more expensive because of feed-grain prices. Yet farmers did not benefit from these prices; it was corporations, especially those in international trade, that profited. Prices fell at the end of the decade, but they remained volatile. 'Food crises' marked by dramatic, sudden price rises have recurred ever since. The world of food became unstable and unpredictable.

The first World Food Summit was held in Rome in 1974 in response to the crisis, launching national and international movements for **food security**. The 'right to food' had been agreed to by governments in 1948 in Article 25 of the Universal Declaration of Human Rights (UNHCR 1948), but had not been top of mind as long as hunger seemed on a steady decline. Agreeing that a food crisis existed, governments signed commitments in 1974 to ensure food security for their populations. Commitments

to reduce hunger have been undertaken again and again (most recently in the United Nations Millennium Development Goals), but have not been met either in Canada or in many other countries (Friedmann 2005). The goal of food security, however, provides focus for social movements advocating social welfare, equality, and justice, including a new set of movements and institutions focused specifically on hunger.

Promoting Food Security

The United Nations World Food Programme (WFP) was founded in 1974 to promote food security through multilateral food aid. Food aid up to that time had been provided from one country to another. As a result, humanitarian motives were mixed with the need to dispose of surplus farm products and requirements that recipients buy farm machines, fertilizers, and pesticides from the donor country. This form of food aid thus did harm as well as good. The WFP is multilateral and focuses on food emergencies. Nonetheless, subsidized exports continue, and the European Union countries joined the United States as major donors of surplus agricultural products. These donations were referred to as 'dumping' rather than 'aid' in international trade negotiations in the 1990s and after (Friedmann 2005)—though it is important to note that emergency aid usually takes the form of buying food from farmers in distressed areas rather than sending food that undercuts their prices and incomes. In response to apparently worsening conditions, small farmers in both the global North and South, including Canada's National Farmers Union, launched the largest social movement in the world, Vía Campesina (McMichael 2010, Patel 2007, Desmarais 2002 and this volume), and defined a new goal of **food sovereignty**. Meanwhile, the goal of ending hunger, despite regular restatements, receded ever farther into the future (Friedmann 2004).

Hunger was hardly restricted to the global South. Food insecurity came to so-called rich countries, including Canada, as incomes grew more unequal. In the 1980s, Canada's first food banks were created (Riches 1986). As hunger worsened, especially among families and children, it became clear that food banks were not, as everyone had hoped, temporary. When politicians noticed that hunger had become a permanent fact for many Canadians, some of the most creative community organizations of our time began to emerge. Notable were FoodShare Toronto and the Toronto Food Policy Council, recognized across North America as pioneer non-profit and municipal organizations. FoodShare was created in 1985 by Toronto mayor Art Eggleton as an alternative to food bank charity, and has fostered innumerable individual and organizational initiatives. The Toronto Food Policy Council, a volunteer citizen council established in 1991 and supported by Toronto Public Health staff, has facilitated and coordinated numerous food-related initiatives in the non-profit, public, and private sectors. Its innovative Food Charter has been adopted by cities across the continent, and now an innovative Food Strategy promises to spark another wave of innovation. Another large non-profit, The Stop, grew from a food bank (which it still is) into a complex organization devoted to empowering people and communities through community food centres. Since agriculture and food are an economic sector as well as a social movement, innumerable creative individuals have formed successful for-profit and non-profit social enterprises (Murray 2009).

Meanwhile, similar initiatives have been growing across the country, showing how regional food systems can pursue goals of sustainability, food security, and food justice. Food Secure Canada was created in 2006, the culmination of almost a decade's efforts to bring together food security initiatives across the country. Soon after, it led a project to update the popular cross-country research of the 1970s called 'The Land of Milk and Money'. The People's Food Project, which was the work of many writers and editors based on 'kitchen table talks' around the country, was launched during the federal

election in 2011. This was the first time that all political parties (except the Conservatives, the party that won!) had a **food policy**. The Greens, with the most extended food policy of any party, elected their first Member of Parliament in that election; the Liberals and New Democratic Party (NDP) each had excellent food policies, which despite some differences shared a focus on health as the link between farming and food.

Promoting Healthy Food

Not only quantity but also quality of food became important in the 1970s. 'Organic agriculture' and 'health foods', as well as concern for global food security, were popularized by writers such as Frances Moore Lappé in *Diet for a Small Planet* (1975 [1971]) and *Food First: Beyond the Myth of Scarcity* (Lappé et al. 1977), Susan George in *How the Other Half Dies* (1976), and Wendell Berry in *The Unsettling of America: Culture and Agriculture* (1977). Of the many youth rebellions against the individualism and alienation of industrial capitalist society, one strand aimed to create communities centred on growing, cooking, and sharing food. Its proponents were early critics of industrial food and agriculture, focusing on soil loss, water pollution, dangers to wildlife from agricultural chemicals (Carson 2002 [1962]), and dangers to human health from additives and increased fats, sugar, and salt in industrial foods. They experimented with conscious ways of returning to farming without chemicals and to cooking fresh meals from scratch. Vegetarianism, hardly a new phenomenon, took on new meaning in an era that also witnessed the emergence and rapid growth of standardized fast-food chains, led by McDonald's and Kentucky Fried Chicken, and early confined animal-feeding operations. People formed food co-operatives as an alternative to the growing dominance of supermarkets which accompanied the growth of suburbs and dependence on cars. Several food co-ops, such as Karma Co-op and the Big Carrot in Toronto, are still active, and the number of health food stores has multiplied. Serving many small co-ops was the Ontario Natural Food Co-op, which still connects small, diversified farms, health-food stores, and consumers.

The Growth of Food Studies

Many researchers became interested in food issues of all kinds. One early paradigm in food studies originated with the French agricultural economists, especially Louis Malassis (1973; Malassis and Padilla 1986) and his concept of the *système agro-alimentaire*, later taken up by other researchers (e.g., Winson 1993) and termed in English the agri-industrial complex or agri-food complex. This paradigm centred on relationships between farming and processing in particular, with Canadian contributions from Tom Murphy (1982), David Glover (1983), Michael Gertler (1991), and Anthony Winson (1988, 1990, 1993). Rather than providing in-depth examination of a single commodity, these studies offer a holistic view of the complex of sectors involved in producing, processing, and retailing food, and the shifting power relationships among these sectors. Around the same time that these Canadian studies were published, a group of American researchers involved in the NC117 project, which focused on the organization and performance of the American food system, made an important contribution to understanding the food system of the world's leading capitalist economy (see, for example, Hamm 1981; Marion 1979, 1986; Connor et al. 1985).

In addition to more popular books, such as those by Michael Pollan (2005, 2008), scholarly food researchers could increasingly communicate their findings in academic collections and in interdisciplinary journals founded in the 1980s and 1990s, such as *Agriculture and Human Values, Journal of Peasant Studies, Journal of Agrarian Change, Food and Foodways,* and *Food, Culture and Society.* Many older journals such as *Rural Sociology,* the *Canadian Review of Sociology and Anthropology,* and the *Canadian Journal of Sociology,* expanded their coverage to include what we now recognize as food studies. These were later joined by a multitude of international journals, notably *International Journal of Sociology of Agriculture and Food.* The Canadian Association essay collections on food studies have proliferated in the United States since the pioneering studies of the 1980s (e.g., Busch and Lacy 1984). The present volume and its contributors are among those defining the field in Canada.

Commodity Studies

The 1980s saw a wave of new research on specific foods. In a groundbreaking article, Counihan (1984) showed how changes in the ways that bread is produced, distributed, and consumed could serve as a 'lens' to understand massive changes in family, community, and work in a small community in Italy. Complementing this microcosmic view, other scholars traced complex global patterns by following a single food making its way through a food system. Two books set the standard for many to come.

In the pioneering work *Sweetness and Power: The Place of Sugar in Modern History* (1985), anthropologist Sidney Mintz shed new light on capitalism and colonialism. Mintz showed how the African slave trade and New World sugar plantations underpinned industrial capitalism in England by making possible new foods for emerging working classes, such as jams, which were rich in calories but poor in nutrition. He showed how sugar reshaped culture both of the rich—for example, through astoundingly complicated giant sugar sculptures for entertaining guests—and the poor—for example, through combining the energy boost of sugar with other colonial imports such as tea and opium to compensate for the suffering caused by appalling living conditions, diets, health, and work. The book is written in a lively, accessible manner, and is still a staple of food courses in history, anthropology, sociology, and other disciplines.

In the same decade, sociologist William Friedland and his colleagues produced a trail-blazing book called *Manufacturing Green Gold: Capital, Labor, and Technology in the Lettuce Industry* (Friedland et al. 1981). Building on Friedland's earlier research into migrant labour in the eastern United States and Carey McWilliams's study of the structure of California agriculture, called *Factories in the Field* (1939), they showed how systems of large-scale crop production in California were fully industrial in their labour relations, finances, and distribution systems. Eventually, industrial organization of large-scale monocropping would overtake California organic produce as well (Guthman 2004).

This work opened up two important directions. First, sociology of agriculture broadened beyond 'family farms' to study all the determinants of agriculture, including inputs, such as machinery and chemicals, and sales, which were coordinated on a continental scale. Lettuce was bred to be easily harvested by machines and shipped across the continent. Labour was not family labour, except that of families of migrant Mexican and Hispanic labourers with limited rights. Canadian contributions to the literature on the role of migrant farm labour include Basok (2002), Wall (1994), and Preibisch (2007, 2010). The low cost made possible by industrial systems (through hidden subsidies of oil and water, as well as through exploited labour) allowed lettuce—and many other crops—to become concentrated in California in large monocropping operations at the expense of small and mixed farms closer to urban consumers. Durability and ease of shipping and storing took precedence over consumption; thus varieties such as iceberg lettuce (rather than multiple varieties better for health or taste) became dominant in supermarkets, shaping consumer choice.

In the second direction, researchers began to reinterpret the history of the capitalist world-system through a food lens, focusing on the worldwide wheat, meat, and dairy trade of the 1800s made possible by European settlement of (mainly) British colonies in North America, Australia, New Zealand, and South America. McMichael (1984) shows how the class structure, land ownership, exports, and eventually independence of Australia were shaped by migration from Britain, British investment, and most important, the monetary system (gold standard) that favoured Britain and underpinned its rule. Friedmann (1978) shows how family farms in Canada, the United States, Argentina, Australia, and other parts of the world were caught up in the changing diets of industrial workers in England—a paradoxical link between family labour on one side of the world and wage labour on the other. This situation was partly due to migration, railway building, new forms of credit, and so on. But it all began with an 1840s policy decision by the British government, then the centre of a dominant world empire, to sacrifice its own farmers for cheaper imports. A world market in staple foods, as Steel (2009) recently emphasized, was something quite new. Not since the Roman Empire, which ended more than a thousand years earlier, had any government felt so confident of its ability to control a world-system that it could risk the food supply of its people. Since then, there have been periods of national management of food and agriculture, followed by periods of increased trade. The present era forced the opening of national markets and a shift towards exports through the World Trade Organization, but these efforts are faltering over agriculture.

Many commodity studies draw on the research tradition of Canadian Harold Innis (1956 [1930], 1940), whose *staples theory* inspired others such as Vernon Fowke (1944), who traced the role of wheat in Canadian political economic history. Commodity or value chain studies are now proliferating, because they allow researchers to follow the food wherever it goes, to understand the food systems at all scales, and thus to discern larger patterns of production, distribution, and consumption (Collins 2005, Bernstein and Campling 2006a, 2006b). Among these are Sanderson's

1986 study of the 'world steer', Wells's 1996 study of strawberries, and DuPuis's 2002 study of milk. In the Canadian context, MacLachlan (2002) has contributed a valuable study on the beef commodity chain. Barndt's 2008 study of the tomato chain from Mexico to Canada is another particularly important Canadian contribution. Barndt connects the gender, race, and class distinctions that underpin transnational tomato chains, from the tomato fields in Mexico, through the trucking industry of North America, to the workers at McDonald's and Loblaws in Canada. Most important, Barndt introduces the key theme of biodiversity, showing that industrial systems select a small number of crop varieties based on production and shipping requirements. But another way is possible: by transplanting tomatoes around the world, gardeners and small farmers have for centuries increased the genetic variety of tomatoes. Seed saving and seed exchanges now preserve the precious heritage of those many varieties.

Food Regimes: Understanding Global Change

Are **commodity chains** related through a global food system? How can analysts link not only all stages of specific production-distribution-consumption of commodities such as wheat, beef, tomatoes, and fish, but all those **commodity systems** too? Commodity studies show how specific changes in food systems happen globally and historically; by tracking commodities along supply chains we get a picture of regional specialization, class relations in production and consumption, and inter-state power, but only as these shape each specific food. Putting them together is an approach to the study of food systems called **food regimes**.

Food regime analysis combines the 'bottom-up' approach of commodity studies with the 'top-down' approach of world-systems theory. In **world-systems theory** (Wallerstein 1974; Arrighi 1978, 1994) it is argued that

capitalism is not something that emerges in any one country and then spreads to others. Rather, the capitalist era began when countries and states became related in a world market through colonial expansion about 500 years ago; the world market ever since is bigger than any state, and the hierarchy of power among states both shapes the market and is shaped by it. In other words, capitalism emerged on a world scale in the years after 1500, because of the *relationships* among industrial wage labour in England, slavery in the Caribbean, servitude in Eastern Europe, and sharecropping in Italy; each region and each commodity complex (sugar, cotton, textiles, iron, wheat) existed only because of the relations among them, including the differences in the powers of states. These relations are the spatial dimension of the world-system. The time dimension of the world-system is equally important. Researchers have documented how the world-system as a whole goes through phases of economic expansion and contraction, and how contractions coincide with shifts in power among states (Arrighi 1994; Arrighi and Silver 1999). These shifts are called *transitions between hegemonic powers*.

Friedmann and McMichael (1989: 85) define food regimes as the link between 'international relations of production and consumption of food' and 'periods of capitalist accumulation' (which are also periods whose rules are set by a hegemonic power). The most important historical food regimes were those centred on imperial power under British hegemony (1870–1914) and on national regulation of food and agriculture under US hegemony (1947–73) (McMichael 2009).

Food regimes built on world-systems theory tend to make two major contributions. First, following the great theorist Polanyi (1944), researchers show through food regime analysis how 'markets' (with their specific mix of commodity prices) are shaped by historically specific rules governing power, money, trade, labour, and more (Magnan in press; Pritchard 2009b). Food regimes are *relatively* stable periods in which all actors, whether they like it or not, can predict the outcome of their actions with reasonable accuracy. There are tensions, even contradictions, but these are stabilized during the regime; but when old tensions and new issues cannot be handled within institutions of the regime, actions become unpredictable, and the regime goes into crisis.

Second, food regime analysis shows that periods of crisis (or 'transition') last as long as periods of stability. The transition between British- and US-centred food regimes lasted more than three turbulent decades. It began in 1914 with the outbreak of the First World War, which disrupted the new world market even as that world market affected the outcome of the war (Offer 1989); encompassed the Great Depression of the 1930s; and ended in 1947. It was brought to an end by the defeat of a wartime plan to manage international food trade, and therefore national production and consumption (Friedmann 1993) and the creation instead of a clause excluding agriculture from the main trade agreement of the era, the General Agreement on Tariffs and Trade.

The Current Transition

The crisis of the US-centred food regime, beginning with the food crisis of 1973–4, has not been accompanied by the dramatic wars and economic depression of the earlier transition. However, no stable, agreed rules and institutions governing global food relations have emerged. Food and agriculture have been a source of conflict and confusion ever since 1973, and, since the creation of both the World Trade Organization (WTO) and the North American Free Trade Agreement in the 1990s, food safety and agricultural trade have been major sources of international and class conflict, especially with the rise of the new food sovereignty movement (McMichael 2010; Patel 2007; Desmarais 2007). Cascading financial, ecological, energy, and health problems have afflicted the food system, and disagreements multiply about what

system is desirable and which rules will secure it (e.g., Campbell 2009; Dixon 2009; Pritchard 2009a; Lang and Heasman 2004). Indeed, Lang and Heasman see 'food wars' between two possible futures: the 'industrial life science' route based on individual consumption and 'functional foods' versus the 'ecological public health' route based on public policies.

This long crisis has led to many changes in the food system since the 1980s. First, new corporate sectors have become powerful. Supermarkets dominate the food sector, and are more influential than branded manufacturers, such as Kraft and Nestlé, which prevailed in all countries in the US-centred food regime. Canadian supermarkets led the trend in offering their own brands such as Loblaws's President's Choice (Winson 1993; Barndt 2008). Since then, supermarkets have moved into financial and real-estate markets, too (Burch and Lawrence 2007, 2009). With social changes in work and family, supermarkets have replaced mothers and grandmothers as a source of advice on what to eat (Dixon 2003). Governments turned over many of the responsibilities for regulating food quality to the ever-larger corporations formed through mergers and acquisitions (Lang et al. 2009; Marsden, Flynn, and Harrison 2000). Supermarkets began to make their own food quality regulations and enforce them on farmers and manufacturers around the world (Friedmann 2005). Other corporations controlling agriculture gained considerable power through new intellectual property rules of the WTO, including rules that, for the first time, allowed patenting of life forms (Tansey and Rajotte 2008). Genetic technologies became a new source of profit and a new basis for mergers and acquisitions, eventually repositioning agriculture with its seeds, chemicals, and pharmaceuticals as part of a new 'life sciences industry' (see Chapter 16 in this volume).

Second, new commodities have become important in international trade, creating new relations between North and South. Debt collection in the 1980s forced countries in Africa, Asia, and South America to shift from national food and agriculture policies to promotion of exports to (privileged) Northern consumers. Fresh vegetables, fruits, fish, and shrimp began to appear year-round in supermarkets, made available through the retailers' transnational commodity chains. Instead of growing food crops for domestic consumption, farmers began to shift to export commodities ranging from mangoes to shrimp to cut flowers, and consumers began to buy imported processed foods rather than fresh local products. In recent years, these supermarkets have been opening stores in poor countries (Reardon et al. 2005; Friedmann 2004).

Third, completely new problems have arisen that cannot be solved by existing divisions of government. The policies of the food regime that lasted until 1973 were designed to address food scarcity for consumers and low prices for farmers during depression and war. The goal was to help farmers produce lots of grains and livestock (and support their prices) to ensure that people would get adequate calories and protein. This goal was achieved: the glut of grains made it cheap to feed them to animals (and eventually to produce fuels for cars), and the hamburger became the iconic food of the regime. By-products of subsidized corn made high-fructose corn syrup a cheap sweetener in processed foods. But the subsidy regime to increase availability of grains and meats succeeded all too well: nutrient-poor products now saturate food environments (Winson 2004, 2008). Costly health problems caused by industrial diets heavy in fats, sugar, and salt have become a burden on individuals and on health-care budgets, while public health and medicine are only beginning to incorporate diet into health care (Baker et al. 2010). Now processed foods, along with chronic diseases related to obesity, are spreading to the global South (Hawkes 2010; Popkin 1998). Most important of all, lapses in food safety have caused public fears and become the focus of consumer politics (Blay-Palmer 2008).

Another new set of problems is the compounding environmental costs of the industrial food system, which now outweigh the advantages of past productivity gains (Sustainable Development Commission 2011). Between the clearing of forests in the Amazon and elsewhere for farming, and the massive use of fossil fuels on industrial farms and feedlots, agriculture is now understood to contribute substantially to greenhouse gases and global warming, to pollution and overuse of water, to loss of precious soil, and to drastic loss of species, both wild and cultivated. Today's farmers, who have inherited the wisdom of those who managed ecosystems and helped crops and livestock co-evolve with humans for ten thousand years, are being displaced in frightening numbers (Araghi 1995). Yet they are also resisting and adapting (van der Ploeg 2008) and have many allies among people advocating for healthy food and farming (IAASTD 2008; De Schutter 2011).

Toward a New Food Regime

Can a new food regime arise to solve these problems? The answer is not yet clear. One area of conflict is certification systems and standards. Certification systems began outside governments, to promote qualities beyond those traditionally regulated by governments such as the permitted levels of contaminants (e.g., from agricultural chemicals or animal manure) in food or water. The earliest certifications were for *organics*, created by 'alternative' farmers to help their customers identify their products, and for *fair trade*, created by social justice organizations to help farmers in the global South get better prices for products such as coffee and cocoa. As demand for these certified, value-based products grew, however, corporations were able to take them over as profitable 'niches' at premium prices (Guthman 2004). And as certifications multiply, from seafood- to forest- to animal-friendly products, consumers are in danger both of 'label fatigue' (Goodman 2003) and uncertainty that any certifications really deliver promised benefits.

As problems of health and environment have multiplied, governments have found it increasingly difficult to keep up. Corporations, led by supermarkets, are taking on the role of making, implementing, and monitoring quality standards, and social movements have shifted their advocacy from public policy to corporations; for instance, Greenpeace and Environmental Defense Fund have pioneered tactics to shame corporations into adopting better practices. In Canada organic farmers and consumers have demanded a higher standard than in the United States for eventual adoption by government (Hall and Mogyorody 2001). Not only do governments lag behind the social and private sectors, but also the certification game is open to anyone to play. Never in history until now have corporations been able to regulate themselves.

Public policy is as important as it is elusive. As mentioned earlier, all parties except the Conservatives adopted food policies in the 2011 Canadian federal election (Leeder 2011), after 20 years of advocacy and food system changes. Of course, a national food policy is still distant, but there are signs that this may come.

Morgan and Sonnino (2008) advocate the 'power of the public plate' to encourage schools, hospitals, and municipal agencies to provide healthy meals for students, patients, and workers, and at the same time create demand for local ingredients grown by sustainable farmers. Alliances between non-profit food advocacy organizations and public institutions are effective means to this end. For example, in Canada, Local Food Plus is one such non-profit that has grown very quickly since its founding in 2006 to facilitate public procurement of local, sustainable foods (Friedmann 2007). And hospitals that are finally preparing fresh meals are discovering along the way that they actually save money through waste reduction.

School meals have been publicly shown to be inadequate and unhealthy in the United States and the United Kingdom, as well as in Canada (see, for example, the work of Marshall 2006, Taylor et al. 2005, and Winson 2008). Shamefully, Canada is the only so-called rich country that has never had a national school meal program; fortunately, if the government creates one now, it can learn from the experiences, good and bad, of all the other countries. As well, FoodShare Toronto is pioneering a multi-stakeholder campaign to make food literacy, including hands-on gardening and cooking skills, part of the school curriculum from kindergarten to graduation.

These are only two of many strategies adopted by a growing food movement to bring together the fragments of a dying food regime to find synergistic solutions to many social problems. Food regimes is a perspective that focuses attention on food as a lens, to see ways to address many social problems at once, from promoting health to managing ecosystems, and to move toward a wise agri-food system as the foundation for a sustainable and just society.

Actor-Network Theory

Actor-network theory became important in food studies in the 1990s as a way to address food challenges. Researchers following the theories of Bruno Latour have made large contributions to agri-food studies (Goodman and Watts 1994). They have gone beyond classical commodity studies to insist on a much more balanced attention to natural processes and natural sciences, what Latour calls 'hybrids' of social and natural 'actants'. Researchers follow specific networks of human and non-human 'actants' to reconstruct relationships, innovations, and discoveries that are not easily contained within other theories. Actor-network theory (and related science and technology studies) initially defined itself in opposition to food regimes and other political economy theories (Goodman and Watts 1997). In fact, however, the two are quite complementary (Wilkinson 2006; Morgan et al. 2006). Actor-network studies follow threads of relationships from the bottom up, much like commodity studies do, and the empirical method yields important insights for food regimes as it moves ever deeper into aspects such as health and eco-systems, which have been the domain of natural science. Food regimes give global and historical shape to the many empirical studies, as food regimes incorporate analysis of biophysical lim-its to the industrial food system (Weis 2007 and this volume). Food regimes also encompass synergistic new combinations of practical know-ledge and formal science that allow ecological farmers to manage ecosystems and create food security (Altieri 1987, Pretty 2002).

Thinking About Food System Change

Analysis of how the food system is changing in Canada, in its regions, and in the world involves at least two questions: What is changing? How does change happen? Both food regimes and actor-network approaches guide research to answer these questions. In addition, we need to think about how economic actors, social move-ment organizations, and public agencies are linked through **communities of food practice**.

What Is Changing?

Food system change is at once a social movement and a set of practical activities to transform the food sector of the economy (Baker 2009). From a food regimes perspective, specific historical social movements have been agents of large-scale change or transitions from one regime to another (Friedmann 2004). Seeing how these changes happened can help us ask useful questions about change today. As mentioned earlier, the first food regime began when the British government removed tariffs on grain in the early 1840s, which sacrificed its own powerful farm sector to imports, and promoted grain production in its colonies, including Canada, by encouraging huge populations to migrate. At one stroke, these two policies created a world market in wheat

and quelled unrest and demands for bread in the working classes of Great Britain. Together, these international movements of wheat and set-tlers created the first food regime of 1870–1914, which, in turn, created new classes of special-ized export wheat farmers in the United States, Canada, and other settler regions.

When the world wheat market collapsed a few decades later, in the 1920s, it heralded a decade of general crisis called the Great Depression. Prairie wheat farmers were hard-est hit, since they depended on export mar-kets which had failed. Farmers created strong social movements, such as the Co-operative Commonwealth Federation in Canada, which later joined with labour to become the NDP. Such political coalitions were key to defining the policies and rules of the second food regime, especially (but not only) in the United States (Winders 2009). These included price supports, marketing boards, supply management, import controls, and the whole array of programs now called subsidies, including export subsidies. In this regime, agri-food corporations became large and powerful through industrialization of agri-culture and food manufacturing with the cre-ation of the GATT in 1947. When in turn the second regime began to falter about 25 years later in 1973, it ushered in another period of transition, in which social movements arose in the 1980s to criticize the industrial food sys-tem, comprising consumers, environmentalists, alternative agriculture practitioners, and advo-cates for food security, food safety, and healthy food. The most important of these is the food sovereignty movement of small farmers around the globe—the largest social movement in the world (Patel 2007; McMichael 2008).

These new movements are studied through food regimes and actor-network theories. They seek creative ways to live within natural limits, which the industrial food system tends to over-ride (Weis 2007). Food scholars study both these change initiatives and the industrial food system itself, examining, for example, how to meas-ure and evaluate risks related to hormones and antibiotics in livestock, to pesticides and genetically modified crops, to food system workers and consumers, and to health systems. These initiatives include certifications for fair trade and organic products, and new networks of production and distribution, such as food co-ops, farmers' markets, and **community-supported agriculture** (CSA). The CSA is an innovation that came of age during the 1990s, in which customers buy a farmer's crops in advance of the growing season and receive produce throughout the season (see Fieldhouse 1996). CSAs help farmers invest and plant without borrowing from a bank, and allow customers to share the risks and benefits of agriculture.

New distribution systems create closer connections—food networks near home for both farmer and eater—and combine social (market) with natural (crops, animals, weather) factors. They support a revival of small, artisanal processors of foods made from local farm products. In other words, they create short, local, alternative supply chains (Marsden, Banks, and Bristow 2000). Social movements recreating the infrastructure of a regional food economy (Baker et al. 2010) thus provide opportunities for entrepreneurs from farm to table. These movements may be the seeds of a new food regime.

How Does Change Happen?

Change always involves tensions. One tension in the food movement exists between alleviating injustices in the current food system and building a new food system. On one side, the food bank communities, which form the front line of emergency help for hungry people, would like to end hunger, and they advocate for better incomes so that everyone can afford to buy food. On the other side, organizations like FoodShare and The Stop, which also guide people to food banks or even operate food banks themselves, nonetheless focus on helping people become self-reliant through education and through community gardens and kitchens. Even 'middle-class' organizations such as Slow Food advocate for food that is 'good, clean, and fair'. But although this tension

persists, most organizations are converging on a concept of food citizenship (Lang et al. 2009; Hinrichs and Lyson 2007).

Another tension exists between farm renewal and meeting the needs of an increasingly urban and diverse population of eaters. Waves of immigrants, from the founding of Canada until the middle of the last century, arrived in a rural country. Many became farmers; the rest were closely connected to the farms and ate what local farmers grew and sold. Historically, most immigrants came from Europe. About 30 years ago, immigrants began to arrive in large numbers from all over the world, mostly settling in large cities. As these cities grew, sprawling across farmland, the new residents found themselves very far from remaining farming areas both geographically and culturally. These recent immigrants began arriving as food markets were becoming global in the crisis of the US–centred food regime. It was easy, therefore, for them to import their familiar cultural foods. Meanwhile, local vegetable farmers, such as those in the fertile Holland Marsh near Toronto, began to specialize in two crops—carrots and onions—and export them, while nearby supermarkets were importing them! As wheat farmers before them had discovered, growing for export is not a reliable livelihood. We now have an economic problem: How can farming be renewed so that farmers can have a decent livelihood? How can good incomes for farmers be reconciled with solving hunger? There is also a cultural problem: How can farmers discover what foods consumers want and learn how to grow them? How can urban cooks, shoppers, and chefs find what they want from local farmers (Friedmann in press)?

Two other important tensions are less frequently noticed. First, much of the revival of local food production has relied on temporary migrant workers. These workers lack the rights of citizens (Sharma 2006; Barndt 2008). Organizations such as Justice for Migrant Workers are just beginning difficult conversations with other food citizenship organizations. Second, Indigenous people, who have been displaced and marginalized since the first food regime, have by far the deepest knowledge of how to live in each ecosystem of Canada. The resurgence of First Nations, both in cities and on reserves, embraces farming and healthy food as part of their pursuit of justice and sustainability. First Nations are potentially the centre in Canada of an emerging circle of food system change.

Communities of Food Practice

Economic and social movement initiatives for food citizenship are linked in communities of food practice (Friedmann 2007). These consist of networks of individuals and organizations—public, private, and non-profit—engaged in creating a regional, integrated, inclusive agri-food economy. A community of food practice is most successful when it is anchored by creative, values-based organizations. Individuals within these organizations—founders, staff, and volunteers—can trust others in the food community even if it is too large for everyone to be personally acquainted. Food change organizations tend to be fluid and to encourage individual creativity, including assisting individuals to move through and beyond them, leaving behind (and taking with them) experiences and projects that foster the movement as a whole. These individuals in turn help the organizations to evolve quickly and encourage others to emulate successful experiments. Many of these organizations are non-profits, with an increasing number of small, values-based businesses that respond to opportunities within an emerging food system based on social economy (Murray 2009).

At the centre of such a network, however, we often find a public organization. For example, the Toronto Food Policy Council (TFPC) is a citizens' council with members from all parts of the food system—including the farm sector—located within municipal government. Staff of Toronto Public Health coordinate the TFPC's volunteer activities. The TFPC thus straddles the line between municipal government and citizen organizations, and facilitates and anchors networks of individuals and organizations. This role has made it an acknowledged pioneer in food

system change. Its own initiatives include the Toronto Food Charter, widely adopted by cities across North America, and most recently, the Toronto Food Strategy, which seeks to take its support for food system change to a new level.

Communities of food practice support creative solutions to a food regime in crisis. The future of food can go one of two ways. Either large-scale food production units will continue to dominate, with their hierarchies of a few good jobs and many poor jobs, including those of migrant workers with few rights; or local communities of food practice will connect and form a 'joined-up food economy' (Roberts 2008).

The growing number of people in communities of food practice cannot know each other—there are too many. But they can easily meet each other and trust each other to work together to improve and innovate (People's Food Policy Project 2011). Trust is especially important in easing the tensions among movements, which will test the communities of food practice in coming years. The most important insight of the concept 'community of food practice' is that by training ourselves to see the links among many diverse initiatives and individuals and organizations, we can discover deep changes underway in the food system.

Conclusion

This chapter has described the food regimes approach to the study of food systems. To provide background to and a holistic view of this approach, the chapter first explored the social context of food systems. The chapter then outlined commodity studies, which provided groundbreaking research on specific foods within a food system. The main focus, however, was on food regimes as a way to understand changes in the global food system. This approach can be complemented by the use of actor-network theory. The chapter concluded by combining these two approaches to help us analyze food system change, and introducing the concept of 'communities of food practice', which support creative solutions to a food system in crisis.

Discussion Questions

1. Why is social context so important to the study of food systems?

2. What are commodity studies? Describe the strengths and weaknesses of using this approach to study food.

3. Define the term *food regime* and explain the advantages of using this approach to study food.

4. How are communities of food practice linked to food system change?

Further Reading

1. Weis, Tony. 2007. *The Global Food Economy: The Battle for the Future of Farming*. London: Earthscan and Halifax: Fernwood.

   Weis uses food regime analysis to show the ecological and social consequences of linking North and South through commodities. Two main commodity chains are the foundation of most global food trade: wheat and livestock. Since most grains in fully commercial systems like North America are fed to animals, corn and soy are part of the livestock complex. In both systems production of grains and meat is concentrated in a few regions, and neither are sustainable. As international trade and investment organize the global South along the lines of the global North, the world food supply becomes increasingly vulnerable.

2. Barndt, Deborah. 2008. (2nd ed). *Tangled Routes: Women, Work, and Globalization on the Tomato Trail*. Lanham, MD: Rowman & Littlefield.

   Using commodity chain analysis, Barndt follows the trail of two tomatoes from field to table through stories and photographs. The first tomato is 'corporate': a standard fruit designed to grow, travel, and be sold in large-scale operations from Mexican fields to Canadian supermarkets. Workers along the commodity chain are organized by gender, race, class, and nationality. The

other tomato is called by the Indigenous word *tomatl*. Today gardeners and small farmers across the world continue the centuries-long adaptation of tomatoes. They save and exchange seeds and thus increase the genetic, cultural, and culinary diversity of the plant.

3. Morgan, Kevin, Terry Marsden, and Jonathan Murdoch. 2006. *Worlds of Food: Place, Power, and Provenance in the Food Chain*. Oxford: Oxford University Press.

   The authors use actor-network theory and political economy to compare three regional farming systems, in California (industrial–export); Tuscany, Italy; and Wales (a 'placeless foodscape' with 'short supply chain' alternatives—much like most regions of Canada). These international comparisons together show how a global economy of values-based, short supply chain, networked regions could work.

4. McMichael, Philip. 2009. A Food Regime Geneaology. *Journal of Peasant Studies* 36(1): 139–69.

   A good place to get an up-to-date overview of food regimes approaches, their origins, and their evolution.

5. Lang, Tim and Michael Heasman. 2004. *Food Wars: The Global Battle for Mouths, Minds and Markets*. London: Earthscan.

Although data are from the United Kingdom, this book offers such a clear analysis of present dilemmas and choices about food systems that it is a good starting point for understanding Canada, too. Lang and Heasman show how the 'productionist paradigm' that dominated national food systems for decades is no longer viable, because it took no direct account of human or ecosystem health. They outline two trajectories for a new food system: the 'life sciences integrated paradigm' and the 'ecological public health paradigm'.

References

Araghi, F. 1995. 'Global De-Peasantization, 1945–1990'. *The Sociological Quarterly* 36(2): 337–68.

Arrighi, Giovanni. 1978. *Geometry of Imperialism: The Limits of Hobson's Paradigm*. London: Verso.

Arrighi, Giovanni. 1994. *The Long Twentieth Century: Money, Power and the Origins of Our Times*. London: Verso.

Arrighi, Giovanni, and Beverly Silver. 1999. *Chaos and Governance in the Modern World System*. Minneapolis, MN: University of Minnesota Press.

Altieri, Miguel A. 1987. *Agroecology: The Science of Sustainable Agriculture*. Boulder, CO: Westview Press.

Baker, Lauren, Philippa Campsie, and Katie Rabinowicz. 2010. *Menu 2020: Ten Good Food Ideas for Ontario*. Metcalf Food Solutions. Metcalf Foundation.

Baker, Lauren E. 2009. *Emerging Biocultural Agrifood Relations: Local Maize Networks in Mexico*. Unpublished PhD thesis. York University.

Barndt, Deborah. 2008. *Tangled Routes: Women, Work, and Globalization on the Tomato Trail*. Lanham, MD: Rowman & Littlefield.

Basok, Tanya. 2002. *Tortillas and Tomatoes. Transmigrant Mexican Harvesters in Canada*. Montreal and Kingston: McGill-Queen's University Press.

Blay-Palmer, Alison. 2008. *Food Fears: From Industrial to Sustainable Food Systems*. Aldershot, England; Burlington, VT: Ashgate.

Bernstein, Henry, and Liam Campling. 2006a. 'Commodity Studies and Commodity Fetishism I: Trading Down', *Journal of Agrarian Change* 6(2): 239–64.

Bernstein, Henry and Liam Campling. 2006b. 'Commodity Studies and Commodity Fetishism II: Profits with Principles'? *Journal of Agrarian Change* 6(3): 414–47.

Berry, Wendell. 1977. *The Unsettling of America: Culture and Agriculture*. San Francisco: Sierra Club Books.

Burch, David, and Geoffrey Lawrence (Eds). 2007. *Supermarkets and Agri-food Supply Chains: Transformations in the Production and Consumption of Food*. Cheltenham/Camberley UK/Northampton MA: Edward Elgar.

Burch, David, and Geoffrey Lawrence. 2009. 'Towards a Third Food Regime: Behind the Transformation'. *Agriculture and Human Values* 26(4): 267–79.

Busch, Lawrence, and William B. Lacy (Eds). 1984. *Food Security in the United States*. Boulder, CO: Westview Press.

Campbell, Hugh. 2009. 'Breaking New Ground in Food Regime Theory: Corporate Environmentalism, Ecological Feedbacks and the "Food From Somewhere" Regime?' *Agriculture and Human Values* 26(4): 309–19.

Carson, Rachel. 2002 [1962]. *Silent Spring*. Boston: Houghton Mifflin.

Collins, J. 2005. 'New Directions in Commodity Chain Analysis of Global Development Processes'. In *New Directions in the Sociology of International Development. Research in Rural Sociology and Development*, ed. F.H. Buttel and P. McMichael. Amsterdam: Elsevier, 3–17.

Connor, John M., Richard T. Rogers, Bruce W. Marion, and Willard F. Mueller. 1985. *The Food Manufacturing Industries*. Toronto: Lexington Books.

Counihan, Carole. 1984. 'Bread as World: Food Habits and Social Relations in Modernizing Sardinia'. *Anthropological Quarterly* 57(2): 47–59.

De Schutter, Olivier. 2011. 'Agroecology and the Right to Food', Report of the United Nations Special Rapporteur on the Right to Food presented at the 16th Session of the United Nations Human Rights Council [A /HRC /16/49]. Accessed 21 June 2011 at www.srfood.org/index.php/en/documents-issued.

Desmarais, Annette Aurélie. 2002. 'Peasants Speak'. *Journal of Peasant Studies* 29(2): 91–124.

Desmarais, Annette Aurélie. 2007. *La Via Campesina: Globalization and the Power of Peasants*. London: Pluto Press.

Dixon, Jane. 2003. 'Authority, Power and Value in Contemporary Industrial Food Systems'. *International Journal of the Sociology of Agriculture and Food* 11(1): 31–9.

Dixon, Jane. 2009. 'From the Imperial to the Empty Calorie: How Nutrition Relations Underpin Food Regime Transitions'. *Agriculture and Human Values* 26(4): 321–33.

Dupuis, Melanie. 2002. *Nature's Perfect Food: How Milk Became America's Drink*. New York: New York University Press.

Fieldhouse, Paul. 1996. 'Community Shared Agriculture'. *Agriculture and Human Values* 13(3): 43–7.

Fowke, Vernon. 1944. *National Policy and the Wheat Economy*. Toronto: University of Toronto Press.

Friedland, William H., Amy E. Barton, and Robert J. Thomas. 1981. *Manufacturing Green Gold: Capital, Labor, and Technology in the Lettuce Industry*. Cambridge/New York: Cambridge University Press.

Friedmann, Harriet. 1978. 'World Market, State, and Family Farm: Social Bases of Household Production in the Era of Wage Labor'. *Comparative Studies in Society and History* 20(4): 545–86.

———. 1993. 'International Political Economy of Food: A Global Crisis'. *New Left Review* 197: 29–57.

———. 2004. 'Feeding the Empire: The Pathologies of Global Agriculture'. In *Socialist Register 2005*, ed. Leo Panitch and Colin Leys. London: Merlin, 124–43.

———. 2005. 'From Colonialism to Green Capitalism: Social Movements and the Emergence of Food Regimes'. In *New Directions in the Sociology of International Development. Research in Rural Sociology and Development*, ed. Frederick H. Buttel and Philip D. McMichael. Amsterdam: Elsevier, 227–64.

———. 2007. 'Scaling Up: Bringing Public Institutions and Food Service Corporations into the Project For a Local, Sustainable Food System in Ontario'. *Agriculture and Human Values* 24(3): 389–98.

———. In press. 'Food Sovereignty in the Golden Horseshoe Region of Ontario', in Hannah Wittman, Annette Aurélie Desmarais, and Nettie Wiebe (Eds), *Food Sovereignty in Canada*. Point Black, NS: Fernwood Publishing.

Friedmann, Harriet, and Philip McMichael. 1989. 'Agriculture and the State System: The Rise and Decline of National Agriculture'. *Sociologia Ruralis* XIX, 2: 93–117.

George, Susan. 1976. *How the Other Half Dies: The Real Reasons for World Hunger*. Harmondsworth/New York: Penguin.

Gertler, Michael. 1991. 'The Institutionalization of Grower-Processor Relations in the Vegetable Industries of Ontario and New York'. In *Towards a New Political Economy of Agriculture*, ed. William Friedland, Lawrence Busch, Frederick Buttel, and Alan Rudy. Boulder, CO: Westview Press, 232–55.

Glover, David. 1983. *Contract Farming and the Transnationals*. Unpublished PhD dissertation, University of Toronto.

Goodman, David. 2003. 'The Quality "Turn" and Alternative Food Practices: Reflections and Agenda'. *Journal of Rural Studies* 19(1), 1–7.

Goodman and Watts (Eds). 1997. *Globalizing Food: Agrarian Questions in Global Restructuring*. London: Routledge.

———. 1994. 'Reconfiguring the Rural or Fording the Divide?: Capitalist Restructuring and the Global Agro-Food System'. *Journal of Peasant Studies* 22(1), 1–49.

Guthman, Julie. 2004. *Agrarian Dreams: Paradoxes of Organic Agriculture in California*. Berkeley: University of California.

Hall, A., and V. Mogyorody. 2001. 'Organic Farmers in Ontario: An Examination of the Conventionalization Argument'. *Sociologia Ruralis* 42(1): 399–422.

Hamm, Larry G. 1981. 'Retailer–Manufacturer Relationships in the Food-Service: Some Observations from the U.S.A'. Working Paper 64, University of Wisconsin, Madison, WI: NC117.

Hawkes, Corinna. 2010. 'The Influence of Trade Liberalization and Global Dietary Change: The Case of Vegetable Oils, Meat and Highly Processed Foods'. In *Trade, Food, Diet, and Health: Perspectives and Policy Options*, ed. Corinna Hawkes, Chantal Blouin, Spencer Henson, Nick Drager, and Laurette Dube. Oxford: Blackwell, 35–59.

Hinrichs, Clare, and Thomas A. Lyson (Eds). 2007. *Remaking the North American Food System: Strategies for Sustainability*. Lincoln, NB: University of Nebraska Press.

IAASTD. 2008. *Agriculture at a Crossroads*. International Assessment of Agricultural Knowledge, Science and Technology for Development. Washington, DC: Island Press.

Innis, Harold. 1940. *The Cod Fisheries: The History of an International Economy*. New Haven: Yale University Press.

Innis, Harold. 1956 [1930]. *The Fur Trade in Canada: An Introduction to Canadian Economic History*. Toronto: University of Toronto Press.

Lang, Tim, David Barling, and Martin Caraher. 2009. *Food Policy: Integrating Health, Environment, and Society*. Oxford: Oxford University Press.

Lang, Tim, and Michael Heasman. 2004. *Food Wars: The Global Battle for Mouths, Minds and Markets*. London: Earthscan.

Lappé, Frances Moore. 1975 [1971]. *Diet for a Small Planet*. New York: Ballantine.

Lappé, Frances Moore, Joseph Collins, and Cary Fowler. 1977. *Food First: Beyond the Myth of Scarcity*. Boston: Houghton Mifflin.

Leeder, Jessica. 2011. 'For the First Time, Food Becomes a Political Priority'. *Globe and Mail*, 11 April. Available at www.globeandmail.com.

MacLachlan, Ian. 2002. *Kill and Chill: Restructuring Canada's Beef Commodity Chain*. Toronto: University of Toronto Press.

Magnan, André. In press. 'Food Regimes'. In *The Handbook of Food History*, ed. Jeffrey M. Pilcher. Toronto: Oxford University Press.

Malassis Louis. 1973. 'Analyse du Complexe Agro-alimentaire d'après la Comptabilité Nationale'. *Economies et Sociétés* série AG (11–12): 2031–50.

Malassis Louis and Padilla Martine. 1986. *Economie agro-alimentaire. III. L'économie mondiale.* Paris: Cujas.

Marion, Bruce W. 1979. *The Food Retailing Industry: Structure, Markets, Profits, and Prices.* New York: Praeger.

Marion, Bruce W. 1986. *The Organization and Performance of the U.S. Food System.* Toronto: Lexington Books.

Marsden, Terry, Andrew Flynn, and Michelle Harrison. 2000. *Consuming Interests: The Social Provision of Foods.* London: UCL Press.

Marsden, Terry, Jo Banks, and Gillian Bristow. 2000. 'Food Chain Supply Approaches: Exploring Their Role in Rural Development'. *Sociologia Ruralis* 40(4): 424–38.

Marshall, Amanda. 2006. *Best Practices in Farm to School.* Report prepared for the Ontario Farm to School Network.

McMichael, Philip. 1984. *Settlers and the Agrarian Question: Capitalism in Colonial Australia.* Port Melbourne: Cambridge University Press.

McMichael, Philip. 2008. 'Peasants make their own history, but not just as they please . . .'. *Journal of Agrarian Change* 8(2/3): 205–28.

McMichael, Philip. 2009. A Food Regime Genealogy. *Journal of Peasant Studies* 36(1): 139–69.

McMichael, Philip. 2010. 'Food Sovereignty in Movement: Addressing the Triple Crisis'. In *Food Sovereignty: Reconnecting Food, Nature and Community*, ed. Hannah Wittman, Annette Aurélie Desmarais, and Nettie Wiebe. Black Point, NS: Fernwood Publishing, 168–85.

McWilliams, Carey. 1939. *Factories in the Field: The Story of Migratory Farm Labor in California.* Boston: Little, Brown.

Mintz, Sidney. 1985. *Sweetness and Power: The Place of Sugar in Modern History.* New York: Viking.

Morgan, Kevin, and Roberto Sonnino. 2008. *The School Food Revolution: Public Food and the Challenge of Sustainable Development.* London: Earthscan.

Morgan, Kevin, Terry Marsden, and Jonathan Murdoch. 2006. *Worlds of Food: Place, Power, and Provenance in the Food Chain.* Oxford: Oxford University Press.

Murphy, Tom. 1982. *The Structural Transformation of New Brunswick Agriculture.* Fredericton: unpublished MA thesis, University of New Brunswick.

Murray, Robin. 2009. *Danger and Opportunity; Crisis and the New Social Economy.* London: National Endowment for Science, Technology, and the Arts (NESTA). Available at www.youngfoundation.org/files/images/Prov_09_-_Danger_and_Opp_v9_methods.pdf.

Offer, Avner. 1989. *The First World War: An Agrarian Interpretation.* Oxford: Clarendon Press.

Patel, Raj. 2007. *Stuffed and Starved: Markets, Power and the Hidden Battle for the World's Food System.* Toronto: HarperCollins.

People's Food Policy Project. 2011. *Resetting the Table: A People's Food Policy for Canada.* http://peoplesfoodpolicy.ca/files/pfpp-resetting-2011-lowres_1.pdf.

Polanyi, Karl. 1944. *The Great Transformation.* New York: Rinehart.

Pollan, Michael. 2005. *The Omnivore's Dilemma: A Natural History of Four Meals.* New York: Penguin.

Pollan, Michael. 2008. *In Defense of Food: The Myth of Nutrition and the Pleasures of Eating.* London: Allen Lane.

Popkin, B.M. 1998. 'The Nutrition Transition and its Health Implications in Lower-income Countries'. *Public Health Nutrition* 5: 205–14.

Preibisch, Kerry. 2007. 'Local Produce, Foreign Labor: Labor Mobility Programs and Global Trade Competitiveness in Canada'. *Rural Sociology* 72(3): 418–49.

Preibisch, Kerry. 2010. 'Pick-Your-Own Labor: Migrant Workers and Flexibility in Canadian Agriculture'. *International Migration Review* 44(2): 404–41.

Pretty, Jules. 2002. *Agri-Culture: Reconnecting People, Land, and Nature.* London/Sterling, VA: Earthscan.

Pritchard, Bill. 2009a. 'The Long Hangover From the Second Food Regime: A World-Historical Interpretation of the Collapse of the WTO Doha Round'. *Agriculture and Human Values* 26(4): 297–307.

Pritchard, Bill. 2009b. 'Food Regimes'. In *The International Encyclopedia of Human Geography*, ed. Rob Kitchin and Nigel Thrift. Amsterdam: Elsevier, 221–5.

Reardon, Thomas, C. Peter Timmer, and Julio A. Berdegue. 2005. 'Supermarket Expansion in Latin America and Asia'. In *New Directions in Global Food Markets*, ed. Anita Regmi and Mark Gehlhar. USDA, 47–61. Available at www.ers.usda.gov/publications/aib794/aib794.pdf.

Riches, Graham. 1986. *Food Banks and the Welfare Crisis.* Ottawa: Canadian Council on Social Development.

Roberts, Wayne. 2008. *The No-Nonsense Guide to World Food.* Toronto: New Internationalist/Between the Lines.

Sanderson, Steven. 1986. The Emergence of the 'World Steer:' Internationalization and Foreign Domination in Latin American Cattle Production. In *Food, the State and International Political Economy*, ed. F.L. Tullis and W.L. Hollist. Lincoln: University of Nebraska Press, 123–47.

Sharma, Nandita. 2006. *Home Economics: Nationalism and the Making Of 'Migrant Workers' in Canada.* Toronto: University of Toronto Press.

Steel, Carolyn. 2009. *Hungry City: How Food Shapes Our Lives.* Vintage.

Sustainable Development Commission. 2011. *Looking Back, Looking Forward: Sustainability and UK Food Policy 2000–2011.* London.

Tansey, Geoffrey. and Tasmin Rajotte (Eds). 2008. *The Future Control of Food: A Guide to International*

Negotiations and Rules on Intellectual Property, Biodiversity, and Food Security. London/Sterling, VA: Earthscan.

Taylor, J.P., S. Evers, and M. McKenna. 2005. 'Determinants of Healthy Eating in Children and Youth'. *Canadian Journal of Public Health* 96(suppl. 3): S20–6.

UNHCR. 1948. Universal Declaration of Human Rights. Accessed 2 April 2011 at http://daccess-dds-ny.un.org/doc/RESOLUTION/GEN/NR0/043/88/IMG/NR004388.pdf?OpenElement.

van der Ploeg, Jan Douwe. 2008. *The New Peasantries: Struggles for Autonomy and Sustainability in an Era of Empire and Globalization*. London/Sterling, VA: Earthscan.

Wall, Ellen. 1994. 'Farm Labour Markets and the Structure of Agriculture'. *The Canadian Review of Sociology and Anthropology* 31(1): 65–81.

Wallerstein, Immanuel. 1974. *The Modern World-System, Volume 1: Capitalist Agriculture and the Origins of the European World-Economy in the Sixteenth Century*. New York/London: Academic Press.

Weis, Tony. 2007. *The Global Food Economy: The Battle for the Future of Farming*. London/Halifax: Earthscan/Fernwood.

Wells, Miriam. 1996. *Strawberry Fields: Politics, Class, and Work in California Agriculture*. Ithaca, NY: Cornell University Press.

Wilkinson, John. 2006. 'Network Theories and Political Economy: From Attrition to Convergence?' In Terry Marsden and Jonathon Murdoch, eds. *Between the Local and the Global*. Amsterdam: Elsevier.

Winders, Bill. 2009. *The Politics of Food Supply: U.S. Agricultural Policy in the World Economy*. New Haven: Yale University Press.

Winson, Anthony. 1988. 'Researching the Food Chain: The Case of Nova Scotia'. *Canadian Review of Sociology and Anthropology* 25(4): 520–58.

Winson, Anthony. 1990. 'Capitalist Coordination of Agriculture: Food Processing Firms and Farming in Central Canada'. *Rural Sociology* 55(3): 376–94.

Winson, Anthony. 1993. *The Intimate Commodity: Food and the Development of the Canadian Agro-Industrial Complex*. Toronto: Garamond Press.

Winson, Anthony. 2004. 'Bringing Political Economy into the Debate on the Obesity Epidemic'. *Agriculture and Human Values* 21(4): 299–312.

Winson, Anthony. 2008. 'School Food Environments and the Obesity Issue: Content, Structural Determinants and Agency in Canadian High Schools'. *Agriculture and Human Values* 25(4): 499–511.

3

Canada's Food History Through Cookbooks

Nathalie Cooke

Learning Objectives

Through this chapter, you can:

1. Recognize cookbooks as offering more than cooking instruction, and look to them for insight into changing social roles (particularly within families and communities) and food tastes over time
2. Through examples of close reading of the titles and cookbook prefaces and introductions provided here, be alert and prepared to recognize moments when cookbooks identify their strategic objectives. After all, cookbooks are addressed to a particular audience for a particular purpose
3. Armed with a brief overview of five periods of Canadian history as seen through Canadian cookbooks, and introduced to some of the most significant Canadian cookbooks, place Canadian cookbooks you encounter going forward into the context of the complex history of Canadian foodways that includes moments of pivotal change often linked to successive waves of immigration

Introduction

What factors have influenced our eating habits over time in Canada? The question is not an innocent one, posed out of idle curiosity. Rather it is an urgent question, posed during a time when, despite the increasing knowledge about nutrition and health, we are unable to stem rising rates of obesity and illnesses born of poor dietary habits. We surely cannot identify how we make **food choices** today and improve our choices without understanding how and why we made food choices in the past. After all, most would agree that the goal of the home food provider is to serve fare that promotes health and well-being. But over the decades of the twentieth century alone, perceptions of how to achieve health and well-being have varied dramatically. For early Canadian settlers, for example, well-being meant a full belly. In the 1920s it depended upon milk, the 'perfect' food. By 1942, when Canada's dietary guidelines were introduced, it was perceived as resulting from a varied, full diet. By the 1980s, cookbook writers were promoting 'lighter fare' and guidelines to limit, rather than increase, Canadians' food intake. For those of us interested in charting the history and shaping of taste, food choices serve as a precise indicator of changing tastes and signal key factors motivating and defining moments of pivotal change. Canadian cookbooks, first published in 1840, serve as a window through which to glimpse changing food tastes and habits during the last 150 years.[1]

Overview

Canadian **foodways** have involved a fine balance between change and continuity, the adoption or refusal of exotic foods, food innovations, or new food traditions. This is true of the earliest days, when Europeans encountered the First Nations who had long made their home in what we now call Canada, to the dawning decades of the twenty-first century when we continue to revisit historical food practices. However, since a comprehensive overview of Canadian foodways is beyond the limited scope of this study, this chapter addresses the opening question—What factors have influenced our eating habits over time in Canada?—by looking closely at cookbooks, which are rich resources of information about foodways at a given time and place.

In À table en Nouvelle-France, Yvon Desloges, looking specifically at the foodways of New France and later Quebec, posits and credibly defends a framework of five periods of culinary practice:

1. 1605 to 1690, beginning when the first French settlers arrived and there was an encounter between French and Amerindian food practices
2. 1690 to 1790, when one ate 'à la française', or in the French style
3. 1790 to 1860, when there was an exchange between French and British foodways resulting from the influx of British in Quebec City following the fateful battle on the Plains of Abraham in 1759 during which both the victorious Britain's General James Wolfe and French General Louis Joseph de Montcalm

were mortally wounded in what is often described as the Conquest of New France
4. 1860 to 1960, when one ate 'à la canadienne', and the Dominion of Canada set about establishing its own distinctive traditions
5. 1967 to the present, when Canadian foodways were shaped by international culinary influences (145)

Desloges's model is effective in part because of its clear focus. However, as one ponders ways to expand the model beyond New France to reference Canadian foodways more generally, the notion of a singular Canadian culture becomes increasingly problematic. Under what conditions can we justifiably use the first person plural—'we Canadians'—about a country of such diversity? With a multicultural population formed by successive waves of immigrants from around the world, as well as the land's First Nations, skepticism about a singular culinary culture is understandable. Nevertheless, Canadian cookbook bibliographer Elizabeth Driver finds considerable evidence of similarity or homogeneity in varying degrees in cookbooks across regions and over time. She writes, 'I looked at over 2,200 individual works and noticed little regional variation in the form and content of the daily meal in works published before 1950' (Driver, Culinary Landmarks, 198). Further, after 1950, considerable energy and emotion have been spent in articulating a distinctively Canadian culinary tradition over the years—with an emphasis on the singular, and the **connotation** of commensality—'eating at the same table'—evoked by such a tradition. As Rhona Richman Kenneally points out, the centennial celebrations of 1967 prompted an outpouring of such nationalistic narratives, ironically at a time when Canada was recognizing not only its multicultural heritage but also its pride in the cultural wealth afforded by such a heritage (168–9). National distinctiveness is evoked in these narratives through reference to shared foodways traditions as well as reliance on specific and readily available ingredients (for example, the bacon colloquially dubbed 'Canadian bacon' outside Canada, salmon, maple syrup). Today, we might add a number of distinctively Canadian foods to the list because of their recent rise to **iconic** status: butter tarts; Nanaimo bars, named after a town on Vancouver Island; poutine, the cheese curd delicacy from Quebec that was the talk of the town in New York in 2007; deep-fried, yeast-raised beaver tails, best enjoyed in winter when skating on the Rideau Canal in Ottawa; or Tim Hortons doughnuts, named after the hockey legend.

The first pulse of Canada's desire to identify distinct food practices was felt in the nineteenth century, with the rise of the printing industry and literacy rates, and the emergence of cookbooks published in Canada and aimed at a specifically Canadian audience. This desire to distinguish things Canadian can be found in the title of one of the earliest cookbooks, *La cuisinière canadienne* (1840), as in many subsequent ones, including the classic 1923 *Canadian Cook Book* (the first edition of many). Also promoting a taste of place were recipes using locally sourced foods, such as those recorded by Lynn Thornton for rhubarb juice and partridge pie in *From the Kitchens of Kings Landing* (1995), a collection of recipes dating from nineteenth-century New Brunswick. This focus on local produce is all the more significant given that ingredients such as pineapple and recipes for curry in the 'Indian mode' in *The King's Daughters Cookery Book* (1904) suggest diverse influences and plentiful supplies of exotic foods very early on, at least on the Pacific coast of British Columbia.

By the mid twentieth century, it seems that many cookbook authors, in addition to assuming or identifying a national cuisine, wanted to share distinctive foodways traditions. Best known, perhaps, are the Mennonite cookbooks of Edna Staebler, including *Food That Really Schmecks* (1968). However, as Elizabeth Driver has found, ethnic foodways traditions began to be defined in cookbooks as early as the 1940s, either in separate sections in mainstream texts or in recipe manuals produced by ethnic groups. By the 1950s, a decade that sees an explosion

of culinary publications, Canada's cookbooks reveal a wealth of diverse food traditions through recipes for distinctive ethnic dishes appearing alongside those for the Anglo-Scots fare familiar to readers of Canadian cookbooks of the early twentieth century (Driver, 'Regional Differences', 206–7). Certainly by 1970, Canadian cookbooks catering to divergent palates and inclinations were the norm, and one must assume that Canadian meals featured an extraordinary diversity of food items as well.

Interestingly, there is considerable evidence to suggest that the sea change in food practice in the mid twentieth century—from homogeneity to diversity or from shared to distinctive tastes and habits—is not uniquely rooted in Canada's growing multiculturalism and its eventual official recognition, but rather to the zeitgeist of the times more generally, both in North America and abroad. In the years following the Second World War, soldiers who had tasted the culinary fare of other countries returned home. At the same time, Canadians prospered and began to travel for leisure; they also began to explore the world through the lens of their television screens. So despite the prescriptive emphasis on the nuclear family and traditional values articulated in magazine articles and advertisements, change was in the air. In an insightful analysis of New Zealand foodways, Michael Symons points to the 1960s as a time when the 'food industry shifted into a new mode' and suggests that 1963 marked a significant turning point in culinary traditions on his side of the world as well as our own (180–1).

Paradoxically, while Canadians increasingly tasted different foods from around the world after the Second World War, the rise of corporate advertising and technological innovation enabled efficient and affordable production of processed foods—big business promoting big brands. This development promoted increased normalization of food tastes and practices. For example, gelatine powder, introduced at the beginning of the twentieth century, dramatically reduced the preparation time of jellies. Not only was the gelatine powder produced and sold in Canada and the United States similar to that in New Zealand, but so too were the little cookbooklets promoting the 'dainty' dishes that could be prepared with this miraculous, versatile product.[2] Similarly, cake mixes were carefully developed to produce a successful cake in a variety of conditions; one wonders if there was a significant distinction between a cake made from a mix north of the 49th parallel and one to the south.

Certainly companies developing packaged foods were often multinational, with satellite or branch offices in various countries. Some companies would use a real or fictitious spokesperson to give themselves a 'human face' and appeal to local consumers. For example, Robin Hood Multifoods used the fictitious Rita Martin to promote its products. In Canada, Mrs. Lereine Ballantyne, who toured Canada under her own name leading cooking demonstrations to promote Robin Hood flour products from 1938 to 1943, was known to Canadians as 'Rita Martin's first assistant in the Dominion'.

Technological change affecting Canadian foodways can be traced through Canadian cookbooks. New cooking technologies were quickly followed by cookbooks to train home food providers in their use, such as *Speed Cooking with Your New General Electric GE Range* (1948), and the many works of Quebecers Norene Gilletz and Jehane Benoît introducing Canadians to cooking methods for the microwave oven and the food processor. Today's readers will find it ironic that *The Modern Cook Book*, compiled in 1923 by the Imperial Order Daughters of the Empire, looks to the past and the future through ads lauding the 'modern' convenience of the electric range in addition to ones extolling the virtues of gas and coal-fired stoves. Perhaps it was 'modern' precisely because the future must be seen in comparison with the past? Canadian cookbooks also record public policy changes, such as Canada's adoption of the metric system in the 1970s.

Similarly, promotional cookbooks document the introduction and use of specific food products.

Companies produced and distributed these cookbooks, incorporating recipes designed to highlight their own products, which were often featured in advertisements with the books. Published by the Kellogg Company, for example, *The Housewife's Almanac: A Book for Homemakers* (1938) advocates a regular diet of Kellogg's All-Bran cereal, along with a number of tips for homemakers in sections entitled 'How to Acquire and Develop Winning Ways' and 'The Canadian Wedding'.

Review of Literature and Commentary

As mentioned earlier, Canada's centennial celebrations in 1967, including Montreal's Expo '67, gave impetus to food studies in Canada by launching a period of intense introspection that continues to our own day. Canadians began to review and revise their culinary practices past and present—to figure food (sometimes retrospectively) as a symbol of self, community, and nation. Cookbooks began to appear on bedside tables and desks as well as on kitchen counters, and gained currency as signifiers of societal change rather than merely culinary handbooks.

During the past few decades, much light has been shed on Canada's food history to identify moments of pivotal change and continuity: first by cookbook writers and cooks in historical kitchens tasked with understanding and reproducing historical recipes; next by bibliographers and **culinary historians**; and most recently, as food studies has moved into colleges and universities, by scholars in such diverse disciplines as anthropology, cultural and communications studies, economics, geography, gastronomy, history, sociology, social studies of medicine, and women's studies.

How can we trace and precisely identify changes in the ways Canadians eat? Exploring the relationship between food choices and larger patterns of taste must rely on a wide and diverse range of cultural artifacts, as well as discursive and visual texts: recipes and cookbooks, novels, journals, maps, menus, product packaging and advertising, photos, postcards, and floor plans, to name only a few. Always present for the researcher is the danger of confusing **prescriptive practice**—what people are told or advised to do—and **descriptive practice**—what they actually do.

While an open set of possibilities is daunting to those determined to categorize and quantify, for those eager to become pioneers in the new field of Canadian food studies and to explore food and the shaping of taste, such breadth of possibility was nothing short of exhilarating. Certainly an enthusiasm for the range of possibilities is evident in the pioneering publication *A Century of Canadian Home Cooking* by Carol Ferguson and Margaret Fraser (1992). Pat Beeson's *Macdonald Was Late for Dinner* (1993) is another labour of love, containing historical photographs, menus, and recipes. Such pioneering enthusiasm was crucial in sustaining Elizabeth Driver in her quest to identify every cookbook longer than 16 pages published in Canada before 1950 (the final count was 2,276 titles, many published in several editions) for *Culinary Landmarks: A Bibliography of Canadian Cookbooks, 1825–1949*.

Enthusiasm also carried the day for librarians who countered institutional tendencies to privilege traditional areas for collection. It propelled Barbara Haber to collect cookbooks at Harvard's Schlesinger Library, for example, at a time when cookbooks and domestic papers were all too often dismissed as trivial, and led Barbara Ketcham Wheaton to embark on her ambitious database of early cookbooks, recipes, and their ingredients, which has grown into an incredibly rich resource. In Canada, also in the late 1970s, McGill University's Rare Books and Special Collections began to gather various kinds of ephemera, particularly from food companies, partially because, as the current librarian Richard Virr says, 'it came very cheap at a time when few recognized its significance'. Today, Montreal is home to two very strong cookbook collections, one in McGill's Rare Books and Special Collections Division, where the corporate ephemera is also housed, and the other at the McCord Museum. The University of Guelph is home to Una Abrahmson's fine private collection and the Canadian Cookbook Collection. Thanks to the foresight of its collections librarians, the Toronto Reference Library also boasts a solid collection of culinary works. But the real treasure trove of Canadian cookbooks and resources lies in private collections, themselves the product of passionate enthusiasm.

That the number of courses, colloquia, and publications relating to food history increased exponentially during the past two decades should not distract from the significant role earlier in the twentieth century of those passionate about food in Canada and its promotion. Well known were individuals who took on iconic status, such as Kate Aitken, Jehane Benoît, Soeur Sainte Marie Edith, Soeur Berthe, Soeur Angele, Elizabeth Baird, Anne Lindsay, and Rose Murray. Others appeared on stage or penned articles using pseudonyms including Edith Adams for the *Vancouver Sun*, Penny Powers for the Saskatchewan Power Corporation, Marie Fraser for the Dairy Food Services Bureau, Brenda York for Canada Packers, and Rita Martin for Robin Hood Multifoods. Food writers and journalists also played a crucial role in cementing the link between food and its various contexts, including Margo Oliver, author of *Classical Canadian Recipes* (1993), and food columnist Julian Armstrong, author of *Taste of Quebec* (1990), one of the best books delineating that province's contemporary cuisine. Incidentally, that Armstrong is a food writer using her own name, while her aunt a generation earlier wrote about food under a pseudonym, indicates the rapidly changing norms surrounding women's role in the workforce in mid-century Canada. *A Taste of History: The Origins of Quebec's Gastronomy* (1989) by historians Yvon Desloges and Marc Lafrance is another important source of information about Quebec foodways. Desloges's recent publication *À table en Nouvelle-France* (2009) mentioned earlier provides watershed insights gleaned from close scrutiny of imports and exports in Quebec's early history.

Publications, though, are only one way of sharing information about historical Canadian foodways. Some scholars, teachers, and enthusiasts also stage re-enactments in the country's many museum kitchens. Dorothy Duncan, co-editor of *Consuming Passions* (1990) and author of *Canadians at Table* (2006), is one such educator. Greater Toronto alone is home to Black Creek Pioneer Village, Montgomery's Inn, Spadina Museum Historic House, Fort York National Historic Site, Colborne Lodge, Scarborough Historical Museum, Mackenzie House, Gibson House Museum, Todmorden Mills Heritage Site, Campbell House Museum— all with active historical culinary recreationists.

Another key forum of discussion was the 1993 conference 'Northern Bounty', which gave rise to a collection of essays by culinary professionals and writers of the same title, edited by Jo Marie Powers and Anita Stewart (1995) and also served to launch the organization Cuisine Canada. Carol Ferguson and Margaret Fraser's *A Century of Canadian Home Cooking* and Dorothy Duncan's *Canadians at Table* represent the most comprehensive discussion of Canadian foodways to date. While Ferguson and Fraser provide an illustrated overview of what was happening in Canadian kitchens through the decades of the twentieth century—in a remarkably handsome book that, admittedly, first piqued my interest in the subject—Duncan provides an accessible and engaging introduction to food's role in directing the course of Canadian history. For example, she explains how the outcome of competition between the two titans of the fur trade—the North West Company and the Hudson's Bay Company— hinged on pemmican, a lowly food substance invaluable to those travelling great distances, made from powdered dried meat mixed with berries and sealed in a bag with grease (49–50). This analysis stands in my mind as one of the best examples of how focusing on an often overlooked food item can give rise to profound insights.[3]

Canada is also lucky to have a number of cookbook writers whose work provides readers with a glimpse into regional history: Marie Nightingale's *Out of Old Nova Scotia Kitchens* (1971) is a fine example. Beulah (Bunny) Barss, through illustrated cookbooks, draws her readers into an understanding of pioneering foodways in Alberta (see, for example, the 1988 *Alberta Pictorial Cookbook*). More recently, in *Flavours of Canada* (2000), Anita Stewart provides an updated and lavishly illustrated overview of Canada's diverse bounty and the recipes developed to celebrate it, a theme emerging as well in *Anita Stewart's Canada—the Food, the Recipes, the Stories* (2008). Rose Murray's *A Taste of Canada* (2008) provides an enjoyable and educational introduction to the regional variety of Canada's foods and fascinating insights into Canada's food history. It is from Murray, for example, that we learn that canning was revolutionized and popularized by the patenting of the Mason jar in 1858 (161) and that buffalo hump and moose nose featured on the Christmas menu served at Fort Edmonton in 1847 (59).

The Form and Function of Cookbooks

Astonishingly, only very recently have commentators in Canada and elsewhere begun to scrutinize the form and function of cookbooks, posing such questions as: What is a cookbook? Is a collection of recipes different in degree or in kind from a single recipe? What kinds of meaning do cookbooks convey?

One wonders whether the lack of a clear definition for the cookbook **genre** is less the result of scholarly trepidation than of scholarly elitism. After all, cookbooks have never ranked in the heady, literary stratospheres of genres like epic or lyric poetry, or even prose fiction. They do not participate in what Anne Bower (1997) calls the 'status-bearing' forms of literature. Nor is a particular cookbook yet identified as a 'classic' in the literary sense: 'a work considered excellent of its kind, and therefore standard, fit to be used as a model or imitated'.[4] Certainly, Ann Mendelson's *Stand Facing the Stove* strives to bestow a particular status upon the American favourite, *The Joy of Cooking*. However, her argument focuses on the attributes of this cookbook that rendered it more popular than its peers, thereby asserting its authority as a bestseller rather than a classic. Further, since cookbooks strive to be timely as well as timeless, it is difficult for such a genre to produce a classic work, which, by definition, transcends time.

Thus positioned outside or, at best, on the margins of the literary taxonomy, cookbooks have not been deemed worthy of literary scrutiny—that is, until recently. Full-length discussions of literary texts containing food scenes have begun to appear.[5] Also, and more importantly for this study, two useful discussions of a key component of cookbooks—the recipe—have surfaced in *PMLA*, the well-respected journal of the Modern Language Association of America. The first was Susan Leonardi's 'Lobster à la Riseholme,' and the second was David Herman's 'Scripts, Sequences, and Stories: Elements of a Postclassical Narratology'. Neither one mentions earlier attempts at defining the recipe, thus clearly distinguishing their particular literary inquiry from earlier approaches. Of these very few earlier commentaries, perhaps the most influential was M.F.K. Fisher's project of describing the three distinct parts of the 'modern' recipe's 'anatomy': the name, the ingredients, and the method (23).

What Is a Recipe?[6]

In her widely influential article, Susan Leonardi looks at the contexts of recipe giving, and in so doing, affords us a sense of what a recipe is. She begins by arguing that recipes are a form of 'embedded discourse' that generally stems from a particular context. She clearly states that her focus is on the 'giving of the recipe' (340) rather than on the list of ingredients and the directions for assembling them because, as she puts it, 'such a list alone is, in fact, surprisingly useless, even for a fairly experienced cook, and surprisingly seldom encountered' (340). This narrative frame is what linguist Colleen Cotter would call 'orientation components' (60). Leonardi points out that 'like a story, a recipe needs a recommendation, a context, a point, a reason to be' (340). For Leonardi, then, the conventions of the recipe genre include

- 'a persona' for the recipe giver with whom 'readers could identify and trust' (347)
- 'the possibility of literalization outside the text' (346)
- the use of second-person address, of the 'you' (347)

While Leonardi focuses on the recipe as a way of connecting people, narratologist David Herman focuses on the recipe as something that can make things happen, that can function as an agent of transformation. For Herman, a recipe, such as:

Remove pizza from box and inner wrapper. . . . [and] place on preheated cookie sheet. Bake for 16–18 minutes or until center cheese is melted and edges are golden brown

is a sequence that can be identified as a recipe because it 'tells not how something happened, in the manner of a story, but rather how to make something (good) happen, in the manner of a prescription or, more precisely, a recipe' (1047). Thus, for Herman, the conventions of a recipe include:

- prescriptive language that anticipates, describes, and directs literalization beyond the text
- like 'telling narratives', 'describing', 'arguing', and 'greeting'—this prescriptive language allows the reader or recipient to reconcile 'emergent with prior knowledge' (1048)

Leonardi and Herman agree that recipes direct attention beyond their own text to the possibility of a future event—the preparation of the described dish. In so doing, they establish an affective relationship with the recipient. Where the two scholars dramatically differ is in their location of agency, that is, their sense of where the action in and of a recipe takes place.

What Is a Cookbook?

Drawing on Leonardi's and Herman's observations, we could define a cookbook as a sequence of prescriptive narratives that

- anticipate culinary realization outside the text
- are disseminated within a particular context that is signalled by the text in the form of an implied author (via the first-person pronoun) and reader (signalled, and called into existence, by the second-person pronoun 'you').

Thus, a primary emphasis on the dissemination of practical information seems to distinguish cookbooks from other forms of food-related texts, including the four categories of 'literary-culinary offspring' informally defined by Anne LeCroy: general histories of human cuisine; essays with illustrative recipes; recipes introduced by metaphysical commentary; and fiction using recipes as vehicles for the development of plot, character, or setting (8). As Lynette Hunter observes, 'any literary study of cookery books comes up against the fact that they exist primarily to communicate information and opinion, not as literary objects in and of themselves' (19). A primary emphasis on prescription, then, seems to distinguish cookbooks from *literary* texts, which privilege aesthetic over practical concerns or, to put it another way, art over science. Nonetheless, commentators cannot ignore how recipes prompt readers to react and to act. Colleen Cotter, for example, acknowledges 'one way to look at a

recipe is as a form of narrative—a particular kind of storytelling—and viewing it formally and structurally as a narrative enriches our reading of it' (52). If a recipe is so framed and mediated, then how much more so must be a collection of recipes, organized by prefatory comments? If a recipe can call up a cast of at least two characters, then how many more can be conjured in a whole cookbook?

If, however, one scrutinizes Canadian cookbooks' own claims about the genre (often articulated in a preface or introduction), one finds claims and aspirations that challenge the privileging of practical and pragmatic concerns over aesthetic ones. The most explicit assertions that cooking is an art, and not a mere skill or craft, appear in the French-language cookbooks. For example, in the 1957 edition of *La cuisine raisonnée*, cooking is described as a science and an art, related to the sciences of anatomy, physics, and chemistry, as well as hygiene. This cooking manual insists that cooking, albeit a science, is also an aesthetic outlet for women, who can exercise their aesthetic tastes (vii). In the tenth edition of the same cookbook, Canadian cuisine is elevated to an art form that takes into account the emergent scientific and nutritional knowledge, as well as cultural values and socioeconomic norms (11).

If *La cuisine raisonnée* seems to put a heavy onus on the woman of the house to practise the art of cooking, it is nothing compared with the responsibilities bestowed by that formidable pillar of virtue, Mère Caron. As the figurehead of the Institute of Providence community at Longue-Pointe, Montreal, Quebec, the Reverend Mother urges women not only to practise the culinary art, but also to become the model of Christian virtue. She stresses that a cook can be 'truly Christian' because cooking requires patience, and that in old religious communities, the cook was the perfect model of all saintly virtues (7). These precepts appear in the 1878 edition, as well as in subsequent editions. In other words, they are aspirations unchanged by changing times.

Aesthetic aspirations, however, are not exclusive to the French-language cookbooks. In her domestic science textbook, Nellie Lyle Pattinson emphasizes the 'art of cooking', instead of positioning cooking as 'only one more job to be done' (v). While English-language cookbooks also claim in their introductions that giving practical instructions is a means to higher ends, these ends are typically ideological rather than purely aesthetic.

One of those ideological ends is certainly the promotion of Canadian nationalism. However, the first Canadian cookbook published (*The Cook not Mad; or Rational Cookery*) was a reprint of an American book, whose authority depended on its wholesome 'Americanness'; it contains 'Good *Republican dishes* and garnishing, proper to fill an every day bill of fare' (7). Another US import was a community cookbook entitled *The Home Cook Book*. It was nonetheless substantially revised by a committee of Toronto ladies and includes an introductory letter to the publisher by prominent Canadian editor and author George Stewart Jr. He suggests that the book has the potential to 'supply the place of the Academy', which is crucial he argues, because 'the subject of cookery is of *national* importance' (v).

These preliminary observations not only suggest that cookbooks lay heavy expectations upon the shoulders of the home food producer, but also signal that Leonardi's sense of recipes as needing 'a recommendation, a context, a point, a reason to be' (127)—rings true for cookbooks as well as recipes. More generally, our understanding of the cookbook genre must as well enable us to understand it as a strategy rather than as a category of textual communication, one that is ideologically loaded rather than neutral.

Exceptions or Further Evidence?

Before accepting the conclusion that cookbooks employ rhetorical techniques to achieve aesthetic or ideological ends rather than merely giving instructions to achieve a tangible and practical goal, we should pause to scrutinize two seeming exceptions, both important to the Canadian cookbook **canon**.

The first of these is a group of cookbooks whose authority resides in the personal cooking experience of their authors, following in the tradition of Catharine Parr Traill's *The Female Emigrant's Guide* (1854). These books carefully resist elevating culinary responsibilities to the realm of higher aesthetic or ideological purposes; yet, they comply with Leonardi's sense that recipes need to be 'given', in that they contextualize their contents in a way that affects the reader. These cookbooks offer knowledge garnered from practical experience, and invite readers to accept their authors as authorities because of that experience. For example, in *Mrs. Clarke's Cookery Book* (1883), Anne Clarke provides recipes that are 'useful'. In *The Dominion Home Cook Book*,[7] the anonymous author provides recipes of 'practical utility' and, ironically, adds that '*every recipe,—every advice—every little piece of information, is the result of personal experience*' (4). Mrs Flynn claims that her Charlottetown cookbook of about 1930 (Driver, *Culinary Landmarks*, 70) is 'thoroughly practical', and provides the 'choicest bits of the best experience of those who have long traveled the daily round of household duties' (Lewis, *Mrs Flynn's Cookbook*, 3). Even the title page of a francophone cookbook, the third edition of *La cuisinière bourgeoise* (first published in 1746), proudly notes that the text has been reviewed by a housewife. In some ways, these claims are far less modest than those made by cookbook authors who invite their readers to join with them in their struggle to achieve religious, aesthetic, and nationalistic goals. But there is something very engaging about the first-person appeal of a cookbook author who claims first-hand kitchen know-how, even if her readers discover that she is skilled working with words as well as with food.

The second exception includes some of the most significant cookbooks in the Canadian canon, that is, if one judges success on the basis of sales and successive new editions alone: namely, the corporate cookbooklets mentioned earlier.[8]

This type of cookbook emerged with the rise of food manufacturing in the twentieth century, and often featured the 'personal' testimonies of fictional corporate 'spokespersons', some of whom, like the well-known North American Betty Crocker, actually 'author' the cookbooks that contain 'their' recipes and advice.[9] Although these were not real people, they served to put a human face on the corporate identity and created the illusion of being trustworthy and personable advisors for the home food provider. Speaking for Maple Leaf Foods, Anna Lee Scott, for example, claimed to have been 'a dietitian, lecturer and adviser on household science' for many years (*51 Ways to a Man's Heart*); while Rita Martin appears as simply an extremely friendly and approachable woman—'just drop me a line. . . . I'd love to hear from you' (*The Velvet Touch*). Martha Logan writes that, 'We . . . and I mean myself and the other Home Economists who assist me. . . . spend most of our time in the kitchen just as you do' (*Meat Complete* 3).

Rather than privileging a particular claim to authority, these cookbooks claim *multiple* authoritative sources such as

- the objective authority of science and innovation
- first-hand experience in the kitchen
- rigorous tests performed in industry food laboratories
- an intimate understanding of the tastes and inclinations of the home food provider and her family

They also take advantage of the affective aspects of conventional cookbooks, and exaggerate them by fabricating a fictional cookbook author. For example, Mary Blake of Carnation explains in 'her' 1924 cookbook: 'My own favorite recipes are contained here-in, one hundred of them, and I can promise that you will find them all thoroughly practical'.[10] The introduction is signed by Blake, who allegedly works for the Domestic Science Department of Carnation Milk Products Company. Mary maintains her

professional role but engages the attention of her readers by employing the first-person singular: 'All of these recipes have been carefully tested in the Carnation kitchen, I am sure you will like them' (2). This sense of certainty results both from the corporate backing of a company that tests its products and recipes extensively, and a culture awed by technology and the promise of modernity. The popular Five Roses cookbooks also tread a fine line between personal experience and corporate collaboration. For example, one notes that recipes are drawn from 'successful users of Five Roses Flour throughout Canada,' but also maintains that they are 'carefully checked and re-checked by [a] competent authority' (*Five Roses Cook Book*). The fictitious Anna Lee Scott is the authority for both Maple Leaf Milling's brand, Monarch Flour, and Purity Flour in the late 1950s. 'She' claims to be an authority not only on baking, but also, as the title of her book *51 Ways to a Man's Heart* suggests, on things beyond the cooking world. A letter on the book's back cover, which bears an illustration of Scott and her 'signature' reads: 'It is many years since I began as a dietitian lecturer and adviser on household science'. Rita Martin, a name that translates into French ever so easily with a shift in pronunciation, plays a similar role for Robin Hood Flour. Only Ogilvie Flour resisted this trend of putting a particular name, signature, or face to a corporation, as the company provided an unnamed 'expert woman' to give advice for *Ogilvie's Book for a Cook* (5). Ironically, Ogilvie claimed to be both the manufacturer of flour of royal households and the publisher of recipes that suit the needs of the 'average housekeeper . . . without calling too much upon her means' (2).

Thus we find two seeming exceptions to the rule that cookbooks are highly mediated forms of communication—the cookbook author's claim to personal first-hand experience, and the multiple, often paradoxically conflicting claims such as those appearing in the corporate cookbooks. But, as further scrutiny here shows, these examples clearly serve to reinforce my suggestion that a cookbook is a strategic offering of a collection of recipes within a particularized context, and further illustrate the constructed and highly contrived nature of that context.

Historical Transformation of the Cookery Books

Armed with the understanding that cookbooks are consciously shaped communications, we can view Canadian history through the lens of these books. When we do so, five different periods emerge—contact and settlement; consolidation; affiliation; articulation; and differentiation[11]—each with its canon of prescriptions for the way a Canadian kitchen and household might best be managed. Rising literacy rates coincided with the first heavy waves of Canadian immigration and settlement; thus cookery that declared itself to be distinctively 'Canadian' was largely founded on the printed page rather than passed down through the generations by word of mouth. As such, its formational history differs significantly from its culinary forebears—the Old World traditions of French and British cuisines, and American cuisine—and indeed from the long transmission of indigenous knowledge of the Aboriginals of North America.

Contact and Settlement

In the mid nineteenth century, the first Canadian cookbooks emerged as guidebooks for newly arrived Canadians, the best-known being Catharine Parr Traill's *The Female Emigrant's Guide* (1854) and A.B. of Grimsby's *Frugal Housewife's Manual* (1840), as well as *La cuisinière canadienne* (May 1840) and *La nouvelle cuisinière canadienne* (1850). While immigrants certainly carried with them cookbooks from the Old World, these first Canadian cookbooks were self-conscious about their role as New World texts constructed for those intending to make a life in the New World. Traill writes, '[I] confine my recipes to dishes that are more

peculiar to the cookery of Canada' (126) and 'This is not a regular cookery book; but is confined to the preparing of food, as practiced in this country' (153).

Consolidation

During the last decades of the nineteenth century, cookbooks served to consolidate knowledge gleaned from various sources for Canadian home cooks. The best known of these include *The Home Cook Book* (1877), *Canadian Housewife's Manual of Cookery* (1861), *Mrs. Clarke's Cookery Book* (1883), and *Directions diverses données par la Rev. Mère Caron* (1878). The consolidation of culinary knowledge in this period was intended to serve the Canadian cook in her kitchen, but it was also the first step in a larger program of consolidation that would both give rise to a sense of a distinctly Canadian cuisine and position cookbooks as useful vehicles for the articulation of Canadian tastes and values. In some ways, then, the period of consolidation might be seen to extend to the latter half of the twentieth century, reaching a crescendo in 1967.

As guides on household management, these books often contain advice on decorum. *The Home Cook Book*, a fundraising project for the Hospital for Sick Children in Toronto, and notable as the first example of the fundraising genre of cookbooks to be published in Canada, has sections on 'Housekeeping', 'Table Talk', 'The Little Housekeepers', and 'Social Observances'. Although intended as practical manuals for household management in the nineteenth century, for twenty-first–century readers they provide valuable insights into domestic ritual, supplies and their availability in different regions of Canada and at different times in its history, advances in technology and nutritional science, and shifts in taste and philosophy.

Affiliation

At the beginning of the twentieth century, many of the cookbooks that emerged were affiliated with institutions rather than individuals. Such corporate cookbooks as *Five Roses Cook Book/La cuisinière Five Roses* (1913), as well as those of the Purity and Ogilvie flour companies, became valued resources in Canadian homes. Further, single-author cookbooks gained credibility from their association with educational institutions. Nellie Lyle Pattinson, for example, developed the trusted *The Canadian Cook Book* (1923) as a textbook for the cooking school of which she was director; similarly, in Quebec the popular *Manuel de cuisine raisonnée* (1919) was used in homes and classrooms.

These textbooks found audiences outside the classroom throughout the twentieth century. In October 2004, the Quebec newspaper *La Presse* surveyed readers about their favourite cookbooks. Both the classic *Five Roses Cookbook* and the 1945 classic *La cuisine raisonnée* made the shortlist, with rationales explaining their trustworthy and timeless recipes. One reader comments:

> My preferred book is *La cuisine raisonnée* by the Congrégation Notre-Dame. I have had it since 1962. I find it practical, with simple and economical recipes. I raised my daughters with this cooking, and if somebody asks me for cooking tips, this is where I find them. This book is invaluable. It is the oldest one I have. (qtd in Marquis, 'The Cookbook Quebecers Prefer', 221)

Articulation

Home economics was professionalized in Canada in 1939. As home economists took up positions not only as teachers and dieticians, but also as corporate and public spokespeople, cookbooks—alongside radio and, later, television shows—served as a conduit for the articulation of Canadian identity. Cookbooks by Kate Aitken (fondly known as 'Mrs A.' to her audiences), such as *Kate Aitken's Canadian Cook Book* (1945), and by Jehane Benoît (or 'Mme B.'), such as *L'encyclopédie de la cuisine canadienne* (1963), stirred an emerging sense of shared national identity. At first glance, then, what characterizes this period is the clearly articulated vision of a distinctively Canadian cuisine. Another form of articulation appeared in this period, one that has received virtually no scrutiny to date. Culinary authorities of this time—and both Mrs A. and Mme B. are excellent examples—began to establish themselves as significant forces in the culinary scene in their own right under their own names, instead of being the public face of a corporate or educational institution, as in the period of affiliation. Kate Aitken, for example, used her own name and became one of the best-known and best-loved cookbook writers and radio personalities of her day. Jehane Benoît was notable for her ability to reach beyond Quebec to an English-language audience; she became a trusted advisor for Canadians from coast to coast. During a period of transition in women's roles during the mid twentieth century, it is fascinating to note that one might see fictional corporate spokespersons sharing the spotlight, quite literally, with their 'real-life' counterparts who worked under their own names. Christine Hindson, who portrayed Swift's Martha Logan, explained to me: 'I did cooking schools in Vancouver [and the] Montreal Forum with Jehane Benoît with 10,000 people at each of those shows. Stores selling our products would give out the tickets, and the grand prize would be a stove. Overhead cameras. . . . a very exciting time. I never imagined myself spinning these wonderful tales and making a pie at the same time'.

Differentiation

During a time of increasing normalization of foodways traditions internationally, the distinctive food traditions of French-speaking Canadians highlighted the differences between Canada and other countries—most obviously its neighbour to the south. Indeed, Canada's centennial celebrations ushered in an era of cultural branding north of the 49th parallel. The appearance of *Canadian* in the titles of cookbooks published around 1967 may have underlined a shared sense of identity, but the 1960s paradoxically ushered in an era of increasing differentiation, evident in cookbooks that focused on regional and cultural variations in foodways practices. These competing drives—towards identification and differentiation—are always at play to some degree in the shaping of foodways, but their co-existence was most acutely visible in Canadian cookbooks of the 1960s and 1970s (Cooke, *What's to Eat?*, 4–6).

Conclusion

Why then should we pay attention to books that describe what Canadians have eaten in bygone days? One compelling answer is surely that cuisine is a story told through the medium of food. Cookbooks, by recording and attempting to shape the cuisine of a community or region at a particular time, tell us the diverse stories of the lived history of a people. If we pay attention to the stories about the foods Canadians have chosen to eat and to share with those around them, and learn to read and make sense of them, then our culinary storytelling will become increasingly rich and complex, as will our sense of who Canadians have wanted to be.

Discussion Questions

1. Identify some key factors influencing Canadians' food choices.

2. How have Canadian cookbooks changed since their first appearance in the mid nineteenth century?

3. What are some of Canada's iconic foods?

4. Give one example of how one might view Canadian history through the lens of a particular food item.

5. How might one define 'Canadian cuisine'?

Further Reading

(listed by date of publication)

1. Ferguson, Carol and Margaret Fraser. *A Century of Canadian Home Cooking: 1900 through the '90s*. Scarborough, ON: Prentice-Hall, 1992.

   An illustrated guide to the shifting food tastes in each decade of the twentieth century.

2. Driver, Elizabeth. *Culinary Landmarks: A Bibliography of Canadian Cookbooks, 1825–1949*. Toronto: U of Toronto P, 2008.

   The first and only bibliography of Canadian cookbooks, this is an indispensible resource tool.

3. Cooke, Nathalie, ed. *What's to Eat?: Entrées in Canadian Food History*. Montreal: McGill-Queen's UP, 2009.

   A collection of articles focusing on Canadian food history—what foods Canadians chose to eat and the meanings ascribed to particular food choices. The introduction offers a way of glimpsing Canadian history through the lens of Canadian cookbooks, developing the five-stage framework introduced here.

4. Desloges, Yvon. *À Table en Nouvelle-France*. Quebec: Septentrion, 2009.

Drawing on primary archival research, Desloges provides a close reading of the foodways of New France from the moment of first contact between North American Aboriginals and European explorers in what is now Quebec through the Conquest of 1760. For those requiring information in English, see Yvon Desloges and Marc Lafrance, *A Taste of History, the Origins of Quebec's Gastronomy— Goûter à l'histoire, les origines de la gastronomie québécoise*. Ottawa: Service canadien des parcs et les Éditions de la Chenelière, 1989.

Notes

1. For additional perspectives on the (hi)stories Canadian cookbooks tell, see Cooke's 'Cookbooks and Culture'.
2. For further scrutiny of similarities and differences between corporate cookbooklets across continents, see Cooke's 'Cookbooklets and Canadian Kitchens'.
3. Bernard Assiniwi's historical perspective on Aboriginal cuisine, the illustrated *Recettes indiennes et survie en forêt*, provides additional insights.
4. See 'classicism, classic' in *The Concise Oxford Companion to English Literature*, ed. Margaret Drabble and Jenny Stringer (New York: Oxford UP, 2007, 139). Originally, the term *classic* referred to the writer rather than to the work. 'A classic, according to the usual definition, is an old author canonised by admiration, and an authority in his particular style' (Charles Augustin Sainte-Beuve, 'What is a Classic?', *Literary and Philosophical Essays*, Vol. XXXII. New York: P.F. Collier & Son, 1909, 14). Interestingly, individuals have been identified as authorities in the culinary world (Julia Child; Fannie Farmer in the United States; Mere Caron and Jehane Benoît in French Canada) in a way that particular cookbooks have not.
5. For example, see Anna Shapiro, *A Feast of Words* (New York: Norton, 1996), Diane McGee, *Writing the Meal* (Toronto: U of Toronto P, 2001), and Sarah Sceats, *Food, Consumption, and the Body in Contemporary Women's Fiction* (Cambridge: Cambridge UP, 2000).
6. For a discussion relating these definitions of the recipe to the genre of poetry, see Nathalie Cooke, 'Recipes and Poems', in Culture savante-culture populaire; reprises, recyclages, récupération, ed. J.J. Chardin, RANAM 43 (Strasbourg, 2010), 87–8.
7. This is the title of some later editions of Clarke's cookbooks, but this particular *Dominion Home Cook Book* is unrelated to Clarke's text.
8. For a discussion of the form and function of the implied author in corporate cookbooks, see also Nathalie Cooke, 'Recipes and Poems', in Culture savante-culture populaire; reprises, recyclages, récupération, ed. J.J. Chardin, RANAM 43 (Strasbourg, 2010), 89–90.
9. For a more detailed discussion of the corporate spokespersons or 'fictional food folk' see Cooke, 'Getting the Mix Just Right for the Canadian Home Baker'.
10. Mary Blake is of course 'American' (if a fictitious person can indeed have a nationality) as indicated by the American spelling of *favorite*; however, through the Carnation Company's publication and dissemination of corporate ephemera in Canada, she was a well-known visitor to Canadian homes.
11. See also the Introduction of Cooke's *What's to Eat?* for a more expansive discussion of this concept and the way it gives rise to our current culinary introspection.

Works Cited

A.B. of Grimsby. *The Frugal Housewife's Manual*. Toronto: 1840.

Aitken, Kate. *Kate Aitken's Canadian Cook Book*. Montreal: The Standard, 1945.

Armstrong, Julian. *A Taste of Quebec*. Toronto: Macmillan, 1990.

Assiniwi, Bernard. *Recettes indiennes et survie en forêt*. Montreal: Leméac, 1972.

Barss, Bunny. *Alberta Pictorial Cookbook*. Halifax: Nimbus, 1988.

Beeson, Patricia. *Macdonald Was Late for Dinner: A Slice of Culinary Life in Early Canada*. Peterborough: Broadview Press, 1993.

Benoît, Jehane. *L'encyclopédie de la cuisine canadienne*. Montreal: Les Messageries de Saint-Laurent 1963.

———. *La cuisine canadienne*. Montreal: Éditions du Jour, 1979.

Berg, Jennifer. 'Icon Foods'. *Encyclopedia of Food and Culture*. Vol. 2. New York: Charles Scribner's Sons, 2002. 243–4.

———. 'From Pushcart Peddlers to Gourmet Take-Out: New York City's Iconic Foods of Jewish Origin, 1920 to 2005'. PhD Dissertation. New York University, 2006.

Blake, Mary. *My Hundred Favorite Recipes*. Toronto: Carnation, 1924.

Bower, L. Anne. 'Bound Together: Recipes, Lives, Stories, and Readings'. Introduction. *Recipes for Reading: Community Cookbooks, Stories, Histories*. Ed. Anne L. Bower. Amherst: U of Massachusetts P, 1997. 1–14.

The Carnation Year Book of Menus and Recipes. Toronto: Carnation, n.d. (likely 1935–1937; see Driver, *Culinary Landmarks*).

Caron, [Emmelie]. *Directions diverses donées par la Rev. Mère Caron pour aider ses soeurs à former de bonnes cuisinières*. 1st edn. Montreal: n.p., 1878.

Clarke, Anne. *Mrs. Clarke's Cookery Book*. Toronto: Grip, 1883.

Clow, Meribeth, Dorothy Duncan, Glenn J. Lockwood, and Lorraine Lowry, eds. *Consuming Passions: Eating and Drinking Traditions in Ontario*. Willowdale: Ontario Historical Society, 1990.

The Cook not Mad; or Rational Cookery. Kingston: James Macfarlane, 1831. Reprint. ed. Roy Abrahamson. Toronto: Cherry Tree Press, 1973.

Cooke, Nathalie. 'Cookbooks and Culture'. *Encyclopedia of Literature in Canada*. Ed. W.H. New. Toronto: U of Toronto P, 2002.

———. 'Getting the Mix Just Right for the Canadian Home Baker'. *Essays on Canadian Writing* 78 (Winter 2003): 192–219.

———. 'Introduction'. *What's to Eat?: Entrées in Canadian Food History*. Ed. Nathalie Cooke. Montreal: McGill-Queen's UP, 2009, 3–17.

———. 'Cookbooklets and Canadian Kitchens'. *Material Culture Review* 70 (August 2010): 22–33.

———. 'Poems and recipes: What do these two magpie modes have in common?' *ranam, recherches anglaises et nord américaines* 43 (September 2010; published by the Université de Strasbourg, France): 65–82.

Cotter, Colleen. 'Claiming a Piece of the Pie'. *Recipes for Reading*. Ed. Anne L. Bower. Amherst: U of Massachusetts P, 1997. 51–72.

La cuisine raisonnée. 8th edn (first edition 1919). Quebec: Congregation de Notre-Dame de Montreal, 1957.

La cuisine raisonnée. 10th edn (first edition 1919). Montreal: Éditions Fides, 1967.

La cuisinière bourgeoise. 3rd edn (first edition 1746). Quebec: Augustin Germain, 1825.

La cuisinière canadienne. Montreal: Louis Perrault, 1840.

Davidson, Alan. *The Oxford Companion to Food*. Oxford: Oxford UP, 1999.

Desloges, Yvon. *À table en Nouvelle-France*. Quebec: Septentrion, 2009.

Desloges, Yvon, and Marc Lafrance. *A Taste of History, the Origins of Quebec's Gastronomy—Goûter à l'histoire, les origines de la gastronomie québécoise*. Ottawa: Service canadien des parcs et les Éditions de la Chenelière, 1989.

The Dominion Home Cook Book. Toronto: Adam Miller, 1868.

Driver, Elizabeth. *Culinary Landmarks: A Bibliography of Canadian Cookbooks, 1825–1949*. Toronto: U of Toronto P, 2008.

———. 'Regional Differences in the Canadian Daily Meal? Cookbooks Answer the Question'. *What's to Eat?: Entrées in Canadian Food History*. Ed. Nathalie Cooke. Montreal: McGill-Queen's UP, 2009. 197–212.

Duncan, Dorothy. *Canadians at Table: Food, Fellowship and Folklore: A Culinary History of Canada*. Toronto: Dundurn, 2006.

Farmer, Fannie. *The Boston Cooking-School Cook Book*. Boston: Little, Brown, 1896.

Ferguson, Carol, and Margaret Fraser. *A Century of Canadian Home Cooking: 1900 through the '90s*. Scarborough: Prentice-Hall, 1992.

Fisher, M.F.K. 'Anatomy of a Recipe'. *With Bold Knife and Fork*. Ed. M.F.K. Fisher. New York: G.P. Putnam's Sons, 1968.

Five Roses Cook Book. Montreal: Lake of the Woods Milling, 1913.

The Grist, Published for all employees by International Milling Company, Robin Hood Flour Mills Limited (Fall 1951), 8.

A Guide to Good Cooking from the Makers of Five Roses Flour. Rev. and enl. edn. Montreal: Lake of the Woods Milling Company, 1938.

A Guide to Good Cooking with Five Roses Flour. Rev. edn. Montreal: Lake of the Woods Milling Company, 1954.

Herman, David. 'Scripts, Sequences, and Stories: Elements of a Postclassical Narratology'. *PMLA* 112.5 (1997): 1046–59.

Hindson, Christine. Interview with the author. 13 September 2003.

The Home Cook Book. Toronto: Belford Brothers, 1877.

The Housewife's Almanac. London: Kellogg Company of Canada, 1938.

Hunter, Lynette. 'Cookery Books: A Cabinet of Rare Devices and Conceits'. *Petits Propos Culinaires* 5 (May 1980): 19–34.

Kenneally, Rhona Richman. '"There *is* a Canadian Cuisine, and it is Unique in All the World": Crafting National Food Culture During the Long 1960s'. *What's to Eat?: Entrées in Canadian Food History*. Ed. Nathalie Cooke. Montreal: McGill-Queen's UP, 2009.167–96.

La nouvelle cuisinière canadienne. Montreal: Louis Perrault, 1850.

LeCroy, Anne. 'Cookery Literature: Or Literary Cookery'. *Cooking by the Book*. Ed. Mary Anne Schofield. Bowling Green: Bowling Green State UP, 1989. 7–24.

Leonardi, Susan. 'Recipes for Reading: Summer Pasta, Lobster à la Riseholme, and Key Lime Pie'. *PMLA* 104.3 (1989): 340–7. Reprinted in *Cooking by the Book*. Ed. Mary Anne Schofield. Bowling Green: Bowling Green State UP, 1989. 126–38.

Lewis, Katherine C. *Mrs. Flynn's Cookbook*. Charlottetown: Ladies of St. Vincent's Orphanage and Society in Aid of St. Vincent's Orphanage. Reprint. Charlottetown: P.E.I. Heritage Foundation, 1981.

Marquis, Marie. 'The Cookbook Quebecers Prefer: More than Just Recipes'. *What's to Eat?: Entrées in Canadian Food History*. Ed. Nathalie Cooke. Montreal: McGill-Queen's UP, 2009, 213–27.

McDougall, Elizabeth J. 'Voices, Stories, and Recipes in Selected Canadian Community Cookbooks'. *Recipes for Reading: Community Cookbooks, Stories, Histories*. Ed. Anne L. Bower. Amherst: U of Massachusetts P, 1997. 105–17.

McMicking, Mrs Margaret Leigton, compiler. *The King's Daughters Cookery Book*. Victoria: Banfield, 1904.

Manuel de cuisine raisonnée adapté aux élèves des cours élémentaires de l'école normale classico-ménagère de Saint-Pascal. Quebec: Imprimerie l'Action sociale ltée., 1919.

Mendelson, Ann. *Stand Facing the Stove*. New York: Scribner, 2003.

Moodie, Susanna. *Roughing It in the Bush; or, Life in Canada*. 1852. Toronto: McClelland & Stewart, 1989.

The Modern Cook Book. Calgary, Alberta: Armistice Chapter I.O.D.E., 1923.

Murray, Rose. *A Taste of Canada: A Culinary Journal*. Vancouver: Whitecap Books, 2008.

Nightingale, Marie. *Out of Old Nova Scotia Kitchens: A Collection of Traditional Recipes of Nova Scotia and the Story of the People Who Cooked Them*. Toronto: Pagurian Press, 1971.

Ogilvie's Book for a Cook. Montreal: Ogilvie, 1905.

Oliver, Margo. *Classical Canadian Recipes*. Montreal: Optimum Publishing, 1993.

Pattinson, Nellie Lyle. *The Canadian Cookbook*. Toronto: McGraw-Hill, 1923.

———. *Canadian Cook Book*. 1923. Rev. edn. Toronto: Ryerson, 1947.

Powers, Jo Marie, and Anita Stewart, eds. *Northern Bounty: A Celebration of Canadian Cuisine*. Toronto: Random House, 1995.

Richards, Henry Ilett, and Elizabeth Richards. *The Canadian Housewife's Manual of Cookery Compiled from the Best English, French and American Works*. Hamilton: William Gillespie, 1861.

Rombauer, Irma. *The Joy of Cooking*. St Louis: A.C. Clayton Printing, 1931.

Sainte-Marie-Edith, Soeur. *The Secrets of Good Cooking*. Montreal: The Canadian Printing and Lithographing Company, 1928.

Scott, Anna Lee. *51 Ways to a Man's Heart*. Maple Leaf Milling, n.d.

Speed Cooking with Your New General GE Electric Range. Toronto: General Electric, 1948.

Staebler, Edna. *Food That Really Schmecks: Mennonite Country Cooking*. Waterloo: Wilfrid Laurier UP, 2006.

Stewart, Anita. *Flavours of Canada*. Vancouver: Raincoast, 2000.

———. *Anita Stewart's Canada—the Food, the Recipes, the Stories*. Toronto: HarperCollins, 2008.

Symons, Michael. 'Grandmas to Gourmets: The Revolution of 1963'. *Food, Culture and Society* 9.2 (2006): 179–200.

Thornton, Lynn. *From the Kitchens of Kings Landing*. Fredericton: Kings Landing Historical Settlement, 1995.

Traill, Catherine Parr. *The Female Emigrant's Guide, and Hints on Canadian Housekeeping*. Toronto: Maclear, 1854. *Early Canadiana Online*. 7 September 2007. www.canadiana.org/ECO/mtg?doc=41417.

The Velvet Touch. Robin Hood: N.p., n.d.

Virr, Richard. Email to the author. 8 October 2010.

4

You Are What You Eat
Enjoying (and Transforming) Food Culture
Josée Johnston and Sarah Cappeliez

Learning Objectives

Through this chapter, you can:

1. Explore the role culture plays in everyday food choices
2. Appreciate the tension between an individual's agency and the influence of cultural and societal norms and prescriptions on food choices
3. Learn how individuals try to reconcile ethical ideals and consumer pleasures in their shopping experiences
4. Recognize that the creation of alternative food cultures rests on a variety of complex motives, including commitments to moral incentives and the pursuit of pleasure

Introduction

It has become a truism that culture shapes how we eat. Our 'culture' tells us how meals are prepared, what foods are enjoyable, and what foods are taboo. We criticize fast-food culture, and praise slow-food cultures that promise meaningful, sustainable sustenance. Culture is the linchpin between the material dimension of food and its ideational existence as norms, ideals, and phobias.

While culture clearly affects how we eat, the meaning of food culture, particularly as it operates in daily life, is nebulous. Does food culture alone dictate our food decisions? To what extent can individuals resist unhealthy or unsustainable food cultures? The idea of food culture is even more perplexing when we consider the highly individualized ideas of eating that dominate the public sphere—ideas that put a pronounced emphasis on choice and personal responsibility. Individuals are encouraged to eat mindfully to avoid overeating (Roth 2010), obese bodies are linked to personal failings (Wood 2009), and individual dietary changes are lauded as solutions to social and environmental problems (Bittman 2008; Pollan 2006). Given the prominence of these individualized understandings, it is important to think about what exactly is meant by food 'culture' and use cultural analyses to move beyond simplistic understandings of individual choice and willpower.

In this chapter we suggest ways to better understand food culture and its transformative potential. Our primary theoretical goal is to introduce conceptual tools that clarify how people use food culture and are in turn used by food culture. This process involves deliberate cultural choices, as well as the less conscious pulls of consumer pleasures and desires. As exemplars of this dialectical approach to culture, we examine data from 40 interviews conducted with consumers at Whole Foods Market (the world's largest natural food retailer) and Karma Co-op (a small consumer-co-op in downtown Toronto).[1] Empirically, we hope to contribute to debates on alternative food cultures by showing how shoppers at these different venues engage with food culture in diverse ways and are influenced by the norms and pleasures of **consumer culture**.

We begin by drawing from debates in cultural sociology and consumer studies to explore ways of thinking about food culture's constraining and enabling features. Next, we use interview data to demonstrate the dialectic of culture in action—how people both are shaped by a dominant food culture and take active steps to transform food cultures. We conclude with a brief discussion of the possibilities of and limits to creating a transformative food culture.

Using (and Being Used by) Food Culture

Cultural sociologists have encouraged movement away from a unified model of culture that straightforwardly determines social action (DiMaggio 1997). Stepping away from such a model requires that we appreciate the creative ways people selectively use cultural elements to make sense of their actions. One influential contribution to this conceptualization of culture is the idea of cultural 'tool kits' or 'repertoires' developed by sociologist Ann Swidler (1986, 2001). For Swidler, 'a realistic cultural theory should lead us to expect not passive "cultural" dopes . . . but rather the active, sometimes skilled users of culture whom we actually observe' (Swidler 1986: 277). Instead of seeing culture as 'the ultimate ends', which implies a cohesive view of culture, Swidler argues that

culture should be viewed as a collection of culturally defined elements (1986: 277). From this repertoire, individuals can pick elements that sustain habitual behaviours (e.g., cooking from an old family recipe) or can select tools to explore new ways of acting in the world (e.g., trying a new cuisine) (Swidler 2001: 24). By viewing culture as a repertoire or tool kit, scholars can appreciate the complex and multidimensional ways culture is used by individuals in daily life.

Insights from cultural sociologists like Swidler match up with the work of food scholars. It has long been recognized that there is no singular food culture dictating diet, and that there is ample room for agency when it comes to making dinner (DeVault 1991: 12). At the same time, it is important not to overstate people's agency—their capacity to actively shape a food culture. As Swidler notes, not only do people use culture, but culture in turn 'uses people' (2001: 24). Applying this idea to food, we see that people have some agency about what they eat, but culinary tastes and ideas about 'good' food are also influenced by broader structural forces, such as ethnic background, social class, family socialization, and gender (see Beagan and Chapman in this volume; Cairns, Johnston, and Baumann 2010; Bourdieu 1984). In addition, food scholars have documented how political-economic and institutional forces powerfully influence food culture (e.g., Winson 1993, 2004; Mintz 1985). Strong political-economic forces shape available cultural repertoires about food (e.g., influencing whether you know how to 'properly' eat sushi, or whether sushi is even available) (Issenberg 2007) and are influential in ways that people cannot always fully articulate. As a result, people's stated ideas and knowledge about food do not always match up with their actual food habits and behaviours (e.g., Caplan 1997: 5–6).

How then does culture work at a less conscious level to influence ideas and actions? Some key theorists have made seminal insights in this direction. Giddens (1984), for example, makes an important distinction between 'practical consciousness', which involves the tacit understandings and intuitive decisions people make as they go about daily routines but which they can't always directly express, and 'discursive consciousness', which involves people's formal articulations and rationalizations for their actions. In *Distinction* (1984), a study of culture and class in France, Bourdieu argues that people's desire to appreciate fine art and good food was not always consciously developed, but reflected a less conscious desire to reproduce their class status. Bourdieu developed the influential concept of the **habitus** to reflect how certain tastes and preferences become 'internalized, and converted into a disposition that generates meaningful practices and meaning-giving perceptions' (1984: 170).

One critique of concepts like Bourdieu's habitus is its 'black box' quality (e.g., Boudon 1998): how do we know if this is how culture works, and what processes are involved in the construction of habitus? Recent research in social psychology gives empirical force to the idea of habitus, and suggests that human cognition has a 'dual process' quality: a deliberate conscious process that is slow and reflexive, and an automatic process that is fast and intuitive (Chaiken and Trope 1999). Building on this literature, sociologist Stephen Vaisey argues that incorporating social-psychological insights about our semi-conscious minds is essential for understanding how culture works in our daily lives (2008, 2009). According to the scholarly consensus on cognitive processes, not only is automatic consciousness influential in what we think, feel, and do, but '*most* of our cognitions occur below the level of conscious awareness' (Vaisey 2009: 1681). A useful metaphor is one of an elephant (the automatic, or practical consciousness) and a rider (the deliberate or discursive consciousness) (Haidt 2001). While the rider might *think* he or she is in charge of the thinking process—training and steering the elephant—the elephant is ultimately 'larger and stronger than the rider and is totally unencumbered by the need, or the ability to justify itself' (Vaisey 2009: 1683). In the context of food

culture, we may feel as though we have complete control over our food preferences, but research on cognitive processes suggests otherwise; when we make food choices, as with other cultural choices, we are both driven by 'deeply internalized schematic processes', and *also* capable of 'deliberation and justification' (Vaisey 2009: 1687).

Research on cognition and consciousness is important for food scholarship because it provides insights on how our food choices may not always be processed at a fully conscious, discursive level. Put simply, what we eat may be based more on habits and hunches than reasoned arguments. To better understand our food hunches, we can think about the role played by cultural 'schemas'. Schemas are not actively 'deployed' like cultural tools, but represent 'deep, largely unconscious networks of neural associations that facilitate perception, interpretation and action' (Vaisey 2009: 1686). Gender schemas, for instance, unconsciously organize thoughts and expectations of how men and women should behave (Bem 1981). Schemas emerge from experience and 'allow a person to respond to stimuli in ways that are automatically generated', keeping people from becoming cognitively over-burdened in daily life (Vaisey 2009: 1686). Like Bourdieu's habitus, schemas are connected to our emotions and motivate actions even if they are not consciously articulated (ibid).

We are particularly interested in the cultural schemas surrounding food and food shopping. While people deliberately and consciously select cultural tools for eating (e.g., intentionally buying vegetables to be healthier), cultural schemas also influence food behaviours at less conscious levels (e.g., an ice cream advertisement can kick-start associations between sugar, pleasure, and self-care). We argue that capitalist consumer culture, with all of its attendant institutions, norms, markets, and habits, is a central and powerful influence on the cultural schemas shaping food choices. At a general level, we can understand consumer culture as emphasizing the satisfaction of private needs and desires through the purchase of commodities

(Sassatelli 2007: 2). Consumer culture tends to de-centre collective modes of action, and focuses on individual consumer choices as a central terrain for cultivating individual pleasures, identities, and the good life in general (Cohen 2003: 18–19; Cross 2000: 135; Soper 2007). Cultural schemas around shopping create norms that are central to consumers' expectations, like the idea that grocery shopping should be aesthetically pleasing, convenient, and cost-effective and involve a wide range of choice (Johnston and Szabo 2011; Johnston 2008).

Critical theorists have long pointed out the ways consumer culture influences and even manipulates desires and behaviour (e.g., Ewen 2001; Adorno 1975), but have been critiqued for depicting consumers as unthinking 'dopes'. Incorporating cultural sociology's insights about cognition (e.g., Vaisey 2008; 2009) can help deflect this critique by shedding light on how consumer culture shapes shopping choices in ways that are not fully understood by consumers, while also recognizing consumers' more deliberate thought processes. Put differently, paying attention to the cultural schemas of consumer culture can help us better understand how food culture gets 'inside us', and serves as a foil to the popular focus on individual agency and personal choice.

Dominant food (and consumer) culture is not static, but continually evolves, and frequently incorporates critical voices into the commercial mainstream (e.g., organic food sold at Walmart) (Frank 1997; Johnston and Cairns 2012; Johnston et al., 2009). We can think about this process of social critique and market adaptation as a fundamental feature of the 'ethical foodscape'—a realm where good food is not simply viewed as an individual indulgence, but connects to collective obligations like sustainability, animal welfare, and social justice (Goodman et al., 2010). Corporate and social movement actors co-exist in the ethical foodscape, sometimes uneasily, making it difficult for consumers and food scholars to identify possibilities for transforming an unsustainable and unjust global food system.[2]

Philosopher Kate Soper identifies such possibilities within an emerging cultural challenge she terms '**alternative hedonism**', which involves 'new conceptions of the good life' that 'appear to be gaining hold among some affluent consumers' (2009: 4). Alternative hedonism implies a 'more questioning attitude towards the supposed blessings of consumerism' (2009: 3–4) and draws attention to the growing dissatisfaction with high-consumption lifestyles (2008). Soper contends that concerns about environmental degradation and social inequalities can overlap with rejection of the displeasures and anxieties associated with consumer culture. In this way, Soper proposes that consuming differently can be the source of pleasures that are neither reducible to the moral satisfactions of 'doing right', nor to the simple fulfillment of self-interested needs. More speculatively, Soper argues that hedonistic approaches are necessary to woo affluent consumers away from unsustainable living standards in affluent societies (2009: 3–4).

In sum, we have argued that sociological debates about culture and **consumerism** can help critical food scholars develop a dialectical view of food culture that people actively use in daily life but that also uses them. In this conceptualization, people have significant agency in selecting the cultural tools that shape how and what they eat, even though they cannot completely control the cultural repertoires available to them. While the deliberate nature of some food choices is important, we equally emphasize how people's food decisions are influenced by less conscious, habitual ways of being that may sustain inequitable social relationships. Bourdieu referred to these influences as the habitus, but we can bolster this important concept by identifying cultural schemas that inform the habitus and shape our intuitions about what feels enjoyable in the realm of food and food shopping. We have argued that contemporary food schemas are centrally influenced by consumer culture and its prioritization of consumer choice, convenience, and sensory pleasures.

This dominant culture of consumerism actively shapes food culture, but it is not unchallenged or static. Critiques continually emerge and are articulated through struggles over food. Market actors incorporate critiques of the food system, and the ethical foodscape represents myriad voices suggesting that individual culinary pleasures can be connected to collective eco-social responsibilities. Sensory food pleasures are not denied, but connected to other civic and environmental responsibilities—Soper's 'alternative hedonism'. In the next section, we employ this dialectical view of food culture to better understand how shoppers at two different sites both stake a claim in debates about how to build a transformative food culture.

Food Culture in Action: Whole Foods Market and Karma Co-op

To better understand the ideas on food culture explored above, we relate them to food consumers in two different settings: Whole Foods Market (WFM) and Karma Co-op. Both stores can be understood as actors within the ethical foodscape, but they operate on different scales and employ very different philosophies. WFM is the world's largest natural food retailer, with over 270 locations in North America and the United Kingdom. This growth-oriented corporation aims to dominate the retail environment for natural foods, while allowing consumers to 'feel good' about where they shop (Johnston 2008). Karma Co-op is a member-owned food cooperative in downtown Toronto that has existed since 1972. Located in a small building sandwiched between two Victorian houses, Karma attempts to satisfy the demands of older members that don't want the co-op to grow or change, while keeping the space attractive enough to draw new members and stay fiscally solvent.

Our comparative analysis offers a window into the meanings held by shoppers at two very different sites in the ethical foodscape—one large-scale and corporate, the other co-operative and small-scale. We do not want to romanticize shoppers at either location (especially since some people shop at both), nor can we offer a comprehensive account of customers' motivations. Instead, our intention is to explore how these shopping spaces encourage different possibilities for a transformative food culture that includes intentionality and pleasure. Based on an interpretive reading of shoppers' own words, we explore the ways deliberative food consciousness can contradict (and affirm) automatic thoughts, habits, and feelings about food shopping.

Whole Foods Market: Enjoying the Pleasures of Consumer Culture (sometimes guiltily)

Situated in the tony Yorkville neighbourhood in Toronto, Whole Foods Market is an epicurean paradise. The produce section has pyramids of brightly coloured fruits and vegetables. Aged balsamic vinegar and Manchego cheese can be found along with eco-friendly laundry soap and organic produce. Despite being located in a busy downtown area, WFM is large and spacious, and offers free parking. The store seems to offer shoppers the possibility to shop ethically, responsibly, and healthily, without sacrificing pleasures like delicious food, choice, and convenience. By examining how people describe their shopping, we aim to better understand how consumers actively seek out the WFM experience while at the same time understand how their experience is shaped by a larger consumer culture. We discuss instances where shoppers talk about intuitive feelings and associations of consumer pleasures at WFM but then express ambiguity about these same pleasures, especially when probing questions lead to discussing them more deliberately and reflexively.

Central to the WFM shopping experience is consumer pleasure (Johnston and Szabo

2011; Johnston 2008). The idea of aesthetically appreciating and prioritizing culinary pleasures in daily life—especially through the pursuit of authentic and exotic foods—is strongly associated with the cultural repertoires that make up today's gourmet or 'foodie' culture (Johnston and Baumann 2010). A majority of shoppers interviewed (18 out of 20) mentioned the aesthetic appeal of WFM, and emphasized the allure of an enjoyable and attractive shopping setting. In the positive descriptions of WFM, the cleanliness, open layout, natural lighting, extensive selection, and the overall play of colours and products were part of participants' pleasurable experience at the store. Not only were these pleasures presented as primary reasons to shop at WFM, they were, along with other consumer values such as convenience and product selection, frequently prioritized over other concerns, like ethically sourced products and environmentally sustainable practices (Johnston and Szabo 2011).

Specific consumer conveniences often bolstered the aesthetically enjoyable shopping experience at WFM. Along with the wide range of specialty products, WFM also supplies basic necessities, as Fred, a 36-year-old music producer and father of two young children, noted: 'if you need a couple of stupid things like sugar or toilet paper, it is actually there. Whereas if you go to a specialty store, it's not going to be there. You don't go to the [organic butcher] and buy a little bit of Ajax, you know? . . . [WFM] is very convenient.' The ability to 'get everything you need' and to 'know that everything's gonna be gorgeous' at WFM, as Mia, a 36-year-old lawyer with a young child puts it, are seen as positive attributes of the shopping experience at WFM.

A particularly prominent element of consumer culture at WFM is the idea of *choice* (Johnston 2008), an ideal that appears central to contemporary cultural schemas of shopping (Slater 1997: 61). Rather than being overwhelmed with the extensive selection of goods on offer (e.g., 72 types of bottled water were available at one store visit), almost all interviewees valued and enjoyed the range of choices

available to them.[3] The importance of plentiful consumer choices was so significant that several shoppers suggested that the selection at WFM was more important than sourcing ethical products. These consumers did not deliberately seek out *unethical* products, nor do we suggest that interviewees were heartless people who lacked concern about other beings or people. Instead, we posit that the idea of maximum choice is so central to underlying cultural schemas of pleasurable shopping that restricting choice in the name of ethics was intuitively understood as diminishing the pleasure and fun of food shopping.

Another key element of cultural schemas around food shopping expressed in our interviews was the valuation of a luxurious and elite shopping experience. This value operated on a relatively intuitive plane; not only was it obliquely referenced, but it frequently co-existed (and contradicted) an egalitarian ethos articulated in other parts of the interviews. Respondents would decry the fact that WFM was too expensive for the average person; at the same time they described the store's luxurious and upscale environment as a key part of its appeal. For example, Steve critiqued WFM for its high prices and elite atmosphere, but also implied that the luxurious setting generates positive affect: 'I like to go to Whole Foods because it makes me feel special', and 'they call me sir—it's much more pleasing'. Mary, a 62-year-old English as a second language (ESL) teacher who had an interest in social justice, insisted 'nobody needs to go to Whole Foods. There's nothing at Whole Foods that anybody couldn't do without', but also used the WFM space to experience a type of lifestyle not readily available to her and feel the thrill of 'rubbing shoulders' with more affluent shoppers in a store that is ostensibly accessible to anyone. While Mary described 'destination' shopping as feeling pleasurable, she also indicated she tries not to think about why she finds it pleasurable: 'I'm trying not to analyze it, I'm not the sociologist doing this research.' Her words suggest that cultural schemas around food shopping can generate strong pleasures, even though conscious thought processes might reject such pleasures as unnecessary and elitist.

Related to the valuation of luxury, the idea of shopping at WFM as an 'escape' from everyday life also appeared central to underlying cultural schemas about shopping. Almost half of the respondents framed shopping at WFM as a leisure activity, using words like *destination, outing, vacation,* and *escape*. However, the idea of a shopping 'vacation' generated feelings that were in tension with idealized visions of leisure and community. Olivia described visiting WFM as a getaway from her normal life:

> If I go on my own, it's like a little mini vacation. . . . I like to troll the aisles and look at the 20 different kinds of teas because that is my outlet right now. Because I'm not going out to a movie, I am not meeting friends for a glass of wine and having a great conversation. So, my outlet right now is shopping. . . . Which is a sad commentary but that is the truth.

Olivia clearly understood shopping at WFM as a form of entertainment; however, her use of derogatory language to qualify this leisure time spent at WFM, as well as her observation that it represents a 'sad commentary', demonstrates her critical interpretation of this shopping experience.

While Olivia and other interviewees acknowledged their attraction to WFM's consumer pleasures, their enjoyment was not without ambiguity, and often contradicted explicitly stated ideals. Put differently, the pleasurable cultural schemas of shopping, so attractively presented at WFM, were often described as intuitively and automatically enjoyable, but critically evaluated when the interviewee was asked to think more deliberately and consciously about the meaning of these pleasures. This juxtaposition of intuitive pleasures and critical thinking was clearly articulated by Julie, a 34-year-old lawyer with one small child, who described a profound enjoyment of the shopping experience at WFM, as long as she minimized 'thinking':

> . . . if I completely divest myself of all political matters and *I don't think about that* . . . what I like about Whole Foods is it does feel . . . quite homey. . . . I just enjoy the whole shopping experience a lot when I go to Whole Foods. It feels like a little bit of an event—a little bit of an outing. It's kind of fun. So, I do. I really enjoy it. It's not something I want to do all the time because politically I have some issues with it. But, *if I feel like not thinking* politically, it's kind of fun. [emphasis ours]

Some respondents, like Julie, were openly skeptical of WFM's corporate practices and questioned the firm's commitment to social and environmental issues, but admitted that they were nonetheless drawn to WFM's pleasurable atmosphere and products. Despite some less agreeable 'political' aspects, the store was associated with 'fun'—a place where 'thinking' could be put on hold. Julie and her husband Hugh describe how they have tried to go to WFM less frequently, but find the store difficult to resist. In Hugh's words, 'You kind of get sucked in'. We interpret the phrase *sucked in* as indicating an intuitive level of attraction based on underlying cultural schemas of shopping as eminently pleasurable. Similarly, Chris, a participant in our sample who was highly politicized about food issues and critical of WFM for 'attracting a certain clientele that makes it very elitist' also articulated this idea of being 'sucked in':

> You walk into Whole Foods and you're in the bakery section and you smell the cookies, you smell the cakes and you see all the breads and all the cheese laid out. You walk in a little further and you see the sushi bar and the hot food and *you're basically sucked into that experience*. [emphasis ours]

Hugh and Chris both allude to the feeling of being compelled by a shopping environment where the pull of consumer pleasures is difficult to resist, even when ideological contradictions and critiques are present at the level of discursive consciousness. While we observed many instances where consumers actively and straightforwardly pursued culinary pleasures and interests at WFM, the excerpts above suggest that ideas of food pleasure are formed neither in a cultural vacuum nor purely at the level of discursive consciousness. Instead, food practices are shaped by influential cultural schemas linked to consumer culture (and its related ideals of choice, luxury, and escape) and generate behaviours and pleasures that can contradict the political and ethical beliefs of some consumers.[4]

Feelings of guilt and anxiety were the by-products of a tension between consumer pleasures intuitively valued at WFM and normative commitments articulated more deliberately at the level of discursive consciousness. For example, Tina, a 55-year-old ESL instructor, had commitments to local eating that kept her away from WFM: 'there are times when I don't go [to WFM] 'cause it just feels—why not just shop in the [neighbourhood] market and support local people in that way. But not 100 percent. I still go there.' For Hugh, a 32-year-old physician who works with economically disadvantaged patients, the abundance and exclusivity that are hallmarks of the consumer culture on offer at WFM created feelings of ambivalence: 'I walk in there and I definitely get a bit of a sick feeling in my stomach and sometimes *a lot* of a sick feeling in my stomach, you know, especially when I walk through and just look at the kind of prices they're charging.' Hugh's remarks stand somewhat apart from those of most of the interviewees, who expressed pleasure at the very elements Hugh found nauseating, but they also bring nuance to our analysis. While most shoppers framed their WFM experience in pleasurable terms, and pointed to the ways that consumer culture contributed to these

enjoyable experiences (e.g., through extensive product selection and feelings of luxurious exclusivity), it is important to note that not all participants wholeheartedly embraced the consumerist experience on offer at WFM. For those who experienced a tension between intuitive pleasures and political beliefs, shopping at WFM was far from being a guilt-free experience.

The ambiguity expressed by some WFM consumers suggests that engagement with food culture is more complicated than a simple enjoyment of consumer pleasures. We observed a complex relationship between the intuitive cultural schemas that generate pleasure through food shopping and the processes of deliberative consciousness that sometimes work to question or even disrupt these pleasures. The attractive shopping environment at WFM is intended to make a banal household task like grocery shopping feel luxurious, fun, and 'guilt-free'. However, this cultural construct can backfire when consumer pleasures are examined at a critical discursive level. Indeed, for a few respondents, the by-products of the food culture on display at WFM—the higher prices, the exclusive atmosphere—were a source of discontent that pushed them to question their decision to shop there. It is precisely this dissatisfaction with consumer culture that Kate Soper proposes is the source of alternative hedonism. In the next section, we will examine how shoppers at Karma Co-op critique conventional consumer food culture but still experience pleasures associated with grocery shopping.

Resistance, Shopping Deliberately, and Alternative Hedonism: Karma Co-op

Member-owned and co-operatively managed, Karma Co-op is situated in a back alley in the Annex neighbourhood in downtown Toronto. The footprint of the store is very small by conventional grocery store standards, but Karma stocks many staples of health-conscious and green lifestyles—soy milks, soba noodles, vitamin supplements, and local fruits and vegetables. Produce and bulk goods are weighed by members, and the checkout—which has a cash register but no product scanners—is usually staffed by a member doing their monthly work-shift. While the space is not luxuriously appointed, Karma Co-op has existed in this guise since 1972 and currently has about 900 active member households.

In this section we examine how some Karma shoppers articulate a conscious decision to oppose the harmful aspects of the food system and consumer culture, and describe their food pleasures as alternatives to conventional consumer culture, a phenomenon we understand through the lens of alternative hedonism (Soper 2008). We argue that Karma shoppers' purposeful decisions to consume differently are sustained by the alternatively hedonistic pleasures they experience in the shopping environment. We also explore some limitations to this consciously transformative food culture—namely, the persistence of dominant cultural schemas around food shopping.

Almost all of the Karma shoppers we interviewed expressed concerns about social and environmental issues in the food system and thought of Karma as a more ethical option than a conventional grocery store. Some respondents talked explicitly about their desire to resist consumer culture through shopping at Karma.[5] For example, Kevin, a 42-year-old father of three, framed his membership as a way to involve his family in alternative forms of consumption: 'I also like the fact that our kids are exposed to Karma and the concept of doing something that's out of the ordinary . . . an anti-consumerism ideal.' Shopping at Karma was also described as a way to avoid the feeling of manipulation in conventional shopping contexts and reclaim a sense of control. Michela, a 31-year-old Italian PhD student, noted:

If I was shopping in a big supermarket I felt I was a puppet. And people will play

with me and make me to buy whatever [they] want and be part of this big game. Where at Karma I feel less I feel . . . it's more: I have my brain, I have my mind, I have my conscience and I feel not anyone is sending me in any direction. Actually, I'm more proactive. . . . I know that there is something, like I'm conscious, like I'm not a puppet—I'm a member. That sounds better, no?

Michela's description of deliberate participation in her food culture contrasts with the remarks of WFM shoppers that describe feeling 'sucked in' to a consumerist culture that some found politically problematic. Lorn, a 51-year-old who works in graphic design, reasoned that his appreciation of Karma resulted precisely from the potential for control, community, and connection: 'It's 'cause I have some control over what's going on in [Karma]. You vote for the board of directors or whatever, you vote for the executive. . . . Like I'm involved and I have a stake and it's part of my community. There's connection there.' As Lorn's words suggest, shopping at Karma involves a continuous renewal of one's engagement with a transformative food culture through membership privileges and responsibilities (e.g., making special orders, volunteering on committees, paying an annual membership fee, and for some members, working shifts in the store). These membership rights and responsibilities impact the balance between deliberate and practical consciousness in shopping decisions at Karma. For many of our interviewees, this involves a relatively high level of deliberate decision making, and fewer automatic, 'non-thinking' pleasures that feel uncomfortable or contradictory.

This is not to say that Karma shoppers were ascetics who described lives devoid of culinary pleasures. A key aspect of alternative hedonism is the idea that disaffected consumers are not simply motivated by the moralistic satisfaction of 'doing the right thing', but that consuming differently generates new pleasures

(Soper 2007: 211). Based on our Karma interviews, we suggest that alternative hedonism involves a dual cognitive process; it involves deliberative thought processes (e.g., intentionally going out of one's way to become a member at Karma, or choosing Karma over a closer or more convenient grocery chain), yet the ensuing pleasures are often experienced at the level of automatic consciousness, and create positive associations with these deliberate practices. Without these automatic pleasures, it is not clear that deliberative consumer practices can be sustained or become routine habits (see Soper 2009: 3–4).

To explore this idea, we examine how Karma shoppers discussed the pleasures of engaging with an alternative food culture. We begin by noting that some Karma shoppers derived pleasure, or at least satisfaction, from *not* consuming. Indeed, alternative hedonism draws attention not only to the pleasures obtained from new forms of consumption, but also to the idea that non-consumption can bring gratification (Soper 2007; 2008). Joschka, an 18-year-old teaching assistant from Germany, displayed this idea when he positively reflected on his consumption practices as '*not* doing stuff, that's basically what my kind of consumption is. Like *not* buying certain things.'

Pleasures at Karma were not just about avoiding or minimizing consumption. For half of the shoppers interviewed, the sense of community and connection at Karma was described as an important source of pleasure, and a primary reason for shopping at the co-op. Karma was described as a friendly place where members and staff greeted each other openly. Renee, a 28-year-old who works at a local college, summed up this commonly articulated sentiment: 'The people [at Karma] are friendlier. . . . And it's a lot easier here to have a quick chat with somebody than it is at Sobey's [a Canadian grocery chain].' Renee also emphasized the intentional quality of the Karma community, framed as a conscious decision by like-minded individuals to fashion a community: 'I think because it's so intentional to be a member here that people can make certain assumptions about who they're meeting in the aisles. You probably share some of the same scruples that I do and you probably have similar political ideas.' Renee explained that this intentionality made Karma *feel* comfortable to her, almost like 'being at home'. For Orly, a 23-year-old student, her desire for a shared community motivated her decision to join the co-op: 'I really, really desire community now which is another reason that I wanted to [join] Karma because you're not just passing through, you know, you're making relationships and you're with people that want to make relationships with you.' In these quotations, we see the dual-process dialectic of food culture at Karma: it is inspired by deliberative thought processes and intentional actions, but sustained and associated with pleasures of community experienced at the level of practical, everyday consciousness.

Related to the social connections at Karma, almost half of participants identified pleasures in the co-op's shopping environment, even though it contrasts with the deluxe environment at WFM. While the Karma experience is less luxurious and more labour intensive (e.g., shoppers weigh produce, pack groceries, and often clean up spills), shoppers identified precisely these characteristics as a source of pleasure. For Joschka, the laid-back attitude at Karma where 'you can just grab a samosa and eat it, you can use the washroom without thinking, you can go into the freezing room, like it's—you own the place and you feel like it', is enjoyable because 'you don't feel so much as a customer as in different stores'. Hong's comments suggest the automatic cognitive processes involved with going to Karma—an environment that, like Renee, he connected with the pleasures of being 'home':

It's just like going home, you know. . . .
I don't know how to explain it. It just

feels right when you go there. You work twenty-four hours a day, your energy's all drained, you go there, you look at the smiling faces, you feel good about it.

Hong's words suggest that his decision to go to the co-op is sustained at the level of practical consciousness: 'it just feels right'. In some ways, Hong's sentiment echoes those of WFM shoppers, for whom shopping at WFM also feels deeply enjoyable. However, Hong emphasizes the 'smiling faces' of people at Karma and how shopping 'feels right', rather than the massive selection or plush environment WFM shoppers enjoy (sometimes guiltily) as a vacation from everyday life. In contrast to our WFM interviews, Karma respondents emphasized the social rather than the aesthetic qualities of the shopping environment. When Karma members did mention aesthetic qualities of Karma, these were often things that *did not align* with conventional aspects of consumer culture such as Karma's less polished decor, complete with mismatched light fixtures and exposed concrete on the floor.

Besides the pleasurable countercultural associations of the shopping environment, another source of pleasure for some Karma participants came from feeling connected to their food source because of the type of products on offer. Respondents spoke enthusiastically about their pleasure in supporting green, local, small producers at Karma, but they also commented about how these foods *tasted* good. By consuming foods that are both 'good to think' and 'good to eat' (Lévi-Strauss 1962), Karma shoppers aligned conscious thought processes to consume differently with more automatic culinary pleasures. For Odette, a 54-year-old counsellor, 'feeling good' about her consumption implied supporting small-scale production *and* eating yummy food: 'I love supporting these small businesses. I just love that it feels so good. Especially when they [taste] *good*'. Other Karma members described how shopping at Karma made them feel more balanced and harmonious.

Moral values linked to 'doing good' were intimately tied to the personal benefits of *feeling* good because of one's actions. In Joschka's words: 'It gives you a new kind of pleasure knowing that you don't have such an impact on the world, meaning like negative impact. . . . generally, you feel more in harmony with the world.'[6]

In short, people's account of why they like Karma Co-op not only is evident at the level of deliberative consciousness—the intentional decision to shop differently—but also is based on pleasures experienced at the level of practical consciousness, which reinforce commitments to Karma shopping. However, these attempts to challenge and transform consumer culture by embracing alternatively hedonistic pleasures were not universally perceived. In some instances, respondents expressed desires for aspects of consumer culture that are *less* available at Karma—elements that we argue are a key part of dominant cultural schemas around food and food shopping.

While Karma's product selection drew many positive comments, it was also the source of some criticism. For Joschka, who was very committed to the co-op and acknowledged that Karma '[has] amazing stuff on the shelves', the choice of produce at Karma was sometimes unsatisfactory: 'Generally [the produce section] could be bigger. When I'm cooking for recipes and I don't find stuff here, it's inconvenient for me because I have to go to another supermarket.' Lorn connected Karma's small space and minimal selection to problems with member retention: 'Karma's doesn't have the space to give members the choices that a lot of them want.' Lorn's words recognize that the alternative pleasures available at Karma may be insufficient to attract and keep members at the co-op. For other members, pricing is an issue, especially for products like organic and free-range meats. Renee mentioned that she finds the high price of 'happy meat' at Karma to be 'quite difficult', and noted, 'sometimes I decide that going conventional—like going to

Sobey's and picking up some chicken breast—is a better option for me that day.'

Some respondents described Karma's shopping space as less convenient and efficient than a regular grocery store. The co-op's restricted store hours,[7] limited parking,[8] and store organization were all identified as problematic. Lara, a 42-year-old who recently joined the co-op, was frustrated by the lack of information about the ordering process: 'I don't have a clue because every time I go [to place a special order], the girl who knows it all isn't there.' Her words show that the limited schedules of the co-op staff responsible for special ordering are difficult to negotiate for a newcomer and a busy professional.

While the majority of respondents expressed positive feelings about shopping at Karma, the comments above show that consumer culture and the cultural schemas around food and food shopping—expectations of convenience, bountiful selection, and inexpensive meat—still reside in the consciousness of Karma members. We argue that the deliberate decision to consume differently at Karma is maintained through alternatively hedonistic pleasures of community and a feeling of hominess. However, dominant cultural schemas around food and shopping also compete for members' attention—especially when they suggest easier, less costly grocery options. In some cases, the alternatively hedonistic pleasures offered at Karma are insufficient, and shoppers make more conventional shopping choices. For these shoppers, the decision to continue shopping at Karma Co-op may be put into question.

Conclusion

Building a more sustainable and equitable food system is an economic and political as well as a *cultural* project. While there is an undeniable agency involved with eating, we have drawn from cultural sociology to suggest that food culture is both enabling and constraining.

More specifically, the cultural schemas of a dominant consumer culture exert tremendous influence on food habits, desires, and preferences—often in ways that reside at the level of practical consciousness, and thus aren't fully examined or articulated by consumers. Challenging the schematic assumptions of the dominant food culture (e.g., that food should be cheap and bountiful regardless of seasonality) is key to food system transformations; however, these challenges take shape within a larger capitalist context where corporate actors have proven able to incorporate cultural resistance into their brands (e.g., Frank 1997; Johnston et al. 2009).

We have looked at two cases that illustrate both sides of a dual-process understanding of culture, and speak to the idea of culture as both constraining and enabling. In the case of WFM, we demonstrated how consumers seek out consumer pleasures at WFM while being shaped by a food culture that prioritizes consumer choice, convenience, luxury, and sensory indulgences. Even highly politicized shoppers found it difficult to resist the pull of WFM, a finding we interpret by examining dominant cultural schemas around shopping. Some WFM consumers experienced a contradiction between their political *ideas* and the sensory pleasures they enjoyed at WFM, and reported feelings of guilt, anxiety, and ambiguity. In these cases, the cultural schemas supporting an automatically pleasurable reaction to WFM are challenged and overshadowed by more deliberative cognitive processes (e.g., asking questions about who can access healthy, sustainable food). Our interviews confirm that consumers experience corporate food cultures in multi-faceted ways that may resist the framing presented by corporate discourse. However, our findings also suggest that corporate food cultures within a broader ethical foodscape can be immensely attractive, even to people who critique these actors at the level of discursive consciousness. In short, the WFM case speaks to how food culture can 'use' us, potentially constraining our desires for social transformation.[9]

Our Karma Co-op interviews prominently featured instances of discursive cognition: members deliberately choose to shop in a less convenient place with less product selection and a less glamorous environment. Karma members described various efforts to resist the dominant food culture, which they understood as unsustainable and unjust, and to create a food culture more in keeping with their political principles. While we observed deliberative consciousness at work, we also saw ample evidence of pleasures automatically experienced—a sense of community among like-minded people, delicious local products, and a feeling of 'harmony' achieved when one's principles matched up with culinary pleasures. While motivations for shopping at Karma varied, the lens of alternative hedonism is an apt concept for understanding many of the pleasures interviewees discussed. As noted, these pleasures were not completely in line with conventional consumer pleasures— they represented an attempt to support a deliberately transformative food culture by consuming differently. However, we are careful not to paint a monochromatic picture of Karma shoppers, since dominant cultural schemas of shopping were evident in some member's critiques of Karma.

The question that our WFM and Karma interviews raise about transformative food cultures is a daunting one: How can the majority of food consumers apply more deliberative, reflexive cognitive processes to food shopping? In popular discourse, this question is often discussed in simple, individualized, and moralistic terms: either you choose 'good food' (e.g., sustainable, non-exploitative, local, organic, grass-fed), or you don't. Looking at the influence of culture on individual food choices allows us to frame the issue with greater nuance, empathy, and sensitivity to culture's constraining dimensions. We have shown that individual food commitments do not always seamlessly match up with food practices and routines, particularly in a context where dominant schemas around food shopping make corporate shopping intuitively attractive. Certainly, the pleasures of alternative hedonism are a hopeful sign in the ethical foodscape, and a necessary fuel sustaining efforts to build a more transformative food culture. Still, Karma is a very small and relatively unusual player in the larger foodscape. This suggests that food scholars need to devote more attention to understanding how alternative hedonism can move beyond specific sub-cultures and become a mass movement of deliberative consciousness and practical culinary pleasures.

Discussion Questions

1. This chapter presents two case studies where culture plays a role defining what people eat. Can you think of an example where particular aspects of culture have influenced what you have bought or chosen to eat? Were you aware of culture's role in your food choices or that culture was working at a less conscious level?

2. Do you agree with Kate Soper that ethical objectives are not enough to change the way people consume, and that *pleasurable* rewards of some kind are necessary to sustain alternative consumer behaviours? Discuss.

3. We use the dual-process model to analyze how WFM and Karma shoppers talk about their shopping experiences at each venue. Find a food consumption example in your own life (e.g., shopping, eating out) that illustrates both aspects of a dual-process model.

Further Reading

Alternative Hedonism

1. Soper, Kate. 2007. 'Re-thinking the "Good Life": The Citizenship Dimension of Consumer Disaffection with Consumerism', *Journal of Consumer Culture* 7(2): 205–29.

This article provides a good introduction to the concept of 'alternative hedonism' and how it fits into the larger context of an analysis of contemporary consumption.

How Culture Works

2. Swidler, Ann. 1986. 'Culture in Action: Symbols and Strategies', *American Sociological Review* 51: 273–86.

In this influential article, Swidler argues that culture is not a singular force, but should be viewed as a mixed bag of tools that individuals select to either sustain habitual or known strategies or to explore new ways of being/acting in the world.

3. Vaisey, Stephen. 2009. 'Motivation and Justification: A Dual-Process Model of Culture in Action', *American Journal of Sociology* 114(6): 1675–715.

Finding the idea of culture as repertoire insufficient, Vaisey develops the dual-process model in this article that posits that culture both motivates (i.e., pushes one toward) and justifies (i.e., explains) action.

Consumer Culture and Ethical Eating

4. Sassatelli, Roberta. 2007. *Consumer Culture: History, Theory and Politics*. Thousand Oaks, CA: Sage.

The book is an 'introduction' to consumer culture, but it is highly nuanced, and masterfully incorporates economic, institutional, historical, theoretical, and political analyses.

5. Johnston, Josée. 2008. 'The Citizen-Consumer Hybrid: Ideological Tensions and the Case of Whole Foods Market', *Theory and Society* 37: 229–70.

This article explores the tensions between the competing and often contradictory dimensions of 'consumerism' and 'citizenship' using the case of Whole Foods Market.

Notes

1. The data referenced in this chapter is based on semi-structured interviews with 20 Karma Co-op shoppers and 20 Whole Foods Market shoppers. The interviews were approximately one hour in length and were recorded and transcribed verbatim.
2. For example, the Slow Food movement's philosophy of 'good, clean and fair' food articulates this merging of political discourse with gastronomic pursuits (see Petrini 2007). Whole Foods Market also suggests (often contradictorily) that shopping at this corporate chain will ameliorate social and environmental problems (Johnston 2008).
3. The one exceptional case involved Nancy, a 34-year-old lawyer who criticized WFM for *not being large enough*. Her criticism speaks to the scale of grocery store now considered routine in contemporary consumer culture.
4. To be clear, we did not observe this tension in all of our interviews with WFM shoppers. About half of the WFM interviewees did not articulate any serious social or environmental concerns in relation to WFM food shopping, and experienced minimal or no contradictions between their stated discursive ideals and the food pleasures at WFM. For more information and analysis of WFM shoppers in the study, see Johnston and Szabo (2011).

5. Just as some WFM shoppers expressed no guilt or contradictions about their shopping practices, some Karma shoppers (3 out of 20) did not explicitly relate their shopping to a critique of consumer culture, and focused on pragmatic considerations (e.g. access to good quality, reasonably priced organic produce).

6. Our goal is not to objectively measure the social or environmental benefits of Karma shopping. We would like to draw readers' attention to the inequalities associated with ethical consumption discourse (e.g., Johnston, Szabo, and Rodney 2011).

7. Current opening hours at Karma are: Monday, 11 a.m.–7 p.m., Tuesday–Friday, 11 a.m. –9 p.m., Saturday 10 a.m.–6 p.m., and Sunday 11 a.m.–5 p.m. Karma's hours have increased over the years since it opened.

8. Karma has only two parking spots, one of which is frequently taken by a delivery truck.

9. To be clear, our goal was not to provide an accounting sheet of WFM's role in the broader food system, but to document the tensions between some consumers' consciousness of political food shopping, and the practices they intuitively enjoy.

References

Adorno, Theodor W. 1975. 'Culture Industry Reconsidered'. *New German Critique* 6: 12–19.

Bem, Sandra Lipsitz. 1981. 'Gender Schema Theory: A Cognitive Account of Sex Typing'. *Psychological Review* 88(4): 354–64.

Bittman, M. 2008. *Food Matters: A Guide to Conscious Eating with More than 75 Recipes*. Toronto: Simon & Shuster.

Boudon, Raymond. 1998. 'Social Mechanisms without Black Boxes'. In *Social Mechanisms: An Analytical Approach to Social Theory*, ed. P. Hedström and R. Swedberg. New York: Cambridge University Press, 172–203.

Bourdieu, Pierre. 1984. *Distinction: A Social Critique of the Judgement of Taste*. Cambridge, MA: Harvard University Press.

Cairns, Kate, Josée Johnston, and Shyon Baumann. 2010. 'Caring about Food: Doing Gender in the Foodie Kitchen'. *Gender & Society* 24: 591–615.

Caplan, Pat. 1997. 'Approaches to the Study of Food, Health and Identity'. In *Food, Health and Identity*, ed. Pat Caplan. New York: Routledge, 1–31.

Chaiken, Shelly, and Yaacov Trope. 1999. *Dual-process Theories in Social and Cognitive Psychology*. New York: Guilford.

Cohen, Lizabeth. 2003. *A Consumer's Republic: The Politics of Mass Consumption in Postwar America*. New York: Knopf.

Cross, Gary. 2000. *An All-consuming Century: Why Commercialism Won in Modern America*. New York: Columbia University Press.

DeVault, M. 1991. *Feeding the Family*. Chicago: University of Chicago Press.

DiMaggio, P. 1997. 'Culture and Cognition'. *Annual Review of Sociology* 23: 263–87.

Ewen, Stewart. 2001. *Captains of Consciousness: Advertising and the Social Roots of the Consumer Culture*. New York: Basic Books.

Frank, Thomas. 1997. *The Conquest of Cool*. Chicago: University of Chicago Press.

Giddens, Anthony. 1984. *The Constitution of Society: Outline of a Theory of Structuration*. Berkeley: University of California Press.

Goodman, Mike, Damian Maye, and Lewis Holloway. 2010. 'Ethical Foodscapes?: Premises, Promises and Possibilities'. *Environment and Planning A* 42(8): 1782–96.

Haidt, Jonathon. 2001. 'The Emotional Dog and Its Rational Tail: A Social Intuitionist Approach to Moral Judgement'. *Psychological Review* 108(4): 814–34.

Issenberg, Sasha. 2007. *The Sushi Economy: Globalization and the Making of a Modern Delicacy*. New York: Penguin.

Johnston, Josée. 2008. 'The Citizen-Consumer Hybrid: Ideological Tensions and the Case of Whole Foods Market'. *Theory and Society* 37: 229–70.

——— and Shyon Baumann. 2010. *Foodies: Democracy and Distinction in the Gourmet Foodscape*. New York: Routledge.

———, Andrew Biro, and Norah MacKendrick. 2009. 'Lost in the Supermarket: The Corporate Organic Foodscape and the Struggle for Food Democracy'. *Antipode: A Radical Journal of Geography*. 41(3): 509–32.

——— and Kate Cairns. 2012. 'Eating for Change'. In Sarah Banet-Wiser and Roopali Mukherjee, eds. *Commodity Activism: Cultural Resistance in Neoliberal Times*. New York: New York University Press, 219–39.

——— and Michelle Szabo. 2011. 'Reflexivity and the Whole Foods Market Consumer: The Lived Experience of Shopping for Change'. *Agriculture and Human Values*. 28(3): 303–19.

———— Michelle Szabo, and Alexandra Rodney. 2011. 'Good Food, Good People: Understanding the Cultural Repertoire of Ethical Eating'. *Journal of Consumer Culture* 11(3): 293–318.

Lévi-Strauss, Claude. 1962. *La pensée sauvage*. Paris: Plon.

Mintz, Sidney. 1985. *Sweetness and Power: The Place of Sugar in Modern History*. New York, NY: Penguin.

Petrini, Carlo. 2007. *Slow Food Nation: Why Our Food Should Be Good, Clean, and Fair*. New York: Rizzoli Ex Libris.

Pollan, M. 2006. *The Omnivore's Dilemma: A Natural History of Four Meals*. New York: Penguin.

Roth, Geneen. 2010. *Women, Food and God: An Unexpected Path to Almost Everything*. Toronto: Scribner.

Sassatelli, Roberta. 2007. *Consumer Culture: History, Theory and Politics*. Thousand Oaks, CA: Sage.

Slater, Don. 1997. *Consumer Culture and Modernity*. Cambridge, MA: Blackwell.

Soper, Kate. 2007. 'Re-thinking the "Good Life": The Citizenship Dimension of Consumer Disaffection with Consumerism'. *Journal of Consumer Culture* 7(2): 205–29.

———— . 2008. 'Alternative Hedonism, Cultural Theory and the Role of Aesthetic Revisioning'. *Cultural Studies* 22(5): 567–87.

———— . 2009. 'Introduction: The Mainstreaming of Counter-Consumerist Concern'. In *The Politics and Pleasures of Consuming Differently*, ed. K. Soper, M. Ryle, and L. Thomas. London: UK: Palgrave, 1–24.

Swidler, Ann. 1986. 'Culture in Action: Symbols and Strategies'. *American Sociological Review* 51: 273–86.

———— . 2001. *Talk of Love: How Culture Matters*. Chicago: The University of Chicago Press.

Vaisey, Stephen. 2008. 'Socrates, Skinner, and Aristotle: Three Ways of Thinking About Culture in Action'. *Sociological Forum* 23(3): 603–13.

———— . 2009. 'Motivation and Justification: A Dual-Process Model of Culture in Action'. *American Journal of Sociology* 114(6): 1675–715.

Winson, Anthony. 1993. *The Intimate Commodity: Food and the Development of the Agro-Industrial Complex in Canada*. Toronto: University of Toronto Press.

———— . 2004. 'Bringing Political Economy into the Debate on the Obesity Epidemic'. *Agriculture and Human Values* 21(4): 299–312.

Wood, Gaby. 2009. 'The Woman Who Hates Fat' *The Observer*, 24 May. Accessed at www.guardian.co.uk/lifeandstyle/2009/may/24/meme-roth-obesity-nutrition.

5

Catalyzing Creativity
Education and Art Feed the Food Justice Movement
Deborah Barndt

Learning Objectives

Through this chapter, you can:

1. Examine your own experiences in growing, purchasing, preparing, and eating food in terms of what they reflect about broader cultural trends
2. Understand the parallels between the commodification of food and the commodification of education and art
3. Consider how reclaiming our capacities to produce food, knowledge, and art can contribute to a more just and sustainable food system
4. Consider how formal education and educational institutions can integrate food literacy (both theoretical and practical) into the curriculum and institutional practices, transforming how learning happens
5. Become more aware of the everyday practices of art making in our families, communities, and cultures that have transformative potential

Introduction

Central to an emerging **food justice movement** are processes of popular, holistic, and place-based education, as well as multiple forms of collective cultural expression through **community arts**; they share with food justice a commitment to a food system that is both equitable and sustainable. As forms of resistance to the interrelated commodification of food, education, and art, these processes seek to reclaim our capacity not only to produce our own food but also to create knowledge and culture. They celebrate both biodiversity and cultural diversity while transforming the food system to one that is more sustainable and just. This chapter probes three stories of cultural reclamation and creative transformation in Toronto, Canada: FoodShare Toronto's Recipe for Change campaign for food literacy in the schools, the West End Food Co-op's participatory democracy through popular education and community food mapping, and the Southern Ontario FoodShed Project's collaborative production of digital stories of local food initiatives. These stories suggest alternative strategies that not only are catalysts for building a multi-sectoral food movement but are ends in themselves.

Circling Round My Neighbourhood

An immense circle of 25 white festival tents reminiscent of a medieval fair, town plaza, or circle of teepees, set up in one corner of Sorauren Park, invites residents of my west-end Toronto neighbourhood to talk with regional farmers, backyard gardeners, organic livestock producers, wild-food foragers, apiarists, bakers, artisans, local ethnic chefs, soap makers, knife sharpeners, chocolatiers linked to an Indigenous cacao co-operative in Oaxaca, Mexico,[1] and more. Every Monday afternoon we become more than mere shoppers; we learn about the food we eat, about the people who produce it, and about how we might preserve, cook, share, and celebrate it. The vast space in the middle of the circle is alive, too, with young and old, individuals and families crisscrossing and greeting each other, pushing strollers and pulling dogs, gathering with friends on a blanket on the ground to share a meal. A few picnic tables in the centre alternately serve as a buffet for a community potluck, invite residents to draw their food sources on a community food map, offer an art project for kids to construct food art with the Greenest City Youth Green Squad,[2] or involve adults and kids alike in making dill pickles or kimchee with Garden Jane.[3] Central to this scene are the musicians of the week—a harpist, a sax and cello duo, a Latin trio with dancer, or a jazz/blues band—often engaging children and encouraging community participation. The music is homegrown and soothing, shifting our energies, slowing us down, connecting us. This is not a place to rush through; I sometimes get so caught up in a stimulating conversation that I forget to fill my basket with the produce I came to buy. In the tradition of slow food, it is 'slow shopping'.[4] But then, much more is happening.[5]

I compare this scene to the typical food shopping experience of the twenty-first century: atomized consumers moving up and down long, straight, narrow, fluorescent-lit supermarket aisles of mostly imported processed and packaged foods, hearing canned music piped in from the ceiling, filling their carts but rarely connecting with each other, let alone with the producers of their food.

In one corner of the farmers' market, we find the tent shared by the Sorauren Farmers' Market and the West End Co-op, whose development since 2008 has overlapped and fed each other. Sally Miller, co-op manager, explains to me that the circle design is no accident; with a doctorate in anthropology, this seasoned popular educator and author of *Edible Action: Food Activism and Alternative Economics* (2008) knows that circles can contribute to the building of democratic communities and processes. Popular education for community development has, in fact, been the major theoretical framework for the organization of the co-op itself, its structure, processes, and programming.

Within two blocks of the park is Fern Avenue Public School, where my son was a student in the 1990s, the decade when the Toronto school board, facing funding cutbacks and responding to corporate pressures, replaced functioning kitchens with vending machines and hot lunches with pizza, chips, and pop.[6] Now almost 20 years later, Toronto Public Health, the school boards, and community organizations work together through the Toronto Partners for Student Nutrition to support 800 meal programs in over 500 schools in Toronto. FoodShare Toronto, the key community partner, helps with the community development components. FoodShare has begun a variety of other school programs, such as the Fresh Produce Program, which sells quality produce to schools at affordable prices; the Good Food Café, a healthy hot lunch program; and Field to Table Schools, which supports school gardens, teacher education, curriculum integration, and community development. In 2009, FoodShare launched the Recipe for Change campaign, aimed at integrating food literacy into all levels of the provincial curriculum. FoodShare's executive director, Debbie Field, whose son also attended Fern

Avenue Public School in the 1990s, observed the decline of school-based food and nurtured the development of this vision of community self-sufficiency within schools, a vision that includes ultimately having a farmers' market at every school.

I have lived in the Roncesvalles–Parkdale neighbourhood for almost two decades, and have witnessed this struggle around school food programs as well as the transformation of a derelict vacant lot into a thriving park with a farmers' market and a field house (where the market is held in the winter). The field house will be the site of a mural, part of Painting Our Stories,[7] a community-based mural project aimed at creating dialogue around the ecological and Aboriginal history of the area, the diverse histories of older and newer residents, and current community activities such as the farmers' market. Fern Avenue Public School was also the site of a Painting Our Stories mural project, which involved classes of all levels in representing their childhood experiences of the neighbourhood on the walls.

Through murals or digital stories, I would like to eventually recount the stories of individuals who live within one block of my house who are creating their own innovative approaches to urban agriculture: the Bay Street banker who has established a plastic container garden and irrigation system on his third floor rooftop; the Chinese corner-store grocer who has lined his concrete lot with 80 pots of Chinese herbs as medicine for his own health; the Indian grandfather whose front-yard patch is a rotating series of intercrops that feed his extended family. Then there are the initiatives within two blocks: Backyard Urban Farmers Company growing and selling heritage seedlings with grow lights in a home basement and Urban Harvest, a more established market of organic seeds and seedlings. These signs of hope are sprouting all around me.

During the 1990s, I gathered stories of women workers in the chemicalized industrial food system, following the journey of a corporate tomato from a Mexican field to a Canadian fast-food restaurant (Barndt 2008). Ironically, the development of this global food system paralleled my own life, which began in a rural farm community at the end of the Second World War. In recent years, through the Southern Ontario FoodShed Project, I have become committed to telling the stories of those grassroots initiatives that are challenging that global food system by creating alternative (and often local) economies based on values of equity, sustainability, democracy, and community. These initiatives, for the most part, fall into what Patricia Allen calls a 'constructivist strategy,' embodied by 'bottom-up efforts to create new, alternative institutions that can serve as the basis for rebuilding the agrifood system' (Allen 2004: 64), and they include farmers' markets, community gardens, urban agriculture, community-supported agriculture, school gardens, food co-operatives, and food-based education. Central to these efforts are popular education and community arts, forms of learning and communicating that draw on diverse knowledges and foster the personal and collective creativity of everyone. Full circle.

Initially, we in the FoodShed Project[8] used the metaphor of the dandelion to talk about this work, referring to the resilience of nature to keep sprouting up amid the cracks in the asphalt. In our first project gathering in 2009, Wayne Roberts, former coordinator of the Toronto Food Policy Council, food writer (see Roberts 2008), and visionary, suggested that the community-based food movement has become more than a tenacious weed pushing through the pavement; rather, we may be at a tipping point (Gladwell 2000), where many initiatives are converging. Alternatives are becoming mainstream[9] as public consciousness about the relationships among food, health, and environment, between biodiversity and cultural diversity, between education, art, and community building is emerging to feed a growing movement. What I am witnessing in my own middle-class neighbourhood may be evidence of a transitional period, with both individual and collective experimentation, but still lacking full state support for an equitable[10] and sustainable food system.

This chapter focuses on the creative educational and arts-based dimensions of these initiatives, telling in depth the stories of the West End Food Co-op, FoodShare's Recipe for Change program, and the FoodShed Project's Digital Storytelling. Representing both informal and formal education, these local initiatives are consciously tapping ways of knowing, learning, and creatively communicating. Popular education and community art are not only means to the goal of a sustainable food system, they are part of the vision of the world we are creating day by day through these simple yet profound gestures. We can reach the stomach through the head and the heart.[11]

Reclaiming Ourselves as Makers: Theoretical Frames for Food Education and Art

The burgeoning **local food movement** is, in part, about reclaiming our capacity to feed ourselves; at least a generation of North Americans has been de-skilled in growing and cooking their own food. A corporate global food system—which depends on agro-exporting southern countries producing for the north (Barndt 2008) and which markets packaged and processed 'food' as well as quick, cheap, and convenient 'fast food' for busy lives—has generated both eaters who are distanced from all aspects of food production (Kneen 2003: 39) and a grazing culture (Reiter 1996) in which people fuel themselves on the run rather than enjoying the process of preparing a meal and gathering around the table to share it (commensality).[12] The new food movement aims to reclaim both self-sufficiency and conviviality.[13] It understands that food is not just food—it is about 'all our relations' (LaDuke 1999) with the land and elements, with the more-than-human, with each other (and across differences), with our own bodies and spirits.

Just as food has become commodified in a market-driven consumer culture, so too has education and art; knowledge is to be digested rather than created, learners are consumers, and art is relegated to the professional, the individual, the producer of advertising (considered the educational arm of capitalism). Countering the **banking model of education**, which perpetuates a static view of knowledge as object or commodity and an individual and competitive notion of learning, are grassroots practices of **popular education**, **holistic education**, and **place-based environmental education**.

Popular education, growing out of social movements in Latin America and articulated by Brazilian educator Paulo Freire, challenges the conventional power relations between teacher and student, starts with the daily experience of the learners, and generates critical dialogue around the social contradictions of their lives to develop their critical consciousness as well as their capacity to act collectively (Freire 2002; Arnold et al. 1991; Barndt 1990). Its practitioners have also appropriated Freire's notion of the 'code' by using various forms of cultural expression—drawing, theatre, music, poetry—as representations of social contradictions and as catalysts for deeper discussion of critical issues as well as a means for developing a vision of alternatives (Barndt 1998). Holistic education[14] promotes a learning process that teaches children about themselves, relationships, emotional and social development, resilience, and beauty. It advocates multi-sensory and interdisciplinary learning, countering the fragmentation of formal schooling, which is often rigidly divided into disciplines and privileges rationalist and technical thinking over the social and emotional dimensions of learning (Anderssen 2010). Place-based environmental education (Gruenewald 2003) honours the particular ecological contexts of learning, shaped by the inseparable biological and cultural diversity.

Each of these three pedagogical approaches counters the conventional dualisms of Western thought: popular education challenges the theory–practice dichotomy; holistic education, the mind–body dichotomy; and place-based environmental education, the nature–culture dichotomy.

I subscribe to an underlying epistemological position, then: The act of knowing is socially and culturally constructed, is multisensory and integrated, is dynamic and creative, and is rooted in our bodies and our environments (natural, social, cultural, and spiritual).

Community-engaged and place-based art offers a similar challenge to conventional notions of art making. While not denying the role of individual artists, community art nurtures the creative capacity of all people to express themselves, their histories, identities, and issues in multiple artistic and cultural forms. It proposes the reintegration of art into everyday life and into rituals that build community, a practice which was and is central to Indigenous cultures and was commonplace in medieval Europe and even early colonial America. Since the capitalist notion of art as commodity is relatively new, the broader framing of art as a way of life[15] or as creative living grounded in ecological context could incorporate food itself—its growing and preparation, presentation and eating—as art. In a recent book, *Random Acts of Culture: Reclaiming Art and Community in the 21st Century*, media professor Clarke Mackey recounts both the unravelling of community in recent decades and the ways that a broader conception of art and culture is being embraced by myriad initiatives responding to the hunger for human interaction and community (Mackey 2010).

The case studies that follow explore some of these notions as they are reflected in attempts to transform the food system while also reforming the school system and local organizations through informal community-based education and arts-based approaches that catalyze creativity; that tap body, mind, and spirit; that enter the stomach through the head and heart.[16]

Stories of Diverse Strategies

I focus on three different strategies represented in Toronto-based local food initiatives in the past year or so, each revealing how education and art are feeding a growing food movement. These strategies include:

- Engaging the next generation: holistic education with kids through FoodShare's Recipe for Change
- Messy democracy: popular education building grassroots food organizations through the West End Food Co-op
- Storytelling in multiple forms: from personal narrative to social action through the FoodShed Project

Engaging the Next Generation

It's a crisp October day in 2010. The Ontario Parliament buildings against a clear blue sky serve as the perfect backdrop for a demonstration unlike any I've ever seen at Queen's Park. Instead of the usual crowd of placard-carrying protesters ranting and chanting in response to a slew of speakers making demands on the government, this is a kind of educational fair, billed as 'Eat-In Ontario'. Over 500 kindergarten through grade 12 students from across the Greater Toronto Area (GTA), accompanied by their teachers, move from one 25-minute workshop to another—ranging from 'Pollination Patrol: Bee Anatomy Dress-Up' for kindergarteners to digital storytelling engaging grade 11 students. The 52 workshops combine hands-on activities with discussion about the broader context: grade 3 students learn about the three sisters of Indigenous interplanting (corn, beans, and squash), for example, while grade 7s discuss the environmental impact of cattle.

Eat-In Ontario is promoted as 'a province-wide fall harvest celebration with fun-filled activities, using fresh local produce to teach students of all ages the joys of cooking, growing and tasting good, healthy food' (FoodShare 2011). As the official launch of FoodShare's Recipe for Change campaign to get the provincial Ministry of Education to integrate food literacy into all levels of the curriculum,[17] Eat-In

Ontario employs the strategy of demonstrating by *proposing* instead of *opposing*.[18] Curriculum-linked workshops are designed for each grade level in four general categories—gardening, soil and composting, food and tasting, and food outside the box (linking food to broader economic, political, and social issues). Teachers can find the workshop designs online, and thus schools across the province can participate in their own classrooms, gyms, and schoolyards. The learning materials are there for future use as well, and fit into the specific curriculum guidelines of the ministry.

The soil has been prepared for this massive effort for more than 25 years; FoodShare was established in 1985 by a group including then–Toronto mayor Art Eggleton in response to increasing hunger. The vision of this non-profit community organization is 'Good healthy food for all', which FoodShare promotes with myriad programs aimed at 'empowering individuals, families and communities through food-based initiatives, while advocating for the broader public policies needed to ensure that everyone has adequate access to sustainably produced, good healthy food' (FoodShare 2010). The many initiatives at all levels of the food cycle that FoodShare has developed in the past two decades reach 145,000 children and adults every month, 'bringing them fresh, nutritious, affordable food, and *cultivating the knowledge and skills that build healthy communities*' (FoodShare 2010, author's emphasis). Good-food boxes and markets, rooftop and community gardens, incubator kitchens for emerging ethnic food businesses, composting and beekeeping, training of immigrant women and at-risk youth—all have served as models emulated in other cities, earning Toronto's food movement a reputation as the most innovative in North America. FoodShare has also taken the lead in bringing together rural and urban actors at many levels of the food movement, hosting its first conference on food sovereignty in the fall of 2009 (Friedmann 2011).

Appropriately, FoodShare's new digs are in a former school, now called the FoodShare Centre

of Innovation and Education, housing a staff of over 50 who represent the great diversity of Toronto's diasporic population. Education has always been central to FoodShare's mission and to the vision of its executive director, Debbie Field. Besides facilitating informal adult education through its many programs, FoodShare has been a leader in promoting public schools as sites of food education and transformation. FoodShare's Field to Table Schools program grew out of a broader network, now known as the Toronto Partners for Student Nutrition (TPSN). Within the TPSN, FoodShare represents community organizations on a steering committee that includes school boards, foundations, and Toronto Public Health. By 2010, FoodShare was coordinating 16 animators doing community development with school coordinators in 500 schools to support their local processes of sourcing and serving 800 breakfast, lunch, or mid-morning meals. While municipal and provincial funding pays about one-third of the costs, parents and teachers have to fundraise to support these initiatives. This is just one reason why the time is ripe for the Recipe for Change campaign.

The ultimate aim of this campaign is to transform the provincial Education Act so that it integrates food literacy into all aspects of the curriculum through the kind of activities demonstrated at the Queen's Park launch. The vision includes establishing a Good Food Café in every school to serve healthy, seasonal food, and having students graduate from grade 12 with the skills to grow and cook their own food. Equally important is the potential of food to infuse, enliven, and ground the entire curriculum and the school itself; students learn about nutrition as they develop cooking skills, they learn about local and global food systems as they till the soil in school food gardens. As the quintessential interdisciplinary subject, food is what I call an entrée or entry point into any other discipline: food can enlighten studies of history, natural sciences, social studies; can be engaged while learning basic numeracy and literacy skills; and can be the subject of music, art, and performance. All these possibilities are, in fact, illustrated in the workshops that FoodShare has offered to schools as samples.

Central to FoodShare's educational campaign is what is often called the 'hidden curriculum' (Snyder 1970) or the *ways* in which students learn about food. The workshops I witnessed on that October day were founded on principles of place-based, holistic, and popular education—place-based, because they involved local food groups in offering the workshops, and promoted local growing, cooking, and eating practices. But these workshops weren't limited to the practices of people born and raised in Ontario, because they often honoured the diverse culinary tastes and cultural rituals of a multicultural population. FoodShare itself has been learning—through its engagement with diverse communities—how to respect the agricultural, cultural, and educational practices of specific communities. For example, the AfriCan FoodBasket, a food organization serving the Caribbean community, was incubated at FoodShare. This community was a pioneer in creating an Afrocentric alternative school in Toronto, where growing food in its own garden and making music in community events was central to the curriculum.

The workshops at Queen's Park were holistic and multi-sensory in engaging students' whole bodies in smelling, tasting, and touching, while tapping emotions and creativity through visual art, music, and drama. One of the best examples of this sensory and experiential approach to learning, FoodShare's Great Big Crunch, initiated in 2008, is a public performance that in 2010 involved 64,000 students across Canada biting into a fresh apple all at the same time. For many kids bred on processed and packaged food this is a novel experience that changes their attitudes toward fresh fruit and vegetables. And, once again, FoodShare uses this moment of simultaneous bites in multiple classrooms to educate about issues related to the apple. A lesson on FoodShare's website, for example, asks students before crunching

to 'imagine what the orchard looked like, the growers who work there, and the workers who harvest and wash the apples'.

This example reveals how critical social analysis can be introduced through a simple celebratory ritual. As well, it points to the popular education potential of Recipe for Change curricula. When students are asked to make links to their own lives, and then to the broader social, ecological, and global context, they have bitten into a richer and deeper learning process. To this end, I have developed a decoding set of questions that can be used with any 'code', such as an apple, or a food map, or a digital story. They can guide a facilitator and a group through a process of what Freire calls 'conscientization', or the development of a critical consciousness, so essential to effective movement building. The questions use a logic that starts with the personal and experiential, and progresses to the collective and active:

1. Description: What do you see/hear/feel?
2. Personal Connection: How does this object/story connect to your personal experience?
3. Common Themes: What are the social issues/themes that emerge from our personal stories? Is there a common issue that we share?
4. Social Analysis: How did this come to be? What are the historical and social processes that created this situation?
5. Planning for Action: What can be done? What can we do?

Ultimately, Recipe for Change is about changing not only the food system but also the dominant pedagogy and a fragmented curriculum disconnected from children's lives, bodies, and communities. In part, it is reclaiming practices such as home economics classes, which used to be integral to Canadian schools, and informal educational programs such as 4-H clubs, which encourage the development of farming, animal husbandry, and housekeeping skills,[19] particularly among rural youth. A program such as Recipe for Change has yet to get the kind of governmental support in Canada that well-known chef Jamie Oliver got in the United Kingdom when the government mandated healthy meals in schools throughout the nation.[20] And even though there have been progressive policies approved, such as the so-called Bondar report, which proposed environmental education be integrated into the entire Ontario curriculum (Working Group on Environmental Education 2007), the structures and processes that hold that curriculum in place are deeply entrenched, and teachers are under tremendous pressure to cover specified subject matter to prepare students for provincial testing.

But if the last 10 years are any indication, FoodShare has developed a strategy that not only focuses on educating the next generation but also engages teachers and parents in schools that are ready to take the lead now in building a movement from the ground up. This momentum, building from the bottom up, is starting to converge with other initiatives like the Toronto Food Strategy and with increasing mainstream media coverage of issues of food sustainability, children's health, and local initiatives.[21] TPSN is one of the **civil society** organizations that is linking school boards, municipal bodies (such as Toronto Public Health, which is championing the food strategy), and community organizations, and that lead by example in challenging the silos of the relevant provincial ministries (Agriculture, Food, and Rural Affairs; Health; Environment; Labour; and Community and Social Services) to consider the need for a coordinated multi-sectoral strategy.

Coalitional work is growing across social movement sectors as well. A Food Chain Workers Alliance was formed in the United States in 2008 to link all the workers 'whose labor grew, picked, processed, cooked, served, shipped, stocked, and sold the food that we eat'.[22] According to Robert Gottlieb and Anupama Joshi, 'food justice' has become 'the governing metaphor for the transformation of the food system that links disparate movements and ideas' (Gottlieb and Joshi 2010: 224). They delineate the connections between food justice and movements of producers, food system workers, consumers, environmentalists, community economic development organizers, public health and nutrition advocates, and human rights and anti-oppression activists promoting equity in terms of race, ethnicity, class, and gender. Popular education and community arts movements share this commitment to challenge and transform power relationships through democratic educational and art-making processes.

Messy Democracy[23]

The development of Toronto's West End Food Co-op (WEFC) was designed as a popular education process, and WEFC has continued to use popular education approaches as it has expanded into the community. Let's consider four moments in its institutional growth: (1) the development of the board, (2) community mapping, (3) the consolidation of a bondholder community, and (4) cannery workshops with a local drop-in centre.

Birthing a Co-op Through Nine Months of Labour

A group of residents in Toronto's west end established the Sorauren Farmers' Market with the vision of eventually forming a food co-op. In late 2008, they hired Sally Miller, a consultant with a rich history in co-op development, to work with them over several months, culminating in incorporation in June 2009. Drawing upon the design and facilitation skills of popular educator Chris Cavanagh of the Catalyst Centre and York University's Faculty of Environmental Studies, Sally moved the group through biweekly strategic planning workshops that excavated their own values, developed their own visions, and explored the models that might embody those values and visions. Sally saw this wrestling with the questions of structure as generating important philosophical and political discussions. 'It was an analysis of power,' Sally concluded, identifying one of the key goals of popular education—to deepen a group's understanding of both broader structural power relations as well as that group's own positions within and in response to those dynamics. And with that layered analysis, a group can go on to develop strategic plans to challenge and transform those power dynamics through the alternatives they create.

In contrast to a top-down model of organizational development, the grassroots process that Sally facilitated took time but resulted in a board deeply committed to a vision of a 'triple bottom line' incorporating economic, social, and environmental goals: 'The collective process they went through together developed a very strong consensus and common vision about what they want to do that has carried them through time with no money.' It also ultimately led Sally to accept the position of coordinator[24] of the new co-op,[25] with the challenge of finding the money. The process fit very well within her own vision of 'messy democracy', a form of participatory social or economic democracy that is built on consensus, or 'feeling, thinking, judging together'. It is different from 'majoritarian voting in an adversarial system', according to Sally, in that 'its emphasis is on having participants make their reasoning accessible and legitimate to each other' (Miller 2008: 169). And popular education is central to this process, as it 'seeks not just moments of democracy, but a time for democracy, perhaps even a whole history' (ibid.: 173).

Community Food Mapping

In the summer of 2009, WEFC ran 12 workshops around the Parkdale and Roncesvalles community that invited residents to map their own food experiences. Hannah Lewis, a food activist from British Columbia, worked as an intern coordinating this process, as part of her master's degree program in environmental studies at York University.[26] The workshops took place in farmers' markets, seniors' homes, English as a second language classes, and community centres. They varied in approach (individual and group sketch mapping, drop-in mapping, and layered sketch mapping), but all asked participants to draw

on a large chart in response to one general question—Where does your food come from?—and three more specific questions: Where do you get your food? How do you get your food? Where do you eat your food?

The decisions about which groups to work with and where to hold the workshops were conscious, reflecting the three principles of community mapping (Parker 2006): transparency (being clear about the purpose and sharing the results), inclusion (of all voices in the community), and empowerment (of community members to act on the information generated).

Hannah brought a popular education perspective to designing and facilitating this process, seeing community mapping as a way of challenging the power of conventional (colonial) maps and allowing people to represent themselves from the inside out. She cautions facilitators of community mapping to be aware of their own privilege and power, as well as the power dynamics within the community. One workshop held in a drop-in centre, for example, brought together mental health consumers/survivors, who were food-insecure, and more affluent residents, whose very presence seemed to silence the low-income community members. While the latter were hosting the event, they sat in the periphery of their own social space, offering the 'guests' the seats in the centre and the most speaking time as well.

The community mapping process is grounded theoretically in *place-based environmental education*, which is, according to Hannah, 'learning that draws upon our experiences, our sense of place and our attachment to place in order to bring about change for the whole world'. Hannah also sees this as part of a process of **decolonization** (identifying issues that operate in our home places) and reinhabitation (addressing these issues by recovering, identifying, and creating ways of living well where we are). The WEFC board realizes the danger of creating a co-op that serves a mainly middle-class white population, and aims to counter that dynamic.

As a culmination of the summer of place-based food mapping workshops, the co-op held a final map tour workshop involving about 25 residents in reviewing and synthesizing the information from the 80 maps produced, as well as suggesting how some of the emerging ideas could be interpreted in a community mural. An exhibit of murals from around the world catalyzed discussion of what a food co-op mural might look like. This visioning of how they wanted to represent themselves revealed clashing cultural aesthetics, as, for example, Chinese seniors responded negatively to murals inspired by a Mexican aesthetic. Community art projects can often provide a forum for dialogue around differences, creation of unique cultural expression, and possible fusions of cultural practices creating new ones. ·

The food maps were finally woven into a paper quilt that was displayed at the official launch of the food co-op in November 2009 at the Gladstone Hotel, a neighbourhood cultural and arts centre and long-time supporter of local food. Directors held workshops for members to practise selling co-op bonds, a major part of the co-op's fundraising strategy, using popular education techniques to help people understand and confront the common fear of asking for money.

Building a Bondholders Group

The WEFC bond structure itself, while influenced by the regulations for non-profit co-operatives in Canada, reflects the community-based principles of the co-operative. In a typical corporate model, a shareholder has a number of votes corresponding to his or her number of shares. In contrast, the bonds respect the 'one member, one vote' model of co-operatives, regardless of the size of the investment. Bonds are sold in hundred-dollar increments, making investment in the co-op widely accessible, while a maximum of $1000 per member per year encourages broad-based community investment, so that the co-op is not merely owned by its members but funded by them as well. The power of these investors is more than symbolic, and the investment is emotional as well as financial.

Tinto's Coffee House, a local café cum cultural centre, was the site of the first gathering of bondholders. Rather than telling them what the plans for building the co-op were, Sally and board members led 25 bondholders in generating ideas for expanding membership. Small groups met around tables and consolidated their ideas, drawing on myriad contacts in the neighbourhood: businesses, local politicians, community centres, schools, social services, and banks. The richness of multiple groups working on this task was clear when they reported back to the gathering, and all ideas were consolidated on flip charts. The process didn't stop there—bondholders were invited to take action: Who will contact each group? Who will offer to promote the idea at that community meeting? As this process illustrates, popular education aims to promote a movement from analysis and planning to action.

Annual general meetings (AGMs) apply this participatory approach in much larger groups. At the June 2010 WEFC AGM, in addition to conventional elections of the board and updates on the co-op's financial situation, the 70 attending members (out of 200)[27] were invited to work in groups to draw on large chart paper their visions of what the co-op 'store' itself might look like. This process gave even quieter participants a 'voice' (or image), allowed members to inspire each other with their visions of the future, and fed into the board's process of seeking an appropriate space. WEFC members also generated ideas about how to get food issues onto the municipal election agenda.

Cannery Workshops: Preserving Our Sanity

In the summer of 2010, the WEFC organized a series of workshops on canning food, charging $30–35 for non-members to attend. The first workshops were held in the kitchen of the Parkdale Activity and Recreation Centre (PARC), both a key partner in the co-op's preserving project and a drop-in centre for mental health consumers/survivors. Over its 25 years PARC has created a model of self-advocacy and integrated economic and cultural activities into its program. Because the PARC kitchen is fully occupied, producing some 300 free meals every day for local residents, subsequent workshops were hosted at the nearby Parkdale Neighbourhood Church (PNC), a street church and drop-in space, which provides numerous services to the community and shares many members with PARC; free spaces were provided for both PARC and PNC members in each workshop. Kitchen crew at PARC were trained by the PARC chef, Michelle Quintal, to host and eventually facilitate workshops. The workshops held at PARC occurred near the beginning of this training; while the kitchen crew hosted the workshops, they were led either by external facilitators or by Michelle. The PARC kitchen continued to host workshops for social service agencies—for instance, Michelle later led a number of workshops for street-involved youth with Eva's Phoenix, a transitional housing and training facility managed by Eva's Initiatives.

For the general community workshops, facilitators used a popular education approach, presenting historical photographs of different kinds of preserving, to use as codes,[28] for example, to tap participant's memories of grandparents who may have canned food, and to generate discussion about how and why we have become de-skilled in this practice. The workshops attempted to grapple with some of the emerging class dynamics of canning, increasingly embraced as a hip hobby but historically grounded in vital self-sufficiency and, often, poverty. They explored what role canning can play in communities today and what kinds of preservation are meaningful and accessible for low-income community members. In a kind of participatory research process, circumstances of participants' lives were revealed that would inform the possibilities and constraints of canning for this population. Many suffered from diabetes, for example, and thus needed to avoid sweet fruit preserves; for those living in boarding-house rooms, a solar dehydrator would be useful, as it doesn't require access to a stove.

The particular experiences of food insecurity experienced by PARC members, as well as organizational efforts to address their food issues, fed into community arts projects produced in the basement of PARC, near the food bank, and in collaboration with the Painting Our Stories community mural project.[29] Two local artists worked with a group of members through the Sand and Water art-making and meditation group to develop stories, images, and photos that drew upon their experiences related to food. These were integrated into collages and displayed in light boxes in the PARC basement. The art project also moved out of the building and into store windows and walls up and down Queen Street; larger-than-life-size photographs of PARC members sitting in meditative poses invited response from passers-by.

Storytelling in Multiple Forms

Storytelling is at the root of all popular education and community art processes; when they are integral to social movements like the food movement, these processes represent efforts to change the dominant story of a globalized, industrialized, and commodified food system.[30] They tap into the tales of courageous and creative people working in their communities to change unjust social structures and unsustainable food production. We've already seen examples of these counter-narratives that challenge official stories: the local stories of both human and non-human (plants, animals) in the Recipe for Change curriculum and workshops and the stories of Parkdale residents represented on community food maps that inform the West End Food Co-op's strategic planning. The FoodShed Project has adopted the tool of digital storytelling to bring to the fore the stories of other local food initiatives in the Southern Ontario **foodshed**, ranging from rare-breed animal producers that challenge dominant factory farming of livestock to community food centres that teach food bank users to grow their own food.

The FoodShed Project

The Southern Ontario FoodShed Project brings together agri-food organizations in the public, private, and non-profit sectors, working collaboratively with food scholars, activists, and students, to excavate, document, and link groups in a community of food practice considered the most innovative in North America. It works toward a vision of a resilient Ontario agri-food system that integrates native and diasporic populations, cuisines, and crops, and is centred on small-scale, networked, culturally diverse enterprises which together promise good jobs and environmental, social, and health benefits for twenty-first-century Ontario.[31] Based on design principles taken from theories of agroecology and food sovereignty,[32] the FoodShed Project aims to collaboratively map the shared history of sustainable, inclusive agri-food initiatives in Southern Ontario, to document innovations of rural and urban ventures, and to create a web platform for self-reflection and strategic analysis. It highlights three important processes: the *organizational ecology* of groups that are creating new forms of local economy; the *generational renewal* of these groups as they promote intergenerational dialogue and mentor new food producers and movement leaders; and the *cultural renewal* of new initiatives that draw upon diverse agricultural and related cultural practices of a diasporic population. Built as a loose network on a model of research constellations,[33] the FoodShed Project has no major funding, but has been responding to issues as they emerge.

While these initiatives represent a desire to reconnect the creative processes of growing, processing, and distributing our food in a more sustainable and just system, the project's methodology similarly represents a desire to reclaim control over the stories about this struggle to transform the food system, and over the forms they take. The research methodology is **participatory action research** (PAR) (Kemmis 1991),

an approach that shifts the power dynamics of conventional research and weds thoughtful reflection and informed action. Through PAR, groups and individuals frame the research and participate in the gathering of data, collective analysis, and creative dissemination of results to feed collaborative actions. Arts-based research methods lend themselves well to PAR projects, as they can open up aspects of peoples' beings, stories, memories, and aspirations in ways that other methods might miss. When people are given the opportunity to tell their own stories—whether through oral traditions, theatre, visual arts, music, or other media—they bring their bodies, minds, and spirits into a process of communicating and sharing their experiences, they affirm their lives as sources of knowledge, and they stimulate each other in a synergistic process of collective knowledge production. Art, education, and research become part of the same dynamic and creative process (Barndt 2011). While the FoodShed Project is cultivating multiple forms of popular creative expression in both the research and dissemination stages, it is digital storytelling that has been most used thus far in the participatory research process.

Digital Storytelling

With the technological advances of the Internet, new social media, user-friendly cameras, and editing software, the possibilities for ordinary people to tell and share their stories in digital form have burgeoned in the past decade. While there are many forms of digital stories, the particular genre adopted and adapted by the FoodShed Project grows out of a practice of the Centre for Digital Storytelling (CDS) in California and its Toronto branch, which has trained FoodShed research facilitators. A three-day workshop leads participants in creating their own digital stories. After working out a personal narrative through a story circle, each produces a three- to four-minute video, driven by the narrator's voiceover and incorporating still and moving images, and, if desired, music. The power of this multi-modal genre (Drotner 2008) derives from the personal stories, their points of view and emotional impact, the exploration of links between self-representation and collective issues in the story circle, and the empowering participatory process—transforming passive consumers of media into active producers. Its broader and deeper potential is that such processes are part of a 'participation revolution', in which 'the balance of power is gradually being shifted to people in the production of knowledge, goods and services' (Benkler 2003). This revolution can be observed within both the community media movement and the local food movement as people reclaim growing and cooking (Uzelman 2005).

The FoodShed Project used digital stories to tell not only personal stories but also organizational ones. Project coordinators also hoped that, as Joe Lambert, founder of the California-based CDS, suggests: 'Story [can be] the critical connection between personal subjective experience and larger political action, between individual and collective action' (Lambert 2002: 137). The goal was to feed the growing food movement, not only through the sharing of stories to provoke public dialogue but also through creating an online platform that would allow participants and groups to connect with each other, analyze and compare their practices, and find the links among them. Researchers were concerned as well not to romanticize or reify any stories—individual or collective—acknowledging that digital stories could reproduce oppressive attitudes and practices as well as helpful ones, and thus needed to be open to critical analysis in both the production process and in their educational use.[34]

Pilot Projects

In the winter of 2010, a public seminar was held at York University in Toronto on the theme of 'Local Food and Food Justice', featuring the work of five partners of the FoodShed Project. The seminar consciously posed some of the contradictions confronting the local food movement,[35] in particular the class and cultural differences perhaps best illustrated by the fact that 'local' food is often picked by Mexican and Jamaican migrant farm workers, who were represented on the panel by their advocates and allies in Justice for Migrant Workers.[36] Following this seminar, 10 students in a graduate cultural production workshop negotiated collaborative projects with six food organizations to produce digital stories on their work. There was great variation on the storytelling process through the different productions: for example, in some the subject was also the storyteller and media producer, while in others, the research facilitators produced stories based on the recorded narrative of a central character in the organization.[37] The following year, four more digital stories were created by students in collaboration with FoodShed partners including Farmstart, the AfriCan FoodBasket, Everdale Environmental Learning Centre, and FoodShare's Recipe for Change program. There was a particular effort to excavate and make visible the stories of new Canadians, of the training of new farmers, and of clear food justice initiatives.

The following five examples illustrate the diversity, challenges, and potential of this tool. 'Land Over Landings', produced by York doctoral student Andrew Bieler, drew on his own family's history on the agricultural land contested for an airport site, highlighting both its Aboriginal history and issues of development in the agricultural belt surrounding the GTA; as an artist, he incorporated collage and focused on artifacts like abandoned barns and farm machinery, along with music that hearkened back to a more active agricultural community. This digital story is being used by the Land Over Landings organization to promote their cause of preserving farmland and is to be used in workshops at local schools.

'Opal's Story: Envisioning Food Sovereignty' was collaboratively produced by York graduate students Magdalena Olszanowski and Sara Udow, and Opal Sparks, a volunteer at The Stop Community Food Centre. The story gives Opal's perspective on The Stop's transition from a food bank to an urban agricultural site that promotes food growing, preparation skills, and self-sufficiency among food bank users. This story deviates from the CDS norm in that Opal was not the media producer, though she did participate in editing her narrative and felt the resulting video fairly represented both her and the organization.

Reclaiming the role of storytellers as producers, but situating their personal stories in a global political context, Sama Bassidj and Erin Wolfson created a dialogue in poetry and image, 'Kitchen Stories', in which each probed the history of conflict in the Middle East as it played out in their diasporic family connections with Iran and Israel respectively. While exposing the broader issue of the construction of the 'other' and stereotypes of both Iranian and Jewish communities in the global media, Sama and Erin focused on the intimate family rituals melding food and religion that centred around the Persian New Year celebration and the Passover Seder. In this case, 'Kitchen Stories' became the starting point for a difficult conversation about commonalities and differences between two people and communities.

Two graduate students, Kellie Scanlan and Ciann Wilson, collaborated with Evelyn Encalada, staff person of Justice for Migrant Workers, to develop a digital story about migrant farm labour brought to Canada through the Seasonal Agricultural Worker Program. Both the gathering and the public showing of these stories is inevitably complex, both logistically and politically; migrant workers often put in 12-hour days, six and a half days a week, so their potential involvement was limited at best. Moreover, having their faces or even their stories in public view is quite threatening, as any critique they make of the program could result in their being sent home at the whim of their patron/employer. This example highlights the greater risks and therefore the greater invisibility of those workers most marginalized in the food system.[38] More time is needed to develop relationships and enter into collaborative production with groups like this, and the project continues.

Finally, in 2011, Caitlin Langlois Greenham worked with Anan Lololi of the AfriCan FoodBasket to tell the story of the struggle to develop an anti-racist food movement, both locally and continentally. 'Growing Food Justice in Toronto' challenges a movement that is still dominated by white middle-class activists to consider not only what is grown and how, but also whose voices are heard in the multi-sectoral efforts to effect food policy change.

Digital Distribution and Critical Use

While the empowering process of composing a personal narrative is emphasized in digital storytelling literature, there is a growing debate about the online use of the stories and their impact on broader movements (Thumin 2008). The FoodShed Project is establishing a web platform, which, among other uses, will host digital stories, building a bank of representations of partner organizations. How can the website encourage connections among groups in the Southern Ontario foodshed and the building of a regional identity and the coalitional capacity to act collectively around common interests and push for policy changes that promote more sustainable and just agri-food practices (Bromley 2010)? If the FoodShed Project becomes part of a regional research hub linked with other hubs across Canada, how can the website encourage connections, comparisons, and debates around strategies to transform not only provincial but also federal policies? The power of the Internet to build movements draws from its rhizome-like quality,[39] in that the technology allows the spontaneous, simultaneous formation of networks in many places, which may then join together into larger networks.

The digital stories themselves are available to a variety of audiences, including schools and community groups. The FoodShed team created a users' guide, 'Telling Stories, Eating Food: Using Digital Stories to Build the Food Justice Movement' to accompany a DVD with 10 digital stories. The guide encourages a critical decoding of the stories, deeper analysis of the forces shaping the personal stories, and the generation of stories by viewers that can be added to a growing collection.

Digital storytelling has taken off in a variety of institutional contexts. Coincidentally, a series similar to the FoodShed stories has been produced by the Centre for Digital Storytelling for Toronto Public Health to document a wide range of local food activity and to promote discussion around the new Toronto Food Strategy. The two efforts converged in a joint conference in April 2011, which launched the digital stories, honoured the subjects of the stories, and invited 200 grassroots food activists to use these short videos as catalysts for sharing their own stories. The conference, 'Our City, Our Food: Building the Food Movement through Digital Stories', encouraged participants in hands-on workshops to start local food initiatives and to join forces in influencing policy makers. In this way, the creative tools are feeding both grassroots movements and policy change.

Bringing Three Strategies Together: The Revival of Festivals

As the FoodShed example shows, there is still the need for face-to-face contact in the building of a movement, even when the main tools are digital and have a global reach. All three of the organizations featured in this chapter converged at the October 2010 'Eat-In Ontario' gathering, organized by FoodShare and also described above. The West End Food Co-op offered a workshop to help kids think about how farmers' markets and co-ops can support farmers and businesses; Carol Ferrari showed images of her Kitchen Bus, a mobile bakery whose outside walls are covered with murals featuring the Florida-based Coalition of Immokalee Workers.[40] They found that many kids were newcomers to Canada who were familiar with markets in their countries of origin but knew little about local alternatives in their new hometown. FoodShed Project researchers/producers led a workshop on digital storytelling, with high school kids taking part in a story circle. Environmental studies and community arts

students contributed to the festive atmosphere of the day through painting banners, dressing as clowns, and performing music. Just as the Sorauren Farmers' Market echoes the medieval markets that gathered together all kinds of creative activity,[41] the Recipe for Change launch was more a festival than a protest on the legislature grounds.

Food-related festivals in parks or in public spaces offer a vision of other ways of being and acting.[42] There has been a proliferation of such gatherings around food in Toronto and the surrounding region, including Feast of Fields, Evergreen's Picnic at the Brickworks and its Pollinator Festival (part of International Pollinator Week), the Conscious Food Festival, and the Vegetarian Food Festival.

Conclusion

Every day, people are creating the kind of society they dream of—not without struggle, but neither waiting for the revolution. They create what Bey calls 'temporary autonomous zones' (1991): prefigurative social movements that are feeding broader movements for social change, ones that move beyond critique of the existing systems to proposing and creating alternatives. Community-engaged art making and popular education bring energy to these spaces and help us imagine the possibilities. They honour us as whole beings—thinking, feeling, and acting—within communities that are constantly reinventing culture. The examples shared here—an educational festival launching a campaign for food literacy, the democratic building of a food co-op through maps and murals, and the communication of local food initiatives through digital stories—all reveal the ways that education and art catalyze creativity in the food justice movement and affirm that another world is possible.

May a thousand roots deepen, may a thousand stories sprout!

Discussion Questions

1. How are the three case studies introduced in this chapter challenging the conventional food system?

2. What are the constraints and possibilities of the Recipe for Change campaign to transform the provincial educational curriculum?

3. How could the popular education processes used in the development of the West End Food Co-op be applied to the development of other grassroots organizations?

4. What are the potential uses of the digital stories collaboratively produced with local food organizations in the FoodShed Project? What are their strengths and limitations?

5. How do you think a food justice movement can be built? What do you think about the strategies proposed in this chapter?

Further Reading

1. Barndt, Deborah with VIVA! Project Partners. Ed. 2011. *VIVA! Community Arts and Popular Education in the Americas.* Albany, NY: SUNY Press.

   The culmination of a five-year exchange among eight partners (both universities and NGOs) in five countries (Panama, Nicaragua, Mexico, the United States, and Canada), this book introduces a rich array of projects that integrate the arts into social-movement building. Framed by notions of place (decolonization), politics (popular education), passion (community arts), and praxis (participatory action research), the projects range from participatory mural production with Indigenous communities in Chiapas, Mexico, to community play productions in multicultural Toronto. Beautifully illustrated with colour photos, the book is accompanied by a DVD of nine videos that bring the projects alive.

2. Gottlieb, Robert, and Anupama Joshi. 2010. *Food Justice.* Cambridge, MA: MIT Press.

   The concept of food justice considers how race and poverty in particular are reproduced and can be challenged in the building of a multi-sectoral food movement. Gottlieb

   and Joshi eschew single-issue organizing and advocate for potential alliances among health, environment, labour, and food organizations organized around food justice.

3. Mackey, Clarke. 2010. *Random Acts of Culture: Reclaiming Art and Community in the 21st Century.* Toronto: Between the Lines.

   How did we get to the place where we see 'art' as the privilege of a few professionals and a commodity for the rest of us to consume? Mackey offers a historical reflection on the emergence of consumer and spectator culture, and advocates for vernacular culture, or the ways that people are daily creating culture and community—through storytelling, family rituals, community singing, street dancing, and making beauty out of objects around us. Food is central to community building, and community gardens and feasts are art in themselves.

4. Smith, Gregory, and David Sobel. 2010. *Place- and Community-Based Education in Schools.* New York and London: Routledge.

   This guide for educators, parents, and community members suggests ways that local and experiential education can be integrated into school curricula, whether through traditional subjects such as social studies and natural sciences or through art and music. Many examples of community-engaged practices are offered, as well as strategies for challenging and transforming school systems that are focused on test-driven studies and text-based learning.

5. Wittman, Hannah, Annette Aurélie Desmarais, and Nettie Wiebe. Eds. 2011. *Food Sovereignty in Canada: An Alternative Food and Agricultural Policy*. Halifax, NS: Fernwood Publishing.

This collection applies the concept of food sovereignty to the Canadian food movement and efforts to change public policy. See especially Harriet Friedmann's chapter 'Food Sovereignty in the Golden Horseshoe Region of Ontario', which examines the challenges of renewing agriculture in both rural and urban contexts in the southern Ontario foodshed, and offers examples of initiatives by many partners in the FoodShed Project, ranging from Farmstart for new Canadian farmers to Local Food Plus scaling up procurement practices, from municipal government initiatives like the Toronto Food Strategy to social enterprises such as Arvinda's Healthy Gourmet Indian Cooking School.

Notes

Special thanks to Katie Sandwell for her support in the research and editing of this chapter, and to Andrew Bieler, Debbie Field, Meredith Hayes, Sally Miller, Magda Olszanowski, and Sara Udow for their thoughtful reading of drafts and helpful editorial suggestions.

1. ChocoSol Traders; see http://chocosol. posterous.com/.
2. See www.greenestcity.ca.
3. See www.gardenjane.com.
4. A 'slow theory' has emerged from the Slow Food movement, based on a critique of globalization, its environmental costs and lost pleasures, and embracing what Nicola Perullo calls 'slow knowledge', which emphasizes 'wisdom, understanding and experience', in contrast to 'fast knowledge' that is technologically driven. See Andrews (2008: 177).
5. Not all vendors are happy when other activities take over and market visitors shop less!
6. With the cutbacks to public education, schools became dependent on deals with corporate beverage companies, creating a cynical competition between 'Coke schools' and 'Pepsi schools', but this sponsorship has become the target of resistance and has been rejected in certain school districts in Canada and the United States.

7. Painting our Stories shares a website portal with the West End Food Co-op at www. paintingourstories.ca.
8. Harriet Friedmann of the University of Toronto and the author are co-coordinators of the FoodShed Project.
9. Patricia Allen (2004: 55) also examines how priorities of sustainable agriculture and community food security are being integrated into dominant agri-food institutions in the United States.
10. Clearly, many of the relocalizing initiatives like my farmers' market serve primarily a middle-class population, with costs being beyond the means of low-income people. But there are many structural obstacles to overcome: for example, lack of support for farmers and an expectation that we spend a smaller percentage of our budgets on food, while we may pay much more for other items such as electronics.
11. I am using these body parts—head, heart, stomach—more as metaphors, very conscious that such use only reinforces a fragmented view of the body and the earth based in Western scientific thought, while I advocate a more holistic 'cosmovision' that emphasizes the connectedness and interrelationships of all living entities.

12. Commensality is the act of eating together, and is increasingly a radical notion, given that we've become a 'grazing culture' with people eating in their cars, in front of the TV, etc.

13. Conviviality is central to the Slow Food movement and to the local group ChocoSol Traders referred to in note 1.

14. For a more detailed overview, see http://en.wikipedia.org/wiki/Holistic_education.

15. Cree and Salish writer Lee Maracle of the Stó:lō Nation offered this definition of art in a workshop on The Art of Decolonization organized by Community Arts Ontario and Jumblies Theatre on 25 November 2010.

16. I recognize that I am reproducing a dichotomy that I am challenging, by talking about 'body, mind, and spirit' and 'head and heart' as though they were separate, when in fact, I agree with eco-philosopher Susan Griffin (1995): 'Of course, the body and mind are not separate. . . . Consciousness cannot exclude bodily knowledge.'

17. An earlier event in February 2010 also launched Recipe for Change with a fundraiser featuring almost 30 of Toronto's top chefs and transforming the FoodShare warehouse into a candle-lit gourmet food–tasting extravaganza. The combination of events like this, aimed at the more affluent of the local food movement with free food events like the FoodShare AGM (feeding 300, including low-income users of the Good Food Markets) and the Eat-In Ontario gathering, reflects a kind of Robin Hood strategy that creates allies of more privileged food activists and provides funds to subsidize initiatives in poorer communities.

18. Judy Rebick (2009: 169–84) quotes FoodShare executive director Debbie Field on this strategy 'to propose rather than oppose'; both build on the use of this mantra of the World Social Forum.

19. 4-H clubs, like home economics classes, were often very gendered, so that girls undertook cooking and sewing projects, while boys cared for animals and built useful objects. 4-H clubs are still operating throughout Canada today and seem to have made some effort to redress gender imbalances: www.4-hontario.ca.

20. Jamie Oliver's 'Feed Me Better' campaign developed as part of the television program *Jamie's School Dinners*, which implemented healthy meals in a school in Greenwich, a London neighbourhood. It became the centre of a significant political campaign, collecting more than 270,000 signatures on an online petition pushing for reforms and increased funding for school meals. Then–prime minister Tony Blair pledged £280 million to improving school meals and promised to set up a School Food Trust. The government went on to adopt stringent new standards for school meals. See www.jamieoliver.com/media/jo_sd_history.pdf.

21. A disappointing exception was a series *The Globe and Mail* newspaper ran in November 2010 focusing on food safety and arguing for a more competitive Canada in the global 'bigger is better' agri-food business, ignoring any discussion of its impact on workers and human and environmental health, and framing 'locavore' initiatives as individual and isolated. www.theglobeandmail.com/news/national/time-to-lead/global-food.

22. See www.foodchainworkers.org.

23. Sally Miller was a major source of information for this section. Interview with author, 17 September 2010.

24. The co-op uses the title 'coordinator' instead of 'manager', which has top-down connotations.

25. Sally Miller resigned as manager in the fall of 2010, but continues to be active in the co-op.

26. See Hannah Lewis's 'Getting There from Here: A Guidebook for Facilitators—Community Mapping for Place-Based Environmental Education, Community Development and Social Change' for a theoretical and methodological introduction to community mapping, and many popular education exercises that can help generate community mapping processes (see http://communitymap.blogspot.com/2010/04/getting-here-from-there-guidebook-for.html).

27. The lifetime membership fee is only $5—very accessible to many local residents. The bond strategy is indeed an explicit response to the question of how to raise funds without relying on membership and therefore excluding lower-income community members.

28. Freirean problem-posing education often used images as catalysts to spark discussion about issues and relate them to their personal experience. See Barndt, 'The World in a Tomato' (1998).

29. See www.paintingourstories.ca.
30. See Patrick Reinsborough and Doyle Canning, *Re:Imagining Change: How to use story-based strategy to win campaigns, build movements, and change the world* (Oakland, CA: PM Press, 2010). Available free at http://inthemiddleofthewhirlwind.wordpress.com/changing-the-story/.
31. Some of this section was drawn from an application for a Community–University Research Alliance grant, written primarily by food scholar Harriet Friedmann of the University of Toronto, with the author.
32. Food sovereignty is increasingly being adopted as a framework for food justice groups in Canada, drawing from a global movement led by Third World peasant and Indigenous groups, who focus on their rights to land and control of the food production process. See Wittman et al. (2010).
33. The Centre for Social Innovation in Toronto promotes a model of research constellations, which is flexible, nimble, and adaptable (Surman and Surman 2008). Those with interest, energy, and commitment collaborate until they are satisfied with results or lose interest. Constellations are self-organizing and self-governing; they arise easily when partners share an overall goal of food system change and have relationships of trust with each other and with the FoodShed Project.
34. In February 2010, we were part of a conference, 'Shooting Back: Photography, Power, and Participation—Celebrating and Challenging Photo Voice and Digital Storytelling Approaches', which brought together practitioners and scholars to critically examine our practices, their organizational contexts, and their ethical tensions.
35. Another contradiction in the local food movement relates to the need to maintain some global trade, but to demand fair trade, while also promoting relocalization.
36. See www.justicia4migrantworkers.org. See also Ramsaroop and Wolk (2009).
37. Six of these digital stories were screened at the Canadian Association for Food Studies in May 2010 in Montreal, and students also presented a critical reflection paper on the methodology itself for other food scholars and practitioners.
38. Nonetheless, creative strategies have been adopted by migrant farm workers organizing all over North America; an inspiring example comes from the Coalition of Immokalee Workers, who have built their coalition through popular education and popular theatre representations of the slave-like conditions of tomato fields in Florida. See www.ciw-online.org/
39. See Scott Uzelman's (2005) adaptation of Deleuze and Guatari's notion of the 'rhizome', often used to describe that emergence of decentralized social movements.
40. See www.ciw-online.org/.
41. For a genealogy of festivals, see Ehrenreich (2006).
42. Robin Kelly (2002) proposes a similar vision, and suggests that 'unless we have the space to imagine and a vision of what it means fully to realize our humanity, all the protests and demonstrations in the world won't bring about our liberation'.

References

Allen, Patricia. 2004. *Together at the Table: Sustainability and Sustenance in the American Agrifood System*. University Park, PA: Pennsylvania University Press.

Anderssen, Erin. 2010. 'Schools Offering Lessons in Emotions, Social Development'. *Globe and Mail*, 18 November. Available at www.theglobeandmail.com/life/family-and-relationships/schools-offering-lessons-in-emotions-social-development/article1804669/.

Andrews, G. 2008. *The Slow Food Story: Politics and Pleasure*. Montreal: McGill–Queen's University Press.

Arnold, Rick, Bev Burke, Carl James, D'Arcy Martin, and Barb Thomas. 1991. *Educating for Change*. Toronto: Between the Lines.

Barndt, Deborah. 1990. *To Change This House: Popular Education Under the Sandinistas*. Toronto, ON: Between the Lines.

———. 1998. 'The World in a Tomato: Revisiting the Use of "Codes" in Freire's Problem-Posing Education'. *Tribute to Paulo Freire* (special issue), *Convergence* 31(1–2): 62–73.

———. 2008. *Tangled Routes: Women, Work, and Globalization on the Tomato Trail*. Lanham, MD: Rowan & Littlefield.

———. 2011. Introduction to *VIVA! Community Arts and Popular Education in the Americas*. Albany, NY: SUNY Press.

Benkler, Yochai. 2003. 'The Political Economy of Commons'. *Upgrade* IV(3) June, 6–9.

Bey, Hakim. 1991. *TAZ: The Temporary Autonomous Zone, Ontological Anarchy, Poetic Terrorism*. Brooklyn: Autonomedia, 1985, 1991.

Bromley, Roger. 2010. 'Storying Community: Re-imagining Regional Identities through Public Cultural Activity'. *European Journal of Cultural Studies* 13 no. 1 February, 9–25.

Drotner, Kirsten. 2008. 'Boundaries and Bridges: Digital Storytelling in Education Studies and Media Studies'. In *Digital Storytelling, Mediatized Stories: Self-Representations in New Media*, ed. Knut Lundby. New York: Peter Lang, 61–85.

Ehrenreich, Barbara. 2006. *Dancing in the Streets: A History of Collective Joy*. New York: Henry Holt and Company.

FoodShare. 2010. Accessed 15 November 2010 at www.foodshare.net.

———. 2011. www.foodshare.net/schools-eatinont.htm.

Friedmann, Harriet. 2011. 'Food Sovereignty in the Golden Horseshoe Region of Ontario'. In *Food Sovereignty in Canada: An Alternative Food and Agricultural Policy*, ed. Hannah Wittman, Annette Aurélie Desmarais, and Nettie Wiebe. Halifax, NS: Fernwood Publishing, 169–89.

Freire, Paulo. 2002. *Pedagogy of the Oppressed*. New York: Continuum.

Gladwell, Malcolm. 2000. *The Tipping Point: How Little Things Can Make a Big Difference*. Boston: Little, Brown.

Gottlieb, Robert, and Anupama Joshi. 2010. *Food Justice*. Cambridge, MA: MIT Press.

Griffin, Susan. *The Eros of Everyday Life: Essays on Ecology, Gender and Society*. New York: Doubleday, 1995.

Gruenewald, David. 2003. 'Foundations of Place: A Multidisciplinary Framework for Place-Conscious Education'. *American Educational Research Journal* 40: 619–54.

Kelley, Robin D.G. 2002. *Freedom Dreams: The Black Radical Imagination*. Boston: Beacon Press.

Kemmis, S. 1991. 'Critical Education Research'. *The Canadian Journal for the Study of Adult Education* 5 (Winter: special issue): 94–119.

Kneen, Brewster. 2003. *From Land to Mouth: Understanding the Food System, Second Helping*. Toronto: NC Press.

LaDuke, Winona. 1999. *All Our Relations: Native Struggles for Land and Life*. Cambridge, MA: South End Press.

Lambert, Joe. 2002. *Digital Storytelling: Capturing Lives, Creating Community*. Berkeley, CA: Digital Diner Press.

Mackey, Clarke. 2010. *Random Acts of Culture: Reclaiming Art and Community in the 21st Century*. Toronto: Between the Lines.

Miller, Sally. 2008. *Edible Action: Food Activism and Alternative Economics*. Black Point, NS: Fernwood Publishing.

Parker, B. 2006. 'Constructing Community through Maps? Power and Praxis in Community Mapping'. *Professional Geographer* 58(4): 470–84.

Ramsaroop, Chris, and Katie Wolk. 2009. 'Can We Achieve Racial Equality in the Food Security Movement?' In *The Edible City: Toronto's Food from Farm to Fork*, ed. Christina Palassio and Alana Wilcox. Toronto: Coach House Books, 252–63.

Rebick, Judy. 2009. *Transforming Power: From the Personal to the Political*. Toronto: Penguin.

Reiter, Ester. 1996. *Making Fast Food: From the Frying Pan into the Fryer*. Montreal: McGill-Queen's University Press.

Roberts, Wayne. 2008. *The No-Nonsense Guide to World Food*. Toronto: The New Internationalist.

Snyder, Benson R. 1970. *The Hidden Curriculum*. New York: Alfred A. Knopf.

Surman, Tonya, and Mark Surman. 2008. 'Open Sourcing Social Change: Inside the Constellation Model'. *Open Source Business Resource*. September. Available at www.osbr.ca/ojs/index.php/osbr/article/view/698/0.

Thumin, Nancy. 2008. '"It's Good for Them to Know My Story": Cultural Mediation as Tension'. In *Digital Storytelling, Mediatized Stories: Self-Representations in New Media*, ed. Knut Lundby. New York: Peter Lang, 85–104.

Uzelman, Scott. 2005. 'Chapter Two: Hard at Work in the Bamboo Garden'. In *Autonomous Media: Activating Resistance and Dissent*, ed. Andrea Langlois and Frederic Dubois. Montreal: Cumulus Press, 17–31.

Wittman, Hannah, Annette Aurélie Desmarais, and Nettie Wiebe, eds. 2010. *Food Sovereignty: Reconnecting Food, Nature and Community*. Black Point, NS: Fernwood.

Working Group on Environmental Education. 2007. *Shaping Our Schools Shaping Our Future: Environmental Education in Ontario Schools*. Report of the Working Group on Environmental Education. Prepared for the Ontario Ministry of Education. June.

PART II

Analytical Perspectives in Food Studies

What are the components of a food system, and how do they relate to each other? What explains some of the food-related problems such as hunger, obesity, and the farm crisis? While answers to these questions are unique to their historical and geographical contexts, there are broader social forces that reveal similarities in patterns and explain interrelations among food-related social problems and various social forces, processes, and institutions. Analytical explanations allow us to understand and explain these broad patterns and interrelations among different parts that compose the whole. In this part we will present four analytical perspectives that have influenced many researchers in food studies.

In Chapter 6, Albritton offers us an account of the historical transformation of the agri-food system from the political economy perspective. Emphasizing the significance of relations of production in human history, the political economy perspective underlines the historical specificity of each epoch with a dominant mode of production and corresponding patterns of class relations and social organization in society. Using this perspective, Albritton examines the impacts of two great revolutions in the agri-food system. The first revolution brought us agriculture and animal husbandry about 10,000 years ago. The second one—the 'agricultural industrial revolution'—combines the mechanical, chemical, and biotech revolutions in agriculture. Albritton argues that the second revolution enabled global capitalism to increasingly enter and control the food system, which explains many of the problems associated with the modern agri-food system.

In Chapter 7, Weis looks at the environmental problems associated with the agri-food system from the political ecology perspective. Political ecology borrows insights from political economy by looking at political-economic tendencies and power imbalances, but also pays special attention to ecological instabilities in how systems operate. Looking through the political ecology lens, Weis identifies the hidden environmental costs of cheap food by focusing on the industrial grain–oilseed–livestock complex and examines how the pressures to standardize and mechanize agriculture magnify biological and physical problems.

Chapter 8 brings a feminist perspective. Feminists pay specific attention to the causes and consequences of inequalities of power between men and women and the division of labour at home and in the workplace. Brady, Gingras, and Power argue that much of the earlier social science literature and the relatively new field of food studies have neglected gender analysis. They contend that scholarly analyses of food must pay attention to gender because of the centrality of women to foodwork and the resulting gender inequalities in matters of food, foodwork, and bodies.

In Chapter 9, Beagan and Chapman outline the importance of discourse analysis in food studies. For these authors, 'discourse' refers to pervasive ways of thinking that over time come to define what can be said about something, or even to define what can be considered possible. Using discourse analysis, they examine the influences on people's everyday food practices by focusing on how people understand what constitutes 'healthy eating'. They argue that the different ways people think, talk, and act in relation to healthy eating are associated with various aspects of their identities. In their view, 'healthy eating' is seen as a 'socially constructed, shifting discourse that shapes and is shaped by what people say and do in relation to food, and that is specifically implicated in the ways people understand and perform their social identities'. Gender, age, ethnicity, and social class play a role in the social construction of reality and the way people understand and speak about their behaviour.

While other analytical perspectives are also used in food studies, this part gives readers a taste of some of the perspectives that prevail in the field.

6

Two Great Food Revolutions
The Domestication of Nature and the Transgression of Nature's Limits
Robert Albritton

Learning Objectives

Through this chapter, you can:

1. Understand the centrality of profit to capitalism and how this centrality affects agricultural production
2. Understand the immense significance of the original domestication of plants and animals in comparison to the previous gathering and hunting
3. Examine manual field labour and conditions for agricultural workers
4. Look at how the increased turnover of agricultural capital may increase profits and examine some of the negative consequences
5. Understand why excluding the costs of externalities from capitalist market prices makes it difficult to address health and sustainability in connection with the food system

Introduction

Historians and anthropologists often claim that the most important change in human history was the domestication of plants and animals that started around 15,000 BCE (before the common era) and was more or less complete by 5000 BCE. The changes in food provision that have occurred since the Second World War, however, may be even more important. I refer to these recent changes as the 'second great food revolution'.

The first revolution gave us agriculture and animal husbandry. It may seem strange to refer to changes that occurred slowly over 10,000 years as a 'revolution', but sometimes deep, restructuring changes that have a monumental impact do take a long time. Fifteen thousand years ago change proceeded very slowly compared to today. The second revolution, which began in 1945 and continues to the present, is both deep and, in world-historic time, quite fast. This revolution combines the mechanical, chemical, and bio-tech revolutions, which together enable global **capitalism** to increasingly enter and control the food system. It is this second revolution, agriculture becoming capitalist, that is the primary focus of this chapter.

The United States's food provisioning system is at the centre of this revolution, and corn is the largest and most important crop grown in the United States. Focusing on corn, therefore, is a good entry into understanding some of the main features of capitalist agriculture. The United States is the *core* of the global food system as the most dominant and most capitalist power within the system. At the same time, other countries within the system have varying degrees of power and practise capitalism to different degrees. Furthermore, different countries are integrated into the system in different ways and to varying extents. For example, Cuba is one of the least integrated into the global capitalist food system, and Canada is one of the most.

While the United States is the core of the increasingly global food system, it is important to remember that because of its proximity to the United States, Canada's food system has many interconnections both with that of the United States and with the larger global system. I hope that this chapter will help readers examine the many Canadian examples in this book and outline a few of the similarities and differences between agricultural production in the United States and in Canada.

The approach to understanding capitalism in this chapter is strongly influenced by Karl Marx's important insights into the nature of capitalism and into how a society could be more egalitarian and democratic (Albritton 2009, 2011). As the analysis unfolds, it will become clearer why I refer to the current food revolution as 'capitalist'.

Gathering and Hunting (2 million BCE to 15,000 BCE)

Food provisioning stands at the very centre of human evolution. Over the millions of years of this evolution, nearly all of what might be called 'work' was preoccupied with satisfying the basic human needs to eat and drink. *Homo*

erectus, one of modern humankind's ancestors, began to slowly move outward from their African home about a million and a half years ago. They remained in the tropics and semi-tropics where food was plentiful year-round and easily extracted directly from nature. For a very long time humans lived in this way, in groups of 25 to 50. When nature's food supply diminished, a group would simply move on to a more plentiful environment. Over most of this evolution there were no techniques for storing or conserving food, so there was no motivation to accumulate more food than could be consumed before it spoiled. Since the tropics were highly productive ecosystems, early hominids and humans had much more leisure time than modern humans. For example, they might very well have taken only two or three days to provide food needed for a week; since they had few needs other than food, the remaining time was leisure time. As anthropologist Marshall Sahlins (1972: 1–5, 14) has claimed, if leisure time is the measure of an affluent society, then, ironically, these early societies were far more affluent than ours. According to Marx and Friedrich Engels (1978: 734–59), the most interesting point about this early period is the general absence of any surplus over and above subsistence and thus the absence of **class relations** that an ongoing surplus makes possible. For once there is a surplus, a dominant class may take control of most of it, and thereby take control of socio-economic life.

It is no accident that *hunting* typically precedes *gathering* in the traditional term *hunting and gathering*; for a long time anthropologists seemed to agree that hunting played a far more important role in human evolution than gathering, and that men did the hunting and women the gathering. On the contrary, we now know that in most cases far more food was supplied by gathering than by hunting, and that sometimes males gathered and women hunted. No doubt hunting did influence human evolution, but it is likely that gathering was more influential.

A more accurate term, then, would be *gathering and hunting*.

The First Great Food Revolution (15,000 BCE to 5000 BCE)

The domestication of plants and animals may be the most important development in human history. Improvements in gathering and hunting would entail simply finding better ways of taking food from the wild; domestication, by contrast, involves the taming and shaping of the wild itself, presumably to better serve human needs. Words like *cultivate* and *agriculture* imply the entry of other living and growing things into human *culture*. Indeed, since its development, agriculture has formed the basis of human food provisioning, though there are exceptions, such as in far northern societies where agriculture is not possible.

The first farmers were groups or extended families who developed more or less co-operative divisions of both the labour and the products. There would have been no strong sense of private property; rather, an extended family or group of families might farm in a particular area, giving it some sense of property based on use, while a particular area might be considered a 'commons' where all families would graze animals or gather wood co-operatively. Thus, while early agriculture might have given rise to the first weak sense of private property, it would not typically be the strong sense that develops later with capitalism, in which a single owner of a piece of land could in principle have a total monopoly over access, control, and use.

As the domestication of plants and animals spread and developed, food productivity gradually increased, generating a relatively stable and growing surplus. It is this surplus that opened the door to radical changes in social and economic structures. First, a food surplus made it possible for increasing numbers of people to be freed from the work of food production, who might then focus on, for example, craft production, art, politics, religion, or war.

Second, surplus food enabled the population to grow in relatively permanent settlements that could trade food and crafts with other settlements and thus develop a degree of specialization. The global population never exceeded 4 million people during the very long era of gathering and hunting. Between 10,000 BCE and 500 BCE, the domestication of nature enabled the global population to increase from 4 million to 100 million; compare this growth to that associated with the post–Second World War capitalist food revolution, which allowed the global population to increase from 2.55 billion in 1950 to 6.8 billion in 2009. Demographers expect the global population to level off at around 9 billion by 2050, though such predictions are always subject to fairly large variations.

Third, food surpluses presented the possibility of class **stratification**. In other words, by systematically taking over most social surplus, one class could come to be dominant. At first this would likely have been a warrior class, institutionalizing itself as an economic master class that also controlled the state.

Fourth, state functions could begin to emerge, as the dominant class generated a key decision-making group that would make and enforce laws, collect taxes, promulgate religion, and make war.

These four changes are fundamental to the evolution of human societies to this day. Today in the most advanced capitalist countries farm productivity is high enough that typically less than 3 per cent of the population work in the farming sector. This percentage is continuously decreasing, particularly in places like the United States and Canada where a long tradition of family farming is being undermined by large corporate-controlled modes of agriculture.

In the ancient world, a major reason for the decline of civilizations was the degradation of soil caused by lack of knowledge of how to replenish the soil's fertility, by deforestation, or sometimes by salination (the buildup of salts in the soil due to irrigation). Today civilization is threatened not only by soil degradation (although this is occurring), but also by global warming, generalized pollution, and the depletion of non-renewable resources, most notably fossil fuels and fresh water, but also many other resources such as helium, phosphorous, and copper.

The Second Great Food Revolution: Capitalism Takes Over Food Production

Though capitalism first developed in England as early as the seventeenth and eighteenth centuries, and has been the predominant economic system globally for at least two centuries, agriculture came under its control in the United States and Canada only after the Second World War (Albritton 1993). Capitalism gained control over agriculture very late in its history because some general features of capitalism do not fit well with agriculture, and because some general features of agriculture in the United States and Canada made it resistant to capitalism until after the Second World War.

Capitalism and Agriculture

The most basic aim of capitalism is to accumulate the greatest **profit** in the least time. This is done by maximizing the spread between the production cost and the selling price of a commodity, by expanding the market for the profitable commodity as quickly as possible, and by increasing the speed at which a unit of capital turns over. Maximizing profit overrides all other goals or values in a capitalist system, for a capitalist's very survival as such depends upon making a profit. A strong though arguable case can be made that ultimately profits depend on getting workers to give maximum effort for minimum pay, so that each worker produces more value than he or she receives back in the form of wages. Marx called the difference between value created by workers and the value they receive back as wages **exploitation**, such that the higher the rate of exploitation, the greater the profits (Marx 1976, Parts II–IV).

Another important dimension of profit making is the speed of **circuits of capital** or **turnover time** between purchase of inputs and sale of outputs (Marx 1978, Part II). For example, if one unit of capital turns over five times a year and a second, similar unit turns over once a year, then the first will earn five times more profit than the second. Each instant that capital is idle or its circuit slows down means profit lost forever. In short, time is money; the goal is the fastest turnover, and hence the greatest profit. There are other important principles inherent to capitalism, but for now we will take these three (profit, exploitation, fast turnover) as central.

These principles can help us understand capitalism's difficulties with agriculture. Suppose a capitalist finds the rate of profit in corn production attractive. Unlike factory production, which in principle requires only buying the needed raw materials, tools, and labour, agriculture poses specific problems. Fertile land may be hard to buy, and access to sufficient water may pose problems. Because temperate farming is seasonal, a given crop can be planted and harvested only once or twice a year (depending on how long it takes to grow); thus there is a natural limit on speeding up turnover time. It may be difficult to find enough workers at harvest time if hand-picking is required. Transportation and storage of crops may be costly. Finally, because agricultural commodities are so dependent upon unpredictable natural forces such as weather, diseases, or insect infestations, prices can vary widely, causing large unexpected losses or gains.

Capitalism's emphasis on profit means human health, environmental health, and social justice are ignored unless they affect profit or unless laws require that these be considered. The problem here is that capitalist markets by themselves do not measure long-term social and ecological costs or benefits, which are dumped into the theoretical black box that economists call **externalities**. If the costs of externalities, such as considerations of long-term human flourishing, far exceed profits, then capitalist markets can be considered irrational, meaning that very large costs and benefits are excluded from prices. And this is precisely what is happening. The growing irrationality of our capitalist economic system needs to be fully recognized if we are to deal with the pressing, mutually exacerbating crises of, for example, economy, health, food, water, petroleum (and other non-renewable resources), and climate change. Long-term, global, systemic problems require long-term, global, systemic solutions, although global solutions may often get their start at a local level.

Let me explain briefly why I prefer to name the main problem *capitalism* and not *globalization* or *industrialization*. If the main problem that agriculture faces is globalization or industrialization, then strategies of change are likely to be different than if the main problem is seen to be capitalism. Globalization emphasizes the spatial aspect, arguing that too much control is wielded at a global level rather than at the state, regional, or local level. Industrialization emphasizes the large factory-like units of production that are coming to dominate in the global food system. While both of these perspectives underline important problems with current agriculture, neither is as broad nor as meaningful as the capitalism perspective.

Arguably it is capitalism that is the main cause of both the globalization and the industrialization of food production. Capitalism emphasizes the profit motive that underlies both the exploitation of workers up and down the food chain and efforts to continuously speed up the food chain. And, as already mentioned, capitalism helps us to understand why long-range social and environmental costs are often ignored in favour of short-term profits. Thus, for example, it may be profitable to replace rain forests with monocultures such as the palm oil plantations now expanding in Indonesia and Malaysia, but the long-term costs of climate change, health problems for plantation workers, species loss, and land degradation make the profits negligible in comparison. If we were more critical of capitalism, we could more

actively intervene in markets to make the prices of commodities reflect real long-term social and environmental costs or benefits. If we did this, palm oil plantations would not exist on the scale and in the locations that they do, because they would not be profitable. In short, we need prices that take into account long-run human and environmental flourishing and that are not based narrowly on short-term production costs and selling prices.

A proto-capitalist agriculture first developed in Britain in the seventeenth and eighteenth centuries, followed by a long history of capitalism's alternating attraction to and repulsion from agriculture. I strongly believe that it makes sense to claim that full-fledged capitalist agriculture first developed in the United States after the Second World War and subsequently has become the dominant type of agriculture globally. While it exists in its most unadulterated form in the United States, the world domination by capitalist agriculture means not only that it is the predominant form of agriculture globally but also that it tends to shape other forms of agriculture more than it is shaped by them. Thus global agriculture is dominated by capitalist corporate farming—controlled by large corporations—which in turn shapes all other modes of farming that still exist to some extent in the world: capitalist collective farming, capitalist state farming, capitalist family farming, capitalist co-operatives, capitalist slavery, and capitalist feudalism (and various permutations and combinations of these). I place *capitalist* in front of each type of farming to emphasize the formative powers of capitalism over it. In other words, each mode of production or set of property relations is modified in varying degrees by the dominant capitalist system. At the same time there are many movements to break free from capitalist agriculture that are gradually gaining strength.

While I focus on US corn production as a particularly revealing case study of some of capitalist agriculture's problems, were I to do a truly global analysis, agriculture would be viewed as having multiple dimensions interconnected by a capitalism that asserts various degrees of control and domination in different parts of the world and in different agricultural and food sectors. Note that the focus here is on agriculture as a whole and not specifically on food provisioning. Agriculture can be considered to consist of 'commodity chains' that start with crop production and end up as cotton shirts, cigars, ethanol, roast beef, or waste.

Agriculture in North America

The family farm rooted itself deeply in the culture of the United States and Canada, where, in contrast to Britain, there was no landlord **class** that centralized landownership into large estates and therefore into a few hands. In the United States and Canada, family farmers, with military backing, pushed the Aboriginal peoples off the land and into reservations, and typically set up farms that one family could manage with existing technology. Further, since much of the soil had not been previously farmed, it tended to be fertile. In the middle of the nineteenth century, North American farms became larger with the introduction of horse-drawn machinery, which was particularly effective on prairie flatlands. Better storage and transportation meant that the increasing grain surpluses could be traded abroad, so that by the second half of the nineteenth century a global market for basic grains was created—for wheat in particular. Prairie grain, with high yields at lower cost, quickly took over the growing global market, and capitalists discovered ways of profiting from family farms from the outside, thereby avoiding the risks and difficulties of farming itself.

Family farmers may have occasionally hired a few farmhands, but for the most part they relied on family labour and not the wage labour that is the basis of capitalist profits. If they exploited anyone's labour it was their own and not that of others. Family farmers may try to maximize

profits, but not by the basic capitalist activity of exploiting wage labour. Also, because family farms are usually relatively permanent settlements, farmers would tend not to maximize short-term profits if in doing so they would undermine the long-term fertility of the soil or other basic conditions of sustainable farming.

A family farm, therefore, would typically not be capitalist unless it were to hire a significant number of wage labourers. Since family farmers are self-employed, their labour cannot be directly exploited by capitalists, but it can be exploited at arm's-length or indirectly. Storage and transportation companies, merchants, and bankers can exploit farmers by charging high fees for their services. Because crops can be wiped out by floods or droughts, because farm machinery can be expensive, and because income arrives in lumps when harvests are sold, farmers are particularly dependent upon banks or other creditors who can ultimately foreclose if debts go unpaid. For these reasons, various economic safety nets have been devised and legislated for farmers, but in many cases they are far less supportive than required, especially when smaller farms need help.

The phase of capitalism that developed after the Second World War is labelled in various ways; the label depends upon the theoretical emphasis. One such label, *Fordism*, emphasizes the mass production and consumption of consumer durables, named for Henry Ford's manufacturing and selling of cars. Mass consumption of such products required significant increases in working-class income. Because mass consumption was a novel economic concept and was so important to this phase of capitalism, I like to use the label *consumerism* (Albritton 1991, ch. 8). In order for consumerism to work, workers needed to spend far less of their total income on food and drink, leaving them more disposable income to buy houses, cars, and appliances. Capitalism had to find ways to decrease the price of food through large increases in productivity, large decreases in production costs (particularly the cost of labour), or both.

The numerous uncontrollable risk factors that always threatened farm profit margins began to be sharply diminished by the mechanization, chemicalization, and biological manipulations that became widespread after the Second World War. Before these innovations, the high risks and low gains of traditional agriculture made it uninviting to capitalists, who had oriented most of their profit-making activities toward factory production. But the technological revolutions after the Second World War promised significant economies of scale (through mechanization and monocultures), less dependence on the weather (through irrigation), less dependence on soil fertility (through petrochemical-based fertilizers), less risk of pest invasions (through petrochemical-based pesticides), more rapid crop turnover (through improved hybrid seeds that sometimes allowed for more harvests in a year). Many of these changes were based on the incredible release of energy made possible by cheap petroleum (as cheap as US$2 a barrel in the 1960s, compared to US$80–$100 today and rising). Today the food system has become so dependent on petrochemicals that the resulting foods have been called 'petro-foods' (meat is particularly 'petroleum dense', and there has been an accelerating and unsustainable 'meatification' of the world's diet). In general, then, cheap energy, control over risk factors, and productivity increases made agricultural profit rates increasingly inviting to capitalism.

Given that agriculture could generate higher profit rates, capital could expand to this sector by creating new corporate farms, buying up family farms and expanding them into corporate farms, or by controlling family farms from the outside. If the family farm becomes simply one link in a very long food chain (or value chain) controlled by large capitalist corporations, then it loses much of its autonomy. In other words, family farms would become almost completely dependent on capitalist corporations: buying all their inputs from them, being guided by their production norms, and selling all their crops to them. It is as if the family

farm becomes one station on a long factory assembly line. To put it strongly but accurately, capitalism's seemingly friendly embrace of family farming is really a strangulation, as on average 20,000 farms go out of business each year in the United States, and between 2006 and 2008, Canada lost 10,000 farmers (Rosset 2006: 49; Cook 2004; Heaps 2010: 30).

Capitalist industry has penetrated the once relatively autonomous family farm in several major ways:

- It provides the farm machinery and the petrochemicals needed to run them. Running a giant high-tech, custom-made combine, sometimes costing more than half a million dollars, requires significant petroleum inputs.
- It provides the petrochemical fertilizers that increase yields and can create a treadmill effect (the more you use, the more you have to increase the use). When a soil's fertility depends on chemicals and little organic matter is returned to it, chemical fertilizers tend to run off as water drains from the soil.
- It provides pesticides, the use of which has skyrocketed, also due to a treadmill effect, as the pests build resistance to them and as huge monocultures set the table for pests to devour their favourite crop.
- It provides seeds that are increasingly costly (especially genetically modified seeds) and that need to be bought anew for every crop. Further, as in many sectors of the food system, a handful of giant corporations control production and marketing. For example, the top three seed companies (Monsanto, DuPont, Syngenta) control 35 per cent of the global seed market (Dalle Mulle and Ruppanner 2010: 3). Such concentration of power is particularly disturbing here, because seeds are fundamental to the whole food system.
- Government subsidies go mainly to the largest farms, thus undermining the smaller family farms.
- Large farms are in a better position to win the lucrative contracts with the suppliers of

supermarkets and fast-food chains that need standardized produce in large quantities, which only large capitalist farms can provide. For example, as is typical in the food system, in 2003 the largest fast-food company in the world, Yum! Brands (which owns KFC, Pizza Hut, Taco Bell, and other restaurants), bought all of its American produce from one company, Unified Foodservice Purchasing Co-op, which in turn bought all of its tomatoes from six growers (Ahn, Moore, and Parker 2004: 3).

In addition to outside control, anything that favours larger farms can ultimately require that farmers hire significant numbers of wage labourers and thus become capitalist farmers. This is particularly the case when a farm is not fully mechanized, and harvesting, packing, or other agricultural processes are done at least partially by hand, as with most fruits and vegetables. The intense competition of capitalism drives the system toward larger units of production. Added to this force is the system of government farm subsidies that rewards sheer size rather than the promotion of human and environmental health.

Corn Production in the United States

Recent archaeological evidence indicates that corn was first domesticated in Mexico as many as 9000 years ago. Today corn is the single-largest crop in the United States, and in many ways it is the foundation of the food system (Pollan 2006). The United States alone grew 39 per cent of the world's corn in 2009. It exported 20 per cent of its crop, constituting 59 per cent of total world corn exports ('Corn' 2010). In 2007, 28.6 per cent of the corn crop was used to produce ethanol for **agrofuel**, 58.6 per cent was used as animal feed by the meat industry, and 4.77 per cent was converted into high-fructose corn syrup (HFCS) ('US Corn Consumption' 2008). If we take 2007 as a typical year, there

was a 17 per cent increase in corn acreage stimulated by the high government subsidies to big corn growers and agrofuel producers ('The Unintended Environmental Impacts of the Renewable Fuels Standard' 2008; Chameides 2008). As long as these subsidies continue, corn acreage is likely to continue to expand. Some of this increase will entail a shift away from other food crops such as soy, and will thus raise their prices due to shrinking supply (Butler 2007).

Corn has numerous uses both visible and invisible to the consumer. It is the primary feed grain in the meat industry, HFCS is the primary sweetener in soft drinks and in many processed foods, corn and its by-products are found in many processed foods, and corn on the cob is a popular dish. Finally, in the United States, corn ethanol is the primary source of agrofuel, used mainly as a fuel for automobiles. Corn agrofuel has created a dangerous link between the energy system and the food system, and we will increasingly be faced with choosing between feeding our trucks and cars or feeding the billions of people who suffer hunger and malnutrition. It is estimated that 3 billion people, nearly half the global population, live on less than US$2.50 per day. Many of these are already malnourished or at risk of malnutrition, and as the price of food goes up, their number will only increase (Shah 2011). Given the importance of corn, it is not surprising that it was one of the first crops to be grown in the United States from genetically modified seed.

Fertile soil is essential to the success of agriculture. Because corn crops take so much fertility out of the soil, it is crucial to find ways of adding fertile organic matter back into the topsoil. Organic matter acts as a sponge that can hold water, prevents erosion, and helps soil maintain its long-term fertility. In the short term, chemical fertilizers are more cost-effective than green manures (crops grown only to enrich the soil) or animal manures, both of which have to be ploughed under. But over-reliance on chemicals depletes the organic content of the soil, leading to erosion and soil degradation. The US

Prairies, often referred to as 'the breadbasket of the world' (Canada's Prairies could be included), have on average lost as much as one-third of their topsoil. The more degraded the soil, the more chemical fertilizers have to be used to get the same results.

Some of the run off of nitrogen fertilizer from Midwest corn crops is gathered by the Mississippi River and deposited in the Gulf of Mexico. Algae love nitrogen-rich water, and, as algae spread, they absorb the oxygen in the water, killing off most water plants and animals that need the oxygen to survive. The result has been labelled **dead zones** in oceans. A rapidly growing dead zone spreads out from the Mississippi delta and is already significantly larger than the state of New Jersey. Some ecologists believe that the continued expansion of the corn production required to meet US ethanol goals will cause the dead zone to expand irreversibly (Keim 2008). Nitrogen fertilizer can also convert into nitrous oxide (N_2O), a long-lived greenhouse gas, or into nitrates that are risk factors for miscarriages and cancer (Roberts 2008: 216).

Corn is a thirsty crop, and farming in general uses 85 per cent of the annual water consumption in the United States. Ninety-seven per cent of accessible fresh water in the world comes from groundwater, which is being rapidly depleted (Arguimbau 2010: 3). In 2003 it took on average 2100 gallons of irrigation water to produce one bushel of corn in Nebraska. The Ogallala aquifer in the US Midwest is thought to be the largest underground lake in the world. At the present rate of use, it has been predicted that the aquifer will run dry in 25 to 30 years (Weis 2007: 32). This would mean that approximately 20 per cent of US grain production would be lost for lack of water.

Corn is the primary feed given to animals in **confined animal feeding operations** (CAFOs), where huge numbers of animals are gorged with corn and other foods in confined spaces, creating significant waste disposal problems. According to the US Environmental Protection Agency, between 1993 and 2003 the number of polluted bodies of fresh water in the United States increased tenfold, and CAFOs, which produce 1.27 billion tonnes (1.4 billion tons) of manure a year, were the highest polluters (Weis 2007: 33).

Corn production depends heavily upon the consumption of petrochemicals, and contributes to two leading ecological problems of our times: the depletion of petroleum and global warming. The increasing size of farm machinery is hardly fuel-efficient. The degradation of topsoil and the growing resistance of pests contribute to a treadmill effect that assures petrochemical fertilizer and pesticide inputs will increase. As well, the use of more and more marginally fertile land becomes profitable through subsidies, which are creating a corn-agrofuel boom. The result is that agriculture contributes 14 per cent of the world's greenhouse-gas emissions (Sharratt 2010), while the food system as a whole may contribute over 50 per cent (GRAIN 2009: 1). Finally, agriculture depends on fossil fuels for over 50 per cent of its productivity (Arguimbau 2010: 7).

The new technology of genetically modifying crops is meant to increase yields and create pest-resistant crop varieties. But recent evidence suggests that genetically modified (GM) corn neither increases yields (Gurian-Sherman 2009) nor necessarily decreases reliance on pesticides even in the short run, much less the long run. For example, between 1985 and 2005 pesticide use in the United States increased 33 times, to 0.54 billion kilograms (1.2 billion pounds) a year (Pfeiffer 2006: 22–3). Roundup Ready GM corn, created by Monsanto and named for its best-selling herbicide (weedkiller), is unaffected by the herbicide. Thus, Roundup can be applied to fields growing Roundup Ready corn to kill weeds without killing the corn. As a result, since the mid 1990s the use of toxic herbicides has been increasing at a dramatic rate, despite recent evidence that relates these herbicides to birth defects and the evolution of 'super weeds' that are resistant to herbicides (Engdahl 2010; Smith 2011).

Another form of GM corn is engineered to contain a bacteria called *Bacillus thuringiensis* (Bt).

This bacteria, which is commonly found throughout the environment, is toxic to some insects. This trait would seem to be desirable to decrease the use of insecticides. However, Bt does not make corn toxic to all insects, and there is reason to believe that in the long run insects will build resistance to it. Should this happen, the effectiveness of the Bt that occur naturally would be destroyed, which could make the insect problem worse than before (Jenkins 2000; Cummins 2004).

High-fructose corn syrup is an important corn product in the United States. Because US sugar corporations are protected by quotas on imported sugar, the price of sugar in the United States is usually two to three times the international price. Thus HFCS, cheaper than sugar, has become the sweetener of choice in processed foods and especially in soft drinks. The tenfold increase in the consumption of HFCS since the early 1970s in the United States is followed closely by the increase in cases of diabetes as a percentage of the population. Indeed, recently an important study suggests that HFCS is a risk factor for high blood pressure, heart disease, cancer, and diabetes (Parker 2010). Thus, on top of the ecological costs of corn production that are not factored in to the market price of HFCS, there are health costs also not factored in. Were they to be factored in, HFCS would be priced out of the market. This, however, is unlikely to occur as long as some very large corporations have the political clout that they do.

Ninety per cent of all US farm subsidies go to only five crops: corn, wheat, cotton, soybeans, and rice. Of these five crops, corn is by far the most heavily subsidized. Note that it is not the environmentally friendly family farm that is subsidized, nor the producer of particularly healthy foods; rather, the larger the farm, the larger its subsidy. In short, according to the existing system of subsidies, the rich get richer simply by producing more, no matter how great the long-term ecological or social costs of their production practices. In 2009 US corn growers received US$4 billion in subsidies,

with 69 per cent of this money going to the top 10 per cent of producers ('The Unintended Environmental Impacts of the Renewable Fuels Standard' 2008). Given the dominant position of the United States in the international corn trade, its big producers tend to establish the international price, which can be lower than their costs of production but still profitable due to subsidies.

The North American Free Trade Agreement (NAFTA) between the United States, Canada, and Mexico, which became effective in 1994, did not require that the United States end its corn subsidies. It is estimated that since 1994, 3 million Mexican corn farmers have gone out of business, and US corn exports to Mexico have increased by 20 times (Relinger 2010; Pechlaner and Otero 2010: 196). Driven off the land, Mexican farmers have migrated either to cities or to other countries in search of work. The farmers who moved to cities have likely not fared well. It has been estimated that one-third of the world's city dwellers now live in slums, and this proportion is likely to soon reach one-half, in large part because of economic policies that are driving small farmers off the land (Davis 2006: 23).

Many Mexican farmers chose to migrate to the United States after NAFTA was implemented. For example, prior to NAFTA there were 900,000 migrant farm workers in the United States and only 7 per cent were undocumented ('illegal'), but by 2004 the number of workers had increased to 2 million, with 50 per cent being undocumented (Ahn, Moore, and Parker 2004: 4). This striking rise in both the total number and the percentage of undocumented workers underscores the very real desperation propelling this northward flow of Mexican workers.

California produces over half of all fruits, vegetables, and nuts consumed in the United States; most people familiar with California's agriculture would agree with the estimate that as many as 90 per cent of California's field workers are undocumented (*The Economist*, 2005). In a study conducted in 2003, their average income was US$7500 a year, or US$3000 below the poverty line, for working in the hot sun in pesticide-drenched fields (Ahn, Moore, and Parker 2004: 2). The death rate for field workers in California is five times higher than that for US industrial workers as a whole.

Lacking the legal status of citizenship, undocumented workers can easily be deported if they complain about low pay, unsafe working conditions, too-long hours, or the intensification (speed-up) of work. In short, they are quasi-slaves. When 35,000 jobs in California's agricultural sector were lost during the three-year drought between 2006 and 2009, Fresno County allotted 20 pounds a week of emergency food rations to undocumented workers who might otherwise have starved (Verma 2009; Holt-Gimenez and Brent 2010). I mention this to illustrate the desperate situation faced by undocumented workers who have no access to the safety nets (such as unemployment insurance) available to citizens.

To take advantage of the subsidies for ethanol production in the United States, many farmers have shifted from crops such as soy to corn. This has raised the price of soy and increased pressure to cut down more of the Amazon rain forest in order to raise more soy. Clearly, then, US subsidies can affect agricultural production both in the United States and in other parts of the world. In this case the impact will have long-run ecological costs, as the Amazon basin is very important in global ecology. More generally, by creating artificially low international prices, US subsidies are not only undermining the small farm everywhere, but also are doing so where it hurts the most—in developing countries where inadequate food supplies and poverty make hunger and malnutrition rampant. Furthermore, it can be argued that the junk-food diet (high in sugar, salt, and fat), which is spreading around the world, is as cheap as it is because of subsidies. For example, HFCS producers saved US$2.2 billion between 1997 and 2005 because of corn subsidies (Philpott 2009). In this case the taxpayer supports a poor

diet, and down the line will pay more taxes to support the health-care system that must deal with the poor health generated in part by the poor diet.

US corn-agrofuel subsidies have been strongly opposed by many scientists, but in this case, as in most others, powerful interest groups and corporations that profit from corn-agrofuel production have gotten their way (Philpott 2006: 5; McKenna 2007). The corn-agrofuel industry would not exist at all were it not for very substantial subsidies, which will cost US taxpayers US$54 billion by 2015 under existing legislation (Cox and Hug 2010). Following are some arguments against corn-agrofuel:

- Ultimately the corn-agrofuel program will tie the price of food to the price of petroleum. As both the supply of petroleum and the supply of cropland for food decrease, the cost of food will skyrocket, significantly adding to the 1 billion people in the world already suffering from hunger. If, as is predicted, the global population eventually levels off at around 9 billion, and both extreme weather and declining supplies of water diminish crops, we will probably need all the arable land on earth to sustainably produce enough food to give everyone access to a good diet.
- As the price of petroleum goes up, so will the price of farmland, making it increasingly difficult for young people to start new farms. This is a serious problem given that in some agricultural regions of the United States the average age of farmers is approaching 60 (*The Economist* 2000: 16).
- Land scarcity is already generating a global **land grab**, part of which involves large agrofuel corporations buying up huge swaths of land in developing countries (*Africa: Up for Grabs* 2010; Daniel and Mittal 2009). In some cases this will lead to deforestation; in others, land desperately needed to produce food for local consumption will be used to produce export crops. For example, in Sierra Leone 40,000 hectares (10 km × 40 km) have been sold to

an agrofuel company that will grow sugar cane for ethanol (Baxter 2010). This not only will require that small farmers be moved off the land and resettled elsewhere, but also will cause pollution and use scarce water resources. In Malaysia and Indonesia the remaining rain forest is rapidly disappearing as it is being cut for giant palm oil monocultures that will be used largely to produce diesel agrofuel (Smolker et al. 2008).

- According to David Pimentel, a leading agricultural ecologist, when all the petroleum inputs required to produce corn are totalled, the production of ethanol takes 29 per cent more energy than is contained in the product (Pimentel and Patzek 2005). While there has been a lot of talk about a 'second generation' of agrofuels that do not use food crops, so far they have not been proven to be environmentally friendly or economically cost effective.

- As currently grown, corn erodes and degrades soil, uses up groundwater, contributes to greenhouse gases, and pollutes the environment. In short, it is not a suitable renewable resource for replacing petroleum. Further, even if all the corn grown in the United States were converted into ethanol, it would replace only 15 per cent of the petroleum currently used in the United States.

- The United States has the largest agrofuel program in the world. If it uses even half of its corn to produce agrofuel, this will likely raise the prices of most foods worldwide, triggering increased hunger and famine.

Conclusion

This chapter can be read as an introduction to a political economy approach to the study of food production. In order to emphasize the immensity of the changes that have occurred in food production since the Second World War, I have compared them to the original development of agriculture and animal husbandry that occurred over a much longer time span far in the past. I have argued that capitalist market prices have become increasingly irrational because they exclude most social and environmental costs, and that capitalism's orientation toward short-term profits is also irrational, when what is needed is long-range democratic planning informed by the best science available to bring prices into line with real social and environmental costs and benefits.

There are many ways of moving forward to deal with the kinds of problems created by capitalist agriculture, which are in most cases similar in the United States and Canada. While it is not my purpose in this paper to present an extended discussion of alternatives, such a critique as this does invite at least some mention of general directions toward alternatives. Many problems would be alleviated if we moved toward more organic forms of production and reduced our dependence on petrochemicals. One of the main arguments against this position is that yields would be reduced. But even assuming this to be the case, do we really need so much corn?

To help achieve a more sustainable food system we could reduce the amount of meat in our diet. More than 60 per cent of the current corn crop goes to the meat industry as animal feed. After all, cattle's natural diet is not corn but grass, so it is not only possible but desirable that farmers raise grass-fed beef. No longer using corn to manufacture agrofuel (a sensible move given that it takes more energy to produce agrofuel than it yields), would free up 30 per cent or more of the corn crop. Radically reducing the amount of HFCS in our diet, which we should do for our health, would free up another 5 per cent. In short, we could easily get by with 40 per cent or less of the current corn crop, an amount that could be grown using farming techniques that either are organic or need far fewer petrochemical or biotech inputs.

If we intervene in markets to make prices approximate real long-term social and environmental costs and benefits, then some prices would go up and others down, and people would consume less of the costly and more of the cheaper food commodities. Let's say for the sake of argument that the price of beef quadruples as a result of pricing that includes externalities. This might mean that only the rich could afford beef, which seems unfair. One way to make fair the including of 'externalities' in market prices is to redistribute wealth on a massive scale in order to promote greater equality. Nationally this could in principle be achieved by highly progressive taxation on incomes, wealth, and profits. Internationally we would need a taxing authority that does not yet exist, but changes could also be made in existing international practices that would make a big difference. For example, we could crack down on the tax evasion arising from one-third of all global assets being held in tax havens (Kohonen and Mestrum 2009, xiii). The resulting funds could contribute to advancing equality by giving everyone a basic income well above the poverty line, and giving anyone who works full-time at least twice the basic income. In our capitalist economy this is a radical proposal, but from the point of view of ethics, it is simply putting into practice the ancient principle that each human life should be equally valued. Further, it is a way of linking sustainability with social justice, a linkage that is essential if we are to avoid advancing sustainability at the cost of social justice or vice versa (Albritton 2011).

It should be possible to devise a system in which subsidies would go to those farmers attempting to use methods that improve the soil, save water, favour local markets, and reduce petrochemical inputs, because these practices would reduce long-run social and environment costs. Similarly, farming practices that increase social and environmental costs could be discouraged by placing surtaxes on them. In this way the price of food could come to approximate its real social costs and benefits, and price structures could actually encourage both a good diet and ecological farming practices. Junk food would become much more expensive, while healthy food would become much cheaper.

This essay has made the great leap from taming the wild through the domestication of plants and animals, to a wildly unsustainable and irrational capitalism, to a bare mention of a socially just and ecologically friendly food system. This happier future is increasingly unlikely unless we mobilize massively to bring about change. To turn things around, we will need to continually expand our scientific knowledge, our practical wisdom, and our ability to mobilize and organize in the face of powers both corporate and political that are caught up in capitalist structures, which tend to undermine the possibilities of a better future.

Discussion Questions

1. How are some of the most important changes in social life made possible by the domestication of plants and animals?

2. What are some of the ways that US domination in the global food system are illustrated by US corn production?

3. What are externalities, and why should they be included in the price of commodities?

4. Discuss the pros and cons of producing corn-based agrofuel.

5. It is argued that US corn production undermines long-term human and environmental health. How are these two kinds of health interconnected, and how are they undermined by US corn production?

Further Reading

1. Magdoff, F., and B. Tokar. 2010. *Agriculture and Food in Crisis: Conflict, Resistance, and Renewal*. New York: Monthly Review Press.

   This is a good collection of different approaches to the political economy of agriculture and food, a collection that is unified by its analysis of many of the currently most crucial crises and their interconnections. Further, there is analysis of efforts toward the sort of radical transformations required to deal with them.

2. Pollan, M. 2006. *Omnivore's Dilemma: A Natural History of Four Meals*. New York: Penguin.

   This is a widely read and influential book on the centrality of corn to the US food system. Readers may be surprised at how much corn and corn by-products are part of most processed food, meat, and soft drinks.

3. Ponting, C. 1991. *A Green History of the World: The Environment and the Collapse of Great Civilizations*. New York: Penguin.

   This classic ecological history is particularly interesting because of its recognition of the role of unsustainable food provisioning in the collapse of great civilizations.

4. Smolker, R., B. Tokar, A. Peterman, E. Hernandes, J. Thomas. 2008. 'The Real Cost of Agrofuels: Impacts on Food, Forests, People, and Climate'. www.globalforestcoalition.org/wp-content/uploads/2010/10/Truecostagrofuels.pdf.

   This is an excellent in-depth study of the short- and long-term impact of the recent turn to agrofuel production as a means of dealing with the looming shortage of fossil fuels and of the power that this shortage gives to petroleum-producing countries.

5. Worldwatch Institute. 2011. *The State of the World: Innovations that Nourish the Planet*. New York: W.W. Norton.

   This is the latest of the valuable annual ecological studies of the planet produced by the Worldwatch Institute. Because food provisioning is so closely tied to ecological issues generally, many of their publications directly or indirectly address food issues. This report is directly focused on the present and possible future of food provisioning.

References

Africa: Up for Grabs. 2010. Friends of the Earth Europe. June. www.foeeurope.org/agrofuels/FoEE_Africa_up_for_grabs_2010.pdf.

Ahn, C., M. Moore, and N. Parker. 2004. 'Migrant Farm Workers: America's New Plantation Workers', *Food First Backgrounder*, 10(2). www.foodfirst.org/en/node/45.

Albritton, Robert. 1991. *A Japanese Approach to Stages of Capitalist Development*. London: Macmillan.

Albritton, Robert. 1993. 'Did Agrarian Capitalism Exist?' *Journal of Peasant Studies* 20: 419–41.

Albritton, Robert. 2009. *Let Them Eat Junk: How Capitalism Creates Hunger and Obesity*. London: Pluto Press.

Albritton, Robert. 2011. 'A Practical Utopia for the 21st Century'. In *Existential Utopia: New Perspectives on Utopian Thought*, ed. M. Marder and P. Vieira. London: Continuum Press.

Arguimbau, Nicholas. 2010. 'Peak Food: Can Another Green Revolution Save Us?' Countercurrents.org, August. www.countercurrents.org/arguimbau310710.htm.

Baxter, Joan. 2010. 'Great African Land Grab'. *Le Monde diplomatique*, English edition, April. http://mondediplo.com/2010/04/10africaland.

Butler, Rhett A. 2007. 'US Corn Subsidies Drive Amazon Destruction'. Mongabay.com. 13 December. http://news.mongabay.com/2007/1213-amazon_corn_sub.html.

Chameides, Bill. 2008. 'Corn Subsidies: How Congress is Shortchanging our Health and Sweetening Things for the Food Industry'. *Grist*, 24 April. www.grist.org/article/the-corn-identity.

Cook, Christopher D. 2004. 'Thanksgiving's Hidden Costs'. Alternet. 23 November. www.alternet.org/story/20556.

'Corn'. 2010. US Grains Council. www.grains.org/corn?tmpl=component&print=1&page=.

Cox, Craig, and Andrew Hug. 2010. 'Driving Under the Influence: Corn Ethanol and Energy Security'. Environmental Working Group. June. www.ewg.org.

Cummins, I. 2004. 'Toxins in Genetically Modified Crops: Regulation by Deceit'. Institute of Science in Society. 23 March. www.i-sis.org.uk/BTTIGMC.php.

Dalle Mulle, Emmanuel, and Violette Ruppanner. 2010. *Exploring the Global Food Supply Chain: Markets, Companies, Systems.* 3D–Trade–Human Rights–Equitable Economy. www.3dthree.org/pdf_3D/3D_ExploringtheGlobalFoodSupplyChain.pdf.

Daniel, S., and A. Mittal. 2009. 'The Great Land Grab'. The Oakland Institute. www.oaklandinstitute.org.

Davis, Michael. 2006. *The Planet of Slums.* London: Verso.

The Economist. 2005. 'The Grapes of Wrath, Again: The Miserable State of California's Farm Workers'. *The Economist*, 8 September. www.economist.com/node/4374316.

Engdahl, F. 2010. 'Study Shows Monsanto Roundup Herbicide Link to Birth Defects'. Geopolitics–Geoeconomics. 30 September. http://oilgeopolitics.net/GMO/Roundup_Study/roundup_study.html.

GRAIN. 2009. 'The International Food System and the Climate Crisis'. *Seedling*, October. www.grain.org/article/entries/734-the-international-food-system-and-the-climate-crisis.

Gurian-Sherman, Doug. 2009. *Failure to Yield: Evaluating the Performance of Genetically Engineered Crops.* Union of Concerned Scientists. www.ucsusa.org/assets/documents/food_and_agriculture/failure-to-yield.pdf.

Heaps, T. 2010. 'The Killer Kernel'. *Corporate Knights* 33 (Fall).

Holt-Gimenez, Eric, and Zoe Brent. 2010. 'Hunger, Jobs and Water Wars'. *Huffington Post*, 7 January. www.huffingtonpost.com/eric-holt-gimenez/hunger-jobs-and-water-war_b_414840.html.

Jenkins, Robin. 2000. 'Agricultural Biotechnology: A Case Study of Bt Crops'. *Association Concentropique*, April.

Keim, Brandon. 2008. 'Corn-Based Agrofuels Spell Death for Gulf of Mexico'. *Wired*, 13 March. www.wired.com/wiredscience/2008/03/corn-based-biof.

Kohonen, M., and F. Mestrum. 2009. *Tax Justice.* London: Pluto Press.

McKenna, Phil. 2007. 'Corn Biofuel "Dangerously Oversold" as Green Energy'. *New Scientist*, 18 July. www.newscientist.com/article/dn12283-corn-biofuel-dangerously-oversold-as-green-energy.html.

Marx, Karl. 1976. *Capital*, Vol. I. New York: Penguin.

Marx, Karl. 1978. *Capital*, Vol. II. New York: Penguin.

Marx, Karl, and Friedrich Engel. 1978. *The Marx-Engels Reader.* Ed. Robert Tucker. New York: W.W. Norton.

Parker, H. 2010. 'A Sweet Problem: Princeton Researchers Find that High-Fructose Corn Syrup Prompts Considerably More Weight Gain'. *News at Princeton,* 22 March. www.princeton.edu/main/news/archive/S26/91/22K07/index.xml?section=science.

Pechlaner, Gabriela, and Gerardo Otero. 2010. 'The Neoliberal Food Regime: Neoregulation and the New Division of Labor in North America'. *Rural Sociology* 75(2): 179–208.

Pfeiffer, D.A. 2006. *Eating Fossil Fuels.* Gabriola Island, BC: New Society Publishers.

Philpott, Tom. 2006. 'How Cash and Corporate Pressure Pushed Ethanol to the Fore'. *Grist*, 6 June. www.grist.org/article/ADM1/PALL/print.

Philpott, Tom. 2009. 'Tufts Study: Corn Subsidies Are a Sop to HFCS Industry, But Don't Alone Make Bad Food Cheap'. *Grist*, 13 February. www.grist.org/article/Farm-subsidies-bitter-and-sweet.

Pimentel, David, and Tad Patzek. 2005. 'Ethanol Production Using Corn, Switchgrass, and Wood; Biodiesel Production Using Soybean and Sunflower'. *Natural Resources Research* 14(21): 65–76.

Pollan, M. 2006. *The Omnivore's Dilemma: A Natural History of Four Meals.* New York: Penguin.

Relinger, R. 2010. 'NAFTA and U.S. Corn Subsidies: Explaining the Displacement of Mexico's Corn Farmers'. *Prospect*, April. http://prospectjournal.ucsd.edu/index.php/2010/04/nafta-and-u-s-corn-subsidies-explaining-the-displacement-of-mexicos-corn-farmers/.

Roberts, P. 2008. *The End of Food.* New York: Houghton Mifflin.

Rosset, Peter. 2006. *Food is Different: Why We Must Get the WTO out of Agriculture.* Halifax: Fernwood.

Sahlins, Marshall. 1972. *Stone Age Economics.* New York: Aldine Press.

Shah, A. 2011. 'Causes of Poverty'. *Global Issues.* www.globalissues.org/issue/2/causes-of-poverty.

Sharratt, L. 2010. 'Biofuels Backfire'. *Common Ground*, July. http://commonground.ca/iss/228/cg228_agrofuels.shtml.

Smith, J. 2011. 'Monsanto's Roundup Triggers Over 40 Plant Diseases and Endangers Human and Animal Health'. Institute for Responsible Technology. www.responsibletechnology.org/blog/664.

Smolker, R., B. Tokar, A. Peterman, E. Hernandez, and J. Thomas. 2008. *The True Cost of Agrofuels: Impacts on Food, Forests, People, and Climate.* Global Forest Coalition. www.globalforestcoalition.org/wp-content/uploads/2010/10/Truecostagrofuels.pdf.

'The Unintended Environmental Impacts of the Renewable Fuels Standard'. 2008. Environmental Working Group. August. www.ewg.org/factsheets/The-Unintended-Environmental-Impacts-of-the-Renewable-Fuels-Standard.

'US Corn Consumption'. 2008. *Fat Knowledge* (blog). http://fatknowledge.blogspot.com/2008_06_01_archive.html.

Verma, Sonia. 2009. 'How Green WAS My Valley: California's Drought'. *The Globe and Mail*, 24 July, F1.

Weis, T. 2007. *The Global Food Economy: The Battle for the Future of Farming.* Halifax: NS: Fernwood.

A Political Ecology Approach to Industrial Food Production

Tony Weis

Learning Objectives

Through this chapter, you can:

1. Understand the problems associated with cheap industrial food and the central place of food and agriculture in global environmental problems and solutions
2. Examine a conceptual framework that sets out the unvalued and undervalued environmental costs (i.e., resource budgets and pollution loads) that are embedded in high-yielding monocultures and factory farms, which are at the heart of the world food system
3. See how this framework extends in a way that simultaneously helps connect cheap food to a range of environmental problems, and explain how the system is becoming increasingly unstable
4. Appreciate the environmental motivations for people turning away from cheap industrial food and seeking to support alternatives that connect them to the earth and to farmers in more sustainable ways

Introduction

Industrial capitalist agriculture has generated ever more and cheaper food. Production comes from fewer and larger farms, while fewer and larger firms dominate agricultural inputs and food processing, distribution, and retail networks. On the consumption side, people's interaction with food in wealthy countries like Canada is overwhelmingly mediated by opaque market forces, from giant supermarkets to super-sized 'value' meals in fast-food restaurants. Together, the low prices, bounty, and opacity of the modern food system have undoubtedly obscured its environmental foundations, limits, and vulnerabilities for many people. The more food gets severed from time and space, the less eating is appreciated as a powerful bodily interaction with the earth, for good or ill.

As with all commodities, food is shrouded in mystery, in that consumers have limited knowledge about the array of social and ecological relations that went into making the things (and their prices) that they encounter in markets, and the many costs that are unvalued or undervalued in this process. The fact that these relations and costs are hidden and largely incomprehensible is something Marx called **commodity fetishism**. Put another way, most consumers see food as having a price, a brand, and a country of origin, but would find it difficult or impossible to answer a host of basic questions about most of what they eat with any precision. What part of the country was it grown in? What agro-inputs were used, how were these made, and where did they come from? How and when was the food harvested and processed? What routes did it travel from land to retail outlet? Beyond these questions lie even more complex ones: How do these matters affect soils, water, biodiversity, energy consumption, and the atmosphere?

To begin to unpack the environmental costs embedded in our cheap food supply, we start by examining how the imperatives of industrial capitalism have transformed agriculture as a biological and physical process. The general approach taken is called **political ecology**, which gives attention to the political economic tendencies, power imbalances, and ecological instabilities in how systems operate.

Agriculture as a Relatively Closed-Loop System

For the vast majority of our history, humans acquired the energy and nutrients produced by photosynthesis and accumulated in plant, animal, and marine life through gathering, hunting, and fishing. In effect, this meant that the products of photosynthesis were harvested from ecosystems, with humans taking a minute part of net primary production. The rise of agriculture 10,000 years ago represented an enormous shift in how human societies obtained energy and nutrients. It meant that the photosynthetic activity of plants was first *organized*—by managing biodiversity, plant and animal interactions, nutrient flows, and water supplies—before the products of photosynthesis were appropriated. While agriculture obviously increased

the usability of these products for humans, the displacement of more biologically productive ecosystems reduced the volume of photosynthetic activity. Over millennia then, agricultural expansion was the biggest factor in the slow but steady increase in the **human appropriation of the net primary product** (of photosynthesis) (HANPP), though this remained very small prior to the modern era.

The limits of technology, surpluses, and storage and the large 'friction of distance'[1] meant that until very recently agricultural societies were predominantly localized. Problems of soil loss, pests, and drought had to be mitigated using nearby resources and by fostering complementary biological interactions, such as **intercropping** patterns (planting multiple crops in mutually beneficial combinations). Agricultural innovation—including, at its core, the selection of seeds geared towards long-term improvements—was deeply rooted in cultures and bioregions, apart from episodic dispersions of seeds and animals. Long-distance trade had to be confined to a small number of commodities, generally those prized for flavouring, preservation, and medicinal effects rather than sustenance.

Another way of understanding the locally oriented nature of agricultural landscapes is that they had to be based upon relatively 'closed-loop' cycles of biological and physical materials:

- most organic wastes and nutrients had to be returned to land close to where they were withdrawn
- biodiversity at the scale of soils enhanced the break-down and recycling of nutrients
- biological approaches (and in some cases extensive terracing) were needed to limit soil erosion and enhance moisture retention
- biological approaches were needed to suppress undesirable organisms
- the sun was the sole external source of energy, fuelling photosynthesis and through it animal power and human labour (Altieri 1999; Jackson 1985)

Although such organization tended to promote crop protection as well as the long-term stability of the resource base, this does not mean that all short-term vulnerabilities were eliminated or that this loop was ever entirely closed, in particular with respect to soil. Soil is the 'living skin of the earth', a combination of biological and physical materials that ultimately underpins all human civilizations; without great care it tends to be lost much more quickly than it develops. Some societies have managed the balance of soil loss versus soil formation more effectively than others, thus enhancing their stability, but failure to maintain soil fertility has had a recurring central role in the decline of civilizations throughout history (Montgomery 2007).

In short, non-industrial agricultural systems contain a range of lessons and applied knowledge about managing diversity, much of which is very valuable in thinking about sustainability, but it does little good to romanticize a pre-industrial golden age.

The Industrial Revolution in Agriculture: Scale, Mechanization, and Standardization

The scope of traded food increased with the onset of European colonialism and the rising movement both of tropical commodities (e.g., sugar, coffee, tea, and cocoa) from parts of the Caribbean, Central and South America, Africa, and Asia, and of temperate grain and livestock products from places such as the United States, Canada, Argentina, and the Punjab region of India. These trade patterns were linked to momentous social and ecological changes and enduring inequalities, as Indigenous peoples across vast areas were displaced by large plantations, farms, and pastures.

While colonialism established new trade patterns and dependencies—and novel long-distance flows of food in bulk—we need to recognize how thoroughly the biological and physical nature of agricultural production has been transformed by capitalist imperatives and industrial methods. The distinctive capitalist imperatives of incessant competition, growth, and accumulation are entwined with the pressure to achieve **economies of scale**: in essence, to increase output per worker in order to reduce the relative cost of labour in production. In uncritical accounts (i.e., mainstream economics), economies of scale are primarily attributed to the wonders of technological innovation, while another crucial element is left out or downplayed: the essential role of fossil fuels in running machines and factories and in reducing the friction of distance in moving commodities around—sometimes described as the compression of time and space. Oil, natural gas, and coal account for roughly four-fifths of the world's total primary energy supply (i.e., the energy used in production, households, and transportation), with oil providing virtually all of the liquid fuel that powers transportation systems (IEA 2008; Heinberg 2005).

Remarkable economies of scale have been achieved in agricultural systems across the industrialized world, with fossil fuel–powered machines, factories, and transportation systems central to the increasing output per worker. Whereas for most of agrarian history a large majority of the population has had to work the land, today farmers make up only about 4 per cent of the workforce across the countries of the Organisation for Economic Co-operation and Development OECD. Economies of scale in agriculture are most advanced in the United States and Canada, the world's largest surplus-producing and exporting region. There farmers make up only 2 per cent of the workforce—and only 1 out of every 400 farmers in the world—yet they account for more than one-eighth of total world agro-exports by value and an even greater volume of basic food staples. In the United States, the number of farms has declined precipitously, together with a remarkable polarization of landholding. Today, two-thirds of all US farmland is controlled by less than one-tenth of its landholders, and more than 80,000 farms are larger than 800 hectares. In Canada the number of farms peaked in 1941, and then fell by more than two-thirds in only 65 years, declining from 732,832 to 229,373 in 2006 (Weis 2009; USDA NASS 2008; Statistics Canada 2007).

In a general sense, in order for technology (and capital) to progressively displace human labour, the production process must be standardized in terms of both physical space and the nature of work. In agriculture, small fields with a range of different crops and small animal populations are obviously not conducive to large, labour-saving machinery. Rather, large machines demand big volumes of the same thing. The basic imperative is thus to reduce **biodiversity** in terms of the numbers of plant and animal species on farms, the ways they interact, and the biological structure of individual species. Thus the loss of biodiversity can be seen from the large scale of **monoculture** (single crop) fields down to the microscopic scale of plant and animal genetics.

Scientific innovation aimed at standardizing plants and animals has been entwined with efforts to increase their size and/or rate of growth, and thus increase their yield. Conventional **genetic enhancement** of seeds and livestock breeds—improvements made by crossing varieties within the same species—is a pivotal dimension of both the biological narrowing and the rising productivity of industrial capitalist agriculture.

The Industrial Grain– Oilseed–Livestock Complex

Today only 10 crops account for roughly three-quarters of humanity's plant-based calories, and only five livestock animals are responsible for virtually all meat, eggs, and milk consumed on a global scale. Industrial agriculture in temperate climates is dominated by a few grain and oilseed monocultures and a few livestock species reared in high-density factory farms and feedlots, and is referred to as the **industrial grain–oilseed–livestock complex** (Weis 2010a, 2007; Friedmann 1993). It is principally focused on

- maize and wheat, and a few secondary grains
- soybeans and secondarily canola (or rapeseed)
- pigs, poultry, and cattle

Industrially reared livestock consume more than a third of the world's grain harvest, and a much greater share of all oilseeds, with the ratios of cycling feed through livestock the highest in industrialized countries. In the United States and Canada, roughly 80 per cent of the total volume of agricultural production comes from the industrial grain–oilseed–livestock complex (Weis 2009; Halweil 2008).

As noted, the separation of livestock from farmland has enabled increasing scale and mechanization, and the productivity gains of industrial grain and oilseed monocultures have allowed livestock populations to grow far beyond their former densities on small integrated farms. At the same time, the cycling of large volumes of grains and oilseeds through livestock greatly expanded profit-making opportunities for cheap surpluses—enhancing markets for grain and oilseed processors and distributors and increasing value-added possibilities in meat, milk, and eggs. Concentrated feed combined with confinement and breeding innovations have also accelerated livestock weight gain and milk and egg productivity, or what might be understood as speeding up the 'turnover time' of animals (Mann and Dickinson 1978).

Thus, while physically separated in landscapes, industrial monocultures and livestock production are bound together by an economic logic that has transformed both (Weis 2007). The industrial grain–oilseed–livestock complex is at the centre of the global **livestock revolution**, a term that marks the dramatically rising scale at which animal flesh and derivatives are produced (Steinfeld et al. 2006). Animal flesh was on the periphery of human diets for most of the history of agriculture, but these transformations have driven it to the centre, a process described as the 'meatification' of diets. Incredibly, the average person on earth today eats twice as much meat as the average person only three generations ago, in spite of the more than doubling of the human population over this period. This colossal shift has, of course, been highly uneven on a world scale, tightly correlated to affluence. The average person in an industrialized country consumes over two and a half times more meat than an average person in a developing country (Weis 2007). The United States and Canada are at the apex of this trend, consuming roughly four times more poultry, three times more beef, and six times more cheese per capita than the world average—along with one-third more calories, 50 per cent more protein, and nearly 100 per cent more fat (Weis 2009). Fast-industrializing countries, foremost China, are moving quickly towards these consumption patterns (Nierenberg 2005).

The United States and Canada illustrate the grain–oilseed–livestock complex in its most productive and technologically developed form. Together, they produce roughly

- one-fifth of the world's total grain production (the United States alone accounts for roughly two-fifths of all maize)
- one-third of the world's oilseed production (mainly soy in the United States and canola in Canada)
- one-sixth of the world's meat by volume (including more than one-fifth of all poultry and beef)

Factory farming and industrial feedlots originated in the United States and are most extensive there. More than four-fifths of all pigs in the United States are confined in operations with more than 5000 animals, and 99 per cent of all meat chickens (called broilers) are raised in operations which sell more than 100,000 birds a year. Roughly 9 billion chickens are killed annually in the United States alone, more in a single day today than were killed in an entire year only 80 years ago (Weis 2009; FAOSTAT 2009; USDA NASS 2008).

Agriculture as a Through-Flow Process

This booming productivity and the accompanying meatification of diets are widely taken for granted across the industrialized world, along with the long-term decline in the average share of income devoted to food. However, this increased output is only one side of the story; on the other side, much less acknowledged, are the increasing external inputs needed to produce this output. To appreciate this, it helps to understand the range of ways that biological and physical problems are magnified or created. Key dynamics include

- reduced fallowing (leaving fields unplanted for a season to let them regain fertility) and shorter time horizons driven by competitive pressures, often linked to the scale of capital investment and debt on farms
- reduced recycling of organic material on farms as a result of the decline in soil biodiversity, fallowing, and scavenging by small livestock populations
- reduced soil moisture retention and increased erosion as a result of the elimination of ground cover between planted rows in monocultures
- damage done to soil biota (the living component of soil) from increased tillage (ploughing) and compaction by large machinery
- increased opportunities for weeds and insects to thrive and spread amid monocultures
- 'thirstier' enhanced seeds, compared with lower-yielding traditional varieties
- increased risks of animal health problems, diseases, and neurotic behaviours as a result

of their intensive confinement and large concentrations in factory farms

- increased food safety concerns associated with food-borne bacteria and viruses in highly concentrated production facilities

The net result is a system with deep biological and physical instabilities—a system that hinges on its ability to override those instabilities with a host of inputs (which therefore might be understood as **biophysical overrides**), such that the system comes to resemble a through-flow process.

As human labour and animal traction are displaced with machinery, the principal source of energy on farms shifts from the sun to fossil fuels—in other words, from renewable stores of photosynthesized solar energy (i.e., plants) to ancient and irreplaceable stores of compressed, photosynthesized solar energy (i.e., oil). The movement of animals into factories further extends this dependence upon external sources of energy (although, as we will see in the following section, the dependence upon fossil fuels and derivatives does not end with the on-farm energy supply).

One of the most fundamental problems in industrial agriculture is the speed at which key nutrients and soil organisms are lost, which has been called **soil mining**. Though soil degradation has an old history, it is greatly accelerated by reduced soil biodiversity and ground cover in monocultures, repeated cycles of tillage and compaction, and heavy chemical use. Soil mining in industrial agriculture is primarily overridden with three fertilizers—nitrogen, phosphorous, and potassium—from inorganic sources (McKenney 2002; Warshall 2002). The increased pest problems also stem from the fact that many organisms that once had complementary, beneficial roles within more diverse agro-ecosystems become problematic within industrial monocultures. The risks are overridden with a large volume of chemical **pesticides**, the umbrella term for herbicides (targeting weeds), insecticides, fungicides, and disinfectants. The voracious appetite for these inputs

in industrial monocultures is reflected in the fact that the United States and Canada together annually account for roughly 15 per cent of global inorganic fertilizer consumption and an even greater share of global pesticide consumption (Weis 2009).

As discussed below, the total volume of fertilizers and chemicals consumed in industrial monocultures expands with the rising volumes of grains and oilseeds fed to growing livestock populations. Further, the health and behavioural problems caused by the unnatural densities of animals in factory farms involve their own chemical override: the proliferation of animal pharmaceuticals (with antibiotics and hormones also serving to enhance yields) and of disinfectants, which are used with large amounts of water to clean factory farms and industrial abattoirs.[2] Behavioural problems are also partially overridden by un-anaesthetized mutilations, as in the rapid de-beaking lines for poultry or tail docking for pigs (Mason and Singer 1990).

While agricultural societies have long relied on irrigation to varying degrees, high-yielding monocultures have significantly increased the scale of irrigation infrastructure and freshwater diversions. Agriculture is by far the largest consumer of water in industrial countries, and its consumption reflects the polarization of productivity described earlier. In the United States, for instance, more than four-fifths of all irrigated land is controlled by less than one-fifth of all landholders (Weis 2009).

In sum, although the industrial revolution in agriculture has brought great gains in terms of output per worker, along with increased yields from each plant and animal, the flipside is that these have been accompanied by tremendous increases in the resources going into farms (Weis 2007; Brown 1996). The dependence upon these biophysical overrides—which must often be sourced across great distances—constitutes a historic rupture of agriculture from relatively closed-loop cycles to a through-flow process, as depicted in Figure 7.1.

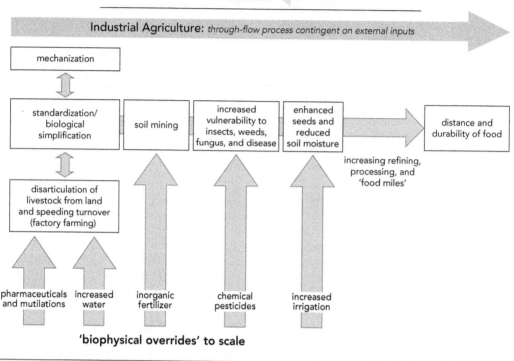

Figure 7.1 The Through-Flow of Industrial Agriculture

The Hidden Environmental Costs of Cheap Food

The previous section examined how industrial capitalism has radically reconfigured agriculture into a through-flow process, with the great productivity gains enabled by a large range of inputs or biophysical overrides. This through-flow process depends upon a large budget of non-renewable resources and is implicated in a multidimensional environmental burden. To appreciate the environmental costs of food, then, it is necessary to understand these overrides both in terms of their resource budget and their pollution burden; that is, to assess what inputs go into the process and what wastes come out of the process. The fact

that this burden does not register as costs within the prevailing economic system—and is largely externalized—is a major reason why industrial food has long been so cheap.

Food Miles

The industrial transformation of agriculture is entwined with the increasing 'distance and durability' of food (Friedmann 1993). As scale and mechanization expand, landscapes are specialized to produce large quantities of a few crops, rural populations decline, communities are separated from their surrounding countrysides, control is centralized in large corporate intermediaries, and food travels further from land to mouth. This distance is popularly referred to as

food miles, and cheap and abundant oil coupled with processing and transportation innovations have been essential to reducing the friction of distance. Much of the growing popular awareness about food miles has focused on the resulting carbon emissions, which makes this concept a very visible marker for how the food system is linked to climate change. Rising concern is reflected in things like the '100 mile diet' (Smith and McKinnon 2007) and related 'locavore' movements to 'eat local' or, as Kloppenberg et al. (1996) put it, to 'move in to the foodshed'.

Soil Mining

If food miles are one of the most popularly recognized environmental costs in the industrial food system, soil mining is one of the least. This is not an entirely new problem; as noted, soil degradation has repeatedly played a significant part in the decline of civilizations, although unfolding too gradually to be appreciated. What is new is that this loss is comprehensively understood and has sped up to an extent that some place this among the most worrisome of all global environmental problems (Shiva 2008; Montgomery 2007; Pimentel 2006; Jackson 1985). But rather than responding to the causes of soil degradation and finding ways to restore organic content and enhance soil formation, the primary industrial response has been the repeated, short-term fix of industrial fertilizers to replace lost nitrogen, phosphorous, and potassium, and these fertilizers involve a host of environmental costs (McKenney 2002; Warshall 2002).

Fertilizers from Production to Farm

Synthetic nitrogen fertilizers are by far the largest soil input by volume. They are primarily manufactured through the Haber-Bosch process of combining atmospheric nitrogen and hydrogen, with natural gas and coal used as the main feedstock, or key resource input. Phosphorous and potassium fertilizers come from phosphate ore and potash mining, which depend upon fossil fuel–powered machinery and refining, and result in a considerable pollution burden. The manufacture of phosphate fertilizer is implicated in highly acidic and toxic wastewater ponds. Potash mining occurs over large areas both above and below ground. Above ground, it leaves behind open-pit wastelands; below ground, extensive mines create risks of water table contamination and land subsidence. In addition to the manufacturing and mining processes, the transportation and application of industrial fertilizers require large volumes of oil, as fertilizers are bulky materials that often travel great distances. When this consumption is added up, from factories and mines to farms and tractor spreaders, fertilizers account for a significant share of both the overall fossil energy budget and of the carbon emissions in industrial agriculture (Pimentel 2006; McKenney 2002). Nitrogen fertilizer is also a major source of nitrous oxide emissions, a significant greenhouse gas (GHG). Thus, if people are concerned about how far their food has travelled (and the energy and atmospheric costs contained in this distance), they might also be asking, 'How local was its fertilizer?' Shiva (2008) argues that there is a central, systematic link between soil degradation, oil dependence, and climate change, and that sustainable and just societies need to be built on the foundation of healthy 'soil not oil'.

Pesticides from Production to Farm

As with fertilizers, the proliferation of chemical pesticides is a short-term fix that not only fails to resolve the basic dynamic of why monocultures face greater pest problems, but worsens it over time. These inputs thus have a treadmill effect. The **pesticide treadmill** means that more or newer pesticides are always needed as natural predators and controls are eliminated, pests and disease organisms develop resistance over time, and localized ecological knowledge and the ability to use non-chemical responses are lost (sometimes referred to as 'knowledge erosion'). In *Silent Spring*, a book which helped give rise to the modern environmental movement, Carson (1962) highlighted the basic dynamics of this treadmill with the powerful metaphor of a low-intensity chemical war on ecosystems and other species. This situation was more than metaphorical: much of the incredible surge in agro-chemicals after the Second World War was manufactured in reconstituted war munitions plants. Many pesticides are petrochemical-based, and like fertilizers involve an energy budget in their manufacture, transport, and application which is seldom recognized (although they are much less bulky than fertilizers). Extensive use of chemical pesticides also contributes to the destruction of soil micro-organisms and thus to the decline of soil fertility.

GMO Risks

In contrast to conventional genetic enhancement where varieties *within* the same species are crossed, **genetic modification** is the term given to the technological combination of genetic traits from different species that could not cross naturally (which is why this process is also described as genetic engineering). Somewhat ironically, the same companies that control pesticide production on a global scale seek to justify the expansion of genetically modified organisms (GMOs), which they also dominate, partly by claiming that this innovation can reduce overall chemical use in agriculture through building pest resistance into the genetic makeup of crops. The predominant corporate actor here is Monsanto. At the same time, the key trait associated with most GMO crops is their tolerance for a particular chemical, which links seed and chemical purchase in a very powerful way—as in Monsanto's Roundup Ready seed varieties.[3]

GMOs pose complex, long-term risks to ecosystem contamination, which has led many countries to take a strong regulatory position against their use. They have also led to a tremendous amount of environmental activism, from public education and lobbying campaigns to direct actions like setting fire to GMO crops. However, permissive regulatory regimes in a few countries have allowed the widespread diffusion of GMOs ahead of comprehensive long-term impact assessments, most notably in the United States, Canada, Argentina, and Brazil, four of the world's most important agro-exporting nations. In these countries, a small number of genetically modified grains and oilseeds now pervade agricultural landscapes and the food system, outside of much public awareness and scrutiny (Kuyek 2007; Mendelson 2002; see also Chapter 16 in this volume).

Factory Farms and Feedlots

Throughout most agrarian history, small livestock populations had roles in nutrient cycles on fallowed land and small pastures, and in scavenging organic wastes on the margins of farm households, by providing fecal matter (manure) for nourishing the soil. Today, in stark contrast, the huge concentrations of animals in factory farms and feedlots produce fecal waste on a scale far greater than what nearby landscapes can absorb. Making matters worse, this waste is also laden with residues from the antibiotics and hormones that the animals are routinely given, and from the agro-chemicals in concentrated feeds (Nierenberg 2005; WorldWatch 2004; Mason and Singer 1990). Landscapes dotted with factory farms and feedlots are marked by 'manure lagoons' of untreated waste, which not only create wretched 'smell-scapes' but also release methane, another potent GHG. The growth of factory farming, with its heating, ventilation, and machinery, also increases energy consumption and GHG emissions (depending on which energy sources supply the local electrical grid).

Factory farms also raise profound questions of environmental ethics, as animals are transformed from sentient beings into pure commodities—inanimate objects whose treatment is shaped almost entirely by market imperatives. This can be seen in the both the episodic violence (e.g., mutilations, transport, fast-paced slaughter lines) and the chronic misery in intensive confinement (e.g., battery cages, broiler houses, gestation crates). The ethical dimensions of these spaces also extends to health concerns facing workers in factory farms and slaughterhouses, who have to cope with the severe psychological trauma of routinely inflicting suffering and death, as well as high incidences of repetitive stress and accidental injuries (Weis 2010b; Midkiff 2004; Eisnitz 1997; Mason and Singer 1990).

The Downstream Pollution Burden

Industrial farms, factories, and feedlots place a large pollution burden on downstream water bodies and groundwater supplies, which necessitate increased investment, technology, and energy in water treatment facilities. However, excess nutrients, chemicals, and pharmaceuticals are much too diffuse to contain, and end up creating untold risks for ecosystems, animal life, and ultimately human bodies from residues on food and in water supplies (Steingraber 2010; Moore 2002). One of the largest burdens on ecosystem health comes from the run off of nutrients from fertilizers and from the waste of concentrated animal populations. These excess nutrients cause widespread **eutrophication** (oxygen-depleting algae blooms) in freshwater bodies and around coastal riverheads, which can have a devastating impact on aquatic life. The most infamous case is the giant dead zone in the Gulf of Mexico, the by-product of run off from the US agricultural heartland deposited by the Mississippi River (MEA 2005; McKenney 2002), but there are now many such zones of varying sizes in coastal areas around the world (Mitchell 2009; MEA 2005).

The persistent toxins that are released into the environment bio-accumulate in higher life forms as they move through aquatic and terrestrial food chains, a problem to which Carson (1962) was the first to draw widespread attention. Though there are more controls on releasing chemicals today than when *Silent Spring* was published (when such controls were virtually non-existent), many would argue that regulatory regimes still generally favour the early release of new chemicals (Moore 2002). Environmentalists argue for chemical regulation to be guided by the **precautionary principle**, which places a strong, pre-release burden of proof on demonstrating that a given chemical is benign in the long term.

Freshwater Diversions and Over-Consumption

On a global scale, agriculture is responsible for almost three-quarters of all freshwater consumption, and irrigated land—although a relatively small percentage of all cultivated areas—accounts for two-fifths of the world's food production. Industrial monocultures are central to this discrepancy, with their heightened productivity enabled, in part, by drawing on freshwater supplies disproportionately to the land area (Briscoe 2002).

Large-scale irrigation projects together with hydroelectricity drove the era of megadam–building in the twentieth century, which wrought massive transformations to riverine ecosystems around the world (McCully 1996). One of the greatest examples of this is in the US West. In *Cadillac Desert*, Reisner (1993) describes how natural watercourses, from the Columbia to the Colorado rivers, were comprehensively transformed by massive engineering schemes to make highly productive industrial agricultural landscapes in areas with little natural irrigation. Other irrigation systems depend upon the unsustainable consumption of underground aquifers, drawing water from them faster than they are recharged. Nowhere is this overdraft more precarious than in the great Ogallala Aquifer, which irrigates much of the arid

US Midwest, the world's most important grain producing and exporting region, and which is being used at a rate that effectively amounts to mining a non-renewable resource (Opie 2000). There is also an energy cost. Although many irrigation diversions are linked to hydroelectric generation at some point in the system, whether on a macro- or micro-scale, much irrigation pumping is powered by fossil fuels.

Prolonged irrigation often contributes to problems of waterlogging, nutrient leaching, and **salinization**. Soil becomes salinized when the dissolved salt in water is left behind after evapotranspiration (water evaporating from the land or transpiring from plants). Salts build up over time, and beyond a certain point salinization has large negative impacts on moisture uptake by plants and thus on crop yields (Briscoe 2002).

Magnifying the Costs: Reverse Protein Factories

A very important dynamic of global agriculture is that rising volumes of monoculture grains and oilseeds are being fed to intensively reared livestock. This trend is led by industrialized countries, where increasingly meat-centred diets are held as one marker of modernization and development (Weis 2010b). The cycling of grains and oilseeds through livestock is an inefficient way to produce food, as large amounts of useable protein, carbohydrates, and fibre are lost in the metabolic process of animals converting grains and oilseeds to flesh. In *Diet for a Small Planet*, Lappé (1971) first drew attention to the environmental implications of this wastefulness, which she called 'reverse protein factories'. Different animals have different conversion ratios, with the pinnacle of inefficiency being the grain-fed steer, but the basic point is that as the proportion of meat rises in a society's diet, so too does the overall land area that must be devoted to grain and oilseed production. Thus, in addition to the direct pollution burden associated

with factory farms and feedlots, the process of cycling of feed through livestock acts like a magnifying lens for the many environmental costs of industrial monocultures (Weis 2010b).

This magnifying lens has a powerful impact on energy consumption and GHG emissions. For instance, it is estimated that eight times more energy goes into a unit of edible protein contained in factory-farmed meat than goes into a unit of edible protein in industrial grain (Nierenberg 2005; WorldWatch 2004). Rising livestock populations are implicated in the carbon emissions from the conversion of biodiverse ecosystems to additional cultivation and pasture, as well as in the resulting reduced capacity for sequestering carbon. The global ruminant population is also a major source of methane emissions. When these atmospheric effects are added up, global livestock production has one of the largest impacts on climate change of all economic sectors (McIntyre et al. 2009; IPCC 2007; Steinfield et al. 2006). Finally, the overall energy and atmospheric budgets are further stretched by the fact that most animal flesh and derivatives have a greater dependence on refrigeration from slaughter to cooking.

The Loss of Biodiversity

The United Nations *Millennium Ecosystem Assessment* (2005: 777) describes agriculture as the 'largest threat to biodiversity and ecosystem function of any single human activity'. This report also highlights how the destruction of natural ecosystems for agriculture accelerated dramatically in the second half of the twentieth century, with more land converted to cropland in only three decades (1950–80) than occurred during a century and a half of widespread colonial transformations (1700–1850) (MEA 2005). Another way of appreciating the scale of agricultural expansion is in terms of the rising human appropriation of the net primary product of photosynthesis (HANPP), of which agriculture is the most important factor. While there are different approaches to calculating the HANPP, one notable recent study found that humans appropriate almost one-quarter of global land-based net primary productivity (Haberl et al. 2007).

The expansive footprint of industrial monocultures in landscapes, magnified by factory-farmed livestock, reduces the space for natural ecosystems and other species. The shrinking of ecosystems and the extirpation, endangerment, and extinction of species have both immeasurable dimensions (What is the ethical cost of a species going extinct?), and ones that more directly impair human economies. These effects on human economies are sometimes discussed in terms of **ecosystem services** to highlight the underappreciated ways in which economies depend upon natural processes, and to translate their degradation into measurable economic costs.[4]

The radical reduction of biodiversity on farms and the consolidation of control over the world's seed markets are destroying the environmental conditions which gave rise to agricultural diversity. Biodiversity loss at the scale of soils has also reduced the nutritional content of industrial foods (Pollan 2008). For most people, however, the biological narrowing of the food supply is partially obscured by the endlessly creative ways it is refined, mixed, coloured, flavoured, and packaged.

From Hidden Costs to Crisis: Accelerating Instabilities

The previous section examined the many hidden environmental costs in industrial capitalist agriculture; these costs effectively subsidize the cheap bounty industrial agriculture generates. A pivotal, recurring aspect is the intractable dependence upon fossil fuels, which can be viewed as a powerful current coursing across the through-flow process (as depicted in Figure 7.2), from the running of heavy machinery and of factory farms, to the production, transport, and application of fertilizers and chemical pesticides, to irrigation pumping and added water treatment, to the increasing processing, packaging, and long-distance movement of food durables. In short, when we eat industrial foods we are 'eating fossil fuels', as many calories of fossil energy are contained in a single calorie of industrial food (Shiva 2008; Pfeiffer 2006; McCluney 2005; Manning 2004). The industrial grain–oilseed–livestock complex and the associated meatification of diets are significant reasons that countries like the United States and Canada have per capita GHG emissions much higher than the world average.[5]

The earth's climate history has had long periods of both major cooling and major warming, a fact which climate change skeptics sometimes cite in order to downplay threats and justify inaction. However, there is overwhelming scientific evidence that the trajectory of current warming falls outside of any natural variability, and is attributable to human economies increasing GHG concentrations in the earth's atmosphere. For a number of reasons, including the persistence of GHGs in the atmosphere, the thermal lag of the oceans,[6] and a variety of positive feedbacks (e.g., less ice in polar and alpine regions means less reflected solar radiation and more absorption of heat), the earth is already committed to a significant amount of warming. The extent of this warming could well be pushing the earth out of the **Holocene**, the short geological period of relative climatic stability in which agriculture and human civilization arose (Rosenzweig et al. 2008; IPCC 2007). In other words, while agricultural societies have always faced climate variability, they have never faced climate change of the magnitude and speed that are projected.

Agriculture is both a major cause of and exceptionally vulnerable to climate change. On balance, climate change is projected to negatively affect agricultural projection on a global scale, but with an incredible regressivity: while rich countries are most responsible, the world's poorest countries (which have by far the highest

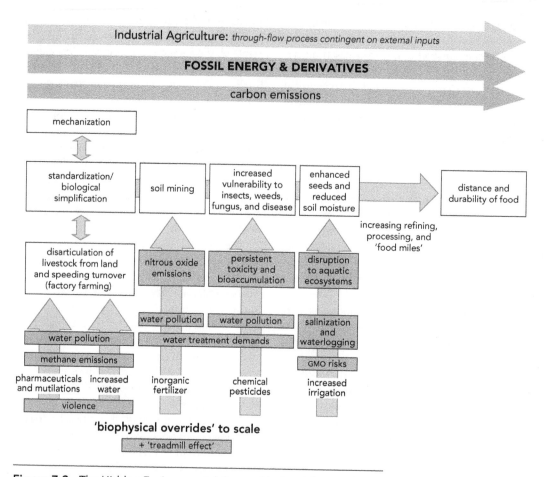

Figure 7.2   The Hidden Environmental Costs of Industrial Agriculture

shares of their population in agriculture) are expected to experience its worst impacts (UNDP 2007). Among projected changes, some of the threats to agricultural production include

- hotter average temperatures, which will cause increased evaporation and reduced soil moisture
- increased heat waves, aridity, and risks of heat stress for crops and animals
- more variable rains
- declining availability of fresh water, due to changing rainfall and ice patterns
- more intense extreme weather events
- enhanced conditions for the movement and reproduction of pests and pathogens

(McIntyre et al. 2009; Schmidhuber and Tubiello 2007; IPCC 2007)

There is, of course, inevitable uncertainty about the magnitude and interactions of different changes. There is also the possibility that warmer temperatures and longer growing seasons could enhance agricultural productivity along the cooler margins of temperate regions, and extend potential arable land northward in a few countries like Canada.

But even in the areas which might benefit, there are fears that gains would be cancelled out by new dynamics, to say nothing of the disastrous climatic implications of further deforestation to expand the land area in cultivation or pasture.

Further, significantly reduced river run off and water availability are anticipated to present a very serious threat to agricultural productivity in the drier mid-latitude regions, which may not be so negatively impacted by warmer temperatures, and there is extensive evidence that this is already unfolding (IPCC 2007). In southern Canada, where 98 per cent of the population lives, overall water yield has declined by almost 9 per cent since the early 1970s (Statistics Canada 2010).

Climate change requires simultaneous action on two fronts: mitigation and adaptation. **Climate change mitigation** means making urgent efforts to reduce the scale of change, first through drastic cuts to GHG emissions and second by increasing GHG sequestration in ecosystems. The immediacy of this challenge is impossible to overstate, as climate scientists are warning of an impending 'point of no return' where positive feedbacks take on an irreversible momentum. The imperative of mitigation challenges the industrial grain–oilseed–livestock complex to its very core. Reflecting this challenge, the global peasant movement Vía Campesina has begun to argue that small-scale, biodiverse farms have a role in 'cooling down the earth' (Vía Campesina 2007), as they produce much less emissions and promote much more sequestration than do industrial farms.

Along with mitigation efforts, there is a need to plan for and respond to the changes which are unfolding and projected, broadly encapsulated in the concept of **climate change adaptation**. In no other sector is adaptation more critical or challenging than in agriculture, as changing physical parameters (e.g., temperatures, evaporation rates, rainfall patterns, watershed yields) affect a range of biological responses (e.g., crops, soil organisms, insects, undesirable and invasive species), which themselves interact in complex ways (Howden et al. 2007). Research and scientific innovation are obviously very important, but ultimately the prospects for adaptation are heavily contingent on the extent of mitigation.

Another dynamic making industrial capitalist agriculture more unstable is the fact that

human economies are at, near, or have just passed the halfway point in the consumption of all global oil reserves—the point of **peak oil**. This implies that

- the world's most accessible (and hence lowest cost) oil reserves have already been discovered
- low-cost oil reserves are all in marked decline
- extracting the remaining reserves will become ever more difficult, costly, and energy-intensive (e.g., Alberta's tar sands, reserves further offshore and at the poles)
- the second half of the world's oil supply will be consumed much faster than the first half was (Heinberg 2007, 2005)

Inevitable cost increases will reverberate in the through-flow process, reducing the implicit subsidy that relatively cheap oil has long provided to cheap food. While oil is the most important limiting factor, the world is also approaching 'peak phosphorous' and peaks and declines in other key resources (Heinberg 2007; Pfeiffer 2006).

However, in the short term the pressure of peak oil has spurred a very contradictory dynamic: a sharp increase in the conversion of grains and oilseeds to agrofuels (or biofuels) over the past decade. On one hand, the agrofuel boom reflects the desire to find new sources of renewable liquid energy as oil declines. On the other hand, nearly as much (or sometimes more) fossil energy goes into the growing and processing of industrial grains and oilseeds as comes out in ethanol or biodiesel (Giampietro and Mayumi 2009). The United States is leading the global surge in agrofuel production, which constitutes an important and growing dynamic influencing the prices of basic foodstuffs.

In the long term, the limits of peak oil and other non-renewable resources will present more foundational challenges to industrial capitalist agriculture as current biophysical overrides become untenable and replacing labour with technology becomes even more problematic.

This is likely to impel either more technological responses or a movement to rebuild agricultural systems in ways that re-centre human labour and skill, localized ecological knowledge, and functional diversity on farms.

Conclusion

This chapter has examined the hidden environmental costs of cheap food by focusing on the industrial grain–oilseed–livestock complex, the productive foundation of the food system in the United States, Canada, and other temperate countries. It explored how the pressures to standardize and mechanize agriculture magnify biological and physical problems and create new ones, how these problems get overridden, and how these overrides involve a large resource budget and pollution burden (amplified by increasingly meat-centred diets), with fossil fuels playing an integral part in all of these matters. When the through-flow process of industrial agriculture is understood, it becomes clear that cheap food depends upon many costs not being counted, and that, in spite of its productive bounty, the system is environmentally unstable. Industrial capitalist agriculture is at once deeply implicated in and threatened by climate change, as well as implicated in soil degradation and the over-consumption and pollution of water. In different ways, climate change and the looming scarcity of oil each present fundamental challenges to the continuation of the system—climate change begs for major restructuring of food economies, and peak oil could well force it.

Fortunately, as people increasingly recognize the environmental costs embedded in cheap food, many are creating alternatives to the industrial grain–oilseed–livestock complex. In the struggles of ecological farmers, consumers' rising demand for local, organic food, and new economic networks linking the two supported by food-centred education and political activism, we find both mounting critical recognition of the problems in the dominant system and hope that it can be rebuilt in more sustainable ways.

Discussion Questions

1. Explain what is meant by the conception of agriculture as a relatively *closed-loop system*, and by agriculture as a *through-flow process*. Discuss what the transformation from closed-loop system to through-flow process has meant for soil in particular, and how ensuing problems have been overridden.

2. Identify and discuss three major aspects of the 'resource budget' of the modern food system.

3. Explain how the modern food system is a major factor in climate change, giving attention to the expansion of livestock production.

4. How will the inevitable scarcity and rising costs of oil affect the modern food system?

Further Reading

1. Kimbrell, A., ed. 2002. *The Fatal Harvest Reader: The Tragedy of Industrial Agriculture.* Washington, DC: Island Press.

    The Fatal Harvest Reader is an edited collection which provides concise, accessible introductions to a range of environmental, health, and social problems associated with industrial agriculture. The chapters are grouped into four parts: (1) deconstructing the 'myths' of industrial agriculture, and problematizing issues such as cheapness and efficiency; (2) exploring the competing ethical and theoretical foundations of low-input versus industrial agriculture; (3) analyzing the technological change and environmental and health hazards; and (4) examining various struggles to re-vision and rebuild alternatives.

2. McIntyre, B.D., H.R. Herren, J. Wakhungu, and R.T. Watson, eds. 2009. *International Assessment of Agricultural Knowledge, Science and Technology for Development: Synthesis Report*. Washington, DC: Island Press.

The International Assessment of Agricultural Knowledge, Science, and Technology for Development (IAASTD) was a three-year project involving more than 400 expert contributors from 110 different countries and a large range of fields. The seven-volume IAASTD report reviews the role of agricultural knowledge, science, and technology (AKST) in shaping development policies over the past half century, and assesses the impacts in terms of hunger, poverty, nutrition, human health, rural development, and the environment. A basic argument is that great productivity gains have many costs, and that AKST must increasingly be approached differently if it is to simultaneously advance development goals like reducing hunger and poverty and build more sustainable agricultural systems.

3. Steinfeld, H., P. Gerber, T. Wassenaar, V. Castel, M. Rosales, and C. de Haan. 2006. *Livestock's Long Shadow: Environmental Issues and Options*. Rome: FAO.

Livestock's Long Shadow is a major FAO report examining the central role of global livestock production in an array of pressing environmental problems, including climate change, land degradation, water pollution, and the loss of biodiversity. It famously calculated (using a Life Cycle Analysis) that on a global scale, livestock has a net greater impact on climate change than does the entire transport sector.

4. Weis, T. 2007. *The Global Food Economy: The Battle for the Future of Farming*. London: Zed Books.

The Global Food Economy analyzes the imbalances, social tensions, and ecological instabilities in the global system of agricultural production and trade. It seeks to understand how this extremely uneven system developed through time, how it has been institutionally entrenched, and how more socially just, ecologically rational, and humane agricultural economies might take shape.

Notes

1. Friction implies that it is hard to move anything in bulk across significant distances when dependent upon human, animal, or wind power, especially something as perishable as food.
2. These fail to override all health risks, however, as disease threats like swine and avian flu, listeriosis, *E. coli*, and mad cow disease persist.
3. A documentary film by Marie-Monique Robin, *The World According to Monsanto* (2008), vividly depicts the nature and scope of its activity.
4. Ecosystem services can be understood through a range of biophysical processes and scales, such as the role that forests play in the carbon cycle; the role that watershed health plays in supplies of fresh water; the role that bees and other pollinators play in agriculture and plant life; and the role that micro-organisms play in soil formation.
5. With this dependence on fossil energy, and in particular oil, industrial agricultural systems are not only tied to climate change but are also indirectly tied to the geopolitics of oil, including the long history of Western political manipulation in the Middle East and the deeply entrenched US military presence there.

Fossil fuels are connected to a different array of unaccounted political, economic, and social costs—or what might be seen as a 'geopolitical externality' (Weis 2010a).

6. 'Thermal lag' means that the world's oceans heat up slowly, due to their enormous thermal mass, and that there is a time lag for rising atmospheric temperatures to translate into rising ocean temperatures. Thus, the extent of atmospheric warming that has already occurred has not yet had its full impact on global ocean temperatures. This concept also relates very powerfully to sea-level rise, since water expands as it warms.

References

Altieri, M.A. 1999. 'The Ecological Role of Biodiversity in Agroecosystems'. *Agriculture, Ecosystems & Environment* 74(1–3): 19–31.

Briscoe, M. 2002. Water: The Overtapped Resource. In *The Fatal Harvest Reader: The Tragedy of Industrial Agriculture*, ed. A. Kimbrell. Washington, DC: Island Press, 181–90.

Brown, L. 1996. *Tough Choices: Facing the Challenge of Food Scarcity*. New York: W.W. Norton.

Carson, R. 1994[1962]. *Silent Spring*. Boston: Houghton Mifflin.

Eisnitz, G. 1997. *Slaughterhouse: The Shocking Story of Greed, Neglect, and Inhuman Treatment Inside the US Meat Industry*. New York: Prometheus.

Food and Agriculture Organization of the United Nations Statistics Division (FAOSTAT) Production Statistics Calculator. 2009. http://faostat.fao.org/site/567/DesktopDefault.aspx?PageID=567.

Friedmann, H. 1993. 'The Political Economy of Food: A Global Crisis'. *New Left Review* 197: 29–57.

Giampietro, M., and K. Mayumi. 2009. *The Biofuel Delusion*. London: Earthscan.

Haberl, H., K.H. Erb, F. Krausmann, V. Gaube, A. Bondeau, C. Plutzar, S. Gingrich, W. Lucht, and M. Fischer-Kowalski. 2007. 'Quantifying and Mapping the Human Appropriation of Net Primary Production in Earth's Terrestrial Ecosystems'. *Proceedings of the National Academy of Science of the United States* 104(31): 12942–7.

Halweil, B. 2008. Meat Production Continues to Rise. In *Vital Signs 2009*, Washington: WorldWatch Institute, 15–17.

Heinberg, R. 2005. *The Party's Over: Oil, War, and the Fate of Industrial Societies*. 2nd ed. Gabriola Island, BC: New Society Publishers.

———. 2007. *Peak Everything: Waking up to the Century of Declines*. Gabriola Island, BC: New Society Publishers.

Howden, M.S., J.-F. Soussana, F.N. Tubiello, N. Chhetri, M. Dunlop, and H. Meinke. 2007. 'Adapting Agriculture to Climate Change'. *Proceedings of the National Academy of Sciences of the United States*, 104(50): 19691–6.

Intergovernmental Panel on Climate Change (IPCC). 2007. *Climate Change 2007: The Physical Science Basis, Contribution of Working Group I to the Fourth Assessment Report of the Intergovernmental Panel on Climate Change*. Cambridge: Cambridge University Press.

International Energy Agency (IEA). 2008. *Key World Energy Statistics*. Paris: IEA Document. www.iea.org/textbase/nppdf/free/2008/Key_Stats_2008.pdf.

Jackson, W. 1985. *New Roots for Agriculture*. San Francisco: Friends of the Earth.

Kloppenberg, J., J. Hendrickson, and G.W. Stephenson. 1996. 'Coming in to the Foodshed'. *Agriculture and Human Values* 13(3): 33–42.

Kuyek, D. 2007. *Good Crop/Bad Crop: Seed Politics and the Future of Food in Canada*. Toronto: Between the Lines.

Lappé, F.M. 1991[1971]. *Diet for a Small Planet*. New York: Ballantine.

McCluney, R. 2005. 'Renewable Energy Limits'. In *The Final Energy Crisis*, ed. Andrew McKillop. London: Pluto Press, 153–75.

McCully, P.M. 1996. *Silenced Rivers: The Ecology and Politics of Large Dams*. London: Zed Books.

McKenney, J. 2002. 'Artificial Fertility: The Environmental Costs of Industrial Fertilizers'. In *The Fatal Harvest Reader: The Tragedy of Industrial Agriculture*, ed. A. Kimbrell. Washington, DC: Island Press, 121–9.

McIntyre, B.D., H.R. Herren, J. Wakhungu, and R.T. Watson, eds. 2009. *International Assessment of Agricultural Knowledge, Science and Technology for Development: Synthesis Report*. Washington, DC: Island Press.

Mann, S., and J. Dickinson. 1978. 'Obstacles to the Development of a Capitalist Agriculture'. *Journal of Peasant Studies* 5(4): 466–81.

Manning, R. 2004. 'The Oil We Eat: Following the Food Chain Back to Iraq'. *Harper's Magazine* 308(1845): 37–45.

Mason, J., and P. Singer. 1990. *Animal Factories*. 2nd ed. New York: Harmony Books.

Mendelson, J. 2002. 'Untested, Unlabelled, and You're Eating It: The Health and Environmental Hazards of Genetically Engineered Food'. In *The Fatal Harvest*

Reader: The Tragedy of Industrial Agriculture, ed. A. Kimbrell. Washington, DC: Island Press, 148–60.

Midkiff, K. 2004. The Meat You Eat: How Corporate Farming Has Endangered America's Food Supply. New York: St Martin's Press.

Millennium Ecosystem Assessment (MEA). 2005. Ecosystems and Human Well-Being: Synthesis. Washington: Island Press.

Mitchell, A. 2009. Sea Sick: The Global Ocean in Crisis. Toronto: McClelland & Stewart.

Montgomery, D.R. 2007. Dirt: The Erosion of Civilizations. Berkeley: University of California Press.

Moore, M. 2002. 'Hidden Dimensions of Damage: Pesticides and Health'. In The Fatal Harvest Reader: The Tragedy of Industrial Agriculture, ed. A. Kimbrell. Washington, DC: Island Press, 130–47.

Nierenberg, D. 2005. Happier Meals: Rethinking the Global Meat Industry. Washington: WorldWatch Paper #171.

Opie, J. 2000. Ogallala: Water for a Dry Land. 2nd ed. Lincoln: University of Nebraska Press.

Pfeiffer, D.A. 2006. Eating Fossil Fuels: Oil, Food and the Coming Crisis in Agriculture. Gabriola Island, BC: New Society Publishers.

Pimentel, D. 2006. 'Soil Erosion: A Food and Environmental Threat'. Environment, Development and Sustainability 8(1): 119–37.

Pollan, M. 2006. The Omnivore's Dilemma: A Natural History of Four Meals. New York: Penguin.

———. 2008. In Defence of Food: An Eater's Manifesto. New York: Penguin Books.

Reisner, M. 1993[1987]. Cadillac Desert: The American West and Its Disappearing Water. 2nd ed. New York: Penguin.

Rosenzweig, C., D. Karoly, M. Vicarelli, P. Neofotis, Q. Wu, G. Casassa, A. Menzel, T.L. Root, N. Estrella, B. Seguin, P. Tryjanowski, C. Liu, S. Rawlins, and A. Imeson. 2008. 'Attributing Physical and Biological Impacts to Anthropogenic Climate Change'. Nature 453 (15 May): 353–7.

Schmidhuber, J., and F.N. Tubiello. 2007. 'Global Food Security Under Climate Change'. Proceedings of the National Academy of Sciences of the United States 104(50): 19703–8.

Shiva, V. 2008. Soil Not Oil. Environmental Justice in an Age of Climate Crisis. Boston: South End Press.

Smith, A., and J.B. McKinnon. 2007. The 100-Mile Diet: A Year of Local Eating. Toronto: Random House.

Statistics Canada. 2007. 'Selected Historical Data from the Census of Agriculture: Data Tables'. 2006 Census of Agriculture, Government of Canada, Ottawa. Accessed 20 April 2009 at www.statcan.gc.ca/pub/95–632-x/2007000/4129762-eng.htm#i.

Statistics Canada. 2010. 'Human Activity and the Environment: Freshwater Supply and Demand in Canada 2010'. Government of Canada, Ottawa. Accessed 31 May 2011 at www.statcan.gc.ca/pub/16-201-x/16-201-x2010000-eng.pdf.

Steinfeld, H., P. Gerber, T. Wassenaar, V. Castel, M. Rosales, and C. de Haan. 2006. Livestock's Long Shadow: Environmental Issues and Options. Rome: FAO.

Steingraber, S. 2010. Living Downstream: An Ecologist's Personal Investigation of Cancer and the Environment. 2nd ed. Cambridge, MA: Da Capo Press.

United Nations Development Programme (UNDP). 2007. Human Development Report 2007–8: Fighting Climate Change: Human Solidarity in a Divided World. New York: Palgrave Macmillan.

US Department of Agriculture, National Agricultural Statistics Service (USDA NASS). 2008. The Census of Agriculture. www.agcensus.usda.gov/Publications/2007/Full_Report/usv1.pdf.

Vía Campesina. 2007. 'Small Scale Sustainable Farmers Are Cooling Down the Earth'. November 2007. www.viacampesina.org/main_en/index2.php?option=com_content&do_pdf=1&id=457.

Warshall, P. 2002. 'Tilth and Technology: The Industrial Redesign of Our Nation's Soils'. In The Fatal Harvest Reader: The Tragedy of Industrial Agriculture, ed. A. Kimbrell. Washington, DC: Island Press, 167–80.

Weis, T. 2007. The Global Food Economy: The Battle for the Future of Farming. London: Zed Books.

———. 2009. 'Breadbasket Contradictions: The Unstable Bounty of Industrial Agriculture in the United States and Canada'. In Food Security, Nutrition and Sustainability: New Challenges, Future Options, ed. G. Lawrence, K. Lyons, and T. Wallington. London: Earthscan, 27–40.

———. 2010a. 'The Accelerating Biophysical Contradictions of Industrial Capitalist Agriculture'. Journal of Agrarian Change 10(3): 315–41.

———. 2010b. 'Our Ecological Hoofprint and the Population Bomb of Reverse Protein Factories'. Review 33(2/3).

WorldWatch. 2004. 'Meat: Now, It's Not Personal! But Like It or Not, Meat-Eating Is Becoming a Problem for Everyone on the Planet'. WorldWatch Magazine July/August, 17(4): 12–20.

Still Hungry

A Feminist Perspective on Food, Foodwork, the Body, and Food Studies

Jennifer Brady, Jacqui Gingras, and Elaine Power

Learning Objectives

Through this chapter, you can:

1. Understand key issues situated at the intersection of food studies and feminism
2. Appreciate the importance of **gender** for food studies
3. Consider how **feminism** could help strengthen, deepen, and politicize the field of food studies

Introduction

Whether feeding themselves or others, women have complicated relationships with food, **foodwork**, and the **body**. At its most elemental level, food nourishes the physical body; however, food is never just about nutrition. Food carries multiple levels of emotional, social, cultural, and political meanings, intertwined with taste, memory, tradition, and ritual. Food marks the body and one's identity in gendered, classed, aged, racialized, ethnic, and other ways. But as much as food carries symbolic meaning, the work of feeding oneself and others can never escape physical or material realities. Everyday foodwork is mundane and repetitive, constrained by affordability and the availability of food and other resources, such as kitchen equipment. It is also central to the rhythms and patterns of everyday life, responding to the body's ongoing need for nourishment.

This chapter introduces the topic of women and food, and the importance to food studies of a feminist analysis. Current food practices do not nourish women well. Despite the rhetoric of a more equal **gender division of household labour**, women continue to do the majority of the foodwork in Canadian families (Beagan, Chapman, D'Sylva, and Bassett 2008). Women also exhibit profound dissatisfaction with their bodies, resulting in high rates of eating problems such as anorexia, bulimia, compulsive overeating, and dieting. Scholarly analyses of food, foodwork, and bodies must pay attention to gender because of the centrality of women to foodwork and the resulting gender inequalities.

Surprisingly, much of the literature in the relatively new field of food studies has neglected gender analysis (Avakian and Haber 2005). Analysis of women's relationships to food, the body, and feeding work in the household would seem a likely focus for feminist scholars, who have been concerned with understanding and changing gender oppression and injustice. Feminists have long taken an interest in the area of the body, critiquing the distorted yet pervasive images of women's bodies and analyzing women's distorted eating practices that result. Feminist scholars have critiqued the dominant (white, upper-middle-class) cultural obsession with thinness and the ways that this obsession keeps women perpetually dissatisfied with their bodies, promotes pathological relationships with food, and benefits capitalism by encouraging women to buy products and services to achieve the elusive 'perfect body' (Avakian and Haber 2005). More recently, feminists have mounted a critique of our body obsession from the perspective of critical fat studies (Hartley 2001; Rothblum and Solovay 2009).

However, feminists have complicated relationships with food and food studies. Many feminists have seen foodwork in the domestic sphere as yet another axis of oppression in the gendered division of labour, in which women's work in social reproduction is largely invisible, unpaid, and undervalued. Some feminists shunned the kitchen and ran away from domestic foodwork (Avakian 1997), spurning scholarly analyses of food and food practices at the same time. Feminist analyses of food practices have barely gained a toehold in the scholarly literature (Avakian and Haber 2005).

Until recently, feminists failed to consider women's participation in unpaid foodwork as a potential source of power, resistance, and creativity rather than as simple oppression (Avakian and Haber 2005; Hollows 2003a). By ignoring food as an area of feminist inquiry, scholars overlooked the important ways in which women produce, reproduce, resist, and transform gender ideologies in their everyday work of feeding themselves and others. Scholars from a wide range of disciplines have begun to bring a feminist lens to the study of food.

However, many feminist analyses of food practices consider gender in isolation from other social positions (Avakian and Haber 2005), neglecting how women's unpaid foodwork is part of the complex 'doing' of *intersecting* identities of gender, class, race, ethnicity, and sexuality. In other words, women do foodwork not just as people with a particular gender identity, but *also* as people of particular classes, races, ethnicities, and sexualities.

As food studies scholars, we are dissatisfied by the dearth of feminist and **embodied** perspectives on food, foodwork, and the body. We ask 'What happens to food studies when we look at it through a feminist lens?' We have three intertwined goals: (1) to draw out using a feminist lens that which is otherwise unseen and unspoken about women, food, foodwork, and the body; (2) to highlight the need to further consider gender in the food studies literature; and (3) to deepen, strengthen, and politicize the emergent field of food studies by drawing lessons from feminism and related critical scholarly fields, and thus to analyze relations of power and understand social inequalities related to food, foodwork, and the body.

In this chapter, we consider the intimate spaces of women's unpaid foodwork, the body, and the household. While recognizing its importance, we leave aside women's paid foodwork in the agri-food system because of the limitations of space. We have endeavoured to iteratively map food, body, and unpaid foodwork using a feminist cartography working from the personal to the political, from the micro to the macro, from the individual to the collective, and weave them together, recognizing that each pole of these analytical dualities contains and constitutes the other. In so doing, the message is clear: people's relationships with food are felt intimately; at the same time these relationships are partly constituted by 'the power that society allocates or denies to men and women through their access to and control of one essential resource: food' (Counihan and Kaplan 1998: 2).

Gender, Food, and the Body

Not surprisingly, many feminist writers have considered the body, because 'feminism is concerned with the historical, social, and political meanings of sexual difference in the human body, and the spectrum of experiences those meanings produce' (Kevin 2009: 1). This section extends previous work in feminist food studies in order to more fully excavate the intersections of gender, food, and the body from a feminist perspective. As we do throughout this chapter, we take a broad view in that we cannot consider food without considering feminism, and we cannot consider feminism without considering the body. Hence the pieces of the triptych (feminism, food, body) are inextricably connected.

Moral Imperatives of Food and Eating

Within our consideration of food studies, we acknowledge how gender as a social construct (not biologically given) establishes differences between men and women in their relations with food (Allen and Sachs 2007). Coveney (2000) aptly describes the dominant contemporary moral imperative facing women: '. . . good food requires one to show less concern with the physical pleasure of eating, and more interest in the good health that results from our dietary habits' which, in turn, serves as '. . . the basis for the moral judgment we make about ourselves and others' (viii). From this moral impetus, it is a small step to consider food strictly in terms of the specific nutrients that promote good health, a preoccupation known as **nutritionism**.

Scrinis (2008) coined the term *nutritionism* to describe the singular preoccupation with the quantification of food—measuring food by its nutrient composition. This reductionist, technical paradigm assumes that food's role in promoting bodily health is the only one that really matters, and leads to highly processed combinations of ingredients being categorized as 'healthy foods' because they are low in fat and have been fortified with key nutrients. Nutrition professionals have been critiqued for perpetuating

and reinforcing these views of food and healthy eating such that the dominant popular culture **discourse** about food is now based in nutritional science and public health, dividing and simplifying foods into those that are healthy or unhealthy and, by extension, good or bad. This dominant approach to food promotes a reductionist, simplistic, technical way of eating that ignores the multiple symbolic dimensions of food and the sheer joy, pleasures, and satisfactions of food, cooking, and eating (Mudry 2009; Parasecoli 2008). Print, digital, and other media have enabled the vast distribution of food knowledge in a simplistic manner, which enables nutritionism's simple message: it is your responsibility to eat right and thus be healthy (Rich 2011).

Nutritionism is thus a component of **healthism**, an overly individualized effort to achieve health while neglecting the complex social determinants that inform health practices (Crawford 1980). In contemporary society, health (at least a narrow conception of health as the well-being of the physical body) acts as a secular religion, justifying the scrutiny of individuals' everyday activities for their health-promoting or health-denying properties, and setting up an associated moral hierarchy of these everyday activities (Crawford 1980). Healthism and its offspring nutritionism are thus vehicles for the implementation of **neo-liberalism**, the dominant political **ideology**. Neo-liberalism emphasizes individual responsibility for security and well-being; promotes cutting back the welfare state activities that formerly ensured collective well-being; and favours the substitution of private market forces for collective government action. Healthism and nutritionism have enabled a neo-liberal form of self-governance, in which 'proper' citizens are expected to govern their own choices and everyday practices in conformity with the latest health and nutrition information about which choices and practices are healthy (Guthman and Dupuis 2006; LeBesco 2010; Lupton 1995). For women who care for others in the household, this means that they are responsible for their loved ones' health and nutrition choices as well.

Nutritionism as a way of understanding food and eating has claimed and disadvantaged the food and body experiences of women. Under nutritionism, eating has taken on a specific, singular, and moralistic purpose: food is a random collection of nutrients that responsible eaters are required to consume in specific, precise, and controlled amounts and combinations to promote health, and that responsible feeders are required to provide to others. Nutritionism requires a sophisticated understanding of the contents of food, from sodium to phytonutrients and micronutrients. It also requires constant surveillance and accounting, to ensure one's own nutritional health and the nutritional health of those being fed. Healthy eating has become eating per se, the implications of which have been taken up elsewhere in this volume (see Chapter 9). To challenge this reductionist and moralistic perspective on food, we encourage a critical feminist theoretical standpoint for food studies scholars, informed by tributary and emergent perspectives from **fat studies**, **critical obesity studies**, and **critical dietetics**.

Emerging Theories of the Body: Fatness and Embodiment

Contemporary fat studies scholars have taken up the feminist challenge of considering the ways in which society's obsession with the thin body has disciplined women and regulated their relationships with food. Rothblum and Solovay's recent edited volume (2009) indicates that fat studies is now on the map as a new interdisciplinary field of study, one which 'is marked by an aggressive, consistent rigorous critique of the negative assumptions, stereotypes, and stigma placed on fat and the fat body' (2). If food studies were to borrow and engage liberally with theories and narratives from fat studies, food and body moralizing could be critically addressed and contested. For example, fat studies offers food studies a means to reconsider the body and gender as performative (Butler 1990, 1988; Colls 2007), avoiding strictly biological understandings of the gendered body and recognizing instead the ways in which each of us repeatedly, and usually unthinkingly,

enact our culture's prescriptions for the body and gender. Fat studies, critical obesity studies, and critical dietetics work to unravel and perturb taken-for-granted notions of the body, pulling back the healthist curtain that has been closed by anti-obesity researchers and public-health practitioners about which bodies are 'worthy' and 'proper'. Fat studies exposes the dominant moralistic, healthist discourse on the body as racist and classist. For example, those who identify with some cultural groups (e.g., those of African descent) put a higher value on rounded, plump bodies than do white people, or at least are less obsessed by thinness (Hughes 1997; Parasecoli 2007). However, there is also evidence that this association is tempered by class. Increasingly, the thin body is a mark of distinction associated with the well-educated upper-middle-class (LeBesco 2004; Sobal and Maurer 1999).

Scholars of fat studies, critical obesity, and critical dietetics urge us to resist the wave of fat panic that is increasingly buttressed by public-health policy (Kirkland 2011; Beausoleil and Ward 2010). Even feminists have been swept up in fat panic, echoing the public-health call for changes to support healthy eating and increased physical activity through urban planning, taxation, agricultural policy, and so on (Yancey, Leslie, and Abel 2006; Probyn 2008). Writing from the context of the United States, Kirkland (2011) is troubled by what seems to be feminists' heart-felt, well-meaning desire to help low-income minority groups, especially women and children, who have poor access to fresh food and recreational facilities, and who have higher rates of fatness. She argues 'It is unethical and self-defeating to ride anxiety about fatness to fulfill political goals that actually call for a sustained commitment to economic redistribution for their long-term success' (481). The public-health stance toward obesity that some feminists have adopted can appear to be caring and compassionate, but their arguments are moralizing and unreflexive, with the unintended consequence of adding another layer of marginalization, i.e., fatness, to bodies that are already marked by poverty and racialization. Kirkland notes an enduring feature of feminist solutions to social problems: 'well-meant efforts to improve poor women's living conditions at a collective level often end up as intrusive, moralizing, and punitive' (464). Fat studies scholars urge us to consider: Why this, why now? Why are we so fixated on body size instead of attending to other more important determinants of health, particularly racism and poverty?

Much like feminism has done, fat studies also offers a way to understand the connections between what we think of as impersonal, large-scale, political forces and discourses, and what we consider to be personal and intimate, the body. For example, a number of authors consider the ways in which the obese body reflects contemporary cultural tensions and anxieties, from the American 'war on terror' to the contradictions of capitalism (Biltekoff 2007; Guthman and Dupuis 2006; LeBesco 2010; Shugart 2010). These authors understand the body to be both material *and* discursive, but move away from the material and physical body to consider metaphor and symbolism, to understand the ways in which our constructions of the fat body tell us about deep and profound underlying political currents in our contemporary society that affect us all, usually without our recognition. For example, Guthman and Dupuis (2006) show how bodies literally take up and manifest the cultural contradictions of global capitalism—on the one hand, as consumers, we are directed to consume endlessly (and, in this case of food, literally) to boost corporate sales and profits; on the other hand, as producers, we are obliged to remain disciplined, healthy workers. In this case, neo-liberalism both produces the problem of obesity (through encouraging over-consumption) and labels obesity as a social problem that individuals must solve by making 'proper' choices, especially in the marketplace.

Gender and Unpaid Foodwork

Just as fat studies scholars have drawn attention to the political nature of the body, feminist activists and researchers highlight the political nature of foodwork, drawing attention to its inequitable distribution, and the resulting gender-based oppression at every level, from the household to global food systems (Allen and Sachs 2007). Given the brevity of this chapter and the breadth of gender and foodwork as a topic, this section focuses on unpaid foodwork to offer one response to the question posed at the beginning of this chapter: What happens to food studies when we look at it through a feminist lens? In this section we move from consideration of the body to examine gender and unpaid foodwork in the home and family.

This section supports our overarching thesis that to contemplate food requires feminist scholarship. We present two arguments that consider unpaid foodwork through a feminist lens. The first challenges the ideology that characterizes the **public sphere** and **private sphere** as separate, dichotomous entities, and illuminates the inequitable distribution of foodwork and the resulting gender inequity that stem from that ideology. The second demonstrates that in doing unpaid foodwork, people, with their inextricably linked identities of gender, class, race, and sexuality, continuously create and recreate both the gendered nature of foodwork *and* their own gender(s). To illustrate, when a woman cooks, she is demarcating herself as a woman because cooking is considered to be a womanly task. On the other hand, because it is a woman cooking, cooking is deemed to be something that women are supposed to do.

In the first part, a review of unpaid foodwork and the contemporary gendered division of labour is presented to support the argument that unpaid foodwork bridges the public and private spheres. This is followed by a brief review of four key theories—relative resources, time constraints, gender ideology, and gender construction theory—to situate unpaid foodwork within the various models proposed to account for the gendered division of unpaid household work in general. This review provides the context for the second part of this section, which begins with a review of feminist scholarship on foodwork and takes a gender construction approach to present the second argument, that unpaid foodwork and identity are iterative processes.

Unpaid Foodwork and the Public–Private Dichotomy

The ideological dichotomy of public and private spheres mirrors dominant gender ideologies and underpins the gendered division of labour. The binary arrangement that organizes gender into two categories, men and women, corresponds with the dichotomy of the public sphere and the private sphere. Dominant gender ideologies associate men and the public sphere with independence, power, paid employment, and financial support of the family. Conversely, women and the private sphere are coupled with dependence, vulnerability, caregiving, and feeding the family (DeVault 1991). The private sphere of home and family has been seen as inherently less important than the public sphere of 'real' work of measurable economic value. Real work is viewed as happening in the public sphere, as remunerated, and as the intuitive purview of men. On the other hand, women are assumed to be innately inclined to nurture, and responsibilities like unpaid foodwork are viewed as a 'labour of love' rather than as the kind of 'real work' done by men (Smith 1987; Swenson 2009). The gender division of labour thus hinges on the socially constructed ideological grouping of men–paid employment–public sphere versus women–unpaid foodwork–private sphere.

Not acknowledging unpaid foodwork as work trivializes the knowledge, skill, and effort it requires and contributes to gender inequality (Oakley 1974). Since unpaid foodwork is not remunerated it is erroneously considered of little economic consequence to family well-being or the functioning of society at large. DeVault (1991) notes that the work of feeding a family is often unnoticed or mistaken for other, more leisurely tasks: 'managing a meal looks like simply enjoying the companionship of one's family . . . and learning about food prices can look like reading the newspaper. The work is noticeable when it is not completed (when the milk is all gone, for example, or when the meal is not ready on time), but cannot be seen when it is done well' (56). This disregard for unpaid foodwork as real work renders the persons held responsible for it (mainly women) of less consequence than those who are ideologically positioned as family breadwinners (mainly men). As Erickson (2005) explains, 'In that women perform more family work than men, failing to characterize these activities as work serves to invalidate women's essential contributions to social and community life and, in this way, contributes to the reproduction of gender inequality' (338).

Feminist scholarship has challenged the ideological dichotomies of gender and social space to argue that 'unpaid foodwork' is indeed real work and invariably bridges public and private space (DeVault 1991; Smith 1987). Unpaid foodwork involves tasks and processes that are carried out in the public sphere and that influence and are influenced by it. To illustrate, unpaid foodwork includes budgeting financial, human, and material resources; purchasing and transporting food; assessing the quality of food for purchase; seeking out and using knowledge of nutrition; planning and preparing meals; juggling the schedules, likes, dislikes, and various health concerns (e.g., diabetes, low-sodium diet) and dietary needs (e.g., allergies, vegetarianism/veganism) of family members; and cleaning up. Clearly, many of these tasks and processes do not occur exclusively within what is usually considered domestic space. Moreover, unpaid foodwork produces goods not only for family members to consume both at home (family meals) and away from home (packed lunches, snacks), but also for extended kinship and community networks (entertaining guests, school bake sales, potlucks). In addition, unpaid foodwork is central to the physical reproduction of family members who live and work outside of the home as well as the reproduction of their social and cultural identities, which marks their membership in a wider community.

For example, the preparation of a Passover Seder, Thanksgiving meal, or Eid feast provides sustenance for family members' bodies and sustains their affiliations with their cultural, religious, and social communities. In this light, the tasks and process as well as the outcomes of unpaid foodwork challenge the notion that the public sphere and the private sphere are distinct realms of activity.

In a recent Canadian study, Beagan, Chapman, D'Sylva, and Bassett (2008) report on data from Statistics Canada that indicate that between 1998 and 2005 the time women spent on cooking and washing up decreased (1.1 to 0.9 hours per day), but it was still more than double the time men contributed to the same tasks (0.4 hours per day, which did not change). The authors conclude, 'For decades, scholarship in the area of domestic labour has assumed gender inequities will diminish over time, yet this does not appear to be happening. Rather, traditional gender roles seem to reinvent themselves in new guises' (668). Why is it that the inequitable division of labour and the resulting gender inequality persist despite predictions to the contrary?

Four main theories have been put forward to elucidate women's markedly larger contribution to household work: relative resources; time constraints; gender ideology; and gender construction theory. Haddad (1996) classifies such theories into two groups: 'pragmatic strategies' and 'patriarchal dynamics' based on the underlying thrust of each theory. The 'pragmatic strategies', which include relative resources and time constraints, propose that co-habiting couples rationally allocate the distribution of household work, including foodwork, based on their relative material and social resources and availability. Relative resources theory is based on the idea that in the interests of maximizing available resources, the partner with greater socio-economic status (financial resources, education, and occupational prestige) will wield greater interpersonal bargaining power to get out of doing household chores (Erickson 2005;

Kroska 2004; McFarlane, Beaujot, and Haddad 2000). The time constraints theory posits that men's and women's participation in unpaid work is a function of the time spent in paid work: as the time spent in paid employment increases, the time spent in unpaid work in the home decreases (Erickson 2005; Kroska 2004; Sayer 2005). Several studies have shown, however, that even in households where both partners spend an equal number of hours per day in paid work, women still contribute substantially more time to unpaid household work (Kamo 1991; Shelton and John 1996; Sullivan 2000).

The problem with the theories of relative resources and time constraints is that neither attends to the underlying ideologies that underpin the inequitable distribution of unpaid work. This is particularly so in light of studies that have found that factors related to the relative resources and time constraints theories do not equally impact men's and women's participation in household work (Bittman, England, Folbore, Sayer, and Matheson 2003; McFarlane, Beaujot, and Haddad 2000). Included in Haddad's (1996) 'patriarchal dynamics' are theories that address other factors that give rise to the inequitable distribution of unpaid work.

Arising from socialization theories, gender ideology theory posits that gender is not determined at birth, but through various socialization experiences is fixed at an early age (West and Zimmerman 1987). Gender ideology theory hypothesizes that in couples that hold more traditional gender ideologies, women perform more of the household work (Erickson 2005; Sullivan 2000). Conversely, partners who hold more liberal gender attitudes will share household work more equally. Studies have shown that men's gender role attitudes have a stronger influence on the division of household work than that of their female counterparts (Kroska 2004; Shelton and John 1996); however, research also indicates that attitudes are generally unreliable predictors of individuals' behaviour (Shelton and John 1996).

The gender construction theory departs from gender ideology theory in seeing gender as an impermanent aspect of identity that is continuously produced through individuals' everyday activities. According to the gender construction theory, performing household work is significant beyond individuals' socio-economic worth, availability, or ideological values because it is implicated in the very constitution of individuals' gender identities (Erickson 2005). That is, gender construction theory proposes that 'the gendered allocation of household labour remains unchanged because it signals the extent to which husbands and wives have constructed gender "appropriately"' (Erickson 2005: 340). In other words, it is (in part) by allocating household work unequally that individuals make themselves out to be proper women and men. Consistency in one's gender identity is achieved by taking on a role in household work that corresponds with other aspects by which individuals constitute their sense of self as gendered subjects, such as style of dress and occupation.

Foodwork and Gender as Iterative Processes

In line with the gender construction theory, some scholars contend that gender is neither a biologically nor a socially fixed identity category, but is a matter of individuals' everyday activities and interactions with their social environments (Butler 1990; West and Fenstermaker 1995; West and Zimmerman 1987). Berk explains, 'Simultaneously, [household] members "do" gender, as they "do" housework and childcare, and what [has] been called the division of labor provides for the joint production of household labor and gender; it is the mechanism by which both the material and symbolic products of the household are realized' (as quoted in West and Zimmerman 1987: 144). In other words, 'it is not simply that household labor is designated as "women's work," but that for a woman to engage in it and a man not to engage in it is to draw on and exhibit the "essential nature" of each' (West and Zimmerman 1987: 144). As one example of individuals' everyday activities, the gender division of labour is not superfluous, but is a purposeful arrangement by which men and women make themselves out as masculine and feminine.

For women, unpaid foodwork is a central part of how they 'do' gender in ways that fit with prevailing gender norms. DeVault (1991) notes that 'It is not just that women do more of the work of feeding, but also that feeding work has become one of the primary ways that women "do" gender. . . . By feeding the family, a woman conducts herself as recognizably womanly' (118). Based on their research of young mothers' dinner practices, Bugge and Almas (2006) support DeVault's (1991) claim in arguing that 'women's dinner practice should be understood not only as an act of caring for others (care work), but also something they do for themselves, a kind of identity work' (204). This view is supported in recent work by others (McIntyre, Thille, and Rondeau 2009). To contravene these normative expectations of being a woman is to risk illegitimacy as a properly gendered individual. By conducting themselves as 'recognizably womanly', women's unpaid foodwork iteratively reinforces the gendered assignment of these tasks as feminine, while also constituting those who perform these tasks as feminine subjects. The iterative construction of foodwork and femininity is also supported by research on same-sex families, where foodwork is seldom equally divided; partners work to protect the masculinity of the primary food provider in gay couples and the femininity of the partner who does less foodwork in lesbian couples (Carrington 2008).

Overall, 'doing' masculinity has received considerably less attention in the literature concerned with gender and foodwork (Julier and Lindenfeld 2005). Of the small pool of published works, many focus on celebrity chefs from television cooking shows (Hollows 2003b; Smith and Wilson 2004; Swenson 2009). For example, Hollows (2003b) explores how celebrity chef Jamie Oliver pulls off an acceptably masculine gender identity while cooking home-style food in the domestic setting of his television kitchen. She says that he accomplishes this by 'disavowing the extent to which cooking is a form of labour and constructing it as a "fun" leisure and lifestyle activity' (229). Hollows (2003b) adds that is it this element of performance that keeps men's cooking at home and for others at a safe distance from the sense of obligation and drudgery associated with women's everyday foodwork. In the domestic sphere, Curtis, James, and Ellis (2010) show how fathers' limited contributions to feeding the family collapse the usual hierarchical and generational boundaries between children and their parents, and re-inscribe the gender division of labour in household foodwork.

Building on West and Zimmerman's (1987) work, others contend that the practices of 'doing' gender actually constitute a multiplicity of gender identities. Swenson (2009) describes gender as 'an activity that is performed in response to institutional and social norms and is capable of pluralities' (39). In other words, the practices by which individuals 'do' gender are not prescribed and, therefore, neither are masculinity or femininity. Moreover, gender identity is cross-cut by the ways in which people simultaneously engage in practices involved in 'doing' other social identities, such as class, race, ethnicity, and sexuality, which further diversifies doable gender identities. Rather than 'doing gender', people's relational and interactive everyday practices may be more aptly described as 'doing gender(s)'.

Bugge and Almas (2006) also found that although women rationalized the unequal distribution of foodwork between themselves and their male partners based on 'pragmatic strategies' (i.e., time constraints) (Haddad 1996), their talk was underpinned by intersecting ideological constructions of gender and class that were enacted by purchasing certain kinds of foods and preparing certain kinds of meals for their families. Study participants explicitly distanced themselves from women seen as not appropriately 'doing' their roles as wives and mothers, that is, from those who purchased and cooked primarily pre-packaged convenience foods. For these women, preparing 'proper meals' and purchasing the right kinds of

high-quality, healthy foods are part of 'doing' a particularly gendered, class identity.

Cairns and colleagues (2010) explored how intersectionalities of gender and class are enacted through 'foodie discourse' by women and men who self-identified as 'foodies' (596). The men and women interviewed spoke similarly about cooking and food as means of seeking pleasure and about which they pursued knowledge and expertise. For women this seems to challenge traditional gender norms that associate femininity with self-denial rather than desire and expertise. While men and women converged on their discussion of food as a source of pleasure, how they talked about feeding others diverged and tended to reinforce traditional gender norms. The women participants described cooking primarily as a means of caring for their partners and children, fostering family connection, and safeguarding family health. Conversely, men discussed cooking as a leisure activity; preparing food for others was performative and used to showcase their talents. For both the women and men, practices of 'doing' class were inseparable from their practices of 'doing' gender. Constructing a foodie identity by spending family resources such as time and money on purchasing certain foods, entertaining guests, and pursuing specialized knowledge and skill iteratively constructs the participants' class privilege.

In another study that highlighted the intersectionalities of gender and race, Beagan, Chapman, D'Sylva, and Bassett (2008) found that while the rationale offered by Punjabi-, African-, and European-Canadian families for the unequal distribution of foodwork among their members differed, the underlying reasons were very similar in that all appealed to traditional notions of gender-appropriate work roles. When asked how foodwork responsibilities are divided among family members, Punjabi families explicitly cited gender role expectations (i.e., foodwork is women's work), while African and European families rationalized men and women's unequal foodwork in ways that concealed the gender discourse that underpinned their reasoning. To illustrate, African and European families often noted women's greater availability of time, despite the fact that in most of these families women were employed full-time. Moreover, their interest in healthier foods, higher standards for cleaning up, and inclination to keep the peace among family members were cited by African and European participants as additional reasons why women were tasked with the majority of foodwork. The authors add, however, that these additional explanations implicitly appeal to gender role expectations, such as women's responsibility for managing the health, well-being, and contentment of family members. These expectations set up standards by which women, not male or teenaged family members, are judged. Based on this research, Beagan, Chapman, D'Sylva, and Bassett (2008) conclude, 'For decades, scholarship in the area of domestic labour has assumed gender inequities will diminish over time, yet this does not appear to be happening. Rather, traditional gender roles seem to reinvent themselves in new guises' (668).

For some marginalized groups, unpaid foodwork may be an important part of resistance to acculturation and oppression by dominant groups. Discussion of resistance movements generally situates action within the public sphere (e.g., protests, demonstrations, labour strikes) rather than in the intimate spaces in the home. For example, Beoku-Betts (2002) explores the unpaid foodwork of Gullah women, African-American women who are descended from slaves, now living along the coast of South Carolina and Georgia. She finds that food preparation, including the type of foods prepared, the methods, and the flavourings used, is part of women's conscious effort to resist the racist past of their ancestors, and demarcate and maintain a group identity distinct from the surrounding dominant culture. Similarly, Narayan (1995) explores the role of food in negotiating Indian identity for expatriates living in Britain and shows how foodwork is a practice of resistance used to set Indians' identities and communities apart from their former colonizers. Taking a slightly different approach to foodwork and resistance, LeBesco (2001) explores the use of Jell-O to resist

the 'drudgery' associated with foodwork and the 'middle-America housewife role' by presumably white, middle-class women (142–3).

However, for women who are economically marginalized, lack of money to feed oneself and one's family adds new levels of complexity and stress to foodwork and contributes to the misery and suffering of poverty. Inadequate money to buy food brings into sharp relief all the invisible work involved in feeding the family and adds to that workload. Food providers who have experienced periods of low income describe the more careful budgeting and planning needed at those times, including checking flyers, clipping and keeping track of coupons, comparison shopping, and keeping a running tally of the cost of the food in the grocery cart so as not to go over budget. With financial constraints, women must be more resourceful in their cooking: cooking more often from scratch; altering menus to 'stretch' the meal; making low-cost meals that use a minimum of ingredients; and serving only food that the family likes so that none is wasted. Under financial duress, women will serve themselves lower-quality food or smaller portions, sometimes skipping meals entirely, to ensure that their children are not hungry or that their male partners are satisfied. They will also swallow their pride and endure the demeaning experience of receiving food from charitable sources such as food banks (DeVault 1991; Hamelin, Beaudry, and Habicht 2002; Power, Beagan, Salmon, and McPhail 2010). Attesting to the invisibility of this work, food providers who had never been short of money for food were asked to imagine what would change if they were. They never mentioned the extra practical work listed above, thinking instead of the food items and restaurant meals they would no longer be able to afford (Power et al. 2010). Layered onto these practical tasks are intense emotions: the worry and anxiety of juggling which bills will get paid and how much money will be left over for groceries; the heartbreak of refusing children's requests so often that eventually they stop asking; the fear of not being able to properly provide for one's children and failing as a mother; the sinking feeling in the gut when what is left in the cupboard and fridge is inadequate to make a satisfying meal (Hamelin et al. 2002; Power et al. 2010; Power 2005). For women living on inadequate incomes, food is hardly the source of pleasure that highly resourced foodies describe (Cairns et al. 2010); instead it is a constant source of stress and anxiety.

Academics working to uncover the theoretical aspects of gender and foodwork rely on previous feminist literatures to highlight the connections between gender inequality, poverty, and policy. These theoretical machinations cannot help but give way to the visceral and very real experiences of the women whose lives constitute these theories. Ongoing activism and feminist scholarship, often conducted coterminously, is required to address persisting inequities.

Conclusion

As we write, in 2012, our world faces a series of crises. The environmental crisis, particularly global climate change, is one of the most prominent, but there are crises in every realm, from the economic and political to the religious, cultural, and social realms. Recent political uprisings in Tunisia and Egypt show the profound longing of ordinary people to create a better world, one of equality, freedom, and democracy. The natural and social worlds cry out for caring and nurturing, values associated with the feminine (in both men and women), and with women's foodwork.

It is our profound hope that food studies can contribute to building a better, more just world,

by analyzing the ways in which food, foodwork, and bodies produce, reproduce, and resist forms of inequality and oppression. We will thus make our scholarship useful, because understanding and analysis is critical to promoting change. To do so, food studies must pay attention to gender as a primary axis of inequality in foodwork. Food studies can also learn from feminism to consider other ways in which power operates to re-inscribe—or resist—relations of inequality and oppression.

On the other hand, perhaps food studies is already helping bring feminists back in touch with food, as highly attuned producers (locavores), distributors (fair trade doyennes), and consumers (customers of organic products and foodies) (Cairns et al. 2010). And, perhaps women are more politically involved in environmental issues (Micheletti 2004), especially those that concern the food supply, bringing feminists and their theories closer to the earth, sustenance, nourishment, and longing. A feminist perspective positions food studies at the promising and visceral edge of integrating embodiment, food, emotionality, and social trust (Beasley and Bacchi 2007; Hayes-Conroy and Hayes-Conroy 2010), a crucial step in doing a better job of caring for and nourishing ourselves, others, and the planet. Lupton (1996) argues that 'devoting attention to embodiment indeed confounds the entire logocentric project of philosophy; the drive to rationalize the emphatic separation of the mind from the body, the elevation of thought over embodiment' (2). Such confounding is exactly what we wish to imagine for future iterations of food studies, theory, and practice.

Discussion Questions

1. A key tenet of feminism is that 'the personal is political', meaning that in addition to the political proceedings we most commonly associate with the public sphere (i.e., policy, laws, government, the economy), the events and relationships that take place in our everyday lives also shape and are shaped by political currents. How do the issues discussed in this chapter affect your everyday life? How is your relationship to food, foodwork, and the body shaped by dominant ideologies about health, nutrition, gender, and class?

2. One goal of this chapter is to deepen, strengthen, and politicize your understanding of the emergent field of food studies by drawing lessons from feminism and other related critical

scholarly fields. If your primary discipline is not gender studies, how does your field of study or area of interest intersect with or contribute to the discussion of feminist perspectives of food studies presented here?

3. The first part of this chapter discusses the impact of healthism and nutritionism on women's relationships to food, eating, and their bodies. How might healthism and nutritionism affect women as those responsible for unpaid foodwork, as discussed in the second part of the chapter?

4. In what ways can you demonstrate the interrelationships among feminism, food, and the body? If you were to propose a means for making visible these interrelationships in order to reduce inequities in foodwork, what advocacy project would you propose?

Further Reading

1. Allen, P., and C. Sachs. 2007. 'Women and Food Chains: The Gendered Politics of Food', *International Journal of Sociology of Food and Agriculture* 15(1): 1–23.

   This article offers a review of the feminist literature on food and gender, and explores the ways in which the contemporary food system begets gender inequality. Allen and Sachs argue that feminist food studies researchers must explore and theorize how the material, socio-cultural, and corporeal domains of the contemporary food system are interconnected and how each is implicated in women's subordination and their acts of resistance. The authors also review how women are organizing to create change within the food system to promote gender equity.

2. DeVault, M. 1991. *Feeding the Family: The Social Organization of Caring as Gendered Work.* Chicago: The University of Chicago Press.

   In this food studies and feminist classic, DeVault reports her analysis of interviews with those most responsible for foodwork (30 women and 3 men) in 30 economically, culturally, and ethnically diverse households in the United States. DeVault sheds light on the often invisible, gendered organization of foodwork and its significance in constructing gender and class identities in the context of the North American family. *Feeding the Family* has stood the test of time

and is an essential resource for food studies students and scholars.

3. Bordo, S. 1993. *Unbearable Weight: Feminism, Western Culture, and the Body.* Berkeley: University of California Press.

   Bordo's *Unbearable Weight* (1993) is a germinal text for those coming to know the (female) body as a social construction. In a collection of poststructural, postmodern, and feminist essays, Bordo brings contemporary philosophy to bear on the cultural, social, and media influences on Western bodies. *Unbearable Weight* makes a significant contribution to our understanding of the body as positioned, mediated, and subjectified.

4. Counihan, C., and S. Kaplan. 1998. *Food and Gender: Identity and Power.* Amsterdam: Harwood Academic Publishers.

   In this edited volume, Counihan and Kaplan present articles that explore various perspectives of food and gender. On the whole, this volume addresses questions about the role of food production, consumption, and distribution in constructing gender identity and the gendered distribution of social and personal power.

5. West, C., and D.H. Zimmerman. 1987. 'Doing Gender'. *Gender and Society* 1(2): 125–51.

In this paper, West and Zimmerman argue that gender identity is not affixed to biological sex nor is gender identity permanent and unchanging. Rather, the authors propose that gender is a socially constructed phenomenon that is 'done', or performed, through the series of individuals' everyday actions and interactions. This is an important text for those seeking to understand critical perspectives of gender.

References

Allen, P., and C. Sachs. 2007. 'Women and Food Chains: The Gendered Politics of Food'. *International Journal of Sociology of Food and Agriculture* 15(1): 1–23.

Avakian, A., and B. Haber. 2005. 'Feminist Food Studies: A Brief History'. In *From Betty Crocker to Feminist Food Studies: Critical Perspectives on Women and Food*, ed. A. Avakian and B. Haber. Boston: University of Massachusetts Press, 1–28.

Avakian, A.V. 1997. *Through the Kitchen Window: Women Writers Explore the Intimate Meanings of Food and Cooking*. Boston: Beacon.

Beagan, B., G. Chapman, A. D'Sylva, and B.R. Bassett. 2008. '"It's Just Easier for Me to Do It": Rationalizing the Family Division of Foodwork'. *Sociology* 42(4): 653–72.

Beasley, C., and C. Bacchi. 2007. 'Envisaging a New Politics for an Ethical Future: Beyond Trust, Care and Generosity—Towards an Ethic of "Social Flesh"'. *Feminist Theory* 8(3): 279–98.

Beausoleil, N., and P. Ward. 2010. 'Fat Panic in Canadian Public Health Policy: Obesity as Different and Unhealthy'. *Radical Psychology* 8: 1. Available at www.radicalpsychology.org/vol8–1/fatpanic.html.

Beoku-Betts, J. 2002. '"We Got Our Way of Cooking Things": Women, Food, and Preservation of Cultural Identity Among the Gullah'. In *Food in the USA: A Reader*, ed. C. Counihan. New York: Routledge, 277–94.

Biltekoff, C. 2007. 'The Terror Within: Obesity in Post 9/11 U.S. Life'. *American Studies* 48(3): 29–48.

Bittman, M., P. England, N. Folbre, L. Sayer, and G. Matheson. 2003. 'When Does Gender Trump Money? Bargaining and Time in Household'. *The American Journal of Sociology* 109(1): 186–214.

Bugge, A.B., and R. Almas. 2006. 'Domestic Dinner: Representations and Practices of a Proper Meal Among Young Suburban Mothers'. *Journal of Consumer Culture* 6(2): 203–28.

Butler, J. 1988. 'Performative Acts and Gender Constitution: An Essay in Phenomenology and Feminist Theory'. *Theatre Journal* 40(4): 519–31.

———. 1990. *Gender Trouble: Feminism and the Subversion of Identity*. New York: Routledge.

Cairns, K., J. Johnston, and S. Baumann. 2010. 'Caring About Food: Doing Gender in a Foodie Kitchen'. *Gender and Society* 24(5): 591–615.

Carrington, C. 2008. 'Feeding Lesbigay Families'. In *Food and Culture: A Reader,* (2nd ed.), ed. C. Counihan and P. van Esterik. New York and London: Routledge, 259–86.

Colls, R. 2007. 'Materialising Bodily Matter: Intra-action and the Embodiment of "Fat"'. *Geoforum* 38: 353–65.

Counihan, C., and S. Kaplan. 1998. *Food and Gender: Identity and Power*. Amsterdam: Harwood Academic Publishers.

Coveney, J. 2000. *Food, Morals, and Meaning: The Pleasure and Anxiety of Eating*. New York: Routledge.

Crawford, R. 1980. 'Healthism and the Medicalization of Everyday Life'. *International Journal of Health Services* 10(3): 365–88.

Curtis, P., A. James, and K. Ellis. 2010. 'Fathering through Food: Children's Perceptions of Father's Contributions to Family Food Practices'. In *Children, Food and Identity in Everyday Life*, ed. A. James, A. T. Kjørholt, and V. Tingstad. New York: Palgrave Macmillan, 94–111.

DeVault, M. 1991. *Feeding the Family: The Social Organization of Caring as Gendered Work*. Chicago: The University of Chicago Press.

Erickson, R.J. 2005. 'Why Emotion Work Matters: Sex, Gender, and the Division of Household Labor'. *Journal of Marriage and Family* 67: 337–51.

Guthman, J., and M. Dupuis. 2006. 'Embodying Neoliberalism: Economy, Culture and the Politics of Fat'. *Environment & Planning D: Society and Space* 24: 427–48.

Haddad, A. 1996. *The Sexual Division of Household Labour: Pragmatic Strategies or Patriarchal Dynamic? An Analysis of Two Case Studies*. PhD thesis: York University.

Hamelin, A.-M., M. Beaudry, and J.-P. Habicht. 2002. 'Characterization of Household Food Insecurity in Quebec: Food and Feelings'. *Social Science and Medicine* 54(1): 119–32.

Hartley, C. 2001. 'Letting Ourselves Go: Making Room for the Fat Body in Feminist Scholarship'. In *Bodies out of Bounds: Fatness and Transgression*, ed. J.E. Braziel and K. LeBesco. Berkeley: University of California Press, 60–73.

Hayes-Conroy, J., and A. Hayes-Conroy. 2010. 'Visceral Geographies: Mattering, Relating, and Defying'. *Geography Compass* 49: 1273–83.

Hollows, J. 2003a. 'Feeling Like a Domestic Goddess: Postfeminism and Cooking'. *European Journal of Cultural Studies* 6(2): 179–202.

Hollows, J. 2003b. 'Oliver's Twist: Leisure, Labour and Domestic Masculinity in The Naked Chef'. *International Journal of Cultural Studies* 6(2): 229–48.

Hughes, M.H. 1997. 'Soul, Black Women and Food'. In *Food and Culture: A Reader*, ed. C. Counihan and P. V. Esterik. New York and London: Routledge, 272–80.

Julier, A., and L. Lindenfeld. 2005. 'Mapping Men onto the Menu: Masculinities and Food'. *Food and Foodways* 13(1): 1–16.

Kamo, Y. 1991. 'A Non-linear Effect of the Number of Children on the Division of Household Labor'. *Sociological Perspectives* 34: 205–18.

Kevin, C. 2009. *Feminism and the Body: Interdisciplinary Perspectives*. Newcastle: Cambridge Scholars.

Kirkland, A. 2011. 'The Environmental Account for Obesity: A Case for Feminist Skepticism'. *Signs: Journal of Women in Culture and Society* 36(2): 463–85.

Kroska, A. 2004. 'Division of Domestic Work: Revising and Expanding the Theoretical Explanations'. *Journal of Family Issues* 25(7): 900–32.

LeBesco, K. 2001. 'There's Always Room for Resistance: Jell-O, Gender, and Social Class'. In *Cooking Lessons: The Politics of Gender and Food*, ed. S.A. Inness. New York: Rowman and Littlefield, 129–49.

LeBesco, K. 2004. *Revolting Bodies: The Struggle to Redefine Fat Identity*. Amherst and Boston: University of Massachusetts Press.

LeBesco, K. 2010. 'Neoliberalism, Public Health, and the Moral Perils of Fatness'. *Critical Public Health*. DOI: 10.1080/09581596.2010.529422

Lupton, D. 1995. *The Imperative of Health: Public Health and the Regulated Body*. London: Sage Publications.

Lupton, D. 1996. *Food, the Body, and the Self*. London: Sage Publications.

McFarlane, S., R. Beaujot, and T. Haddad. 2000. 'Time Constraints and Relative Resources as Determinants of the Sexual Division of Domestic Work'. *Canadian Journal of Sociology/Cahiers Canadiens de Sociologie* 25(1): 61–82.

McIntyre, L., P. Thille, and K. Rondeau. 2009. 'Farmwomen's Discourses on Family Food Provisioning: Gender, Healthism, and Risk Avoidance'. *Food and Foodways* 17: 80–103.

Micheletti, M. 2004. 'Why More Women? Issues of Gender and Political Consumerism'. In *Politics, Products, and Markets: Exploring Political Consumerism Past and Present*, ed. M. Micheletti, A. Folesdal, and D. Stolle. New Jersey: Transaction Publishers, 245–64.

Mudry, J. 2009. *Measured Meals: Nutrition in America*. Albany, NY: State University of New York Press.

Narayan, U. 1995. 'Eating Cultures: Incorporation, Identity and Indian Food'. *Social Identities* 11: 63–86.

Oakley, A. 1974. *The Sociology of Housework*. New York: Random House.

Parasecoli, F. 2007. 'Bootylicious: Food and the Female Body in Contemporary Black Pop Culture.' *Women's Studies Quarterly* 35(1/2): 110–25.

Parasecoli, F. 2008. *Bite Me: Food in Popular Culture*. Oxford and New York: Berg.

Power, E. 2005. 'The Unfreedom of Being Other: Canadian Lone Mothers' Experiences of Poverty and "Life on the Cheque"'. *Sociology* 39(4): 643–60.

Power, E., B. Beagan, N. Salmon, and D. McPhail. 2010. '"And then the Broccoli Crept into our Life": Imagined and Real Impacts of Changes in Income on Food & Eating Practices'. Paper presented at the Association for the Study of Food and Society. 3–6 June, Bloomington, IN.

Probyn, E. 2008. 'Silences behind the Mantra: Critiquing Feminist Fat.' *Feminism and Psychology* 18(3): 401–4.

Rich, E. 2011. '"I See Her Being Obesed!": Public Pedagogy, Reality Media and the Obesity Crisis'. *Health* 15(1): 3–21.

Rothblum, E., and S. Solovay, eds. 2009. *Fat Studies Reader*. New York: New York University Press.

Sayer, L.C. 2005. 'Gender, Time and Inequality: Trends in Women's and Men's Paid Work, Unpaid Work and Free Time'. *Social Forces* 84(1): 285–303.

Scrinis, G. 2008. 'On the Ideology of Nutritionism'. *Gastronomica* 8(1): 39–48.

Shelton, B.A., and D. John. 1996. 'The Division of Household Labor'. *Annual Review of Sociology* 22: 299–322.

Shugart, H. 2010. 'Consuming Citizen: Neoliberating the Obese Body'. *Communication, Culture & Critique* 3: 105–26.

Smith, D.E. 1987. *The Everyday World as Problematic: A Feminist Sociology*. Boston: Northeastern University Press.

Smith, G.M., and P. Wilson. 2004. 'Country Cookin' and Cross-Dressin': Television, Southern White Masculinities, and Hierarchies of Cultural Taste'. *Television & New Media* 53: 175–95.

Sobal, J., and D. Maurer, eds. 1999. *Weighty Issues: Fatness and Thinness as Social Problems*. New York: Aldine de Gruyter.

Sullivan, O. 2000. 'The Division of Domestic Labour: Twenty Years of Change?' *Sociology* 34(3): 437–56.

Swenson, R. 2009. 'Domestic Diva? Televised Treatments of Masculinity, Femininity and Food'. *Critical Studies in Media Communication* 26(1): 36–53.

West, C., and S. Fenstermaker. 1995. 'Doing Difference'. *Gender & Society* 9(1): 8–37.

West, C., and D.H. Zimmerman. 1987. 'Doing Gender'. *Gender & Society* 1(2): 125–51.

Yancey, A.K., J. Leslie, and E.K. Abel. 2006. 'Obesity at the Crossroads: Feminist and Public Health Perspectives'. *Signs: Journal of Women in Culture and Society* 31(2): 425–43.

9

Constructing 'Healthy Eating'/Constructing Self

Brenda L. Beagan and Gwen E. Chapman

Learning Objectives

Through this chapter, you can:

1. Understand 'healthy eating' as diverse ways of thinking about and relating to food, influenced by media, government policies, and the food industry as well as by personal and cultural traditions
2. Reflect upon how food practices are one of the ways people 'produce' or portray their social identities as men and women, teens and adults, and members of ethnic, racial, or class groups
3. Reflect upon how social identities—such as gender, ethnicity, social class, age—influence people's relationship to healthy eating

Introduction

A Canadian national newspaper recommends that to avoid the health hazards that accompany the consumption of trans fatty acids, one should 'simply eat fewer processed foods and restaurant meals, and instead emphasize home-prepared meals made with whole grains, legumes, fruits, and vegetables' (Beck 2006: A13). A research article in *Circulation: Journal of the American Heart Association* reports that women who eat less red meat and more nuts, poultry, fish, and low-fat dairy products have significantly lower risk of coronary heart disease (Bernstein et al. 2010). Health Canada advises that 'A healthy diet rich in a variety of vegetables and fruit may help reduce the risk of some types of cancer' (Health Canada 2007).

These kinds of messages from the media, researchers, government websites, and nutrition and health educators are everywhere, constantly informing Canadians that the food choices we make as individuals affect our health. Most Canadians understand basic nutrition, are confident in their knowledge, and take healthfulness into consideration when deciding what to eat (DiFrancesco 2008). Nonetheless, Canadians' diets do not measure up to current nutrition recommendations (Garriguet 2006).

Clearly, there is no simple relationship between what people think and know about nutrition and what they actually eat. Health educators have developed a variety of models to understand the complexity of this relationship. The population health approach points to a variety of individual, interpersonal, and environmental factors that determine **healthy eating**

(Raine 2005). The Food Choice Model describes how food decisions are shaped by values and beliefs, as people balance food preferences, cost, convenience, healthfulness, and social relationships (Sobal and Bisogni 2009). For social scientists, healthy eating is understood as a socially constructed, shifting **discourse** that shapes and is shaped by what people say and do in relation to food, and that is specifically implicated in the ways people understand and perform their social identities. For example, women and men think and talk about healthy eating differently, largely because social definitions of masculinity and femininity construct certain ways of being in relationship to food. Similarly, being a teenager means talking and acting in relation to healthy eating in different ways than adults.

This chapter explores relationships between healthy eating and how people construct and convey their social identities. We argue that contemporary understandings of healthy eating influence the ways Canadians engage with food and eating through discourses that link health and eating practices to **identity** categories defined by **gender**, life stage, **ethnicity**, and social class. We draw on a number of qualitative studies we have conducted, exploring how everyday food practices and concerns are shaped by understandings of food, health, bodies, and identities. While other discourses, social structures, and systems—such as food policies and characteristics of the food system—are equally important influences on food practices, here we focus only on discursive social influences, specifically the relationships among healthy eating, food practices, and social identities. How Canadians simultaneously 'do food', 'do health', and 'do self' are central to everyday eating practices.

The chapter begins with an introduction to healthy eating discourses and a discussion of the nature and content of contemporary healthy eating discourses in Canada. We then discuss how people's engagement with healthy eating is implicated in the construction of four identity categories: gender, life stage (teen/adult), ethnicity, and social class. Although we treat each

of these facets of identity in separate sections of the chapter, obviously they intersect within each individual, shifting people's everyday experiences and practices.

Healthy Eating—Discourses of Food, Consumption, and Health

When we interview people in our research about food, almost everyone refers at some point to the healthfulness of food patterns—accepting messages about healthy eating, adapting those messages, refuting them, or resisting them—but nevertheless engaging with the idea of healthy eating. Other ideas about food also come up, such as ethical or environmental concerns about food production, processing, and transportation (Beagan, Ristovski-Slijepcevic, and Chapman 2010), but these issues are raised less frequently, and many people do not address them at all. Healthy eating is currently one of the dominant discourses—if not *the* dominant discourse—concerning food.

'Discourses' refers to pervasive ways of thinking that over time come to define what can be said about something, or what can even be considered possible. Discourses influence, shape, and determine how people think and act, or how they are expected to think or act, in a given society (Foucault 1979). Media play a significant role in dispersing discourses throughout a society, and thus in solidifying their power to set social standards that influence behaviour and ways of thinking. In terms of food, healthy eating discourses construct some foods and practices as 'healthy' or 'unhealthy', 'good' or 'bad'. These assessments of particular foods and particular ways of eating are promoted through avenues like Canada's Food Guide and nutritional advice from the Heart and Stroke Foundation, the Canadian Diabetes Association, and other health agencies. Nutritional guidelines are then dispersed through newspapers, television, magazines, the Internet, and educational institutions. Discourses are further promoted through informal channels as they are enacted and reproduced through people's everyday social relationships. As people talk with each other about food and health, and as they observe others practising or resisting healthy eating habits, these discourses are promoted.

The discourses that are used most frequently, that are most widespread in a particular place and time, are considered dominant. The dominance of healthy eating as a way of thinking and talking about food in Western societies is well documented (e.g., Henson, Blandon, and Cranfield 2010). The effect of this dominant discourse on what people eat, however, is not simple. Sociological theories maintain that the relationship between discourses and individual actions is not unidirectional. While social structures and discourses shape and constrain individual actions, those actions (and inactions) simultaneously shape social structures, expectations, and institutionalized practices (Giddens 1984). As people take up, alter, or actively resist thinking and acting in ways that conform to dominant discourses, alternative discourses take shape and circulate through society, and may gradually shift the dominant discourse. These alternative discourses may be related to, supportive of, or even opposed to the dominant discourse. More marginal discourses may gain strength in different times or places, or may dominate for specific social groups according to age, ethnicity, gender, education, or social class.

It would therefore be expected that multiple discourses relating to healthy eating will circulate within a society at any given time. Our research has explored this expectation through two studies. In the first (Chapman and Beagan 2003), 61 adult women in Vancouver were asked about their eating habits and their beliefs about relationships among diet, health, and breast cancer risk. Analyzing the ways in which the women discussed healthy eating, we identified three different perspectives or discourses. About half of the women articulated what we call a 'mainstream' healthy eating discourse, emphasizing consumption of fruits and vegetables; grains; and low-fat meat, poultry, and dairy products. These women also talked about broad nutrition principles of balance, moderation, and variety, as well as the importance of being physically active. This perspective fit well with current official nutrition guidelines. About a quarter of the women, however, expressed a more 'traditional' discourse of healthy eating that emphasized consumption of home-cooked meals based on meat, potatoes, and vegetables, as well as unprocessed foods. The clearest distinction between traditional and mainstream discourses was in how meat was described: while the traditional view saw meat as a key component of healthy eating, the mainstream view saw meat, particularly red meat, as unhealthy. Finally, about a quarter of the women described an 'alternative' discourse of healthy eating that focused more on toxins and carcinogens in food, as well as protective factors such as micronutrients and phytochemicals. As one woman said:

> We're really poisoning the planet and poisoning ourselves. You know, all the processed foods and additives, and they shoot up the animals with all these chemicals. . . . You've got to cut all of that out of your life. Avoid any refined and processed foods. . . . Eat and buy organic. (Chapman and Beagan 2003: 138)

The alternative discourse aligned with the mainstream discourse in promoting consumption of fruits and vegetables, and with the traditional discourse in emphasizing natural rather than processed foods. It differed from both, however, in its emphasis on organic food production, the risks of synthetic pesticides and fertilizers, and the compounds in particular foods that boost the immune system or combat environmental toxins.

The second study, in which we identified variations of healthy eating discourses, explored family food decision-making processes with families from Vancouver and Halifax. Participants included Canadian-born European-heritage families from British Columbia and Nova Scotia, Punjabi–British Columbians, and African–Nova Scotians. Analysis of interviews with 105 adults again showed three distinct ways of knowing about healthy eating. As with our earlier study, both mainstream and traditional perspectives were apparent. The mainstream discourse mimicked official nutrition guidelines, describing healthy eating as 'all four food groups, low in fat, and high in fruit and vegetables . . . more fibre' (Ristovski-Slijepcevic, Chapman, and Beagan 2008: 172). Some participants—especially women and those with higher education—discussed food and eating with a level of precision that included identifying specific nutrients and food components such as protein, vitamins, and minerals. Themes of control and monitoring were prominent. In contrast, participants who engaged with the traditional healthy eating discourse emphasized eating foods associated with traditional cultural cuisines, foods produced in natural, simple ways, and the positive strength-giving properties of foods. Food was rarely dissected into component nutrients or associated with specific health risks. These participants learned about healthy eating from the way they had eaten as children, from their elders, and from their own bodily experiences. While the mainstream discourse was articulated by participants from both regions and all three ethnocultural groups, the traditional discourse was more commonly used by older African–Nova Scotians and Punjabi–British Columbians, as well as more recent Punjabi immigrants and a small number of European–Nova Scotians.

The third healthy eating discourse was similar to the alternative discourse identified in the study with Vancouver women, but greater emphasis was placed on moral and ethical values relating to the food system, with less concern articulated about toxins (the focus on breast cancer in the previous study may have influenced participants' concerns about toxins in the food supply). We therefore called the third discourse 'complementary/ethical', to reflect these participants' prominent emphasis on natural and organic food, in addition to concerns about ethical treatment of animals, environmental sustainability, and relationships with local people. This discourse was primarily used by some European–British Columbian women.

Other research supports our findings of multiple meanings of healthy eating, with mainstream understandings being dominant. The mainstream healthy eating discourse appears to be widely known and understood in Canada, among adults, youth, and children as young as 11 years (e.g., Pacquette 2005; Protruder et al. 2010). For example, when asked to categorize foods into groups of their choice, children and teens tend to use some version of the food groups defined in Canada's Food Guide, and simply dichotomize foods as either healthy or junk foods, or both (Chapman and Maclean 1993). When asked for details, they demonstrate more refined understandings of healthy eating discourses, identifying fruits and vegetables as healthy foods, and high-fat, high-sugar foods as detrimental to health, while also speaking about benefits of 'protein and dairy' as well as micronutrients such as 'calcium and iron' (Protruder et al. 2010). With regard to support for traditional understandings, researchers in the United States, the United Kingdom, and Europe have noted that some people emphasize the importance of natural or unprocessed foods in their definitions of healthy eating (e.g., Margetts et al. 1997). Alternative or ethical concerns as components of healthy eating discourses have received less attention, although there is a growing literature on ethical food consumption, and research examining consumers' motivations for purchasing organic food have noted that some people conflate health and food system concerns (Shepherd, Magnusson, and Sjödén 2005).

The production and dissemination of healthy eating messages tend to position health and nutrition professionals against the food industry (Nestle 2007; Pollan 2008). The emphasis on over-consumption that dominates the food industry in developed countries is in direct opposition to the overall healthy eating message of 'eat less'. Any dietary advice to eat more or less of particular foods has a direct impact on food producers. Thus governments attempting to satisfy both the food industry and health and nutrition professionals have been accused of producing official healthy eating guidelines that are unclear and politically compromised. At the same time, fearful of healthy eating cutting into profits, the food industry has responded by entering the health-food market, fortifying, supplementing, and transforming foods into vitamin-enriched, low-fat, high-fibre, cholesterol-free facsimiles. This approach begins to borrow from the alternative healthy eating emphasis on micronutrients and phytochemicals promoted through popular media as well as by complementary and alternative health practitioners (Chapman and Beagan 2003; Novak and Chapman 2001).

Healthy eating discourses are strongly connected to body weight. Currently, a major focus in North America concerns body weight and the 'obesity epidemic' (World Health Organization 2006). A variety of health promotion initiatives encourage Canadians to take responsibility for preventing future health problems by achieving and maintaining a 'healthy' body weight. Not surprisingly, Canadians tend to conflate healthy bodies with slender ones, and healthy eating with maintaining low body weight. Healthy eating is seen as a lifestyle that entails 'watching what you eat' as a never-ending practice of self-surveillance (Chapman 1999). Critical research in a number of fields challenges the taken-for-granted 'truth' that obesity is directly linked with poorer health, though these messages are far less available through mainstream media (Colls and Evans 2010). Such accounts point to the socially constructed nature of current approaches to health and body weight.

In this section, we have introduced the notion of healthy eating discourse: multiple, shifting understandings of how eating practices affect well-being. These understandings are socially constructed through the ways people engage with, support, and resist messages promoted by government, science, health professionals, the media, and each other. What we have particularly explored here are some variations in how healthy eating is currently understood in Canada. We have mentioned in passing that certain ways of thinking about healthy eating seem to be articulated more or less frequently by certain groups of people, for example by women versus men, or by people from different ethnic groups. We explore these differences in more depth in the remainder of this chapter, examining how people interact with healthy eating discourses differently as they construct and convey self-identities through food practices and their interactions with healthy eating discourses.

Gendered Interactions with Healthy Eating Discourses

Canadians tend to believe that gender does not shape our lives or our practices, including our food practices. As in all liberal democracies, there is a strong impetus to believe that individuals exercise free choice in the context of equal opportunity. Thus any inequalities are individualized, seen as the result of individual choices rather than systematic and historically rooted oppressions. Denying the potential impacts of gender, then, becomes part of constructing images of ourselves as liberal, equal-minded individuals (McPhail, Beagan, and Chapman 2012).

Yet decades of scholarship have shown that food practices are highly gendered. Many foods are well-understood to be 'feminine' (e.g., ice cream, chocolate, salads, vegetables, and 'light' foods) or 'masculine' (e.g., steak and other red meat, 'heavy', and rich foods). Jeffrey Sobal maintains that associating men with meat consumption positions them as self-sufficient, independent, and ostensibly able to provide for their families through 'the particularly masculine activity of hunting' (2005: 138). The relationship between women and 'light' foods largely centres on the desire to maintain low body weight (Chapman 1999). While some have argued that obsession with body image is a distinctly feminine preoccupation, others have countered that men's body image concerns are simply less well understood, and that it is less socially acceptable for men to admit to concern over body image (Gough 2007; Monaghan 2008).

In a recent study, we explored how men, women, and teens of both genders engaged with food discourses by asking them about their own food habits and preferences, then asking them to categorize photographs of a variety of foods as 'men's' or 'women's' foods (McPhail, Beagan, and Chapman 2012). Regardless of age or gender, the participants strongly denied that foods were in any way gendered, then proceeded to sort the photographs into highly consistent categories of masculine (bacon cheeseburger, beef Wellington, pot roast, hotdog, pizza, and macaroni and cheese) or feminine (sushi, stir fry, couscous, chicken soup, Korean food, fish, and spring green salad). Women's foods were seen as prettier, fancier, more 'delicate', and healthier. Masculine eating was described as centred on meat, heavy and filling, and unconcerned with health. Further exploring participants' own eating practices revealed that most did in fact adhere to at least some aspects of the stereotyped gendered food practices they denied.

The association of women's eating with health concerns and men's eating as unconcerned with health demonstrates the significant interactions between gender and healthy eating discourses. Numerous studies have shown that men typically are uninterested in healthy eating, and in fact lack of concern for healthy eating is almost a defining characteristic of masculinity (Gough and Conner 2006). Engaging in healthy eating, then, especially for weight loss, can threaten a man's portrayal of masculinity (Lyons 2009). Given the association of red meat with masculinity, it is not surprising that in one large Canadian survey, men had a harder time than women adhering to the healthy eating recommendation

to limit meat consumption (Henson, Blandon, and Cranfield 2010).

While a particular idealized version of masculinity tends to predominate in any one place and time ('hegemonic masculinity'), just as there are variations in healthy eating discourses, there are always variations of masculinity in circulation, depending on class, education, location, ethnicity, and other factors (Connell and Messerschmidt 2005). For example, a study of well-educated, higher-income single men in Vancouver found a higher than usual degree of concern for healthy eating—though the men did not necessarily follow healthy eating guidelines in practice, preferring to eat out or prepare convenience foods rather than cooking for themselves (Sellaeg and Chapman 2008). Often men who are dieting emphasize other aspects of masculinity, such as re-asserting their heterosexuality and the gendered division of labour, through describing their female partners as 'in charge' of their food restriction, thus maintaining the notion that dieting is feminine (de Souza and Ciclitira 2005). For example, in one study, men who had been diagnosed with cancer became more involved in food preparation and in healthy eating, yet they and their female partners actively constructed this as non-feminine, depicting the men as 'helpers' in the kitchen, less skilled cooks, and less knowledgeable about health and nutrition (Mróz et al. 2011). The research evidence, then, suggests that men choose not to engage with healthy eating discourses to portray a particular version of masculinity—unless they can afford to demonstrate 'feminine' healthy eating concerns because their masculinity is assured in some other way.

Women, too, can use interactions with healthy eating discourses to construct or convey particular versions of femininity, most notably through supervising healthy eating within the family. Mothers are understood to have a critical role in children's nutrition education; preparing meals and insisting children and teens eat family meals is purported to encourage healthy eating habits (Hannon et al. 2003). In our study with Vancouver and Halifax families from three ethnocultural groups (above), teenagers described their mothers as enforcing healthy eating in the family, as well as teaching them about nutrition. Similarly, fathers tended to name women as responsible for family health and nutrition. As one father said, '[My wife] does the whole home health and safety thing and I do the work and things. . . . She is always concerned about healthy eating, healthy lifestyle, making sure the kids are active' (Ristovski-Slijepcevic, Chapman, and Beagan 2010: 472). Other research has also found that men attribute healthy eating within families to their female partners (de Souza and Ciclitira 2005).

The expectation that mothers will influence children and teens toward healthy eating positions them as the healthy eating experts within the family. Through learning a range of healthy eating messages and supplying that information to families, women can constitute themselves as 'good mothers', knowledgeable about and responsible for healthy eating. 'Feeding the family' has long been understood as a means of constructing not just family, but also oneself as woman and mother (DeVault 1991). Today there is an added requirement of healthy eating expertise. Just as 'good families' are those who sit down to nutritious meals together 'like a family' (Coveney 2000), so 'good mothers' are those who care for their children's health by providing healthy food, learning about healthy eating, educating family members about it, monitoring what is eaten, guiding their children toward healthy influences, and protecting them from unhealthy ones. Women, then, can construct themselves as good mothers—good women—through healthy eating within the family.

In summary, it is clear that the different ways that individuals engage with and resist healthy eating practices are strongly implicated in how they develop and portray social identities as men or women.

Age and Family Stage—Interacting with Healthy Eating Discourses

Living with even one other person tends to affect eating patterns (Kemmer, Anderson, and Marshall 1998). On average, those who live alone spend more on food and on eating out, consume less nutritionally adequate diets, and eat more processed convenience foods (Blisard and Stewart 2007). Even when people hold fairly strong beliefs in healthy eating, they may have little motivation to uphold healthy eating ideals when there is no one else to cook for, or even to notice.

Commensality—eating together—requires negotiation concerning food practices. When adults marry or cohabit, the change in eating habits that almost inevitably occurs marks a new stage of adulthood and a new partnered identity. Eating at least the evening meal together seems to be understood as an ideal (Bove, Sobal, and Rauschenbach 2003), and people in couples are more likely than single adults to prepare and consume 'proper meals' (Beagan and Chapman 2004). In one of our studies we interviewed seven cohabiting heterosexual couples in Vancouver to explore how they negotiated healthy eating. When partners differed significantly in their values or approaches, they needed to negotiate their identities as individuals and as a couple. One participant reflected:

> I worry about [healthy eating] more now. I think it's just, I don't know if you could attribute that to being married, I am sure that sped up the process, but I am just getting older, so, those care-free days are starting to disappear now. (Ristovski-Slijepcevic and Chapman 2005: 306)

In some couples, one partner tried to change the other's food choices; in others, both partners compromised; and some couples chose to eat separately, at least sometimes. Conflict could arise if one or both partners preferred to eat together as part of constructing a 'coupled' identity, yet their individual food identities differed substantially. As one woman said, her partner 'first became a vegetarian and then he wanted to become vegan and not eat dairy at all. And I just said "that's just ridiculous"' (Ristovski-Slijepcevic and Chapman 2005: 306). Healthy eating, then, can be part of constructing an adult, coupled identity, yet differing individual identities constructed in relation to healthy eating may conflict with constructing a coupled identity.

In households with children, early research showed that women tended to cater to the food preferences and habits of men and (to a lesser extent) children (DeVault 1991). Children are routinely described as 'picky eaters' whose narrow food repertoires require considerable managing in relation to healthy eating (Dovey et al. 2008). As children age, parents struggle to enforce healthy eating standards, while granting increasing autonomy to adolescents (Bassett, Beagan, and Chapman 2008), who often prefer to seek out 'junk foods'.

An early study exploring the ways young women aged 11–18 categorized foods indicated healthy eating discourses were prominent. Teens dichotomized between 'healthy foods' (associated with parents, meals, and eating at home) and 'junk foods' (associated with friends, snacks, eating away from home, 'doing whatever you want', and being 'normal') (Chapman and Maclean 1993: 111). Participants were ambivalent about both groups, identifying conflicts regarding maintaining family relationships and gaining autonomy as adults. Eating junk food was a way to demonstrate increasing independence from family and allegiance to their peer group. Yet, family continued to be important to them, and eating healthy food was one way to maintain family ties.

We further explored the interaction of healthy eating discourses and adolescent identities in our study with Vancouver and Halifax families described above, which included

47 teenagers aged 13–19 years (Bassett, Beagan, and Chapman 2008). They and their parents engaged in complex negotiations, through which parents (especially mothers) tried to encourage the teens to eat healthy foods. As discussed, enforcing healthy eating may be one means for parents to establish themselves as 'good parents'. The parents' strategies for encouraging healthy eating included coaching, coaxing, and coercing, though they also controlled consumption to some extent through food purchasing and meal preparation. They made space for teens to develop a growing sense of autonomy by allowing them to choose from the foods in the house, while enforcing healthy eating by purchasing predominantly healthy foods. Many parents emphasized they would never force their teens to eat particular foods, establishing themselves as 'good parents' through granting teen autonomy, a particular approach to parenting.

Meanwhile teens pestered, cajoled, coaxed, and manipulated parents to get foods they liked. They were forging autonomous identities in relation to healthy eating, at times ignoring their parents' healthy eating advice, at times taking up healthy eating as their own responsibility. One 14-year-old said, 'I don't think, "Should I be eating this?" or "Could I find a better restaurant?" I'll get whatever tastes good and probably with the highest fat content on the menu' (Bassett, Beagan, and Chapman 2008: 329). In contrast, an 18-year-old stated, 'I definitely keep learning things [about healthy eating]. Mom mentions things and I pick up on them' (Bassett, Beagan, and Chapman 2008: 329). Some teens in our study refused outright the foods served at family meals, preferring to fend for themselves at home or by eating out. Some frustrated parents reported that their teens seemed to use food to convey an adult identity only outside the home:

There's things, like, that [my son has] learned to like that he would never have tried here. I could strangle him. He complained and complained when we'd have them. Next thing he'd say, 'Oh, I had such-and-such at somebody's house and it was really good.' (Bassett, Beagan, and Chapman 2008: 329)

Whether perpetuating or resisting healthy eating discourses, relating to them provides one means of constructing teen and parent identities.

In this section we have explored some of the tensions experienced as family members negotiate individual and collective identities through the ways they take up or resist specific healthy eating practices. For coupled adults, when eating together is part of a couple's identity, yet their approaches to healthy eating diverge, eating patterns may require considerable negotiation. Teens convey adolescent identities through resisting healthy eating in some settings and adopting it in others. They and their parents negotiate around healthy eating, as adults may attempt to convey a 'good parent' identity through encouraging healthy eating while still allowing teens autonomy in food choices.

Ethnicity and Race Interacting with Healthy Eating

Food is a highly significant cultural symbol of ethnicity, and an important means for constructing ethnic identities. For many members of migrant communities, traditional foods from their country of origin are a 'taste of home' (Harbottle 1996). Food and food preparation are central mechanisms in the transmission and maintenance of culture as well as in the process of acculturation—adaptation to the new culture (e.g., Lawton et al. 2008). Women often pass along cultural values, norms, expectations, stories, and skills through cross-generational work in the kitchen. Many families experience tensions between the desire to maintain traditional foods as part of ethnic identity and the desire to incorporate 'new' foods (D'Sylva and Beagan

2011; Vallianatos and Raine 2008). There are often intergenerational conflicts, as youth seek to solidify Canadian identities through eating 'Canadian' foods, while elders may prefer to eat the foods of 'home'.

In one of our studies, we conducted qualitative interviews with 11 Filipino-Canadian women aged 19 to 30 years old to explore their beliefs and practices relating to bodies, food, and health. Participants expressed both 'Canadian' and 'Filipino' beliefs. 'Canadian beliefs' included the desirability of thinness, 'watching' dietary fat, reducing intake of rice and 'junk' food, and eating healthful foods to lower disease risk. 'Filipino beliefs' included valuing fatness as an indicator of health and self-care, 'just eating' without monitoring and restricting intake, and using food to maximize disease resistance. One woman spoke about bringing sandwiches rather than rice for lunch, in order to fit in more easily. Another described Canadians: 'They're afraid of getting fat, and they are afraid of having more cholesterol. . . . you will get this kind of sickness if you eat this kind of food' (Farrales and Chapman 1999: 189). Participants vacillated between cultural beliefs, using food and differing discourses of healthy eating to portray Canadian or Filipino identity.

Several studies have suggested that eating in ways that maintain ethnic identity may conflict with healthy eating, while others have suggested that Western diets adopted after migration significantly increase prevalence of nutrition-related illnesses (e.g., McDonald and Kennedy 2005). What seems clear is that the meanings of food in relation to health differ by ethnicity—which means relationships to healthy eating discourses also differ.

For example, in our study described earlier with Vancouver and Halifax families, Canadians of European heritage in both cities thought about food and eating primarily through a lens of mainstream healthy eating discourses, with an emphasis on minimizing risk of chronic diseases. Punjabi-Canadians who were relatively recent migrants (one to three generations) and African-Canadians whose families had been in Canada for centuries tended to employ broader understandings of health and well-being in relation to food. While the latter two groups knew and understood dominant discourses, many of them focused on positive attributes of foods, rather than depicting certain foods as increasing disease risk. Foods were described as strength-giving, energy-providing, healing, and improving resistance to disease. As one elder Punjabi woman said, 'Roti has a lot of strength in it. Dahl and subjee. They have a lot of strengths. . . . It is very good for the health' (Chapman, Ristovski-. Slijepcevic, and Beagan 2011: 106). Healthy eating knowledge was not only that learned in school or through the media, but also that passed down through generations. As one elder said, 'It's been like this from the very beginning' (Ristovski-Slijepcevic, Chapman, and Beagan 2008: 171). In both the Punjabi- and African-heritage groups, health and well-being were understood to incorporate more than prevention of physical illnesses—they included spiritual wellness, family and community well-being, and cultural well-being.

In the Punjabi families, the young people particularly sought out 'Western' foods, and understood healthy eating in terms of dominant discourses, highlighting Canadian identity. It is interesting to note the contrast to our earlier discussion of how teens may demonstrate independence from family through rejecting healthy eating; some Punjabi-Canadian teens may reproduce mainstream healthy eating discourses as a means to differentiate themselves from family. Punjabi elders tended to think about healthy eating in more traditional terms, focusing on cultural heritage. Participants in the middle generations generally moved smoothly between traditional and scientific discourses of healthy eating, displaying a truly hybrid identity (Chapman, Ristovski-Slijepcevic, and Beagan 2011). In the African-Canadian families, fewer generational differences were apparent, perhaps

because that community is not made up of recent migrants, but rather has been in Nova Scotia for over 400 years. The adults and youth all showed familiarity with mainstream healthy eating discourses, yet also displayed resistance to them. As one man argued:

> Whether other people want to realise it or not, certain things aren't meant for Black folk . . . and that has to do with the structure of their body. . . . We forget how we are supposed to eat, and we sort of start Westernising it, as some people put it, and that's when we start having health problems. We start getting away from who we are and what it is that we would normally eat. (Ristovski-Slijepcevic, Bell, Chapman, and Beagan 2010: 322)

For some participants, resisting mainstream healthy eating seemed to be a way of portraying an African-Canadian identity.

Similar resistance appeared in relation to healthy eating messages concerning body size or weight. Just as the Filipino-Canadian women discussed above were influenced by cultural beliefs valuing fatness as a sign of health, so some African-Canadian participants reported a preference for a larger body size. Many saw the slender body type promoted in the media and through healthy eating discourses as too thin for health. One woman said, 'I'm supposed to be like 150 pounds. I don't want to be no 150 pounds. . . . It's too small . . . you need something to lean on when you get sick' (Ristovski-Slijepcevic, Bell, Chapman, and Beagan 2010: 323). This resistance to mainstream discourses of healthy body weight has been documented in other studies with African-Americans, though there is evidence that both African-heritage and European-heritage women monitor their own bodies, attempting to shape their bodies to fit with cultural standards (Reel et al. 2008). Thus, constructing a particular body weight, and engaging in resistance to the dominant discourses, can be a means of constructing a racialized identity (Rubin, Fitts, and Becker 2003).

In summary, while much of the literature on ethnicity and food focuses on continuity and change in eating patterns, here we focus on how ethnic identities are negotiated through engagement with healthy eating discourses. The mainstream discourse is associated with the dominant culture and 'Canadian' ethnic identity. Young people from migrant families may be quick to adopt much of this dominant discourse as part of a Canadian identity, but this is in tension with traditional food discourses associated with their cultural heritage. Elders and relatives 'back home' may use a different set of understandings about food and health. In the case of long-standing racial minority communities, cultural healthy eating discourses may be employed as a form of resistance to assimilation.

Social Class Interactions with Healthy Eating Discourses

Interactions with healthy eating differ significantly by income and social class. Social class concerns not only income but also education and type of job—in particular, white collar or mental labour versus blue/pink collar or manual labour. While the upper class may live on inherited wealth, the middle class has high school or higher education and works in professional or semi-professional jobs. The working class conducts manual labour in skilled or unskilled trades, labour, retail, service, or clerical jobs. The underclass works one or more minimum wage jobs or may receive income assistance such as disability pensions or welfare.

In Europe, the United States, Australia, and Canada, people from higher social classes have consistently been shown to have diets closer to standard healthy-eating recommendations (e.g., Ricciuto and Tarasuk 2007). Below a certain

point, income is the most important determinant of consumption of fruit, vegetables, and dairy products. In some provinces minimum wage simply does not provide enough income for a nutritious diet. The lowest-cost diets are least healthy, featuring energy-dense, shelf-stable foods (such as pasta) rather than nutrient-dense foods (Darmon and Drewnowski 2008). Many of the underclass rely upon food banks as a regular strategy for procuring food.

While it is commonly believed that lower income groups lack nutrition knowledge and cooking skills, several studies contest this. Research in the United Kingdom, France, and Canada suggests that in fact higher-income groups are more likely to eat out and purchase prepared foods than are lower-income groups. In the underclass, lack of access to cooking facilities, lack of time if parents are working multiple jobs, or both may mean reliance on prepared foods. Nonetheless, it is clear that access to material resources—money or the time and space to grow and prepare food—directly affects access to healthy eating. Darmon and Drewnowski conclude in an exhaustive review of existing literature, 'The promotion of high-cost foods to low-income people without taking food costs into account is not likely to be successful' (2008: 1113).

More recently, researchers have focused on intersections of the local food environment and social class. It is clear that supermarkets carrying fresh produce, meats, and fish tend to cluster in affluent neighbourhoods, while fast-food outlets and convenience stores (where food quality is lower and prices are higher) predominate in lower-income neighbourhoods (Larson, Story, and Nelson 2009). Areas lacking supermarkets and access to healthy foods are often called **food deserts**. Lower-income persons are also less likely have access to transportation and often cannot afford the costs associated with getting to a supermarket outside of their immediate neighbourhood, forcing them to sacrifice cost and quality for convenience (Walker, Keane, and Burke 2010).

As a consequence of greater access to nutrient-dense foods, higher social classes tend to be less obese than lower social classes, though this varies slightly for men—higher-income men are more likely to be obese (Godley and Mclaren 2010). To account for this apparent anomaly, it has been proposed that thinness is a more important status marker for women than for men, and that higher-income men work longer hours at more sedentary jobs. This latter notion highlights the potential for culturally distinct approaches to food and bodies in upper and lower classes.

Studies of food and class indicate that food has meant very different things to different social classes: for lower classes it has been a means of sustenance, while for upper classes it has been an aesthetic, in the presentation of food and in a focus on self-discipline to maintain a particular body aesthetic. In his systematic study of culture and class in France, Pierre Bourdieu (1984) found that consumption of 'highbrow' culture (foods, art, music, sports, etc.) was a way that elites demarcated and maintained their social status. More recently, in North America the 'cultural omnivore' has become a more significant marker of high social class: 'The cultural omnivore thesis suggests that elites can be distinguished from members of lower classes by the breadth and variety of their preferred cultural tastes and practices rather than by possession of some specified set of highbrow tastes' (Veenstra 2010: 104). In terms of food, there is growing evidence that openness to and knowledge about a vast variety of foods, both highbrow and lowbrow, from a variety of ethnic cuisines, emphasizing authentic and exotic foods, is connected with upper classes and urban environments (Johnston and Baumann 2010). In contrast, rural and working-class individuals may display more 'food conservatism', preferring traditional, familiar fare (Lupton 2000). While these class differences in food preferences may link to different understandings of healthy eating, our research has tended to show no clear class differences in approaches to healthy eating

(Beagan, Ristovski-Slijepcevic, and Chapman 2010; McPhail, Chapman, and Beagan 2011).

In short, social class interacts with eating practices in multiple ways—through financial access to healthy and high-quality foods, through environmental or geographic access to such foods, and through differing class-based relationships to food and bodies. Food practices, then, not only are shaped by social class, but also can become a means of conveying social class identities.

Conclusion

In this chapter, we have argued that healthy eating discourses play a major role in shaping how Canadians engage with food and eating and that the ways people think, talk, and act in relation to healthy eating are entwined with various facets of their identities. We have specifically explored variations in how healthy eating is currently understood, including mainstream discourses that reflect nutritional science approaches, discourses grounded in tradition and cultural histories, and alternative/ethical discourses that emphasize food system concerns. We have examined the interplay of food with gender, demonstrating how healthy eating is socially constructed as a feminine pursuit, placing demands on women not only to take care of their own bodies (especially bodily appearance) but also to manage their families' nutritional well-being. The gendered nature of healthy eating discourses appears to limit men's uptake of healthy eating, since lack of interest and expertise in food and nutrition in part define dominant constructions of masculinity. We have also explored how healthy eating discourses are negotiated within families. While youth may seek to be 'independent teens' through resisting parental influence over eating patterns, adults may strive to establish themselves as 'good parents' through promoting healthy eating. We then examined how ethnic identities are preserved and shifted by the different ways people 'do' healthy eating, and through relationships to health and well-being. Finally, we explored the ways income and social class intersect with food practices.

It is not possible, of course, to address in one chapter all of the ways healthy eating discourses intersect with social identities. However, the examples that we have chosen illustrate multiple complex influences of the social on people's everyday food practices. One of our aims in presenting this argument has been to challenge individualistic assumptions about nutrition behaviours. Both the lay public and health professionals often assume that what people eat is shaped primarily by individual factors such as nutrition knowledge, beliefs, and motivations. There is less understanding of how food practices and ideas about healthy eating are structured by social identities and discourses. The study of food practices is a fruitful venue for exploring how the social world works. As a core part of our everyday lives, we think about, talk about, and consume food multiple times a day, alone or with others. Food is pragmatic but also symbolic, individual yet social, mundane yet also tied to ritual and occasion. The ways we use food, express who we are within a society and, in turn, shape the way a society understands food and food practices, make food practices a valuable lens through which to examine how social forces operate.

Discussion Questions

1. How does healthy eating influence your family and friends differently, depending on age, gender, race or ethnicity, and social class?

2. If food is so strongly influenced socially, how is it we all believe ourselves to have individual food tastes and preferences?

3. In what ways do you and the people you know use food to convey particular social identities?

4. Working in a group, make a list of 25 foods; next to each item individually note whether that food is associated with males or females, teens or adults, higher or lower social classes. Discuss your differences and agreements.

Further Reading

1. Colls, R., and B. Evans. 2010. 'Challenging Assumptions: Re-thinking the Obesity "Problem"'. *Geography* 95: 99–105.

   An excellent overview of critical obesity research, which challenges the medical science linking obesity to ill health, and questions how obesity is measured and characterized.

2. Darmon, N., and A. Drewnowski. 2008. 'Does Social Class Predict Diet Quality?' *American Journal of Clinical Nutrition* 87: 1107–17.

   An exhaustive review of research connecting social class and diet, examining possible reasons why lower-class and lower-income groups tend to have less healthy diets.

3. Delormier, T., K.L. Frohlich, and L. Potvin. 2009. 'Food and Eating as Social Practice—Understanding Eating Patterns as Social Phenomena and Implications for Public Health', *Sociology of Health & Illness* 31: 215–28.

   An excellent discussion of sociological theories that are useful for understanding the routine food choice practices of families, including the adoption or non-adoption of healthy eating.

4. Johnston, J., and S. Baumann. 2010. *Foodies: Democracy and Distinction in the Gourmet Foodscape.* New York: Routledge.

   Based on analyses of food writing and interviews with self-identified 'foodies', an engaging analysis of those who prioritize culinary pleasures and gourmet eating, even when consuming 'lowbrow' foods.

5. Power, E.M. 2005. The Determinants of Healthy Eating Among Low-Income Canadians. *Canadian Journal of Public Health* 96: S37–42.

A valuable review of literature concerning healthy eating for low-income Canadians, addressing material resources and access, as well as cultural approaches to food.

References

Bassett, R., B.L. Beagan, and G.E. Chapman. 2008. 'Autonomy and Control: Parents, Teens & Resistance'. *Appetite* 50(2/3): 325–32.

Beagan, B.L., and G.E. Chapman. 2004. 'Family Influences on Food Choice: The Context of a Breast Cancer Diagnosis'. *Journal of Nutrition Education and Behavior* 36: 320–6.

Beagan, B.L., S. Ristovski-Slijepcevic, and G.E. Chapman. 2010. '"People Are Just Becoming More Conscious of How Everything's Connected": Ethical Food Consumption in Two Regions of Canada'. *Sociology* 44(4): 751–69. doi: 10.1177/0038038510369364

Beck, L. 2006. 'Getting the Lowdown on Hidden Fats'. *The Globe and Mail*, 12 July: A13.

Bernstein, A.M., Q. Sun, F.B. Hu, M.J. Stampfer, J.E. Manson, and W.C. Willett. 2010. 'Major Dietary Protein Sources and Risk of Coronary Heart Disease in Women'. *Circulation: Journal of the American Heart Association.* Published online before print 16 August 2010. doi: 10.1161/CIRCULATIONAHA.109.915165

Blisard, N., and H. Stewart. 2007. 'Food Spending in American Households, 2003–04'. *Economic Information Bulletin No. 23.* USDA Economic Research Service.

Bourdieu, P. 1984. *Distinction: A Social Critique of the Judgement of Taste.* Cambridge, MA: Harvard University Press.

Bove, C.F., J. Sobal, and B.S. Rauschenbach. 2003. 'Food Choices among Newly Married Couples: Convergence, Conflict, Individualism, and Projects'. *Appetite* 40: 25–41.

Chapman, G.E. 1999. 'From "Dieting" to "Healthy Eating": An Exploration of Shifting Constructions of Eating for Weight Control'. In *Interpreting Weight: The Social Management of Fatness and Thinness,* ed J. Sobal and D. Maurer. New York: Aldine de Gruyter, 73–87.

Chapman, G.E., and B.L. Beagan. 2003. 'Women's Perspectives on Nutrition, Health and Breast Cancer'. *Journal of Nutrition Education and Behavior* 35(3): 135–41.

Chapman, G., and H. Maclean. 1993. 'Junk Food and Healthy Food: Meanings of Food in Adolescent Women's Culture'. *Journal of Nutrition Education* 25: 108–13.

Chapman, G.E., S. Ristovski-Slijepcevic, and B.L. Beagan. 2011. 'Meanings of Food, Eating, and Health in Punjabi Canadian Families'. *Health Education Journal* 70(1): 102–12.

Colls, R., and B. Evans. 2010. 'Challenging Assumptions: Re-thinking the Obesity "Problem"'. *Geography* 95: 99–105.

Connell, R.W., and J.W. Messerschmidt. 2005. 'Hegemonic Masculinity: Rethinking the Concept'. *Gender & Society* 19(6): 829–59.

Coveney, J. 2000. *Food, Morals and Meaning: The Pleasure and Anxiety of Eating.* London: Routledge.

D'Sylva, A., and B.L. Beagan. 2011. '"Food Is Culture, But It's Also Power": The Role of Food in Ethnic and Gender Identity Construction Among Goan Canadian Women'. *The Journal of Gender Studies* 20(3): 279–89.

Darmon, N., and A. Drewnowski. 2008. 'Does Social Class Predict Diet Quality?' *American Journal of Clinical Nutrition* 87: 1107–17.

de Souza, P., and K.E. Ciclitira. 2005. 'Men and Dieting: A Qualitative Analysis'. *Journal of Health Psychology* 10(6): 793–804.

DeVault, M.L. 1991. *Feeding the Family: The Social Organization of Caring as Gendered Work.* Chicago: University of Chicago Press.

DiFrancesco, L. 2008. 'Tracking Nutrition Trends VII. Highlights from the Canadian Council of Food and Nutrition Survey of Food and Nutrition Knowledge, Attitudes and Behaviours of Canadians in 2008'. *Canadian Journal of Dietetic Practice and Research* 69(4): Insert.

Dovey, T.M., P.A. Staples, E.L. Gibson, and J.C.G. Halford. 2008. 'Food Neophobia and "Picky/Fussy" Eating in Children: A Review'. *Appetite* 50: 181–93.

Farrales, L.L., and G.E. Chapman. 1999. 'Filipino Women Living in Canada: Constructing Meanings of Body, Food, and Health'. *Health Care for Women International* 20(2): 179–94.

Foucault, M. 1979. *Discipline and Punish: The Birth of a Prison.* New York: Random House. (French original published in 1975.)

Garriguet, D. 2006. *Nutrition: Findings from the Canadian Community Health Survey. Overview of Canadians' Eating Habits 2004.* Ottawa: Health Statistics Division,

Statistics Canada. Report No. 2: Catalogue no. 82–620-MIE.

Giddens, A. 1984. *The Constitution of Society: Outline of the Theory of Structuration*. Cambridge: Polity Press.

Godley, J., and L. Mclaren. 2010. 'Socioeconomic Status and Body Mass Index in Canada: Exploring Measures and Mechanisms'. *Canadian Review of Sociology* 47: 381–403.

Gough, B. 2007. '"Real Men Don't Diet": An Analysis of Contemporary Newspaper Representations of Men, Food and Health'. *Social Science & Medicine* 64: 326–37.

Gough, B., and M.T. Conner. 2006. 'Barriers to Healthy Eating Amongst Men: A Qualitative Analysis'. *Social Science & Medicine* 62(2): 387–95.

Hannon, P.A., D.J. Bowen, C.M. Moinpour, and D.F. McLerran. 2003. 'Correlations in Perceived Food Use between the Family Food Preparer and Their Spouses and Children'. *Appetite* 40: 77–83.

Harbottle, L. 1996. '"Bastard" Chicken or *Ghormeh-sabzi*? Iranian Women Guarding the Health of the Migrant Family'. *Sociological Review Monographs: Consumer Matters*. London: Blackwell.

Health Canada. 2007. 'Canada's Food Guide'. Accessed 25 August 2010 at www.hc-sc.gc.ca/fn-an/food-guide-aliment/choose-choix/fruit/index-eng.php.

Henson, S., J. Blandon, and J. Cranfield. 2010. 'Difficulty of Healthy Eating: A Rasch Model Approach'. *Social Science & Medicine* 70: 1574–80.

Johnston, J., and S. Baumann. 2010. *Foodies: Democracy and Distinction in the Gourmet Foodscape*. New York: Routledge.

Kemmer, D., A.S. Anderson, and D.W. Marshall. 1998. 'Living Together and Eating Together: Changes in Food Choice and Eating Habits During Transition from Single to Married/Cohabiting'. *Sociological Review* 46: 48–72.

Larson, N.I., M.T. Story, and M.C. Nelson. 2009. 'Neighborhood Environments: Disparities in Access to Healthy Foods in the U.S.' *American Journal of Preventive Medicine* 36: 74–81.

Lawton, J., N. Ahmad, L. Hanna, M. Douglas, H. Bains, and N. Hallowel. 2008. '"We Should Change Ourselves, But We Can't": Accounts of Food and Eating Practices Amongst British Pakistanis and Indians with Type 2 Diabetes'. *Ethnic Health* 13: 305–19.

Lupton, D. 2000. '"Where's Me Dinner?" Food Preparation Arrangements in Rural Australian Families'. *Journal of Sociology* 36(2): 172–86.

Lyons, A.C. 2009. 'Masculinities, Femininities, Behaviour and Health'. *Social and Personality Psychology Compass* 3/4: 394–412.

McDonald, J.T., and Kennedy, S. 2005. 'Is Migration to Canada Associated with Unhealthy Weight Gain? Overweight and Obesity among Canada's Immigrants'. *Social Science & Medicine* 61: 2469–81.

McPhail, D., B.L. Beagan, and G.E. Chapman. 2012. '"I Don't Really Want to be Sexist But–": Denying Gender, Reinscribing Gender Through Food'. *Food, Culture & Society* 15(3).

McPhail, D., G.E. Chapman, and B.L. Beagan. 2011. "Too Much of That Stuff Can't Be Good": Canadian Teens, Morality, and Fast Food Consumption. *Social Science & Medicine* 73: 301–7.

Margetts, B.M., J.A. Martinez, A. Saba, L. Holm, and M. Kearney. 1997. 'Definitions of "Healthy" Eating: A Pan-EU Survey of Consumer Attitudes to Food, Nutrition and Health'. *European Journal of Clinical Nutrition* 51, Suppl 2: S23–9.

Monaghan, L.F. 2008. *Men and the War on Obesity: A Sociological Study*. London: Routledge.

Mróz, L.W., G.E. Chapman, J.L. Oliffe, and J.L. Bottorff. 2011. 'Gender Relations, Prostate Cancer and Diet: Re-inscribing Hetero-Normative Food Practices'. *Social Science & Medicine* 72: 1499–506.

Nestle, M. 2007. *Food Politics: How the Food Industry Influences Nutrition and Health*. 2nd edn. Berkley: University of California Press.

Novak K.L., and G. E. Chapman. 2001. 'Oncologists' and Naturopaths' Beliefs and Practices Regarding the Role of Diet in Breast Cancer Prevention and Treatment'. *Cancer Practice* 9: 141–6.

Pacquette, M.C. 2005. 'Perceptions of Healthy Eating: State of Knowledge and Research Gaps'. *Canadian Journal of Public Health* 96, Supplement 3: S15–9.

Pollan, M. 2008. *In Defense of Food: An Eater's Manifesto*. New York: Penguin.

Protruder, J.L.P., G. Marchessault, A.L. Kozyrskyj, and A.B. Becker. 2010. 'Children's Perceptions of Healthful Eating and Physical Activity', *Canadian Journal of Dietetic Practice and Research* 71: 19–23. doi: 10.3148/71.1.2010.19

Raine, K.D. 2005. 'Determinants of Healthy Eating in Canada: An Overview and Synthesis'. *Canadian Journal of Public Health* 96: S8–14.

Reel, J.J., S. SooHoo, J.F. Summerhays, and D.L. Gill. 2008. 'Age Before Beauty: An Exploration of Body Image in African-American and Caucasian Adult Women'. *Journal of Gender Studies* 17(4): 321–30.

Ricciuto, L., and V.S. Tarasuk. 2007. 'An Examination of Income-related Disparities in the Nutritional Quality of Food Selections among Canadian Households from 1986–2001'. *Social Science & Medicine* 64: 186–98.

Ristovski-Slijepcevic, S., K. Bell, G.E. Chapman, and B.L. Beagan. 2010. '"Being 'Thick' Indicates You Are Eating, You Are Healthy and You Have an Attractive Body Shape": Perspectives on Fatness and Food Choice amongst Black and White Men and Women in Canada'. *Health Sociology Review* 19(3): 317–29.

Ristovski-Slijepcevic, S., and G.E. Chapman. 2005. 'Integration and Individuality in Healthy Eating Meanings, Values, and Approaches of Childless, Dual Earner Couples'. *Journal of Human Nutrition and Dietetics* 18: 301–9.

Ristovski-Slijepcevic, S., G.E. Chapman, and B.L. Beagan. 2008. 'Engaging With Healthy Eating Discourse(s): Ways of Knowing about Food and Health in Three Ethnocultural Groups in Canada'. *Appetite* 50(1): 167–78.

———. 2010. 'Intergenerational Transmission of Healthy Eating Knowledge in Three Ethnocultural Groups in Canada'. *Health: An Interdisciplinary Journal for the Social Study of Health, Illness and Medicine* 14(5): 467–83.

Rubin, L.R., M.I. Fitts, and A.E. Becker. 2003. '"Whatever Feels Good in My Soul": Body Ethics and Aesthetics among African American and Latina Women'. *Culture, Medicine and Psychiatry* 27: 49–75.

Sellaeg, K., and G.E. Chapman. 2008. 'Masculinity and Food Ideals of Men who Live Alone'. *Appetite* 51(1): 120–8.

Shepherd, R., M. Magnusson, and P. Sjödén. 2005. 'Determinants of Consumer Behavior Related to Organic Foods'. *Ambio* 34(4/5): 352–9.

Sobal, J. 2005. 'Men, Meat, and Marriage: Models of Masculinity'. *Food & Foodways* 13: 135–58.

Sobal, J., and C.A. Bisogni. 2009. 'Constructing Food Choice Decisions'. *Annals of Behavioral Medicine* 38, Suppl 1: S37–46.

Vallianatos, H., and K. Raine. 2008. 'Consuming Food, Constructing Identities: A Symbolic Analysis of Diet among Arabic and South Asian Immigrant Women'. *Food, Culture & Society* 11: 355–73.

Veenstra, G. 2010. 'Culture and Class in Canada'. *Canadian Journal of Sociology* 35: 83–111.

Walker, R.E., C.R. Keane, and J.G. Burke. 2010. 'Disparities and Access to Healthy Food in the United States: A Review of Food Deserts Literature'. *Health & Place* 16: 876–84.

World Health Organization. 2006. 'Obesity'. Accessed 15 September 2010 at www.who.int/topics/obesity/en/.

"BE THE CHANGE YOU WANT
TO SEE IN THE WORLD."
MAHATMA GANDHI

PART III

Crises and Challenges in the Food System

As food issues come to be central in public discourse, it is clear that part of the reason for this focus is the perception of a crisis in our food system. The most recent manifestation of this crisis is the escalation of food prices around the globe, particularly in 2010–11. The dramatic price increases we have recently witnessed in a whole range of food commodities have aggravated the misery of hundreds of millions of the poorest people around the globe and are credited with providing oxygen to the ongoing democratic struggles in the Middle East characterized as the 'Arab Spring'. Price spikes for food commodities are essentially 'conjunctural' crises, that is, of a limited time frame. Prices for raw food commodities will likely trend down again before too long, as they typically have in the past. This is not to say that retail food prices will decline though—at least not in any significant way—because of powerful actors in the food system who are often able to prevent price declines in raw commodities from being transferred to consumers. The issue of powerful actors in the food system is dealt with in more detail in Chapters 10 and 12 in particular.

In addition to conjunctural crises, the food system is beset with other crises that are arguably much more serious. These crises are of a more *structural* nature, in that they are rooted in the very structures that make up the food economy as we know it. In other words, they are more deep-seated—embedded in the way in which our economy and society are organized, and require careful analysis to really understand how they are generated and what their consequences are.

In this part the various contributors have provided multiple insights into a number of structural crises that characterize our food system today. Wiebe provides in Chapter 10 a clear analysis of how our political economy is shaping the prospects for those producing food on the land—farm operators and their families. The 'cost–price squeeze' is a central process negatively impacting agricultural producers and leading to extraordinary debt loads in recent times.

In Chapter 11, Sundar examines the serious degradation of our marine environment and of the populations of animal species that we depend upon for foods that emanate from the sea. She also considers the problems associated with aquaculture as a solution to the decline in wild marine-food species, as well as more long-term solutions to the ongoing crisis in global fisheries.

Moving away from the production of food, Winson, Martin, and Suschnigg each discuss separate dimensions of the crisis that characterizes some aspect of food consumption. Among the crises characterizing our food system is a crisis of nutrition. While a growing number of Canadians are facing an insecure food supply, the majority of adult Canadians are now overweight or obese, and dramatic increases in weight gain have occurred among children and youth. This situation is especially disturbing because of the host of chronic diseases that medical science has established are associated with being overweight. In Chapter 12 Winson brings a political-economic perspective to the analysis of food environments to shed light on this situation, and to help us understand why these food environments are so saturated with nutrient-poor 'pseudo-foods' and junk foods. He brings to bear empirical evidence from two key food environments—supermarkets and schools—to support his argument.

Martin probes the nutritional transition taking place in Canada's Aboriginal communities and the heavy burden of chronic disease that has been associated with this transition in Chapter 13. She presents a strong case for the need to consider the social, economic, and political context as crucially shaping this nutrition transition and, in particular, to consider the impact of *colonization* on the way this nutrition transition has unfolded in these communities. Stressing the traditional importance of food in the production of community among Aboriginal cultures, she argues that respect for the traditional cultural practices around food must be part of the nutritional solutions so badly needed in many Aboriginal communities.

The crisis in food security is explored in Chapter 14 by Suschnigg, who notes the alarming rise of *food insecurity* in Canada and the increasing recourse to food banks for a growing number of Canadian adults and their children. She considers two perspectives that offer differing explanations of food insecurity—the anti-poverty perspective and the food sovereignty perspective. Via an analysis of three case studies of corporate donors to Canadian food banks, Suschnigg explores the problematic nature of food banks as a 'solution' to hunger in Canada, and argues that major corporate donors to food banks are also significant contributors to the undermining of food security among certain groups.

These chapters do not exhaustively explore the crises facing our food system, but they do give the reader a good idea of their breadth, provide crucial analytical tools for understanding their root causes, and offer some revealing insights into the policy initiatives that will have to be vigorously pursued if viable solutions are to be found.

10

Crisis in the Food System
The Farm Crisis[1]
Nettie Wiebe

Learning Objectives

Through this chapter, you can:

1. Gain a critical understanding of the key forces that have changed farming and food production in Canada
2. Evaluate the advantages and dangers posed by the transition from family farming to corporate dominance in the food system
3. Articulate the primary causes of the farm crisis
4. Name some ecological and social advantages of small-scale farming

Introduction: Images of Farming

A summer drive through the countryside in much of settled Canada offers a picturesque and reassuring view. The landscape is dotted with farmsteads, and herds of cattle and even the occasional flock of sheep can be spotted, along with a variety of field and horticultural crops. The practised eye might observe some abandoned farms, clusters of grain bins without buildings nearby, or nearly empty villages, especially on the Prairies. But for the most part, 'farming country' looks as if it is doing just fine.

These impressions are reinforced by any food-product advertising that links food to its sources. The key images connecting food to farming in the popular imagination are rustic, serene, and healthy. Wholesome healthy food, whether butter, burgers, lettuce, or breakfast cereal, is

claimed to come from grandpa and grandma's **family farm** where you are apt to see chickens running in the yard, apples hanging from trees in the garden, or golden wheat waving in the prairie wind. The farming folk are hard-working, hearty, and honest. The countryside might be rugged in places, but it's mostly benign and welcoming.

The publicity directed at farmers themselves, however, has an entirely different tone. The prevalent advertising for farm products such as chemical pesticides, herbicides, fungicides, and farm machinery is overwhelmingly focused on their awesome power and efficacy. The images tend to be masculine and victorious, portraying wiping out the 'enemy' weeds or pests and getting the job done. Chemical names include Avenge, Achieve, Fulfill, Fortress, Leader, Liberty,

Pinnacle, Sharpshooter, and Touchdown. To farmers who often feel oppressed and financially insecure, chemical companies market promises of power and profit.

The story of agriculture and farming in Canada is a story of change and movement. From the immigrant farmers for the most part displacing hunter–gatherer food systems (Hurt 1987) to the current high-tech, high-input, corporate-controlled agriculture in turn displacing family farming,[2] the food system has changed more fundamentally than most sectors of our society and economy. These changes have largely been driven by technology, trade, urbanization, and the politics of agriculture. People and jobs have moved from rural to urban areas, reducing the social, economic, and political importance of rural populations. And the political and economic power within the sector has shifted from the family farm and rural community to corporate agribusiness and international markets.

This chapter examines the values and forces driving some of the key changes that have occurred in Canadian agriculture, focusing on what these changes have done to the family farm. I begin with an overview of the trade and technology agendas that have moved food production from small family-owned businesses to corporate enterprises. Far from benefiting family farms, increases in food production and trade, greater efficiencies, and more investments have led to higher debt loads, lower net earnings, and a shrinking, aging farming population. Understanding the causes and outcomes of the crisis in farming explored in this chapter can help us see how to stem and reverse many of the other crises in our current food system. In the final section of this chapter I argue for a fundamental reorientation of food production—food sovereignty. This initiative moves control over food-producing resources and markets back into local domains, where the primary responsibility for and control over food is in the hands of small-scale growers and those who put this food on our tables.

Redesigning Canadian Farming: External Forces

The industrialization of farming, which began more than two centuries ago in Western economies, gained velocity and momentum as horses were replaced by tractors in many parts of North America. This trend began in the decades following the First World War, with particularly rapid changes occurring during and immediately after the Second World War (Olmstead and Rhode 2001; Winson 1985). As in other sectors, replacing animal power with engines increased the speed, power, and output of farm operations exponentially. A team of horses could cultivate a few acres in a day of hard work; tractors raised that limit dramatically with far fewer person-hours required, and made larger farms possible. Exchanging the hay and grain that fed horses for tractor fuel had several other effects on the farm. What was essentially solar power was displaced by oil, increasing greenhouse gases and making food production vulnerable to the risks inherent in dependence on non-renewable resources.[3] Also, the breeding and feeding of draft horses was agricultural work, mostly done on the farm. By contrast, tractors are designed and built in industrial plants, and the oil that runs them is extracted and refined by oil companies. The cost of purchasing these sources of power made larger farms necessary. A more subtle cost of technological advances is farmers' loss of self-reliance as farming increasingly depends on the industrial corporate sector for key inputs. This shift has had dramatic effects on family farming, rural communities, the environment, and rural cultures, as discussed below.

The changes that came with the adoption of engine-driven farm equipment were rapidly augmented by the widespread introduction of hybrid seeds and chemical fertilizers, herbicides, and pesticides. These technological advances fundamentally changed farming and food production methods. For example, planting farm-saved seed or seed acquired through purchase or exchange within farming communities had been the norm since the beginning of cultivated crop production; new technologies and regulatory regimes changed those practices. Seed is increasingly purchased from seed companies, who own **patent** rights to the new varieties. Plant breeders' rights legislation enacted in Canada in 1990 curtailed farmers' rights to sell seeds to each other and gave powerful new profit-protection tools to seed development companies. New, stricter versions of that legislation—introduced twice in Canada in recent years but pushed back each time by farmer and citizen outcry—would largely extinguish farmers' abilities to save and reuse their seeds (Canadian Organic Growers 2005). Hybridization, long used in breeding corn, is now being expanded to canola and other crops; farmers must purchase new hybrid seed each year, because subsequent generations of the seed lose their 'hybrid vigour'. The most recent shift to **genetically modified (GM) seeds** and their patented genes, which began with the commercialization of Roundup Ready canola in 1996, has eliminated the option to save or trade seeds altogether for farmers who use this seed. The purchase of GM seeds (mostly canola, corn, and soybeans in Canada) comes with a technology-use agreement prohibiting the planting of seeds harvested from these crops. New seed must be purchased from the patent-holding corporation every year.

Much of the touted efficiency of high-input, intensive agriculture stems from its ability to produce a uniform, standardized product with greater speed and in higher volume than would be possible on smaller-scale diversified farms. Industrial production demands standardization. But food comes from living organisms, and biological diversity can be forced into uniformity only with a great deal of control and manipulation. The drive to achieve massive production of uniform product, whether pigs or tomatoes, can be successful only if genetic diversity is suppressed or eliminated, growing environments are artificially controlled, and all inputs such as feed or fertilizer are standardized and uniform. In short, the natural diversity of living, interacting organisms has to be ruthlessly thwarted to achieve the industrial uniformity desired for the shelves of the supermarket. In contrast, small-scale farmers can work within more natural contexts and enhance the diversity of the food they produce. They seldom have the capacity to impose the strict controls of industrial-scale operations, even if they should wish to do so.

The introduction of chemicals to the farm has driven major changes in on-farm practices and in the way food is produced. The promise of greater control and higher productivity, coupled with little critique about environmental impacts or long-term outcomes for biodiversity, non-targeted species, soils, and water, has won the day. Canadian farming now relies very heavily on chemical interventions to control diseases in livestock, poultry, and crops of every variety. The use of broad-spectrum and targeted herbicides, along with fungicides and insecticides, is an integral part of conventional farming. The sprayer has become as essential for crop and horticultural operations as the seeding and harvesting implements. The push for higher yields requires increasing use of chemical fertilizers, so that Canadian farmers are using 36 per cent more fertilizer today than they did 20 years ago (AAFC 1998: table 2.12; Statistics Canada CANSIM 001-0065 and 001-0068). Nationwide, Canadian farmers now apply just over three megatonnes per year. Pesticide purchases are up sixfold between 1971 and 2005, according to *Agriculture and Agri-Food Canada* (AAFC), and fertilizer purchases are up about three and one-half times (Qualman, 2011). Farmers have become so reliant on chemical inputs that many can no longer conceive of farming without them. When we converted our own prairie grain and cattle farm from conventional to organic production more than a decade ago, many of our farming neighbours and peers expressed skepticism that it would even be possible to grow crops without the use of chemicals.

The key objective for redesigning food production, as articulated in much of the information, advertising, and agriculture policy directives, is to increase efficiency and maximize production and thereby enhance profitability. Canadian farms have certainly become steadily more efficient as measured by output per farm, farmer, hour, animal, and acre. With the use of sophisticated technologies such as automatic steering global positioning systems for tractors, robotic milking machines, and computerized feed ration mixers, productivity has risen while the number of farms and farmers has declined. In the 20 years between 1989 and 2009 the production of Canada's corn, wheat, barley, canola, soybeans, and other major grains increased by 24 per cent (Statistics Canada 2010e). Canada has increased production of beef cattle by 28 per cent over the same period (Statistics Canada 2010i) while hog production has doubled (AAFC 2005). In dollar terms, Canadian farm production (not counting support program payments) has nearly doubled in two decades: $38.5 billion in 2010 versus $20.3 billion in 1990 (Statistics Canada 2010a; AAFC 2010b).

The drive to greater efficiency and productivity, which in very simple terms are labour expended and volumes produced, has necessarily led to greater specialization. Instead of producing a variety of plants and animals, efficiency and productivity dictate that only those products which can be produced with the highest yields or fastest gain should be grown in any one operation. Not only is it too labour-intensive to have a variety of production systems on one farm, but also neither economies of scale nor adequate investment in new technologies is likely to be achieved in any one of those endeavours. A few chickens, a pen with a half-dozen pigs, and a small dairy herd along with field crops and gardens—the kind of 'mixed' family farm that I grew up on—cannot compete on price in any one of those products. Intensive chicken or hog operations housing tens of thousands of birds or thousands of pigs have lower costs per pound of meat raised. Thus we see the end of the mixed farm and the growing trends towards large-scale operations and monocultures.

Abandoning or being forced out of mixed farming has changed the life of farming families. The increased use of technology has lightened the physical labour demanded by farming and changed the nature of the work. The sheer range of skills and knowledge required for raising a variety of animals and crops is no longer demanded. However, new skills for operating equipment, mixing chemicals, advanced accounting, navigating government programs, and running computers are now required along with the general traditional knowledge about soils and climate conditions. As well, producing fewer products on larger farms has undermined on-farm food self-sufficiency. Prairie farm families that produce thousands of tonnes of canola or barley are as reliant on the grocery store for food as any household living in an inner-city apartment.

Technology advances have made many of the changes in farming possible. But the rate of uptake and the usage of new technologies is a function of the values, politics, and culture of a society. The shift in Canadian agriculture away from small-scale, family farms to large-scale, intensive, high-input operations bespeaks a change in how food and farming is viewed and valued. Viewing the growing of food primarily as the production of commodities for profit and trade, rather than as an essential ingredient in nurturing people, catapults agriculture into the marketplace on a par with other commodities. The pressures for competitiveness and increased market share militate against small-scale, diverse, ecologically and culturally sensitive farming practices in favour of concentrated industrial operations maximizing the production of standardized products. This focus on maximizing production, lowering price per unit, and increasing market share reflects and enhances the global neo-liberal trade agenda.

Policy Changes: Trade-Driven Agriculture

When the first farming settlers arrived in Canada early in the seventeenth century, they concentrated on subsistence agriculture, but even then fishing for export on the Grand Banks near Newfoundland was already underway. Vast food-producing resources of fertile land, fresh water, and well-stocked fisheries coupled with sparse populations resulted in a pattern of surplus food production. Much of western Canada was settled with the express purpose of developing agriculture for export out of the region or across the ocean. Thus growing more food than we need for our own consumption and exporting the surplus is not a new phenomenon.

However, the more recent shift to growing food primarily for export while importing food from other countries to meet our own needs has changed the focus of agriculture policy and purpose. The inclusion of agriculture in the General Agreement on Tariffs and Trade negotiations in the 1980s made this changed perspective official and global. This move was welcomed by food-exporting countries such as Canada and the United States and advocated by agribusiness corporations. But it proved to be contentious as many countries balked at the risks of putting such a key sector under the control of external markets. Farmers and peasants protested the extreme dangers the liberalization of agriculture trade posed for local markets, rural livelihoods, cultures, and environments (Vía Campesina 1996). However, the forces pushing for the liberalization of trade in agricultural goods prevailed. Agricultural goods have become one of the key commodities in the global marketplace, although this trade remains subject to an array of concessions, exceptions, qualifications, and distortions. The new trade policies signalled the changing place of food and farming and the attendant displacement of farmers, both here in Canada and elsewhere.

Although Canada has been an exporter of grains and other foods for a long time, the trade agreements opened a new era. The rate of export growth increased dramatically and Canadian agri-food exports quadrupled following the 1989 implementation of the Canada–United States Free Trade Agreement, the 1994 implementation of the North American Free Trade Agreement, and the 1995 implementation of the World Trade Organization Agreement on Agriculture. These pacts have been followed by the implementation of numerous other bilateral and multilateral investors' rights and trade agreements that are aimed at gaining greater market access and erasing whatever barriers to trade in foodstuffs remain. Current negotiations on a trade agreement with the European Union entail even more measures, such as further curtailing farmers' rights to save and reuse seeds (Boehm 2010).

Individual farmers do not trade in the global marketplace. They are excluded by the scope, risks, expertise, and power required. Nor, for the most part, do nations trade. Agricultural trade is largely given over to agribusiness corporations operating in multiple jurisdictions. Thus, it is not Canada versus Brazil versus the United States when it comes to international agricultural trade, but rather Cargill Canada, Cargill Brazil, and Cargill US 'competing' against each other to make a sale.

One exception within this transnational-controlled trading system has been the **Canadian Wheat Board (CWB)**—the western Canadian farmers' collective marketing agency. The CWB markets wheat and barley on farmers' behalf. Although this impediment to the transnational grain-marketing corporations has been repeatedly challenged at trade negotiation tables, it has been successfully defended there (Magnan 2011; Pugh and McLaughlin 2007). However, if current domestic policy changes aimed at destroying the CWB are enacted, the prairie grain trade will also be controlled by a handful of global corporate giants. The only other sectors of Canadian food production that operate as exceptions to the dominant liberalized trade rules are poultry, egg, and dairy farms. Canadian farmers collectively secured their domestic market for these products with a legislated **supply management** system that matches production to the needs of that market. Under this system farmers are rewarded for the discipline of limiting their production with the assurance that their production costs are met by the prices they receive. This is possible only because of negotiated trade restrictions prohibiting the importation of cheaper products, which would undercut the domestic prices based on production costs and displace Canadian products. It is noteworthy that supply-management farms maintain high productivity, adopt new technological advances, and produce high-quality foods without being subjected to the global market forces. Furthermore, these farms are among the few in Canada that despite increasing in size continue to operate as family farms, successfully managing generational transfers, attracting younger farmers, and garnering viable farm incomes.

Under the neo-liberal policy agenda, Canadian agriculture is subsumed under trade policy whose key goal is to increase both the volume and value of exports. Ensuring that Canadians enjoy food security, that farmers prosper, or that food-producing resources are protected and enhanced may figure as subsidiary interests in agriculture policy, but these are overridden by the primary goal of increasing production, global market share, and trade. This goal is being successfully met. Over the past two decades, Canadian governments and transnational agribusiness corporations have set aggressive food-export targets, and they have met them—nearly quadrupling our agri-food exports between 1989 to 2009 (AAFC 2010c; AAFC 2010a).

Canadian agricultural trade policy is developed in concert with transnational agribusiness corporations whose interests in increasing trade are clearly linked to their own profitability and global market power. Corporate profitability is a function of buying products at the lowest price, processing and transporting them, and then selling them into the highest-paying market available. So, with the exception of intellectual property rights, where patent holders profit from the restrictions imposed, agriculture clauses in trade agreements have focused almost exclusively on deregulating the industry and removing domestic restrictions on exporting or importing food.

The overarching goal for Canadian agriculture, as set out by governments and industry organizations, is to increase production, competitiveness, exports, and market share. Agriculture policies and trade agreements are shaped to achieve this goal. The project has been a brilliant success on all these counts. As Agriculture Canada boasts:

> Almost 45 per cent of [Canada's] domestic food and agricultural production . . . is exported either directly as primary products or indirectly as part of processed products. In 2008 we exported $42.8 billion (Cdn) worth of food and agriculture around the world! We were also the 4th largest exporter in the world! (AAFC 2010d)

These statistics, highlighting the achievements of growth and competitiveness in the agriculture industry, might evoke the skeptical question: What crisis?

Down on the Farm: Growing More, Losing Ground

The phenomenal growth in investment, productivity, and trade in agriculture is mirrored by an equally dramatic decline in the fortunes of family farms in Canada. As the 'agricultural industry' is doing better and better, its primary stakeholders, farmers, are doing worse and worse. Export success, for example, has not benefited farmers. In fact, as Figure 10.1 illustrates, net farm income has fallen as agriculture exports have risen.

To understand the apparent paradox of higher productivity and more trade resulting in lower farm incomes, we must consider how the structural changes in agriculture marginalize and exploit small and medium-sized farms to the advantage of intensive, large-scale production and corporate profit. A complex array of interrelated factors could be named, but the most destructive ones are the **cost–price squeeze**, (higher input costs coupled with lower farm-product prices), overweening corporate power within the food system, and hostile agriculture policies that aid and abet the forces undermining family farming and local food systems.

Cost–Price Squeeze

Canadian farmers have been and continue to be willing adopters of new technologies. These include ever-larger and increasingly complex (and expensive) machinery, new seed varieties, updates to and new inventions of chemicals, antibiotics, animal health and growth products and sophisticated computerized farm management and accounting systems. All of these items are manufactured externally to the farm and are costly purchases. Higher yields, better production and growth rates, and labour savings are all incentives for making these expenditures.

The financial problems on many farms stem from the imbalance between the cost of these technical advances and inputs and the

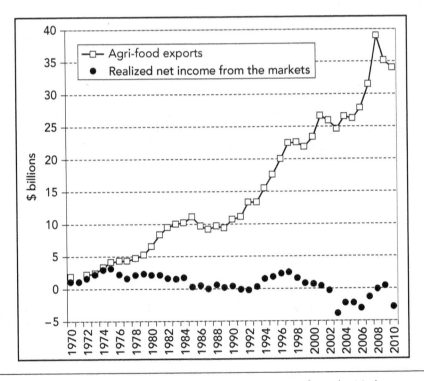

Figure 10.1   Canadian Agri-Food Exports and Realized Net Income from the Markets: 1970–2010

Source: NFU Union Farmer Monthly, Vol 60, Issue 2.

remuneration received from selling the farms' products. While the prices paid for inputs continually rise, the farm-gate price of many of the key products has either remained stagnant or fallen. For example, over the past 50 years, farm-input prices have increased nearly twice as fast as farm-product prices (e.g., fertilizer and chemical prices have gone up twice as much as corn and feeder-calf prices) (AAFC 2009: 115). Prices for grains, livestock, potatoes, and other farm products are well below even the most efficient farmer's costs of production. This is the cost–price squeeze that is eliminating many family farms.

Writing about agriculture policy, US economist Richard Levins says: 'The shortest possible economic history of . . . agriculture during the twentieth century would be this: non-farmers learning how to make money from farming' (Levins 2000: 8). This quip sums up the past 25 years of Canadian farming. From 1985 to 2010, Canadian farmers, employing world-leading productivity and efficiency, managed to produce and sell $723 billion worth (government payments excluded) of grains, livestock, potatoes, vegetables, milk, and other farm products—nearly three-quarters of a *trillion* dollars in gross revenue. But over that same period, farmers' net farm income (again, government payments excluded) was less than zero. All of the money farmers generated as gross revenue, the entire three-quarters of a trillion, was captured by the agribusiness transnational corporations that sell farmers fuel, chemicals, fertilizer, veterinary drugs, machinery, technology, and other products and supplies (Qualman 2011: 26). To survive financially, most farm families have been forced to rely on off-farm income, taxpayer-funded farm-support programs, and borrowed money. The cost–price squeeze has reached an excruciating intensity.

Downsides of Trade Dependence

Most non-farming people hear about variable weather and its effects, such as droughts, floods, or early frosts, reducing the quality and quantity of harvests. However, the weather risks are paralleled by growing uncertainty about markets and fluctuating prices. While farmers can buy crop insurance to help them survive weather-related yield losses, farmers have few tools to deal with market risks. Price fluctuations are considered useful 'price signals' for farmers to use in their production decisions. But as more Canadian products move into a global marketplace, the vicissitudes of global demand and pricing can come home to roost on the farm with dire results. For example, when the United States closed its border to Canadian beef in 2003 due to the discovery of a cow in Alberta with bovine spongiform encephalitis (BSE), the farm-gate price for prairie beef cattle plummeted, throwing many cattle farmers and ranchers into a financial crisis (NFU 2008). With the exception of the supply-managed sectors, marketing uncertainties and product price fluctuations have to be absorbed on the farm.

As the BSE example shows, greater reliance on offshore markets, even a nearby market such as the United States, increases the risks for farmers. The underside of the glowing agricultural export numbers and increased reliance on exports is the higher risks that farmers face in these markets. As well, in the global agricultural marketplace Canadian farmers are competing with growers who produce in more favourable climates using low-cost farm labour and production systems and, in some cases, with government-subsidized producers. All these factors contribute to low and declining farm-gate prices.

Sized to Succeed?

In the face of this economic reality, governments and agricultural economists advise farm families to make up for the lower margins by making the farms bigger and producing more. This advice is based on the view that economies of scale deliver efficiencies that can compensate for lower prices. Canadian farmers have complied. Whether it is potato farms in Prince Edward Island, orchards in British Columbia's Okanagan

Valley or greenhouses in Essex County in southwestern Ontario, every kind of farm has increased in size. Whereas a large cow-calf operation might have had 100 cows a generation ago, today 300-cow operations are not uncommon. Feedlots are even larger; several single-location feedlots in Canada boast throughput of 100,000, 200,000, or more cattle per year. Grain and oilseed farms, especially in western Canada, routinely encompass thousands of acres, with some very large farms covering 10,000 or 20,000 acres or more.

Farms with $1 million or more of annual revenues produce 40 per cent of Canadian food. Those million-dollar-plus farms make up just 3 per cent of farms overall (AAFC 2009: 105). Thus, approximately 7500 production units produce 40 per cent of Canadian food output. The focus on expanding and intensifying production has worked—but not for family farms. While some of these large operations, such as the intensive hog barns, are owned by individuals or communally on Hutterite colonies, most of the large intensive operations are owned by outside investors and rely on hired labour and management. These investor and management structures are characteristic of industrial plants, not family farms.

Perverse Programming

The productivity of large-scale operations succeeds in driving down prices per unit and driving out smaller-scale producers. For example, intensive hog operations in the Prairie region have succeeded in displacing virtually all family-farm hog production—two-thirds of Canada's independent family-farm hog producers have been forced to cease production over the past 14 years.[4] But this has resulted in neither profitability nor stability. The farm types that have been most aggressive and successful in expanding, such as grain and oilseed farms and hog farms, also suffer the largest farm losses (Statistics Canada 2009). Large farms are getting billions of dollars in tax-funded farm-program payments in order to remain solvent. Based on

Statistics Canada farm tax-filer data from 2004 to 2008, approximately 64 per cent of program payments—about $2.2 billion annually—went to the 27 per cent of Canadian farms with gross revenues over $250,000 per year (AAFC 2009: 105). The payment imbalance becomes even more disproportionate when we consider the number of really big operations. Approximately 28 per cent of program payments—about $1 billion annually—went to the 5 per cent of Canadian farms with gross revenues over $1 million per year (Statistics Canada 2009). Canada's largest farms are by far the largest recipients of publicly funded farm-support payments, presumably because they are the neediest. It may seem counter-intuitive that these large operations are granted public money while family farms are suffering severe losses. However, because agriculture subsidy programs are primarily based on payment per unit of production, with very high caps on the total amount of program money any single operation can receive, the largest producers get the majority of the funds.[5] Federal and provincial governments have increased caps on maximum payments to agricultural operations; they now stand at $3 million per year. As this policy of 'backing the winners' subsidizes products that will be exported, it enhances agribusiness profitability while in effect subsidizing foreign buyers of our pork, soybeans, wheat, and other farm products. A further perverse outcome for family farms is the added resources and incentives that these subsidies provide for further buyouts and displacement of small farms.

Killer Debts

To pay for rising input, machinery, and land costs, to expand operations, or to simply stay in farming, families are borrowing money. Canadian farm debt is increasing rapidly and now stands at about $64 billion.[6] It is rising by about $2.7 billion per year, and it has doubled in the past 12 years. The debt loads on many farms make them very vulnerable to rises in interest rates—and contributes to a great deal of anxiety. The farm financial crisis of the 1980s was brought on by sharp increases in interest rates, which made farm debts unpayable. Thousands of farm families saw generations of their work, history, and hopes disappear in the wake of fore-closures and forced sales (Pugh 1987).

Family farms are even more vulnerable now than they were in the 1980s because the current ratio of debt to net income is higher. In the 1970s farm families bore $3.40 worth of debt for each dollar of net income. By the 1980s, the ratio had risen to $7.42 of debt for each dollar of net income. In the 1990s, for each dollar of net income, farmers carried $10.47 in debt. During the first decade of the twenty-first century, farm-ers were carrying more than $23 in debt for each dollar of net income. Because, in effect, farm families must borrow and risk seven times as much debt as in the 1970s, and three times as much as in the 1980s, they are that much more vulnerable to losing the farm if interest rates go up, prices go down, or they suffer a bad crop year (Qualman 2011).

Corporate Takeover

As farm families struggle to make ends meet, other parts of the food system are highly prof-itable. Farmers buy fuel, fertilizers, chemicals, antibiotics, seeds, and equipment from cor-porations at the demanded prices. These inputs are sold by some of the world's most powerful and profitable corporations: fuel by Exxon and Shell; fertilizer by Potash Corporation, Cargill, Mosaic, Yara, and Agrium; chemicals by Bayer, Syngenta, Dow, Monsanto, and DuPont; and seeds by Monsanto, DuPont, Syngenta, and Bayer. Farmers have virtually no bargaining power on any of those items.

The industrialization and globalization of agricultural trade has also been a bonanza for the agribusiness transnationals such as Monsanto, Cargill, ADM, and others who buy, process, market, and increasingly produce agricultural products. Although they tend to eschew the risks and low returns of actually producing raw foodstuffs, corporations are making some stra-tegic intrusions into production where upstream profitability can be enhanced. For example, beef processors are taking ownership of more of the cattle being finished in feedlots for slaughter in order to use this captive supply to depress the price of cattle they have to buy for their pack-ing plants. Farmers delivering cattle to the auc-tion ring have no choice but to sell at the prices offered. With two beef packers, Cargill and XL Foods (Nilsson Brothers), owning almost 90 per cent of the industry in Canada, their mar-ket power allows them to keep the prices low. So, while the price you are paying for ground beef in the grocery store has more than doubled since 1988, the price farmers are getting paid for slaughter cattle and feeder calves has declined during that same period (NFU 2010). As cor-porate power becomes more concentrated, the handful of transnational agribusiness firms that farmers rely on are able to extract all of the potential revenue from farming (Qualman 2001). As these corporate players are thousands of times bigger than the biggest family farm, the market–power imbalance is overwhelming.

Policy Failure

Although farm families cannot successfully challenge large corporate interests, government policies can rebalance the relative power and profitability of farmers vis-à-vis the large corpor-ate players in the system. Unfortunately, despite rhetoric touting support for farmers, agriculture policies over the last three decades have done much to undermine and erase family farming in Canada.

Program payments, the most obvious and public 'aid to farmers', fail to secure small- and medium-scale farms, although they are clearly a crucial component of net farm income. As noted above, the money goes disproportionately to large-scale operations when the payouts are based on production and revenues.

But the government failure to limit corporate power and regulate the industry to support family farming has had devastating effects on farming families and rural communities. Instead of instituting policies to achieve such goals, the government has created a regulatory framework that is entirely and increasingly hostile to small-scale diversified farms. For example, the re-regulation of grain transportation in the latter half of the 1990s, giving Canada's two major railways leave to offer favourable rates to unit trains (large blocks of cars) and abandon branch lines, had a domino effect throughout the rural Prairies. Grain co-operatives and companies that had located elevators in hundreds of communities along these branch lines consolidated their operations. Functioning elevators in many communities were demolished in order to force grain into higher-throughput, centralized elevators. This forced grain from railcars onto trucks, adding road costs and greenhouse gas emissions to the equation. These regulatory changes have also had multiple on-farm effects. Along with making transportation one of the highest expenses for grain farms, the trucking requirements have forced farmers either to invest in larger trucks or to hire truckers to haul their grain. The policy changes did not offer any new revenue streams to compensate for these added expenses.

Farmers were supposed to be able to share the benefits of these so-called efficiencies. Canadian legislation sets the amounts Canadian National and Canadian Pacific railways can charge farmers for transporting western grain. These rates are fixed at levels that cover railway costs and allow for appropriate profits for the rail companies. Moreover, those regulated rates increase each year to account for inflation. In addition to this inflation-adjustment mechanism, however, a second mechanism—a costing review—is supposed to assess actual railway costs and to reduce rates as efficiency gains and other cost-saving measures lower the actual costs of moving grain. In effect, costing reviews are meant to ensure both that railways

continue to earn reasonable profits and that farmers share in system-wide efficiency gains. The federal government has refused, however, to hold a costing review since 1992. Thus, farmers' freight rates have increased year after year. A recent independent study (Travacon 2010) has calculated that the lack of such a review is costing western grain farmers an extra $200 million per year—money transferred from hard-pressed farm families to railway executives and shareholders.

Regulations on meat processing offer another example of how policy undermines small-scale, local food production. Most local abattoirs in Canada have gone out of business. Along with price competition from large corporate processors selling through supermarkets and under-cutting smaller operations, further impediments introduced as food-safety requirements make it virtually impossible for many to continue. In response to the food dangers inherent in large plants, many food-safety regulations have been imposed that are both inappropriate and unaffordable for smaller operations. By opting for a 'one size fits all' regime, the Canadian Food Inspection Agency has in fact harmed local butchers and taken away a market option for small-scale farmers. As these examples illustrate, hostile agriculture policies that increase costs and fail to enhance revenues harm the prospects of making a living on the family farm.

The cost–price squeeze has meant that farmers' net incomes from the marketplace have been negative in most of the first decade of the twenty-first century. Farm families are caught in the tightening grip of the cost–price squeeze. Extraordinary commitment, adaptability, some government aid, and, most importantly, non-farm income, account for the survival of those families who continue in farming. Because the market fails to allow farmers to profit from producing food, off-farm income and farm-support payments now make up 100 per cent of most farm families' net income. This is the reality for farm families in every part of the country, although not in every sector—supply-managed farms are consistently the exceptions. In general however, the investments in, labour for, and costs of growing food do not return enough for farmers to live on, so wages from other employment are needed to meet family living expenses.

Sadly, working longer hours and doing more jobs, along with getting the farm work done, hasn't been enough to save many farms. Agriculture census data indicate that Canada lost 22 per cent of its farms and farm families between 1986 and 2006 (Statistics Canada 1987, 2007). However, this number does not tell the whole story. It leaves out the troubling fact that many of the surviving farms are in a holding pattern with little likelihood of a long-term future. This situation is reflected in the statistics on young farmers, on whom that future depends. According to Statistics Canada's Census of Agriculture, in 1991 (the first year for which we have data), Canada had 77,910 young farmers (those aged under 35). Fifteen years later, in 2006, we had just 29,920—a drop of 62 per cent. In 1991, there was a young farmer on one farm in every four; today, just one farm in eight supports a young farmer. Aspiring young farmers are faced with almost insurmountable obstacles. The high debt loads required to start farming coupled with the lack of potential net earnings to meet those debts makes it virtually impossible for people to enter farming. And it is obvious that an aging farm population that is not being replaced by the next generation of young farmers spells the end of many family farms.

Rural Communities: Change and Decline

The aging farmer demographic affects not only the prospects of particular family farms, but also the dynamics, culture, and prospects of farming communities. The boarded-up buildings along the main streets of towns and villages stand as stark testimony to both the economic and the social losses of these communities. My own nearby village has declined from a thriving community, that in the 1940s boasted five grain elevators, stores, a church, an arena, a restaurant, and a bank, to a nearly deserted site today where the collapsing roof of the church and its precariously tilting steeple graphically paint the picture of the fate of many such communities. Small-town businesses that rely on farm trade become unviable unless non-farming customers move into the area to make up for the diminished and aging farm populations. Without young families to use the services, the schools, sports arenas, and social organizations in many rural communities have become unsustainable. Boarded-up hardware stores, defunct arenas, and empty schoolyards illustrate the lack of youth and renewal in many towns and villages.

Women in farming and rural women in general are differentially affected by the decline of rural communities and the loss of young people from these communities. As primary family caregivers, women often invest energy in maintaining the social and cultural life of their communities. The absence of young families and young women in rural communities is felt especially acutely. Although rural families share with their urban counterparts the common experience of having their own children move away from home when they reach adulthood, the move away from rural areas represents not only that particular loss but also a more general one. While urban centres experience an influx of young people seeking jobs and education, the departure of most rural youth from their homes and communities leaves a gap that is unlikely to be filled with incoming young people. This means that the energy and forward-looking dynamic of young people is permanently gone. It makes the social life, such as community events and services that rely on buoyant community spirit and volunteer energy much more difficult to initiate and maintain. As women are often key initiators and volunteers for family-oriented community life and celebrations, the absence of young neighbours makes this social and cultural work more challenging, if not impossible, in aging and dying rural communities.

The cultural losses in rural communities, though most acutely experienced in those communities, accrue to the whole country. Just as biological diversity is necessary for healthy and sustainable biological life, so cultural diversity contributes to making societies more adaptive and sustainable. The displacement of traditional farming knowledge and skills has practical consequences. So does the loss of the wisdom and cultural nuances that are developed by communities of people who share a unique physical place and have learned to grow food, create meaning, and build social spaces adapted to and shaped by that particular place.

Conclusion: Changing Menus and Relationships

Farming does not have to be ecologically destructive and financially ruinous. Since the long-term sustainability of our food system affects us all, positive change is in our collective interest. Far more food could be grown and purchased locally. Prosperous, ecologically sound family farms could produce healthy food, and eaters could know what they are eating and where it comes from. Public policy could support and enhance small-scale farming, local food production, and markets rather than shoring up transnational agribusiness. All of this is possible.

In this final section of the chapter I argue that the restoration, re-invigoration, and re-invention of small-scale family farming is at the crux of the solutions to many of the ecological, health, and social ills of our current food system.

Mixed family farms can use resources in an integrated way that enhances diversity, works with natural biological cycles, and decreases pollution. For example, raising cattle as well as cropping land allows us to integrate hay crops into our crop rotations, adding fertility to soils, controlling weeds, and producing feed for the animals. The cattle, while being fed to produce beef, generate manure which does the work of fertilizer. The hay rotation and manure eliminate

the need to bring in external chemical inputs that require fossil fuels both to manufacture and to transport. Where the waste products from **intensive livestock operations** create dangerous water, soil, and air pollution and require careful management, less concentrated animal waste on small-scale integrated farms is a welcome resource. This is only one example of the complex ecological services small-scale, multipurpose, integrated food production offers.

In contrast to agricultural production that is owned by outside investors primarily interested in profits, family farms are, as the name indicates, *family* enterprises as well as business ones. Not only does the enterprise rely on family labour, management, and commitment, but its long-term success depends on cross-generational co-operation. Without generational transfers, either within or outside of the family, the individual farm disappears as a distinct entity. The tradition of retaining farms within families over many generations has various roots and reasons, not the least of which is the valuable local knowledge about growing food and living well in a particular place, which takes generations to accumulate. Also, knowing that the livelihoods and well-being of one's children and grandchildren depend on the condition of the farm is a great incentive to carefully enhance ecological resources for the next generation rather than depleting them for current profits.

Beyond the ecological benefits, family farms and local food production offer important benefits to everyone who eats. Many of the health and dietary problems caused by the current food system are explored in other chapters of this volume. Solutions and improvements are possible only if those who work for them have the power to effect changes. As long as agriculture is controlled by corporations and investors and regulated by governments to support corporate interests, the fundamental transformations that are needed for sustainable, healthy food production cannot be implemented. In order to re-orient priorities and make the food system responsive to nutritional, cultural, environmental, and social needs, control of food-producing resources and markets must be handed back to local farmers, communities, and citizens. That is, food sovereignty must be achieved (see Chapter 21 in this volume).

But in order to get there we need to be able to imagine and articulate new relationships to food, community, and ultimately the earth. Instead of the system where farmers are producing commodities that are transformed and transported to distant markets, the relationships among farmers, food, and eaters must be re-established. Food sovereignty begins from the position that citizens can and must be engaged in decisions about a life-sustaining good—food—within an ecological, social, and cultural context. It recognizes that the growing, buying, preparing, and eating of food are embedded in social and ecological relationships, rather than primarily functioning under market determinants.

Changing the role, purpose, and structure of agriculture by reasserting the importance of ensuring that everyone has healthy, culturally appropriate food produced in ecologically and socially sustainable ways requires the engagement of a movement of citizens. Although the number of family farms is declining, a growing number of non-farming people are engaging in actions that focus on food and farming issues, from buying local food at farmers' markets, to gardening, to social movement activism. More eaters are recognizing that family farming and local food are linked to eating well and having access to sustainably produced food from a known source. Solving the farm crisis requires many major changes in the food system. It begins with a new understanding of the key role of family farmers in solving many of the other crises in the food system.

Discussion Questions

1. How have industrialization and liberalized trade benefited the agriculture industry?

2. What benefits and harms have industrialization, technical advances, and liberalized trade afforded family farms?

3. How is it possible that the agriculture industry is experiencing growth and enhanced profits while family farms are suffering decline and financial losses?

4. Could Canadian agriculture policy support small-scale farming? If so, how?

5. What is the role of family farming in a sustainable food system?

Further Reading

1. Diaz, Harry P., Joanne Jaffe, and Robert Stirling, eds. 2003. *Farm Communities at the Crossroads: Challenge and Resistance*. Regina: Canadian Plains Research Center.

   Essays on the politics, economics, and culture of rural communities.

2. Epp, Roger. 2008. *We Are All Treaty People: Prairie Essays*. Edmonton: University of Alberta Press.

A personal and political exploration of rural communities and farm people whose livelihoods are under intense economic and cultural pressure.

3. Epp, Roger, and Dave Whitson, eds. 2001. *Writing off the Rural West: Globalization, Governments, and the Transformation of Rural Communities*. Edmonton: University of Alberta Press & Parkland Institute.

Essays on the changes and prospects for agriculture-, resource-, and tourism-dependent rural communities.

4. Ervin, Alexander M., Cathy Holstlander, Darrin Qualman, and Rick Sawa, eds. 2003. *Beyond Factory Farming: Corporate Hog Barns and the Threat to Public Health, The Environment, and Rural Communities.* Saskatoon, SK: Canadian Centre for Policy Alternative—Saskatchewan.

Experts and activists present a critical analysis of the impact of intensive hog operations.

5. Wittman Hannah, Annette Aurélie Desmarais, and Nettie Wiebe, eds. 2010. *Food Sovereignty: Reconnecting Food, Nature and Communities.*

Halifax: Fernwood, Oakland: Food First, Cape Town: Pambazuka.

Experts present in-depth analysis of key issues and trends in the global food system and explore the radical alternative options that a food sovereignty framework affords.

6. Wittman, Hannah, Annette Aurélie Desmarais, and Nettie Wiebe, eds. 2011. *Food Sovereignty in Canada: Creating Just and Sustainable Food Systems.* Halifax: Brunswick.

Canadian authors explore the current state of the Canadian food system offering ways in which adopting food sovereignty as the operative framework would resolve key problems.

Notes

1. I want to thank Darrin Qualman for the key research and analysis he contributed to this chapter.
2. The term *family farm* denotes a farming operation where the labour and management and much of the ownership investment is supplied by family members.
3. Wendell Berry notes that fossil-fuel–driven agriculture turns food production into an industrial project based on a non-renewable source of energy that uses up 'in our own time the birthright and livelihood of posterity' (2009: 59).

4. Statistics Canada, Historical Overview of Canadian Agriculture, Cat. No. 93–358-XPB; Statistics Canada CANSIM table 003–0089; and Statistics Canada, 'Hog Statistics,' Cat No. 23–010, 28 October 2010 ('Third quarter 2010').
5. Margin-based programs such as AgriInvest pay on the basis of whole farm losses which advantages single commodity operations.
6. Statistics Canada, 'Farm Debt Outstanding—Agriculture Economic Statistics', Cat. No. 21–014-X, November 2010. 2010 value of $64 billion is an estimate based upon the 2009 value of $62.7 billion.

References

Agriculture and Agri-Food Canada (AAFC). 1998. *Fertilizer Pricing in Canada.* June.

———. 2005. *A Statistical Profile of the Pork Supply Chain.* December. Updated data by request.

———. 2009. *An Overview of the Canadian Agriculture and Agri-Food System: 2009.* May.

———. 2010a. *Medium Term Outlook for Canadian Agriculture: International and Domestic Markets.* January.

———. 2010b. *Canada's Farm Income Forecast for 2009 and 2010.* February.

———. 2010c. Canadian Trade Highlights. (Agri-Food Trade Service). Available at ats-sea.agr.gc.ca.

———. 2010d. 'Canada Brand International, Market Research in Key Export Markets'. Available at marquecanadabrand.agr.gc.ca/research-etudes/research-etudes-eng.htm.

Berry, Wendell. 2009. 'Energy in Agriculture'. In *Bring It to the Table: On Farming and Food.* Berkeley: Counterpoint.

Boehm, Terry. 2010. 'Canada-EU Trade Agreement Damaging'. *Western Producer,* 29 April: 11.

Canadian Organic Growers. 2005. 'A Response to the Proposed Amendments to Plant Breeders Rights Legislation and the Seed Sector Review'. Available at www.cog.ca/documents/COGrespPBRseeds_001.pdf.

Ervin, Alexander M., Cathy Holstlander, Darrin Qualman, and Rick Sawa, eds. 2003. *Beyond Factory Farming: Corporate Hog Barns and the Threat to Public Health, The Environment, and Rural Communities*. Saskatoon, SK: Canadian Centre for Policy Alternative—Saskatchewan.

Hurt, R. Douglas. 1987. *Indian Agriculture in America: Prehistory to the Present*. Lawrence, KS: University of Kansas Press.

Levins, Richard. 2000. *Willard Cochrane and the American Family Farm*. Lincoln, NB: University of Nebraska Press.

Magnan, André. 2011. 'The Limits of Farmer-Control: Food Sovereignty and Conflicts over the Canadian Wheat Board'. In *Food Sovereignty in Canada: Creating Just and Sustainable Food Systems*, ed. Hannah Wittman, Annette Aurélie Desmarais, and Nettie Wiebe. Halifax: Fernwood, 114–33.

National Farmers Union (NFU). 2008. 'The Farm Crisis and the Cattle Sector: Towards a New Analysis and New Solutions'. Report by the National Farmers Union (Canada). 19 November.

———. 2010. 'Free Trade: Is It Working for Farmers? Comparing 1988 to 2010'. *Union Farmer Monthly* 60: 2.

Olmstead, Alan L., and Paul W. Rhode. 2001. 'Reshaping the Landscape: The Impact and Diffusion of the Tractor in American Agriculture, 1910–1960'. *Journal of Economic History* 61(3): 663–98.

Pugh, Terry, and Darrell McLaughlin, eds. 2007. *Our Board Our Business: Why Farmers Support the Canadian Wheat Board*. Halifax: Fernwood.

Pugh, Terry, ed. 1987. *Fighting the Farm Crisis*. Saskatoon, SK: Fifth House.

Qualman, Darrin. 2001. *The Farm Crisis and Corporate Power*. Ottawa: Canadian Centre for Policy Alternatives.

———. 2011. 'Advancing Agriculture by Destroying Farms? The State of Agriculture in Canada'. In *Food Sovereignty in Canada: Creating Just and Sustainable Food Systems*, ed. Hannah Wittman, Annette Aurélie Desmarais, and Nettie Wiebe. Halifax: Fernwood Publishing, 20–42.

Statistics Canada. 1987. *Census, Canada 1986, Agriculture*. Cat. No. 96-102, December. Ottawa: Ministry of Supply and Services.

———. 2007. '2006 Census of Agriculture: Farm Data and Farm Operator Data'. Cat. No. 95-629-XWE, 16 March. Available at www.statca.gc.ca/pub/95-629-x/2007000/4123856-eng.htm.

———. 2009. *Statistics on Income of Farm Families*. Cat. No. 21–207-E. 26 June.

———. 2010a. *Farm Cash Receipts—Agriculture Economic Statistics*. Cat. No. 21–011-X. May.

———. 2010b. *Farm Debt Outstanding—Agriculture Economic Statistics*. Cat. No. 21-014-X. November.

———. 2010c. *Agricultural Economic Statistics*. Cat. No. 21-603-E. November.

———. 2010d. *Farm Income—Agriculture Economic Statistics*. Cat. No. 21-010-X. November.

———. 2010e. CANSIM Table 001–0017. 'Estimated Areas, Yield, Production, Average Farm Price and Total Farm Value of principal Field Crops, in Imperial Units, Annual'. All CANSIM tables available at www5.statca.gc.ca/cansim/a01?lang=eng.

———. 2010f. CANSIM Table 001–0065. 'Fertilizer Shipments to Canadian Agriculture Markets, by Nutrient Content and Fertilizer Year, Annual'.

———. 2010g. CANSIM Table 001–0068. 'Fertilizer Shipments to Canadian Agriculture and Export Markets, by Product Type and Fertilizer Year, Cumulative Data, Annual'.

———. 2010h. CANSIM Table 001–0069.

———. 2010i. CANSIM Table 003–0026. Cattle and Calves, Farm and Meat Production, Annual (Head).

———. 2010j. CANSIM Table 003–0089. 'Hogs Statistics, Number of Farms Reporting and Average Number of Hogs per Farm, Quarterly (Number)'.

———. 2010k. 'Historical Overview of Canadian Agriculture'. Cat. No. 93–358-XPB.

———. 2010l. 'Hog Statistics'. Cat No. 23–010. Third quarter 2010. 28 October.

Travacon Research Limited. 2010. *Estimating Contributions Earned by Railways from Handling of Statutory Grain and Grain Products 2007/2008 and 2008/2009*. Prepared for the Canadian Wheat Board. May.

Winson, Anthony. 1985. 'The Uneven Development of Canadian Agriculture: Farming in the Maritimes and Ontario'. *Canadian Journal of Sociology* 10(4): 411–38.

Vía Campesina. 1996. 'The Right to Produce and Access to Land'. Available at www.viacampesina.org.

The Crisis in the Fishery
Canada in the Global Context
Aparna Sundar

Learning Objectives

Through this chapter, you can:

1. Understand the nature of the food system in the fishery, in Canada, and globally
2. Understand the relationship of food security, sustainability, and social justice in the fishery
3. Understand the multiple dimensions of the crisis in the fishery
4. List the main institutions and actors involved in fisheries governance
5. Become familiar with key frameworks and approaches to dealing with the crisis in the fishery

Introduction

The fishery is in the news frequently these days, as are discussions of whether fish are still safe to eat, and which ones are safe. There is growing concern that the world's marine fisheries are in a state of crisis with the decline of significant marine fishing stocks and a levelling off of total catches since the early 1990s. Powerful works by popular writers such as Canadian journalist Alanna Mitchell (*Sea Sick*), American journalist Charles Clover (*The End of the Line*), and Canadian novelist Taras Grescoe (*Bottomfeeder*) have begun to bring the extent of the crisis to the attention of the North American public. Yet fish and seafood retain the popularity they have acquired in wealthy countries over the last decade as healthy sources of protein and omega-3 acids, or as 'brain food'. They also continue to be the major source of animal protein for low-income populations across the global South. Fish and seafood are among the most highly traded food commodities; this trade continues to rise despite declining stocks. The gap between the growing demand for fish and the decline of wild stocks is being met by the growth of **aquaculture**, which now supplies some 46 per cent of all fish and seafood and is the fastest-growing form of agriculture in the world. Aquaculture, however, raises a whole new set of problems related to food safety and environmental impact.

The crisis in the fishery is multi-dimensional, having to do with food supply and food security, and also with food safety, the North–South dimension of the food trade, the survival of livelihoods and communities, biodiversity, and ecosystem stability. Both because fish do not respect national boundaries, and because of the highly globalized trade in fisheries products, local and national approaches to fisheries sustainability must necessarily have a global perspective. Even more fundamentally, the state of the fishery forces us to confront larger questions about our relationship to nature as the source of our food and about how we might draw upon it more sustainably in the future.

This chapter seeks to provide an understanding of the multiple dimensions of the crisis in the fishery. The first two sections describe the nature and extent of the declining fisheries, along with an overview of the fisheries food chain. The third section traces the history of the current crisis, and the fourth discusses various solutions to it. The final section before the conclusion focuses on the growing importance of aquaculture as one solution.

Defining the Crisis

The growth rate of global marine fish catches, after rising rapidly through the 1960s and 1970s, began to slow in the 1980s, reaching its peak at the end of that decade. In Canada, this decline came dramatically to national attention when the Atlantic cod was declared 'commercially extinct' by the end of the 1980s, and the East Coast cod fishery was closed in 1992.

Fisheries scientists work with the concept **maximum sustainable yield (MSY)** to determine the size of the catch of a particular species of fish in any one year that will not impair its ability to reproduce itself and generate the same level of catch in subsequent years. If fishing has exceeded this level, the stock is deemed to have exceeded its MSY, and is declared overfished or over-exploited. When the drop in catches is so significant that the catch is unlikely to recover to financially viable levels in the foreseeable future, the species is declared 'commercially extinct', a point reached well before that of biological extinction.

The 2010 *State of World Fisheries and Aquaculture* report of the United Nations Food

and Agriculture Organization (FAO) estimates that in 2008 about 15 per cent of the stock groups monitored by FAO were under-exploited (3 per cent) or moderately exploited (12 per cent), meaning that catches had not yet reached the MSY levels established for those species and could perhaps produce more. Some 53 per cent were fully exploited and therefore were producing catches at or close to their MSY, with no room for further expansion. The other 32 per cent were either over-exploited (28 per cent), depleted (3 per cent), or recovering from depletion (1 per cent) and thus yielding less than their maximum potential owing to excess fishing pressure in the past. With these stocks, there was no possibility in the short or medium term of further expansion, but instead, there was an increased risk of further decline. Thus, overall, only 15 per cent of global stocks still have room to provide increasing catches in coming years, while 85 per cent of the world fish stocks for which data are available are fully exploited or over-exploited. This is especially true for high-sea fish resources. The report notes with concern that the figure for over-exploited, depleted, or recovering stocks was the highest since the 1970s, while that for stocks still capable of being exploited further was the lowest.

A recent study (Devine et al. 2006) classified five popular North Atlantic deep-sea species as biologically endangered, since these species grow and mature slowly and have been fished to the point where there are few juvenile fish left. The overfishing of the larger predator fish such as cod has complex impacts (Myers and Worm 2003). A phenomenon called **fishing down the marine food web** has been noted: as larger fish are depleted, a greater proportion of the catch consists of smaller fish of lower weight and density. Excessive fishing of these smaller fish in turn takes away the food source of the larger fish and prevents their regeneration, as well as threatening the food source of human populations who eat the smaller fish (Pauly et al. 1998). It also creates uncertainty about how different stocks will fare, and points to the importance of biodiversity.

Marine biodiversity is increasingly recognized as valuable for reasons other than sustaining food supply, such as helping with waste detoxification and reducing floods. The Halifax-based authors of an important recent study conclude: 'marine biodiversity loss is increasingly impairing the ocean's capacity to provide food, maintain water quality, and recover from perturbations' (Worm et al. 2006: 787), although their data suggest that these trends are as yet reversible. As Alanna Mitchell found to her astonishment when talking to a marine biologist, 'Life on land is utterly dependent on the life and chemistry in the ocean.' Ocean plankton are 'the real lungs of our planet', producing half the oxygen we breathe. 'The ocean controls climate and temperature and the carbon and oxygen cycles of the planet, as well as other chemical systems that give all living creatures life—including us' (Mitchell 2009: 12). Loss of ocean biodiversity due to overfishing might have graver consequences for us than we realize.

The social costs of the commercial or biological extinction of a species are complex and uneven. In Canada, when 30,000 fishermen in Newfoundland found themselves thrown out of work upon the collapse of the cod fishery, the Department of Fisheries and Oceans (DFO) encouraged a shift to harvesting shellfish such as lobsters and crab. Shellfish fetch a high price, and now compensate to a large extent for the decline of groundfish such as cod in national

production figures (DFO 2008). In this case, the crisis affected those dependent on the cod fishery for their livelihood more than it affected the Canadian economy as a whole. Canadian consumers are also sheltered from the effects of the crisis by the almost immediate availability of new species in the market when a popular species becomes rare (Jacquet and Pauly 2007, 2008), by their ability to buy food produced in all parts of the world, and by the increasing supply from aquaculture. Thus the social effects of the fisheries crisis are felt unevenly across regions and nations, and can be understood only by paying attention to the various points of the fisheries food chain.

The Fisheries Food Chain

This section paints a broad brushstroke picture of production, trade, and consumption patterns in the fishery. Table 11.1 provides an overview of production and employment in the different sectors of Canada's fishery.

Canada ranks twentieth globally in terms of its fish landings, which represent 1 per cent of the global total; the top producers are China, Peru, Indonesia, and the United States. The proportion of marine versus inland catch in Canada is similar to the global pattern, where 88 per cent of all fish captured is from the seas, and only 12 per cent from inland waters (FAO 2010).

Table 11.1 Employment and Production Value of the Commercial Fisheries, Aquaculture, and Processing in Canada, 2006

Industry	Gross Production Value (millions of dollars)	Employment Estimates
Marine Fisheries	1,922	51,462 (including freshwater)
Freshwater Fisheries	68	
Aquaculture	913	3,970
Processing	4,197	28,587
Total	7,100 ($7 billion)	84,019

Source: Adapted from Tables 1.1 and 1.2, DFO 2008.

Discussions on the fisheries crisis tend to focus on the marine fishery because of its overwhelming dominance and because available figures suggest that inland overfishing has generally not been a problem. We must nevertheless remember that inland water bodies are also complex ecosystems and susceptible to a range of pressures, most notably pollution.

The fisheries as a whole employ some 180 million people around the world. In 2006, an estimated 51 million people were directly engaged in primary production of fish, either in capture from the wild or in aquaculture, with employment in the secondary sector—processing, marketing, and service industries—making up the rest. Counting families of employees, there are about 540 million people dependent on the sector, or nearly 8 per cent of the world population (FAO 2010: 29–30).

In Canada, the industry's economic contribution, including employment, is relatively more important at the regional and community levels than nationally: 35 per cent of the value of all landed fish catches in 2006 was from Nova Scotia, 24 per cent from Newfoundland and Labrador, and 13 per cent from British Columbia. Fish processing further contributes to the economy and to employment. Three-quarters of the country's total exports of fish and fish products originate from the Atlantic region, where the seafood sector is the second-largest exporting industry in terms of value, after refined petroleum products (DFO 2004).

Most fishers and fish farmers around the world are small-scale fishers. In Canada too, about 91 per cent of fishing vessels are inshore vessels less than 45 feet long that each have two to three crew members including the skipper. However, larger vessels that operate further out in the ocean capture a far greater proportion of the catch by value because of the types of gear they use and their ability to traverse greater distances; large vessels made up only about 8 per cent of all vessels but took 43 per cent of all catch in Canada in 2006 (DFO 2008: 7). This is an important statistic to keep in mind in our subsequent discussion about how to achieve a sustainable fishery.

Fish and seafood are among the most-traded food commodities, with 39 per cent of all production entering international trade (FAO 2010: 9). The highly globalized nature of fish can be seen at the Tsukiji market in Tokyo, the world's largest wholesale seafood market, where almost $6 billion worth of fish changes hands every year. Here tuna from Massachusetts is sold beside octopus from Senegal, eel from Guangzhou in China, crab from the Russian island of Sakhalin, salmon from British Columbia and the Japanese island of Hokkaido, and abalone from California (Bestor 2004; Grescoe 2008). Bestor (2000) provides a fascinating account of the trading process for bluefin tuna, a fish that on average weighs 500 pounds, and which in the late 1990s sold at over US$35 wholesale per edible pound. He describes how, in a fishing village in Maine, 20 tuna buyers, half of them Japanese, inspect three bluefin tuna caught by local fishermen. The buyers check the tuna, call Japan by cellphone to get the morning prices from the Tsukiji market, then place their bids on the fish. Once the deals are made, the fish are loaded onto trucks in crates of crushed ice, driven to New York's John F. Kennedy International Airport, and air-freighted to Tokyo. The prepared sushi using these fish may be shipped to restaurants in New York or elsewhere.

It is not only high-value fish like bluefin tuna that are globally traded. Small, low-value fish such as anchovies, which are used for fishmeal in aquaculture, animal feed, and pet food, are also a highly traded item. The high volume of trade in fish raises two kinds of concerns: traceability and food security.

The concern over traceability arises because globalization in the fish trade occurs not only at the point of sale, but also further back in the production chain. Fish caught in one place might be processed in a quite distant place: a significant amount of Canadian imports come directly to the processing plants, where they are processed, packaged, and re-exported. In such cases, the label might be quite confusing. For example, cans of 'wild Alaska salmon' found in US supermarkets have been found to be labelled 'product of Thailand' (Jacquet and Pauly 2008: 310). The labelling of fish by their country of processing rather than of capture may disguise the fact that they were caught in a declining fishery. In other cases, fish that are on 'red lists' (lists of endangered fish species) may be served up under another name, or an unfamiliar and lower-value species may be deliberately mislabelled as a popular, higher-value fish. For instance, American restaurant-goers continued to be served fish passed off as grouper long after the fish itself disappeared from American waters, leaving them oblivious to the fact that overfishing had destroyed grouper stocks (Jacquet and Pauly 2007, 2008). Mislabelling and the lack of traceability reduce consumers' ability to make choices around food safety and sustainability.

The role of fish and seafood in food security, especially as sources of animal protein and other important micronutrients, varies by region based on location, availability, and traditional patterns of food consumption. Canada imports far less fish than it exports, ranking as the world's eighth-largest fish and seafood exporter (DFO 2008; FAO 2010). (In 1990, Canada was the second-largest seafood exporter in the world,

behind the United States, but the collapse of the groundfish catches in Canada, combined with increased aquaculture production in China and elsewhere, has led to a drop in Canada's rank.) Despite Canada being a net exporter of fish, the quantity of fish and seafood available for consumption to the average Canadian in 2006 was 24.1 kg, close to the 29.3 kg per capita available across the industrialized nations of the world. This is in contrast to the 8.3 kg per capita available in the Low-Income Food-Deficit Countries (LIFDCs), or the 16.2 kg in the developing countries excluding the LIFDCs. Although smaller amounts of fish are consumed per capita in the LIFDCs, the high cost of other animal meats means that on average fish is a greater source of animal protein in those countries than in wealthy industrialized countries like Canada and the United States (FAO 2009).

Even though fish is an important source of animal protein for LIFDCs, these countries are net exporters of fish. Because they are not highly industrialized, they rely heavily on agricultural exports for their foreign exchange earnings, and fisheries products are now the single-most valuable agricultural commodity exported by developing countries, as demonstrated in Figure 11.1 (FAO 2009: 49). The LIFDCs alone

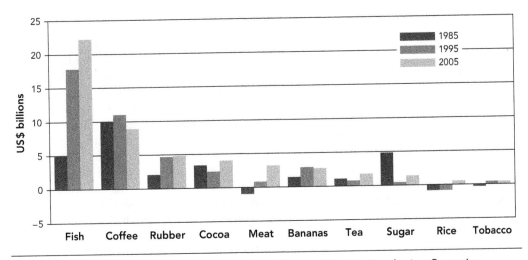

Figure 11.1   Net Exports of Selected Agricultural Commodities by Developing Countries

Source: State of World Fisheries and Aquaculture, 2008. © Food and Agriculture Organization of the United Nations.

supplied 20 per cent of the total value of world fish exports in 2006, up from 10 per cent in 1976 (FAO 2009: 49).

Some 19 per cent of fish production is directed to non-food uses (FAO 2010). Fish such as sardines, anchovies, mackerel, and other small pelagic fishes (those that live at the ocean's surface) are fit for human consumption and are relatively cheap in LIFDCs, but are often converted to fishmeal because of the global demand for fishmeal for animal feed, including in aquaculture, and for uses such as pet food (Pauly 2009), demonstrating that domestic animals in the global North have greater purchasing power than humans in the South.

The Origins of the Crisis

There is historical evidence of excessive fishing leading to the decline and even extinction of fish species, such as in the Wadden Sea off northwest Europe between the fifth and the fifteenth centuries (Mitchell 2009: 125). But there is no historical parallel to the speed and scale of the decline witnessed over the last century. The factors leading to the falling catch figures and virtual extinction of some species are a complex interplay of modern production technologies, growing demand, and inadequate governance structures, all based on the dangerous assumption that marine resources are virtually inexhaustible.

European fishers and sailors coming to Newfoundland in the 1600s wrote of seas so thick with cod that the fish could be scooped up in baskets (Kurlansky 1997: 49). The Aboriginal fishery that sustained numerous communities across what is now Canada was for the most part a freshwater fishery, fishing salmon in rivers such as the Fraser River in British Columbia (Claxton 2008: 52). Mark Kurlansky (1997) documents the role of the cod fishery in the development of an increasingly international pattern of settlement, colonization, and trade. The arrival of the Spanish, the French, and especially the English,

led to the establishment of seasonal settlements in what is now Newfoundland, and permanent settlements in the more temperate climate of New England. Here, cod fish was caught and dried by European fishing expeditions and supplied initially to Europe and later also to feed England's colonies in the Caribbean.

The expansion of markets and the increased profitability of the fishery led to two new developments in the industrial and scientific revolution of the nineteenth century. One was the technological development of craft and gear, and the other was the establishment of fisheries science. The need to better predict the returns for capital invested in the fishery put pressure on governments to focus scientific efforts on the study of fish patterns. This requirement became urgent by the middle of the 1800s, as catches began to fluctuate dramatically, and fishers reported the disappearance of cod from inshore waters and the need to go further offshore. Techniques based on human demography and statistics were used to establish the dynamics of particular fish species (Bavington 2010: 18–35).

The use of steam to power fishing craft by the late 1800s in Europe, the development of freezing technology, and the invention of the bottom trawling net all served to revolutionize fishing (Kurlansky 1997: 112–25). The combination of more 'efficient' craft (able to travel longer distances faster and with less human effort) and more 'efficient' gear such as the trawl net (able to scoop up larger quantities of fish faster and with less human effort) marked a qualitative and quantitative shift in the nature of fishing in the early decades of the twentieth century, from a reliance on 'passive' technologies that had to wait for the fish, to more 'active' ones by which fish could be chased and scooped up aggressively.

The greatest expansion in fishing took place following the Second World War, when the fishery became harnessed to the goal of national economic development, both in Europe, North America, and Japan, and in the newly independent nations of Asia, Africa, and the Caribbean. In these latter parts of the world, the fishery had been carried on for centuries using craft with limited propulsion power, using wind and human effort. Under the modernization approach that shaped most post-colonial development plans, efforts were made to introduce mechanized, fuel-dependent propulsion craft and fishing gear like trawlers and purse seiners (Kurien 1985).

In the decades following the Second World War the industrial fishery expanded and became firmly established. During the war, the three innovations—powerful ships, onboard freezing facilities, and massive dragging nets—had come together in the huge factory ship. Today's factory ship may be 450 feet or longer, powered by twin diesel engines of more than 6000 horsepower, pulling a trawl net with an opening large enough to swallow a jumbo jet. The trawl net is hauled up every four hours, 24 hours a day. 'Tickler chains' hang from the net to stir up the bottom, making noise and clouding the water, thus forcing the groundfish such as cod that hide at the bottom of the ocean to flee into the net. The net catches everything in its way, and leaves behind a desert on the ocean floor (Kurlansky 1997: 139–40). Modern devices such as global positioning systems and echo-sounders further enable ships to chase and locate fish more efficiently.

The postwar expansion took place along three dimensions—*geographical*, to more coastlines and continental shelves; *bathymetric*, to greater depths, especially in the high seas, due to new technologies like trawlers and long lines; and *taxonomic*, to include all kinds of new species, several of which were earlier rejected for food purposes (Pauly 2009: 216). Also, as Pauly notes, at this time the fishery appeared to behave like any other sector of the economy, with increased inputs leading to increased outputs. Catch figures grew exponentially around the world. In Atlantic Canada, annual cod catches that had fluctuated from less than 100,000 tonnes to a maximum of 300,000 tonnes up to the 1940s expanded to a historical high referred to as the 'killer spike' in 1968, when over 800,000 tonnes of cod were landed (Bavington 2010: 17).

The emphasis on the fishery as a source of national revenue led to another development. The freedom of the seas (*mare liberum*), a key principle of the international law that had evolved in Europe since the seventeenth century, had allowed ships belonging to European and other fishing nations like Japan to fish unchallenged in seas distant from their own coasts. But with fish and mineral resources under the sea becoming important national assets, more and more nations declared sovereignty over their territorial seas. This became codified in the UN **Convention on the Law of the Sea (UNCLOS)** of 1982, under which each nation-state had sovereignty over an **exclusive economic zone (EEZ)** extending 200 miles from its coast. The EEZ boundaries enclosed some 90 per cent of the world's fishing grounds, and coastal states were given the responsibility for their conservation (Allison 2001: 937–9). But, as Seckinelgin (2006: 15) notes, the facts that 'throughout the convention, marine living resources are recognized as an agent of development' and that the 'ecological life of the resources is subsumed under the *raison d'état* in relation to "development"' meant that maximizing the exploitation of fisheries resources, rather than conservation, became the primary goal of states.

With the declaration of EEZs, countries acted swiftly to evict foreign fishing vessels from their territorial waters, as Canada did with the French and Spanish fleets fishing in the Grand Banks off Newfoundland. Canada then encouraged domestic investment to enable exploitation of the resources, because the UNCLOS dictated that fish within an EEZ should be harvested at their maximum sustainable yields. Any country unable to do so should allow other states access to their waters (Bavington 2010: 32).

This requirement to harvest fish at their MSYs within an EEZ also set in motion a North–South dynamic peculiar to the fishery. Most newly independent states in the South lacked both the fishing capacity to harvest their own resources fully and the data collection and surveillance capacity to keep poachers out of the vast

200-mile EEZ. Many of them therefore signed Fisheries Access Agreements with countries of the North, such as that between the African–Caribbean–Pacific Group of States (ACP) and the European Union, inviting the EU's distant-water fleets to continue to operate in ACP waters in exchange for a fee. These agreements enable industrialized countries to use their advantages in technology and finance to keep their access to developing countries' fisheries (Kaczynski and Fluharty 2002; O'Riordan 2000).

The UNCLOS fails at conservation also because it attempts to manage ecological zones through the creation of political boundaries, whereas living resources have their own spatial extents and logics that do not always follow national EEZ boundaries (Seckinelgin 2006). This can be seen in the challenge of managing deep-sea species that straddle EEZs or are highly migratory, such as the world's highest-value fish, the bluefin tuna: the Atlantic bluefin tuna ranges from the equator to Newfoundland, from Turkey to the Gulf of Mexico (Bestor 2000); a single Pacific tuna was tracked crossing the Pacific Ocean three times, covering a distance of 25,000 miles (Grescoe 2008). The International Commission for the Conservation of Atlantic Tunas, which has representation from all states that fish in the Atlantic or trade in its fish, has failed miserably to manage the tuna sustainably. This failure is due to the low deterrence cost of violating quotas compared to the potential profit from this highly valuable species.

The difficulties of international coordination can also be seen in the problem of **illegal, unregulated, and unreported (IUU) fishing**, especially in the high seas. Catch may be landed on shores of countries where regulation is minimal, or processed off-shore on factory ships. Where there is a fixed quota of a species, by-catch of lower-value fish other than the target species may be dumped at sea. Part of the recent growth in IUU fishing is due to large factory ships subsidized by rich states but unable to find enough fish in their own waters (Jacquet and Pauly 2007: 310; Pauly 2009; World Bank and FAO 2009).

Factors other than overfishing also contribute to the depletion of marine life. These include chemical and organic pollution and the destruction of habitats, such as mangroves and other coastal wetlands, for agriculture, aquaculture, urbanization, and industrialization. The effects of climate change are also beginning to be seen in the heating of the ocean, rising acidity levels, and falling metabolism rates of marine life. Yet, as Ward and Myers (2005) demonstrate, compelling evidence shows that the advent of industrial fishing and the intensification of fishing around the world have been the largest factors in the declining catches beginning in the early 1990s. Since that time, efforts have been underway to arrest this decline and address the growing crisis in the fishery. The next section will review some of these efforts and their effectiveness.

Solutions to the Crisis: Dilemmas of Scale, Authority, and Knowledge

The above sections indicate some of the specific requirements of fisheries governance, given the mobile and complex nature of the resource and the variety of scales—international, national, and local—at which there has to be coordination. The challenge is not simply to sustain the fish stocks and the marine ecosystem, but to do so in a way that continues to provide a healthy source of protein for millions and employment to large numbers of relatively low-income people around the world.

Part of the complexity of governance also arises from the fact that different actors involved in the fisheries bring very different, often conflicting, perspectives on the causes of declining catches and on how best the goals of providing food and jobs might be met. The fishery is studied by ecologists, marine biologists, economists, fisheries scientists (who combine biological knowledge and statistical skills), and social scientists such as anthropologists and geographers.

Fishers and the community organizers who work with them are also important sources of knowledge. The chief debates occur along two related questions: Where should the locus of governance lie—in the state and its experts, the market and consumers, or producers and their communities? What knowledge is needed for effective governance?

The traditional approach to fisheries governance, especially in advanced industrial countries like Canada, placed it in the hands of the government. Government ministries like Fisheries and Oceans Canada (DFO) employ fisheries scientists to work out the MSY and **total allowable catch (TAC)** for particular species, monitor the catch, and set other regulations such as closed seasons. The TAC is then divided up between individual fishers in the form of an individual quota (IQ): the right to catch a certain quantity of each species each year within a given area. Since the 1980s, these quotas have been designated as assets that can be bought, sold, or transferred. Management through quota systems is the dominant mode in the Atlantic and Pacific fisheries in Canada, where quotas are sold for all the major fisheries, such as cod, salmon, and snow crab (Bavington 2010; DFO 2008).

Individual quotas are a form of private property rights in the fishery, created in response to an influential argument made by economists that overfishing occurs because of the absence of those rights in the fishery, or what they call the 'tragedy of the commons' (Hardin 1968; Scott 1955). As Bavington (2010) argues, however, the Atlantic cod fishery was managed according to these measures—was not an unmanaged or open fishery—and yet it collapsed, in part because there is nothing in the logic of IQs to prevent overfishing. Quota owners may find it makes more economic sense during a bumper harvest to exceed the quota and pay the fine. The species-specific approach means that there is no way of measuring the harm done to non-target species (by-catch) which are often dumped in order to meet the quota of the target species (Copes 1999).

The difficulties of state-controlled fisheries management, coupled with the rise of neo-liberal policies that entail a reduced role for the state in the economy, have engendered three parallel shifts since the late 1980s: adoption of international codes and conventions, increased influence of consumers and the marketplace, and increased influence of fishing communities and organizations.

International Codes and Conventions

The first shift is the adoption of new international codes and conventions that recognize the role of non-state actors in the fishery. These include Chapter 17 of Agenda 21, the plan of action adopted at the first UN Conference on Environment and Development (UNCED) held in Rio de Janeiro in 1992; the 1993 Convention on Biological Diversity; the **FAO Code of Conduct for Responsible Fisheries** of 1995; and the 2001 **UN Fish Stocks Agreement** on Straddling Stocks and Highly Migratory Fish Stocks. These, along with the UNCLOS and many bilateral and multilateral regional fisheries agreements, constitute the normative framework for the management of marine resources.

These international agreements have led to the establishment of regional fisheries management organizations such as the International Commission for the Conservation of Atlantic Tunas, mentioned earlier in the chapter, and are especially important in trying to address problems related to straddling and highly migratory stocks and to IUU fishing. But they are non-binding for the most part and, like all international treaties and agreements, very hard to enforce. Nevertheless, these agreements—the FAO Code of Conduct in particular—are significant in enshrining two important principles that have become the reference point for sustainable fisheries: the **precautionary principle**, which states that 'the absence of adequate scientific information should not be used as a reason for postponing or failing to take conservation and management measures' (Article 7.5); and the **ecosystem approach**, which moves away from modelling individual stocks to recognizing the interdependence of marine flora and fauna and their sensitivity to many influences from destructive fishing gear to land-based pollution.

Consumers and the Marketplace

The second shift is seen in consumers' greater role in regulating fishing practices through the mechanism of the market. This is appropriate to the fishery, given that fish and seafood are now the most-traded food commodities in the world, and that half of all food production in this sector enters international trade. Campaigns around overfishing led by NGOs like Greenpeace combined with growing consumer concern about the health effects and sustainability of fishing and aquaculture have led to consumer-driven sustainability campaigns. In Europe recently, after Greenpeace launched its sustainable seafood campaign ranking supermarkets on the basis of their seafood sourcing policies, many of the largest supermarkets adopted seafood procurement policies which make sustainability a key criterion in their sourcing (Hunter and King 2008: 31). Three years into Greenpeace's campaign in Canada, only three of the nine supermarkets that control 60 per cent of Canada's grocery market had passing marks on their sustainable sourcing efforts (Leeder 2011).

Consumer consciousness has led to the emergence of an increasingly popular form of labelling: **certification** or **eco-labelling**. This form of marketing incentive promotes consumer demand for fish caught or raised in environmentally and/or socially sustainable ways, and rewards producers for using responsible fisheries practices. The certifiers may be independent bodies such as the Marine Stewardship Council or large supermarket chains such as Carrefour, a transnational chain based in France, which has its own *peche responsable* label (Sharma 2009).

However, market-based certification is no guarantee of reliable information for consumers or of sustainability. Certification bodies

and schemes proliferate with no unanimity of criteria among them; some take into account only environmental sustainability, while others include food safety and social criteria such as labour standards (FAO 2009: 96). The use of a quota system is often taken as evidence of sustainable management by certifying bodies; most fisheries certified as sustainable are industrial fisheries under quota management, rather than small-scale, community-based fisheries. Importantly, as Jacquet and Pauly (2007) note, in an era of increasing awareness that fisheries management must be ecosystem based, the rhetoric of seafood campaigns based on a species-specific approach may represent a step backward.

Fishing Communities and Organizations

The third shift is toward a greater role for fishing communities and organizations in managing the fishery. Organizations such as the Maritime Fishermen's Union in New Brunswick and Nova Scotia, the Canadian Council of Professional Fish Harvesters, the International Collective in Support of Fishworkers, and the World Forum of Fisher Peoples firmly assert a role for small-scale, community-based producers in fisheries production and governance (Sall et al. 2002). They argue that their reliance on smaller vessels that are less dependent on fossil fuels; their labour-intensive techniques that generate greater employment; their interest in the long-term survival of the fishery; and their holistic, inherited, and experiential knowledge of the ecosystem allow for a more sustainable and equitable development of the fishery than the destructive and overly efficient fishing techniques and the concentration of profits that characterize the industrial sector (Pauly 2007).

Small-scale fishers challenge the knowledge and approach underlying scientific fisheries management. The first element of this approach is the economists' assumption that the absence of private property rights is the chief cause of overfishing. The fishers' argument, backed by anthropological studies, is that much of the inshore fishery was historically governed by various community-based **common property resource** management regimes that regulated access and extraction (McCay and Acheson 1987; Cordell and McKean 1992; Bavinck 1996), many of which were delegitimized as a direct outcome of the state's harnessing of fisheries management to national economic development after the Second World War (Allison 2001: 938).

Fishers have also criticized the assumption, expressed in measures such as the MSY, TAC, and IQ, that increasingly sophisticated modelling and forecasting tools enable scientific prediction and control of the fishery. The failure of scientists to explain the recent disappearance and reappearance of the Fraser River salmon (Hume 2010; Hunter 2010) seems to back this critique. Fishers have argued instead for an ecosystem approach and an increased role for their own experiential knowledge in dialogue with the 'expert' knowledge of scientists (Mathew 2010). Fishing people have historically held the sea in respect, seeing it as a powerful entity that must be propitiated and cared for in order for it to provide. The Aboriginal approach to the fishery (Claxton 2008; Metallic 2008) exemplifies this deep respect and sense of relationship. In Claxton's words (2008: 54):

> The WSÁNEĆ people successfully governed their traditional fishery for thousands of years, prior to contact. This was not just because there were laws and rules in place, and that everybody followed them, but there was also a different way of thinking about fish and fishing, which included a profound respect. At the end of the net, a ring of willow was woven into the net, which allowed some salmon to escape. This is more than a simple act of conservation. . . . It represents a profound respect for salmon. It was believed that the runs of salmon were lineages, and if some were allowed to return to

their home rivers, then those lineages would always continue. . . . The salmon are our relatives.

The outcome of the sustained advocacy by the small-scale producers can be seen in agreements such as the FAO Code of Conduct, which recognizes their important contributions to employment and income and food security, and includes sections on the precautionary principle, the ecosystem approach to management, the mandatory use of selective fishing gear, and the traditional knowledge of fishers. Small-scale producers have also spearheaded attempts to evolve a form of collaborative or **co-management** between the state and fishing communities (World Bank 2004: 37); sought to intervene in market-based management, proposing certification schemes in which the advantages of the small-scale sector, such as the use of less destructive gear, unique processing techniques, and sails (i.e., using wind power rather than fossil fuels), are given credit (Vandergeest 2007; Sharma 2009); and initiated experiments in **community-supported fishery** whereby producers directly supply consumers who wish to support sustainable fishing practices (Moore 2010).

Is Aquaculture a Solution?

Aquaculture is a broad term that refers to a range of practices including the centuries-old carp farming in small ponds across China, the conversion of rice fields into shrimp farms across south and southeast Asia, the highly controlled marine salmon farms in Canada, and the marine pens in the Mediterranean where juvenile bluefin tuna captured in the wild are held and fattened for export to the Japanese market.

The FAO 2010 report notes that the supply from aquaculture more than compensates for the stagnation of capture fisheries and the growth of human population. Global per capita supply from aquaculture increased from 0.7 kg in 1970 to 7.8 kg in 2008, an average annual growth rate of 6.9 per cent. Aquaculture now accounts for 46 per cent of all fish and seafood production for food and is set to overtake capture fisheries as a source of food fish, propelled by increased investment and further decreases in the stocks of wild fish. Globally, the number of people engaged in capture fisheries has declined while the number in aquaculture has gone up. Since 1980, employment in the aquaculture sector has grown faster than both the world's population and employment in traditional agriculture.

In Canada, aquaculture is a relatively new commercial activity, but by 2005 it already made up approximately 25 per cent of all Canadian fish and seafood production. The leading farmed marine species are Atlantic salmon, blue mussels, chinook salmon, Pacific oysters, and American oysters. Inland species like trout are also farmed (DFO 2008).

Some forms of aquaculture, especially that described as **intensive aquaculture**, where fish and shrimp are raised in industrial conditions, have proven to have several harmful effects. The high price fetched by shrimp in global markets has spurred the conversion of rice fields into shrimp farms across coastal south and southeast Asia, with obvious implications for the supply of rice (Flaherty et al. 1999). There, and in other places such as Ecuador, fragile coastal ecosystems such as mangroves and estuaries have been destroyed when converted to shrimp farms (Stonich et al. 1997). Problems with salination of inland areas and pollution by antibiotics and other organic pollutants have been noted in several parts of the world, including salmon farms in British Columbia and Atlantic Canada. There are also concerns around escaped farmed fish carrying sea lice and diseases into the wild (Young and Mathews 2010; Halweil 2008). Finally, the raising of carnivorous fish like salmon and tuna have created a phenomenon parallel to 'fishing down the food web'—which has been labelled 'farming up the food web' (Pauly 2009: 219)— the use of captured smaller, lower-value fish to feed and fatten higher-value predator fish. Given that the smaller fish are often exported

from LIFDCs where they would otherwise have been eaten, the net impact of this kind of aquaculture on global food security seems to be negative. But there are also examples of organic marine salmon farms that pay far greater care to ecosystem impacts (Halweil 2008).

There are fewer concerns with the **extensive aquaculture** that takes place in inland water bodies such as lakes, rivers, and ponds. The fish raised in these farms are largely herbivorous, and tend to be less vulnerable to disease, thus requiring fewer antibiotics and chemicals. The bulk of the aquaculture carried out in China is of this kind, as is the trout farming in Canada's lakes.

For many, the shift to the culture rather than the capture of fish is the natural and long-overdue last step in our evolution from hunters and gatherers to settled agriculturalists. This progression is valid to the extent that it helps take pressure off marine stocks and gives them a chance to regenerate. However, our existing levels of urbanization and industrialization leave too little land for the amount of aquaculture necessary to substitute for the entire marine capture fishery. Nor are there obvious solutions to the pollution, salination, and disease associated with intensive aquaculture. Further, a sustainable capture fishery remains vital for the employment and food security of millions of producers. An organic, ecologically friendly extensive system of farming small herbivorous fish in existing inland water bodies (an approach that Grescoe [2008] labels 'bottomfeeding') is probably the best option, but we must also reconcile ourselves to eating far smaller quantities.

Conclusion

As long as demand for fish and seafood remains high in world markets, production will continue to attempt to cater to it. Developing countries in particular are likely to direct more and more of their fish production to export in search of foreign currency. Fishing access agreements and the reflagging of fishing vessels under the national flag of developing countries owning large fisheries resources are the equivalent of the purchase or lease of land in Latin America and Africa by agro-industrial corporations to supply food to wealthier countries. Unless serious attempts are made at generating alternative sources of employment and national income, the risk is that the fisheries resources of developing nations will remain under high pressure from international markets and the contribution of fish to local food security may decrease. Globally, as noted in the FAO's 2010 *The State of World Fisheries and Aquaculture* report, the growth in the proportion of over-exploited or depleted fisheries is a matter of urgent concern. On the other hand, there is new evidence that management measures have worked in some areas (Worm et al. 2009; FAO 2010: 42), and the rate of decline has been arrested.

It is possible that with increased consumer awareness of the need to limit demand, states' commitment to stop subsidizing large factory fleets and to regulate destructive technology more stringently, the shift to a governance approach that gives a leading role to small-scale fishers and to a perspective that respects the force and cunning of nature, and the judicious combination of capture fishery with extensive inland aquaculture of herbivorous species, we may yet be able to turn back the crisis before it is too late.

This chapter has provided a picture of the crisis in the fisheries, arguing that it can be fully understood only in a global context. The crisis is multidimensional, and affects not only food security but also ecological sustainability and social justice. While multiple factors have led to the crisis, central among them are the burgeoning demand for fish as both luxury food and fishmeal and the dominance of an industrial fishery using highly destructive craft and gear. The chapter explored diverse approaches to governing the fishery and managing the crisis, and argued that an approach that gives priority in production and management to small-scale community-based fishers is most likely to achieve the related goals of food security, environmental sustainability, and equitable development. It concluded with a section on aquaculture, noting that while an extensive inland aquaculture of small, herbivorous fish could help compensate for the decline of the capture fishery, it should not, for ecological and social reasons, be expected to replace it entirely.

Discussion Questions

1. What does 'crisis in the fishery' refer to?

2. What factors led to the decline of the cod fishery in Atlantic Canada?

3. To what extent can aquaculture replace a capture fishery?

4. At what scale should the fishery be managed—internationally, nationally, or locally?

5. What are the most promising solutions to the crisis in the fishery?

Further Reading

1. For statistics and occasional reports on trends and current issues in the fishery, good sources are the website of Fisheries and Oceans Canada (www.dfo-mpo.gc.ca/), and the FAO's *The State of World Fisheries and Aquaculture* report which is released every two years (www.fao.org/fishery/sofia/en). A gold mine for documents and resources on the fisheries worldwide is the website of the International Collective in Support of Fishworkers (http://icsf.net/) and their journal, *Samudra Report*.

2. Mark Kurlansky's *Cod: A Biography of the Fish that Changed the World* is a highly readable, non-academic account of the rise and fall of the North Atlantic cod fishery. Dean Bavington's *Managed Annihilation: An Unnatural History of the Newfoundland Cod Collapse* is a more academic, but very accessible, study of fisheries policy and scientific management which makes a passionate argument for a less managerial approach to fishing and to nature.

3. Daniel Pauly's 'Beyond Duplicity and Ignorance in Global Fisheries' and James McGoodwin's classic *Crisis in World Fisheries; People, Problems, and Policies* provide excellent overviews of the complex web of technology, markets, and management regimes that have contributed to the global crisis in the fishery. On the limits and successes of actual consumer campaigns around the fishery, see Hunter and King's (Greenpeace) *Out of Stock: Supermarkets and the Future of Seafood*. Taras Grescoe's *Bottomfeeder: How to Eat Ethically in a World of Vanishing Seafood* tries to help us think practically through a question that many of us are concerned with.

4. Specifically with regard to whether aquaculture is a sustainable and healthy alternative, see Brian Halweil's 'Farming Fish for the Future'.

References

Allison, E.H. 2001. 'Big Laws, Small Catches: Global Ocean Governance and the Fisheries Crisis'. *Journal of International Development* 13: 933–50.

Bavinck, Maarten. 1996. 'Fisher Regulations along the Coromandel Coast: A Case of Collective Control of Common Pool Resources'. *Marine Policy* 20(6): 198–200.

Bavington, Dean. 2010. *Managed Annihilation: An Unnatural History of the Newfoundland Cod Collapse*. Vancouver: UBC Press.

Bestor, Theodore C. 2000. 'How Sushi Went Global'. *Foreign Policy* 121 (November/December). Available at www.foreignpolicy.com/articles/2000/11/01/how_sushi_went_global.

———. 2004. *Tsukiji: The Fish Market at the Center of the World*. Berkeley: University of California Press.

Claxton, N. X. 2008. 'ISTÁ SĆIÁNEW_, ISTÁ SX_OLE 'To Fish as Formerly': The Douglas Treaties and the WSÁNEĆ Reef-Net Fisheries'. In *Lighting the Eighth Fire: The Liberation, Resurgence and Protection of Indigenous Nations*, ed. Leanne Simpson. Winnipeg: Arbeiter Ring Publishing, 47–58.

Clover, C. 2004. *The End of the Line: How Overfishing Is Changing the World and What We Eat*. London: Ebury Press.

Copes, Parzival. 1999. 'Coastal Resources for Whom?' *Samudra*, September 1999.

Cordell, John, and Margaret A. McKean. 1992. 'Sea Tenure in Bahia, Brazil'. In *Making the Commons Work: Theory, Practice and Policy*, ed. Daniel W. Bromley. San Francisco: Institute for Contemporary Studies, 183–205.

Devine, J.D., K.D. Baker, and R.L. Haedrich. 2006. 'Fisheries: Deep-Sea Fishes Qualify as Endangered'. *Nature* 439 (5 January). Available at www.nature.com/nature/journal/v439/n7072/abs/439029a.html.

DFO. 2004. '2004 Costs and Earnings Survey, Atlantic Region'. Accessed 10 October 2010 at www.dfo-mpo.gc.ca/stats/commercial/ces/content-eng.htm#n10AtlanticFishingIndustryOverview.

———. 2008. *Canadian Fisheries Statistics 2006*. Ottawa: Fisheries and Oceans Canada.

Flaherty, M., P. Vandergeest, and P. Miller. 1999. 'Rice Paddy or Shrimp Pond: Tough Decisions in Rural Thailand'. *World Development* 27: 12.

FAO. 1995. *Code of Conduct for Responsible Fisheries*. Rome: FAO.

———. 2009. *State of World Fisheries and Aquaculture 2008*. Rome: FAO.

———. 2010. *State of World Fisheries and Aquaculture 2010*. Rome: FAO.

Grescoe, Taras. 2008. *Bottomfeeder: How to Eat Ethically in a World of Vanishing Seafood*. New York: Bloomsbury.

Halweil, Brian. 2008. 'Farming Fish for the Future'. *Worldwatch Report* 176, Washington, DC: Worldwatch Institute.

Hardin, Gareth. 1968. 'The Tragedy of the Commons'. *Science* 162: 1243–8.

Hume, Mark. 2010. 'Commission into Sockeye Salmon Stocks Releases Areas of Inquiry'. *The Globe and Mail*, 9 June. Available at www.theglobeandmail.com/news/national/british-columbia/commission-into-sockeye-salmon-stocks-releases-areas-of-inquiry/article1597924/.

Hunter, B., and S. King. 2008. *Out of Stock: Supermarkets and the Future of Seafood*. Greenpeace Canada. Accessed 10 October 2010 at www.greenpeace.org/canada/en/campaigns/Seafood/resources1/documents/out-of-stock/.

Hunter, J. 2010. 'Surprising Salmon Run Masks an Industry in Crisis'. *The Globe and Mail*, 26 August. Available at www.theglobeandmail.com/news/national/british-columbia/surprising-salmon-run-masks-an-industry-in-crisis/article1686603/.

Jacquet, J.L., and D. Pauly. 2007. 'The Rise of Seafood Campaigns in an Era of Collapsing Fisheries'. *Marine Policy* 31: 308–13.

———. 2008. 'Trade Secrets: Renaming and Mislabelling of Seafood'. *Marine Policy* 32: 309–18.

Kaczynski, V.M., and D.L. Fluharty. 2002. 'European Policies in West Africa: Who Benefits from Fisheries Agreements?' *Marine Policy* 26: 75–93.

Kurien, John. 1985. 'Technical Assistance Projects and Socio-economic Change: Norwegian Intervention in Kerala's Fisheries Development'. *Economic and Political Weekly* 20, 25/26: A77–9.

Kurlansky, Mark. 1997. *Cod: A Biography of the Fish that Changed the World*. New York: Walker and Company.

Leeder, Jessica. 2011. 'Grocers Get Mild Praise for Seafood Practices'. *The Globe and Mail*, 7 July, A8.

Mathew, Sebastian. 2010. 'Fishery-Dependent Information and the Ecosystem Approach: What Role Should Fishers and their Knowledge Play?' Keynote address to the FDI 2010 conference, Galway, Ireland, August. http://icsf.net/icsf2006/uploads/resources/presentations/pdf/english/1282814022643***Sebastian_Mathew_Keynote_Address_FDI_2010_fINAL.pdf.

McCay, B.J., and J.M. Acheson. 1987. 'The Question of the Commons: The Culture and Ecology of Communal Resources'. Tucson: The University of Arizona Press.

McGoodwin, James R. 1990. *Crisis in World Fisheries; People, Problems, and Policies*. Stanford: Stanford University Press.

Metallic, Fred (Gopit). 2008. 'Strengthening our Relations in Gespe'gewa'gi, the Seventh District of Mi'gma'gi'. In *Lighting the Eighth Fire: The Liberation, Resurgence and Protection of Indigenous Nations*, ed. Leanne Simpson. Winnipeg: Arbeiter Ring Publishing, 59–72.

Mitchell, Alanna. 2009. *Sea Sick: The Global Ocean in Crisis*. Toronto: McClelland & Stewart.

Moore, Oliver. 2010. 'Shoal Survivors'. *The Globe and Mail*, 21 July, L3.

Myers, R.A., and J. Worm. 2003. 'Rapid Worldwide Depletion of Predatory Fishing Communities'. *Nature* 423(15 May): 280–3.

O'Riordan, Brian. 2000. 'Fisheries Agreements: Socializing Costs, Privatizing Benefits'. *Samdura* 26(August): 16–22.

Pauly, Daniel. 2007. 'Small but Mighty: Elevate the Role of Small-scale Fishers in the World Market'. *Conservation Magazine* 8(3): 25.

———. 2009. 'Beyond Duplicity and Ignorance in Global Fisheries'. *Scientia Marina* 73(2): 215–24.

Pauly, D., S. Christensen, J. Dalsgaard, R. Froese, and F.C. Torres Jr. 1998. 'Fishing Down Marine Food Webs'. *Science* 279: 860–3.

Sall, Aliou, Michael Belliveau, and Nalini Nayak. 2002. *Conversations: A Trialogue on Power, Intervention and Organization in the Fisheries*. Chennai, India: International Collective in Support of Fishworkers.

Scott, A. 1955. 'The Fishery: The Objectives of Sole Ownership'. *Journal of Political Economy* 63(2): 16–124.

Seckinelgin, H. 2006. *The Environment and International Politics: International Fisheries, Heidegger, and Social Method*. London and New York: Routledge.

Sharma, Chandrika. 2009. 'Market-Driven Conservation: Social issues in Certification Schemes for Capture Fisheries'. Presentation to the National Seminar on Conservation and Sustainability of Coastal Living Resources of India. http://icsf.net/icsf2006/uploads/resources/presentations/pdf/english/1259903293538***CIFT_ICSF2.ppt.

Stonich, S., J.R. Bort, and L.L. Ovares. 1997. 'Globalization of Shrimp Mariculture: The Impact on Social Justice and Environmental Quality in Central America'. *Society and Natural Resources* 10.

Vandergeest, Peter. 2007. 'Certification and Communities: Alternatives for Regulating the Environmental and Social Impacts of Shrimp Farming'. *World Development* 35(7): 1152–71.

Ward, P., and R.A. Myers. 2005. 'Shifts in Open-Ocean Fish Communities Coinciding with the Commencement of Commercial Fishing'. *Ecology* 86(4): 835–47.

World Bank. 2004. *Saving Fish and Fishers: Towards Sustainable and Equitable Governance of the Global Fishing Sector*. Washington, DC: The World Bank, Agriculture and Rural Development Department.

World Bank and FAO. 2008. *The Sunken Billions: The Economic Justification for Fisheries Reform*. Washington, DC: The World Bank, Agriculture and Rural Development Department.

Worm, Boris, Edward B. Barbier, Nicola Beaumont, et al. 2006. 'Impacts of Biodiversity Loss on Ocean Ecosystem Services'. *Science* 314: 787–90.

Worm, Boris, Ray Hilborn, Julia K. Baum, et al. 2009. 'Rebuilding Global Fisheries'. *Science* 325: 578–85.

Young, Nathan, and Ralph Matthews. 2010. *The Aquaculture Controversy in Canada: Activism, Policy and Contested Science*. Vancouver: UBC Press.

12

Spatial Colonization of Food Environments by Pseudo-food Companies

Precursors of a Health Crisis[1]

Anthony Winson

Learning Objectives

Through this chapter, you can:

1. Better understand the socio-economic and political determinants of key food environments such as supermarkets and schools
2. Become acquainted with some novel conceptual tools that help in understanding what drives unhealthy eating among Canadians

Introduction

Canadian society today, like that of most other developed countries, is facing a looming health crisis related to the characteristics of diets and lifestyles as they have evolved over the last several decades. The incidence of weight gain and obesity has reached levels never before seen, as has the incidence of diseases such as diabetes, which is closely associated with excessive weight (Statistics Canada 2002; Tremblay and Willms 2000).[2] The recent Canadian Health Measures Survey provides data on measured (as opposed to self-reported) body composition,[3] and gives us the most accurate picture in this regard to date. It indicates that between 1981 and 2009, among 15- to 19-year-old boys, those classified as overweight or obese rose from 14 per cent to 31 per cent. Among girls in the same age group, that category increased from

14 per cent to 25 per cent. Moreover, between 2007 and 2009, about 1 per cent of adult Canadians were underweight, 37 per cent were overweight, and 24 per cent were obese. The survey also notes dramatic declines in fitness levels among adults aged 20 to 39. The percentage of these adults whose waist circumference places them at high risk for health problems more than quadrupled in this period, from 5 per cent to 21 per cent among men, and from 6 per cent to 31 per cent among women.[4]

Serious chronic diseases such as type II diabetes are strongly correlated with excess weight and sedentary lifestyle. Canada, like many other countries, has seen a disturbing increase in the incidence of type II diabetes in recent years and there is evidence that its rate of increase has been seriously underestimated (Lipscombe and Hux 2007). The tendency of governments so far, to the extent that they have come to terms with this serious issue, has largely been to focus on issues related to sedentary lifestyles and to encourage greater physical activity for different segments of the population. Our problematic contemporary food environment has not been tackled by policy makers, with very few exceptions. Undoubtedly this inaction is at least partly due to the political sensitivity of the issue, and the powerful vested interests that control our food system.

While various factors shape eating behaviour, including individual psychological factors, family influences, peer pressures, the physical environment, and so on (see Raine 2005), political economic determinants of diet have yet to receive the full attention they warrant. As Power argues, 'it is important to explore how the food industry shapes social norms around eating in Canada; how those in different positions in social space (e.g., class, sex, ethnicity, age, etc.) are targeted by food marketers; and how people take up and act on those marketing messages and thus produce and reproduce food norms and culture' (2005).

This chapter considers the contemporary food environment as a problematic subject in need of critical analysis. It examines Canadian institutional food environments with a view to understanding the key factors shaping the nutritional content of their offerings. The focus here is on two institutional domains—the supermarket chain store and the high school food environment. It draws on the author's own recent research and that of others to make the case that the degradation of contemporary food environments in Canada plays a significant role in exacerbating widespread weight gain and obesity and their related serious health outcomes.

Conceptual Issues

In previously published research I argue for the use of several concepts that aid in understanding the present content and factors shaping

contemporary food environments, which are also discussed here: **pseudo-foods, differential profits, corporate concentration, mass advertising and product differentiation**, and **spatial colonization** (Winson 2004). In addition I will attempt to clarify the concept of **food environments** and show how the earlier concepts can be used in exploring food environments.

Food environments, as termed here, are those institutional spheres where food is displayed for sale and/or consumed.[5] Until the not-too-distant past, food was largely produced and consumed within the household in the countryside. This unity of production and consumption prevailed for thousands of years, although food markets have existed at least as early as the Incan, Mayan, and classical Greco-Roman civilizations (see Garnsey 1999, ch 2). However, the rise of industrial capitalism undermined this unity in what became the developed world, as masses of people were forced off the land and into the industrializing cities. (This pattern has been the recent experience of much of the global South as well.) The household unity of production and consumption that was a central institution of agrarian societies for millennia has largely been broken. This fact alone has been fundamental to the development of the food industry. It has also allowed processors, and more recently retailers, to dramatically shift food consumption patterns and shape mass diets.

Today some noticeable differences distinguish the procurement of food from its consumption. Foodstuffs today are among the world's most valuable commodities to be bought, transported, and sold, and indeed a very significant proportion of our labour force is in some way involved with these commodity chains. For most people, in keeping with the long-standing evolution of capitalist economies all over the world, food is procured from private, for-profit institutions, which are now dominated by supermarket chain-store operations that increasingly operate on a global scale. It had been thought that this situation characterized only the developed countries, but recent research has made clear the major inroads of supermarket chains in the global South as well, particularly in Asia and Latin America (Reardon and Berdegué 2002; Reardon et al. 2003).

Unlike procurement, food consumption is still characterized by the continuing existence of not-for-profit institutional spheres. At-home consumption is one of the most obvious and important of these, and in this sphere market pressures are not yet as intrusive in shaping the foods we consume. Another significant not-for-profit sphere of food consumption is the school, where food environments traditionally were run on a not-for-profit basis, although this situation is rapidly changing in many jurisdictions, with notable consequences. But even in institutional spheres where profit-making constraints do not hold sway the influence of market pressures may be felt, as I argue below. Overall, however, consumption is increasingly taking place in *for-profit* institutional settings; time constraints on family life, both parents working away from home, the loss of culinary skills, and other influences determine that more and more people find they must eat away from home, or eat food prepared by others elsewhere that is then brought home. As Austin et al. (2005: 1575) note, Americans now spend almost half of their food expenditures away from home, and 'among youths aged 12 to 18 years, the percentage of total energy intake consumed from fast-food and other restaurants has increased from 6.5 per cent in 1977–1978 to 19.3 per cent in 1994–1996'. This situation implies loss of control over nutritional content, as decisions around ingredients (e.g., quantities of sugar and salt) and preparation techniques (e.g., deep-frying versus steaming vegetables) are alienated to other actors in the food system.

Pseudo-foods

Pseudo-foods are those nutrient-poor edible products that are typically high in fat, sugar, and salt and often provide over-abundant calories. They are notably low in nutrients such

as proteins, minerals, and vitamins essential for health. Pseudo-foods are typically an important component in what has been termed in Britain the high fat, salt, and sugar (HFSS) foods, which are the subject of recent legislation that restricts advertising them to children and youth (OfCom 2006). While pseudo-foods include products more commonly known as 'junk foods' (candy bars, chips, soft drinks, and the like), they also include products not usually thought of as a junk food. For example, many of the juice 'beverages' sold today qualify as pseudo-foods because of their high sugar content and absence of the nutrients associated with products made from pure juices. Many of the frozen dairy products that are proliferating in supermarkets in recent years can be considered pseudo-foods, because of their high fat and sugar content and low levels of essential nutrients. Ice cream, the dominant frozen dairy product in supermarkets and one that now occupies more shelf space than fluid milk, typically has around 50 per cent of its calories coming from fat, although in some varieties this figure is as high as 70 per cent (Nutribase 2001: 309–12).[6] These and other high-profile supermarket products such as pre-sweetened breakfast cereals, plus the copious quantities of soft drinks, confectionaries, and sugar- and trans fat–laden baked goods, as well as the proliferation of salty snack products (which average 50 per cent calories from fat [Nutribase 2001: 460–3]), constitute a substantial part of the modern supermarket food environment and are also ubiquitous in other food environments. Table 12.1 provides a graphic illustration of the nutritional differences underlying the pseudo-food/food divide.

Differential Profits

Differential profit is a concept that attempts to account for the fact that where foodstuffs are very highly commoditized, some food and beverage products attract higher returns, or profits, for their sellers than others. In a capitalist economy, profit, and the rate at which it

Table 12.1   Nutrient Comparison of Pseudo-food Beverages with Real Food Beverages per 0.35 L (12 oz.) serving

	Coca-Cola	Pepsi	Orange Juice	1% Milk
Calories	154	160	168	153
Sugar, g	40	40	40	18
Vitamin A, IU	0	0	291	750
Vitamin C, mg	0	0	146	3
Folic acid, µg	0	0	164	18
Calcium, mg	0	0	33	450
Potassium, mg	0	0	711	352
Magnesium, mg	0	0	36	51
Phosphate, mg	54	55	60	353

Source: Adapted from Nestle (2002), Table 23, 198.

can be accumulated, is the prime mover, the master compass that orients flows of investment, whether in the food business or in any other sector where market forces prevail. The rate of profit, or the more commonly used business euphemism 'earnings', plays a fundamental role in shaping the organization of food environments.

Generally speaking, highly processed foodstuffs, goods with much 'value added', have more attractive rates of return for retailers and processors. Foodstuffs that have undergone minimal levels of transformation, such as table potatoes, fluid milk, eggs, flour, and tomato paste, referred to in the food business as 'commodity' products, typically have thin profit margins, and indeed some, like fluid milk, are often sold below cost as 'loss leaders' solely to attract customers to the store. On the other hand, products created out of inexpensive (often subsidized, as with corn and sugar) raw ingredients such as sugar, potatoes, wheat, and corn, and processed with inexpensive chemical additives to create 'value added', can be very profitable commodities. Their success in the market depends heavily on advertising, however, as I shall explain below.

Reports in the trade journals of the retail food industry give some idea of the profitability of pseudo-food products. *Canadian Grocer*, for example, reports that confectionary has grown to

be one of retailers' largest categories in Canada, at $2 billion in sales annually and growing at 5 per cent a year. This category consistently has one of the highest gross margins, averaging 35 per cent. The journal quotes an executive of one retail chain saying about confectionary, 'healthy markups, good profits, reliable sales—there aren't many other grocery categories that can make the same claim' (Kohane 2000: 59). Potato and corn chip products and the like, which the industry refers to as 'salty snacks', are another high-profit product category in the food business. The main trade journal of the American grocery industry, *Progressive Grocer*, reports that food retailers have indicated that salty snacks are the second-most profitable product category for them, outpaced only by bakery products (Anonymous 1998). The profitability of these pseudo-foods is corroborated by a representative of one of the world's largest salty snack manufacturers—PepsiCo's Frito Lay—who claimed that while the company's products represented only about 1 per cent of supermarket sales in 1998, they accounted for about 11 per cent of operating profits and 40 per cent of profit growth for the average American supermarket (cited in Wellman 1999).

The argument that pseudo-foods are especially profitable is further corroborated by industry data from companies that control convenience chain stores in the United States, reported in *Canadian Grocer*. While gross margins for all merchandise averaged 33 per cent, the gross margins for pseudo-foods were notably higher: 35 per cent for cookies, 37 per cent for salty snacks, 39 per cent for ice cream, 43 per cent for candy and gum, and up to 59 per cent for soft drinks served in-store (Shoesmith 1992). Finally, it is noteworthy that in Canada the snack-food industry has experienced much more rapid growth than has the food industry as a whole. In fact, its growth from 1988 to 1997, measured in constant 1992 dollars, was 56 per cent, compared to overall growth of only 6 per cent for the entire food and beverage industry (Food Bureau 1998).

Corporate Concentration

Corporate concentration helps to explain *why* these nutrient-poor products are so lucrative, beyond the fact that many of them are fabricated largely from cheap commodities like sugar and wheat.[7] The snack-food industry, for example, is controlled by a very few multinational food manufacturers. In Canada the federal government reported that by the mid 1990s only four firms controlled about 90 per cent of the value of all shipments of snack foods (Food Bureau 1998). Sugar-laden pre-sweetened breakfast cereals, for example, are produced by a sector of the food industry that has been heavily concentrated for decades. Even by 1970 only four firms— Kellogg's, General Mills, General Foods, and Quaker Oats—controlled 91 per cent of the sales (Scherer 1982: 195). A key benefit of this oligopolistic situation, at least to these companies, is in pricing.

Frederic Scherer's well-known study of the breakfast-cereal industry some years ago illustrates how oligopolistic pricing works, and illustrates the gap between the idealized world of competitive pricing in free markets, as touted by orthodox economists, and the real world of

business today. This study shows us that the Kellogg Company, the most powerful player for many decades, appears to have successfully imposed a high degree of 'price discipline' on its few competitors. Essentially, Kellogg's typically set the pattern of price changes, almost always upward, and the other firms followed. Scherer noted,

> Out of 15 unambiguous price increase rounds between 1965 and 1970 . . . Kellogg's led 12. Kellogg's price increase was followed nine times by General Mills and ten times by General Foods. On only one occasion did neither follow. . . . *Leadership was sufficiently robust to permit price increases in times of both booming and stagnant demand.* (1982: 203–4, my emphasis)

Through the mechanism of a price leader in a heavily concentrated sector, then, these firms were able to avoid much of the price competition that is supposedly at the core of a 'free market' economy. It is notable that of the 1122 price changes in the industry between 1950 and 1972, only 1.5 per cent were list-price reductions, with about half of these occurring in a single incident (ibid.).

One would expect this situation to benefit the companies involved, and indeed it did. After-tax returns for the top five cereal manufacturers were an impressive 19.8 per cent for the period 1958–70, when returns for manufacturing as a whole were only 8.9 per cent (ibid. 211). Moreover, the US Federal Trade Commission stated that overcharging by the few firms controlling this one sector of the food and beverage industry was costing consumers US$100 million a year by the late 1970s (*Consumer Reports* 1981: 76).[8]

We can extrapolate the results of this exposé of the breakfast-cereal industry some decades ago to other product categories where pseudo-foods prevail, such as soft drinks, salty snacks, and chocolate bars and confectionaries. These categories tend to be even more tightly controlled today by a few corporate players than was the breakfast-cereal industry at the time of Scherer's study. Moreover, it is seldom recognized that the corporate players that largely control the production and marketing of nutrient-poor pseudo-food products are among the largest of all companies in the food and beverage sector. PepsiCo, for example, with worldwide sales of $35 billion in 2006 (*Advertising Age* 2007: 75), makes more in profits each year than the total sales of many prominent food companies. The power of these giants has been enhanced even further of late by corporate alliances between some of the largest players to more efficiently carve up global markets. One such alliance is Snack Ventures Europe, formed between PepsiCo and the snack-food division of General Mills in the early 1990s, which then became the largest European snack-food company (General Mills 2003).[9]

Mass Advertising and Product Differentiation

Mass advertising is the process whereby one particular firm's product becomes differentiated in the marketplace. This product differentiation has been the mechanism in the food system and in the wider economy that has allowed some companies to develop branded products which, in turn, have historically allowed them to dominate their competition.[10] In the post–Second World War era, those food processors that successfully established branded products via massive advertising expenditures achieved a favoured position in the food economy, relative both to other processors and also to food retailers, which were becoming more concentrated and powerful (Connor et al. 1985: 79).

Mass advertising and corporate concentration in the food business thus go hand-in-hand—they are mutually reinforcing processes. The high cost of mass advertising on such media

as network television means that only the largest companies have the deep pockets to afford access in the first place. The benefits of such advertising can be immense, however, and its ability to create and strengthen a brand has made these same corporations even more powerful over time. Furthermore, there are economies of scale for companies that do the most advertising, enabling them to get discounts from media corporations and thus gain a market advantage over their competitors. This process had progressed sufficiently far during the twentieth century that by the early 1980s, of the 1100 food companies that were using major media sources to advertise their products, only 12 firms accounted for 45 per cent of all advertising expenditures (Connor et al. 1985, ch. 3).

Intensive advertising is a key means by which pseudo-food companies have boosted their products into their current prominent position in our lives. Food companies have always been among the most advertising-intensive of industries. For decades advertising expenditures by food processors exceeded those of any other broad manufacturing category (ibid., 80–2). Of the total advertising expenditure by food companies, spending on pseudo-foods takes priority. As Taylor et al. (2005, S22) note, research supports the view that 'food advertising promotes more frequent consumption of less healthy foods, including higher-fat, energy-dense snacks and rarely features healthy choices such as fruits and vegetables.' According to Marion Nestle, of the astounding $33 billion spent by food companies on all their promotional campaigns by 2000, almost 70 per cent was spent on convenience foods, candy and snacks, alcoholic beverages, soft drinks, and desserts, whereas just 2.2 per cent was for fruits, vegetables, grains, or beans (2002: 22).

Despite the fact that such products are unnecessary and arguably quite harmful from a nutritional point of view, a small number of corporations that market well-known branded pseudo-food products spend a huge amount of

Table 12.2   Ten Largest Pseudo-food Manufacturers: United States and World Sales and Expenditures on Advertising in the United States, 2004, 2006[1]

Company	US Sales 2004 (millions)	US Sales 2006 (millions)	% change	World Sales 2004 (millions)	World Sales 2006 (millions)	% change	US Ad Expenditures 2004 (thousands)	US Ad Expenditures 2006 (thousands)	% change
Burger King	7,700	8,392	9	n/a	2,048	n/a	542,143	379,459	–30
Coca-Cola	6,643	6,662	0.30	21,962	24,088	9.70	540,551	740,824	37
General Mills	9,441	9,803	3.80	11,070	11,640	5.10	912,455	920,466	0.90
Kellogg's	5,968	7,349	33.20	9614	10,907	13.40	647,097	765,089	18.20
McDonald's	6,525	7,464	14.40	19,065	21,586	13.20	1,388,862	1,748,345	25.90
Nestlé[2]	22,444	24,889	10.90	70,114	78,327	11.70	1,028,295	1,314,975	27.90
Pepsi	18,329	22,178	21	29,261	35,137	20.10	1,262,160	1,322,721	4.80
Wendy's (Tim Hortons)	2,475	2,197	11.20	3,635	2,349	32.90	435,776	435,209	–0.10
Yum! Brands[3]	5,763	5,603	2.80	9,011	9,561	6.10	779,396	902,047	15.70

1. Figures in US dollars. Mars Inc. is a major manufacturer of pseudo-foods but data on sales was not available.
2. Sales are for North and South America. Ad expenditures are for the United States.
3. Yum! Brands owns KFC, Taco Bell, Pizza Hut, and A&W restaurants.

Source: Advertising Age, *Special Report: Profiles Supplement*, 25 June 2005, 2007.

money each year to keep these products front and centre in the minds of consumers. In 2005, just the 10 most powerful companies marketing pseudo-food products spent a total of roughly US$7.62 billion on advertising their brands in the United States—an amount 119 times greater than the entire advertising budget for the US federal government's Department of Health and Human Services (*Advertising Age* 2007). Table 12.2 provides a breakdown of sales and ad expenditure by company, as well as advertising dollars spent per dollar of sales, for this group.

Spatial Colonization

The concept of spatial colonization helps us understand how differential profits, corporate concentration, mass advertising, and market power come to affect the geography of food environments and the prominent role of pseudo-foods within them. For profits to be realized, product must be sold. While intensive, incessant advertising has become a necessary investment for corporations marketing pseudo-food products to maintain and expand their markets, such advertising is not sufficient on its own. Translating manufactured demand into sales requires securing the *physical visibility and availability* of the product within a particular food environment. Spatial colonization then, essentially refers to the power of food processors to place product *in the most visible and effective selling spaces* in a food environment. An industry spokesperson summed up this process concisely when commenting on the marketing of confectionary in supermarkets:

> Confectionary sells confectionary—you must have a variety of products and you must have a variety of locations in your store. You should use a combination of feature and display for maximum impact. . . . If it's not in the face of customers, it can't sell well. (Kohane 2000: 59)

Ensuring a product's physical visibility and availability can take different forms. For fast-food corporations, spatial colonization is more about securing desirable real estate in high-traffic urban locations, whether on city streets, in shopping malls, or in airports, or even today in public sector–controlled spaces such as schools, universities, and hospitals. For most pseudo-food manufacturers, on the other hand, product visibility has to be secured first and foremost in the supermarket food environment, although other marketing channels, including convenience store chains and vending machine sales in a variety of institutional settings, are very important as well. In the telling words of a Coca-Cola Company executive, '[T]o build pervasiveness of our products, we're putting ice-cold Coca-Cola classic [sic] and our other brands within reach, wherever you look: at the supermarket, the video store, the soccer field, the gas station—everywhere' (cited in Nestle and Jacobson 2000: 19).

In the remainder of this chapter I discuss some of my recent empirical research that examines the spatial colonization of pseudo-foods in the context of two essential institutional food environments: supermarkets and high schools.

Pseudo-foods in the Supermarket

As the most important food environment in terms of sales, supermarkets and their shelves are much-sought-after locations for pseudo-food processors. Supermarket chain-store companies, on the other hand, function as shelf-space 'landlords', renting out space in their stores to those companies that can afford to pay. The fact that the supermarket retail sector has seen dramatic concentration in a number of countries, particularly in Canada, gives the few retailers that dominate this sector a good deal of power over processors and the price supermarkets can demand for displaying products (Howe 1983: 113).[11] The special deals, discounts, rebates, and allowances that processors pay to 'rent' the shelf space from the supermarket chains and to facilitate marketing of their products have, according to one analyst, allowed US food retailers to make up to one-third of their profits solely from these kinds of trade payments (Shapiro 1992: 5). In Canada, in the late 1980s, an industry analyst for *The Globe and Mail* estimated that these payments amounted to $2 billion of the $32 billion in annual food sales at that time (Matas 1987: 1). Given the secretive nature of these payments, current data on them is hard to find, but it can be assumed that they have grown as overall food sales have grown.

There is thus a considerable cost for products to be prominently displayed in the supermarket food environment. Increasingly fewer and fewer food processors are able to pay, and as a result in most categories the products of smaller firms have all but disappeared. Hastening this trend has been the push since the early 1980s by most supermarket chain-store companies to develop and market their own store brands (e.g., Loblaw's President's Choice brand) in the supermarkets they control. In this context, few companies can compete with the market power of the large concentrated corporations that dominate the production of pseudo-foods.

The relationship between supermarket chain and processor is not simply a 'landlord–tenant' relationship; it is more complex than that. The success of transnational processing giants in transforming the supermarket food environment also appears to have much to do with their active promotion of the mutual benefits of pseudo-food sales to the retail chain stores. The largest companies, Nestlé and Coca-Cola among them, communicate regularly to retailers in such key trade journals as *Progressive Grocer* about preferred retail strategies to maximize sales. For their part, retailers seem eager to steal business away from other non-food chain-store operations, including drugstore chains, when it comes to selling confectionary products, for example.

How is spatial colonization manifested in the geography of the supermarket? To begin with,

supermarket layout, the overall positioning of product categories, is noteworthy. Low-profit 'commodity' items that most shoppers will purchase no matter what else they buy (milk, butter, margarine, eggs, and often bread) are placed at the back of the store, as far as possible from the entrance, so that customers will have to first pass by less essential but more profitable products. Favoured locations in the supermarket include the eye-level shelf (as opposed to the much less favoured bottom shelf); 'special displays'—unique product positioning that sets a product apart from competing brands and heightens visibility; and areas that the customer must pass by, with the checkout counter being the most significant. In today's supermarket, particularly in the 'superstore' format, spatial colonization can take the form of a massive island display of a single product that is virtually impossible to ignore.

It might be asked, does the spatial manipulation of product have any real significance? Market research suggests that it indeed does. Research indicates the powerful effect of shelf position on sales, for example, and studies have suggested that the use of special end-of-aisle displays in supermarkets can boost unit sales by several hundred per cent, even when no price reduction occurs (see Chevalier 1975: 426; Cox 1970).

In 2001 and 2002 I conducted a study that involved visits to a number of supermarkets in the cities of Kitchener, Waterloo, Cambridge, and Guelph in south-central Ontario. At that time, 24 supermarkets existed in the region, of which 12 were studied. While anecdotal evidence suggested that low-nutrition products had become more significant in modern retailing, there was little research to document the situation. This study attempted to provide some data on the spatial colonization of pseudo-food products in the supermarket food environment. The stores surveyed included stores owned by the three main supermarket chain-store companies operating in Ontario. The study included both the smaller, more traditional supermarket format stores and the largest superstore format that contains in-store pharmacy, florist, and electronic shops; furniture; and so on. It also included the lower-price 'no frills' store format. Because the industry is dominated by so few players, and because store organization tends to follow fairly standard formats, the stores included in the study are believed to reasonably represent what is happening in the industry.

Measurements were taken of the linear shelf space devoted to all food items in each of the main product categories (e.g., breakfast cereals, juices, bottled beverages, salty snack products, bakery products, dairy products, meats, fresh, frozen, and canned fruits and vegetables, etc.). The linear shelf space devoted to nutrient-poor pseudo-food products in each category was also measured. (Shelf space for non–food and beverage items was not measured.) In the end, for each store there were data on both the total linear shelf space devoted to food and beverages and that devoted to pseudo-foods. The data also showed the relative proportion of foods and pseudo-foods in each major product category. In some product categories, such as bottled beverages, most of the shelf space was devoted to soft drinks. In others, such as breakfast cereals, a smaller portion of shelf space was devoted to nutrient-poor products, in this case pre-sweetened cereals. In each store the number and content of all special displays were recorded, but the linear footage of these was not recorded. Since most of these displays market pseudo-food products, the overall measure of pseudo-food shelf space is therefore a conservative one.[12]

Findings

In the 12 supermarkets surveyed the mean linear footage devoted to pseudo-foods ranged from 26 per cent to 37 per cent of the total of all linear footage devoted to edible goods. The average proportion of shelf space for pseudo-foods was 31 per cent of that for all foods. On the shelves in the central area of each store, the proportion of pseudo-foods was considerably higher, ranging from 35 per cent to 44 per cent. This is the part of most supermarket food environments where, for example, entire aisles are devoted to bulk candies and chocolates, cookies, soft drinks, and potato and corn chip products. The area surrounding the central aisles is typically a healthier place to shop, although this is changing with the rapid growth of extensive high-fat and/or high-sugar ice-cream snack displays, as well as those of high-fat prepared foods, both of which tended to be located outside the central area in our sample.

Interestingly, there was no clear relationship between the prevalence of pseudo-foods in the store and store ownership. All the chain-store companies appeared to use the same marketing strategies as far as pseudo-foods were concerned. There was, however, evidence that the newest stores in the study employed more prominent mechanisms to promote pseudo-foods. This typically entailed the use of massive special displays to market nutrient-poor products rather than having a higher proportion of them on the regular store shelves. This development seems to suggest the future direction of food retailing.

It is interesting to note that in the supermarkets studied, an entire shelf extending the full length of the central retail space, and in the larger stores the equivalent of two such shelves, was typically devoted to candies and chocolate bars, and these items were conspicuously displayed in many other locations in the store as well. In most stores a dairy case occupying an entire aisle was devoted to high-fat and/or high-sugar ice creams and other high-fat and high-sugar dairy products. This situation reflects the efforts by manufacturers and retailers to extend the consumption of 'frozen snacks' from the traditional summer months to the entire year (Maclean 1992). The newer the store, typically the more extensive the ice-cream case.

The breakdown within some major product categories reveals some interesting findings.

It was typical, for example, that over 90 per cent of the linear footage devoted to frozen juice drinks was occupied by high-sugar beverages that contain 25 per cent or less, often much less, real fruit juice. The situation with juices in cans and Tetra Pak containers was not much different. In the ready-to-eat breakfast-cereal category, from 55 per cent to 80 per cent of total shelf space was devoted to pre-sweetened cereals, which are a potent vehicle for getting sugar into children's diets.[13] The readiness of retailers to aggressively market pre-sweetened cereals is not surprising given that this type of cereal is the fastest-growing segment of the fastest-growing category of 569 product categories tracked by The Neilsen Company (Burn 1999).

With consumer research indicating that as much as two-thirds of brand selection decisions are made *in the store* (Nielsen Marketing Research 1992: 20), and impulse purchases being a significant part of overall profits for retailers, it is not surprising that stores, in conjunction with leading processors, increasingly use special displays. It is well known that supermarkets place high-profit impulse items at the checkout; indeed, in our survey, candies, chocolate products, and salty snacks were present at 80 per cent or more of the checkout counters in a typical store. Impulse sales are promoted throughout the modern supermarket today. Special display stands, hooks, and strips are now commonly positioned in the most visible locations throughout the store.

While special display devices can hypothetically be used to market any manner of goods normally found in supermarkets today, in practice we found they were overwhelmingly dominated by nutrient-poor products. The number of special displays of these pseudo-foods in the sampled stores ranged from 8 to a high of 26, with the average being 19. Figure 12.1 gives an idea of the extensive use of special displays in one of the supermarkets sampled, which was fairly typical of other stores as well. It also lists the products that were featured in these special displays.

The supermarket food environment today carries a range of foods from all parts of the globe that is unprecedented in human history. For those concerned with the lack of healthy nutritional offerings available to the poor and marginal populations in even the richest societies, the availability of a supermarket is often seen as a benefit for inner-city populations and poor rural communities where little other than fast-food restaurants and convenience stores are to be seen (Cummins and MacIntyre 2006).[14] Yet despite the real diversity of available foods and beverages in the supermarket food environment, we have seen that certain types of products receive privileged treatment in terms of visibility and promotion. These products are too often nutrient-poor edible commodities high in sugar, fat, and salt. Their presence in the supermarket is vastly disproportionate to their nutritional contribution to our lives.

High corporate concentration in the food industry allows a few firms in each sector to saturate target markets with mass advertising to successfully differentiate their products in the minds of consumers. Nutrient-poor edible commodities, or pseudo-foods, are especially profitable for processors and retailers alike, and this differential profit motivates powerful actors in the food business to ensure the spatial colonization of these edible commodities in the supermarket food environment.

Pseudo-foods and Public Sector Institutions: The High School

The high school is another institutional sphere worthy of study because of the evidence that youth today get a large portion of their daily energy needs while at school (French et al. 2004: 1507), and, indeed, it is argued

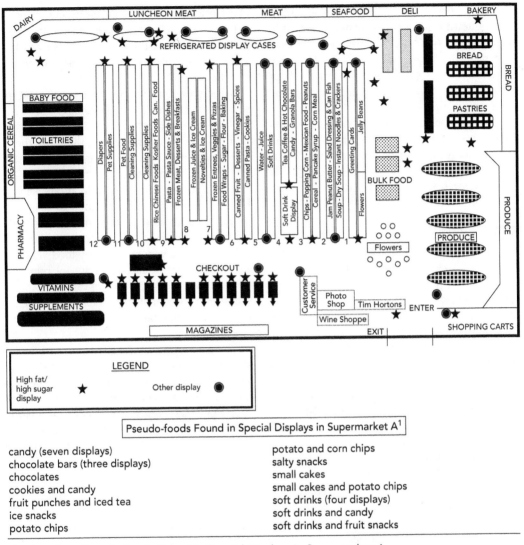

Pseudo-foods Found in Special Displays in Supermarket A[1]

candy (seven displays)	potato and corn chips
chocolate bars (three displays)	salty snacks
chocolates	small cakes
cookies and candy	small cakes and potato chips
fruit punches and iced tea	soft drinks (four displays)
ice snacks	soft drinks and candy
potato chips	soft drinks and fruit snacks

Figure 12.1   Pseudo-foods Found in Special Displays in Supermarket A

1. Each listing represents a separate display in the store. Displays at checkout counters are *not* included.

that nutrient needs are higher in adolescence than at any other time (see Story et al. 2002: S40). It has been noted that relatively little research has examined factors influencing adolescent eating behaviour (Shannon et al. 2002: 229) particularly in the Canadian context (see Taylor et al. 2005). Food choices and eating patterns developed at this time of life are likely to influence long-term behaviour and help determine a person's vulnerability to chronic diseases such as heart disease and osteoporosis, as well as to certain cancers, later in life (Centre for Disease Control 1997). Nutritional authorities argue that schools can play a key role in reversing the trend toward childhood obesity (American Dietetic Association 2003: 506). For these reasons it is useful to know more about the role of pseudo-foods in the high school food environment.

Given the relative dearth of concrete knowledge about the content of high school food environments in Canada and students' purchasing patterns of food and beverages while at school, my research assistant and I undertook a pilot study of public high school food environments in 2004–5. The study had three basic objectives: (1) to provide some insights into the kinds of foods being purchased in Ontario schools; (2) to gain insights into the factors that shape the high school food environment; (3) to discover whether formal or informal initiatives exist to improve the nutritional standard of the high school food environment.

The design of the study is reasonably similar to that of one completed by Carter and Swinburn (2004) in New Zealand, which examines the extent to which primary schools there can be considered 'obesogenic', or obesity-promoting. Our study took place in a school district encompassing three small cities and adjacent rural areas about one hour's drive west of Toronto, Ontario. A key reason this school district was chosen for study was that most of its schools still controlled their cafeteria operations and thus offered better chances of access than a situation where these operations were largely privatized.[15] In the end, interviews took place in 10 of the 12 schools in this school district.

To find out what kinds of foods were being purchased in these high schools (objective 1) face-to-face interviews solicited detailed information regarding the quantities of various kinds of foodstuffs and beverages purchased over the course of a week in each school cafeteria. At a minimum this allowed us to estimate the relative proportions of foods and beverages of differing nutritional values being purchased by students (seasonal variations in food offerings were also recorded). Interviews

took place with respondents overseeing cafeteria and vending-machine operations in high schools, teachers with special duties as 'student activity directors', and/or cafeteria managers, depending on the school.

We surveyed all vending machines found in each school, as well as any tuck shops, because the food environment of high schools includes more than cafeteria fare. Early in the study, these interviews yielded evidence suggesting that the food environment *external* to the school is an important determinant of what foods are sold in the schools. We thus endeavoured to map out the locations of food vendors near the school, and those of fast-food vendors in particular. For each school, the variety of nearby food vendors and the distance of each from school property were noted. The significance of this mapping is discussed below. Finally, we noted any implicit[16] or explicit nutritional policies that a school may have adopted.

The data were organized by nutritional content. Data for units sold of various edible products on a daily basis were gathered from cafeteria staff. These data were placed into four basic categories: main meals (e.g., pasta plate, hamburger, stir-fry, panzerotto), side dishes (e.g., french fries, cut vegetables, salad), desserts and snacks (e.g., cookies, muffins, fresh fruit, fruit salad, brownies), and beverages (e.g., soft drinks, chocolate milk, white milk, pure fruit juice, juice beverage, water).[17] These data were then organized according to three basic nutritional categories—'maximum', 'moderate', and 'minimum' nutrition—suggested by the Ontario Society of Nutrition Professionals in Public Health in an important report addressing nutrition in Ontario schools: (OSNPPH 2004, Table 7). Foods in the 'moderate' category were considered to have some positive nutritional value, but also to have higher-than-desirable levels of fat, sugar, and/or salt, often as a result of processing. Those in the 'minimum' category are products typically high in sugar and fat and low in most nutritional areas—products I have earlier termed *pseudo-foods*.

Findings

A broad nutritional assessment of the food-purchasing patterns at the high schools surveyed revealed several notable findings. The popularity of high-sugar and/or high-fat foods such as french fries, cookies, muffins, soft drinks, and fruit beverages was evident; all of these were purchased in large quantities relative to other items in virtually all of the schools studied. These products are judged to be of 'minimum' nutritional value (see OSNPPH 2004). Typically, these products were found as cafeteria side dishes, desserts, or snack items. Outside school cafeterias, these nutrient-poor offerings dominated vending machines found in all schools, available to students at any time of the school day.

Only main-meal items were likely to be judged of 'maximum' or 'moderate' nutritional value, and cafeteria staff typically made an effort to have nutritious options offered daily. Nevertheless, staff often felt obliged to cater to student demand for fast-food items as well (e.g., pizza, hamburgers), particularly when such items were very often easily available a short walk from the school (see below).

We also found that the purchases of fresh fruit and vegetables were extremely low in almost all cases, particularly those of fruit. For example, in several of the surveyed high schools of 1000 or more students, where fruit was always available in the cafeteria, as few as three to five pieces of fruit *in total* per week were purchased. All too often, when other low-nutrition snacks and desserts were available, the vast majority of students opted for them instead of fruit.

Students in the schools we studied purchased more products high in saturated fats and hydrogenated fats (trans fats) than desirable for a couple of reasons. One was the popularity of such main-meal items as hamburgers, which are high in saturated fat. Another was the popularity of industrial baked goods (cookies, muffins, brownies, etc.) made with hydrogenated oils, which contain trans fats. Research over a number of years has established that trans fats are even more harmful to health than saturated fats (Mozafarrian et al. 2006).

While a number of these schools had facilities to prepare baked goods from scratch on-site using unsaturated and non-hydrogenated oils, and in fact had done so in the past, staff shortages in recent years made this impossible. Time constraints on staff forced the preparation of such items using semi-processed products made in factories elsewhere. One positive feature of cafeteria kitchens in our study was that consumption of saturated fats in such perennial-favourite side dishes as french fries was reduced because of decisions in most of the schools surveyed not to purchase a deep fryer. Hamburgers, another popular main-meal item, were mostly baked rather than fried. Nevertheless, these items are still high in saturated fat.

Variations in the Schools

Some schools performed less well in the main-meal category because they typically offered more fast-food items that were high in fat and refined carbohydrates (e.g., hamburgers, pizza) and fewer of the healthier main meals. In the side-dish and desserts-and-snacks categories, where pseudo-foods tended to dominate, a couple of schools did relatively better in nutritional terms. These schools had decided not to offer such items as french fries and onion rings, but had placed more than typical emphasis in offering well-prepared salads, cut-up vegetables, and healthier side dishes such as egg rolls instead. The factors behind these nutritional decisions are discussed below.

With respect to beverages sold in cafeterias, we recorded a relatively high volume of 'healthy' beverages sold compared to the less-nutritious items. This is *not* an accurate reflection of beverage purchases in the schools, however. Rather, in nearly all cases a decision had been made

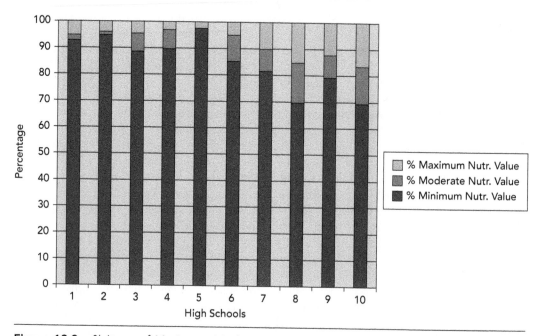

Figure 12.2   % Items of Maximum, Moderate, and Minimum Nutritional Value in High School Vending Machines

not to offer soft drinks in the cafeteria, which in itself is commendable, but in all but one case soft drinks were readily available in vending machines outside the cafeteria and sometimes in tuck shops. Evidence linking soft drink consumption to childhood obesity was emerging over a decade ago, it should be noted (Ludwig et al. 2001). The results of our survey of vending machines in high schools, and the dismal nutritional picture they depict, is illustrated in Figure 12.2. Vending machines are a major mechanism for pseudo-food manufacturers to market their products in these schools, a finding that Taylor et al. (2005) note has been reported in other Canadian research.

Determinants of the High School Food Environment

Why do students' food-purchasing patterns in our study diverge so widely from what would be considered nutritionally ideal? Part

of the explanation lies outside of the realm of schools entirely and has to do with the effects of aggressive mass advertising targeting children and youth by the corporate purveyors of junk foods and fast foods. Such advertising is a powerful force creating demand for these products, and students do not, of course, cease to be influenced by such advertising once they enter the school. However, other factors seem to reinforce present food-purchasing patterns.

Among the most important factors are those that shape what food and beverages high schools *offer* students. Since the era of provincial government cutbacks to education in the mid 1990s, school cafeterias and vending machines have been expected to generate revenues to pay for a host of student activities, equipment, and even what might be considered essential parts of school infrastructure.[18] According to interview respondents in our study, fiscal restructuring by the provincial government under Progressive Conservative

Table 12.3   Extra–school Food Environment (n=10 schools)

| | Number of Fast-food Outlets and Distance from School | | | | |
	0–5 min	6–10 min	11–15 min	16–20 min	5-min drive
Total All Schools	16	25	3	1	10

Party rule (1995–2003) largely eliminated monies coming from school boards for such expenses. Given the current fiscal realities, several schools have now assigned a teacher to spend significant time organizing the school food environment and accessing students' disposable income. As one of these teachers told me, 'All the money you need for student activities walks in the door each day, and walks right out again [to purchase food and drinks] unless you can capture it in the school'. Today, schools are left to fend for themselves to cover many of their costs. In effect, they have been forced to view their students as customers and cafeterias and vending machines as profit centres to make up for revenues no longer coming from the provincial government via the school board.

Our interviews made it clear that other factors shaped the in-school food environment as well. A crucial one is the food environment found in the immediate area *outside* the school. Respondents indicated to us that these food venues were well patronized by students. Mapping this outside-school food environment was clearly necessary to understanding what was happening to food in the schools. When we did so, we found that most schools, except for two suburban schools and one rural school, were within easy walking distance of several fast-food outlets (see Table 12.3). Why consider only walking distance? Our reasoning was that with the elimination of grade 13 in Ontario schools, only a few students are now of driving age and able to drive to school.

Do purveyors of nutrient-poor foods such as fast-food corporations explicitly target high schools as part of their locational strategies? This is an important question that has not been well studied. Our findings do reflect a pattern found in one of the few other studies that has considered the relationship between schools and the fast-food industry. As Austin et al. (2005: 1578) wrote in their study of fast-food outlets and schools in Chicago,

> we found that although fast-food restaurants are located throughout the city, they are clustered in areas within a short walking distance from schools. We estimate that there are 3 to 4 times as many fast-food restaurants within 1.5 km from schools than would be expected if the restaurants were located around the city in a way unrelated to schools. Nearly 80 per cent of schools in Chicago had at least 1 fast-food restaurant within 800 m.

One inner-city school we studied that was close to several fast-food outlets and a deli in a large grocery store demonstrates the effects of nearby off-site fast-food vendors on the in-school food environment. The school has to compete with outside vendors on price and offerings in order to capture student disposable income, according to the respondent in this school. This, in turn, had implications for the in-school pricing of pseudo-foods and beverages, which were purposefully priced below that of outside vendors to capture revenue that would otherwise be lost to the latter. Research has shown the sensitivity of this age group to price with respect to different food and beverage offerings in schools (see Shannon et al. 2002). It seems likely that skewing the prices of unhealthy food and beverages in this manner is influencing food-purchasing patterns in the schools and contributing to unhealthy eating.

A further determinant of the in-school food environment is the reduction in cafeteria staff deemed necessary because of provincial funding cuts. Respondents in most schools reported that staff reductions made it difficult or even impossible to prepare meals, side dishes, and desserts from scratch, leading to a dependence on prepared or semi-prepared industrial food and a sacrifice in the nutritional quality of the food offered. When schools relied more on an outside supplier of a main dish, it was typically a 'finger food' item (e.g., panzerotto, pizza) of only 'moderate' nutritional value. Cafeteria desserts prepared or semi-prepared off-site tend to contain excess trans fats and saturated fats.

The Struggle to Promote Healthy Eating in Schools

When this study was undertaken, broad government initiatives to deal with serious nutritional issues in high schools were largely non-existent;[19] it was left to *local* initiatives to improve the situation. One such initiatives was the decision of staff in most of the schools surveyed not to purchase a deep fryer, to avoid the health perils of deep-fried food. Among the boldest of local initiatives was the elimination in one school of *all* soft drinks. This required the purchase of new vending machines (because the soft-drink supplier had provided the machines), a considerable expense, so that healthier options could be offered. It is notable that the respondent at this school reported that no complaints had been received from students over the year since this change was made. While revenues from vending machines did decline with this decision, the healthier options that now filled the machines offset most of the decline.

There were a few other informal nutritional policies initiated by staff. These included concerted efforts to promote salad and vegetable options to students, and to minimize junk foods in the cafeteria. Unfortunately these efforts to expand healthy eating in the schools were undermined by other factors. One was

the perceived need for revenue generated from vending machines to cover a host of student activity expenses and even the cost of some basic infrastructure. Vending machines are presently the main mechanism for pseudo-food companies to enter public high school food environments.

Finally, a key factor appearing to undermine healthier eating in schools is the corporate food environment surrounding most schools. As with the Chicago schools studied by Austin et al. (2005), our schools were for the most part surrounded by several nutrient-poor fast-food vendors within easy walking distance.

Conclusion

I have argued that a powerful segment of the food industry controlling the production and promotion of nutrient-poor products I call pseudo-foods has an inordinate impact on the content of contemporary food environments. The mutually reinforcing effects of corporate concentration and mass advertising in the food business, via the process of spatial colonization of food environments by pseudo-food–producing corporations, is implicated in undermining healthy eating behaviours in society. We have examined two significant institutional food environments in the Canadian context—the supermarket chain store and the high school food environment—with a view to understanding the key factors shaping their nutritional content. In the supermarket realm, our research suggests that both powerful pseudo-food corporate processors and highly concentrated supermarket chain-store companies engage in mutually beneficial behaviour to aggressively promote nutrient-poor products in the supermarket food environment. The spatial colonization of pseudo-foods was well advanced in the sample of stores we studied.

In the public sector institutions represented here by the high school, our survey of schools in one district in southern Ontario indicated a high degree of penetration of pseudo-foods as well, despite apparent efforts to encourage healthy eating there. Vending machines were a key vector for the entrance of pseudo-foods into the schools, but not the only one. Others included school tuck shops, and even cafeteria fare that was replete with nutrient-poor products, especially snack foods and side dishes. Important factors shaping the high school food environment were (1) previous rounds of cut-backs by the Ministry of Education, which encouraged the use of vending machines to make up needed revenue; (2) kitchen-staff shortages, also due to cutbacks, which resulted in the use of trans fat–laden baked goods prepared off-site; and (3) the food environment adjacent to schools, which was dominated by fast-food outlets and vendors of nutrient-poor products, which informants told us affected the types of foods that schools could offer in order to compete effectively for students' disposable income, and which also affected the prices charged for pseudo-foods available in school tuck shops.

Discussion Questions

1. What are key consequences of the rapidly increasing phenomenon of people eating away from home?

2. How does the concept of 'pseudo-foods' differ from the commonly used term 'junk foods'?

3. How does the concept of 'spatial colonization' help us understand how powerful corporate pseudo-food processors maintain and expand their dominance in our food environments?

4. What aspects of high school food environments were found to be most dominated by edible products of minimal nutritional value?

5. What were found to be the key determinants of the quality of high school food environments? Discuss how each had an influence on that food environment.

Further Reading

1. Kessler, David. 2009. *The End of Overeating*. Toronto: McClelland and Stewart.

   A remarkably accessible book that considers how the profit motive distorts modern restaurant meals and processed foods more generally. Kessler has interviewed a wide variety of people, from food scientists to executives of leading food corporations, to understand what has happened to processed food. The book is particularly illuminating on the role of added salt, fats, and sugars in making processed foods so palatable, with an excellent and very readable discussion of the powerful neurological effects of these substances.

2. Nestle, Marion. 2007. *Food Politics: How the Food Industry Influences Nutrition and Health*. Berkeley: University of California Press.

   Probably the most widely known writer on nutritional matters in the world today, Nestle established her reputation with the earlier version of this book. With a title that says it all, Nestle details the way the food industry has shaped the various dimensions of our contemporary food environment, with excellent chapters on shaping the diets of children and youth, school foods, and the role of food corporations in influencing the science of nutrition itself.

3. Pollan, Michael. 2006. *The Omnivore's Dilemma: A Natural History of Four Meals.* New York: Penguin Press.

This book begins with an exposé of corn, which as it turns out is, in its various forms, at the core of the modern industrial food system. Pollan's account of the transformation of this onetime mainstay of the Mexican diet into a feedstock of the contemporary food economy is exceptionally engaging, and leads to his examination of the meat industry as well. This book has influenced the thinking of many about the dilemmas of our present day food economy.

4. Schlosser, Eric. 2001. *Fast Food Nation: The Dark Side of the All-American Meal.* New York: Houghton Mifflin.

This remarkably successful book shines a critical light on the various components of the corporate complex that is fast food. The book is very readable and entertaining as well as being informative about a phenomenon that is a critical part of modern food environments the world over.

5. Simon, Michele. 2006. *Appetite for Profit.* New York: Nation Books.

This book examines American food companies and their claims that they are offering healthier foods. Considering the nutritional offerings in such institutional spheres as the fast food restaurants and schools, and the quality of processed food more generally, Simon examines the phenomenon she calls 'nutriwashing' in the American food system.

6. Wright, Wynne, and Gerard Middendorf. 2008. *The Fight Over Food: Producers, Consumers, and Activists Challenge the Global Food System.* University Park: University of Pennsylvania Press.

This is one of the first books to focus on social agency in the reshaping of the food system. It reports on the research of some leading writers on the food economy and their findings regarding efforts to establish a safer, more sustainable, and more equitable agri-food system.

Notes

1. I would like to thank Maxine Fung, Chris Valiquet, and Anita Mahadeo for assistance with this research.
2. For an extensive recent survey on the science examining the relationship between weight and mortality see Fontaine and Allison (2004), Manson et al. (1995), and Marks and Allegrante (2005). For recent surveys of literature examining the relationship between obesity and disease, see Manson et al. (1995), Saltzman and Benotti (2004), Pi-Sunyer (2002), and Ko and Lee (2004).
3. Body composition includes measures of body mass index, waist circumference, and skin-fold tests. Previously Canadian data consisted largely of self-reported information, with the inherent biases this entails.
4. A summary of the Canadian Health Measures Survey: Cycle 1 Data Tables, 2007 to 2009, was reported in Statistics Canada, 2010, 'Health, 2007 to 2009', *The Daily*, Wednesday, 13 January, accessed 6 January 2011 at www.statcan.gc.ca/daily-quotidien/100113/dq100113a-eng.htm.
5. While this term is used in the literature, it is not treated as a concept but typically used solely as a descriptive term.
6. 'Light' ice creams tend to have substantially lower fat levels.
7. Low prices for sugar were historically sustained by slave labour until the mid nineteenth century, and after that by below-subsistence wages in many parts of the world where it was produced. More recently pseudo-food manufacturers, and in particular the soft-drink corporations, have benefited from developments in biotechnology allowing the cheap production of high-fructose corn syrup as an inexpensive

sweetener made from a heavily subsidized crop—corn. Wheat production has historically been heavily subsidized by government as well, and chronic over-production has helped to depress prices to the advantage of processors.

8. Fortunately for consumers, in recent years corporate concentration in the supermarket chain-store end of the food economy has opened up opportunities for the latter to market store brands of breakfast cereals that have undercut somewhat the prices established earlier by the breakfast-cereal processing giants. This retail concentration has not always had positive outcomes for consumers, however. In this regard, see Winson (1993, ch. 7, 'Food Retailers: New Masters of the Food System').

9. This alliance was dissolved in 2005.

10. For a fuller discussion of this process, see Winson (1993: 122–7).

11. The leverage that retailer concentration gives them has been recognized for some time. As Howe noted in the early 1980s, 'the dominance of the large food distributors vis-à-vis manufacturers is evidenced by the additional discounts these mass distributors are able to extract from processors despite the market concentration among the latter' (1983: 113).

12. For more details on the methodology of this study, see Winson (2004: 305).

13. These cereals, a breakfast favourite of North American children and bestsellers in the prepared cereal category, have on average between four and five teaspoons of sugar for each single-serving equivalent. Four grams of sugar are taken to be equivalent to one teaspoon (see Larsen 2003).

14. For more discussion of these 'food deserts' see Alwitt and Donley (1997) and Nayga and Weinberg (1999).

15. In 2004 most but not all of the school boards in Ontario were phoned to assess the degree of privatization of food services. The great majority of those contacted had privatized their operations.

16. By 'implicit' policy I mean a decision regarding food and beverage offerings and/ or their preparation that was made in the school and that was not explicitly designated as a nutritional policy, but which had obvious nutritional and therefore health implications for students.

17. What we have categorized as side dishes, snacks, and beverage items were almost always offered on a regular daily basis. Main meals, on the other hand, were typically rotated through the week according to a fixed schedule in nearly all the schools sampled. Calculating units sold per day was thus not as straightforward with main meals. Calculations were made on the following basis: if a pasta dish, for example, was usually offered once a week throughout the school year and typically sold 50 units on that day, we considered this as having sold 10 units per day (50 units/5 days= 10 units/day).

18. In one school, for example, vending machine revenues went to replace the school clocks and to completion of the parking lot.

19. This is beginning to change, as new guidelines on school food came into force in Ontario in the fall of 2011. How effective they will be remains to be seen.

References

Advertising Age. 2007. 'Special Report: Profiles Supplement'. 27 June.

Alwitt, L.F., and T.D. Donley. 1997. 'Retail Stores in Poor Urban Neighbourhoods'. *Journal of Consumer Affairs* 31(1): 139–64.

American Dietetic Association. 2003. 'Nutrition Services: An Essential Component of Comprehensive School Health Programs'. *Journal of the American Dietetic Association* 103(4): 505–14.

Anonymous. 1998. 'Scrutinizing Snacks'. *Progressive Grocer* 10–11.

Austin, S. Bryn, Steven J. Melly, Brisa N. Sanchez, Aarti Patel, Stephen Buka, and Steven L. Gortmaker. 2005. 'Clustering of Fast-Food Restaurants Around Schools: A Novel Application of Spatial Statistics to the Study of Food Environments'. *American Journal of Public Health* 95(9): 1575–81.

Burn, Douglas. 1999. 'Thriving on Consumers' Hand to Mouth Existence'. *Food in Canada* 59(1): 16–17.

Carter, Mary-Ann, and Boyd Swinburn. 2004. 'Measuring the "Obesogenic" Food Environment in New Zealand Primary Schools'. *Health Promotion International* 19(1): 15–20.

Centre for Disease Control. 1997. 'Guidelines for School Health Programs to Promote Lifelong Healthy Eating'. *The Journal of School Health* 67(1): 9–26.

Chevalier, Michel. 1975. 'Increase in Sales Due to In-Store Display'. *Journal of Marketing Research* 12: 426–31.

Connor, John M., Richard T. Rogers, Bruce W. Marion, and Willard E. Mueller. 1985. *The Food Manufacturing Industries*. Toronto: Lexington Books.

Consumer Reports. 1981. 'Monopoly on the Cereal Shelves?' February: 76–80.

Cox, Keith. 1970. 'The Effect of Shelf Space on Sales of Branded Products'. *Journal of Marketing Research* 7: 55–8.

Cummins, Steven, and Sally MacIntyre. 2006. 'Food Environments and Obesity—Neighbourhoods or Nation? *International Journal of Epidemiology* 35: 100–4.

Fontaine, Kevin R., and David B. Allison. 2004. 'Obesity and Mortality Rates'. In *Handbook of Obesity: Etiology and Pathophysiology*, 2nd edn, ed. George Bray and Claude Bouchard. New York: Marcel Dekker, 767–86.

Food Bureau. 1998. *The Canadian Snack Food Industry*. Ottawa: Market and Industry Services Branch. Accessed April 2003 at www.agr.ca//food/profiles/snackfood/snackfood_e.html.

French, S., M. Story, J.A. Fulkerson, and P. Hannan. 2004. 'An Environmental Intervention to Promote Lower-Fat Food Choices in Secondary Schools: Outcome of the TACOS Study'. *American Journal of Public Health* 94(9): 1507–12.

Garnsey, Peter. 1999. *Food and Society in Classical Antiquity*. Cambridge: Cambridge University Press.

General Mills. 2003. *General Mills: 75 Years of Innovation, Invention, Food and Fun*. Accessed 27 December 2011 at www.generalmills.com/~/media/Files/history/history_book.ashx.

Howe, D. 1983. 'The Food Distribution Sector'. In *The Food Industry: Economics and Politics*, ed. Jim Burns. London: Heinemann, 113.

Ko, C., and S. Lee. 2004. 'Obesity and Gall Bladder Disease'. In *Handbook of Obesity: Etiology and Pathophysiology*, ed. G. Bray and C. Bouchard. New York: Marcel Dekker, 919–34.

Kohane, Jack. 2000. 'Sweet Opportunities: Maximize Your Profits in Confectionery'. *Canadian Grocer* (September): 57–61.

Larsen, Joanne. 2003. 'Ask the Dietician: Junk Food'. Accessed May 2003 at www.dietitian.com/junkfood.html.

Ludwig, David S., Karen Peterson, and Steven Gortmaker. 2001. 'Relations Between Consumption of Sugar-Sweetened Drinks and Childhood Obesity: A Prospective, Observational Analysis'. *Lancet* 357: 505–8.

Lipscombe, Lorraine L., and Janet E. Hux. 2007. 'Trends in Diabetes Prevalence, Incidence, and Mortality in Ontario, Canada 1995–2005: A Population-Based Study'. *Lancet* 369: 750–6.

Maclean, Susan. 1992. 'Cold Comfort: A Frozen Novelty Is No Longer Just a Summertime Treat'. *Canadian Grocer* 106(3): 15–21.

Manson, JoAnn E., Walter Willett, Meir Stampfer, Graham Colditz, David Hunter, Susan Hankinson, Charles Hennekens, and Frank Speizer. 1995. 'Body Weight and Mortality Among Women'. *The New England Journal of Medicine* 333(11): 677–85.

Marks, Ray, and John P. Allegrante. 2005. 'Health Outcomes of Child, Adolescent and Adult Obesity: A Review of the Literature'. In *Body Mass Index: New Research*, ed. Linda A. Ferrera. New York: Nova Biomedical Books, 13–43.

Matas, Robert. 1987. 'Stocking Shelves Has a Hidden Cost'. *The Globe and Mail*, 28 February, A1.

Mozaffarian, Dariush, Martijn Katan, Alberto Ascherio, Meir Stampfer, and Walter Willett. 2006. 'Trans Fatty Acids and Cardiovascular Disease'. *New England Journal of Medicine* 354: 1601–13.

Nayga, Rodolfo, and Zy Weinberg. 1999. 'Supermarket Access to the Inner City'. *Journal of Retailing and Consumer Services* 6(3): 141–5.

Nestle, M. 2002. *Food Politics: How the Food Industry Influences Nutrition and Health*. Berkeley: University of California Press.

——— and Michael Jacobsen. 2000. 'Halting the Obesity Epidemic: A Public Health Policy Approach'. *Obesity* 115(1): 12–24.

Neilsen Marketing Research. 1992. *Category Management: Positioning Your Organization to Win*. Chicago: NTC Business Books.

Nutribase. 2001. *Nutritional Facts: Desk Reference*. New York: Penguin Putnam.

OfCom. 2006. *Television Advertising of Food and Drink Products to Children—Statement and Further Consultation*. Accessed 14 March 2007 at www.ofcom.org.uk/consult/condocs/foodads_new/summary/.

Ontario Society of Nutrition Professionals in Public Health (OSNPPH). 2004. *Call to Action: Creating a Healthy School Nutrition Environment*. School Nutrition Workgroup Steering Committee. Available at www.osnpph.on.ca.

Pi-Sunyer, F. Xavier. 2002. 'The Obesity Epidemic: Pathophysiology and Consequences of Obesity'. *Obesity Research* 10: 97S–104S.

Power, Elaine. 2005. 'Determinants of Healthy Eating Among Low Income Canadians'. *Canadian Journal of Public Health* 96: S37–S43.

Raine, K.D. 2005. 'Determinants of Healthy Eating in Canada'. *Canadian Journal of Public Health* 96 (supplement 3): S8–S14.

Reardon, Thomas, and Julio Berdegué. 2002. 'The Rapid Rise of Supermarkets in Latin America: Challenges and Opportunities for Development'. *Development Policy Review* 4: 371–88.

Reardon, Thomas, Peter Timmer, Christopher Barrett, and Julio Berdegué. 2003. 'The Rise of Supermarkets in Africa, Asia, and Latin America'. *American Journal of Agricultural Economics* 85(5): 1140–6.

Saltzman, E., and P. Benotti. 2004. 'Effects of Obesity on the Cardiovascular System'. In *Handbook of Obesity: Etiology and Pathophysiology*, ed. G. Bray and C. Bouchard. New York: Marcel Dekker, 825–44.

Scherer, Frederic F. 1982. 'The Breakfast Cereal Industry'. In *The Structure of American Industry*, 6th edn, ed. Walter Adams. New York: Macmillan, 191–217.

Schlosser, Eric. 2001. *Fast Food Nation: The Dark Side of the All-American Meal*. New York: Houghton Mifflin.

Shannon, Christine, Mary Story, Jayne A. Fulkerson, and Simone French. 2002. 'Factors in the School Cafeteria Influencing Food Choices by High School Students'. *Journal of School Health* 72(6): 229–34.

Shapiro, Eben. 1992. 'P&G Takes on the Supermarkets with Uniform Pricing'. *The New York Times*, 26 April.

Shoesmith, John. 1992. 'Changing the Way C-stores Do Business: Gas, Deli, Fresh and Prepared foods. Is This a Supermarket or a Convenience Store?' *Canadian Grocer* 106(10): 30–4.

Statistics Canada. 2002. 'National Longitudinal Survey of Children and Youth: Childhood Obesity, 1994–1999'. *The Daily*, 18 October.

Story, M., D. Neumark-Sztainer, and S. French. 2002. 'Individual and Environmental Issues on Adolescent Eating Behaviors'. *Journal of the American Dietetic Association* 102(3): S40–S51.

Taylor J., S. Evers, and M. McKenna. 2005. 'Determinants of Healthy Eating in Children and Youth'. *Canadian Journal of Public Health* 96 (supplement 3): S20–S26.

Tremblay, M.S., and J.D. Willms. 2000. 'Secular Trends in the Body Mass Index of Canadian Children'. *Canadian Medical Association Journal* 163: 1429–33.

Wellman, David. 1999. 'The Big Crunch'. *Supermarket Business* 54(3): 46–8.

Winson, Anthony. 1993. *The Intimate Commodity: Food and the Development of the Agro-Industrial Complex in Canada*. Toronto: Garamond Press.

———. 2004. 'Bringing Political Economy into the Debate on the Obesity Epidemic'. *Agriculture and Human Values* 21(4): 299–312.

13

Nutrition Transition and the Public-Health Crisis

Aboriginal Perspectives on Food and Eating

Debbie Martin

Learning Objectives

Through this chapter, you can:

1. Develop a critical understanding of the nutrition transition as it relates to Aboriginal communities
2. Become aware of the role that culture plays regarding food choices, and thus, in health and well-being
3. Understand the diverse ways in which Aboriginal peoples understand foods and the important role that foods hold for expressions of culture

---

Introduction

The **nutrition transition** characterizes populations that have experienced growing rates of overweight, obesity, and related chronic diseases as a result of the increased consumption of 'unhealthy' foods such as those high in saturated fats, refined sugars, and sodium (Bjerregaard 2010; Kuhnlein et al. 2004). The nutrition transition has, by and large, been conceptualized by nutritional scientists as an inevitable by-product of 'development' that includes changing employment patterns, technological advancements, and other associated measures of 'progress' within a society (Kuhnlein et al. 2004; Lambden et al. 2006; Thow 2009; Winson 2004). This assumption has been called into question more recently as food researchers ranging from

nutritionists to political economists have argued that the nutrition transition must encompass the socio-political context in which foods are eaten. A more nuanced understanding sheds light on how an individual's food 'choices' are often the product of government policies and marketing strategies that promote processed and refined foods to the exclusion of more traditional or unprocessed foods (Thow 2009; Winson 2004). Although no research has conclusively explained the causes and consequences of the nutrition transition, it is posited by growing numbers of nutritional scientists (as well as food researchers from diverse disciplines) that the nutrition transition is not simply an inevitable by-product of development, nor is it simply a matter of individual food choice (Delormier et al. 2009; Thow 2009). It is argued that a more complex understanding of the nutrition transition, based on cultural awareness and its implicit effects on food availability and choices, is warranted.

Canada's Aboriginal peoples are undergoing a nutrition transition (Bjerregaard 2010; Kuhnlein 2009, 2004). Although the diverse First Nations, Inuit, and Métis who make up Canada's Aboriginal peoples live within one of the most 'developed' nations of the world (ranked sixth on the United Nations Human Development Index), many Aboriginal communities across Canada are reminiscent of what one might find in a much less developed country (United Nations 2011). These communities are characterized by poverty, overcrowded housing, poor water quality, and in some cases, hunger (King et al. 2009; Loppie-Reading and Wien 2009; Power 2008). The nutrition transition has been deemed a public-health crisis within Aboriginal communities (Kuhnlein 2004), although it seems counter-intuitive that communities experiencing hunger and poverty might also face problems typically associated with overeating and obesity. However, if we view the nutrition transition from a perspective that understands food and eating as inseparable from the social, cultural, political, and natural environment in which foods are procured and consumed, then the nutrition transition, despite its name, is about much more than simply nutrition.

The conventional definition of the nutrition transition views chronic health conditions as being *caused* by poor food choices; the word *choice* implies that individuals have complete control over what, how much, when, and why certain foods are eaten over others. As well, rising rates of chronic disease and obesity cannot be explained by diet alone, since many Aboriginal peoples have historically had high-fat diets; for instance, chronic diseases associated with high-fat foods, such as cardiovascular disease, diabetes, and certain cancers, were virtually absent from Aboriginal communities until the past 50 or so years

(Delormier et al. 2009; Bjerregaard 2010). Clearly, we need to look beyond simply what is being eaten by individuals and toward a perspective on food and eating that reflects upon the role of the socio-cultural and political environment in influencing the types, amounts, and nature of foods being eaten. In response to this awareness, research conducted within Aboriginal communities has noted that the nutrition transition is marked by a shift *away* from eating **traditional foods**—those that are procured locally from the land and sea and whose procurement, preparation, and consumption are closely linked to expressions of culture—and a trend *toward* replacing traditional foods with **market foods**, or those foods that can be purchased through the market economy (Lambden et al. 2006). It is important to explore the changing nature of foods eaten (i.e., from traditional to market foods) if we are to understand the nutrition transition.

In communities where Aboriginal peoples have replaced much of their traditional diets with market foods, there are exponential increases in chronic conditions such as diabetes and cardiovascular disease, and in many cancers—all of which correspond to the nutrition transition (Bjerregaard 2010; Kuhnlein et al. 2004; Sharma et al. 2010). Similarly, communities where Aboriginal peoples have maintained traditional practices to access and procure traditional foods have not experienced the nutrition transition to the same extent (Damman et al. 2008; Kuhnlein 2009; Lambden et al. 2006; Samson and Pretty 2003). Partial explanations of the nutrition transition exist: the lack of affordable, nutritious market foods; lack of consistent access to the same (Sharma et al. 2010); their high cost for those with low incomes or on social assistance; poverty; high unemployment; and the exclusion of Aboriginal peoples' perspectives about how they understand food, eating, and the importance of both within their communities.

Positioning the nutrition transition as a more complex concept than nutritional content alone generates a broad debate about the socio-cultural and political environment in which foods are eaten. This environment is constructed and shaped increasingly by those who control the production and distribution of market foods, who may know nothing about the Aboriginal communities in which these foods are being eaten (Delormier et al. 2009). The systematic exclusion of Aboriginal peoples from discussions about food systems, including decisions about when, how much, how often, and even what types of food can be eaten, means that Aboriginal peoples often exercise very little control or decision-making power over their food choices. This represents a significant shift from a generation ago, when communities and families relied upon their own wherewithal to acquire, prepare, and store all of the foods that were needed to live healthfully within a particular geographic area (Martin 2009). The blame for subsequent public-health crises related to the nutrition transition is laid on individuals and communities with little or no direct control over the crises being experienced (Carter 1990; Delormier et al. 2009; King et al. 2009; Wheatley 1998).

It is thus critical to begin to explore the nutrition transition from a perspective that acknowledges the role of historical and continued **colonization**—that is, the dismissal, under-representation, or complete undermining of Aboriginal knowledge(s) regarding the important role of food within their communities in any discussions about Aboriginal peoples' food systems (Smith 1999). In Aboriginal communities within Canada, for example, various health and social issues can be traced back to the arrival of the European colonizers in the Americas, since it was at this time that Aboriginal peoples were introduced to diseases to which they had never been exposed, as well as to imported foods that differed significantly from the diets to which they had grown accustomed. The impact of historical colonial encounters cannot be understated in any attempt to grasp the complexity of the nutrition transition as it continues to shape the types and amounts of foods that are eaten within Aboriginal communities. It is also important to

remember that colonization continues to exist, and is often expressed differently. For example, Aboriginal peoples within Canada currently face struggles in accessing and using their traditional territories for food procurement activities like hunting, fishing, trapping, and agriculture. These struggles occur because of strict government regulations that inhibit traditional food-gathering practices, economic development processes that affect Aboriginal communities but do not include them in decision making, environmental destruction resulting from unfettered development, and moral opposition to traditional food-gathering practices from non-Aboriginal people who are unfamiliar with Aboriginal livelihoods (Lynge 1992; Nuttall et al. 2005; Panelli and Tipa 2009; Radkau 2008; Samson and Pretty 2003). Pursuing the (relatively recent) agenda of nutritional science while simultaneously failing to account for the existing wealth of knowledge about food and eating from the perspective of Aboriginal people perpetuates colonial assumptions about the unworthiness of Aboriginal knowledge(s) (Smith 1999). Continued forms of colonization present new challenges for Aboriginal peoples in procuring and consuming foods necessary to uphold and strengthen their diverse Aboriginal cultures.

This chapter will critically explore how the nutrition transition has been explained (through the lens of nutritional science), and how diverse Aboriginal perspectives can contribute to our collective understanding of the nutrition transition. The key argument is that diverse approaches to food and eating, when woven together, have the potential to offer a more complete understanding of how the nutrition transition unfolds within Aboriginal communities.

The Culture of Nutrition

Conventional nutrition research has attempted to explain the nutrition transition within Aboriginal communities by describing the nutrient content of the various foods that Aboriginal peoples eat, comparing those foods with nutrition guidelines, and suggesting how Aboriginal peoples whose diets have shifted can learn to eat in a modern world. Canada's Food Guide has recently been adapted for First Nations, Inuit, and Métis communities to provide Aboriginal peoples with guidelines about portion sizes, caloric content, and healthy food combinations using examples featuring traditional foods such as wild meats and berries (Health Canada 2007). Although efforts to change individual diets represent a step forward in recognizing the importance of providing culturally appropriate nutrition education within Aboriginal communities, these efforts have met with limited success (Delormier et al. 2009), due in part to the nutritional lens through which approaches to food and eating are viewed. As contemporary researchers seeking to engage community members have repeatedly demonstrated, encouraging Aboriginal populations to simply eat 'right' is fraught with concern, as it presupposes that nutritional science can adequately address all of the nutrition problems within Aboriginal communities. Moreover, it ignores the fact that Aboriginal communities already have millennia-old traditional food systems in place to provide themselves with the nutrients they need to live and thrive.

In her book *Food Politics*, Marion Nestle (2007) argues that different cultures understand their relationships to food differently. Nestle contends that there are distinct belief systems that guide how people think about food and that nutritional science represents one such belief system. Nutritional science, like all belief systems, is based upon a particular point of view. Thus, what constitutes 'sound nutritional advice' according to the scientific standards set by nutritional scientists may or may not resonate with the way that diverse cultures, which hold very different belief systems, conceptualize and understand their relationships to food. With the understanding that there are many different ways to conceptualize food, it becomes necessary to learn about the cultural perspectives on the nutrition transition from those who are actually experiencing it.

The French Paradox and the Culture of Nutrition

Conventional approaches to nutrition research have almost synonymously linked food with nutrition, to the extent that alternative belief systems about food often fail to be incorporated into food research at all (Nestle 2007). Whereas the goal of food and eating within many Aboriginal communities is to provide a means to express culture, uphold cultural traditions, and strengthen cultural knowledge about the world (Willows 2005), the goal of conventional nutritional science research reduces foods to their biochemical properties and categorizes them according to their chemical compounds (Lupton 1996; Scrinis 2002; Warde 1997). These categories are then quantified in order to project measureable amounts of each category that should be consumed every day to remain 'healthy'. Nutritional science advocates for the use of these 'nutritional requirements' as dietary guidelines to which individuals should adhere in order to achieve optimal health.

The problem is that some people who might strictly follow these guidelines might still become ill, while others who do not follow the guidelines might remain very healthy (Cannon 2003; Pollan 2008). This dietary conundrum has posed such a grand problem within the field of nutrition that it has even been given a name: the French Paradox (Cannon 2003). The French Paradox describes French peasants, who often smoke, drink excessively, and eat copious amounts of saturated fats. According to the rationale of nutritional science, French peasants should be among the unhealthiest people on the planet; however, they have historically had among the lowest rates in the world of obesity, cardiovascular disease, and certain types of cancers (Cannon 2003).

As the French Paradox suggests, conventional nutritional science offers only one way of understanding the relationship between people and food. In his book *In Defense of Food*, Michael Pollan (2008) argues that while conventional nutritional scientists spend copious amounts of time and energy searching for a 'magic bullet'—the key to the 'best' and most healthful diet that will alleviate increasing burdens of disease—it is not the scientific accuracy of the arguments with which we need to be concerned. Rather, he argues that in addition to looking at how the nutrients within foods biochemically react with our internal bodily systems and organs, we also need to pay attention to the broader context outside of our bodies that influence our health, including our social, cultural, political, and physical environments (Pollan 2008).

The idea that the foods we eat are linked to our health can be traced back thousands of years to cultures that identified eating certain foods with preventing, curing, or enhancing one's overall health and sense of well-being (Trivedi 2006). Historically, however, the link between food and health has focused less on understanding how foods react within the body and more on learning about the types of foods that would prevent hunger or nutritional deficiencies (Cannon 2003; Hanrahan 2008). As such, what was known about food was also closely related to each culture's locale: through trial and error, experience and circumstance, people engaged with their surroundings to grow, harvest, pick, hunt, and gather foods as they were available. Food allowed diverse cultures to survive in their particular localities and also to develop relationships with their surroundings that are expressed through culture (Willows 2005). The ways in which people gather, prepare, and consume food give rise to diverse expressions of culture; thus, the study of food involves the study of culture (Counihan 1999; Pannelli and Tipa 2009).

As a symbol of culture, food provides a means to understand the health of particular cultural groups, including social, emotional, spiritual, and physical health and well-being. Aside from the information our foods can provide about nutritional health, foods and food-related cultural activities and processes also provide insight into other aspects of health (Kuhnlein et al. 2004). For example, the ceremonies and activities related to acquiring, processing, and consuming food might also be important for reinforcing cultural practices and norms that are important for social, emotional, and/or spiritual health. In this sense, food presents a way to understand health (broadly defined) through the lens of culture that includes but extends beyond its importance for nutrition.

The French Paradox indicates that it is perhaps insightful to look at the social, political, and cultural context in which eating occurs. Indeed, the French Paradox is not limited to the French, since there are many cultures who continue to eat foods that are considered to be 'traditional' who do not experience the same rates of non-communicable diseases as those who follow a 'Western' diet—that of the industrialized world (Cannon 2003). Whether or not these diets are considered 'healthier' than those advocated by nutritional guidelines, it appears that the interactions between culture and health might provide some insight into the overall health and well-being of particular populations.

Aboriginal Peoples and the Culture of Nutrition

If issues of food and health are viewed through the lens of culture, meaning that we take into account how diverse groups of people use food to express their relationship to one another and to the earth, we can begin to see how foods eaten by a particular culture affect the overall health of the ecosystems in which their foods originate. When people rely upon their natural surroundings for food, as is the case in many Aboriginal communities, and those surroundings become compromised, this can have devastating impacts upon key food sources, which can also influence social, physical, mental, and spiritual health (Shiva 2000; Willows 2005). As a result, changes to the availability or accessibility of food can be particularly harmful to local economies, affecting two determinants of health, namely, employment and income (Berkman and Kawachi 2000; Raphael 2004; Wilkinson and

Marmot 2003). Similarly, if a cultural or spiritual event depends upon the availability of a particular type of traditional food, then the loss of that resource may also represent a cultural loss for a community. This, in turn, may affect the social, emotional, and/or spiritual well-being of community members in addition to the overall health of communities and individuals (Berkman and Kawachi 2000; Pannelli and Tipa 2009; Power 2008; Raphael 2004).

Nutrition research that accounts for the wealth of knowledge held by Aboriginal peoples who remain rooted to their traditional territories has arrived at interesting findings: Aboriginal peoples who obtain the bulk of their nutrient energy from traditional sources get more essential nutrients than those who substitute market foods for traditional foods (Egeland et al. 2009; Hanrahan 2008). Although market foods tend to provide more energy, they have an overall lower density of essential nutrients than that in traditional foods (Egeland et al. 2009). This data thus supports the consumption of traditional foods.

Other nutrition research conducted with Aboriginal communities has shown that even 'sound' nutritional advice at best may be ignored if messages are not tailored to the communities they are directed to, or at worst may lead to poorer nutritional outcomes if the scientific advice counters cultural beliefs about food. Kuhnlein and Chan (2000) provide a poignant example of this situation in their research on the nutritional implications of environmental contaminants in certain foods. Previous research had indicated dangerously high levels of the contaminant toxaphene in burbot liver, consumed by the Indigenous people in the Northwest Territories. A resultant food advisory limiting consumption of burbot liver to one liver per person per week failed to account for the seasonal availability of burbot livers, making the food advisory inapplicable to the people it was meant to protect. Well-intentioned food advisories might create skepticism and unnecessary worry about eating traditional foods. Additionally, Kuhnlein and Chan point out that

research regarding contaminants in Aboriginal peoples' traditional food should not only identify contaminants that can be harmful to health, but also account for 'non-nutritional' values assigned to food that might outweigh the risks of eating it: time spent outdoors, passing along generational knowledge to children, and reinforcing values of conservation and environmental responsibility (Kuhnlein and Chan 2000).

Aboriginal Peoples' Understandings of Food and Eating

Although Aboriginal collectives within Canada share a historical connection to the land and are each influenced, historically and presently, by the Canadian state, Aboriginal peoples within Canada are incredibly diverse. In fact, **Indigenous peoples** worldwide, meaning all those who continue to hold an ancestral connection to a particular territory—Canada's Aboriginal peoples included—share some imperatives regarding the role of humans in relation to the world around them. These imperatives have to do with an intimate connection and belonging to the environment, a sacred responsibility to the earth, and a respect for all things living and non-living, including family and community. Each of these beliefs and values manifests itself differently depending on the origins and experiences of particular Indigenous groups, but they all nevertheless reflect overarching themes consistent with Indigenous peoples worldwide (Clarkson et al. 1992). These values and beliefs all position food and eating as more meaningful than nutritional requirements suggest. Each of these imperatives will be explored in turn as they relate to the Aboriginal peoples of Canada.

Connection and Belonging

Aboriginal peoples' knowledge of the natural world has frequently arisen in response to the need to find ways of addressing problems of hunger, thirst, shelter, and clothing. Learning about one's natural surroundings and how its bounties can provide for one's family and community was integral to life itself (Radkau 2008). The connection and belonging that Indigenous peoples have to their natural surroundings is born not of romantic notions of 'living close to nature', as is often assumed, but rather is viewed as a reciprocal relationship, where the earth provides resources for survival as long as the people take care not to deplete their surroundings (Turner 2005). Similarly, the greater the awareness that people have in caring for the lands and waters around them, the greater the likelihood that the earth will continue providing food and other necessities for survival. This understanding of the fragile relationship between humans and nature created an indisputable maxim for sustainability that not only was premised on *not depleting* resources, but in fact was dedicated to improving the amounts and types of resources available for future generations (Turner 2005).

For many Aboriginal cultures, humans form an inseparable part of their physical surroundings; thus all foods that are eaten reaffirm a direct and intimate connection to the earth and all things living and non-living. Among the Inuit, for example, there is a belief that the foods you eat become a part of you, and therefore, you are, literally, what you eat. Respecting the sacrifice that an animal makes to provide food is recognized as a necessary part of life and, thus, overall health and well-being (Hanrahan 2008). Indigenous peoples often do not separate the plants and animals used for food from those used in other daily practices such as making clothing and shelter, heating homes, making medicines, and so on (Condon et al. 1998; Hanrahan 2008; Willows 2005). For the Inuit, in particular, the practice of ensuring that all parts of an animal or plant were used largely stemmed from times when foods were scarce. The foods eaten, therefore, are intimately connected to health; since foods come from lands and waters, the health of individuals and communities is dependent upon the health of those resources. Essentially,

what we do to our physical surroundings, we ultimately do to ourselves. This very holistic definition of health accepts the interrelatedness of all things, since we all form an integral part of the ecosystems that make up our surroundings (Henderson 2000).

Foods and the natural surroundings in which they are obtained also provide important ingredients for medicines, clothing, shelter, and indeed, for overall health and well-being. In fact, the physical world acts as a 'natural pharmacy' in many respects, allowing Aboriginal peoples to develop an extensive range of medical therapies and treatment procedures over centuries of living in direct contact with the natural world (Samson and Pretty 2003; Turner 2005). For example, both Ackroyd (1930) and Howell (1998) have noted that Labrador Inuit women developed tonics of cod liver oil, bog bean, and various other locally derived remedies, undoubtedly preventing certain nutrition deficiencies. Indeed, Ackroyd (1930) found that compared with their non-Aboriginal counterparts in northern Newfoundland, the Inuit of the south coast of Labrador exhibited far fewer incidents of food-deficiency diseases such as beriberi, rickets, and scurvy, despite less access to fresh fruits and vegetables, and despite higher levels of poverty (Ackroyd 1930).

Another example of the way in which the procurement of plants and animals provided medicinal uses far beyond that of 'food' can be seen in Samson's impressions of his time spent 'on the land' with some members of the Labrador Innu.

> The first animal that was killed after I joined the camp was a beaver. On the way back to camp in the canoe, Dominic said that the film on the scrotum of the beaver can be used as a balm for earaches. For certain infections, a muskrat's fur can be used to clean the pus, after which sap or gum can be applied. Another Tshenut, Pien Penashue, told me that medicines can be obtained from all of the animals in

the country. Sponges can be made from caribou skin, diaper rash and skin irritations can be treated with the soft shavings from dead spruce trees. For toothaches and teething babies, the gums should be scratched with a pine needle, and then applied with berries. If the arm is infirm, one can eat the arm of a bear to regain strength, and similarly with other limbs. Other more psychological problems can be dealt with by substances found in the country as well as physical exercise, dreaming, and communicating with others. (Samson 2003: 262)

Food not only protected against nutritional deficiencies, but also reinforced a collective solidarity, fostering emotional and mental health and well-being. For example, among the Inuit of southern Labrador there was always a tradition of sharing the first salmon caught in the spring with all members of a community (Hanrahan 2000; Martin 2009). This practice, arising from a collective history of benevolence and respect for others, ensured that even the young and frail had a meal, and provided an important means to protect against hunger at a time of year when supplies of food were at their lowest, in addition to fostering an atmosphere of sharing and cohesion among community members.

Sacred Responsibility

Only after the last tree has been cut down.
Only after the last river has been poisoned.
Only after the last fish has been caught.
Only then will you find that money cannot be eaten.

—Cree Prophecy

In her book *The Earth's Blanket*, ethnobotanist Nancy Turner (2005: 24) states that the 'rich are those people who balance the benefits they receive in life with the responsibilities they assume for themselves, their families

and communities and their environment'. In the Western world, wealth is measured by the accumulation of possessions and less and less frequently by the value placed upon traditions or the ability to care for and benefit from natural surroundings (Turner 2005), yet many Aboriginal societies have held onto perspectives that do not deviate substantially from the original teachings of their ancestors (Clarkson et al. 1992). Such teachings suggest that 'wealth dwells in people who know about, appreciate and respect the other life forms around them and who understand the importance of habitats for people and all living things' (Turner 2005: 24–5).

Turner describes a letter written by James Douglas, who later became governor of the colony of Vancouver Island, upon his first arrival at what is now the city of Victoria. He described the landscape that he first saw as 'a perfect Eden in the midst of the dreary wilderness of the Northwest Coast' (as quoted in Turner 2005: 147). Turner argues that like so many who came before and after him, James Douglas assumed that the vistas he was admiring were untouched by humans, when in fact the landscapes he was referring to were actually moulded and developed by Coast Salish people, who tended and cared for the land using centuries-old practices of burning, clearing, and harvesting. These practices were not simply done for the purpose of creating an 'Eden' that would be left unexplored and untouched; rather, they were enacted to satisfy the needs of the people who lived there and enable trade for faraway resources.

Europeans' historical accounts about the land now known as Canada noted dramatically varied landscapes and climates, suggesting that diverse adaptations must have evolved among Aboriginal peoples in order to survive in these varied locations. These adaptations corresponded with the biodiversity of the geographic regions, which is evidenced by the diversity of foods, languages, songs, clothing, ceremonies, and other practices that emerge directly from the intimate knowledge of the world around them. Important for understanding the nutrition transition are the historical accounts that demonstrate the European colonists' commonly held assumption that the lands and waters upon which they arrived were undiscovered and untouched by humans, *terra nullius*, and were therefore awaiting human intervention in the form of 'development'. Turner (2005) suggests that the 'untouched' wilderness on Canada's west coast was interpreted as prime real estate by Europeans, who could not comprehend that such bounty was the result of years of careful resource management practices. Not unlike the west coast, the 'barren and inhospitable' landscape of the northeast coast of Canada was also interpreted as 'untouched', when in reality, diverse groups of Aboriginal peoples had thrived there for thousands of years (Fitzhugh 1999). The concept of *terra nullius* has been used to justify the appropriation, development, and exploitation of Aboriginal lands, signalling the assumption that Aboriginal lands were unoccupied prior to European settlement. From this perspective, food for Aboriginal peoples acts as much more than a means to ensure nutritional health or provide sustenance. Traditional practices of hunting, fishing, picking, trapping, and other forms of harvesting are also used to demonstrate a historical and ongoing connection to the land that has never been ceded.

Since Aboriginal peoples have historically viewed the foods they eat as being central to many of their daily activities, definitions of what constitutes 'food', 'sustenance', and 'subsistence' are much less clearly defined than those cited by Western nutritionists, health researchers, medical experts, government administrators, and wildlife regulators. According to a study conducted by Condon et al. (1998) among Inuit subsistence hunters, aside from the economic benefits of harvesting a particular food resource, most of the informants in their study mentioned other aspects of harvesting that had very little to do with economics or nutrition in a Western sense. Many mentioned the rest and

relaxation associated with living on the land, the continuation of Inuit hunting activities, and the importance of re-establishing ties with the land. These statements suggest the depth of cultural identity that can be exhibited through subsistence lifestyles, as well as the important role that foods and their associated activities play in maintaining and protecting the health and well-being of Aboriginal peoples. As Willows (2005: S33) suggests,

> Of importance to understanding the role that culture plays in determining food choice in Aboriginal communities is that the activities required to procure traditional food are not merely a way of obtaining food but, rather, a mode of production that sustains social relationships and distinctive cultural characteristics. This is because the consumption of traditional foods is more than just about eating; it is the endpoint of a series of culturally meaningful processes involved in harvesting, processing, distribution and preparation of these foods. For many Aboriginal peoples, these processes require the continued enactment of culturally important ways of behaving, which emphasize cooperation, sharing and generosity.

Respect

Respect for the earth is a natural extension of responsibility, surpassing the respect for one's natural or physical surroundings to include the importance of one's family and community (Knudtson and Suzuki 1992). In a report written for the International Institute for Sustainable Development, three Indigenous authors point out that in order to survive, historical Indigenous peoples had a responsibility to treat all life—plants, animals, minerals, and humans—with the utmost respect (Clarkson et al. 1992). Their rationale was based upon neither aesthetic choices nor resource conservation; rather, treating the natural world with respect meant engaging with the earth in ways that ensured one could meet all of the needs of one's family and community—harvesting, hunting, and shaping the environment in ways that would ensure that the earth would continue to provide (Clarkson et al. 1992; Turner 2005). Failure to do so could mean hunger or starvation. As such, the responsibility to the earth was based on the survival of future generations (Clarkson et al. 1992). In this sense, it is the duty of Aboriginal peoples to tend and care for the earth so that it can allow future generations to live in a world whose resources remain bountiful.

Ensuring the replenishment of resources required many Aboriginal groups to adopt nomadic lifestyles to avoid depleting the resources in a particular area (Carter 1990). How groups of Aboriginal peoples organized themselves varied according to geographic location, the ages and genders of the group members, and the roles and responsibilities assigned to each member. The pragmatic nature of Aboriginal survival on the land demanded clearly defined roles for each group member, as people depended upon one another for the group's survival. In fact, many pre-Columbian Aboriginal peoples of Canada did not exhibit signs of the social stratification and hierarchies that are common in Western society today (Cruickshank 1998; Samson 2003). Although each member of a community or tribe had specific roles and responsibilities, none were given priority over others (Cruickshank 1998; Gunn Allen 1986; Kelm 1998). Women, men, the young, and the elderly were all given respect because they all played equally important roles in the survival of the community.

Men and women, for example, had roles and responsibilities that were clearly divided by gender, yet unlike the Western world's gendered divisions of labour today, these roles were equally valued (Gunn Allen 1986). As the only ones able to bring life into the world, women were given special status in communities as caregivers and creators of life (Graveline 1998).

Women were also charged with preparing meals and clothing for men, enabling the men to hunt, trap, and fish, and thus provide the family and community with food (Goudie 1983; Hanrahan 2001). If anyone failed to accomplish his or her assigned duties, or did so inadequately, the entire family and perhaps community might go hungry or starve. Young people were given the important role of gathering fuel and food for the family, and as they got older and learned about their environments, were expected to impart their knowledge to the next generation (Cruickshank 1998).

Community elders have always been given a special place in Aboriginal communities (Knudtson and Suzuki 1992). As the keepers of legends and stories, elders were considered the very transmitters of culture and were expected to pass on their knowledge to younger generations through advice and guidance (Knudtson and Suzuki 1992). The accumulated wisdom and teachings of the Indigenous ancestors tell much about how to encourage plant and animal resources to thrive, so that they can continue to give life and support the needs of current and future generations (Knudtson and Suzuki 1992). Thus, interactions with the earth and its resources must be carefully considered in order to ensure the survival of future generations.

This sense of responsibility for future generations has guided previous generations and offers guidance to the current generation (Clarkson et al. 1992). Respecting and honouring elders and ancestors means listening carefully to their teachings, learning from their mistakes, and living in step with their wisdom. Accordingly, there is a responsibility for us all to take care to respect and honour the generations of the future, just as previous generations have honoured us by giving us life and taking care of our resources. Thus, the knowledge passed on through generations, whether through actions or words, must be given privilege and respect if there is to be greater understanding of the nutrition transition. When we think about the nutrition transition from this perspective, we can begin to think about food and eating as a series of processes that are profoundly infused with the culture in which they occur, and which cannot be understood outside of a social, cultural, and political context. As the following quotation about the annual seal hunt in south-eastern Labrador suggests, viewing traditions and practices outside of their contexts causes misinterpretation of important cultural practices, which are challenged by those who do not fully understand them.

> If you're living in the city and have never been exposed to [our] way of life, then you probably might think that it's disgusting or that you're trying to destroy the environment. It's like those seal protestors. Like they have absolutely no idea what a seal meant to people . . . they have no idea . . . they don't know how dependent we were on nature. To survive. And I think that it still holds true in our culture today. Probably depend on it just to keep our traditions alive. Not so much if people need it to survive like we used to, but I think we need it to maintain our connection with our past and with our culture . . . (Martin 2009: 140)

Conclusion

Throughout the world, concern about the nutrition transition is escalating rapidly for both Indigenous and non-Indigenous populations, particularly with respect to the burden of chronic diseases related to overeating. In 2004, the World Health Organization (WHO) developed a *Global Strategy on Diet, Physical Activity and Health*, based on the recognition that the current worldwide burden of disability, mortality, and morbidity is directly related to chronic diseases acquired through unhealthy eating and physical inactivity. In this report, the WHO notes that 47 per cent of the global burden of disease is directly attributed to

rising rates of obesity, cardiovascular disease, diabetes, and various cancers, all of which are preventable through changes in diet and regular physical activity. In addition, the WHO acknowledges that given the exponential rise in the rates of chronic diseases over the past 30 years, having the appropriate resources in place to deal with the associated health-care costs, policy changes, and targeted interventions represents a major challenge to global public health (WHO 2004).

Some of the biggest population and public-health concerns being faced today are linked to over-consumption of food, and yet the world is actually experiencing an unprecedented global food shortage that is contributing to the number of the world's hungry (United Nations 2008, 2009). A February 2009 fact sheet issued by the World Food Programme notes that the current global economic downturn has increased the number of the world's hungry to nearly 1 billion people. It might appear counter-intuitive to assert that the number of hungry people in the world is growing at the same time that people are experiencing unprecedented burdens of disease related to overeating. If we look at these two health concerns as each representing part of a growing crisis related to the nutrition transition, we can begin to view food as being about much more than providing people with too much or too little to eat, and more in terms of how social, economic, political, environmental, and cultural circumstances beyond the control of individuals affect how, how much, when, and even why certain foods are being eaten or not eaten across diverse populations. Thus, understanding the role that food plays in our health and well-being is about more than simply having 'enough' to eat or calculating the nutritional content of the foods that are being eaten; instead, it is essential to understand the social, economic, political, environmental, and cultural context in which foods are accessed and consumed.

Even though mounting concerns about the diminishing food supply and the increasing burden of disease are attracting attention from researchers all over the world, there is little conversation among researchers from diverse disciplines regarding potential solutions to some of these major shared ecological and human crises (Saul 2008). Nutritionists remain isolated from sociologists and anthropologists, and public health officials are largely unaware of their counterparts who work in political economy and environmental stewardship. The result is that policies and programs that rely upon the research advances within specific disciplinary fields are overlooking key areas of concern that exist across multiple disciplines. Although certain policies and programs may legitimately address the concerns within a particular discipline, such as the need to develop public health interventions that halt growing rates of diabetes, the application of these policies may undermine, ignore, or contradict some of the fundamental concerns that exist within a different discipline or policy field. For example, when government policies regarding resource conservation infringe upon Aboriginal peoples' right to access their traditional livelihoods and sources of income, the result may be an increased burden on health care as Aboriginal peoples experience higher rates of chronic disease such as obesity and diabetes resulting from physical inactivity and poor food choices (Damman et al. 2008). In effect, policies and programs meant to address problems of environmental devastation or population health may contribute to the harm affecting the overall health of the environment and the people who live in it, when they do not seek to more broadly understand issues that affect health outside of specific disciplinary silos.

The nutrition transition from land foods to market foods indicates a shift away from the traditional practices and the corresponding knowledge that is involved in the procurement, preparation, and consumption of these foods. Many Aboriginal peoples are facing a veritable onslaught of circumstances that are conspiring to end traditional practices of food gathering. These circumstances arise from all directions—the appropriation of Indigenous lands for industrial development, conservation policies that undermine traditional practices of food gathering, and the continued globalization of the market economy, which undermines the value of traditional food-gathering practices (Damman et al. 2008). First-hand accounts of this onslaught can be found within Canada's diverse Aboriginal communities.

Scratching the surface of the broader social, economic, political, and environmental crises in which the nutrition transition is occurring raises many more questions than answers for Aboriginal communities. As Aboriginal youth grow up to learn that traditional land use is regarded as contributing less to the economy than conventional Western agricultural or industrial uses, our children, our most precious resource, become discouraged and are pressured to abandon the ways of their elders. Indeed, it is difficult for elders to suggest otherwise, as they witness any direct dependence upon the natural world as making their people more vulnerable. Their vulnerabilities prevent their knowledge from becoming part of the discourse about food systems (Damman et al. 2008).

The promotion and protection of Aboriginal food systems and the food systems of Indigenous peoples all over the world need to happen through the promotion and protection of diverse Indigenous cultures and the practices and knowledge that are part of cultural traditions about food. This must occur through the inclusion of Indigenous peoples as a fundamental part of the decision-making process around food systems. Only when Indigenous peoples are included as full and equal partners in discussions that affect their access to traditional foods might we recognize that creative solutions to worldwide food shortages and over-consumption all hinge upon the preservation of the cultural diversity of our world's Indigenous peoples.

Discussion Questions

1. How might understanding Aboriginal cultures promote a better understanding of the nutrition transition?

2. Think about the apparent contradiction between global food shortages and rising rates of obesity. What might Aboriginal perspectives on food offer in terms of understanding the complexity of this contradiction?

3. Many Aboriginal communities in Canada are fighting for greater control over their lands and resources. How and why might traditional food use be an important part of this fight?

Further Reading

1. Kuhnlein, H.V., B. Erasmus, and D. Spigelski, eds. 2009. *Indigenous Peoples' Food Systems: The Many Dimensions of Culture, Diversity and Environment for Nutrition and Health*. Rome: Food and Agriculture Organization of the United Nations.

   This book is a collection of 12 case studies from around the world that share the perspectives of Indigenous community knowledge-holders and international scientists regarding the importance of preserving and protecting Indigenous knowledge, biodiversity, and the richness of food resources. It presents a critique of modern technological developments that value mono-cultural food production over the people and cultures who are the main producers and consumers of those foods. Importantly, this book emphasizes the critical importance of valuing and preserving Indigenous peoples' knowledge about traditional food systems.

2. Loppie-Reading, C., and F. Wien. 2009. *Health Inequalities and Social Determinants of Aboriginal Peoples' Health*. Vancouver, BC: National Collaborating Centre for Aboriginal Health.

   This report presents a conceptual framework for understanding the relationship between the social determinants of health and health disparities that are experienced by Aboriginal people and communities, as compared to their non-Aboriginal counterparts. The conceptual framework is called the Integrated Life Course and Social Determinants Model of Aboriginal Health, which examines the proximal, intermediate, and distal determinants of health. Using available data to describe health inequalities, the report presents potential trajectories of health across the life course and suggests ways in which the social determinants may act as barriers to addressing health inequalities.

3. Martin, D.H. 2009. 'Food Stories: A Labrador Inuit-Métis Community Speaks about Global Change'. Unpublished doctoral dissertation. Halifax, NS: Dalhousie University.

   This qualitative study explores how people who live in one Inuit–Métis community experience and understand their relationships to food in a context of global change. Using 'food stories' collected from eight elders, eight middle-aged adults, and eight young adults, the study discusses changes to peoples' relationships to food and how these changes are influencing the health and well-being of both people and communities. Findings from the study demonstrate how the introduction of both government services and the market economy has led to the creation of certain policies and programs that undermine or ignore established social and cultural norms. The study ends with suggestions of how Indigenous knowledge should work alongside non-Indigenous approaches to policy and program development in order to protect and promote the health of Indigenous people and communities.

References

Ackroyd, W.R. 1930. 'Beriberi and Other Food-Deficiency Diseases in Newfoundland and Labrador'. *Journal of Hygiene* 30: 357–86.

Berkman, L., and I. Kawachi. 2000. *Social Epidemiology.* New York: Oxford University Press.

Bjerregaard, P. 2010. 'Nutritional Transition—Where Do We Go from Here?' *Journal of Human Nutrition and Dietetics* 23, suppl. 1: 1–2.

Cannon, G. 2003. *The Fate of Nations: Food and Nutrition Policy in the New World.* The Caroline Walker Lecture. London, UK: Royal Society.

Carter, S. 1990. *Lost Harvests: Prairie Indian Reserve Farmers and Government Policy.* Montreal: McGill-Queen's University Press.

Clarkson, L., V. Morrissette, and G. Regallet. 1992. *Our Responsibility to the Seventh Generation: Indigenous Peoples and Sustainable Development.* Winnipeg, MB: International Institute for Sustainable Development.

Condon, R., P. Collings, and G. Wenzel. 1998. 'The Best Part of Life: Subsistence Hunting, Ethnicity and Economic Adaptation among Young Adult Inuit Males'. *Arctic* 48(1): 31–56.

Counihan, C. 1999. *The Anthropology of Food and Body: Gender, Meaning and Power.* NY: Routledge.

Cruikshank, J. 1998. *The Social Life of Stories: Narratives and Knowledge in the Yukon Territory.* Vancouver: University of British Columbia Press.

Damman, S., W.B. Eide, and H.V. Kuhnlein. 2008. 'Indigenous Peoples' Nutrition Transition in a Right to Food Perspective'. *Food Policy* 33: 135–55.

Delormier, T., K.L. Frohlich, and L. Potvin. 2009. 'Food and Eating as Social Practice—Understanding Eating Patterns as Social Phenomena and Implications for Public Health'. *Sociology of Health and Illness* 31(2): 215–28.

Egeland, G.M., G. Charbonneau-Roberts, J. Kuluguqtuq, J. Kilabuk, L. Okalik, R. Soueida, and H.V. Kuhnlein. 2009. 'Back to the Future: Using Traditional Food Knowledge to Promote a Healthy Future among Inuit'. In *Indigenous Peoples' Food Systems: The Many Dimensions of Culture, Diversity and Environment for Nutrition and Health,* ed. H.V. Kuhnlein, B. Erasmus, and D. Spigelski. Rome: United Nations Food and Agriculture Organization, 9–22.

Fitzhugh, L.D. 1999. *The Labradorians: Voices from the Land of Cain.* St John's, NL: Breakwater.

Goudie, E. 1983. *Woman of Labrador.* Agincourt: Book Society of Canada.

Graveline, F.G. 1998. *Circle Works: Transforming Eurocentric Consciousness.* Halifax, NS: Fernwood.

Gunn Allen, P. 1986. *The Sacred Hoop: Recovering the Feminine in American Indian Traditions.* Boston: Beacon Press.

Hanrahan, M. 2000. *Brooks, Buckets and Komatiks: The Problem of Water Access in Black Tickle.* St John's, NL: Faculty of Medicine, Memorial University of Newfoundland.

———. 2001. 'Salmon at the Centre: Ritual, Identity, and the Negotiators of Life Space in Labrador Métis Society'. In *From Red Ochre to Black Gold,* ed. D. McGrath. St John's, NL: Flanker Press, 146–65.

———. 2008. 'Tracing Social Change among the Labrador Inuit and Inuit-Metis: What Does the Nutrition Literature Tell Us?' *Food, Society and Culture* 11(3): 315–33.

Health Canada. 2007. 'Eating Well with Canada's Food Guide: First Nations, Inuit and Métis'. Available at www.hc-sc.gc.ca/fn-an/alt_formats/fnihb-dgspni/pdf/pubs/fnim-pnim/2007_fnim-pnim_food-guide-aliment-eng.pdf.

Henderson, J.Y. 2000. 'The Context of the State of Nature'. In *Reclaiming Indigenous Voice and Vision,* ed. M. Battiste. Vancouver: University of British Columbia Press, 11–38.

Howell, J., transcribed by M. Hanrahan. 1998. 'Taking Care of Each Other: The Relationship between the Labrador Metis and the Environment'. *Terra Borealis* 1: 26–8.

Kelm, M.E. 1998. *Colonizing Bodies: Aboriginal Health and Healing in British Columbia, 1900–50.* Vancouver: University of British Columbia Press.

King, M., A. Smith, and M. Gracey. 2009. 'Indigenous Health Part 2: The Underlying Causes of the Health Gap'. *Lancet* 374(9683): 76–85.

Knudtson, P., and D. Suzuki. 1992. *Wisdom of the Elders: Native and Scientific Ways of Knowing about Nature.* Vancouver: Greystone.

Kuhnlein, H.V. 2009. 'Why Are Indigenous Peoples' Food Systems Important and Why Do They Need Documentation?' In *Indigenous Peoples' Food Systems: The Many Dimensions of Culture,*

Diversity and Environment for Nutrition and Health, ed. H.V. Kuhnlein, B. Erasmus, and D. Spigelski. Rome: United Nations Food and Agriculture Organization, 1–8.

Kuhnlein, H.V., and H.M. Chan. 2000. 'Environment and Contaminants in Traditional Food Systems of Northern Indigenous Peoples'. *Annual Review of Nutrition* 20: 595–626.

Kuhnlein, H.V., O. Receveur, R. Soueida, and G.M. Egeland. 2004. 'Arctic Indigenous Peoples Experience the Nutrition Transition with Changing Dietary Patterns and Obesity'. *The Journal of Nutrition* 134(6): 1447–53.

Lambden, J., O. Receveur, J. Marshall, and H.V. Kuhnlein. 2006. 'Traditional and Market Food Access in Arctic Canada is Affected by Economic Factors'. *International Journal of Circumpolar Health* 65: 331–40.

Loppie-Reading C., and F. Wien. 2009. *Health Inequalities and Social Determinants of Aboriginal Peoples' Health*. Vancouver: National Collaborating Centre for Aboriginal Health.

Lupton, D. 1996. *Food, the Body and the Self*. London: Sage.

Lynge, F. Translated by M. Stenbaek. 1992. *Arctic Wars, Animal Rights, Endangered Peoples*. Hanover, NH: University Press of New England.

Martin, D.H. 2009. 'Food Stories: A Labrador Inuit-Metis Community Speaks about Global Change'. Unpublished doctoral dissertation. Halifax, NS: Dalhousie University.

Nestle, M. 2007. *Food Politics: How the Food Industry Influences Nutrition and Health*. Berkeley, CA: University of California Press.

Nuttall, M., F. Berkes, B. Forbes, G. Kofinas, T. Vlassova, and G. Wenzel. 2005. 'Hunting, Herding, Fishing and Gathering: Indigenous Peoples and Renewable Resources Use in the Arctic'. In *Arctic Climate Impact Assessment Scientific Report*, ed. C. Symon, L. Arris, and B. Heal. London: Cambridge University Press, 662–95.

Panelli, R., and G. Tipa. 2009. 'Beyond Foodscapes: Considering Geographies of Indigenous Well-being'. *Health Place* 15: 455–65.

Pollan, M. 2008. *In Defense of Food: An Eater's Manifesto*. London: Penguin.

Power, E. 2008. 'Conceptualizing Food Security for Aboriginal People in Canada'. *Canadian Journal of Public Health* 99(2): 95–7.

Radkau, J. 2008. *Nature and Power: A Global History of the Environment*. New York: Cambridge University Press.

Raphael, D. 2004. *Social Determinants of Health: Canadian Perspectives*. Toronto: Canadian Scholar's Press.

Samson, C. 2003. *A Way of Life that Does Not Exist: Canada and the Extinguishment of the Innu*. St John's, NL: Institute for Social and Economic Research.

Samson, C., and J. Pretty. 2003. 'Environmental and Health Benefits of Hunting Lifestyles and Diets for the Innu of Labrador'. *Food Policy* 31: 528–53.

Saul, J.R. 2008. *A Fair Country: Telling Truths about Canada*. Toronto: Viking.

Scrinis, G. 2002. 'Sorry, Marge'. *Meanjin* 61(4): 108–16.

Sharma, S., J. Gittleshon, R. Rosol, and L. Beck. 2010. 'Addressing the Public Health Burden Caused by the Nutrition Transition through the Healthy Foods North Nutrition and Lifestyle Intervention Programme'. *Journal of Human Nutrition and Dietetics*, 23, suppl. 1: 120–7.

Shiva, V. 2000. *Stolen Harvest: The Hijacking of the Global Food Supply*. Cambridge, MA: South End Press.

Smith, L.T. 1999. *Decolonizing Methodologies: Research and Indigenous Peoples*. New York: Zed Books.

Thow, A.M. 2009. 'Trade Liberalization and the Nutrition Transition: Mapping the Pathways for Public Health Nutritionists'. *Public Health Nutrition* 12(11): 2150–8.

Trivedi, B. 2006. 'The Good, the Fad and the Unhealthy'. *New Scientist* 191(2570): 42–9.

Turner, N. 2005. *The Earth's Blanket: Traditional Teachings for Sustainable Living*. Vancouver: Douglas and McIntyre.

United Nations. 2008. *Assessment of the World Food Security and Nutrition Situation*. 34th Committee on World Food Security. Rome: United Nations Food and Agriculture Organization.

———. 2009. *The State of Agricultural Commodity Markets 2009: High Food Prices and the Food Crisis—Experiences and Lessons Learned*. Rome: United Nations Food and Agriculture Organization.

———. 2011. *Human Development Report 2011. Sustainability and Equity: A Better Future for All*. New York: United Nations Development Programme.

Warde, A. 1997. *Consumption, Food and Taste*. London: Sage.

Wheatley, M.A. 1998. 'Social and Cultural Impacts of Environmental Change on Aboriginal Peoples in Canada'. *International Journal of Circumpolar Health* 57 Suppl. 1: 537–41.

Wilkinson, R., and M. Marmot. 2003. *Social Determinants of Health: The Solid Facts*. Copenhagen: World Health Organization.

Willows, N.D. 2005. 'Determinants of Healthy Eating in Aboriginal Peoples in Canada'. *Canadian Journal of Public Health* 96: S32–S36.

Winson, T. 2004. 'Bringing Political Economy into the Debate on the Obesity Epidemic'. *Agriculture and Human Values* 21: 299–312.

World Health Organization (WHO). 2004. 'Global Strategy on Diet, Physical Activity and Health'. Accessed 16 August 2009 at www.who.int/dietphysicalactivity/strategy/eb11344/strategy_english_web.pdf.

14

Food Security?
Some Contradictions Associated with Corporate Donations to Canada's Food Banks
Carole Suschnigg

Learning Objectives

Through this chapter, you can:

1. Understand the concepts of 'food security' and 'food sovereignty'
2. Examine how food insecurity has increased exponentially across Canada since 1980
3. Review two main perspectives on 'food insecurity'—the anti-poverty approach and the food sovereignty approach

Introduction

Food insecurity is a major social problem in Canada. In March 2010, almost 870,000 people sought assistance from a local **food bank** or an affiliated emergency food program.[1] This figure represents a 28 per cent increase from March 2008 and is 'the highest level of food bank use on record' (Food Banks Canada 2010a).

Without doubt, Canada's food banks are helping to ameliorate the symptoms of food insecurity nationwide. But is it possible they are perpetuating the need for such services? Critics have long complained that food banks are a 'band-aid solution' to a fundamentally flawed economic system—that by taking the edge off people's suffering, food banks thereby help keep a lid on civil unrest. However, little attention has been paid to food banks' dependence on corporate donations of food and money, and to the fact that some of those donors are contributing to food insecurity on a grand scale: what they give with one hand they take with the other. Exposing this contradiction from the **food sovereignty** perspective is the main goal of this chapter.

I begin with a summary of the rise of food banks in Canada and an explanation of this phenomenon from an anti-poverty perspective. After that I expand my analytic gaze to examine the recent global food crisis from the food sovereignty perspective. Returning to the subject of Canada's food banks, I describe our National Food Sharing System and, using three major corporate donors as examples, demonstrate how Food Banks Canada's solicitation of such donors is, albeit inadvertently, undermining food sovereignty and thereby also undermining **food security** in Canada and abroad.

The Rise of Food Insecurity in Canada

Long after the Depression of the 1930s, Canada's first food bank opened in 1981 (Riches 1997: 49). A decade later the number of food banks had swelled to almost 300 (ibid.). By 2002 there were an estimated 620 food banks and over 2000 affiliated organizations providing so-called 'emergency' food services to people nationwide. In March of that year, these services fed almost three-quarters of a million people across the country (Wilson and Toas 2002: 3–4).

The number of food recipients peaked during 2003–5, had dropped slightly by 2008, but was on the rise again by 2009 (Food Banks Canada 2009: 4; Food Banks Canada 2010b: 2). In March 2010, 38 per cent of food recipients were children, 51 per cent of recipients were dependent on social assistance, 15 per cent of recipients were dependent on a disability pension, and 11 per cent of recipients reported their main source of income was from employment (ibid.).

From 2009 to 2010, the two provinces that experienced the greatest increase in numbers of people turning to food banks were Saskatchewan (20.1 per cent) and Manitoba (21 per cent). In Alberta, Saskatchewan, and Manitoba, a large proportion of people assisted by food banks self-identified as Aboriginal (51 per cent, 52.2 per cent, and 38.4 per cent respectively) (ibid.: 6–7). In Canada's largest metropolitan region, the Greater Toronto Area, there were nearly 1.2 million visits to the Daily Bread Food Bank and its partner organizations—a 15 per cent increase from the year before. Almost half of these food recipients were dependent on social welfare, and almost a quarter were dependent on a disability pension. Among those who had been coming to a food bank for six months or less, 46 per cent said they came because they had lost their job or their hours of employment had been reduced (Matern 2010).

Outside cities, 'food bank use in Canada's small towns and rural areas increased by 13% between 2009 and 2010' (Food Banks Canada 2010b: 9). In part this may be a consequence of the 7.1 per cent drop in the number of rural farms from 2001 to 2006 along with a 2.7 per cent increase in the total rural population (Statistics Canada 2008). As well, increased transportation costs are contributing to higher food prices in some rural and northern areas (Food Banks Canada 2010b: 25).

Despite the proliferation of emergency food services across Canada over the past 30 years, many households' nutritional needs remain unmet, in part because food banks are not publicly funded: their (mostly volunteer) staff members depend on charitable donations from individuals and corporations. In turn, irregular and limited resources mean that food banks are obliged to ration the amount of food they distribute. Interviews with food bank managers in my own community of Sudbury, Ontario, for instance, revealed that most were limiting households to one visit per month and to about three days' worth of emergency food per visit. Furthermore, limited on-site storage—especially a lack of refrigeration facilities—was preventing most local food banks from providing fresh items such as vegetables, fruit, milk, eggs, and meat. Mostly what they could offer were non-perishables such as canned soup, jars of peanut butter, and boxes of macaroni and cheese (Suschnigg et al. 2002).

Interviews with food recipients themselves serve to reinforce this picture. Results for a non-random, convenience sample of 92 people seeking assistance from food banks in 2003 revealed that, on average, they had run out of money to buy food on 6 out of the previous 28 days.[2] Even then, access to a food bank was no guarantee that their nutritional requirements were being met. For instance, 41 per cent of people interviewed (n=37) said they rarely had access to fresh or frozen vegetables; 54 per cent (n=49) said they rarely had access to fresh or canned fruit; and 76 per cent of parents (n=35) said they had gone without food in order to feed their children (Suschnigg et al. 2003).

Linking Theory and Practice

Someone once said, 'There's nothing as practical as good theory'. The literature on food insecurity tends to fall into two camps: I will call them the 'anti-poverty camp' and the 'food sovereignty camp'. Each camp has a different set of explanations as to why food insecurity exists, and each has a different set of recommendations to help solve the problem.

The Anti-Poverty Perspective

From the anti-poverty perspective, Canada has more than enough food to feed all of its inhabitants, but some people simply cannot afford to buy what they need. In 2007, for example, just over 9 per cent of people in Canada were living below the poverty line. Particularly hard-hit were unattached individuals and lone-parent families headed by females: poverty rates for these groups were 26.6 per cent and 27.5 per cent respectively (Statistics Canada 2010).[3]

One of the main factors contributing to food insecurity has been the inadequacy of social assistance payments. As Table 14.1 illustrates, in Ontario in 2007 the average total welfare payment to a lone parent with one child was 75 per cent of the poverty line income; for a person with a

disability it was 69 per cent; for a couple with two children it was 62 per cent; and for a single employable adult, it was a mere 40 per cent (National Council of Welfare 2008: 45).

A major reason for the inadequacy of welfare benefits is the federal government's decision to alter its policy for transferring money to the provinces. For 30 years a federal–provincial agreement, the Canada Assistance Plan, had obliged the federal government to pay 50 per cent of a province's costs for social programs so long as that province upheld certain standards: that people in need be given financial assistance, regardless of cause; that financial assistance be based on a person's basic cost of living; and that no one be compelled to work in order to qualify for social assistance (Riches 1997: 67). However, this agreement led to the federal government having no control over its own budget: whatever a province spent on social programs the federal government was obliged to match.

Faced with spiralling costs, in 1996 the federal government replaced the Canada Assistance Plan with the Canada Health and Social Transfer (CHST). This newly adopted system of 'block funding' to the provinces enabled the federal government to regain some control over its budget, but for the provinces it resulted in 'cutbacks of $7 billion (15 per cent over three years) for health, education and welfare' (ibid.).

The federal government had promoted the CHST on the grounds it afforded the provinces more autonomy: provincial governments

Table 14.1 Adequacy of Welfare Incomes, Ontario, 2007

Household Type	Total Welfare Income, 2007	After-Tax LICOs, 2007	Welfare Income as % of Poverty Line[1]
Single employable adult	$7,204	$17,954	40
Person with a disability	$12,382	$17,954	69
Lone parent and one child	$16,439	$21,851	75
Couple and two children	$21,058	$33,946	62

1. Based on after-tax LICOs.

Source: Adapted from Table 2.2-b, National Council of Welfare (winter, 2008:45).

no longer were required to ensure welfare payments reflected residents' basic cost of living, and henceforth they were free to oblige welfare recipients to work for the financial assistance they received (Oliphant and Slosser 2003: 5–6).

According to critics the CHST proved to be 'a significant precursor to emerging food insecurity and hunger in Canada' (Wilson and Toas 2002: 15). Take the province of Ontario as an example. During the late 1990s the cost of living began rising dramatically. From 1997 to 2001, for instance, shelter costs rose 10 per cent; food costs, 14 per cent; clothing costs, 15 per cent; transportation costs, 23 per cent; and education costs, 47 per cent (Statistics Canada 2002).

While shelter costs in general rose by 10 per cent from 1997 to 2001 in Ontario, the average *rent* increased by 17.4 per cent from 1998 to 2002 (Oliphant and Slosser 2003: 9). Compared to other necessities, even a 1 per cent increase in the cost of shelter tends to have a relatively large impact on a household's budget, and since people on low incomes are more likely to rent than to own their home, any increase in rent is likely to make their accommodation less affordable. Indeed, Ontario's ongoing 'Pay the rent or feed the kids' campaign was born of this very problem (Ontario Non-Profit Housing Association 2004).

The dramatic increase in the cost of rental accommodation occurred after the elimination of rent controls when, in 1998, Ontario's Progressive Conservative government replaced the Landlord and Tenant Act with the so-called Tenant Protection Act. This new Act precipitated a housing crisis across the province. Many young adults found themselves unable to afford to leave home, people who tried to reduce costs by sharing accommodation found themselves living in overcrowded and stressful conditions, tenants who could not meet their rent found themselves evicted, and increasing numbers of people found themselves homeless (Ontario Tenant Toronto Tenants 2003).

Social assistance payments did not just fail to keep pace with the increased cost of living at this time; they were cut back substantially. In 1993 the Progressive Conservatives had chastised the New Democratic government for increasing welfare benefits by a mere 1 per cent (Oliphant and Slosser 2003: 3). Once elected, however, the Progressive Conservatives chose to *reduce* those same benefits by more than a fifth. They also introduced the Ontario Works Act, a law that continues to require 'employable' people who receive welfare benefits to work for them.

In May 2004, Ontario's newly elected Liberal government announced an increase in social assistance payments—but this increase was only 3 per cent of the previous rate and did not take effect until early 2005. For a sole-support parent with one child the increase provided a maximum of $29.91 more per month; for a single adult on welfare it provided a maximum of $15.60 more per month. In order to close the gap between welfare income and the poverty line, however, welfare payments would have had to increase substantially—to more than double in the case of payments to single employable adults. Not surprisingly, by March 2008 in Ontario, 43.1 per cent of people turning to food banks were on social assistance (Cernik and Spence, cited in Food Banks Canada 2009: 24).

Ontario's social safety net for people with disabilities is looking rather tattered as well. Ostensibly a person whose disability prevents him or her from finding employment is eligible for social assistance under the Ontario Disability Support Plan (ODSP). Up until 2005, a single person with a disability was eligible to receive up to $930 per month under this plan—very little when one considers the many additional costs such a person may incur when it comes to support for independent living.[4] Unfortunately, however, compared to the Family Benefits Act it replaced in 1998, the ODSP Act has made it much more difficult for individuals to apply for and receive disability payments (Daily Bread Food Bank 2001). If a person's application for a disability benefit proves unsuccessful then she or he is left to survive on the much lower Ontario Works benefit. Of particular concern, research shows that 'many people are refused [the ODSP] through the inaccessible and confusing application process and through strict ODSP eligibility requirements'. The government, in the meantime, 'saves almost $5,000 per person denied ODSP each year' (ibid.). The 3 per cent increase in ODSP benefits as of February 2005 has done little to solve these problems: in March 2008, 23.1 per cent of people seeking assistance from food banks in Ontario were on a disability pension (Food Banks Canada 2009: 24).

Also under the Progressive Conservative government, Ontario's minimum wage rates remained frozen for nearly a decade. In 2000 there were over 220,000 minimum-wage workers in the province; 40 per cent of them were employed full-time and the majority were adults (Battle 2003). Employed at $6.85 per hour, their pay was worth 18.5 per cent less than it had been eight years earlier. And while $6.85 per hour had represented 43 per cent of average earnings in the province back in 1995, by 2001 it had dropped to 38.5 per cent of average earnings (ibid.).

In February 2004 the Ontario government raised the general minimum wage from $6.85 to $7.15 per hour. However, this increase generated only about $10.50 more per week, before taxes, for full-time workers. Further increases were introduced over the next few years, and as of the end of March 2010 the province's general minimum wage stood at $10.25 per hour (Ontario 2008; Ontario 2010). However, these increases have been 'too little too late' to eliminate workers' dependence on food banks: in March 2010, 11 per cent of people seeking assistance from food banks in Ontario reported that their primary source of income was from employment (Food Banks Canada 2010b: 28).

To summarize the situation for Ontario: despite the increased cost of living from the 1990s on, the provincial government eliminated rent controls, it legislated minimum wage rates that have continued to keep even full-time workers in poverty, it maintained social assistance payments at a fraction of the poverty line,

and it made it increasingly difficult for people with disabilities to obtain adequate financial support. These policies have contributed to harsh economic circumstances that, in turn, have left many thousands of people unable to purchase the food they need.

From the anti-poverty perspective, then, the most expedient solution is to introduce policies that ensure a living income for all. In particular, welfare payments, disability payments, and the minimum wage should be raised substantially. Everyone should be assured access to affordable housing, and publicly funded daycare should be made available to all who need it. Until these changes occur, food banks and other types of emergency food services must continue to exist in order to provide at least some food security for the poor.[5]

The Food Sovereignty Perspective

I turn now from the anti-poverty perspective to the food sovereignty perspective. Food sovereignty means everyone has 'the right to healthy and culturally appropriate food produced through ecologically sound and sustainable methods, and the right to define their own food and agricultural systems. It puts the aspirations and needs of those who produce, distribute and consume food at the heart of food systems and policies rather than the demands of markets and corporations' (Forum for Food Sovereignty 2007).

From the food sovereignty perspective, the anti-poverty perspective is short-sighted insofar as it conveys the impression that only poor people are vulnerable to food insecurity: from the food sovereignty perspective the entire world is at risk. Another criticism is that the anti-poverty perspective separates consumption issues from production issues and renders the latter invisible. Furthermore, food sovereignty advocates say the anti-poverty approach 'runs the risk of reducing the issue of hunger and malnutrition to a humanitarian problem for rich countries to solve, a prospect unacceptable to societies with long and rich agrarian histories' (Mazhar et al. 2007). Generally speaking, then, food sovereignty advocates in Canada and elsewhere tend to have a much wider analytic lens—one that brings global food production and distribution systems into focus.

The recent food crisis that saw hunger revolts break out in various countries around the world helps illustrate this point. From 2005 to 2006, the number of 'structurally undernourished' people in the world rose from 842 million to 875 million. While 34 million of those people were living in the global North, the rest were in the global South, especially sub-Saharan Africa, Haiti, and several countries in Asia (Ziegler 2009: 3). The vast majority were living in rural areas: 'The rural poor suffer from hunger because they lack access to resources such as land, do not hold secure tenure, are bound by unjust share-cropping contracts, or have properties that are so small that they cannot grow enough food to feed themselves' (ibid.).

More recently the number of structurally undernourished people rose very quickly to 925 million in 2008. This phenomenon was observed to be affecting the urban poor, not just the rural poor, in the global South. The immediate cause of the crisis was skyrocketing prices on the international market for rice, soya, maize, and especially wheat. While some countries temporarily could afford to subsidize the cost of food to consumers, others such as Haiti could not (ibid.: 6). High transportation costs served to exacerbate the situation for countries that by then had become heavily dependent on imported food.

Several factors are considered to have contributed to the rapid increase in food prices. The first factor, following the collapse of the world's financial markets in late 2007, was a massively increased investment in agricultural products with speculators seeking to buy low and then sell high to countries experiencing food shortages due to crop failures. 'One firm calculates that the amount of speculative money in commodities futures—markets where investors do not buy or sell a physical commodity, like rice or wheat, but merely bet on the price movements—has ballooned from US$5 billion in 2000 to US$175 billion in 2007' (GRAIN 2008).

A second factor was the conversion of vast amounts of agricultural land to grow crops for the production of biofuels. In some regions non-edible seed crops such as jatropha, castor, and candlenut are being grown; in other regions biofuels are derived from food crops such as wheat, maize, soya, corn, and sugar (Kagolo 2010). The subsequent reduction in food crops available for sale on the world market is another reason why food prices have increased. Of particular concern, since the production of biofuels in some countries is insufficient to meet increased internal demand, those countries are taking over fertile land elsewhere for the sole purpose of growing fuel crops. For example, 'European biofuel companies have acquired or requested about 10 million acres in Africa . . . displacing farmers and food production' (Rice, cited in Vidal 2010). More generally this process 'pits peasant farmers and Indigenous communities against massive agribusiness corporations and large investors who are already buying up large swathes of land or forcing people off their land' (Ziegler 2009: 9–10).

A third factor contributing to the food crisis was the structural adjustment policies imposed by the International Financial Institutions (IFIs) on indebted countries in the global South. These policies obliged countries to prioritize cash-crop production for export over food for local consumption, to privatize state-owned enterprises such as water supply systems, to reduce public spending on unprofitable public services like health and education, to eliminate price controls on basic necessities, to reduce the value of the local currency in relation to the American dollar, to eliminate import quotas and tariffs, and to encourage foreign investment. These policies have caused widespread impoverishment, with fewer people able to grow their own food and fewer people able to afford to purchase food they cannot grow for themselves.

Likewise the creation of conservation areas in certain parts of the world has caused thousands of Indigenous people and peasants to be evicted and their means of livelihood to be lost (Pimbert 2009), sometimes as a consequence of carbon-offsetting agreements that benefit corporations in the global North (Isla 2009).

While much of the food sovereignty literature focuses on processes affecting small farmers and peasants in the global South, similar neo-liberal economic policies have been undermining family farms here in Canada. Just as with the so-called Green Revolution that occurred in countries like India and the Philippines in the 1960s, farmers in Canada were encouraged to take out loans and adopt industrial agricultural practices: expand the area of land under production through the use of expensive complex machinery, purchase hybrid seeds from newly emerging biotech corporations, engage in monocropping, and maximize production through the application of chemical fertilizers and large-scale irrigation. Exports to hungry Third World countries were anticipated to guarantee profits.

However, as countries in the global South were sinking deeper and deeper into debt (partly due to having adopted similar agribusiness practices) many farmers in Canada were finding their production costs were exceeding their returns on the world market (Haley 1987). Starting in the early 1980s farm bankruptcies became commonplace, peaking at 551 in 1984 and remaining above 200 per year until 2006 (Canada 1997; Alberta 2008). From 2001 to 2006 the number of family farms in Canada dropped by 7.1 per cent. Among small farmers remaining on the land, many have been obliged to find off-farm work in order to supplement their income; others have gone into debt or sold off property in an effort to survive (Oser, cited in Food First 2006).

Yet, while the average annual income for small farmers has been declining, most major fuel, seed, grain, and fertilizer corporations have been enjoying high profits. In 2007, for example, Potash Corp (Canada) made a profit of US$1.1 billion on its sales of fertilizer, up 72 per cent from the year before; Cargill (US) made a profit of US$2.34 billion *in grain trading alone*, up 36 per cent from the year before (GRAIN 2008).[6]

> It seems that nearly every corporate player in the global food chain is making a killing from the food crisis. . . . Monsanto, the world's largest seed company, reported a 44% increase in overall profits in 2007. DuPont, the second-largest, said that its 2007 profits from seeds increased by 19%, while Syngenta, the top pesticide manufacturer and third-largest company for seeds, saw profits rise 28% in the first quarter of 2008. (ibid.)

In regard to solving the complex problems presented above, supporters of the food sovereignty movement argue that food security can best be achieved by promoting and protecting small-scale food production and distribution systems—whether a country's population be mostly urbanized as in Uruguay (Oliver 2006), or still highly rural as in India (Nayak 2009). At the Forum for Food Sovereignty in 2007 in Mali, for example, hundreds of representatives from more than 80 countries acknowledged that small-scale food producers—especially Indigenous people and women—are 'critical to the future of humanity'. These producers must be assured access to the land and resources they need to feed their communities. Unfortunately, however, their traditional 'capacities to produce healthy, good and abundant food are being threatened and undermined by neo-liberalism and global capitalism' (Forum for Food Sovereignty 2007).

Local markets thus need to be protected from the unfair competition associated with cheap imported food (under free trade agreements) and food dumping disguised as food aid. Also important, industrial farming methods must be relinquished and environmentally sustainable methods of food production promoted. Ultimately, people's right to food must be prioritized over export-oriented trading policies designed to maximize corporate profit (Forum for Food Sovereignty 2007; Vía Campesina 2009; Ziegler 2009; GRAIN 2008).

How are such goals to be achieved? In his report to the Human Rights Council Advisory Committee on the Right to Food, Special Rapporteur Jean Ziegler (2009: 18–19), recommended the following top-down initiatives. First, he insisted that 'staple foods should not be subjected to speculation on the stock exchange, but should be fixed by international agreement between producer countries and consumer countries'. Second, he called for a stop to the conversion of food crops to biofuels: 'The ease of mobility brought about by the use of hundreds of millions of cars in the northern hemisphere should not be paid for by hunger and undernourishment in the Southern hemisphere.' Third, he stressed that international trade agreements should not have negative consequences for any country's food security. Fourth, he criticized the IFIs' agribusiness agenda and urged those institutions to 'give absolute priority to investments in subsistence agriculture and local production'.

While these top-down solutions make eminent sense to food sovereignty advocates, the most promising solutions are being initiated from the bottom-up. Far from a one-size fits all approach, such solutions are born of each region's pre- and post-colonial/colonizing history, its ecological niche(s), its culture, and its cosmology. Pimbert (2009), for example, writes about Indigenous peoples' adaptive management of food production in 'fragile ecosystems' such as the Andes of South America, the circumpolar regions of North America, and the tropical forests of the Congo Basin. Rosset (2010: 196–8) makes a compelling case for 'land reform from below', citing the highly organized re-appropriation of land by Brazil's Landless Workers Movement (MST). According to Rosset, the MST 'has set the standard for other

landless people's movements around the world' by demonstrating how properly managed land redistribution and a small-farm economy can reduce household poverty, increase crop productivity, stimulate local economic development, and contribute to environmental sustainability.

In Canada, similar advantages have been noted in urban consumers' support of local farmers (Roberts, cited in Bell-Sheeter 2004: 25). Examples of such initiatives include, but are not limited to, farmers' markets and community-supported agriculture (CSA). CSAs involve people in the community paying farmers a membership fee to help cover the up-front cost of production in return for a share of the harvest on a weekly or bi-weekly basis. The objectives of such schemes include encouraging sustainable farming practices, ensuring the survival of family farms, having consumers share the risks associated with farming, enhancing the local economy, improving people's access to fresh, wholesome foods, and reducing transportation costs and dependence on fossil fuels (Pimbert 2009).

For Canada's First Nations, assimilation and the destruction of many Indigenous food systems—whether farming, hunting, gathering, trapping, or fishing—make it difficult to restore traditional forms of self-sufficiency in many areas.[7] In Alberta, for example, subsistence food activities are being destroyed due to tar sands development. More generally, 'the failure of federal programs to include or support the continued use of traditional foods has contributed to Native American's reliance on less healthy foods and culturally inappropriate patterns of consumption'— a problem exacerbated by the geographic isolation of many reserves and the availability of mainly high-cost, poor-quality, processed foods on the shelves of local stores (Bell-Sheeter 2004: 7). Nevertheless, efforts are being made to promote food sovereignty in these areas: 'While traditional foods may restore physical health, they are equally important for the revitalization and continuation of Native American cultural and spiritual traditions' (ibid.: 9).

Somewhat different again is the situation faced by many of Canada's Inuit: food insecurity for them is related to pollution drifting in from thousands of miles away, increasingly unpredictable weather patterns, and the impact of global warming on their access to country (traditional) foods.[8] Restoring food sovereignty for them will be a long process requiring major changes to the way industrialized countries burn fossil fuels and manage their ecosystems. In the meantime some Inuit communities are calling for more weather stations to give them updates on local conditions, and shorter call-out times for rescue teams to begin searching for stranded hunters (Higgins 2006).

Canada's Food Banks

What relevance does the food sovereignty perspective have for people in Canada who cannot afford to purchase enough food to feed themselves and their families and who depend on food banks?

Depending on one's analytic lens, Canada's food banks may be viewed as a charitable contribution to the deserving poor, a necessary evil, or a curse. In this section I argue, from the food sovereignty perspective, why Canada's food banks—insofar as they accept contributions from certain corporations—are a curse. I begin by summarizing some general criticisms of food banks. I move on to describe Canada's little-known National Food Sharing System, paying particular attention to some of the self-serving aspects of corporate participation. Then I examine three corporate donors in more detail: I demonstrate how these corporations, while appearing to promote food security via their charitable donations, do the very opposite through their undermining of food sovereignty at home and abroad.

Some General Criticisms of Canada's Food Banks

Clearly, the proliferation of food banks across Canada has let politicians 'off the hook' for taking

responsibility for the health and well-being of their constituents. Furthermore, as food banks have settled in for the long haul, there have been increased surveillance and regulation of food recipients via registration records, eligibility criteria, and documentation of visits. This development has been prompted in part by concerns about people visiting more than one food bank per month (so-called 'double-dipping'), lying about the number of their dependents, and selling emergency food aid to maintain an addiction.[9] Increasingly, then, food recipients have been obliged to demonstrate they are among the deserving poor. Their personal records, in the meantime, are vulnerable to unauthorized access, theft, and even court subpoena.

Canada's National Food Sharing System

In recent years a very large and complex system has evolved that now embraces most of Canada's small-scale local emergency food programs. The National Food Sharing System (NFSS) is a nationwide web of food collection and distribution operated by Food Banks Canada—formerly the Canadian Association of Food Banks—the umbrella organization for 10 provincial or territorial associations and their affiliated food banks across the country.

The NFSS is highly dependent on corporate donations of food, money, transportation, and services in kind. Take food as an example. These days millions of kilograms of food each year are donated by the food industry itself. In 2007, for instance, over 3.6 million kilograms of food and drink were donated to the NFSS by corporate giants such as Kraft, Proctor and Gamble, Coca-Cola, Kellogg's, General Mills, ConAgra, Tyson Foods, Nestlé, and Starbucks (Canadian Association of Food Banks 2007: 6).

Basically, the system works as follows. If a corporate food or beverage donation fills 10 pallets or more it is shipped by train, truck, or ship across country to a major distribution centre in Toronto or Montreal. Here the items enter a warehouse, are divided into smaller portions, and subsequently are shipped back out to regional 'hubs' across the country. 'Donated product is shared in a fair and equitable way, based on the number of people being served by food banks in each province' (ibid.: 5).

If one contemplates the ratio of calories-in to calories-out associated with the NFSS its overall inefficiency is colossal: the energy it takes to produce, process, package, transport, and re-distribute donations is far greater than the number of calories eventually made available to food recipients. When discussing this issue with me in 2003, staff members at the Canadian and Ontario food bank associations were well aware of this contradiction. Nevertheless, they felt they had no option but to solicit corporate donations when so many people are going hungry.

Another issue to consider is the benefits that accrue to the food industry through their participation in the NFSS. First, dumping fees are saved when food that otherwise would end up in landfill sites can be redirected to food banks. And as it turns out, most of the industry-donated food falls into this category: the goods donated may be close to, or past, their expiration dates; they may be the surplus created through over-production of a certain item; their containers may be dented or lack labels; or they may contain 'formula errors' (Daily Bread Food Bank, n.d.). Food recipients, to put it bluntly, have become a relatively cheap way to dispose of some forms of industrial waste.

Then there is the fact that food companies gain free advertising by donating food, most of which they would not be able to sell anyway. Moreover, being seen to help 'feed the poor' is particularly good for a company's marketing image. At a publicity event I attended in 2003, for example—just prior to a major food drive sponsored by the Canadian Association of Food Banks—corporate logos were on display while the director of the organization was being interviewed and filmed by the local media. At the time of writing, Food Banks Canada's website displays the logos of its major corporate donors

and lauds their efforts to help end hunger in Canada.

Corporations Undermining Food Security: Three Examples

For some corporations, donations to Food Banks Canada help distract public attention from the ways in which they create food insecurity by undermining food sovereignty elsewhere. The next section of this chapter is devoted to three examples that serve to support this claim.

Kraft Foods Inc.

Kraft Foods Inc. is the third-largest food and beverage company in the world. From 1988 to 2007 it was a major subsidiary of Philip Morris (now known as Altria), the biggest cigarette producer on the planet, whose profits reached $10.6 billion in 2000 (Campaign for Tobacco Free Kids 2001: 7).

Along with other major tobacco companies, Philip Morris has been shifting tobacco production to the global South because production costs are lower there. As well, in the South the market for manufactured cigarettes is growing the fastest: 'Where once the rich countries exported death and disease, increasingly these are manufactured locally' (World Health Organization 2004: 51). For instance, China and India are now the top two countries in the world in the amount of land devoted to growing tobacco, the number of people working in the tobacco industry, and the average number of manufactured cigarettes consumed per male each year (ibid.: 31–49).

Small farmers, having been persuaded that tobacco is a more profitable crop, have switched from growing food for local consumption to growing tobacco for export. In the process they have become far more dependent on cash to buy the food they need. A glut on the world market, however, has seen the selling price of tobacco drop. Consequently, many of these farmers have ended up in a perpetual cycle of debt to tobacco leaf–purchasing companies. In this manner,

Philip Morris has undermined food sovereignty and thereby contributed to food insecurity in its pursuit of profit:

> Many tobacco farmers are now stuck producing a crop that is labor and input intensive and brings with it a host of health and environmental dangers. Meanwhile, the cigarette companies continue to downplay or ignore the many serious economic and environmental costs associated with tobacco cultivation, such as chronic indebtedness among tobacco farmers (usually to the companies themselves), serious environmental destruction caused by tobacco farming, and pesticide-related health problems for farmers and their families. (Campaign for Tobacco Free Kids November 2001: 2)

When it was a major subsidiary of Philip Morris, Kraft nevertheless was hailed as one of Canada's most generous food donors and a 'partner' in the struggle to end hunger. Indeed, the Canadian Association of Food Banks praised companies like Kraft for helping to raise public awareness about food insecurity: food industry donors 'help us educate our members, government, the media and the general public about the hunger issue in Canada' (Canadian Association of Food Banks N.d.a).

Petro-Canada

In 2007, the Canadian Association of Food Banks touted Petro-Canada as one of its 'Top Financial Donors' (Canadian Association of Food Banks 2007: 7). This corporation is one of five major oil companies operating in Alberta to recover oil from Canada's tar sands. These tar sands are located in the northeastern part of the province and cover more than 140,000 square kilometres, most of it boreal forest and muskeg (Alberta Energy 2009). The tar sands are a mix of sand, clay, silt, water, and bitumen—a very thick form of oil. To achieve a usable product, the bitumen

has to be separated out and then refined. In 2006, oil production from tar sands was over 1 million barrels per day—almost half the oil produced in Canada. Production is expected to triple by 2020 (ibid.).

Some of Alberta's tar sands are located close to the earth's surface and are relatively easy to reach. However, before mining can start, 'the boreal forest must be clear-cut, rivers and streams diverted, and wetlands drained' (Woynillowicz 2007). Surface rocks and peatbog must then be removed—about 3.6 tonnes for every barrel of bitumen collected (ibid.). After that, the raw tar sands are scooped up from huge open-pit mines and trucked elsewhere for processing. The consequent scarring of the landscape is enormous, and the impact on the region's ecosystem has been devastating.

The majority of tar sands, however, are found far underground, and thus different mining processes are required. With steam-assisted gravity extraction, for example, partial processing of the tar sands is achieved by pumping steam underground to liquefy the bitumen, and then drawing it up to the surface (ibid.).

Regardless of the mining method used, large volumes of water are required to process the bitumen found in the tar sands. The main source of this water—the mighty Athabasca River—runs right through the tar sands region. Approximately 65 per cent of the oil industry's water is taken from this river: 'every day as much water is taken from [it] as would serve a city of a million people' (Edemariam 2007). This high uptake has reduced the water level in the river, depleted groundwater, and caused a lowering of the water table in some areas (Woynillowicz 2007).

Enormous amounts of waste are created as a result of the extraction processes used by the industry. Known as 'tailings', this waste is a slurry of waste water, sand, fine clay, and remnants of bitumen; even with recycling efforts, 'up to five barrels of tailings water is left after one barrel oil is produced' (Canadian Broadcasting Corporation 2009a). The slurry is stored in vast reservoirs euphemistically called 'tailing ponds'.

Some tailing ponds are so large they are visible from space (Woynillowicz 2007). They are also highly polluted with mercury, arsenic, naphthenic acids, and polycyclic aromatic hydrocarbons (ibid.; Canadian Broadcasting Corporation 2009a). Leaks from these tailing ponds are polluting rivers and groundwater sources.

What is the connection between Petro-Canada and food insecurity? The area in which the tar sands are located is home to a number of Aboriginal communities—Dene, Cree, and Métis. Traditionally, these communities have been self-sufficient, supporting themselves through hunting, fishing, and trapping. In Fort Chipewyan, for example, until recently about 80 per cent of the community's food needs were being met through subsistence activities (Thomas-Müller 2008). However, the oil industry's practice of clear-cutting, mining, and pipeline construction has destroyed much of the area's wildlife habitat. As well, the depletion and contamination of natural water sources has caused the demise of subsistence and commercial fishing (Woynillowicz 2007). A recent study of the drinking water in one community has confirmed the presence of toxins at a level not safe for human consumption. The unexpectedly high rate of a particular type of cancer in that community most likely is due to this pollution (Thomas-Müller 2008; Canadian Broadcasting Corporation 2009a).

Disregarding its impact on local food sovereignty, in 2008 Petro-Canada was planning to spend another $26.2 billion to expand its tar sands project at Fort Hills, Alberta, with an anticipated 280,000 barrels of oil a day being produced by 2014 (Tar Sands Watch 2007). Meanwhile the corporation's charitable donations to Canada's NFSS continue to convey the impression it is striving to end hunger in our country. Instead, by undermining Indigenous peoples' food sovereignty, it is doing the very opposite.[10]

Syngenta

In past years, the Food and Consumer Products Manufacturers of Canada has been listed as one of the NFSS's 'in-kind' supporters (Canadian Association of Food Banks N.d.b). Affiliate members of this organization have included major biotechnology companies like Bayer CropScience Canada, Dow AgroSciences Canada, Monsanto Canada, and Pioneer Hi-Bred. All of these companies market genetically modified (GM) seeds.

Syngenta is a large agribusiness corporation with operations in over 90 countries; in 2008 it made US$1.4 billion dollars in profit (Syngenta 2009b). The corporation's main products are GM corn and soybean seeds and so-called 'crop protection' chemicals—herbicides, fungicides, insecticides, and seed treatments. The corporation's Canadian head office and research farm are located in Arva, Ontario, and its seed production facility is located in Cottam, Ontario (Syngenta 2008).

According to its corporate website, Syngenta is 'committed to sustainable agriculture' and to 'delivering better food for a better world through outstanding crop solutions' (Syngenta 2009a). In a surrealistic video clip, the corporation's Foundation Acre website (Syngenta 2009c) makes exhortations such as 'Equal rights for every acre of land'—a slogan reminiscent of the civil rights movement—and 'No field left behind'—a slogan adapted from Project Headstart for underprivileged children in the United States. The message conveyed is that farmers who fail to see the benefit of using Syngenta products are environmentally irresponsible and intellectually stunted.

When one cruises through Syngenta's website, it is difficult to find any mention of GM seeds let alone what their associated risks might be. Outside of the biotech industry, however, there is widespread recognition that production of these crops is putting our health, our environment, and our entire food system in jeopardy (Altieri 2000; Kneen 1999; Paul and Steinbrecher 2003; Pringle 2003; Teitel and Wilson 2001; Tokar 2001). Loss of biodiversity, gene pollution, the emergence of 'super weeds', the patenting of seeds, terminator technology, biopiracy—these are just a few of the ways in which the world's food production systems increasingly are being taken over and put at risk by biotech corporations like Syngenta.

As an example, among Syngenta's 28 new corn hybrids is one called Agrisure Viptera 3111. This hybrid has been genetically modified to resist a variety of pests both above and below ground and to tolerate glyphosate-based herbicides such as Roundup (Syngenta 2010a). Similarly, the corporation has produced a new soybean that is both aphid-resistant and glyphosate-tolerant (Syngenta 2011a). However, farmers in North America are discovering weeds that have developed resistance not just to glyphosate-based herbicides but to other types of herbicides as well. In parts of Illinois, for example, a weed called common waterhemp is now resistant to five different herbicide families (Hager 2011).

In response to this emerging crisis, Syngenta is advocating a series of farm management practices to help solve the problem. Strategies recommended include applying a diverse range of herbicides (rather than planting a diverse range of crops!), scouting fields for evidence of herbicide-tolerant weeds, performing mechanical weed control, planting cover crops, and 'using a diverse crop/fallow rotation to extend the range of available herbicides'(Syngenta 2011b). Ironically, some of these strategies sound eerily similar to traditional, non-chemical forms of farm management.

While Syngenta continues to promote unsustainable farm practices in Canada and elsewhere, food bank use in rural areas of our country has been increasing. Indeed, in 2010, approximately 45 per cent of food banks in Canada were located in municipalities with populations under 10,000 (Food Banks Canada 2010b: 9). Syngenta trumpets itself as a major supporter of Food Banks Canada. In 2001, for example, the corporation initiated the Syngenta Rural FoodShare Initiative and donated $500,000 to America's Second Harvest and the Canadian Association of Food Banks. This money was used to purchase around 6.75 million kilograms

of food and distribute it to the rural hungry (Laws 2001; Syngenta 2009d and 2010b).

Further afield, Syngenta has been operating in Brazil since 1981. The corporation has been conducting experiments with GM soy and corn in an area close to Iguaçu National Park—a UNESCO World Heritage Site and an important nature reserve. Despite a legally defined buffer zone around the park, Syngenta transgressed the law by planting GM crops close to the park's boundary. More recently, in 2007, Syngenta and several other biotech companies successfully lobbied to have the width of that buffer zone reduced from 10 kilometres to 500 metres (Vía Campesina 2008: 2–3).

In protest, 70 peasant families occupied Syngenta's test site for 16 months from March 2006 to July 2007. On 21 October, 2007, 200 peasants returned to reoccupy the site. That afternoon about 40 heavily armed security guards arrived on the scene and began shooting.[11] One protester was killed and four others were injured.

Meanwhile Syngenta continues to promote itself as a compassionate corporation dedicated to ending world hunger. Unfortunately, information on Food Banks Canada's website serves to reinforce that impression.

Discussion

Across Canada, local resistance to industrial farming and GM foods is spreading. Interest in small-scale organic farming and access to organically grown food is increasing. Organizations like FoodShare are encouraging people to grow their own food in community gardens, to appreciate and safeguard seed diversity, to buy locally produced food, and to engage in non-market-based forms of food distribution. Participation in programs like Worldwide Opportunities on Organic Farms is growing.

What about supermarkets? Are they getting on the 'eat local' bandwagon? Several supermarket chains in the United States claim to be promoting this principle. For example, Wegmans and King Kullen—two family-owned chains—are making an effort to purchase directly from local growers: depending on the season, these chains sell locally produced fruits and vegetables side-by-side with those purchased from wholesale distributors (Miller 2004; Mininni 2008; *Progressive Grocer* 2008). The benefits are said to include fresher produce, a wider variety of produce, reduced transportation costs, less pollution due to the shorter distance travelled between farm and store, benefits to the environment due to reduced packaging, improved ability to track down the source of any contaminated products, and more money remaining in the local economy.

One must be careful, however, to check what a supplier means when it claims to be selling food grown 'close to home'. For most food sovereignty advocates, the term means that the food must have been grown within a 100–150 mile radius of its point of sale. In the United States the Wegmans and King Kullen supermarket chains appear to be adhering to this principle. But when Walmart advertises produce 'Grown Close to Home' this simply means its food was grown within the same state it is sold in—that it was not imported from elsewhere. This practice does not prevent the corporate giant from 'buying from a single large farm' and 'locking out smaller operations' (Pirog, cited in CBS News 2008).

In Canada the Loblaw supermarket chain has received similar complaints about its 'Grown Close to Home' campaign because the company's definition turns out to be so broad. For example, peaches grown in Ontario and 'shipped to the Western or Atlantic provinces' nevertheless have been advertised as 'Grown Close to Home' (Weeks 2010). Moreover, most of the supermarket's suppliers of so-called 'local' produce are 'large operations encompassing hundreds, or even thousands, of hectares' (ibid.). Concerned consumers, then, must be vigilant to ensure they don't end up supporting the very corporate monopolies they had hoped to see eliminated.

Conclusion

From an anti-poverty perspective, the social problem of hunger and food insecurity in Canada is entirely preventable: there is enough food to go around but thousands of people can't afford to buy it. To solve the problem, Canada's social safety net must be improved and the general minimum wage increased substantially. Strict controls must be placed on increases to basic cost-of-living expenses, especially rent. Major investments must be made in affordable housing and publicly funded daycare.

On the face of it, these recommendations pose little or no threat to capital. Indeed, if instituted they mainly would help ameliorate the worst impacts of neo-liberal monetarist policies and leave an increasingly exploitative economic system intact. But even if there were the political will to implement these anti-poverty recommendations, the structural constraints on our government would be considerable. In a world where multinational corporations have more wealth and wield more power than many nations do, welfare states such as Canada's are becoming an anachronism (Teeple 1995). Corporate pressure is on all levels of government to reduce social spending and to privatize state-owned enterprises; so-called 'free trade' policies are being pursued despite their obvious social costs.

In the Canadian context, food sovereignty advocates would not be opposed to the income-security measures recommended by anti-poverty activists: clearly, people who have fallen off the cliff shouldn't be abandoned while the fence at the top is being constructed. However, unlike the anti-poverty approach, the food sovereignty movement poses a direct challenge to capital. Canada's federal and provincial governments would face formidable constraints if they tried to implement the anti-corporate agenda put forward by food sovereignty advocates: to do so would be to acknowledge, expose, and undermine the class-based origins on which the state's own survival depends.[12]

In closing, across Canada and around the world, people are becoming increasingly aware of the threat that multinational monopolies pose to global food security. For now it is mainly poor people who are experiencing food insecurity. But in the not-too-distant future, we may all be experiencing food insecurity and finding ourselves hostage to corporations like Syngenta and Monsanto. In the words of Vía Campesina (2009), 'This is the battle of modes of production'.

Discussion Questions

1. What do anti-poverty advocates argue are the main causes of food insecurity in Canada?

2. Why are food sovereignty advocates critical of the anti-poverty approach to understanding and addressing the root cause of food insecurity?

3. What do food sovereignty advocates argue are the main threats to food security worldwide?

4. What is the National Food Sharing System (NFSS), and how does it operate?

5. How do the charitable donations of some major corporations help conceal their undermining of food security at home and abroad? Explain using three examples.

Further Reading

1. Food Banks Canada, http://foodbankscanada.ca/main.cfm.

   Food Banks Canada probably is the best resource for anyone who wants to have up-to-date information on hunger statistics in Canada. Every year the organization publishes a HungerCount report based on data collected from a survey of member food banks across the nation. As well as demographic details, each HungerCount report includes recommendations for addressing the problem of hunger and food insecurity in Canada.

2. Madeley, John. 2000. *Hungry for Trade. How the Poor Pay for Free Trade*. London: Zed Books.

   This book helps explain how trade liberalization—so-called free trade—has undermined food security for people in the global South. Huge amounts of cheap, subsidized food from the global North have been imported into countries in the global South. Unable to compete, small-scale rural farmers have been rendered bankrupt; and local self-sufficiency has been undermined. Hunger and malnutrition have been on the rise, especially among the landless poor.

3. Magdoff, Fred, John Bellamy Foster, and Frederick H. Buttel, eds. 2000. *Hungry for Profit. The Agribusiness Threat to Farmers, Food, and the Environment*. New York: Monthly Review Press.

   The overarching analytic perspective for this edited compilation is 'the political economy of agriculture, food, and ecology'. The book's main focus is the paradoxical increase in rates of hunger around the world despite increases in the world's production of food. It's in this context that the destructive environmental and social consequences of industrial-scale agribusiness are considered for the global North and South.

4. Paul, Helena, and Ricarda Steinbrecher, with Devlin Kuyek and Lucy Michaels. 2003.

Hungry Corporations: Transnational Biotech Companies Colonise the Food Chain. London: Zed Books.

This book examines strategies such as vertical and horizontal integration that have enabled a few transnational corporations to increase their control over the world's food production and distribution systems. Particular attention is paid not only to the environmental but also to the social implications of genetically engineered food crops and their undermining of food self-sufficiency in the global South.

5. Salleh, Ariel, ed. 2009. *Eco-sufficiency and Global Justice: Women Write Political Economy*. London: Pluto Press.

Readers looking for a theoretical framework that enables them to link political economy, gender analysis, and environmentalism will find this book useful. Regarding food sovereignty issues, Chapter 11 by Ana Isla ('Who Pays for the Kyoto Protocol?') is especially insightful. She explains how carbon-offsetting policies that benefit the global North undermine food security for peasants in Cost Rica, thereby leaving many rural women no choice but to enter the urban sex industry.

Notes

1. Affiliated food programs include services like food pantries (smaller versions of food banks), meals-on-wheels to people who are housebound, soup kitchens serving daily meals to people on low incomes, and school breakfast and lunch programs.

2. Face-to-face interviews were conducted at food banks in Greater Sudbury in early 2003 using a structured questionnaire. The household composition of respondents was as follows: 33 per cent contained a single adult; 24 per cent contained a sole support parent with one or more children; and 19 per cent contained two adults with one or more children (Suschnigg et al. 2003). As a comparison, Food Banks Canada (2009: 7) reported 38.5 per cent, 27.3 per cent, and 23 per cent respectively for March 2008.

3. These figures are based on a quantitative, relative measure of poverty, that is, on a set of 35 after-tax, low-income cut-offs (LICOs) produced by Statistics Canada. LICOs are calculated for seven different family sizes and five different community sizes and are adjusted each year to reflect changes in the cost of living. While Statistics Canada avoids using the term 'poverty line', the National Council of Welfare and many other organizations deem any household falling below its applicable LICO

to be living in poverty. For information on how LICOs are calculated see www.statcan.gc.ca/pub/75f0002m/75f0002m2006004-eng.pdf.

4. In 2003 the federal government introduced a new income tax act called the *Medical Expense and Disability Tax Credits and Attendant Care Expense Deduction* (Canada 2003). While ostensibly providing financial relief to people with mental or physical disabilities or to those with a dependent having such a disability, this Act contains a dizzying set of limitations and provisos.

5. It is worth noting that people's right of access to medical care in Canada, regardless of their ability to pay, is enshrined in law through the Canada Health Act (1984). However people's right of access to food—a far more fundamental determinant of health—has no such guarantee. Yet along with 186 other countries participating in the 1996 World Food Summit in Rome, the federal government acknowledged that food security is a fundamental human right, that emergency food programs address only the symptoms of widespread hunger, and that poverty is the root cause of food insecurity at home and abroad (Canada 1998: 6).

6. Donating a drop from its immense financial bucket, in 2009 Cargill contributed $1 million to the Global Food Banking Network, of which Food Banks Canada is a member.

7. In the United States 'Native Americans own over 54 million acres . . . making them collectively the single largest private owner of agricultural land'. But this does not mean they have control over their own food production processes. Most of their land is leased out to non-Natives; any land that remains under Indigenous control tends to be 'highly fractionated' and difficult for individuals to contemplate cultivating (Bell-Sheeter 2004).

8. Land animals and waterfowl are becoming scarce, are moving away from their normal habitats, or are becoming more diseased. Hunters find they must travel further afield to acquire food, often under treacherous conditions. Furthermore, warmer weather is making it difficult to preserve food using traditional methods. 'The cumulative effect of all these factors has meant fewer successful hunts, smaller harvests, and an increased dependency on store-bought food' (Murphy and Hsu 2008).

9. To be fair, increased record keeping also has been prompted by concerns about people with 'multiple needs' who might benefit from referrals to other support services. Most

important—in their effort to eliminate the very need for food banks—many workers are determined to document the size and severity of the hunger crisis in our country; hard evidence, they argue, is an essential tool when it comes to educating the public and lobbying politicians.

10. In March 2009, Petro-Canada and Suncor announced they were merging to form Canada's largest oil company. They have since decided 'to put off building massive oilsands projects due to languishing commodity prices and rattled financial markets' (Canadian Broadcasting Corporation 2009b).

11. The armed guards were hired by a security company under contract to Syngenta and some other landowners (Vía Campesina 2008: 6). Syngenta maintained 'it did not know the security guards were armed, and that its contract with NF prohibited guards from using arms on the site; however, there are clear indications in the police investigation that the company knew the guards were armed' (ibid.: 9).

12. See Renaud's (1975) account of the structural constraints on the state when it comes to reforming the mainstream health system.

References

Alberta. 2008. Table 16: 'Farm Bankruptcies, Canada and Provinces, 1991–2008'. *Alberta Agricultural Statistics Yearbook, 2008*. Edmonton: Alberta Agriculture and Rural Development, Statistics and Data Development Branch.

Alberta Energy. 2009. 'Oil Sands'. Accessed 2 April 2009 at www.energy.gov.ab.ca/OurBusiness/oilsands.asp.

Altieri, M.A. 2000. 'Ecological Impacts of Industrial Agriculture and the Possibilities for Truly Sustainable Farming'. In *Hungry for Profit. The Agribusiness Threat to Farmers, Food, and the Environment*, ed. F. Magdoff, J. Bellamy Foster, and F.H. Buttel. New York: Monthly Review Press, 77–92.

Battle, K. 2003. *Ontario's Shrinking Minimum Wage*. Ottawa: The Caledon Institute of Social Policy.

Bell-Sheeter, Alicia. 2004. *Food Sovereignty Assessment Tool*. Fredericksburg, VA: First Nations Development Institute.

Campaign for Tobacco Free Kids. 2001. *Golden Leaf Barren Harvest: The Cost of Tobacco Farming*. Washington, DC: CTFK. Accessed 8 February 2009 at www.tobaccofreekids.org/campaign/global/FCTCreport1.pdf

Canada. 1997. *Farm Income and Financial Conditions and Government Assistance*. Economic and Policy Analysis Directorate, Policy Branch. Ottawa: Publications Section, Agriculture and Agri-Food Canada.

———. 1998. *Canada's Action Plan for Food Security: A Response to the World Food Summit*. Ottawa: Publications Section, Agriculture and Agri-Food Canada.

———. 2003. 'Medical Expense and Disability Tax Credits and Attendant Care Expense Deduction.' Canada Revenue Agency. Accessed 10 August 2010 at http://www.cra-arc.gc.ca/E/pub/tp/it519r2-consolid/.

Canadian Association of Food Banks. 2007. *Annual Report*. Accessed 8 January 2008 at http://foodbankscanada.ca/documents/2007AnnualReport(EnglishB).pdf.

———. N.d. a. 'Supporters'. Accessed 12 July 2003 at www.cafb-acba.ca/supporterse.cfm.

———. N.d. b. 'In-Kind Supporters'. Accessed 12 July 2003 at www.cafb-acba.ca/supporters_inkind_e.cfm.

Canadian Broadcasting Corporation. 2009a. 'Water Pollution'. Accessed 12 June 2010 at www.cbc.ca/edmonton/features/dirtyoil/waterpollution.html.

————. 2009b. 'Suncor, Petro-Canada Announce Merger'. 23 March. Accessed 19 June 2009 at www.cbc.ca/money/story/2009/03/23/suncor-petro-canada-merge.html.

CBS News. 2008. 'Wal-Mart Switches to Local Fruit, Veggies'. 2 July. Accessed 28 December 2010 at www.cbsnews.com/stories/2008/07/02/business/main4227280.shtml.

Daily Bread Food Bank. 2001. *Disabled Benefits*. Toronto: Report prepared for the Ontario Association of Food Banks.

————. N.d. 'Corporate Food Donations'. Accessed 12 July 2003 at www.dailybread.ca/donate/donate_corp.html.

Edemariam, A. 2007. 'Mud, Sweat and Tears'. *The Guardian*, 30 October. Accessed 2 March 2010 at www.guardian.co.uk/environment/2007/oct/30/energy.oilandpetrol.

Food Banks Canada. 2009. *HungerCount 2008*. Accessed 1 June 2009 at http://foodbankscanada.ca/documents/HungerCount_en_fin.pdf.

————. 2010a. *HungerCount 2009*. Accessed 20 July 2010 at http://foodbankscanada.ca/documents/HungerCount2009NOV16.pdf.

————. 2010b. *HungerCount 2010*. Accessed 6 May 2011 at www.foodbankscanada.ca/documents/HungerCount2010_web.pdf.

Food First. October 2006. 'A Vision of Food Sovereignty: Farmers Speak Out'. Report on the second day of a plenary session at the Bridging Borders Conference for Community Food Security. Accessed 5 May 2011 at www.foodfirst.org/node/1526.

Forum for Food Sovereignty. 2007. *Declaration of Nyéléni*. Nyéléni Village, Sélingué, Mali, 23–7 February. Accessed 31 March 2009 at www.foods-overeignty.org/public/new_attached/49_Declaration_of_Nyeleni.pdf.

Global FoodBanking Network. 2009. 'Donor Spotlight. Cargill's Major Gift'. Accessed 5 May 2011 at www.foodbanking.org/partners/spotlight/.

GRAIN. 2008. 'Making a Killing from Hunger'. Accessed 25 April 2011 at www.grain.org/articles/?id=39.

Hager, Aaron. 2011. 'Herbicide-Resistant Weeds in Illinois: A Cause for Concern'. *The Bulletin*, No. 3, Article 6, 22 April. Accessed 6 May 2011 at http://bulletin.ipm.illinois.edu/article.php?id=1466.

Haley, Ella. 1987. 'Hard Times for Farm Women'. *Canadian Women Studies* 8(4): 62–6.

Higgins, Jenny. 2006. 'Signs of Difference: Climate Change in Labrador'. *Newfoundland Quarterly* 5: 44.

Isla, Ana. 2009. 'Who Pays for the Kyoto Protocol? Selling Oxygen and Selling Sex in Costa Rica'. In *Eco-Sufficiency and Global Justice: Women Write Political Ecology*, ed. Ariel Salleh. London: Pluto Press, 192–217.

Kagolo, Francis. 2010. 'Hunger Looms as Biofuels Take Root in Uganda'. *New Vision Online*, 19 January. Accessed 2 May 2011 at www.newvision.co.ug/D/9/37/707552.

Kneen, B. 1999. *Farmageddon: Food and the Culture of Biotechnology*. Gabriola Island, BC: New Society Publishers.

Laws, Forrest. 2001. 'Merger Giant Syngenta Donates to FoodShare'. Western Farm Press, 3 March. Accessed 25 April 2011 at http://westernfarmpress.com/merger-giant-syngenta-donates-to-foodshare.

Matern, Richard. 2010. *Who's Hungry: 2010 Profile of Hunger in the GTA*. Toronto: Daily Bread Food Bank.

Mazhar, F., D. Buckles, P.V. Satheesh, and Farida Akhter. 2007. *Food Sovereignty and Uncultivated Biodiversity in South Asia*. International Development Research Centre. Accessed 12 September 2010 at www.idrc.ca/fr/ev-110418–201–1-DO_TOPIC.html.

Miller, Lynne. 2004. 'King Kullen Spotlights Locally Grown Produce.' *Supermarket News*, 24 June. Accessed 28 December 2010 at http://subscribers.supermarketnews.com/mag/king_kullen_spotlights_2/.

Mininni, Ted. 2008. 'Wegman's Going Local'. MarketingProfs, 3 September. Accessed 28 December 2010 at www.mpdailyfix.com/wegmans-going-local/.

Murphy, Ava, and Shi-Ling Hsu. 2008. 'Climate Change Litigation. Inuit v. the U.S. Electricity Generation Industry'. University of British Colombia Faculty of Law. Accessed 28 December 2010 at www.law.ubc.ca/files/pdf/enlaw/climatechange_04_24_09.pdf.

National Council of Welfare. 2008. *Welfare Incomes, 2006 and 2007*. Winter. Ottawa: National Council of Welfare.

Nayak, Nalini. 2009. 'Development for Some is Violence for Others'. In *Eco-sufficiency and Global Justice: Women Write Political Ecology*, ed. Ariel Salleh. London: Pluto Press, 109–20.

Oliphant, M., and C. Slosser. 2003. *Ontario Alternative Budget 2003: Targeting the Most Vulnerable: A Decade of Desperation for Ontario's Welfare Recipients*. Ottawa: Canadian Centre for Policy Alternatives.

Oliver, Beatriz. 2006. *A Place for Family Farming: Food Sovereignty in Uruguay*. PhD dissertation. Department of Anthropology. Montreal: McGill University. Available at http://digitool.library.mcgill.ca/webclient/StreamGate?folder_id=0&dvs=1293474581794~900.

Ontario. 2008. 'Ontario's Minimum Wage Increases 2007 to 2010'. Toronto: Ontario Ministry of Labour. Accessed 3 March 2009 at www.labour.gov.on.ca/info/minimumwage/.

————. 2010. 'Minimum Wage'. Toronto: Ontario Ministry of Labour. Accessed 12 August 2010 at www.labour.gov.on.ca/english/es/pubs/guide/minwage.php.

Ontario Non-Profit Housing Association. 2004. 'What's Wrong with This Picture?' Newsroom 21 July. Accessed 6 November 2004 at www.onpha.on.ca.

Ontario Tenant Toronto Tenants. 2003. *New Ontario rental Housing Statistics and Their Meaning*. Accessed 10 August 2010 at www.ontariotenants.ca/research/rents-vacancy.phtml.

Paul, H., and R. Steinbrecher. 2003. *Hungry Corporations: Transnational Biotech Companies Colonise the Food Chain*. New York: Zed Books.

Pimbert, Michel. 2009. *Towards Food Sovereignty: Reclaiming Autonomous Food Systems*. London: The International Institute for Environment and Development.

Pringle, P. 2003. *Food, Inc: Mendel to Monsanto—the Promises and Perils of the Biotech Harvest*. New York: Simon and Schuster.

Progressive Grocer. 2008. 'Wegman's Touts "Locally Grown" Program'. 9 June. Accessed 28 December 2010 at www.progressivegrocer.com/top-story-wegmans_touts__locally_grown__program-24072.html.

Renaud, M. 1975. 'On the Structural Constraints to State Intervention in Health'. *International Journal of Health Services* 5(44): 559–73.

Riches, G. 1997. 'Hunger in Canada: Abandoning the Right to Food'. In *First World Hunger: Food Security and Welfare Politics*, ed. G. Riches. London: Macmillan Press, 46–77.

Rosset, Peter. 2010. 'Fixing our Global Food System: Food Sovereignty and Redistributive Land Reform'. In *Agriculture and Food in Crisis: Conflict, Resistance, and Renewal*, ed. F. Magdoff and B. Tokar. New York: Monthly Review Press, 189–205.

Statistics Canada. 2002. *Survey of Household Spending–3508. Table 203–0001: Household Spending, Summary-Level Categories by Province and Territory, Computed Annual Total*. December. Accessed 7 July 2003 at http://cansim2.statcan.ca/cgi-win/CNSMCGI.EXE.

——. 2008. *Farm Population and Total Population by Rural and Urban Population, by Province (2001 and 2006 Census of Agriculture and Census of Population)*. November. Accessed 6 May 2011 at www40.statcan.gc.ca/l01/cst01/agrc42a-eng.htm.

——. 2010. 'Persons in Low Income after Tax'. Derived from CANSIM Table 202–0802. 17 June. Accessed 12 September 2010 at www40.statcan.gc.ca/l01/cst01/famil19a-eng.htm.

Suschnigg, C., with C. Bowes, P. Cannon, F. Wang, and C. Riggi. 2002. *Survey on Food Bank Use, Sudbury and Region, 2002*. Sudbury, ON: Department of Sociology, Laurentian University.

Suschnigg, C., with L. Alexander, L. Carter, D. Cudney, and K. Whitfield. 2003. *Dependence on Food Banks, Greater Sudbury, 2003*. Sudbury, ON: Department of Sociology, Laurentian University.

Syngenta. 2008. 'About Syngenta Seeds'. Syngenta Seeds Canada Inc. Accessed 25 April 2011 at www.nkcanada.com/en/About.aspx.

——. 2009a. 'About Syngenta'. Accessed 31 March 2009 at www.syngenta.ca/en/about/about.aspx.

——. 2009b. *Annual Results 2008*. Accessed 31 March 2009 at www.syngenta.com/en/media/pdf/mediareleases/en/20090206_ENGLISH_Syngenta_Full_Year_Results_2008.pdf.

——. 2009c. 'About the Syngenta Foundation'. Accessed 31 March 2009 at www.syngenta.ca/foundationacre/.

——. 2009d. *Giving Back to Agriculture Report*. Accessed 25 April 2011 at www.syngenta.ca/en/about/GivingBack2009_E.pdf.

——. 2010a. 'Canada Approves New Syngenta Corn Trait Stack'. Syngenta Seeds Canada Inc. Accessed 25 April 2011 at www.syngentaebiz.com/DotNetEBiz/ImageLIbrary/CANADA_VIPRELEASE_100510.pdf.

——. 2010b. 'Syngenta Celebrates Ten Year Anniversary with $500,000 Milestone Donation to Food Banks Canada'. Syngenta Crop Protection Canada Inc. Accessed 25 April 2011 at www.syngenta.ca/en/media/article.aspx?media_type=2&article_id=946.

——. 2011a. 'Syngenta Seeds Canada Adds the First Aphid Resistant Variety to Its High-Performing Glyphosate Tolerant Soybean Line-up'. Syngenta Seeds Canada Inc. Accessed 25 April 2011 at www.syngentaebiz.com/DotNetEBiz/ImageLIbrary/Syn%20Seeds%20Canada%20Media%20Release%20Mar%209%202011.pdf.

——. 2011b. Resistance Fighter. Management Practices. Accessed 6 May 2011 at http://resistancefighter.com/products/cropstrategies.aspx.

Tar Sands Watch. 2007. 'Petro-Canada Plans C$26.2 Billion Oil-Sands Project'. Accessed 9 April 2009 at www.tarsandswatch.org/petro-canada-plans-c-26-2-billion-oil-sands-project.

Teeple, G. 1995. *Globalization and the Decline of Social Reform*. Toronto: Garamond.

Teitel, M., and K. Wilson. 2001. *Genetically Engineered Food: Changing the Nature of Nature*. Vermont: Park Street Press.

Thomas-Müller, C. 2008. 'Tar Sands: Environmental Justice, Treaty Rights and Indigenous Peoples'. *Canadian Dimensions Magazine*, March/April 2008. Accessed 15 March 2009 at http://stoptarsands.wordpress.com/2008/03/10/tar-sands-environmental-justice-treaty-rights-and-indigenous-peoples/.

Tokar, B. 2001. *Redesigning Life? The Worldwide Challenge to Genetic Engineering*. London: Zed Books.

Vía Campesina. 2009. *Statement at the UN General Assembly on the Global Food Crisis and the Right to Food*. Accessed 10 August 2010 at http://viacampesina.org/en/index.php?option=com_content&view=article&id=698:via-campesina-statement-at-the-un-general-assembly-on-the-global-food-crisis-and-the-right-to-food&catid=19:human-rights&Itemid=40.

———. 2008. *The Case of Syngenta: Human Rights Violations in Brazil, 2008.* Accessed 10 August 2010 at http://viacampesina.org/en/index.php?option=com_content&view=article&id=565:the-case-of-syngenta&catid=14:publications&Itemid=30.

Vidal, John. 2010. 'Billionaires and Mega-Corporations behind Immense Land Grab in Africa'. *Mail & Guardian Online*, 10 March. Accessed 4 May 2010 at www.alternet.org/story/145970/.

Weeks, Carly. 2010. 'What Exactly Does Produce Grown Close to Home Mean?' *The Globe and Mail*, 18 August. Accessed 28 December 2010 at www.theglobeandmail.com/life/what-exactly-does-produce-grown-close-to-home-mean/article1677842/.

Wilson, B., with E. Toas. 2002. *Hungercount 2002: Eating Their Words: Government Failure on Food Security.*

Toronto: A report prepared for the Canadian Association of Food Banks.

World Health Organization. 2004. *The Tobacco Atlas.* Accessed 27 December 2010 at www.who.int/tobacco/statistics/tobacco_atlas/en/print.html.

Woynillowicz, D. 2007. 'How Canada Went from 21st to 2nd in World's Oil Reserves'. Accessed 9 April 2009 at www.alternet.org/environment/62325/how_canada_went_from_21st_to_2nd_in_world's_oil_reserves.

Ziegler, Jean. 2009. *Preliminary Report to the Drafting Group of the Human Rights Council Advisory Committee on the Right to Food.* Human Rights Council Advisory Committee, Second session, 26–30 January.

PART IV

Challenging Food Governance

Although the term *governance* had become obsolete by the 1950s, it has made a comeback in the age of globalization. Considered by some to be synonymous with *government*, the term however, is generally understood to have a broader meaning that encompasses power both within and beyond the nation-state. From a critical perspective, the rejuvenation of governance highlights a shift in the patterns and processes of governing from the public sector to the private sector. The rise of public–private partnerships, free-trade agreements, codes of corporate social responsibility, and non-democratic, supranational institutions like the World Trade Organization are all evidence of a structural shift to create the infrastructure to support a liberalized market economy that denounces social and environmental considerations as barriers to trade. This shift is opposed by social movements around the world that have sprung up in resistance to the marketization of all aspects of life.

Not surprisingly, the tensions of governance are evident in the area of food and food systems. The enclosure of common land, the rise of fast food, the effects of industrial agriculture, the spread of global food and the consolidation of the food system under corporate control are all opposed by grassroots food movements such as the international peasant movement called Vía Campesina, the Slow Food movement, the organic farming movement, and the local food movement.

The chapters in Part IV reflect the tensions surrounding food system governance and raise questions about who wins and who loses in the new governance climate. In Chapter 15, Knezevic examines food labelling as one contentious area in food system governance. Rather than informing consumers so they can make rational choices in the marketplace, labels hide more than they reveal. In essence, the chapter argues that labels serve to subdue consumer questions and concerns while perpetuating a questionable food system that has been criticized for myriad social and environmental costs.

Chapter 16 addresses another area of struggle—genetically modified organisms (GMOs). In Canada, the federal system for regulating GMO environmental safety does not have specific provisions that protect farmers dealing with the harms caused by genetic contamination. Consequently, legal challenges have served as one arena where organic farmers have tried to defend their interests, but to date, they have been unable to obtain legal protection against genetic drift. In effect, Abergel proposes that localized struggles about GMO contamination and opposition between farmers and powerful multinational corporations are emblematic of wider issues about the future of the global food system. Despite important limitations, legal challenges help uncover important governance gaps in the food system.

In Chapter 17, Clapp covers the challenges to food system governance arising from the global economic forces that shape food systems at a variety of levels and in many important ways. Through financial and investment policies and international trade, these forces profoundly affect both trends in food prices and access to food. Clapp cautions that while 'market fundamentals' are important considerations, broader international macroeconomic factors must also be analyzed, particularly as they shape international governance responses to food crises. These factors have played a major role in not only precipitating the recent food price volatility, but also shaping the longer-term vulnerability to price swings in the world's poorest countries.

Urban food systems is Mendes's subject in Chapter 18. In cities around the world, millions of hungry people depend on food that has often travelled thousands of kilometres to reach supermarket shelves. Until recently, however, few of us questioned the conditions under which that food was grown, processed, and transported in and out of our cities, let alone considered the far-reaching social, economic, and environmental impacts on our communities and our planet. Today, Mendes maintains, food is reappearing on the agenda of a growing number of municipal governments, becoming an issue for city planners, and emerging as a pressing concern for urban dwellers. As a result, new forms of municipal governance are being expressed through urban food system policies and programs.

Chapter 19, the final chapter in Part 4, centres on the tensions in food system governance involving food policy. Arguing that food policy has not been designed and implemented to reflect the fact that food is a biological requirement for life, MacRae puts forward a set of principles, values, and goals that would be consistent with a coherent, joined-up food policy. The chapter also provides a broad but comprehensive accounting of the policy instruments, structures, and governance models that need changing to achieve such a transformation.

Labels and Governance
Promises, Failures, and Deceptions of Food Labelling
Irena Knezevic

Learning Objectives

Through this chapter, you can:

1. Consider food labelling through a critical lens
2. Examine connections between the **industrial food system** and public policy
3. Explore the links between food, advertising, and health

Introduction

As we wade through the problems of the contemporary global **foodscape**, as in this volume, many of the criticisms seem to identify the same culprit. Whether the critiques address environmental problems of food production, the alarming trends in human health, or the inequities inherent in the dominant food economy, they all point to the industrial food system as being largely responsible for these woes. The model is profit-driven, is based on free-market principles of efficiency, and, critics argue, treats food as just another commodity (Winson 1993; Shiva 1999; Lang and Heasman 2003). In contrast, the critiques call for a recognition that food is a human right as well as a social and cultural artifact and thus should not be merely a commodity (Shiva 1999; Kent 2005; Patel 2007; Tansey and Rajotte 2008). Because of its free-market foundations, the industrial food system is incapable of accommodating such demands. It is likewise inadequate in addressing the concerns regarding its social and

environmental costs, except to the extent that sometimes changing practices to accommodate those concerns can mean profits, when such changes allow price premiums.

Large-scale food scares have plagued the industrial food system in recent years with everything from mad-cow disease to *E. coli* outbreaks. The spread of the problems brought into question the overall safety of the wide geographical distribution of food that is essential to the industrial model. Questionable practices abroad, such as the melamine contamination of some pet foods manufactured in China, discovered in 2007, also prompted consumers to distrust the global economic system that brings food from all corners of the world to the North American consumer. Such incidents were accompanied first by a flood of academic literature, and now a growing body of popular literature, exposing problematic industry practices and their consequences (e.g., Schlosser 2001; Pollan 2006; Patel 2007;

Kenner 2008). In turn, these exposés resulted in a better-informed public and a new breed of discriminating consumers who demand more information about their food (Caswell 1998; Hobbs 2002; Roosen et al. 2003).

In addition to years of tweaking mandatory nutritional information requirements, governments are now also overseeing an increasing flow of information from the food industry to the consumer. In a system where the supplier of food is most commonly a vague corporate entity, **food labels** are the link between that entity and the consumer, and this link is becoming increasingly complex. Consumer demand has led to a greater number of more detailed labels on industrial food. Yet, as this chapter reveals, rather than holding the industrial food system to account, labels are themselves tools of the industry. They ensure that while small adjustments are implemented, the system's foundations remain intact and unchallenged. The symbolic power of labels shapes our **discourse** on food and hence our understanding of it. Sophisticated marketing practices ensure that the products are always presented in a positive light, so labels commonly advertise much more than they reveal.

In shaping the discourse, labels also play political and ideological roles by helping the industry appear properly regulated, thus making radical policy changes appear unnecessary. Finally, in their role as representations of standards and regulation, labels assist the industry in **co-opting** and commercializing alternative food models. In doing so, labels minimize the effects of alternatives on the industry. As this chapter demonstrates, labels help turn those alternatives from attempts at undermining the industrial food system into profitable niche markets. A selected sample of a broad set of data on food labelling and advertising (collected randomly over the last decade), including a brief discussion of organic labelling, is used to illustrate the complex nature of labels and the way in which they mediate the relationships between food and consumers.

Labels as Discourse

In 2009, a provincially run liquor store in North York, Ontario, featured an end-of-aisle display that exclaimed 'GO LOCAL!' to advertise a celebrity-label wine from the Niagara region. While the winery was a mere 130 kilometres from North York, the product on display was only 'cellared in Canada'. In other words, up to 70 per cent[1] of the wine in the bottles was not from Canada, but from some other part of the world where labour and grapes are cheaper. 'Cellared in Canada' is a legitimate label, but it does misleadingly suggest that the wine is Canadian, and teamed with the distributor's shameless advertising, is a perfect ploy to attract consumers looking for wine from local vineyards. The irony of this marketing move is that the label was in fact addressing those who could be seen as discriminating customers.

A variety of 'in Canada' labels target consumers looking for Canadian products. Following several 2007 media exposés of the problematic 'product of Canada' label, the Canadian government changed the label regulation. Previously that label meant only that more than half of production capital was supplied by a Canadian company, allowing Russian fish processed in China and then packaged in Canada to be labelled 'product of Canada' (CBC 2007). The public outcry following the media reports caused the Canadian Food Inspection Agency to stipulate that for the label to be used 'all or virtually all of the significant ingredients, components, processing and labour used in the food product must be Canadian' (2008: 1). Instead of causing the industry's practices to change, the new labelling regulation resulted in a number of new variations of the claim—'prepared in Canada', 'manufactured in Canada', and so on. Such vague and misleading claims are not exceptions in the world of food labels, and they are commonly used to attract consumers to products about which they essentially know nothing.

Labels on food products are the communicative bridge between the producer/processor and the consumer in a food system in which the two may never otherwise communicate. While most effective when presented as simple and straightforward messages, labels are inherently never just that. As Cook and O'Halloran write, 'food labels bring together within a very small space and short text, the interests of major discourse communities. On a food label, the discourses of business, marketing, aesthetics, law, science, health, environmentalism, and the family, all meet, intermingle and compete' (1999: 148). The content of a label then, complex as it is, is never a simple message, and its loaded meaning is further complicated by its interaction with other labels on the same product. In theory, labels inform and reassure the consumers that their food is monitored, nutritionally analyzed, and held to a variety of safety and quality standards. In practice, they are more of an opportunity to advertise and make glowing claims about products. They are the tool of the packaged food industry, necessitated and developed by it, and as such can really serve only one master faithfully—the industry that needs them for its very existence.

And labels do more than just promote and perpetuate the processed food industry. They also determine the boundaries of discourse. By giving us 'need to know' information, they also indicate what should not be of concern to us. The messages conveyed by labels obscure more than they declare, by selectively providing the information the manufacturers want us to know. They shape our understanding of the food items we buy and consequently our understanding of the food system. They tap into what we want to hear (and read) by providing constant reassurance that the food system is under control and functioning. In the long run, they assist the industrial food system in minimizing criticism and challenges. For most consumers, who can devote only a fraction of their time to making food-purchasing decisions, they provide a sense of security and knowledge and at the same time discourage questioning of the food system. Most of all they assure us that is acceptable to not know where our food comes from.

Distancing from Food

In his *Scavenger's Guide to Haute Cuisine* Steven Rinella writes, 'A historian could make a good argument that human history is just a long story of depersonalization of food production' (2005: 12). Critiquing the food system in which consumers have little or no personal connection to their food is not a nostalgic cry for pastoral images of agrarian idyll. Rather, it is a warning bell to citizens who want to eat fresh and healthy foods produced in a sustainable manner, within the context of a system where few food items can be described as such. Various chapters in this volume outline the shortcomings of the dominant food system. Other critiques of the industrialized, intensive mass production of food also encompass a range of concerns relating to the health of societies: human (Nestle 2002; Pilcher 2005), environmental (Altieri and Nicholls 2005), and economic (Perelman 2003). Those problems persist virtually unchallenged in large part because they happen outside of consumers' immediate environments.

Brewster Kneen uses the term **distancing** to describe the process of 'separating people from the sources of their food and nutrition with as many interventions as possible' (1995: 11). Distance is both physical and informational. Consequently, consumers' purchasing decisions are informed mainly through the labels on the packaging. Without any connection to the field or the farmer who produced the food, consumers are prompted to associate their food with brands, such as the friendly faces of Aunt Jemima and the Pillsbury Doughboy. They are also prompted to rely on the labels to tell them how one product can be a better choice than the next, and to assure them that the product meets some set of standards of quality and safety. The industrial food system depends on these messages to communicate with consumers and provide them with a sense of trust and reassurance. It also depends on them to maintain the distancing without major objections.

Food labels can be mandatory or voluntary, and both types can distance people from their food. Mandatory labels are the ones required by the extensive regulatory framework imposed on the agri-food companies to ensure certain standards are met and that certain information (such as the nutritional breakdown or expiry date) is available to the consumer. The regulatory framework is overseen by government agencies (such as Health Canada and the Canadian Food Inspection Agency) who set the standards, and while it determines many of the safety and quality requirements, it does nothing to remedy the 'distance'. Instead, the regulatory framework provides us with what Laura B. DeLind describes as a 'surrogate for trust', explaining that

> Standards and certification processes, whatever their scope, cut two ways. They are restrictive as well as enabling. While they function as a form of interest-group insurance and assurance, they also insert themselves between individuals and direct experience and responsibility. They substitute for, indeed, they become a surrogate for personal awareness and judgement. In what we are told is an ever expanding universe, we are continually asked to place our trust in standards and certification processes at the expense of our trust in interpersonal relationships and daily interactions informed by wisdom locally generated and grounded in place. . . . Even at the local level there is a tendency for standards and certification to become more significant than the principles they are designed to uphold. (2002: 200)

In other words, labelling (and its regulation) not only fails to address many of the shortcomings of the industrial food system, it also facilitates the system by providing few and easily surmountable obstacles, which, rather than significantly challenging the system, actually provide it with a cloak of legitimacy. Whereas a mandatory label such as a nutrition table can tell us about the level of sodium in a food item, the manufacturer is not required to explain how it treats its labour force or how it disposes of its waste. In fact, the existence of standards and labels that represent manufacturers mediate the economic and environmental consequences of industrial food production (Deaton and Hoehn 2005). What labels do not tell us can sometimes be even more significant than what they say.

Voluntary labelling, on the other hand, refers to the labels that the manufacturer can choose to apply, usually because such a label extols some virtue of the product, such as 'low in fat', 'no sugar added' or the above-noted labels of origin. They can also be labels associated with a certification process that differentiates the product from others in the same category, for instance 'organic' or 'fair trade'. Voluntary labels are still somewhat regulated—though not required, their use is restricted at times and some of the claims are carefully defined. Government agencies, industry associations, and advertising councils all have a say in what voluntary labels can claim and under what circumstances. Certification procedures for voluntary labels are often designed by third parties (e.g., Fairtrade International) or a combination of third-party and industry collaboration (e.g., the Rainforest Alliance) and in some cases by producer associations and government agencies (e.g., Canada Organic). Often associated with noble causes and aimed at consumers concerned with the shortcomings of industrial food production, voluntary labels nevertheless, as the next section describes, are often used to advertise rather than inform.

Moreover, voluntary labels fragment the information surrounding food. They can really convey only one or two messages at a time, allowing for distancing to continue. Fair-trade certification says nothing about pesticide use, organic labelling says nothing of food miles, food miles/carbon footprint labels tell us nothing of labour conditions, and so on. Even in cases of multiple labels, the distance remains, because the labels themselves are merely representations of those interventions. They tell the concerned consumer that the interventions are up to their higher-than-average standards, deflecting suspicion that the interventions themselves may be problematic.

Advertising and Labels

Through their selective nature food labels try to highlight information that can sell the product while obscuring the information that may make us question the product. Packages of Kraft Singles processed cheese, for example, emphasize the product's calcium content, and each package bears a very visible stamp stating that the product is 'A source of calcium'. The product is indeed a source of calcium, providing 6 per cent of recommended daily value in one slice, compared to a cup of average yogourt which provides nearly 50 per cent. It is also a source of saturated fat (13 per cent), sodium (15 per cent), and cholesterol (3 per cent), and half of the total calories in a slice come from fat. This information, though available in the nutrition table, is something that the potential buyer has to look for, as it is less immediately visible than the calcium-boasting claim. Similarly, Nature Valley granola bars packaging touts a 'Made with 100% whole grains' label in addition to its healthy-sounding name, but tells us in small print that the whole-grain oats are in fact only the second ingredient; the first is corn syrup, and the third and fourth are sugar and glucose-fructose. The whole grains in the product provide only 1 gram of fibre in a 35 gram bar, compared to 14 grams of sugar, and the entire nutrition table suggests that the nutritional value of a Nature Valley granola bar is about the same as that of 35 grams of the proverbial junk snack—the Pop Tart.[2]

Nutrition tables are still useful for the concerned consumer, but a 2008 US Department of Agriculture (USDA) Economic Research Service study indicates that fewer than two-thirds of consumers use nutritional information in making their purchasing decisions, and that even

those numbers have been declining, particularly among young adults. While the numbers may indicate consumer skepticism, they also mean that flashy messages are more likely to reach consumers than the information provided in mandatory nutrition tables.

In addition to this imbalance in how messages are conveyed, some labelling can confuse the consumer when, instead of informing, it actually creates new questions. For instance, a package of seasoned Ontario-processed shish kebabs informs the buyers that the product is of 'Mediterranean quality' and that it is 'authentic'. There is nothing that explains what is authentic about it, nor what 'Mediterranean quality' means, and there is certainly no standardized meaning for those labels in the food industry.

In all of the above examples, while the mandatory information is still provided to the consumer, the voluntary labels that cast the product in a positive light are significantly more pronounced and more likely to be noticed by the potential buyer. On a bottle of PurOliva cooking oil, for instance, the large-letter product name is accompanied by a similarly large picture of olives, and it is only in much a smaller and quite ornamental (and therefore more difficult to read) font that the product admits to being 'A perfect blend of canola oil & extra virgin olive oil'. A consumer may wonder what the perfect blend is (the package lists canola and olive oils as ingredients, but says nothing about the proportions of each), but that question will arise only upon close reading of the labels.

Moreover, while mandatory information is required it is also often helpful to the manufacturer, since it doubles as litigation insurance. Should a consumer complain about being fooled by PurOliva's packaging, the company is protected by that very ingredient list that is mandated by government agencies. Mandatory labels in the end are the insurance policy for the larger, louder, more colourful voluntary labels that are commonly placed on the front of the package.

Selling Health

The growing evidence that the industrial food system is associated with climbing rates of obesity and diet-related disease prompts many consumers to seek out healthier alternatives. Long-term effects of additive-laden processed foods are becoming impossible to hide among the increasingly unhealthy populations of the industrial world. Consumer demand for better food and growing pressures from health practitioners and government agencies have compelled manufacturers to convince their consumers that they can respond to those concerns. Food labels are now commonly communicating misleading messages of health, such as the previously described labels of Kraft Singles processed cheese and Nature Valley granola bars. That the messages are effective marketing strategies is made possible by the cunning work of manufacturers as well as by the fragmented understandings of food and nutrition.

Scientific studies have pointed to specific ingredients as being 'bad' or 'good' for human health, making nutritional makeup the sole determining factor in whether foods are bad or good. When avoiding particular nutrients and choosing others is so often equated with health, the door to misleading marketing is wide open. If a consumer's main concern is getting enough calcium, overlooking all the other nutritional facts is easy. This fragmented understanding of nutrition also fails to take freshness, sustainability, and nutrient interactions into consideration. Michael Pollan (2007, 2008) describes this understanding as **nutritionism**.[3] Although the term was coined only in 2002 by Gyorgy Scrinis (Pollan 2008: 27), the trend of nutritionism started in the early 1980s with scientific codification of dietary components, which has over the years transformed food into 'nutrients'. Pollan writes: 'Drink coffee with your steak, and your body won't be able to fully absorb the iron in the meat. The trace of limestone in the corn tortilla unlocks essential amino acids in the corn that would otherwise remain unavailable'

(Pollan 2007: 7). Nutritionism in its cultural context is merely another form of **scientific reductionism**, the attempt to reduce complex interactions to isolated simple relations.

The scientific reductionism in treating food as nutrients results not only from reductionist nutritional science, but also from a particular advertising discourse that has for decades attempted to sell health through reducing the human body to a machine. 'The term "body maintenance" indicates the popularity of the machine metaphor for the body', wrote Mike Featherstone in his 1982 discussion of body image and commercialism (24), arguing that the phenomenon was a direct product of consumer culture and its aggressive discourse of advertising. Whereas industrial food is largely responsible for increased levels of sugars, fats, sodium, and chemical preservatives in North American diets (as they are all used in large quantities to improve taste, appearance, and/or shelf life of food), once the awareness of the health effects of processed foods arose, the same manufacturers started cashing in on consumers' apprehensions. Health claims of all sorts are made for marketing purposes, although they frequently highlight a product's levels of one or two nutrients and in effect only obscure other ingredients. These claims also obscure the production and processing aspects of food, and in their selection of information to be emphasized, they imply that any other information is unnecessary. Meanwhile, reductionist claims are also the mainstay of the weight-loss industry whose worth is estimated to be in the tens of billions of dollars (BBC 2003). Ironically, most of those profits go to the pockets of the very food-manufacturing giants associated with the highly processed and additive-laden foods that cause weight problems in the first place. The Jenny Craig weight-loss brand, for example, is owned by Nestlé, and Slimfast is a part of the Unilever empire (Patel 2007).

One of the more troubling examples of how the reductionist approach is exploited by the food industry is evident in the Health Check approval program. Run by the Heart and Stroke

Foundation of Canada (HSFC), the program promotes heart-healthy foods by giving products a stamp of approval. In addition to about 15,000 products in Canadian stores, HSFC also approves menu items in restaurants. HSFC evaluates the foods based on Canada's Food Guide, but it measures only certain individual nutrients—sodium and fat—and until very recently it did not even evaluate added sugar content (sugar criteria are currently under review). A 2008 CBC exposé claimed that many nutritionists and dietitians questioned the nutritional value of some Health Check–approved foods, and that many non-approved foods had much better nutritional values. By singling out only a handful of nutrients, HSFC effectively allows food manufacturers to promote their products as healthy when in fact those products have reduced levels only of certain nutrients. Moreover, the stamp comes with an annual licensing fee of $1,225 to $3,625 per product and is promoted by the HSFC as a business- and brand-building strategy (Health Check 2010). The label that appears to be a shortcut to healthy eating is, in reality, both a marketing tool and a stamp of approval for the depersonalized industrial food system.

Responsibility

Labels provide information, however selective, but by doing so, they also individualize responsibility for eating habits. Once the information has been conveyed to the consumer, responsibility has been transferred with it, which helps circumvent demands for better policy options. Recent research on the social determinants of health indicates that the most important determinant of an individual's poor health is poverty (Mikkonnen and Raphael 2010). Food insecurity and poor nutrition are both associated with lower socio-economic status (Tarasuk 2001). Healthy foods are more expensive per calorie (Derwnowski and Darmon 2005), and choosing them requires at least some knowledge of nutrition, thus linking healthy food choices to social factors such as education and income levels.

Food labels, however, communicate with the individual consumer, not society. As such, they suggest that healthy diets are determined at the individual level. Most critics of industrial food see reform and modification of politics and policy as the most effective changes (see Koç and Dahlberg 1999), calling for economic policy reform (Qualman 2007) and a wide range of public-health policy improvements that would include everything from municipal planning to education programs (see Nestle and Jacobson 2000). The industry, however, has resisted such change (Nestle 2002), repeatedly invoking the free-market principles of consumer demand and individual choice as the justifications for its problematic practices. Labels, in their service to the industry, indicate that eliminating unhealthy food items need not happen at the processing or regulatory level, but should be left to the workings of individual choice. Making health an individual responsibility lets both the industry and public policy–makers off the hook (Nestle 2009). This individualization of diet choices downloads the responsibility from the industry, which continues to profit, to the consumer, who is faced with limited and at times confusing information.

One of the most heated debates in contemporary food studies (as well as in policy-making) centres around the issues of responsibility and choice. The popularity of Michael Pollan's work, the Slow Food movement (Petrini and Waters 2007), and alternative food options causes ripples in the food system and also highlights the importance of being an informed consumer and making the right purchasing choices. But this shift has incited a reaction from critics such as Julie Guthman, who advocates political and policy reform, and sees the shift to 'informed consumer' as a 'highly privileged and apolitical idea' (2007a: 78), and declares 'I am fed up with the apolitical conclusions, self-satisfied biographies of food choices, and general disregard for the more complex arguments that scholars of food bring to these topics' (2007b: 264).

The road to a better food system is probably somewhere in the middle and includes individual choice, which once organized—as the effectiveness of historical mass boycotts tells us—can turn itself into a formidable political force. But choice is difficult in a complex, problematic food system, and it can be effective only when combined with appropriate policy changes.

Labels, however, shift all the responsibility to the consumer; moreover, they imply that the industry is quite capable of communicating with the consumer, and that policy change is not needed. The inadequacy of this implication is evident in a recent labelling initiative. Much has been made of the recent New York city law requiring fast-food chains to label their items with calorie counts, but the move does not affect the ingredients nor the way the items are prepared. Instead, the new label suggests to the consumer that if eating cheap chain food makes them overweight, it is their own fault. Additionally, a survey of low-income minority communities in New York city found that most consumers paid no attention to the labels and that even those who read them still did not change their purchasing habits (Elbel et al. 2009).

In the perverse reach of industrial food the focus on individual responsibility also encompasses the responsibility for others. The above-described case of Kraft Singles is a great example because, in addition to associating the product with healthy eating, it plays into parental responsibility with the slogan 'good food to grow up on'. Even the choices that are not nutrition-related, such as choosing fair-trade products, imply that the individual consumer bears the responsibility for the ills of the industrial food system. Hence some critiques of ethical consumer choices have addressed the marketing power of guilt and the role of products as status symbols (Guthman 2003, 2007a). Whatever the case, food labelling clearly does little to change the food system itself, and by providing the industry with the veil of honesty it actually reinforces the status quo.

Alternative Food Choices— The Organic Example

As fragmented as it may be, consumer resistance to the industrial food system runs deep in the industrialized world. Consumers who can afford to choose alternatives are redefining themselves as food citizens and are making choices that chip away at the system. From organic and vegetarian purchases to the Slow Food movement and fair-trade products, consumers choose not to support the kind of production that characterizes the global industrial food system (Allen 2008; DuPuis and Gillon 2009). By reclaiming the power to make decisions about food, citizens are shaking a metaphorical fist at industrial food and its ideological foundations. In doing so they create new spaces for production, exchange, and consumption of food upon which other social relationships can be built (Blay-Palmer 2007), and they open new understandings of food and food economy.

Some alternatives, such as community gardens and community-supported agriculture, take approaches that place food more or less outside of the dominant economy. However, much of the resistance has been unable to step outside of consumer culture and the free-market economic framework. In the spirit of individual choice and responsibility, many of the alternatives demonstrate the 'voting with your dollar' concept, promoting improvements to certain aspects of the food economy, but leaving the underlying economic underpinnings intact. As such, many of the alternative food choices have failed to substantially alter the foodscape and instead have lent themselves to the very system they once sought to oppose.

Organic foods may be the most salient example of this co-opted resistance. For several decades organic foods in North America represented a full-fledged alternative, a product of chemical-free, small-scale, diverse farming, which relied on social relationships for marketing and manifested the 'back-to-the-land' resistance to the dominant ideologies and economic system. Organic foods for many years meant shrinking the gap between the consumers and the sources of their food. But as the popularity of organic foods grew, instead of presenting a greater challenge to the industrial food economy they became a new marketing opportunity for large industrial players. The greater demand in fact allowed for greater distancing, and set in the landscape of consumer culture, organic foods quickly fell into the trap of certification, standardization, and labelling shortcuts. Labels replaced interpersonal trust and helped to reduce organics from more sustainable alternatives to merely chemical-free foods within the industrial food system. With most organic brands now owned by industry giants (Howard 2008) and sold through chains like Loblaws and Walmart, organics are now largely a part of the very system they once opposed.

Now mostly produced and distributed on a large scale, organics have become industrial food, albeit grown without pesticides, chemical fertilizers, and artificial hormones. Labelling regulation has helped this process by providing communicative shortcuts through standardized certification. Buying organic in Canada now means that the consumer needs to look for only one logo—Canada Organic—a standardization move ensuring that organic foods can be produced and sold within the industrial system and that the consumers need not know where or how their organic food was grown. For instance, a package of organic soy milk available at a Canadian dollar store bears the Canada Organic logo, but also states that the product was 'prepared and packaged in Canada' giving no indication of where in Canada it was prepared and by whom, and, more important, no indication of the source of the organic ingredients. The label effectively reduces 'organic' to 'chemical-free', rendering all other aspects of the organic philosophy irrelevant. By making it easier for consumers to identify organic products, the logo in essence restates that the distancing is fine and need not

be revisited. As David Conner writes of organic labels:

> The information on the label is restricted to how the food was produced, and at best is a proxy for the on farm environmental impacts of production. It provides no information on how the producer treats his or her labor force, how many miles the food has traveled, how the farm contributes to the community and local economy, etc. . . . It does nothing to address the 'corporatization' and consolidation of the food system. (2004: 31)

In removing all the other, once-important, characteristics of organic foods, organic standardization and the labels that represent it imply that the consumers' demand for organics is only about removing the potentially harmful chemicals from their diets. The emphasis on individual health trumps environmental and social well-being and contributes to further fragmentation of food information. The connection between socio-economic status and health—whether real or perceived—and premium prices on organics have also turned organic food into a symbol of social status (Guthman 2003), making it desirable for more than just its nutritional value.

The environmental benefits of eliminating chemicals may still be significant on an industrial organic farm, and thus may help promote the foods as 'greener' options. But industrial farms, characterized by intensive and specialized production, are not good for ecosystems even if elimination of chemicals makes them more acceptable than their chemical-using counterparts. As well, processing and distribution in the industrial model cause problems associated with packaging and transportation, which organic products still require.

Most of all, national organic labels do nothing to shrink the distance between the consumers and the source of their food. To those who have the luxury of choosing organics, the labels offer an opportunity for self-congratulatory purchases marked by a stamp that tells little and obscures much. They also allow for responsible decision making with respect to individual health and strengthen the relationship between the industry and the consumer. Indeed, they open doors to industrial organics that may be chemical-free but are far from being socially or environmentally sustainable.

Meanwhile, the small, diverse organic farms that nurtured organic agriculture over the years have now become secondary to industrial organics. Having practised comprehensively sustainable farming that made organics popular in the first place, those producers now have to play by the rules of the industrial food system—the very system they once resisted. By reducing organics to a label, the industrial food system has managed to co-opt a sustainable alternative.

Conclusion

Food labelling has had its bright moments and many attempts have been made to make labelling more honest, transparent, and informative. Government agencies and consumer groups alike have occasionally tried to hold the food industry more accountable, and many of the labelling guidelines have been designed in response to consumer demands. But even when successful, such attempts seem to only promote the idea that the system is working like a well-oiled machine. In September 2010, *The Globe and Mail* reported that the US Food and Drug Administration (FDA) issued a warning to Dr Pepper Snapple Group and Unilever, asking the companies to stop making 'unsubstantiated nutritional claims about their green tea-flavoured beverages', part of their respective Canada Dry and Lipton product lines. The companies are expected to remove the labels that claim the beverages contain antioxidants, and failing to do so may result in a court appearance. Their misleading labelling already helped launch the products onto the market, yet they are expected only to stop making such claims,

without being subjected to any fines or other penalties unless they ignore the FDA's warning.

Similarly, the makers of Ben & Jerry's ice cream recently succumbed to pressure from the Center for Science in the Public Interest to stop using the 'all natural' labels on their products that contain alkalized and partially hydrogenated ingredients (Fulton 2010). But the move ultimately benefited the company by creating a media blitz and allowing them to brag about the quality of their products while reiterating the vagueness of the 'all natural' label.

These instances not only reinforce the impression that the food system is under control, but also remind us that it is only the big players in the system that matter. Effectiveness of labelling regulation is measured by industry's compliance; small producers hardly ever make the news. Additionally, the big players wield a great deal of influence—partly through lobbying (Nestle 2002), but also partly through their ability to shape voluntary labelling. In Canada, for example, large grocery chains refuse to carry products labelled 'non-GMO'. The argument is that such labels imply that products free from genetically modified organisms (GMOs) are somehow superior, thereby threatening the sales of products that cannot make such claims. With the decision to shun products labelled 'non-GMO', the grocery chains effectively declared the label nonsensical, and, perhaps more importantly, re-established the hierarchy of power in the system.

While making minor corrections to the foodscape, labels still operate within the confines of the industrial system. They serve the industry much more than they control it. Their ultimate message is that the food system as a whole cannot be changed and neither can the workings of the global economy, with all its negative environmental and social consequences. The best we can hope for, labels seem to say, is to get selected information and have faith that we can make the right choices within the existing system. The more we rely on labels, the more we accommodate the problematic industrial food system and the less likely we are to act as agents of real change. A truly re-imagined food system would not need an ever-increasing number of labels, because certifications, standards, and labels are the front line of the industrial food system. Labels are not needed for food grown in community gardens, preserves purchased from a friend, or bread bought from a neighbour's bakery. Ensuring the availability of food that is economically fair, socially responsible, and environmentally sound will require us to become active agents in the system—both as individuals and as communities. A sustainable food system entails informed and responsible choices made within a context of comprehensive well-being. Labels, as communicative shortcuts across numerous interventions, are but reminders that such a context does not exist. They provide a bandage for all that is wrong with the industrial food system, but they cannot fix its fundamental problems. If they did, labels would render themselves obsolete.

Discussion Questions

1. What are the connections between food labelling and advertising?
2. Can food labels be useful in countering problems associated with food and social determinants of health?
3. Can alternative food choices be useful in countering problems associated with food and social determinants of health?
4. How do labels facilitate 'distancing' in the food system?

Further Reading

1. DeLind, Laura B. 2002. 'Transforming Organic Agriculture into Industrial Organic Products: Reconsidering National Organic Standards'. *Human Organization* 59(2): 198–208.

    DeLind discusses standardization of food production as a tool of commerce and trade that runs counter to diverse, locally based food systems. Using the example of national organic standards in the United States, DeLind challenges 'green' consumption and standardized alternative food choices.

2. Drewnowski, Adam and Nicole Darmon. 2005. 'The Economics of Obesity: Dietary Energy Density and Energy Cost'. *American Journal of Clinical Nutrition* 82(1): 265S–73S.

    This study looks at the cost of nutrient-dense foods in comparison to low-nutrient calorie-dense foods and argues that the problem of obesity is highly correlated to poverty, and that this correlation is growing as price disparity between healthy and unhealthy foods grows.

3. Guthman, Julie. 2007. 'Commentary on Teaching Food: Why I Am Fed Up with Michael Pollan et al.' *Agriculture and Human Values* 24: 261–4.

    This is one of Guthman's several pieces to offer a scathing critique of the self-congratulatory approach to alternative food choices, and writings that present those choices as the individualized and often apolitical and class-biased solutions to the problems of the industrialized food system.

4. Kneen, Brewster. 1995. *From Land to Mouth: Understanding the Food System*. 2nd edn. Toronto: NC Press.

Kneen's book offers a good primer to the free-market logic of the industrial food system. The book deals with distancing, concentration of power, and the ideology that accompanies the system.

5. Winson, Anthony. 2004. 'Bringing Political Economy into the Debate on the Obesity Epidemic'. *Agriculture and Human Values* 21: 299–312.

Winson examines food environments, making a compelling argument about how the spatial and economic organization of supermarkets and fast-food outlets play a role in diet-related health outcomes.

Notes

1. In Ontario, at least 30 per cent of the wine has to be from Ontario to be labelled 'cellared in Canada'. In British Columbia, however, a 'cellared in Canada' wine can be made with 100 per cent–imported wine.

2. The nutritional comparison is based on the manufacturer-provided nutritional information on the packaging for both products.
3. Pollan did not coin the term (and he freely acknowledges that fact), but he greatly popularized it.

References

Allen, Patricia. 2008. 'Mining for Justice in the Food System: Perceptions, Practices, and Possibilities'. *Agriculture and Human Values* 25: 157–61.

Altieri, Miguel A., and Clara I. Nicholls. 2005. *Agroecology and the Search for the Truly Sustainable Agriculture*. Mexico: United Nations Environment Programme.

BBC. 2003. 'The Diet Business: Banking on Failure'. BBC, 5 February. Accessed 27 July 2010 at http://news.bbc.co.uk/1/hi/business/2725943.stm.

Blay-Palmer, Alison. 2007. 'Relational Local Food Networks: The Farmers' Market @ Queen's'. In *Interdisciplinary Perspectives in Food Studies*, ed. Mustafa Koç, Rod MacRae, and Kelly Bronson. Toronto: McGraw-Hill Ryerson, 111–17.

Canadian Food Inspection Agency. 2008. *Guidelines Defining Product of Canada and Made in Canada on Food Labels and Advertising*. Accessed 15 September 2010 at www.inspection.gc.ca/english/fssa/labeti/inform/prodcane.shtml.

Caswell, Julie A. 1998. 'How Labeling of Safety and Process Attributes Affects Markets for Food'. *Agricultural and Resource Economics Review* 27(2): 151–8.

CBC. 2007. 'Marketplace: Product of Canada, eh?' Video. CBC, 27 October.

———. 2008. 'Marketplace: Does HealthCheck Logo Hype Health or Sell Food?' Video. CBC, 23 January.

Conner, David S. 2004. 'Expressing Values in Agricultural Markets: An Economic Policy Perspective'. *Agriculture and Human Values* 21(1): 27–35.

Cook, Guy, and Kieran O'Halloran. 1999. 'Labels Literacy: Factors Affecting the Understanding and Assessment of Baby Food Labels'. In *Language and Literacies: Selected Papers from the Annual Meeting of the British Association for Applied Linguistics*, ed. Teresa O'Brian. Clevedon, UK: Short Run Press, 145–56.

Deaton, B.J., and John P. Hoehn. 2005. 'The Social Construction of Production Externalities in Contemporary Agriculture: Process Versus Product Standards as the Basis for Defining "Organic"'. *Agriculture and Human Values* 22(1): 31–8.

DeLind, Laura B. 2002. 'Transforming Organic Agriculture into Industrial Organic Products: Reconsidering National Organic Standards'. *Human Organization* 59(2): 198–208.

Drewnowski, Adam, and Darmon, Nicole. 2005. 'The Economics of Obesity: Dietary Energy Density and Energy Cost'. *American Journal of Clinical Nutrition* 82(1): 265S–73S.

DuPuis, E. Melanie, and Sean Gillon. 2009. 'Alternative Modes of Governance: Organic as Civic Engagement'. *Agriculture and Human Values* 26: 43–56.

Elbel, Brian, Rogan Kersh, Victoria L. Brescoll, and L. Beth Dixon. 2009. 'Calorie Labeling and Food Choices: A First Look at the Effects on Low-Income People in New York City'. *Health Affairs* 28(6): web exclusive w1110–21.

Featherstone, Mike. 1982. 'The Body in Consumer Culture'. *Theory, Culture and Society* 1(2): 18–33.

Fulton, April. 2010. 'Ben & Jerry's Takes "All Natural" Claims off Ice Cream Labels'. National Public Radio, 27 September. Accessed 27 September 2010 at www.npr.org/blogs/health/2010/09/27/

130158014/ben-jerry-s-takes-all-natural-claims-off-ice-cream-labels?sc=fb&cc=fp.

Globe and Mail. 2010. 'FDA Slams Lipton, Canada Dry for Nutritional Claims'. *The Globe and Mail*, 7 September. Accessed 7 September 2010 at www.theglobeandmail.com/life/health/fda-slams-lipton-canada-dry-for-nutritional-claims/article1698274/. Now available at http://www.ctv.ca/generic/generated/static/business/article1698274.html.

Guthman, Julie. 2003. 'Fast Food/Organic Food: Reflective Tastes and the Making of "Yuppie Chow"'. *Social and Cultural Geography* 4(1): 45–58.

——. 2007a. 'Can't Stomach It: How Michael Pollan et al. Made Me Want to Eat Cheetos'. *Gastronomica* 7(2): 75–9.

——. 2007b. 'Commentary on Teaching Food: Why I Am Fed up with Michael Pollan et al.' *Agriculture and Human Values* 24: 261–4.

Health Check. 2010. *Food Manufacturers: Help Your Customers Make Healthy Food Choices*. Accessed 27 August 2010 at www.healthcheck.org/page/licensee-overview-0.

Hobbs, Jill E. 2002. *Consumer Demand for Traceability*. Paper presented at the International Agricultural Trade Research Consortium Annual Meeting, December. Accessed 13 April 2011 at http://ageconsearch.umn.edu/bitstream/14614/1/wp03–01.pdf.

Howard, P. 2008. *Who Owns What in the Organic Food Industry*. Accessed 23 September 2010 at www.certifiedorganic.bc.ca/rcbtoa/services/corporate-ownership.html.

Kenner, Robert (Dir.) 2008. *Food, Inc*. Video. Los Angeles: Participant Media.

Kent, George. 2005. *Freedom from Want: The Human Right to Adequate Food*. Washington, DC: Georgetown University Press.

Kneen, Brewster. 1995. *From Land to Mouth: Understanding the Food System*. 2nd edn. Toronto: NC Press.

Koç, Mustafa, and Kenneth A. Dahlberg. 1999. 'The Restructuring of Food Systems: Trends, Research, and Policy Issues'. *Agriculture and Human Values* 16: 109–16.

Lang, Tim, and Michael Heasman. 2003. *Food Wars: The Global Battle for Mouths, Minds and Markets*. London: Earthscan/James & James.

Mikkonnen, Juha, and Dennis Raphael. 2010. *Social Determinants of Health: The Canadian Facts*. Toronto: York University School of Health Policy and Management.

Nestle, Marion. 2002. *Food Politics: How the Food Industry Influences Nutrition and Health*. Berkeley, CA: University of California Press.

——. 2009. *Food Politics: Personal Responsibility vs. Social Responsibility*. Lecture at the University of Toronto, 21 January 2009.

Nestle, Marion, and Michael F. Jacobson. 2000. 'Halting the Obesity Epidemic: A Public Health Policy Approach'. *Public Health Reports* 115: 12–24.

Patel, Raj. 2007. *Stuffed and Starved: Markets, Power and the Hidden Battle for the World's Food System*. Toronto: HarperCollins.

Perelman, M. 2003. *The Perverse Economy: The Impact of Markets on People and the Environment*. New York: Palgrave Macmillan.

Petrini, Carlo, and Alice Waters. 2007. *Slow Food Nation: Why Our Food Should Be Good, Clean, and Fair*. New York: Rizzoli Ex Libris.

Pilcher, Jeffrey M. 2005. 'Industrial *Tortillas* and Folkloric Pepsi: The Nutritional Consequences of Hybrid Cuisines in Mexico'. In *The Cultural Politics of Food and Eating*, ed. James L. Watson and Melissa L. Caldwell. Malden, MA: Blackwell Publishing, 235–50.

Pollan, Michael. 2006. *The Omnivore's Dilemma: A Natural History of Four Meals*. New York: Penguin.

——. 2007. 'Unhappy Meals'. *New York Times*, 28 January. Accessed 26 August 2010 at www.nytimes.com.

——. 2008. *In Defense of Food: An Eater's Manifesto*. New York: Penguin.

Qualman, Darrin. 2007. 'The Farm Crisis & Corporate Profits'. In *Interdisciplinary Perspectives in Food Studies*, ed. Mustafa Koç, Rod MacRae, and Kelly Bronson. Toronto: McGraw-Hill Ryerson, 95–110.

Rinella, Steven. 2005. *The Scavenger's Guide to Haute Cuisine*. New York: Miramax Books.

Roosen, Jutta, Jayson L. Lusk, and John A. Fox. 2003. 'Consumer Demand for and Attitudes toward Alternative Beef Labeling Strategies in France, Germany, and the UK'. *Agribusiness* 19(1): 77–90.

Schlosser, Eric. 2001. *Fast Food Nation: The Dark Side of the All-American Dream*. New York: Houghton Mifflin.

Shiva, Vandana. 1999. *Stolen Harvest: The Hijacking of the Global Food Supply*. Cambridge, MA: South End Press.

Tansey, Geoff, and Tasmin Rajotte. 2008. *The Future Control of Food: A Guide to International Negotiations and Rules on Intellectual Property, Biodiversity and Food Security*. London: Earthscan.

Tarasuk, Valerie. (2001). *Discussion Paper on Household and Individual Food Insecurity*. Ottawa: Health Canada. Accessed 9 September 2010 at www.hc-sc.gc.ca/fn-an/alt_formats/hpfb-dgpsa/pdf/nutrition/food_sec_entire-sec_aliments_entier-eng.pdf.

USDA Economic Research Service. 2008. 'Use of Nutrition Labels Declining, Especially among Young Adults'. *USDA Amber Waves*. Accessed 28 August 2010 at www.ers.usda.gov/AmberWaves/September08/PDF/NutritionLabels.pdf.

Winson, Anthony. 1993. *The Intimate Commodity: Food and the Development of the Agro-Industrial Complex in Canada*. Toronto: University of Toronto Press.

16

The Paradox of Governing Through the Courts
The Canadian GMO Contamination Debate
Elisabeth A. Abergel

Learning Objectives

Through this chapter, you can:

1. Understand the complex problems posed by genetically modified crops
2. Become familiar with the governance of genetically modified organisms in Canada and globally
3. Learn about the issue of genetic contamination and its impact on farming
4. Learn about the agency of local farmers in global debates
5. Understand the broader social function of legal challenges

Introduction

Canada is the world's fifth-largest producer of **genetically modified** (GM) crops after the United States, Brazil, Argentina, and India (James 2009). The worldwide agri-**biotechnology** sector was worth an estimated US$10 billion in 2009. The combined global value of biotech crops since their introduction in 1996 has reached over US$62.3 billion, and it is expected to increase as more developing countries invest in GM agriculture. Meanwhile, another industry is also on the rise. Since 1995, the Canadian organics industry has grown 15–20 per cent annually and its retail value reached CAD$2 billion in 2008 (AAFC 2008). Organics is the fastest growing sector of the global food system and, unlike biotechnology, which is industry driven, organics is consumer driven. To be certified organic, food cannot contain **GM organisms (GMOs)**. However, biotechnology is poised to take over the world's agriculture with new products awaiting market approvals. Expansion of GM acreage is expected to come mostly from developing countries, where production of GM crops is tied to global trade in food biotech. In addition, it is thought that as more varieties of GMOs are approved and released for commercial planting, the rate of genetic contamination of organic crops will increase, affecting not only the availability and quality of organic foods but also the economic viability of the organics market.

The rapid global commercialization of GM crops, from zero to 134 million hectares in approximately 15 years, has caused widespread genetic contamination via **transgene** escape or **genetic drift**. Meanwhile, worldwide demand for organic foods poses two possible scenarios: first, that contamination of crops such as corn and canola will erode the strict organic certification standards; and second, that large-scale organic farming will conform to an industrial model of agriculture. Already in Canada, the organic production of some crops such as canola in Saskatchewan and Alberta has become practically impossible. Both the organic and the biotech industries have reached a critical juncture of key domestic and international decisions that will determine their future viability.

One of the most strategic areas concerning agriculture biotechnology is the debate over coexistence—the idea that conventional (i.e., non-GM and organic) and GMO crops can be grown commercially side by side and that different types of agricultural practices can be accommodated. The European Union (EU) has historically taken a cautious approach to GMOs, and has very strict regulations around the planting and use of GM crops. Only a few GM crops have been allowed to be grown in or imported to its member countries. Recently, the EU introduced plans for its members to establish clear coexistence policies amid vocal opposition by conventional and organic farmers and anti-GM protesters. These policies would enable organically grown crops to contain up to 0.9 per cent GMOs. Many environmentalists have suggested that this would effectively allow GM crops into the EU through the back door. Critics also think that GM and non-GM agricultural systems are fundamentally incompatible and that coexistence between organics and biotech is a practical impossibility.

At first glance, it appears that widespread genetic contamination of crops such as canola denies the possibility of establishing coexistence regimes that would enable GMO, conventional, and organic agricultural systems to subsist commercially and environmentally. Moreover, recent large-scale contamination events in the Canadian Prairies provide evidence that coexistence is not an option for non-GM farmers. However, many in the EU, where some farmers are ready to grow GM crops commercially, believe that with proper measures, different cropping systems can coexist and that farmers will be 'free to choose' between GM and conventional crops. Coexistence may be the latest strategy devised by the biotech industry to pursue its goals of expanding the worldwide acreage of GM crops.

By claiming that agricultural systems of all types may coexist, proponents of transgenic technology evade the problem of contamination, and dealing with it becomes subsumed under the costs of doing business. Hence, the economic burden of contamination and cleanup is borne not by those causing the problem but by non-GM and organic farmers and consumers; as well, the environment may suffer costly or even irreversible effects. The trade-off behind 'peaceful coexistence' is an inequitable sharing of rights and duties when a farmer chooses to grow GM crops. The burden is placed on those defending organic and non-GM agriculture to safeguard their production systems, way of life, and markets against the damages caused by transgenic contamination.

The goal of this chapter is to examine and link the implications of two emblematic case studies that signal the future of GM crops in the Canadian Prairies. Saskatchewan is a testing ground for the future of coexistence and contamination, and events there set the stage for studying how non-GM farmers are coping with widespread contamination in the absence of comprehensive regulatory measures and the ways in which they may secure their livelihoods, including options for maintaining organic products free of transgenic materials.

The broader objective of this chapter is to examine how legal action between farmers and biotechnology multinational corporations can create a counter-hegemonic space. The concept of **counter-hegemony** is based on the writings of

Antonio Gramsci, who believed that 'hegemony pertains to the condition in which the dominant classes utilize the state to both coerce and at the same time achieve consent to their dominance within civil society' (Katz 2006: 336). Social change can be effected only through a historic counter-hegemonic bloc of people challenging the status quo: a coalition of diverse forces working to develop local and global solidarity movements that resist the ideology of the dominant classes. This chapter examines how these two localized struggles can be seen as catalytic confrontations with actors representing the dominant classes—catalytic in that they galvanize worldwide opposition to GMOs. Through these cases we can identify multiple forms of social action and assess their 'oppositional promise' (Shreck 2005). Thus it is hoped that the lack of adequate governance systems for dealing with widespread contamination be revealed and that ways of coping with this serious ecological, economic, political, and social issue be found.

The Case Studies

The first case study involves the outcome of the *Monsanto Canada Inc. v. Schmeiser* landmark legal decision, which carries serious implications concerning farmer **liability** and transgenic contamination in Canada and elsewhere. Monsanto initiated the court action, alleging that Percy Schmeiser had illegally obtained and planted Monsanto's patented Roundup Ready (RUR) canola.[1] The Canadian Supreme Court, in a very close judgment, decided in favour of Monsanto and focused the case on the rights of patent holders. As a result, the Schmeiser case was instrumental in securing patent rights on higher life forms, in this case plants, despite the fact that Canadian law does yet not grant these types of patents.

The second case study examines the provincial court challenge between the Saskatchewan Organic Directorate (SOD) against Monsanto Canada and Bayer CropScience to compensate for the loss of canola as an organic crop and to prevent the commercial release of RUR wheat in

Canada. This case, initiated in 2002, highlights first the lack of adequate post-approval mechanisms to deal with the damages caused by the large-scale commercialization of GM crops in the Canadian Prairies and second the distribution of rights and obligations between multinational corporations and farmers using alternative production systems (Phillipson 2005). The Saskatchewan organic farmers tried to challenge multinational corporations in order to protect their livelihoods and more specifically to hold corporations accountable for widespread ecological damage. Transgenic contamination has made it now impossible to obtain organic certification for canola grown in Saskatchewan. Organic farmers failed to obtain legal recognition as a class when they tried to file a class-action lawsuit. Ultimately, a Supreme Court of Canada ruling denied their application for an appeal in December 2007. In 2008, Larry Hoffman and Dale Beaudoin announced their decision not to proceed with their individual claims against Monsanto and Bayer for losses resulting from their contaminated canola crop (SOD 2008). Meanwhile, in May 2004, after massive opposition from farmers, consumers, and international wheat buyers, Monsanto issued a press release saying the company would temporarily suspend its plans to commercialize Roundup Ready wheat. On 21 June 2004 Monsanto officially withdrew its application for its regulatory approval in Canada.

Monsanto Canada, a division of a multinational corporation, sued Percy Schmeiser because he allegedly made illegal use of patented technology; Larry Hoffman and Dale Beaudoin sued Monsanto Canada and Bayer CropScience for compensation for the loss of their organic canola crop. These cases are linked in that the *Schmeiser* decision recognizes the rights of patent owners over their creations, while the SOD case questions the responsibilities and duties of these same patent owners when their products cause widespread damages via contamination. These court cases are about new forms of control by biotech companies as well as the companies' simultaneous attempts to escape or limit their responsibilities (Müller 2006). The issue of **intellectual property rights** via patenting of life forms in relation to genetic contamination provides a window into the most contentious issue facing farming communities today.

Ultimately, linking these two cases grants us two insights. First, it allows us to analyze how market actors frame GM risk, especially genetic contamination, and the possibility of 'coexistence'. Second, it allows us to assess the merits of the legal arena not only in obtaining justice but also in creating a potential space of resistance against biotechnology.

Chapter Organization

The chapter is organized into four main parts: the first outlines some background on the case studies, including the Monsanto case against Percy Schmeiser and the SOD case against Monsanto. The second part examines disputes over the risks posed by GM crops, focusing on risk disputes in both the Schmeiser case and the SOD case. The third part discusses risk disputes as fields of contestation in transgenic contamination, taking into consideration the competing hegemonic discourses between science and the law, the issue of asymmetric power and resources between corporate actors and farmers, and the question of the independence of the judiciary. The fourth part explores resistance and the problem of legal protection of the rights of organic and non-GMO farmers.

Ultimately, it is hoped that local farmers' strategies to protect their interests against the damages caused by GM contamination render them 'knowledge brokers' and agents of change in anti-hegemonic movements (Escobar 2004). More generally, by uncovering the connections between these two legal challenges in their expression of deeply embedded public concerns about agricultural biotechnology and transgenic contamination, this chapter shows the strengths and weaknesses of both cases in two ways. First, they publicly raised objections to GM

crops. Second, they revealed the inadequacies of existing legal institutions to deal with genetic contamination. It then becomes easier to see how lawsuits involving farmers and biotech corporations can become political arenas that 'stage' issues of risk yet fail to provide adequate spaces for counter-hegemonic resistance.

Background on the Case Studies

Monsanto Canada Inc. vs. Schmeiser

Percy Schmeiser has farmed in Saskatchewan for over 50 years, growing conventional canola. In the 1990s, many of Schmeiser's neighbours started to grow Roundup Ready canola, a **herbicide-tolerant** (HT) canola containing a gene patented by Monsanto.[2]

In 1997, Monsanto inspectors obtained samples from various parts of Schmeiser's fields and along ditches outside them and found evidence of RUR canola. Monsanto accused him of illegally growing canola containing a patented gene, without licence or permission. Monsanto representatives visited Schmeiser in 1998 and put him on notice based on these findings. Mr. Schmeiser had his harvest treated for use as seed, which he used to plant in nine fields (approximately 400 hectares).

Monsanto launched its lawsuit in 2000; expert testimony was presented during a three-week trial at the Federal Court in Saskatoon. The Court issued its judgment in March 2001 in favour of Monsanto's patented technology; Justice William McKay dismissed Schmeiser's claims that the dispersal of the patented gene was uncontrollable. In May 2002, Schmeiser launched an appeal, which was rejected by the Federal Court of Appeal. He then asked for leave to have his case heard by the Supreme Court of Canada. Leave was granted in May 2003 and the case was heard in January 2004.

During the Federal Court hearing in Saskatoon, samples from Schmeiser's fields were taken and analyzed, some under court order and some not. The seed-treatment plant also kept back some of Schmeiser's seed and gave it to Monsanto without his knowledge. Tests conducted by Monsanto revealed that over 90 per cent of Schmeiser's 400 hectares of canola crop was derived from RUR plants. The fact that his plants survived spraying with Roundup indicated that they contained the patented genes.

What remains unclear is how the RUR seed originally got into Mr. Schmeiser's field. Details of the case suggest that RUR plants may have grown as a result of RUR seed that blew onto his land; reports published by the federal government's appointed scientific panel, the Royal Society of Canada, describe adventitious presence as 'technically unavoidable', and in this way, the issue of seed dispersal was established prior to this case. However, seed was then collected from plants that survived after Schmeiser had applied Roundup in ditches, along the road, and around poles adjacent to his fields. The trial judge rejected Schmeiser's explanations of how RUR seed might have gotten into his crops and based his decision on the concentration and extent of RUR canola found, which was considered of 'commercial quality'.

Clearly, the case revolved around patent infringement and what remedies Monsanto could claim. How the seed got into Schmeiser's fields was considered irrelevant—the facts and scientific evidence presented during court proceedings were not central to the judge's decision.

The Supreme Court of Canada's judgment was released in May 2004. After six years of legal battles, the Court in a 5–4 decision found Schmeiser guilty of infringing Monsanto's patent rights by illegally saving and planting canola seed containing the RUR gene. The five judges of the majority decision ruled that Monsanto was entitled to the full benefits of their biotechnological monopoly (De Beer and McLeod-Kilmurray 2007). However, the four judges of the minority decision rejected the patent claim made on higher life forms and refuted the idea that plants are simply compositions of matter.

They recognized that granting patents on higher life forms means granting ownership rights to all offspring of this organism and declared that this 'represents a significant increase in the scope of rights offered to patent holders. It also represents a greater transfer of economic interest from the agricultural community to the biotechnology industry than exists in other fields of science' (quoted in Müller 2006).

The Saskatchewan Organic Directorate or *Hoffman vs. Monsanto Canada Inc.*

In 2002, the Saskatchewan Organic Directorate (SOD), an umbrella group representing over 1000 organic producers, certifiers, and processors, initiated a class-action lawsuit against agri-biotech companies Monsanto Canada and Bayer CropScience, seeking damages for economic losses caused by transgenic contamination by GM canola. Two plaintiffs, Larry Hoffman and Dale Beaudoin, both certified organic farmers, were named in the class-action lawsuit (*Hoffman vs. Monsanto Canada Inc.*).

Since 2002, SOD has sought compensation for the damages incurred from the commercial planting of GMO crops developed and owned by US–based Monsanto and Germany's Bayer CropScience. A class action suit was launched by two plaintiffs from Saskatchewan on behalf of all Canadian organic farmers.

In 2004, the battle to block the commercialization of RUR wheat ended when Monsanto withdrew its application to have it commercially approved in Canada. The company stated that it would continue to pursue other genetic modifications in several wheat varieties, which has left many of the farmers involved in the SOD case thinking that the fight is far from over.

In May 2005, the Saskatchewan lower court rejected the group's class action status. Appeals were denied by the Saskatchewan Court of Appeal in May 2007 and by the Supreme Court of Canada in December 2007, leaving no other legal recourse in this case. Even though class status was repeatedly denied to farmers, the final ruling opens the door for individual court cases to be filed. However, as stated earlier, the two plaintiffs in the case decided not to pursue their individual claims against the two multinational corporations.

Disputes over Risks

At the heart of each of these cases is dispute over what risks are posed by GM crops. Canada's regulatory position features prominently in each case, and each reveals serious weaknesses in the governance of agricultural biotechnology. These weaknesses create openings for critical analysis of the global restructuring of agriculture and the survival of organic farming within this system. At the same time, however, the limited scope of these two cases as public spaces of resistance uncovers the inadequacy of risk disputes in resolving political questions or addressing major governance gaps. Each case, seen as a key moment in the globalization process, is played out in undemocratic structures that both restrict and create new forms of political action. Studying how various actors frame risk in these conflicts reveals the limits of governing institutions, the law, and science for reconciling opposing world views, and reveals as well ways to undermine their authority. According to Nelkin and Marden (2004) the common questions pervading risk disputes are about choice and control rather than science.

Conflicting perspectives about the future of food and agriculture, technology, and nature underlie current responses by governments, industry, and non-governmental actors, both domestic and international. Studies suggest that national regulatory approaches to risk reflect differing political assumptions about the economic importance of the disputed technology and about the ability of science to provide definitive and conclusive evidence of the dangers of biotechnology. Risk disputes over GM crops rely on the scientific assessment of risk. These disputes become entangled in the 'global' context of biotechnology, which is largely driven by industry and government in the global North. Disputes over risk uncover marked differences among the perceptions of industrialists, regulators, and opposition groups about the role of biotechnology in solving the world's most pressing problems and about alternative systems of agriculture. These categories provide a powerful framework within which to study the deeper issues emerging from these legal disputes.

Conflict over risk is not merely obstructive but also productive (Rajan 2003), as it represents 'speed bumps' in the fast-paced process of globalization. These speed bumps act as catalysts: they draw attention to the practices of multinational corporations and mobilize people and groups to oppose harmful practices. In addition, these legal challenges produce important flows of information and knowledge in defence of local places, which then become enacted globally (Escobar 2004). As we shall see, in these legal terrains of conflict, farmers and farming organizations involved in similar struggles tend to form unpredictable means of co-operation. Prairie farmers thus can become agents of global mobilization against dominant forms of power–knowledge (ibid.).

Risk Disputes in *Schmeiser*

In *Schmeiser*, the trial focused on private property and the rights of property owners without any discussion of responsibilities and duties associated with ownership rights.

According to Arnold Taylor, president of SOD, Schmeiser was never charged with stealing anything. In fact, in the pre-trial phase of the Federal Court case Monsanto withdrew its claim that he had stolen the technology and that he had bought or collected the seed illegally. So, the trial revolved around a very narrow piece of patent legislation which focused attention on the illegal use of the HT seed as opposed to how it was obtained.

This focus was clearly expressed when the judge completely dismissed scientific evidence about the different ways that canola seed and pollen can travel from one field to another. How the GM seed got into Schmeiser's field was irrelevant; what mattered was that it got there without Monsanto's permission. The biological facts about contamination (transgenic escape and travel) and the realities of farming (seed falls off trucks, equipment shared between farmers may not be clean, etc.) were not considered determining factors in the case. As Cathy Holstlander (a member of the SOD Organic Agriculture Protection Fund Committee) put it, the scientific information presented in support of Schmeiser's claim of contamination ended up being 'pure theatrical performance' (2008). It was not taken into account and as a result had no direct bearing on the outcome of the case.

Farmers are at a clear disadvantage when presenting evidence and in particular scientific data. Schmeiser provided detailed farm-based evidence that his fields contained seeds he did not knowingly acquire and that the presence of HT canola was due to contamination from a neighbouring field. His data were verified by independent studies performed at the University of Manitoba. Monsanto's tests were performed in-house or by experts hired by the company and were not independently verified. The results of the two series of tests were significantly different. The University of Manitoba tests found that the presence of RUR canola in Schmeiser's fields varied between 0 per cent and 68 per cent depending on the proximity to the road and his neighbour's field; fields closest to the road had the highest levels of RUR canola. Monsanto found that samples from all of Schmeiser's fields (regardless of distance from the road) contained more than 90 per cent commercial-quality RUR canola.

The stigma of the farmer as a non-expert was manifest during proceedings, when Monsanto lawyers and scientists, backed by official government reports, argued their case. What is striking here is that pragmatic common sense, situated and grounded in experience, engaged directly with expert scientific knowledge with varying degrees of success. Moreover, the scientific evidence farmers relied on for their defence vitiated their case, whereas Monsanto's use of scientific expertise was given full legitimacy by the courts. Nevertheless, the trial showed that such critical engagement is possible and is in fact desirable, as we shall see later.

Risk Disputes in the SOD Case

According to Phillipson (2005), the favoured approach in Canada for dealing with cases of genetic contamination is best described as 'laissez-faire'. Canada chooses to rely on existing laws and regulations not designed to deal with contamination to handle the conflict and interaction between GM crops and organic crops, as the SOD case illustrates.

The loss of organic certification for organic canola in Saskatchewan has discouraged many farmers from investing in this crop. They have lost the price premium associated with organic production as well as their markets in the EU and elsewhere. Canola has been sacrificed on the altar of genetic technology in the Prairies, as the level of GM pollen and seed is now impossible to control. Clean-up costs cannot even be estimated for the province, and contaminated canola is the new norm.

In the Hoffman lawsuit, the failure to have organic farmers recognized as a class was a major setback. When the request was filed in 2005, Justice Gene Anne Smith of the Saskatchewan Court of Queen's Bench turned down the application for certification of the class-action lawsuit. Justice Smith rejected Hoffman's claims on the basis that he had no cause for action. Her decision was appealed in 2006, because the plaintiffs perceived that she misinterpreted her role during the certification process.

In their statement of appeal, SOD lawyers claimed that Justice Smith discussed the merits of the case in a manner that clearly influenced her decision not to certify the action as a class proceeding. Rather than recognizing organic farmers as a 'class' by virtue of the fact that they shared the same interest in the resolution of the common issue (i.e., contamination and damages incurred), she instead based her ruling on the lack of sufficient evidence 'that members of the class shared the damages claimed' (Stevenson et al. 2006).

Based on their critique of the Smith decision, the organic farmers then filed for leave to appeal to the Supreme Court of Canada; this application was denied on 13 December 2007. This denial blocked the case from moving forward as a class-action lawsuit, but it has not deterred SOD from pursuing other legal and non-legal options in the struggle against transgenic contamination.

According to Phillipson (2005), the laissez-faire approach means that legal institutions in Canada are set up to formally prevent organic farmers from attempting to protect their right to (co-)exist. As Justice Smith said in her decision to deny class status to organic farmers, the case would make corporations liable 'for an undeterminable amount for an undeterminable time to an undeterminable class', which would interfere with 'commercial freedom and economic interests' (quoted in Müller 2006). Many studies in other jurisdictions (e.g., the United States and the EU) also contend that legal institutions fail to adequately address liability and compensation for the contamination of organic crops by GMOs.

Risk Disputes as Terrains of Contestation in Transgenic Contamination

Competing Hegemonic Discourses between Science and the Law

The problem of determining liability and responsibility for genetic pollution shows the ways in which scientific and legal discourses diverge. Because the environmental and health risks posed by GMOs are impossible to prove, scientific uncertainty undermines the possibility of resolving these cases in the legal arena. Lack of scientific knowledge about risk, however, is not proof that GMOs are safe. Besides, science may

not provide significant guidance for managing environmental and health risks at the political level. The fact that regulatory structures consider HT canola to be safe complicates matters, since these legal proceedings were not intended, and indeed were not able, to put the Canadian regulatory system on trial. Instead, the failings of the system are reinforced, since regulations served to adjudicate these cases, as in Justice Smith's decision in the SOD case. Similarly in *Schmeiser*, the rights of patent holders were strengthened, as was the possibility for higher life forms to become patentable in Canada.

The plaintiffs in the SOD case sought common-law damages for negligence, strict liability, trespass, and nuisance. They also asked for damages under the Saskatchewan Environmental Management and Protection Act. However, common law is limited, because it requires plaintiffs to impose obligations on the manufacturers of GM crops and not on their neighbours who planted GM canola. Ultimately, common law cannot address the challenges posed by genetic technologies; to do so, actions would have to be brought against individual GMO farmers rather than directly confronting the biotech industry. Hence, this form of resistance to GMOs is severely constraining and divisive. It tends to once again 'stage' the issues farmers are facing but evades their collective rights.

Asymmetric Power and Resources between Corporate Actors and Farmers

Phillipson believes that in Canada the producers of GM crops have at their disposal a significant arsenal of legal rights and are at the same time relatively unburdened by legal obligations (2005). In fact, he states that the gap between rights and obligations is most apparent in the post-approval phase of GM products. This is obvious in both the Schmeiser and the SOD cases.

Failure to obtain class certification for organic farmers is a major setback. Class-action lawsuits are an affordable and efficient way for farmers such as Larry Hoffman and Dale Beaudoin to seek compensation from multinational corporations such as Monsanto and Aventis. Without this legal avenue, individuals will have to bring cases to justice, with no guarantee of the same outcome in each case.

In their description of the proposed class-action lawsuit, Monsanto referred to members of SOD as 'activists', stripping them of their credibility as experts in farming and agricultural biotechnology. The false dichotomy between farming expertise and scientific knowledge was also problematic throughout the Schmeiser proceedings—it served to reinforce the power–knowledge nexus. However, in an interview produced by the Kootenay Co-op Radio (*Deconstructing Dinner* 2008), SOD president Arnold Taylor claimed that Larry Hoffman and Dale Beaudoin were not activists—they were ordinary farmers protecting their position in the marketplace. Their lives had been damaged by the technology and they were taking legal action. The suggestion that SOD members are activists implies that environmental groups such as Greenpeace are funding them. But Taylor claims that SOD funding comes from organic farmers in communities across Canada. The 'activist' label also suggests that organic farmers cannot fight effectively against biotech companies on their own—that they are not a credible force. However, the label can also be seen to pose a serious threat to corporations such as Bayer and Monsanto. As such, the term 'activist' can either strengthen or undermine the cause defended by organic farmers. When it is used by pro-GMO forces, it tends to give SOD a negative public image; it implies that they are 'anti-science' and diminishes the value of organics as a legitimate and profitable sector of the Canadian economy. However, when anti-GMO forces invoke the term, it has a strong political connotation associated with resistance to various forms of domination; it can thus have a double meaning, depending on the strategic context.

Schmeiser's appeal to the Supreme Court of Canada allowed for submissions from Canadian and international civil society groups such as the Council of Canadians, the National Farmers Union, the ETC (Erosion, Technology and Concentration) Group, the International Center for Technology Assessment, and Vandana Shiva's Research Foundation for Science, Technology and Ecology (Schmeiser 2003). These groups intervened in this case because the Court's decision in the Schmeiser appeal extends far beyond western Canada to the rest of the world—it could affect the ability of farmers to save seed at all. Thus the Supreme Court's ruling was seen as playing a key role in the international debate about the patenting of life forms (Fanning 2004).

If one considers farmers in Saskatchewan to be part of a global campaign against biotech, then what happens there is of great consequence to the rest of the world. Clearly, the industry is attempting to strip farmers of their agency as legitimate players in the globalization process by characterizing organic farmers as tied to the past, backward-looking, anti-progress, and anti-technology. The Saskatchewan lawsuits presented the biotech industry with a serious challenge, even though the outcomes failed to protect the rights of farmers. Nevertheless, they were close calls; in *Schmeiser*, the Supreme Court decision was 5–4. Although they were but speed bumps on the road to spread GM crops globally, these challenges—pitting the rights of corporations against those of organic farmers—exposed the fallacy of 'peaceful coexistence'. They also enabled the formation of support and solidarity networks between Saskatchewan farmers and global civil society. Although it is important to analyze court proceedings and their outcomes, what happens outside of the courtroom is also significant for understanding how new forms of social resistance develop and evolve.

In the Schmeiser case, the disparity between legal teams was apparent. Monsanto could afford to let the case drag on at relatively little cost to itself, while for Schmeiser finance was a major constraint. During the six years of legal wrangling, Monsanto obtained a Federal Court of Appeal ruling against Schmeiser to cover their legal expenses plus some fines totalling over $1 million (Fanning 2004). Fortunately, in the Supreme Court decision the judges turned down Monsanto's request that Schmeiser pay damages. Schmeiser subsequently obtained $650 from Monsanto through small-claims court to cover the costs of cleaning up (hand 'roguing') a quarter of his fields contaminated by RUR canola.

A major problem in the Federal Court hearing of the Schmeiser case in Saskatoon was that the presiding judge was not familiar with farming and different types of farming systems. Nor did he appear interested in scientific facts, as his demeanour during the presentation of scientific evidence made abundantly clear. This attitude was especially apparent when, during court proceedings, a canola expert in an affidavit for Monsanto claimed that 'Schmeiser's theories of cross-pollination by wind and bees did not make sense to him' given the purity of the canola plants found in his fields. Monsanto supported this argument with wind data from Saskatchewan weather stations and government climate reports. The Schmeiser team, armed with common sense— situated and place-based experience—tried to convince the presiding judge that canola seed could in fact be propagated and blown into fields quite easily during the normal course of farming and during the transportation of harvested seed. Coincidentally, this evidence was presented at the same time that a powerful windstorm hit the Saskatoon area; this storm blew barbeques off people's decks into their neighbour's yards, and yet the judge dismissed the possibility of HT canola seed propagation between neighbouring fields (Holstlander 2008).

Geography Matters: Independence of the Judiciary in the Schmeiser and SOD Cases

Saskatchewan is the epicentre of Canada's biotech industry; it is also a world leader in agricultural research and development, and is the location of most of the large agri-biotech industries

and associated research centres. The province's economy largely depends on the biotech industry, and the political climate is such that governments are pro-innovation and promote investment in high technology. The proceedings in the Schmeiser case obviously favoured Monsanto. During the SOD certification hearings, the lawyers defending the organic farmers found that Justice Smith inappropriately discussed the merits of the case, using arguments that demonstrated a clear bias towards industrial interests. SOD members are very critical of the independence of the judiciary in Saskatchewan. In fact, it was suggested that other Canadian jurisdictions might be better suited to pursue their cause (Holstlander 2008). Clearly the political and legal landscapes were important in how these cases played out. The adoption rate of RUR canola among Saskatchewan farmers is approximately 80 per cent; those fighting biotechnology are at a clear disadvantage. The province has invested public money and infrastructure to support the biotechnology industry and is now a worldwide leader in the agri-biotech field in terms of its research and development policies. These lawsuits clearly put Saskatchewan on the biotech map; while decisions in both cases reinforced the domination of biotech in that province, they also focused worldwide attention on the devastating consequences of widespread transgenic agriculture for non-GMO farmers and the lack of effective measures to protect against contamination.

Spaces of Resistance: Legal Protection of Organic and Non-GMO Farmers

It appears that the Schmeiser and SOD lawsuits failed to protect the rights of farmers against those of multinational corporations, and that such lawsuits cannot constitute a viable resistance strategy against GM agriculture. The legal arena dismisses the complexity of issues faced by organic and non-GMO farmers by focusing narrowly on liability cases. Even if it were possible to arrive at a compensation value for damage and loss caused by contamination, it is doubtful that the organics industry in the province could be saved. As was mentioned, certification of canola as an organic crop is no longer available to some prairie farmers due to the massive amounts of GM pollen and seed dispersed throughout the countryside. Hence, compensation in liability cases fails to address real issues of livelihoods and of the sustainability of the global food system. These court cases serve to stage the plight of these farmers but they also work to keep their concerns out of public view, since the legal arena has limited scope and compensation rulings are undisclosed.

The legal framework ultimately fails farmers because it focuses on the protection of private property. GM crops are considered the private property of the patent holders in the Schmeiser decision, whereas in the SOD case the obligations and duties that come with property ownership (that is, those of corporate patent holders) are minimized. Monsanto initiated court action in the Schmeiser case after making repeated threats. Schmeiser's appeal to the Supreme Court was unsuccessful, but it was a narrow escape for Monsanto in the closeness of the decision. In each case, economic imperatives and hegemonic power prevailed, and farmers' demands for redress were not legitimized.

What remains hidden from these court cases and the legal process is market logic and the various institutional strategies devised either to perpetuate (Rajan 2003) or to get around the impediment that organic farmers represent for the biotech industry. In fact, in the process of upholding their own property rights, organic farmers are simultaneously and ambiguously defending and negating market logic. They are working both 'in and against' the same global capitalist market they are trying to change (Shreck 2005). In this manner, when market logic is a terrain of hegemonic contestation, those making arguments on either side do not closely analyze how they use it, but redefine it for the purposes of organic market opportunities

or biotech crop expansion. Market logic also assumes that these two types of agriculture can co-exist and compete within the same productive spaces when in fact they may not. The stage is set yet again for counter-hegemonic potential, but it ends up being buried in the legal process.

To conclude that these cases do not provide any possibility for resistance, however, would be simplistic. In the Schmeiser case, and in similar cases involving farmers threatened by Monsanto, there was enormous pressure to settle out of court, essentially rendering the plight of farmers invisible. Fortunately, the Schmeiser and SOD cases received worldwide media attention and public exposure of the problem of genetic contamination. Since 1998, numerous delegations of farmers, regulators, and politicians from around the world have visited Saskatchewan to learn about and witness first-hand the impact of contamination on farmers. Percy Schmeiser has become a powerful symbol of the global struggles that farmers face in their fight against GMOs. The publicity surrounding these cases formed an important channel for exposing such struggles, allowing solidarity networks of rural communities around the world to emerge. By giving farmers a voice, these lawsuits identified multinational corporations as the main culprits of genetic pollution. Rather than pitting farmers against each other, Saskatchewan farmers uncovered the ways in which biotech corporations evade their responsibilities and tried to hold them publicly accountable.

Had the class-action lawsuit been successful in *Hoffman vs. Monsanto*, liability would have posed a real threat to Monsanto and Bayer CropSciences. The world was closely watching the outcome of this precedent-setting case. One of the most important victories in the SOD case was an injunction against the introduction of GM wheat in the Prairies. In January 2002, farmers initiated a class-action lawsuit aimed at stopping the introduction of GM wheat and limiting the spread of GM canola, both of which were alleged to be harmful to the interests of organic grain farmers and therefore unlawful. A short time later, Monsanto withdrew (or delayed) its application for regulatory approval of HT wheat. Thus the basis of the lawsuit intended to protect the wheat crop from contamination was removed, but the group could still claim damages for the loss of organic canola. In late 2010, Bill C-474 was introduced in the Canadian Parliament by the Liberal opposition's agriculture critic. This bill would have required that 'an analysis of potential harm to export markets be conducted before the sale of any new genetically engineered seed is permitted' (Sharratt 2010). The direct impact of the bill, which underwent extensive review by a House of Commons committee, would have effectively prevented the introduction of GM wheat and alfalfa in Canada. Unfortunately, in February 2011, the bill was defeated in a final vote at third reading. If passed, this bill would have provided some legal protection against GM contamination for Canadian farmers and filled an important governance gap.

Conclusion

The court cases presented here are symptomatic of how genetic contamination concretely and symbolically has come to represent a wide range of socio-cultural conflicts and clashing worldviews about agricultural production techniques and the future of the food supply. GM crops are excluded by all major organic certification bodies because of their incompatibility with organic standards of production. Legal action to resolve fundamentally intractable problems such as the coexistence of GM and non-GM agriculture seems to create a political 'dead end' for biotechnology opponents. Lawsuits are the last resort for these farmers to have their claims officially recognized in light of inadequate regulatory systems. However, the narrow scope of the legal system, which focuses on liability and compensation, represents a real danger to the broader ecological and socio-cultural values that organic agriculture aims to defend. Even if the SOD lawsuit had gone ahead and compensation had been obtained, organic farmers would thus have legitimated

the rights of multinational corporations to 'cause' widespread contamination by accepting compensation and assigning value to a harmful yet acceptable practice. Nevertheless, with the failure of the class-action lawsuit, organic farmers succeeded in drawing attention to the breakdown of both the regulatory system and the law to address the protection of their livelihoods. Most important, these cases illustrate how events on Canadian farms are distorted when presented in the courts; at the time of writing, no effective measures to limit GM contamination have been adopted, and gene introgression is an ecological as well as an economic disaster.

The decision to include an injunction against GM wheat in the civil lawsuit was significant; wheat is a major prairie crop and a universal symbol of peasant struggles. Monsanto realized that the stakes would be high if wheat were the focus of the court case and decided to withdraw its application for regulatory approval. The canola challenge posed a clear threat to biotech corporations and its resolution was 'an intensely political matter', as Müller suggests (2006).

Legal actions against biotech corporations draw attention to the inadequacies of current systems of regulation. They challenge the hegemony of risk and hold biotech companies accountable for their actions. More broadly, both Saskatchewan cases highlight issues that have been ignored, underplayed, or inadequately addressed in biotechnology regulatory frameworks—liability concerns, post-market surveillance, biodiversity losses, widespread contamination via genetic drift, the displacement of alternative farming practices, and the elimination of producer and consumer choice in the food system. These cases expose important governance gaps in the GM debate and, as a result, perform broader political functions. The judicial arena is limited in scope and process, and therefore may not be the proper forum for evaluating the social desirability of GM crops. However, attention must be paid to the many smaller spaces of public discourse that open up around these events. Percy Schmeiser and others who travel the world and share their stories actively participate in the global fight against GM crops. In addition, the legal arena may not be an important terrain of contestation, yet the contradictions and challenges it embodies represent a unique opportunity to analyze novel forms of resistance. As we can see, these failed attempts to obtain justice often pave the way for further legal or parliamentary actions such as a recent GM alfalfa ban in the United States and the introduction of Bill C-474 in Canada, which serve to raise public awareness of the need for stringent regulation of GM crops. In the case of GM alfalfa, regulatory inaction prompted citizens to use the court system to intervene when the US Department of Agriculture neglected its duty to produce an Environmental Impact Statement proving the ecological safety of this crop. In Canada, the design and purpose of the existing regulatory system—to facilitate commercialization and trade of GM crops—has left GM contamination unaddressed. Since attempts to politicize the problems caused by the loss of organics and conventional international markets

have been forestalled by economic actors and private interests, thus preventing wider public debate, these court cases are important symbolic, strategic moments in the global fight against GM crops and in the defence of diverse rural livelihoods. The problems caused by transgene escape will worsen as GM crop production intensifies around the world, increasing concerns about the survival of biodiversity in wild ecosystems. The interplay between intellectual property rights over GMOs and transgene contamination requires courts and governments to pay specific attention to allowing alternative, non-GM agricultural practices to survive. The limitations of legal and policy processes on contamination were obvious in both the Schmeiser and the SOD examples, as courts and regulatory authorities failed to anticipate claims and provide adequate protection against ecological damages and market losses. It is unclear how Canada will deal with GM contamination in the future, since important regulatory and policy gaps remain and GM crops continue to occupy more of the prairie landscape.

Discussion Questions

1. Why does the author claim that the development of agricultural biotechnology has taken place outside of democratic structures? What might be some concrete examples of this in Canada?

2. In what ways were the two court cases discussed in this chapter 'counter-hegemonic'?

3. What is the relationship between intellectual property rights and transgene contamination?

4. What are the implications of genetic drift for farmers involved in either organic or conventional agriculture, both locally and globally?

5. What effect might the presence of transgenes in organic crops have on the organics industry? On the food system as a whole?

Further Reading

Barrett, K. and Abergel E. (2002). 'Defining a Safe Genetically Modified Organism: Boundaries of Scientific Risk Assessment'. *Science and Public Policy* 29(1): 47–58; and Barrett, K. and Abergel, E. (2000). 'Breeding Familiarity: Environmental Risk

Assessment for Genetically Engineered Crops in Canada'. *Science and Public Policy* 27(1): 2–12. Both these articles explain how the regulatory process for approving the safety of GM crops works in Canada and provide a comprehensive background of the development of the regulatory system and of the scientific concepts used to determine the environmental safety of GM herbicide-tolerant canola. They also present the weaknesses of such a system.

For a critical analysis of the Canadian regulatory framework for dealing with GMOs, refer to the Royal Society of Canada's 2001 'Elements of Precaution: Recommendation for the Regulation of Food Biotechnology in Canada', www.rsc.ca/files/publications/expert_panels/foodbiotechnology/GMreportEN.pdf. This report was produced by Canada's expert scientific panel and includes information about how the regulatory system works in practice while questioning some of its scientific basis and ability to quantify and predict risk.

Deconstructing Dinner. (2008). 'The Colonization of the Canadian Farmer: Saskatchewan Organic Farmers vs. Monsanto/Bayer'. Broadcast produced by the Kootenay Co-op Radio on 4 January 2008, www.cjly.net/deconstructingdinner/010308.htm. While this is not an academic source, it is a very informative radio broadcast which deals with GM contamination from the farmers' perspective. More generally, this program covers a wide range of the issues facing Canadian farmers and Canadian farms today and is a very valuable resource.

For more information on GM contamination globally, the *GM Contamination Register* (available at www.gmcontaminationregister.org) provides an online database which documents the extent of the contamination problem worldwide. The information collected by GeneWatch UK and Greenpeace International tracks contamination incidents that can be searched by region, year, and/or by GM organism.

To learn more about the global status of commercialized Agri-Biotech crops and their development worldwide, the International Service for the Acquisition of Agri-Biotech Applications (ISAAA) publishes a yearly report which collects statistics and provides maps about the various regions of the world where GM crops are grown. The ISAAA is a non-profit organization that is pro-biotechnology. Older yearly reports are available online; more recent ones need to be purchased (www.isaaa.org).

For a more critical perspective on GM crops, the UK's Soil Association published a report entitled 'Seeds of Doubt' which draws from North American farmers' experiences of GM crops. The report aims to challenge the positive claims made about GM crops through interviews with growers of GM soya, maize, and canola as well as through their impacts on yield, agro-chemical use, and farmer income. The report is available at www.soilassociation.org.

Notes

1. Roundup is the trademark name for Monsanto's broad-spectrum herbicide glyphosate. In Roundup Ready crops, the genes encoding for glyphosate resistance are engineered inside the DNA of plants such as canola and soy so that they can resist applications of the herbicide killing weeds without incurring any significant losses to the crop.

2. Farmers wishing to grow RUR canola must sign a Technology Use Agreement (TUA) and attend a Grower Enrollment Meeting, which explains the technology and the licensing terms. Signing the TUA means that farmers can purchase RUR canola from an authorized seed agent. The TUA stipulates that only one crop may be planted and it must be sold to a commercial purchaser

authorized by Monsanto. Seeds cannot be saved for another planting; they may not be sold or given to a third party. The TUA also gives Monsanto the right to inspect the fields of the contracting farmer and to take samples that verify compliance with the agreement. Farmers pay a licensing fee for each acre planted with RUR seed. In 1998, the licensing fee was CAD$15.

References

Agriculture and Agri-Food Canada (AAFC). 2008. 'Canada's Organic Industry at a Glance 2008'. Accessed 25 October 2010 at www.agr.gc.ca.

Barrett, K., and E. Abergel. 2002. 'Defining a Safe Genetically Modified Organism: Boundaries of Scientific Risk Assessment'. *Science and Public Policy* 29(1): 47–58.

Barrett, K., and E. Abergel. 2000. 'Breeding Familiarity: Environmental Risk Assessment for Genetically Engineered Crops in Canada'. *Science and Public Policy* 27(1): 2–12.

Cullet, Philippe. 2005. '*Monsanto v Schmeiser*: A Landmark Decision Concerning Farmer Liability and Transgenic Contamination'. *Journal of Environmental Law* 17: 83–108.

De Beer, Jeremy, and Heather McLeod-Kilmurray. 2007. 'Commentary: The SCC Should Step up to the Environmental Plate'. *The Lawyers Weekly*, 5 October, 7.

Deconstructing Dinner. 2008. 'The Colonization of the Canadian Farmer: Saskatchewan Organic Farmers vs. Monsanto/Bayer'. Broadcast produced by the Kootenay Co-op Radio. 4 January. Accessed 8 August 2010 at www.cjly.net/deconstructingdinner/010308.htm.

Escobar, A. 2004. 'Actor Networks and New Knowledge Producers: Social Movements and the Paradigmatic Transition in the Sciences'. In *Para Além das Guerras da Ciência: Um Discurso sobre as Ciências Revisitado*, ed. Boaventura de Sousa Santos. Porto, Portugal: Afrontamento. Draft/translation available at www.unc.edu/escobar.

Food and Agriculture Organization (FAO). 1999. *Glossary of Biotechnology and Genetic Engineering*. Accessed 12 December 2010 at www.fao.org/docrep/003/x3910e/x3910e00.htm.

Fanning, Uncle Don. 2004. 'Schmeiser Stands up to Biotech Tyrants'. *Synthesis/Regeneration 34*.

Glover, Dominic, and Peter Newell. 2005. 'Business and Biotechnology: Regulating GM Crops and the Politics of Influence'. In *Agribusiness and Society: Corporate Responses to Environmentalism, Market Opportunities and Public Regulation*, ed. Kees Jansen and Sietze Vellema. London: Zed Books.

Holstlander, Cathy. 2008. Personal communication.

James, Clive. 2009. Global Status of Commercialized Biotech/GM Crops: 2009. ISAAA Brief No. 41. Ithaca, NY: International Service for the Acquisition of Agri-Biotech Applications (ISAAA).

Katz, Hagai. 2006. 'Gramsci, Hegemony, and Global Civil Society Networks'. *Voluntas* 17: 333–48.

Kimbrell, Andrew. 2010. 'Supreme Court Case a Defeat for Monsanto's Ambitions'. *The Huffington Post*. Accessed 24 October 2010 at www.huffingtonpost.com/andrew-kimbrell/supreme-court-case-a-defe_b_620087.html.

Müller, Birgit. 2006. 'Infringing and Trespassing Plants: Patented Seeds at Dispute in Canada's Courts'. *Focaal: European Journal of Anthropology* 48: 83–98.

Nelkin, Dorothy. 1992. *Controversy: The Politics of Technical Decisions*, 3rd ed. Newbury Park: Sage.

Nelkin, Dorothy, and Emily Marden. 2004. 'The Starlink Controversy: The Competing Frames of Risk Disputes'. *International Journal of Biotechnology* 6(1): 20–42.

Newell, P. 2003. 'Globalization and the Governance of Biotechnology'. *Global Environmental Politics* 3(2): 56–69.

Phillipson, Martin. 2005. 'Giving Away the Farm? The Rights and Obligations of Biotechnology Multinationals'. *King's College Law Journal* 16: 362.

Rajan, Kaushik Sunder. 2003. 'Genomic Capital: Public Cultures and Market Logics of Corporate Biotechnology'. *Science as Culture* 12(1): 87–121.

Reincke, Wolfgang. 1998. *Global Public Policy: Governing without Government?* Washington, DC: Brookings Institution Press.

Royal Society of Canada's Expert Panel Report on the Future of Food Biotechnology. 2001. *Elements of Precaution: Recommendations for the Regulation of Food Biotechnology in Canada*. Ottawa: Canada. Accessed 28 October 2010 at www.rsc.ca/files/publications/expert_panels/foodbiotechnology/GMreportEN.pdf.

Sassen, Saskia. 2003. 'The Participation of States and Citizens in Global Governance'. *Indiana Journal of Global Legal Studies* 10(5): 5–28.

Saskatchewan Organic Directorate (SOD). 2008. 'Individual Action Not the Way to Go'. SOD Press Release. Accessed 27 October 2010 at www.saskorganic.com/oapf/.

Schmeiser, Percy. 2003. 'NGO's Seek Standing in Monsanto v. Schmeiser'. Accessed 21 December 2010 at www.percyschmeiser.com/NGO.htm.

Sharratt, Lucy. 2010. 'Final Vote on Bill C-474: Dec. 7 (Subject to Change)'. Accessed 27 October 2010 at www.cban.ca/Take-Action/Act-Now.

Shreck, Aimee. 2005. 'Resistance, Redistribution and Power in the Fair Trade Banana Initiative'. *Agriculture and Human Values* 22: 17–29.

Stevenson, Hood, Thornton, Beaubier LLP, Barristers and Solicitors. 2006. 'Factum on Behalf of the Appellants: Larry Hoffman, L.B. Hoffman Farms Inc. and Dale Beaudoin and Monsanto Canada Inc. and Bayer CropScience Inc'. Saskatoon, Saskatchewan.

Winham, G. 2003. 'International Regime Conflict in Trade and Environment: The Biosafety Protocol and the WTO'. *World Trade Review* 2(2): 131–55.

Winickoff, David et al. 2005. 'Adjudicating the GM Food Wars: Science, Risk, and Democracy in World Trade Law'. *The Yale Journal of International Law* 30: 81–123.

Wynne, B. 2001. 'Creating Public Alienation: Expert Culture of Risks and Ethics of GMOs'. *Science as Culture* 10(4): 445–81.

Who Governs Global Food Prices?

Jennifer Clapp

Learning Objectives

Through this chapter, you can:

1. Understand the various factors that contributed to the recent episode of food price volatility, in particular the international economic forces beyond supply and demand for food
2. Become aware of why developing countries are particularly vulnerable to sharp changes in food prices on international markets
3. Consider the various responses to the food price crisis that might be required at the international level

Introduction

The global economic context is important in any analysis of food policy and politics, even at a very local level. Global economic relationships—including international trade, finance, and investment flows—shape food systems at all scales and in many important ways that go beyond simple supply and demand for food. These relationships, and the policies under which they operate, profoundly influence both trends in food prices and access to food. In developing countries that depend on food imports for a significant portion of their food consumption, food security is especially sensitive to changes in the global economy. But even the food systems of countries such as Canada that produce an abundance of food, including significant quantities for export, are affected by global economic forces.

The sharp food price rises in late 2007 and the first half of 2008 are an important illustration of the ways in which international economic

relationships affect food security and farmer livelihoods, particularly in developing countries. Suddenly higher food prices hit poor countries hard as food import bills rose quickly and widespread civil unrest ensued. Farmers did not necessarily see enormous benefits from food price rises, as prices for agricultural inputs such as seeds and fertilizer rose just as quickly. This food price crisis was abrupt and severe, but by late 2008, food prices had fallen back sharply, although they were still well above pre-2007 levels (FAO 2008a). Despite lower prices by late 2008, the number of hungry people on the planet climbed; it topped 1 billion by mid 2009 as farmer incomes fell (FAO 2009a). In late 2010 and early 2011 food prices spiked again, fuelling fears of yet another food crisis on top of what was already a fragile global hunger situation. The extreme **food price volatility** between 2007 and 2011 was highly unusual, following years of relatively low and stable food prices. Understanding the range of factors contributing to food price volatility is important for assessing whether it will continue, what impacts it will likely have on the world's poorest countries and low-income people, and how the international community should respond.

At the height of the food price rises in mid 2008, most analysts focused on supply and demand for food as the key cause. Jeffrey Sachs, prominent economist and UN advisor, explained the emergence of the crisis to European Union (EU) Members of Parliament in May 2008 in very basic terms: 'World demand for food has outstripped world supply' (Sachs 2008). Since that time, questions have emerged about whether the crisis was simply a product of a mismatch of **market fundamentals**—that is, supply and demand for food—alone.

The volatility of food prices between 2007 and 2011, first rising, then falling, then rising again, has led several analysts to argue that market fundamentals alone cannot explain the rapid shifts in food prices. Supply and demand are important, but broader economic relationships—particularly those related to financial, trade, and investment policies—must also be taken into account. Taking this wider view is especially important in shaping responses to the food crisis. Cranking up supply, in other words, will not resolve the problem unless other policy changes are also made. In this chapter, I argue that broader global economic relationships—especially international financial, agricultural trade, and investment policies—played a prominent role not only in precipitating the recent food price volatility, but also in influencing the longer-term vulnerability to food price swings in the world's poorest countries. Yet the role of these global economic relationships has not featured prominently in international governance responses to the food crisis. Failure of the international community to take these broader international economic factors fully into account when formulating responses to the global food situation risks a continuation of both volatility and vulnerability in the world's poorest countries.

Initial Focus on Supply and Demand

As food prices began to rise quickly in late 2007 and early 2008, most official analyses targeted market fundamentals—supply and demand for food—as the key culprits. Reports by organizations such as the Food and Agriculture Organization (FAO), World Bank, Organisation for Economic Co-operation and Development (OECD), and US Department of Agriculture (USDA), as well as think tanks such as the International Food Policy Research Institute (IFPRI) all took this approach (e.g., FAO 2008b; UN High Level Task Force 2008; World Bank 2008a; World Bank 2008b; OECD 2008; USDA 2008; Von Braun et al. 2008).

Mainstream reports on the crisis pointed to rising demand for food in countries such as India and China that were experiencing rapid economic growth (Von Braun et al. 2008: 4; USDA 2008: 12; OECD 2008: 2; IMF 2008: 7). It was assumed that people's rising incomes would mean greater demand for meat and dairy products, thus putting pressure on demand for grain to feed animals. And while demand was rising, supply was constrained. Drought in Australia as well as bad harvests in Europe in 2007–8 were blamed for production drops (FAO 2008b: 5; OECD 2008: 2; USDA 2008: 2). Indeed, the amount of grain in storage and the 'stock-to-use ratio' (the amount of grain stocks on hand as a percentage of overall use of grains per year) were at very low levels in early 2008 (FAO 2008b: 5; OECD 2008: 2; USDA 2008: 21).

Most reports also pointed out that a rising demand for grain-based biofuels from 2006 to 2008 had greatly exacerbated the situation, leading to a large proportion of maize production being diverted from the food supply (OECD 2008: 2; FAO 2008b: 7–8; Rosegrant 2008). Diversion of grains into biofuel production affects both the demand for grain and the supply of food, and as such, can influence prices. Almost all of the grain production increases in the United States between 2004 and 2007 went into biofuel production, and around 12 per cent of world maize production in 2007 was used to produce ethanol (World Bank 2008a: 1). The diversion of grain for biofuel production was estimated to be responsible for around 30 per cent to 70 per cent of the change in food prices (Rosegrant 2008; World Bank 2008).

Do these basic supply and demand explanations tell the entire story of food price rises? The demand arguments are perhaps the least convincing. Increasing demand for food in India and China did not suddenly appear. Rather, it has been gradually growing over the past few decades, and did not increase sharply in 2007–8. Moreover, these countries are self-sufficient in food, and as such have not been major buyers on global food markets (Headey and Fan 2008: 377). In terms of supply, although world cereal production fell short of utilization in 2005 and 2006, food production increased to record levels in both 2007 and 2008. In fact,

stock-to-use ratios actually rose by the end of 2008 (see Figure 17.1) (FAO 2008b: 6–8). This increase in global production occurred despite droughts and other bad weather. Moreover, food prices rose in 2007 at the same time that production was on the rise. Low levels of grain stocks could still affect prices, even if production had been climbing. But similar levels in the stock-to-use ratio for cereals in 2003 occurred without a sharp price jump This variation in the relationship between stock-to-use ratios and price changes raises questions about the impact of stock-to-use ratios on food prices (Dawe 2009).

Some have pointed out that there were reasons for lower grain stock holdings that did not necessarily relate to supply and demand forces. With low food prices for most of the prior two decades, governments moved away from storing grain in order to save on the high costs of storage. This approach made sense so long as food was widely available at a low cost. Many food processors adopted a 'just in time' inventory system, and did not invest in storage. Lower

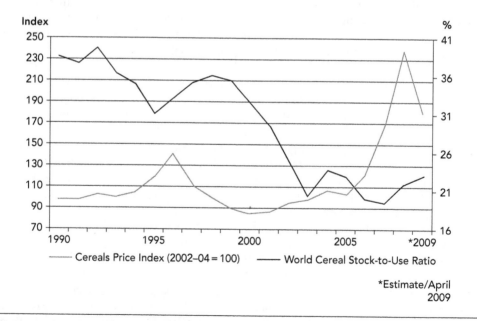

Figure 17.1   World Cereal Stocks-to-Use Ratio and Cereal Price Index, 1990–2008

Source: High-Level Conference on World Food Security: The Challenges of Climate Change and Bioenergy. © Food and Agriculture Organization of the United Nations, 2008.

amounts of grain held in storage, then, had little to do with the amount of food produced. Rather, it was more closely tied to the rising costs of storage (FAO 2008b: 5–6). For example, China deliberately reduced its stocks after 2000 (Headey and Fan 2008: 381; Dawe 2009: 4–5). China, however, is not a major player on world grain markets and thus the drawdown of its stocks had little, if any, impact on prices. World stock-to-use ratios excluding China have been steady in recent years (Dawe 2009).

By mid 2008, the FAO noted that the underlying forces of supply and demand could not account for a significant portion of the price volatility in international food markets. Futures prices for wheat, for example, had gone 60 per cent beyond what the market fundamentals would dictate in March 2008, while prices for maize had gone 30 per cent beyond the underlying expected value in April 2008 (FAO 2008c: 55–7). In the second half of 2008, just as the broader financial crisis took hold, food prices fell back sharply. Then, in 2010, they began to climb again, despite that year's harvest being the third-largest on record (FAO 2010). It is important to identify the source of this significant price volatility on world food markets if effective international governance responses are to be developed.

Beyond Supply and Demand: Other Factors Behind Food Price Volatility

Food prices dropped sharply in the fall of 2008, just as world financial markets were experiencing a significant collapse. This rapid price adjustment suggests that food supply and demand alone were not the only forces determining food prices. It is now increasingly understood that global financial markets and agricultural trade policies played an important role in influencing food prices in this period.

The value of the US dollar on financial markets plays a role in commodity pricing. Generally,

when the US dollar falls, commodity prices rise, because food on international markets is typically priced in US dollars. Demand also tends to rise for US grain when the dollar falls, because it appears to be 'cheap' for those buyers whose currencies are now worth more against the dollar. Foreign agricultural producers, whose commodities are priced in dollars, may also raise prices to compensate for the declining dollar (Elliott 2008). The dollar's value against other currencies depreciated by 22 per cent from 2002 to 2007, which likely was a factor in gradually rising food prices over this period (Abbot, Hurt, and Tyner 2008: 28; see also Timmer 2008). The US Federal Reserve deliberately kept the dollar value low by keeping interest rates low in 2007–8, due to the US mortgage crisis. Indeed, the US dollar depreciated a full 8 per cent against the euro in April 2008 alone (Abbott, Hurt, and Tyner 2008; Lustig 2008).

Because their prices tend to rise when the dollar falls, commodities are particularly attractive investments in such a context. Investors in such circumstances often move their money into **commodity futures contracts** and **commodity index funds**, because these are seen to be a higher-return investment, as indeed they were after 2007. Investors increased their purchases of commodity-linked financial products in 2007–8, including products involving agricultural commodities. It was exactly at this time that food prices began to rise. **Commodity speculation**, or a 'bubble' linked to shifts in financial investment, coincided with the food price rises, raising questions about causality and whether food prices were simply a product of supply and demand. Peter Timmer noted the separation between real and financial factors: 'Price formation in organized commodity markets depends on financial factors as well as 'real' supply and demand factors' (Timmer 2008: 8).

It is difficult to determine the precise impact on food prices of speculative financial investment in agricultural commodities. In the past 30 years there has been scant attention to the impact of agricultural commodity speculation, perhaps because most of those investing in commodity futures markets were largely the direct users or producers of the commodities (known as 'physical traders' or 'commercial speculators'). These physical traders use commodity futures markets to hedge against their risks. In this way, commodity futures markets play an important role in mitigating risk in the agricultural sector. But in the past few years, investors with no direct interest in the commodity in its physical form (known as 'non-commercial speculators') have entered futures markets in unusually large numbers (Clapp and Helleiner 2011). Non-commercial speculators invest in commodities as a financial investment, typically with 'long' positions (i.e., holding on to them for long periods of time), betting that prices will rise over time, and take their profits only when market conditions dictate (see IATP 2008).

Investment in commodities generally has grown dramatically in recent years. The amount invested in commodity futures contracts doubled to an estimated US$400 billion between the start of 2005 and March 2008, rising by US$70 billion in the first three months of 2008 alone (Young 2008: 9). Most of this investment originates from banks and other large-scale investors such as sovereign wealth funds, pension funds, hedge funds, university endowments, and other institutional investors. These investors typically purchase investment products called commodity index funds (CIFs). These funds bundle together a range of commodities, including agricultural commodities (typically around 30 per cent of the commodities in the bundle), into a single financial instrument that pays out according to price changes in those commodities. Banks sell these products, and, in order to cover their own risks, actively engage in the futures markets. CIFs have become very popular with investors, and investment in CIFs alone increased from US$13 billion in 2003 to US$260 billion in March 2008 (Masters 2008).

In addition to the weak dollar and rising commodity prices, loopholes in the regulatory framework for commodity futures markets in the United States also encouraged this activity.

Investors who are 'non-commercial' participants in futures markets, meaning they are not farmers, grain elevator operators, or physical grain traders, have long been subject to regulations that limited how many futures contracts they could hold in agricultural commodities. These regulations were intended to control purely speculative trades on agricultural futures markets by investors, including banks, whose main motivation was profit. In the late 1990s, however, these regulations were relaxed, and large-scale investors were then allowed to invest huge sums in commodities futures via large Wall Street banks who acted as brokers. These financial investors are not interested in the physical commodity they purchase. Rather, they move their money in and out of commodity markets largely in reaction to market algorithms based on broader macroeconomic conditions (Clapp and Helleiner 2011; IATP 2008). It is difficult to know which comes first, the speculation or the higher prices, as they are tightly linked. The result, however, is the same: large swings in the prices of agricultural commodities, including those of basic food staples, in response to movements of investment money on futures markets.

With the falling dollar, other commodity prices also rose, including oil. The price of a barrel of oil reached nearly US$150 in mid 2008 before it began to drop significantly when the financial markets collapsed. Oil prices have a direct influence on food prices by increasing the cost of production. Farm inputs such as pesticides and fertilizers are petroleum based, and prices for these inputs have closely tracked changes in oil prices. Oil prices also affect food prices through their influence on the demand for biofuels which divert grain from food markets. As oil prices rise, biofuels become more economically viable, and investment money flows into their production, further driving up grain prices (see Weis 2009).

Trade policies as well played a role in the food price spikes. As food prices rose precipitously early in 2008, some developing countries, including Vietnam, India, China, Argentina, and Egypt, began to impose trade restrictions on agricultural exports (World Bank 2008b: 2; Von Braun et al. 2008: 5). Largely a response to already rising food prices, these restrictions were intended not only to keep foodstuffs at home, but also to insulate each country's economy from further price increases on international markets. Although attempts to control exports can help with food availability and keeping prices low at home, they can cause further volatility in food prices on international markets because they disrupt usual trade patterns. The largest food price spikes for wheat and rice, for example, occurred on days when **export restrictions** were announced in major food-exporting developing countries.

There has been a growing acknowledgement of the importance of financial, investment, and trade policies in determining food prices, especially since financial markets collapsed in late 2008 and food prices began to fall and then rise again without apparent changes in production or stocks (Timmer 2008: 7; Kerckhoffs et al. 2010; IATP 2009). Food price spikes in mid 2010 and early 2011 raised new concerns about the role of export restrictions, as Russia imposed an export ban in the wake of bad harvests.

Increased attention has been paid to the role of commodity speculation as well in this period, as stock levels did not drop significantly and grain harvests were at record high levels in 2010, as noted above.

Vulnerability of Developing Countries to Food Price Volatility

Although all countries can be affected, food price volatility of the sort experienced from 2007 to 2010 is particularly problematic for the world's poorest countries, which are typically agriculture-based and dependent on food imports. There are over 80 countries in the category of 'Low-Income Food-Deficit Countries' (LIFDCs), and these countries are especially vulnerable to sharp movements in international food prices.[1] The least developed countries (LDCs)—most of which are also currently LIFDCs—were net agricultural exporters in the 1960s. Today, as a group they are net agricultural importers (see Figure 17.2). Several international economic

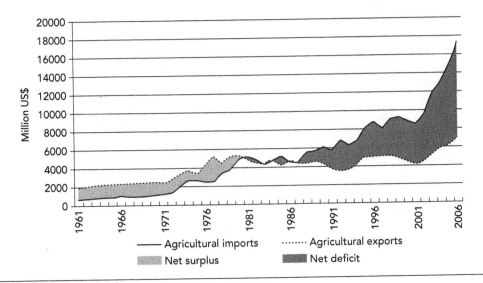

Figure 17.2 Agricultural Trade Balance of Least Developed Countries, 1961–2006

Source: Clapp (2012a).

factors have contributed to import dependence of LIFDCs, thus creating vulnerability to changes in international food prices. These factors are complex and wide-ranging, and only a brief overview is provided here.

Agricultural trade policy in industrialized countries is widely seen to have had a negative impact on agriculture in developing countries. Agricultural subsidies of over US$300 billion per year in the industrialized countries, for example, is one policy that has had a negative impact. For most of the 30 years prior to the recent food price spikes, rich-country subsidies have encouraged the dumping of cheap agricultural products on world markets, depressing world agricultural commodity prices (Oxfam 2005; Murphy, Lilliston, and Lake 2005). Industrialized countries also protected their own markets from agricultural products exported by developing countries through raising tariff barriers on tropical products. In the 1980s and 1990s, most developing countries already liberalized their trade policies under structural adjustment programs. As a result they cannot afford to subsidize their own farmers or raise their own tariffs to counteract the trade practices of the industrialized countries, because such rules were locked in as part of the 1994 Uruguay Round Agreement on Agriculture, adopted at the time that the World Trade Organization (WTO) was created. This highly uneven playing field in international agricultural trade has been identified by many analysts as a key cause of reduced incentives for agricultural production in developing countries in the past two decades (see Khor 2005; Weis 2007).

The lopsided nature of international agricultural trade rules were recognized at the launch of the **Doha Round** of WTO trade talks in 2001. The Agreement on Agriculture was to be renegotiated under the Doha Round as a means by which to rectify these imbalances. But thus far a deal has not been reached after 10 years of contentious negotiations over agriculture, with disagreements both among rich countries and

between rich and poor countries. The United States and the European Union in particular have not made any commitments to significantly reduce their domestic support subsidies to their own farmers. Yet at the same time, both have pushed hard for greater access to markets in developing countries (Clapp 2006; Rosset 2006). The talks have been stalled since 2008 over the details of a special safeguard mechanism that developing countries insist on, to protect themselves from import surges of low-priced agricultural imports that threaten their own farmers' livelihoods.

Investment in agriculture in those developing countries also declined over the past 30 years. The World Bank's lending for agriculture, for example, dropped from 30 per cent of its overall lending in 1980 to just 12 per cent in 2008. Similarly, the percentage of official development assistance earmarked for agriculture fell from a high 18 per cent in 1979 to just 3 per cent in 2008 (World Bank et al. 2009). Governments of developing countries also did not invest heavily in the agricultural sector, constrained by high levels of international debt that cut their budgets. This sharp decline in agricultural investment over the past 30 years coincided with historically low world food prices, as noted above. With cheap food imports available during that time, there was little incentive for developing countries and donors to improve agricultural productivity.

Food crises that periodically emerged since the 1980s in developing countries were largely addressed via food aid from the rich industrialized countries. This aid provided a stopgap rather than a viable long-term investment for the agricultural sector. The manner of providing food aid has only exacerbated the situation. Food aid that is tied—food that must be purchased within the donor country—has dominated for much of the past 50 years. Tied food aid, however, can create disincentives for local production and can also disrupt local markets in recipient countries (Barrett and Maxwell 2005). Since the 1990s a number of donors have moved to cash-based food aid provision, including the European

Union, Canada, and Australia. Untying food aid allows donors to purchase food in developing countries. This practice is seen to be less disruptive: food reaches hungry recipients faster because it is sourced closer to them, and it provides incentives for farmers in poor countries. But the United States, which provides nearly 50 per cent of all international food aid, maintains a nearly 100 per cent tied food aid policy (OECD 2005). Since 2008 the United States has implemented some policy changes that allow it to untie a small portion of its food aid, but the amounts involved are extremely small compared to its overall food aid program (Kripke 2009; Clapp 2012b).

Over the past 30 years, these various international economic policies contributed to weak agricultural performance and growing dependence on imported food, including food aid, in the world's poorest developing countries. Rural poverty, import dependency, and heightened vulnerability to food price shocks on international markets have resulted from these policies. In such a context, suddenly higher food prices were devastating to poor countries that had become dependent on food imports. And while higher prices might potentially benefit farmers in poor countries, this did not occur. Most poor farmers in developing countries are still net purchasers of food, and the cost of their inputs and transportation also rose sharply. In other words, both rural farmers and urban dwellers were hard hit by rising food prices.

International Governance Responses to the Crisis

The global community responded with a number of distinct yet overlapping initiatives in the wake of the 2007–8 food price spikes and the further volatility in food prices since that time. These initiatives have come in two major phases: those that were implemented quickly in 2008 in the atmosphere of crisis, which focused on emergency relief; and those implemented in

2009 and beyond that focused on longer-term efforts to promote food security. In neither phase was attention primarily focused on the broader international economic factors—that is, factors beyond the simple food supply and demand equation. Instead, emergency food aid and loans dominated the first phase, and increasing agricultural production through new technologies dominated the second.

When the extent of the price crisis became apparent in early 2008, UN Secretary General Ban Ki-Moon immediately established the High-Level Task Force [HLTF] on the Global Food Crisis. The HLTF initial report, *Comprehensive Framework for Action* (CFA) was circulated at the High-Level Conference on World Food Security in early June 2008 (UN High Level Task Force 2008). The G8 met in July 2008 in Hokkaido, Japan, and released the Leaders' Statement on Global Food Security, which noted that members had already in 2008 pledged US$10 billion in assistance to developing countries to cope with the crisis (G8 2008).

In this early phase of the international response to the crisis, the focus was on providing emergency funding and loans to meet short-term food needs in order to stem civil unrest sparked by food prices. This phase included increased funding for food aid programs as well as emergency balance-of-payments loans to enable food-deficit countries to pay for food imports. These measures were welcomed by multilateral agencies and recipient countries. The rapidly rising price of food increased procurement costs significantly for the World Food Programme, which found itself short by over US$755 million to meet its existing obligations to feed over 70 million people in 2008. Donor governments pledged additional funding for food aid, including a US$500 million untied cash donation from Saudi Arabia. But the food aid from the United States was still largely tied, rather than in the form of cash. The 2008 US Farm Bill—passed in the midst of the food price crisis in June 2008—included a modest pilot project of cash food aid for local and regional food purchases in developing countries. This project was smaller than it could have been; at that important time, the international community could have put much more pressure on the United States to thoroughly reform its food aid policies. Such reform would reduce market distortions and remove conditions on food aid that weaken domestic production incentives in developing countries.

The early initiatives in this phase of the international community's response also called for tempering demand for grain by rethinking biofuel policies. But the initiatives stopped short of calling for mandatory measures, and instead proposed further study on the issue. IFPRI suggested specific policies, such as imposing a moratorium on biofuels based on grains and oilseeds until prices dropped and increasing support to non-food-based biofuels (Von Braun et al. 2008). The CFA suggested an International Biofuel Consensus to ensure broad support for less damaging biofuel policies (UN High-Level Task Force 2008: 24–5). But as grain prices eased in late 2008, these suggestions were abandoned.

With respect to broader factors contributing to the crisis, the various initiatives in this phase of response called for an end to export bans in developing countries and a swift completion of the Doha Round, neither of which were achieved. No doubt export restrictions exacerbated the price spike, but it is unclear whether they caused the initial sharp price rises. Developing countries largely responded to the international context in which global prices for foodstuffs were rising quickly. Further, the call for a swift completion of the Doha Round could have benefited long-term food security only if it were more balanced toward the needs of the developing countries.

Missing from these early international initiatives was any effort to regulate commodity markets to limit speculation by non-commercial market participants. The CFA did note that agricultural commodity speculation merited further study and that regulatory measures might be considered. But there was little concrete effort

on this front, as some think tanks such as IFPRI warned of the risk of over-regulation and called for 'market-oriented' measures (Von Braun et al. 2008: 9). This position contrasted sharply with recommendations at the time from more critical organizations. The Institute for Agriculture and Trade Policy, for example, immediately called for multilateral efforts to reduce agricultural commodity speculation (IATP 2008: 10).

As food prices temporarily eased somewhat in 2009 (though they were still higher than pre-2007 levels), the international community began to consider longer-term policies. At a major meeting on food security in Madrid in early 2009 a Global Partnership on Agriculture and Food Security (GPAFS) was formed to coordinate global efforts. The July 2009 G8 meeting in L'Aquila, Italy produced a further statement on food security that included a pledge to invest US$20 billion over three years in sustainable agriculture in developing countries as part of this broader partnership (G8 2009). The September 2009 G20 meeting in Pittsburgh reiterated the US$20 billion pledge and endorsed the establishment of the Global Agriculture and Food Security Program (GAFSP), which would be housed in the World Bank, as a primary channel for these funds (G20 2009; World Bank et al. 2009). In October 2009 the FAO significantly reformed the Committee on World Food Security to better enable it to take a key role in coordinating global efforts on food security with enhanced participation of civil society as part of the broader GPAFS (FAO 2009b).

The World Summit on Food Security, held in Rome in November 2009, promoted these various efforts, and adopted the Five Rome Principles for Sustainable Global Food Security (FAO 2009c). These principles include a focus on country-owned plans for food security (viewing food security as a national responsibility), strategic coordination from the local to the global levels, both short- and long-term measures to promote food security and the right to food, multilateral involvement in food security initiatives, and a commitment by all partners to substantially invest in agriculture, food security, and nutrition (FAO 2009c). The various above-mentioned initiatives adopted in 2009 were reinforced at the 2010 G8 and G20 meetings held in Canada, although food security played a less prominent a role at these meetings than in the previous two years.

Although these later initiatives, underpinned by the Rome Principles, promote integrated food security, involving both developing countries and multilateral partners, they tended to focus primarily on investment to boost agricultural production rather than addressing the international economic dimensions, especially trade and financial policies, that contributed to the crisis. The renewed focus on agricultural investment is important, especially given its drastic decline over the previous three decades as noted above. Indeed, even before the price spikes occurred some analysts had been calling for this trend to be reversed.

Two major reports on revitalizing agricultural investment were published just as food prices began to rise and shaped international responses to the crisis. One was the World Bank's World Development Report 2008, *Agriculture for Development*, which mapped out a strategy that included the promotion of new agricultural technologies, agricultural biotechnology among them, as its key component. As well, it advocated further trade liberalization in developing countries to integrate small farmers into global markets, deemed a more pressing measure than reducing agricultural subsidies in industrialized countries. Taking a different approach, the International Assessment of Agricultural Knowledge, Science and Technology for Development (IAASTD) report was released in April of 2008 (IAASTD 2008). This report was the result of a multi-year, multi-institution, government-supported effort to rethink how best to revitalize agriculture. The report was skeptical of the benefits of GMOs in agriculture and instead promoted investment in small-scale agro-ecological agriculture. It also was cautious about agricultural trade liberalization,

recommending that the agreement be more balanced and allow developing countries the policy space to protect their agricultural markets when their own farmers' livelihoods are threatened.[2]

It is interesting to note how the divergent recommendations in these reports were taken up in the various initiatives to address the food crisis. The UN-based HLTF's CFA document and the Committee on World Food Security reflect the IAASTD position, recommending more equitable trade practices such as reducing rich-country agricultural subsidies and advocating caution in the promotion and adoption of new agricultural technologies (HLTF 2008: 21–3). The CFA also notes the importance of looking further into agricultural commodity speculation as one cause of the food-price rises (HLTF 2008: 23). The G8 and G20 policy initiatives, on the other hand, are linked to the GAFSP at the World Bank; thus it is not surprising that these initiatives focus primarily on promoting new technologies for increasing agricultural production, linking farmers to markets through trade liberalization in developing countries, and introducing private-sector insurance and commodity exchanges to reduce risk and vulnerability caused by price volatility (World Bank et al. 2009). Because most of the multilateral funding for global food security following the food crisis has been directed to the GAFSP, the bulk of the efforts are likely to follow the World Bank's focus on increasing agricultural production with new technologies and further trade liberalization.

Because most funding is channelled through the World Bank's GAFSP, the broader economic dimensions of the crisis, including rich-country agricultural subsidies that contributed to long-term global trade inequities, and agricultural commodity speculation that contributed to short-term price volatility, are largely ignored in global efforts to cope with the crisis. Also missing from the various initiatives is much mention of the role of corporate concentration in the global food system.[3] The World Bank GAFSP does call for increased private-sector investment in agribusiness to encourage more production in developing countries. But little has been said in any of the initiatives about how corporate concentration might hinder developing-country production incentives and retail market access for their agricultural goods. As global corporations come to dominate most aspects of global food supply chains, it is important to carefully consider the impact of this trend on developing country agricultural systems.

When food prices began to climb again in the second half of 2010 and early 2011, food price volatility once more took centre stage in global economic discussions. As host of the G20 in 2011, France featured the issue on the group's agenda (Benedetti-Valentini 2010; Farchy 2010). The outcome, however, was disappointing. The final communiqué from the November 2011 leaders' meeting failed to make any significant recommendations on the regulation of financial markets to curb food price speculation or to curb biofuel subsidies. Instead, the G20 put most of its efforts regarding food prices on a new initiative called the Agricultural Market Information System (AMIS) which seeks to smooth food prices by making more information available to market participants. With the G20 countries as host to most of the world's financial markets and the principal players with respect to biofuel subsidy provision, AMIS was politically much easier for this group to endorse than financial regulation or biofuel policy changes. While AMIS may result in some smoothing of food prices on agricultural commodity markets, it does not move the global economy any closer to the kinds of structural economic reforms that many see as necessary to rein in food price volatility.

Conclusion

In a global economy, economic shifts in one part of the world can have unexpected repercussions elsewhere. Unexpected food price spikes in the international arena not only can wreak havoc in developing countries by deepening poverty, hunger, and political unrest, but also impact developed countries in unforeseeable ways. Since 2007, food price volatility has been particularly intense and it is not clear that these price swings result only from the simple market fundamentals of supply and demand. Broader economic factors, including agricultural commodity speculation on financial markets and trade restrictions, appear to have played a large role in feeding this volatility in food prices. At the same time, developing countries have been especially vulnerable to sharp food price swings due to long-term inequities in international trade and investment that have encouraged them to become increasingly reliant on food imports.

International responses to the situation thus far have largely focused on supply and demand as causes of the food price rises, and as such have given priority to short-term emergency aid, and to long-term investment for boosting agricultural productivity in poor countries with new technologies. These responses, however, have downplayed broader economic factors that have encouraged both food price volatility and developing countries' vulnerability to that volatility. Boosting production and further integrating developing countries into an already inequitable global agricultural trade system, without rectifying inequities and tempering speculative forces in global financial markets, may do little to avert future food crises in the world's poorest countries.

Discussion Questions

1. Who or what is to blame for the 2007–8 food price crisis?

2. What might account for the widely diverging viewpoints on the role of speculation on commodity futures markets in the food price crisis?

3. What accounts for developing countries' high vulnerability to food price fluctuations on international markets?

4. What governance measures at the international level will best help to prevent future food crises?

Further Reading

1. Clapp, Jennifer and Eric Helleiner. 2012. 'Troubled Futures? The Global Food Crisis and the Politics of Agricultural Derivatives Regulation'. *Review of International Political Economy*. In press.

   This article provides an overview of the role of commodity futures markets and financial investment in the food price crisis, and efforts to regulate it.

2. Headey, Derek, and Shenggen Fan. 2008. 'Anatomy of a Crisis: The Causes and Consequences of Surging Food Prices'. *Agricultural Economics* 30: 375–91.

   This article provides a general overview of the many factors involved in the 2007–8 food price crisis.

3. IAASTD. 2008. *Executive Summary of the Synthesis Report*, 1–11. www.agassessment. org/reports/IAASTD/EN/Agriculture%20 at%20a%20Crossroads_Executive%20 Summary%20of%20the%20Synthesis%20 Report%20(English).pdf.

   This report provides an overview of the IAASTD viewpoint on the policies required to improve the state of agriculture in developing countries.

4. Weis, Tony. 2007. *The Global Food Economy: The Battle for the Future of Farming*. London: Zed Books.

   This book provides an overview of the key forces that explain vulnerability of developing countries in the global food economy.

5. World Bank. 2007. 'Overview'. *World Development Report 2008. Agriculture for Development*, 1–25. http://siteresources. worldbank.org/INTWDR2008/ Resources/2795087–1192112387976/ WDR08_01_Overview.pdf.

   This report provides an overview of the World Bank's perspective on agriculture's role in developing countries.

Notes

1. This group includes most countries in sub-Saharan Africa, much of Asia including India, China, Philippines, Bangladesh, Pakistan, and Indonesia, as well as several countries in Central America and the Caribbean.

2. For a comparison of these two documents, see Clapp 2009b.

3. An earlier IFPRI document, however, does mention this factor (Von Braun 2007).

References

Abbot, Philip, Christopher Hurt, and Wallace Tyner. 2008. *What's Driving Food Prices?* Oak Brook, IL: Farm Foundation.

Barrett, Christopher, and Daniel Maxwell. 2005. *Food Aid After Fifty Years: Recasting Its Role*. London: Routledge.

Benedetti-Valentini, Fabio. 2010. 'France Wants G-20 to Limit "Monetary Disorder," Speculation on Commodities'. Bloomberg, 26 September. At: www.bloomberg.com/ news/2010–09–26/france-wants-g-20-to-limit-monetary-disorder-speculation-on-commodities.html.

Clapp, Jennifer. 2006. 'WTO Agriculture Negotiations: Implications for the Global South'. *Third World Quarterly* 27(4): 563–77.

———. 2009a. 'Food Price Volatility and Vulnerability in the Global South: Considering the Global Economic Context'. *Third World Quarterly* 30(6): 1183–96.

———. 2009b. 'The Global Food Crisis and International Agricultural Policy: Which Way Forward?' *Global Governance* 15(2): 299–312.

———. 2012a. *Food*. Cambridge, UK: Polity Press.

———. 2012b. *Hunger in the Balance: The New Politics of International Food Aid*. Ithaca, NY: Cornell University Press.

Clapp, Jennifer, and Doris Fuchs (eds.) 2009. *Corporate Power in Global Agrifood Governance*. Cambridge, MA: MIT Press.

Clapp, Jennifer, and Eric Helleiner. 2011. 'Troubled Futures? The Global Food Crisis and the Politics of Agricultural Derivatives Regulation'. *Review of International Political Economy*. In press.

Dawe, David. 2009. 'The Unimportance of "Low" World Grain Stocks for Recent World Price Increases'. ESA Working Paper No. 09–01. February. Rome: FAO.

Elliott, Larry. 2008. 'Against the Grain: Weak Dollar Hits the Poor'. *The Guardian*, 21 April.

Farchy, Jack. 2010. 'Merkel Weighs in Over Reforms to Regulation'. *Financial Times*, 5 October.

Food and Agriculture Organization (FAO). 2008a. *Crop Prospects and Food Situation*. No. 4, October. Available at www.fao.org/docrep/011/ai473e/ ai473e00.htm.

———. 2008b. 'Soaring Food Prices: Facts, Perspectives, Impacts and Actions Required'. Paper presented at the High-Level Conference on World Food Security: The Challenges of Climate Change and Bioenergy. 3–5 June, Rome. Available at ftp://ftp.fao.org/docrep/fao/ meeting/013/k2414e.pdf.

———. 2008c. *Food Outlook*. June. Available at ftp://ftp. fao.org/docrep/fao/010/ai466e/ai466e00.pdf.

———. 2009a. *More People than Ever Are Victims of Hunger*. Rome: FAO. Available at www.fao.org/fileadmin/ user_upload/newsroom/docs/Press%20release%20 june-en.pdf.

———. 2009b. 'Reform of the Committee on World Food Security'. Committee on World Food Security, 35th Session, 14–17 October, Rome. Available at ftp://ftp. fao.org/docrep/fao/meeting/017/k3023e3.pdf.

———. 2009c. 'Declaration of the World Summit on Food Security'. World Summit on Food Security, 16–18 November, Rome. Available at www.fao.org/fileadmin/ templates/wsfs/Summit/Docs/Final_Declaration/ WSFS09_Declaration.pdf.

———. 2010. 'No Food Crisis Seen, but Greater Market Stability Needed'. *Global Food Security Crisis*. Available at www.un-foodsecurity.org/node/765.

Group of Eight (G8). 2008. 'G8 Leaders Statement on Global Food Security', July. Available at www. canadainternational.gc.ca/g8/assets/pdfs/G8_Leaders_ Statement_Global_Food_Security-eng.pdf.

Group of Eight (G8). 2009. '"L'Aquila" Joint Statement on Global Food Security: L'Aquila Food Security Initiative (AFSI)'. July. Available at www.g8italia2009.it/static/ G8_Allegato/LAquila_Joint_Statement_on_Global_ Food_Security%5B1%5D,0.pdf.

Group of Twenty (G20). 2009. 'G20 Leaders Statement: The Pittsburgh Summit'. September. Available at www.g20. utoronto.ca/2009/2009communique0925.html.

Hatanaka, Maki, Carmen Bain, and Lawrence Busch. 2005. 'Third Party Certification in the Global Agrifood System'. *Food Policy* 30(3): 354–69.

Headey, Derek, and Shenggen Fan. 2008. 'Anatomy of a Crisis: The Causes and Consequences of Surging Food Prices'. *Agricultural Economics* 30: 375–91.

Heffernan, William. 2000. 'Concentration of Ownership and Control in Agriculture'. In *Hungry for Profit: The Agribusiness Threat to Farmers, Food and the Environment*, ed. Fred Magdoff, John Bellamy Foster, and Frederick H. Buttel. New York: Monthly Review Press, 61–75.

International Assessment of Agricultural Knowledge, Science and Technology for Development (IAASTD). 2008. 'Executive Summary of the Synthesis Report'. Washington DC: Island Press. Available at www. agassessment.org/docs/IAASTD_EXEC_SUMMARY_ JAN_2008.pdf.

Institute for Agriculture and Trade Policy (IATP). 2008. *Commodities Market Speculation: The Risk to Food Security and Agriculture'*. Minneapolis. Available at www.iatp.org/tradeobservatory/library. cfm?refID=104414.

———. 2009. *Betting Against Food Security: Futures Market Speculation*. Minneapolis: IATP. Available at www.iatp. org/documents/betting-against-food-security-futures- market-speculation.

International Monetary Fund (IMF). 2008. *Food and Fuel Prices—Recent Development, Macroeconomic Impact and Policy Responses*. Washington DC. 30 June. Available at www.imf.org/external/np/pp/eng/2008/063008.pdf.

Kerckhoffs, Thijs, Roos van Os, and Myriam Vander Stichele. 2010. *Financing Food: Financialisation and Financial Actors in Agriculture Commodity Markets*. April. Amsterdam: Centre for Research on Multinational Corporations.

Khor, Martin. 2005. *The Commodities Crisis and the Global Trade in Agriculture: Problems and Proposals*. Malaysia: Third World Network.

Kripke, Gawain. 2009. 'The Uses of Crisis: Progress on Implementing US Local/Regional Procurement of Food Aid'. In *The Global Food Crisis: Governance Challenges and Opportunities*, ed. Jennifer Clapp and Marc J. Cohen. Waterloo, ON: Wilfrid Laurier University Press, 113–26.

Lustig, Nora. 2008. 'Thought for Food: The Challenges of Coping with Soaring Food Prices'. Working Paper 155. Washington, DC: Center for Global Development.

Masters, Michael. 2008. 'Testimony Before US Senate Committee on Homeland Security and Governmental Affairs'. Washington, DC. 20 May.

Murphy, Sophia, Ben Lilliston, and Mary Beth Lake. 2005. *wto Agreement on Agriculture: A Decade of Dumping*. Minneapolis: Institute for Agriculture and Trade Policy.

Organisation for Economic Co-operation and Development (OECD). 2005. *The Development Effectiveness of Food Aid: Does Tying Matter?* Paris: OECD.

———. 2008. 'Rising Agricultural Prices: Causes, Consequences and Responses'. *OECD Observer*, Policy Brief. August.

Oxfam. 2005. *A Round for Free: How Rich Countries Are Getting a Free Ride on Agricultural Subsidies at the WTO*. Oxfam Briefing Paper 76. June. Available at www.maketradefair.com/en/assets/english/aroundforfree.pdf.

Rosegrant, Mark. 2008. 'Biofuels and Grain Prices: Impacts and Policy Responses'. Testimony to the US Senate Committee on Homeland Security and Governmental Affairs. 7 May. Washington, DC: International Food Policy Research Institute.

Rosset, Peter. 2006. *Food Is Different: Why the WTO Should Get out of Agriculture*. London: Zed Books.

Sachs, Jeffrey. 2008. 'Speech to the European Parliament Committee on Development'. Brussels. 5 May.

Timmer, C. Peter. 2008. *The Causes of High Food Prices*. Asian Development Bank Working Paper No. 128. Manila: Asian Development Bank. Available at www.adb.org/Documents/Working-Papers/2008/Economics-WP128.pdf.

United Nations High-Level Task Force on the Global Food Crisis (UN HLTF). 2008. 'Elements of a Comprehensive Framework for Action'. New York: United Nations. June.

United States Department of Agriculture (USDA). 2008. 'Global Agricultural Supply and Demand: Factors Contributing to the Recent Increase in Food Commodity Prices'. Washington, DC: USDA Economic Research Service. May.

Von Braun, Joachim. 2007. *The World Food Situation: New Driving Forces and Actions Required*. IFPRI Food Policy Report. Washington, DC: International Food Policy Research Institute. Available at www.ifpri.org/pubs/fpr/pr18.pdf.

Von Braun, Joachim, Akhter Ahmed, Kwadwo Asenso-Okyere et al. 2008. 'High Food Prices: The What, Who and How of Proposed Policy Actions'. IFPRI Policy Brief. Washington, DC: International Food Policy Research Institute. Available at www.ifpri.org/PRESSREL/2008/pressrel20080516.pdf.

Weis, Tony. 2007. *The Global Food Economy: The Battle for the Future of Farming*. London: Zed Books.

———. 2009. 'Fossil Energy and the Biophysical Roots of the Food Crisis'. In *The Global Food Crisis: Governance Challenges and Opportunities*, ed. Jennifer Clapp and Marc J. Cohen. Waterloo, ON: Wilfrid Laurier University Press, 145–59.

World Bank. 2008a. 'Rising Food Prices: Policy Options and World Bank Response'. Washington, DC: World Bank. Available at http://siteresources.worldbank.org/NEWS/Resources/risingfoodprices_backgroundnote_apr08.pdf.

———. 2008b. 'Double Jeopardy: Responding to High Food and Fuel Prices'. Paper presented at the G8 Hokkaido-Toyako Summit. 2 July. Available at http://siteresources.worldbank.org/INTPOVERTY/Resources/335642-1210859591030/G8-HL-summit-paper.pdf.

World Bank, International Fund for Agricultural Development, Food and Agriculture Organization, and the World Food Programme. 2009. 'Framework Document for a Global Agriculture and Food Security Program'. Draft. 6 November.

Young, John. 2008. 'Speculation and World Food Markets'. *IFPRI Forum*. July.

18

Municipal Governance and Urban Food Systems

Wendy Mendes

Learning Objectives

Through this chapter, you can:

1. Understand and define what constitutes a food system
2. Distinguish what makes a food system urban
3. Identify who makes decisions about urban food systems, and why this matters in the context of broader food system goals
4. Explain the ways that food has returned to the agendas of municipal governments, urban planners, and interested citizen groups
5. Understand how new forms of municipal governance are expressed through urban food system policies and programs

Introduction

Every day in cities around the world, millions of hungry mouths depend on food that has often travelled thousands of kilometres to reach supermarket shelves. Yet many of us remain unaware of how this happens. Until recently, few of us questioned the conditions under which food is grown, processed, and transported in and out of our cities, let alone the far-reaching social, economic, and environmental impacts on our communities and our planet. As Carolyn Steel reminds us:

> When you think that every day for a city the size of London, enough food for thirty million meals must be produced, imported, sold, cooked, eaten and disposed of again, and that something similar must happen

every day for every city on earth, it is remarkable that those of us living in cities get to eat at all. (Steel 2008: ix)

The 'gargantuan effort' required to feed cities has played a central part in the rise and fall of urban civilizations from the time of the ancient Romans to the present day (ibid.). Over the course of the twentieth century, global changes placed unprecedented pressure on cities and their food systems, including intensive rural-to-urban migration, loss of farmland, the rise of technologies such as intensive mechanized farming, and refrigeration allowing for long-distance food transportation (Mougeot 2006; Pothukuchi and Kaufman 1999, 2000; Mendes 2007a, 2008;

Morgan 2009). These changes, along with the effects of climate change, environmental degradation, and public health crises, have drawn our focus back to food and food systems as issues of major importance to cities.

Today, food is reappearing on the agendas of a growing number of municipal governments and emerging as a pressing concern for the many urban dwellers who are flocking to community gardens, engaging in urban farming, shopping at farmers' markets, planting urban orchards, educating themselves about the sources of their food, participating in community kitchens and community food events, and serving on **food policy councils**. A food system includes all of the activities and processes by which people produce, obtain, consume, and dispose of their food. It also includes the inputs and outputs that make the system run. But what exactly makes a food system urban? Who makes decisions about **urban food systems**, and why does 'urban' matter in the context of broader food system goals? This chapter examines these questions by tracing some of the ways that food has returned to the agendas of municipal governments, urban planners, and interested citizen groups. We then explore how new forms of municipal governance are expressed through urban food system policies and programs.

Feeding Twenty-First Century Cities

After decades of neglect, municipal governments in cities worldwide are increasingly developing **food policy** commitments (Koç, MacRae, Mougeot, and Welsh 1999; Mendes 2006, 2007a, 2007b, 2008; Mendes, Balmer, Kaethler, and Rhoads 2008). Canadian cities such as Vancouver, Victoria, Toronto, and Ottawa, and US cities such as Seattle; Philadelphia; Madison, Wisconsin; Baltimore; New York; San Francisco; and Portland, Oregon have significant food policy commitments as part of their formal mandates. Cities in the global South

take an equally active interest in **food systems**; many of these are emerging as global leaders and innovators in municipal food policy. For instance, Belo Horizonte, Brazil, has been implementing policies based on the principle of food security as a right of citizenship since 1993. Its programs reach over 800,000 people daily, or close to 38 per cent of the total municipal population at a cost of less than 1 per cent of the city's total budget (Rocha 2001). Rosario, Argentina, has been recognized for its food-policy development with a United Nations Best Practice Award for its Urban Agriculture Programme.[1] This program arose from Argentina's 2001 economic crisis, which caused poverty levels in Rosario to reach 50 per cent (Spiaggi 2005).

Before we examine in detail the implications of the return of food to municipal agendas, it is first helpful to define some of our central concepts, beginning with food policy. Food policy can be defined as those policies that affect who eats what; when and how food is produced, processed, distributed, consumed, and recycled; and what impacts (social, environmental, and economic) result from these activities (Iowa Food Policy Council 2005: 1). Food policies involve a range of issues and jurisdictions: municipal—determining where grocery stores are located, how food waste is disposed of, what opportunities are available for urban agriculture, how emergency food is distributed, how the local food economy is developed, etc.; regional and national—regulating public health, nutrition, agriculture, natural resources, fisheries, etc.; and global—establishing international trade agreements, managing food aid, mitigating climate change and its impacts on agriculture, etc.

Food policies are an interconnected set of subsystems ranging from the household to the global level (Dahlberg 1992, 1994). By extension, a systems approach reflects the need to holistically address problems in the ways that food is produced, processed, distributed, consumed, and recycled, instead of addressing individual problems of the food system in isolation (Garrett and Feenstra 1997). Although we might think that the most far-reaching food-policy decisions are made in international or national arenas (in debates over food aid, international trade, or genetically modified organisms, for example), many observers argue that the most profound changes are in fact taking place in cities. This makes sense in light of the estimate that half the world's population lives in urban areas (United Nations 2007). The question then becomes: What makes food policies urban? The Food and Agriculture Organization (FAO) of the United Nations describes **urban food policy** as:

> . . . a set of goals, objectives, strategies or programs designed to improve access of urban households to stable supplies of good quality food through efficient, hygienic, healthy and environmentally sound food supply and distribution systems. (Argenti 2000: 12)

Urban food policies are those decisions and actions that fall within the jurisdiction of municipal governments, whether addressed through zoning, by-laws, or other forms of land-use regulation, or through partnerships with other levels of government. Another common characteristic of present-day urban food policies is their association with broader goals of social, environmental, and economic sustainability in cities (Koç and Dahlberg 1999). Concretely, urban food policies that are couched in terms of sustainable food system goals might include policies that

- Support opportunities to grow food in the city (e.g., community or rooftop gardens, urban farms, community orchards, urban aquaculture)
- Encourage reduced distance between food production and consumption (e.g., policies supporting farmers' markets, community-supported agriculture, local food procurement policies)

- Give a city's most vulnerable populations improved access to nutritious and affordable food (e.g., free or low-cost food and food recovery programs)
- Ensure that neighbourhoods have grocery stores or farmers' markets within walking or cycling distance
- Create infrastructure and education on food-waste management (e.g., medium- and large-scale food composting, food-waste diversion, community composting programs)
- Nurture citizen-based groups to advise on municipal food policy issues (e.g., food policy councils, neighbourhood food networks)
- Support food celebrations that enhance social inclusion and community capacity building
- Integrate food policies into comprehensive or neighbourhood plans (IDRC and UMP, 2003; Mendes 2007a, 2008; HB Lanarc 2009)

Policies alone do not automatically result in sustainable urban food systems. Policies must be 'put to work' by the authority that creates them or the practitioners (and community partners) who are guided by them. One group that often works closely on the design and implementation of urban food policies is urban planners. Professional **land-use planning** is concerned with the spatial organization of the city: how it is used, by whom, and for what purposes. Planning the ways cities are built and lived in has been done for millennia. However as a profession, land-use planning (sometimes called 'urban planning' or 'town planning') is relatively new. Planners use tools including zoning; by-laws (or ordinances, as they are called in some places); building codes and other standards for housing; transportation, sanitation, water supply, and sewage systems; and public health policies. Planners also use facilitation techniques to bring together grassroots, non-profit, and private sector stakeholders to formulate solutions to common problems.

Urban planners are far from the only professionals involved in decisions about urban food systems. Others include engineers, architects, and urban designers, all of whom can help shape our urban foodscapes, whether by building infrastructure for large-scale composting of food waste, designing buildings to enable rooftop gardening, or ensuring that cities' transportation networks and storage facilities support efficient movement and storage of enough food to supply the population.

In recent years, many emerging issues have found their way on to the agendas of urban planners and related professionals. These include

- Sustainability
- Climate change mitigation
- Environmental protection
- Bio-diversity and habitat protection
- Social inclusion and community services
- Managing cultural and heritage resources
- Creating economic capacity in local communities

This shifting agenda reflects a change from previous understandings of the typical urban systems or areas of urban responsibility, such as housing, transportation, and regional economic development. Although food was conspicuously absent from urban planning in the latter half of the twentieth century, there are many signs that food system issues are returning to city planning in both the global North and the global South (Pothukuchi and Kaufman 1999, 2000; Morgan 2009; FAO 1998, 2000a, 2000b). Food system planning, as it is sometimes called, is perceived in some jurisdictions as a planning sub-discipline in its own right. In food system planning, such issues either are urban planners' primary focus or are integrated into more traditional areas of planning. For example, an urban planner focusing primarily on housing might use food system planning 'tools' or approaches by incorporating community garden plots into a housing development, building facilities for residents to compost their food waste, or ensuring that there are grocery stores within walking or cycling distance.

Among the signs that food system planning is becoming more common in municipal governments is the 2007 American Planning Association (APA) policy on community and regional planning. This policy encourages APA members to help build stronger, sustainable, and more self-reliant local food systems. The APA maintains that a city that can supply and control its food needs will have more influence over what its residents eat, will provide greater availability of fresh foods, and can protect itself against disruptions in food distribution (APA 2007). In addition, the report points out that dollars spent on locally produced food have a greater chance of cycling back through the community, and that growing food closer to its points of sale reduces greenhouse gases released in transport (ibid.). Examples of APA policy guidelines include:

1. Develop plans, regulations, and economic incentive programs to provide accessible and well-serviced sites for public markets, farmers' markets, small-scale processing facilities, and distribution centres for food produced in the region.

2. Encourage mixed-use neighbourhood design and redevelopment to include small and mid-sized grocery stores, farmers' markets, and community gardens to allow residents to grow their own food.

3. Prepare comprehensive plans and neighbourhood plans that recognize community gardens, farm/garden stands, and farmers' markets uses that enhance overall community vitality.

4. Support development of vegetable gardens, edible landscaping, and related infrastructure on publicly owned lands, such as schoolyards, parks, and greenways, and tax-foreclosed properties.

5. Provide incentives and special zoning provisions to integrate locally supported agriculture (e.g., community gardens, urban agriculture, small farms) into existing settlements and new areas of residential development.

6. Explore possibilities for recycling food wastes through composting and biofuel development (ibid.).

At the same time, food system planning should be understood as one 'ingredient' in more comprehensive policies and plans to create healthier, more resilient cities. Urban development models such as 'healthy cities', 'green cities', 'walkable cities', and 'sustainable cities' offer visions for integrating food system issues into city planning and design. For example, improving access to nutritious, locally produced food through farmers' markets can be one aspect of broader strategies for alleviating poverty and improving the health of urban populations. Promoting urban agriculture can form part of more encompassing policies that aim to 'green' the city, protect urban biodiversity, and provide vibrant public gathering spaces and opportunities for recreation. Food system planning in cities can also form part of strategies to reduce CO_2 emissions by reducing dependence on long-distance food transportation. Support of economic activities such as small-scale food processing, food business incubation, and street-food vending can strengthen the local economy.

Table 18.1 provides a helpful illustration of the interactions between elements of the urban food system and areas of responsibility of local governments (land use and growth management, transportation, urban design, energy and infrastructure, buildings and housing, parks and open space, waste management, and social/economic development).

Table 18.1 demonstrates the extent to which food system planning is a matter of city and municipal authorities 'doing what they already do in a better way' (Argenti 2000: 3). Or, as Toronto's consultation report 'Food Connections: Toward a Healthy and Sustainable Food System for Toronto' (City of Toronto 2010: 15) describes it:

The goal is not to make food a priority that competes against other issues for resources but to identify opportunities where food can address and enhance local government objectives.

In this way, rather than 'What can a city do for its food system?' the question is, 'What can a more resilient food system do for a city?' (Mougeot 2006).

What Does Municipal Governance Have To Do with It?

So far we have seen how food and food systems are once again recognized as issues of great importance to the functioning of cities and the well-being of urban dwellers. We also learned what makes *urban* food policy distinct, and the role of urban planners as one profession (among others) closely involved in developing and implementing urban food policies. However, a broader question remains: Who exactly is responsible for making decisions about urban food systems? At one time we might have answered 'government', but recent decades have seen important shifts in this assumption where food systems and many other issues are concerned.

While **government** can be understood to refer to the exercise of authority over a political jurisdiction by the 'state' (whether a municipality, region, or country), **governance** broadens this understanding to refer to a more transparent and participatory process of decision making, involving not only the formal institutions of the state ('government') but equally those in civil society.

The shift from *government* to *governance* signals a recognition that multiple groups and interests are (or should be) meaningfully involved in identifying a community's concerns and proposing solutions to address them. This trend is seen frequently in areas related to sustainable development where consultations, action planning, and visioning exercises are the

Box 18.1 Defining Civil Society

Civil society refers to the arena of uncoerced collective action around shared interests, purposes and values. In theory, its institutional forms are distinct from those of the state, family and market, though in practice, the boundaries between state, civil society, family and market are often complex, blurred and negotiated. Civil society commonly embraces a diversity of spaces, actors and institutional forms, varying in their degree of formality, autonomy and power. Civil societies are often populated by organisations such as registered charities, development non-governmental organisations, community groups, women's organisations, faith-based organisations, professional associations, trades unions, self-help groups, social movements, business associations, coalitions and advocacy groups. (London School of Economics: 2004)

Source: from London School of Economics. 2004. 'What is Civil Society?'

legitimizing 'stamp of approval' on any policy exercise (Dorcey and McDaniels 2001).

Issues of governance and participatory decision making are particularly important where urban food systems are concerned, because decisions about food systems often involve many stakeholders with varying interests. The 'food movement' draws together a wide range of perspectives from citizen groups, including public-health advocates who focus on nutrition education and community-based strategies to address food insecurity; sustainable agriculture activists who express concern about food safety, the disappearance of productive land, increasing distances between producer and consumer, environmental degradation, and corporate concentration of agribusiness; anti-poverty advocates who want to reduce hunger and disadvantage; and anti-globalization activists who protest the homogenization of culture, goods, and services, including food (Bouris 2005).

Such a wide range of stakeholders, combined with a common focus on social justice and a commitment to including the voices of marginalized groups, have led some observers to assert that this broad and active participation in decision making is not merely a preferable approach, but an *essential* aspect of addressing food systems (Wekerle 2004; Barling, Lang, and Caraher

2002). As a result, urban food initiatives lead the way in innovation in municipal governance with strong citizen participation, inclusiveness, broad accountability, and cross-cutting approaches to food system issues that simultaneously benefit the economy, the environment, and public health (Wekerle 2004; Toronto Food Policy Council 2002; MacRae 1999; Welsh and MacRae 1998). While these claims are not without their detractors and criticisms, we can identify a number of examples of the principles of participatory decision making and new forms of governance being expressed through urban food system policies and programs. We will briefly review three such examples: (1) municipal food charters and multilateral agreements; (2) food policy councils; and (3) neighbourhood food networks. Important to keep in mind is the extent to which these example reflect a specific focus on the interests and jurisdictional powers of *municipal* governments and their methods of governance.

Municipal Food Charters and Multilateral Agreements

The United Nations International Covenant on Social, Economic and Cultural Rights includes 'the fundamental right of everyone to be free from hunger' (1966). But what does this statement

Table 18.1 The Food System: Opportunities for Integrating Food and Agriculture into Sustainable Community Planning

Agriculture & Food System Elements	Key Performance Areas of Local Government							
	Land Use & Growth Management	Transportation	Urban Design	Energy & Infrastructure	Buildings & Housing	Parks & Open Space	Waste Management	Social/Economic Development
Production	• Contain urban growth and protect agricultural land • Permit community gardens as a use in all land use designations	• Provide end-of-trip cyclist facilities (secure, weather-protected bike storage) near community gardens	• Enhance the public and private realms through food amenities, including community and private gardens, edible landscaping, green roofs, etc.	• Use production space to manage storm water • Use waste heat from infrastructure (e.g. sewer lines) and other as an energy source for greenhouses	• Insulate buildings and provide urban habitat through the use of green roofs and vertical landscaping	• Integrate edible landscaping and permit gardening as a use and recreation opportunity in parks and public open spaces • Ensure required gardening infrastructure including water hook-up and secured sheds	• Provide for composting space in gardening areas to help divert waste from the landfill	• Utilize all food system elements in social programming (e.g. skills development and education) and as part of a larger economic branding/marketing strategy (e.g. food precincts and related destinations)
Processing	• Permit context appropriate scales	• Provide end-of-trip cyclist facilities (secure,	• Provide community-scale processing options (e.g.	• Use waste heat as an input into processing	• Design community centres to accommodate	• Provide community-scale processing options (e.g.	• Support food processing waste	

Table 18.1 (Continued)

Agriculture & Food System Elements	Key Performance Areas of Local Government							
	Land Use & Growth Management	Transportation	Urban Design	Energy & Infrastructure	Buildings & Housing	Parks & Open Space	Waste Management	Social/Economic Development
	of food processing as a use in all land use designations	weather-protected bike storage) for processing facilities • Ensure good transit access to processors	bread ovens, fruit presses) as amenities in private and public developments	activity, and/or as an output for other processing or industrial uses	community kitchens for processing activity (canning, preserving, etc)	bread ovens, fruit presses) in parks and public open spaces, where appropriate	diversion programs to reduce organic waste	
Transport	• Cluster various food-related uses (e.g. processing, retail, etc) to reduce transportation pressures for goods movement, and to increase walkability	• Ensure Transportation Master Plans include a food transport component	• Design for convenient yet pedestrian-friendly food drop-off/loading areas at the rear of buildings containing food retailers and restaurants	• Promotion of biodiesel or other alternative energy powered vehicles (including people powered) for the local transport of foods?	• Provide food drop-off and distribution areas in multi-family and possibly other buildings (e.g. Community Supported Agriculture drop-off points)	• Provide end-of-trip facilities (secure, weather-protected bike storage) near gardens in parks • Ensure good transit service to garden areas	• Support waste collection efforts that also rescue quality organic waste from retailers and restaurants (i.e. unused nearly expired food) for food emergency organizations	

(Continued)

Table 18.1 (Continued)

Agriculture & Food System Elements	Key Performance Areas of Local Government							
	Land Use & Growth Management	Transportation	Urban Design	Energy & Infrastructure	Buildings & Housing	Parks & Open Space	Waste Management	Social/Economic Development
Storage	• Permit food storage in all land use designations as part of food-secure/resilient neighbourhoods	• Create multi-functional underground parking areas for cool storage (e.g. root cellars, beer cellars, etc.)	• Include food storage components in site and neighbourhood design (e.g. root cellars, beer cellars, etc.)	• Use renewable and/or waste energy to cool large food storage areas	• Provide food storage areas in units and buildings (e.g. pantries)	• Consider integrating community root cellars into parks and other public spaces	• Co-locate or incorporate waste diversion facilities/areas near/in food storage areas	
Retail, Wholesale & Marketing	• Support food retailers as important uses in complete, mixed-use neighbourhoods	• Provide end-of-trip cyclist facilities (secure, weather-protected bike storage) in food retail areas • Ensure good transit access to food retailers	• Ensure food retailers are designed to a scale and character appropriate for walkable, vibrant neighbourhoods	• Use renewable or waste heat from infrastructure as an energy source for retailers/wholesalers	• Incorporate food retailers (e.g. grocery stores) into residential developments as part of complete, mixed-use neighbourhoods	• Co-locate food retailers and parks to support complete, vibrant communities	• Support food retailer waste diversion programs to reduce organic waste	

Table 18.1 (Continued)

Agriculture & Food System Elements	Key Performance Areas of Local Government							
	Land Use & Growth Management	Transportation	Urban Design	Energy & Infrastructure	Buildings & Housing	Parks & Open Space	Waste Management	Social/Economic Development
Eating & Celebration	• Support restaurants and other eating venues as important uses in complete, mixed-use neighbourhoods	• Provide end-of-trip cyclist facilities (secure, weather-protected bike storage) at eating establishments/venues • Ensure good transit access to eating establishments/venues	• Encourage sidewalk cafes and other opportunities for food celebration in the public and private realms through pedestrian-oriented design guidelines	• Use renewable or waste heat from infrastructure as an energy source for eating establishments	• Ensure community centres are designed to accommodate community kitchens for processing (canning, preserving, etc.)	• Design and integrate celebration opportunities (e.g. picnic tables for food fairs, community dinners, etc) into parks and other public open spaces	• Support restaurant waste diversion programs to reduce organic waste	
Nutrient Recycling & Waste Management	• Support composting as an important activity in all land use designations	• Utilize biodiesel and/or waste oil as a transportation fuel (e.g. green fleet)	• Design composting facilities into the public realm (e.g. appropriate receptacles) to divert organic waste from the landfill	• Utilize waste oil (e.g. vegetable oil) in a digester for power generation	• Ensure all multi-family and other buildings in which food is consumed include organic waste separation stations and/or storage	• Use composted organic waste as a fertilizer in parks and other public areas	• Utilize bio-diesel and/or waste oil as part of garbage pick-up/delivery fleet	

Source: de la Salle, J., and Holland, M., (Eds). (2010). Agricultural Urbanism: Handbook for Building Sustainable Food and Agriculture Systems for 21st Century Cities. Winnipeg, Manitoba: Green Frigate Books, pp. 44–7.

Box 18.2 Vancouver Food Charter

January 2007

The Vancouver Food Charter presents a vision for a food system which benefits our community and the environment. It sets out the City of Vancouver's commitment to the development of a coordinated municipal food policy, and animates our community's engagement and participation in conversations and actions related to food security in Vancouver.

Vision

The City of Vancouver is committed to a just and sustainable food system that
- contributes to the economic, ecological, and social well-being of our city and region;
- encourages personal, business and government food practices that foster local production and protect our natural and human resources;
- recognizes access to safe, sufficient, culturally appropriate and nutritious food as a basic human right for all Vancouver residents;
- reflects the dialogue between the community, government, and all sectors of the food system;
- celebrates Vancouver's multicultural food traditions.

Preamble

In a food-secure community, the growing, processing and distribution of healthy, safe food is economically viable, socially just, environmentally sustainable and regionally based.

Some members of our community, particularly children, do not have reliable access to safe and nutritious food. In addition, much of the food we eat travels long distances from where it is grown and processed and is dependent on fossil fuels at every stage. Dependency on imports for our food increases our impact on the environment and our vulnerability to food shortages from natural disasters or economic set-backs. Overall food security is increasingly influenced by global factors that affect our community's ability to meet our food system goals.

Community food security needs the involvement of all members of our community, including citizens, consumers, businesses and governments. When citizens are engaged in dialogue and action around food security, and governments are responsive to their communities' concerns and recommendations, sound food policy can be developed and implemented in all sectors of the food system and the community.

In 2002, the City of Vancouver adopted sustainability as a fundamental approach for all the City's operations. The goal of a just and sustainable food system plays a significant role in achieving a "Sustainable Vancouver".

Principles

Five principles guide our food system:

Community Economic Development

Locally-based food systems enhance Vancouver's economy. Greater reliance on local food systems strengthens our local and regional economies, creates employment, and increases food security.

Ecological Health

A whole-system approach to food protects our natural resources, reduces and redirects food waste, and contributes to the environmental stability and well-being of our local, regional, and global communities.

Social Justice

Food is a basic human right. All residents need accessible, affordable, healthy, and culturally appropriate food. Children in particular require adequate amounts of nutritious food for normal growth and learning.

Collaboration and Participation

Sustainable food systems encourage civic engagement, promote responsibility, and strengthen communities. Community food security improves when local government collaborates with community groups, businesses, and other levels of government on sound food system planning, policies and practices.

Celebration

Sharing food is a fundamental human experience. Food brings people together in celebrations of community and diversity.

To create a just and sustainable food system, we in Vancouver can

- Be leaders in municipal and regional food-related policies and programs
- Support regional farmers and food producers
- Expand urban agriculture and food recovery opportunities
- Promote composting and the preservation of healthy soil
- Encourage humane treatment of animals raised for food
- Support sustainable agriculture and preserve farm land resources
- Improve access to healthy and affordable foods
- Increase the health of all members of our city
- Talk together and teach each other about food
- Celebrate our city's diverse food cultures

Source: City of Vancouver Food Charter - http://vancouver.ca/commsvcs/socialplanning/initiatives/foodpolicy/tools/pdf/Van_Food_Charter.pdf.

mean for cities, and how can such a covenant be enforced by a municipal government? In recent years a new type of 'rights' document has emerged that is specific to cities and their food systems: the municipal food charter. A **food charter** is a municipally endorsed policy document that expresses key values and priorities for improving a city's food system. Typically, a food charter combines vision statements, principles, and broad action goals supporting a municipal government's food strategy. A number of municipal governments currently have food charters; Canadian examples include Toronto and Sudbury in Ontario; Saskatoon and Prince Albert in Saskatchewan; and Kamloops, Merritt, and Vancouver in British Columbia.

Food charters are a good example of participatory governance because they are often created through community-based processes involving a local food policy council and other citizen groups in partnership with a municipal government. In this way, a food charter embodies principles of participatory decision making: the process of creating the charter is just as important as the charter itself. For instance, the Vancouver Food Policy Council found that the process of formulating a food charter engaged individuals and organizations from all aspects of the food system in finding creative solutions to local food challenges (City of Vancouver 2007a). Before presenting the proposed food charter to Vancouver City Council for formal endorsement, the Vancouver Food Policy Council held many workshops and public forums with a wide range of community groups and organizations throughout the city. The result was a food charter that reflected a food system vision and the goals of a broad cross-section of the city's residents, while providing opportunities to educate people and raise awareness about food system issues. By the time the Vancouver Food Charter was officially enacted, it reflected meaningful citizen 'ownership' resulting from its wide-ranging input.

A municipal food charter can embody a range of food system goals. For example, the Vancouver Food Charter identifies five principles of a 'just and sustainable food system': community economic development, ecological health, social justice, collaboration and participation, and celebration (City of Vancouver 2007b). Other food charters, such as Toronto's, identify a host of commitments including 'championing the right of all residents to adequate amounts of safe, nutritious, culturally-acceptable food without the need to resort to emergency food providers', and 'encouraging community gardens that increase food self-reliance, improve fitness, contribute to a cleaner environment, and enhance community development' (City of Toronto 2010).

Far from being merely a symbolic gesture, a municipal food charter can be a powerful statement used to justify and legitimize further policy development. Or, it can be a building block for more encompassing policy. For instance, a food charter that identifies the goal of encouraging more community gardens (as Toronto's does) might be used to justify an urban agriculture strategy or incentives for builders to include community gardens or urban orchards in their development applications. The role of a food charter in enabling further policy making is apparent in comprehensive city-wide food strategies that bring together a range of food policy goals under one umbrella, along with visions, goals, and targets for a city's food system. In Toronto, where a municipal food strategy has been proposed (City of Toronto 2010), and Vancouver, where one is being developed, each city's food charter is an important policy context and a justification for further work.

Another form of food charter is a multilateral agreement, which includes inter-municipal agreements to address food policy concerns. For instance, the regional seminar Feeding Asian Cities, held in Bangkok, Thailand, in November 2000, declared as its premise that city and local authorities can play a key role in enhancing access to food, especially in the context of continuing urbanization and decentralization (Yasmeen 2001). Furthermore, a commitment was made to develop better awareness, understanding, and appreciation among decision-makers of the need to integrate urban food security with sustainable social, economic, and environmental development (ibid.).

In Latin America, the Caribbean, and Africa, multilateral commitments to achieve food system goals are enshrined in agreements including the April 2000 Declaration of Quito. The declaration commits 33 cities and local governments to the goal of:

> . . . replicating and improving Urban Agriculture municipal policies and actions developed in Latin American and Caribbean cities as to enhance food security, address urban poverty, improve urban environment and health management, and develop more participatory and less excluding governance processes, as well as to protect urban biodiversity with the support of the Urban Management Program for Latin America and the Caribbean. (Declaration of Quito 2000: 3)

Like food charters, multilateral agreements between cities can aim to create more resilient food systems and ensure more participatory and inclusive mechanisms to achieve them.

Food Policy Councils

A food policy council (FPC) is one of the most common citizen-led vehicles for influencing urban food policies and embodying a more participatory approach to municipal governance. An FPC is an officially sanctioned voluntary body made up of stakeholders from various segments of a state/provincial or municipal food system (Borron 2003: 4). MacRae (1999: 195) describes FPCs as

> . . . multi-sectoral roundtables . . . where many interests are represented and many different kinds of sectoral resources can be offered to solve problems.

FPC membership might include representatives from various sectors and organizations, including gardeners, producers, processors, distributors, grocers, restaurateurs, environmentalists, anti-hunger activists, business people, educators, health and nutrition professionals, school administrators, and food waste disposal experts (Dahlberg 1994; Yateman 1994). One of the defining functions of an FPC is to create working collaborations between citizens, community agencies, and government officials that give voice to food-related concerns and interests. An FPC is asked to examine the operation of an urban food system and provide ideas or recommendations on improving it. While the contributions of citizen advisory committees may at times be largely symbolic, FPCs, in contrast, are often one of the more dynamic innovations in city governments across North America and beyond (Borron 2003; MacRae 1999; Dahlberg 1994; Yateman 1994). Reinforcing this view, it is often claimed that an FPC is uniquely positioned to contribute directly to policy development and municipal governance, to increase the capacity of the city to act on sustainability principles, and to

> . . . increase public and City understanding of the synergies flowing from the linkages of programs directed towards food security, healthy public policy, and social, economic and environmental sustainability. (Toronto Food Policy Council 2002: 9)

This unique positioning of FPCs stems from a number of elements including strong citizen participation, broad accountability, and active working committees. Perhaps more suggestively, however, FPCs also claim distinctive characteristics such as the ability to lobby and advocate for food issues, and a cross-cutting approach to food system issues (ibid.). As the Toronto FPC describes it:

> [Food policy councils are] an exciting experiment in working through an

emerging 21st century set of relationships between politicians, government staff and engaged citizens. Perhaps [they] anticipate what some have called the reinvention of government. (ibid.: 17)

While the goals of advocacy and direct citizen involvement might be expected from the groups outside of local government, what makes an FPC so compelling is that it claims to represent a reconfigured approach to food issues drawing from the expertise of both governmental and non-governmental actors. Some food system scholars theorize FPCs as exemplary 'networked movements' (Wekerle 2004; MacRae 1999; Welsh and MacRae 1998). As such, the ways that an FPC informs programs and policy and participates in other networked activities from positions in civil society and in partnership with the local state is the subject of growing interest to scholars and practitioners (Wekerle 2004).

Food system scholar Mark Winne estimates that over 100 jurisdictions in the United States and Canada have established food policy groups to provide a systematic focus on food system issues (Mendes and Nasr 2011). While food policy councils continue to develop in many regions, an equally interesting trend is emerging at an even smaller scale in cities: the neighbourhood.

Neighbourhood Food Networks

As many scholars and policy makers observe, food system initiatives often originate from the local communities they serve. In many cases, it is individuals, community groups, or local non-profit organizations that spearhead food policy efforts 'in their own backyard'. We see this place-based tendency in a host of food system initiatives ranging from urban agriculture and farmers' markets to community kitchens and emergency food distribution (Wekerle 2004; Clancy 2004; Welsh and MacRae 1998). Often in defence against what are perceived to be the homogenizing effects of globalization and the breakdown of a sense of community, neighbourhood food initiatives typically emphasize inclusiveness, equity, empowerment, community action, local decision making, and defining a sense of place. The localization of food system issues is thought to provide 'deep social benefits' to communities as a whole (Norberg-Hodge, Merrifield and Gorelick 2002: 79). As one food system scholar notes, 'the ideas that "place matters" and "[local] scale matters" have been argued to be crucial to the community food security approach' (Allen 1999: 119).

For many years, projects such as community kitchens, neighbourhood food celebrations, and community gardens have been initiated and led by local communities. In some cities, the

---

Box 18.3 Grandview Woodland Food Connection

Initiated in 2004, Grandview Woodland Food Connection is a neighbourhood organization dedicated to supporting the health and well-being of [vulnerable populations] in the Grandview Woodlands neighbourhood by promoting an accessible, just and sustainable food system for our community. We seek to build capacity of the neighbourhood through [sustainable leadership development and support around] grassroots initiatives to address food security and justice issues.

[http://gwfoodconnection.wordpress.com/2011/06/]

Projects include: food celebrations, community gardens and orchards, canning workshops, arts-based food projects, and aquaponics.

Source: from http://gwfoodconnection.wordpress.com/2011/06/.

sheer number of projects in some neighbour-hoods, combined with high community capacity and funding support from public, private, and non-profit sources, has led to the 'scaling up' of individual projects into formal neighbourhood-based networks where different projects, and the groups responsible for them, are connected. The rationale for creating larger networks is often that food system strategies and solutions must move beyond single organizations or groups of residents. This approach has the double bene-fit of taking a more encompassing systems approach to food issues while building social networks and community capacity.

An example can be found in Vancouver, British Columbia, where at least five neighbourhood food networks (NFNs) operate in different areas of the city. These include the Grandview Woodland Food Connection, Renfrew Collingwood Food Security Institute, Downtown Eastside Right to Food Network, Trout Lake Cedar Cottage Food Security Network, and the Westside Food Security Collaborative. NFNs tend to share some characteristics in their composition and

broad mandates. They are typically coalitions of individual residents, community leaders, workers from health and other social agencies, municipal staff, and representatives from faith-based organ-izations, with a goal of identifying and address-ing food system priorities in their respective communities. At the same time, NFNs may have distinctive methods for and approaches to tack-ling issues in their neighbourhoods depending on local conditions and the needs and abilities of residents. A comprehensive study of Vancouver's current and emerging neighbourhood food net-works has been undertaken by Fodor (2011).

In Vancouver, NFNs are looking beyond the boundaries of their respective neighbourhoods by creating a 'network of neighbourhood food networks' that will not only connect the existing NFNs with each other to share knowledge and ideas, but equally help guide the development of new NFNs in parts of the city where they do not yet exist. The NFNs and their work to create a network of food networks are being supported by a range of organizations includ-ing the municipal government, the Vancouver

---

Box 18.4   Goals for the Renfrew Collingwood Food Security Institute:

- Develop multi-cultural community leadership teams who will organize around creative food sharing and organic food growing.
- Increase learning, leadership and connections in the community by supporting commun-ity residents and organizations in creating their own food sharing, growing programs and projects.
- Develop a system of coordination, efficiencies in distribution of food and information regarding food within the community.
- Develop evaluative research methods in which food related needs and resources are identified, better coordinated and successes documented.
- Develop a sustainability food security plan based on identified local assets, social enter-prise opportunities and available funding.

Projects include: community gardens and orchards, rooftop gardening, native berry trail, food workshops, breakfast and shower program, community kitchen, plant and seed swaps, food celebrations and leadership development.

Source: from www.cnh.bc.ca/foodsecurity/aboutus.htm.

Health Authority, the Vancouver Food Policy Council, and other partners. In this sense, NFNs offer a compelling illustration of a more participatory form of municipal governance that combines grassroots citizen-led initiatives, city-wide citizen advisory groups (food policy councils), municipal planning departments, and health or social agencies. Together, this blend shows how addressing food system issues at different scales within the city itself can inspire a new way of approaching not only food but also a host of emerging concerns for which we will require complex and agile solutions as we progress into the most urbanized century in history.

Conclusion

This chapter examined the ways in which food and food systems are once again being recognized as issues of great importance to the functioning of cities and the well-being of urban dwellers. We learned what makes *urban* food policy distinct, and about the role of urban planners as one profession (among others) closely involved in developing and implementing urban food policies. As well, we examined shifts in municipal governance towards more participatory and inclusive methods for improving the resilience of the urban food systems upon which so many of us rely.

Discussion Questions

1. What is a food system?

2. What makes a food system urban?

3. Who makes decisions about urban food systems, and why does this matter in the context of broader food system goals?

4. What are some indications that food is returning to the agendas of municipal governments, urban planners, and interested citizen groups?

5. What are the links between participatory governance and food system planning in cities?

Further Reading

1. Born, B. & Purcell, M. 2006. 'Avoiding the Local Trap. Scale and Food Systems in Planning Research'. *Journal of Planning Education and Research* 26: 195–207.

   A reading that advances food system planning analyses by challenging the tendency to assume that 'local' is necessarily preferable.

2. City of Toronto. 2010. *Cultivating Food Connections: Toward a Healthy and Sustainable Food System for Toronto: A Consultation Report*, May 2010. Available at http://wx.toronto.ca/inter/health/food.nsf/Resources/340ACEEDBF1B2D608525773

8000B22F2/$file/Cultivating%20Food%20Connections%20report.pdf.

   A policy document illustrating how one local government (the City of Toronto) proposes to advance its urban food system goals.

3. Mendes, W. 2008. 'Implementing Social and Environmental Policies in Cities: The Case of Food Policy in Vancouver, Canada'. *International Journal of Urban and Regional Research* 32(4): 942–67.

   An article that analyzes the challenges of *implementing* food system agendas within local governments using the case of the City of Vancouver, Canada.

4. Mougeot, L. 2006. *Growing Better Cities: Urban Agriculture for Sustainable Development*. Ottawa: International Development Research Centre.

Redwood, M. 2009. *Agriculture in Urban Planning: Generating Livelihoods and Food Security*. Ottawa: International Development Research Centre.

Two books that focus on one specific dimension of food system planning, urban agriculture, within the context of the developing world (or 'global South').

5. Pothukuchi, K. and J. Kaufman. 2000. 'The Food System: A Stranger to the Planning Field'. *Journal of the American Planning Association* 66(2): 112–24.

Pothukuchi, K. and J. Kaufman. 1999. 'Placing the Food System on the Urban Agenda: The Role of Municipal Institutions in Food Systems Planning'. *Agriculture and Human Values* 16(2): 213–24.

Two foundational readings that were among the first to identify and analyze the absence of food system issues from urban agendas, and examine the opportunities and challenges posed by the 'return' of food to urban planning.

Note

1. Urban agriculture refers to the practice of growing plants and raising animals in and around cities. A more comprehensive definition describes urban agriculture as: 'An industry located within (intra-urban) or on the fringe (peri-urban) of a town, a city, or a metropolis, which grows or raises, processes, and distributes a diversity of food and non-food products. It (re)uses on a daily basis human and natural resources, products, and services largely found in and around that urban area and, in turn, supplies on a daily basis human and material resources, products, and services largely to that urban area' (Mougeot 2006: 82). Throughout history, urban agricultural practices have been an integral part of city life. Over the course of the twentieth century, as 'urban' and 'rural' land uses became more separated, urban agriculture became a less accepted activity that in some cases was deemed illegal. Recent decades have seen a strong revival of urban agriculture, with food growing in cities once again becoming a widespread and legitimate activity. Factors explaining the renewed interest in urban agriculture include rapid urbanization, food shortages, 'peak oil', economic crises, and large-scale impacts of climate change. The 'return' to urban agriculture has also been linked to a recognition that it can act as a catalyst for community capacity building, promoting health and nutrition, increasing social inclusion, and creating vibrant public gathering places.

References

Allen, P. 1999. 'Reweaving the Food Security Safety Net: Mediating Entitlement and Entrepreneurship'. *Agriculture and Human Values* 16: 117–29.

American Planning Association. (2007). 'Policy Guide on Community and Regional Food Planning'. Washington, D.C.: APA. Available at www.planning.org/policy/guides/adopted/food.htm.

Argenti, O. 2000. *Food for the Cities: Food Supply and Distribution Policies To Reduce Urban Food Insecurity.*

A Briefing Guide for Mayors, City Executives and Planners in Developing Countries and Countries in Transition. Rome: Food and Agriculture Organization of the United Nations, Food into Cities Collection, DT/430–0E.

Atkins, P., and I. Bowler. 2001. *Food in Society: Economy, Culture, Geography*. London: Arnold.

Barling, D., T. Lang, and M. Caraher 2002. 'Joined up Food Policy? The Trials of Governance, Public Policy and the Food System'. *Social Policy & Administration* 36(6): 556–74.

Borron, S.M. 2003. 'Food Policy Councils: Practice and Possibility'. Unpublished report. Eugene, OR: Congressional Hunger Center.

Bouris, K. 2005. 'Examining the Barriers and Opportunities to Local Food System Planning in the Georgia Basin: Of Planners, Politics and the Public'. Unpublished masters' thesis. University of British Columbia, School of Community and Regional Planning.

———. 2001. *Toronto Food Charter*. Accessed 6 September 2010 at www.toronto.ca/food_hunger/pdf/food_charter.pdf.

City of Toronto. 2010. 'Food Connections: Toward a Healthy and Sustainable Food System for Toronto'. Unpublished report.

City of Vancouver. 2007a. *Vancouver Food Charter: Backgrounder*. Accessed 6 September 2010 at http://vancouver.ca/commsvcs/socialplanning/initiatives/foodpolicy/tools/pdf/Van_Food_Charter_Bgrnd.pdf.

———. 2007b. *Vancouver Food Charter*. Accessed 6 September 2010 at http://vancouver.ca/commsvcs/socialplanning/initiatives/foodpolicy/tools/pdf/Van_Food_Charter.pdf.

Clancy, K. 2004. 'Potential Contributions of Planning to Community Food Systems'. *Journal of Planning Education and Research* 23(4): 435–8.

Dahlberg, K. 1992. 'Report and Recommendations on the Knoxville, Tennessee Food System'. Unpublished report.

———. 1994. 'Food Policy Councils: The Experience of Five Cities and One County'. Paper presented at the Joint Meeting of the Agriculture, Food and Human Values Society and the Society for the Study of Food and Society, Tucson AZ, 9–12 June.

Declaration of Quito. 2000. Accessed 6 September 2010 at www.ruaf.org/sites/default/files/Quito%20Declaration-Ingles.pdf.

de la Salle, J., and Holland, M. (eds). 2010. *Agricultural Urbanism: Handbook for Building Sustainable Food and Agriculture Systems for 21st Century Cities*. Winnipeg, MN: Green Frigate Books.

Dorcey, A.H.J., and T. MacDaniels. 2001. 'Great Expectations, Mixed Results: Trends in Citizen Involvement in Canadian Environmental Governance'. In *Governing the Environment: Persistent Challenges, Uncertain Innovations*, ed. E.A. Parson. Toronto: University of Toronto Press, 247–302.

Fodor, Z. 2011. *People Systems in Support of Food Systems: The Neighbourhood Food Justice Network Movement in Vancouver, British Columbia*. Unpublished final project. University of British Columbia, School of Community and Regional Planning.

Food and Agriculture Organization of the United Nations (FAO). 1998. 'Feeding the Cities'. Excerpt from: *The State of Food and Agriculture*. Food into Cities Collection DT/399–8E. Rome: FAO.

———. 2000a. *Agriculture towards 2015–30*. Technical Interim Report.

———. 2000b. 'Seminar Addresses Feeding Asia's Cities'. *FAO News Highlights*, 30 November.

Garrett, S., and G. Feenstra. 1997. *Growing a Community Food System*. Community Ventures series. Puyallup, WA: Washington State University Cooperative Extension, Puyallup Research & Extension Center.

HB Lanarc. 2009. 'Food & Agriculture Brief'. Unpublished document.

International Development Research Centre & Urban Management Program for Latin America and the Caribbean (IDRC and UMP). 2003. *Guidelines for Municipal Policymaking on Urban Agriculture*. Accessed 6 September 2010 at www.idrc.ca/en/ev-296882–011–DO_TOPIC.html.

Iowa Food Policy Council. 2005. 'Food Policy Council Questions and Answers'. Drake University Agricultural Law Center. The State and Local Food Policy Project. Accessed 29 May 2007 at www.iowafoodpolicy.org/qanda.htm.

Koç, M., and K. Dahlberg. 1999. 'The Restructuring of Food Systems: Trends, Research, and Policy Issues'. *Agriculture and Human Values* 16: 109–16.

Koç, M., R. MacRae, L.J.A. Mougeot, and J. Welsh. 1999. 'Introduction: Food Security as a Global Concern'. In *For Hunger-proof Cities: Sustainable Urban Food Systems*, ed. M. Koç, R. MacRae, L.J.A. Mougeot, and J. Welsh. Ottawa: International Development Research Centre, 1–7.

London School of Economics. 2004. 'What Is Civil Society?' Accessed 6 September 2010 at www.lse.ac.uk/collections/CCS/what_is_civil_society.htm.

MacRae, R. 1999. 'Policy Failure in the Canadian Food System'. In *For Hunger-proof Cities: Sustainable Urban Food Systems*, ed. M. Koç, R. MacRae, L.J.A. Mougeot, and J. Welsh. Ottawa: International Development Research Centre, 182–94.

Mendes, W. 2006. 'Creating a "Just and Sustainable" Food System for the City of Vancouver: The Role of Policy, Partnerships and Policymaking'. Unpublished doctoral thesis. Simon Fraser University, Department of Geography.

———. 2007a. 'Negotiating a Place for "Sustainability" Policies in Municipal Planning and Governance: The Role of Scalar Discourses and Practices'. *Space & Polity* 11(1): 95–119.

———. 2007b. 'Creating and Implementing Food Policies in Vancouver, Canada'. *RUAF Magazine* (Resource Centres on Urban Agriculture and Food Security) 16: 51–3.

———. 2008. 'Implementing Social and Environmental Policies in Cities: The Case of Food Policy in

Vancouver, Canada'. *International Journal of Urban and Regional Research* 32(4): 942–67.

Mendes, W., K. Balmer, T. Kaethler, and A. Rhoads. 2008. 'The Role of Urban Agriculture in Enhancing Green Communities: Experiences from Portland, Oregon and Vancouver, British Columbia'. *Journal of the American Planning Association* 74(4): 435–49.

Mendes, W., and J. Nasr, with T. Beatley, B. Born, K. Bouris, M. Caton Campbell, J. Kaufman, B. Lynch, K. Pothukuchi, and G. Wekerle. 2011. 'Preparing Planners to Address Emerging Planning Issues: Reflections on Teaching about Urban Food Systems'. *Journal of Agriculture, Food Systems, and Community Development* 2(1): 15–52.

Morgan, K. 2009. 'Feeding the City: The Challenge of Urban Food Planning'. *International Planning Studies* 14(4): 429–36.

Mougeot, L. 2006. *Growing Better Cities: Urban Agriculture for Sustainable Development*. Ottawa: IDRC.

Norberg-Hodge, H., T. Merrifield, and S. Gorelick. 2002. *Bringing the Food Economy Home: Local Alternatives to Global Agribusiness*. London: Zed Books.

Pothukuchi, K., and J. Kaufman. 1999. 'Placing the Food System on the Urban Agenda: The Role of Municipal Institutions in Food Systems Planning'. *Agriculture and Human Values* 16(2): 213–24.

———— and ————. 2000. 'The Food System: A Stranger to the Planning Field'. *Journal of the American Planning Association* 66(2): 112–24.

Rocha, C. 2001. 'Urban Food Security Policy: The Case of Belo Horizonte, Brazil'. *Journal for the Study of Food and Society* 5(1): 36–47.

Spiaggi, E. 2005. 'Urban Agriculture and Local Sustainable Development in Rosario, Argentina: Integration of Economic, Social, Technical and Environmental Variables.' In *Agropolis: The Social, Political and Environmental Dimensions of Urban Agriculture*, ed. L.J.A. Mougeot. Ottawa: International Development Research Centre, 187–202.

Steel, C. 2008. *Hungry City: How Food Shapes Our Lives*. London: Random House.

Toronto Food Policy Council. 2002. 'Introducing the Toronto Food Policy Council: Who We Are, What We Do, and How We Do It'. Unpublished report.

United Nations. 1966. 'International Covenant on Social, Economic and Cultural Rights'. Accessed 6 September 2010 at www2.ohchr.org/english/law/pdf/cescr.pdf.

————. 2007. 'World Urbanization Prospects'. Accessed 6 September 2010 at http://esa.un.org/unup/.

Wekerle, G. R. 2004. 'Food Justice Movements: Policy, Planning, and Networks'. *Journal of Planning Education and Research* 23(4): 378–86.

Welsh, J., and R. MacRae. 1998. 'Food Citizenship and Community Food Security: Lessons from Toronto, Canada'. *Special issue of Canadian Journal of Development Studies* 19: 237–55.

Yasmeen, G. 2001. *Feeding Asian Cities: Proceedings of the Regional Seminar*. Food into Cities Collection AC/370–1E (Rome: Food and Agriculture Organization of the United Nations). Accessed 6 September 2010 at www.fao.org/DOCREP/003/X6982E/x6982e05.htm#TopOfPage.

Yateman, H. 1994. *Food Policy Councils in North America: Observations and Insights*. Final Report: World Health Organization's Travelling Fellowship.

19

Food Policy for the Twenty-First Century[1]

Rod MacRae

Learning Objectives

Through this chapter, you can:

1. Discover how policy has previously determined, and could determine in the future, food system functions and activities
2. Understand how current food policy is deficient
3. Examine the range of policy changes required to create a sustainable and health-promoting food system

Introduction

Without food, air, and water, most organisms, including humans, cannot survive. As other chapters have described, the health of hundreds of millions is compromised by the way the dominant food system operates. The recovery thresholds of many environments on which humans depend have already been surpassed (e.g., in many fisheries) and others are significantly compromised, particularly those with unproductive soils associated with salinization and degradation, agriculturally contaminated water courses and bodies, and species decline associated with agriculturally altered habits. Individual and social identities and cultures are also intimately connected to food (see chapters 4 and 9 in this volume). Food policy must now be designed and implemented to reflect fully the essential reality of our dependence on food.

Policy is the set of rules, spoken or unspoken, that determines how things are run. In this chapter, I focus on government policy, because, if properly designed and implemented, it can influence the policies of everyone else operating in the food system (see chapters 1 and 2 in this volume). In the industrial world, private firms are the key 'expressions' of food system thinking, but they are unlikely to modify their approaches unless forced to by other actors. Government policy change is potentially one of these influencing forces.

During the twentieth century, the dominant thinking about markets framed our rules about food (see chapters 1 and 6 in this volume). Food was largely something to be bought and sold in the marketplace rather than a biological and cultural necessity (to appreciate its cultural importance, imagine a social event without food). Although many people still had gardens, and some still hunted and fished, the days of providing almost everything for ourselves were largely gone. Government farm policy primarily supported the buying and selling of food, especially in international markets. Farm overproduction served the interests of food firms because it helped to keep prices paid to farmers and processors low. And the food system was actually designed to encourage people to over-consume to generate profits for the same food companies benefiting from low farm prices. This consumption and the diseases it produced appeared to be economically positive because they drove up health care costs and made our economic accounts, especially the gross national product (GNP), look better. In the twenty-first century, all this must change.

A Quick Historical Review of Canadian Food Policy

Similar to most industrial countries, Canada has never had a coherent and integrated national food policy. Agricultural production has been the primary driver of food-related policy since Canada's founding. In the nineteenth century, agricultural policy was mostly about Canada's obligations to Britain and efforts to establish national boundaries, particularly by attracting new farmers to the Prairies (Skogstad 1987). Agricultural historian Vernon Fowke stated in the 1940s, 'government assistance has been typically extended to agriculture because of what agriculture was expected to do for other dominant economic interests in return for assistance, rather than for what such assistance might do for agriculture' (Fowke 1946: 272). The political influence of the grain and livestock sectors on eating patterns and nutrition recommendations originates in this period, a time when governments began providing significant supports (Fowke 1946).

The relationship between food and health received some attention from policy makers in the first part of the twentieth century. Early efforts to regulate food focused on sanitation and prevention of adulteration (MacDougall 1990): important work, but not reflecting the importance of nourishment to health. There is little indication, for example, that the pioneering work of some UK medical doctors (McCarrison 1943; Picton 1946), examining the relationship between food production systems, food quality, and health, had any impact on Canadian policy makers. Food also received some favourable attention from health professionals after vitamins were discovered in the 1920s, but even then, certain food industries had significant influence on the kinds of eating patterns advocated by health professionals (Ostry 2006).

Canadian food regulations remain, however, rooted in a traditional food safety and fraud prevention framework. Hedley (2006) links this approach to the thinking of political philosopher John Stuart Mill:

> governments ought to confine themselves to affording protection against force and fraud: that these two things apart, people should be free agents, able to take care of themselves and that so long as a person practices no violence or deception to the injury of others in person or property, legislatures and governments are in no way called upon to concern themselves about him. (Mill 1965: 800)

This thinking, modified by Keynesian economic analyses on the food production side, remains firmly in place on the food consumption side (Hedley 2006), meaning that governments are very reluctant to intervene in food consumption.

As industrial approaches to agriculture took hold in North America and Europe after the Second World War, and the number of diversified farms declined, farmers increasingly organized around the dominant crops and animals they produced. Divisions along commodity lines were created and solidified. Farm organizations evolved to dominate farm-level input into the policy system (Forbes 1985; Skogstad 1987). Consequently, there were and remain few voices speaking to the need for systems approaches to policy development, and even fewer people in policy circles to hear the message.

There was, though, a brief period in which food policy and the language of food systems were considered. The federal government in the late 1970s was influenced by Norway's work on food policy development (Norwegian Ministry of Agriculture 1975); by the Nutrition Canada National Survey of 1970–1972 (Sabry 1975); the Lalonde Report on health promotion (Lalonde 1974); and by the Report of the Committee on Diet and Cardiovascular Disease (Health Canada 1976). Financial problems for farmers and dramatic food price increases also applied pressure.[2] The federal government's food strategy was consequently developed in 1977–8. Led by Agriculture Canada and Consumer and Corporate Affairs, there was a Deputy Ministers' Committee on Food Policy and an Interdepartmental Steering Group on Food Policy.

But their work was confined to seven major policy areas: income stabilization and support; trade policy and safeguards; research, information, and education; marketing and food aid; the processing, distribution, and retailing sectors; consumer concerns; and price stability, nutrition, and food safety. And their philosophy did not significantly depart from earlier approaches to agricultural policy. For example: 'Government policies must continue to develop and expand Canada's production and export strengths to ensure the adequacy of safe and nutritious food supplies for the domestic and export markets at reasonable prices which are responsive to competitive forces over time' (Interdepartmental Steering Group on Food Policy 1978).

To their credit, policy makers were concerned that national nutritional priorities should not

be overridden by the economics of agriculture. They asked that Nutrition Impact Statements be prepared for policy initiatives related to food.[3] Yet, still, they believed that efficient operation of the marketplace was the best way to meet policy objectives.

Aside from the limitations and contradictions inherent in this emerging policy, and the struggles of interdepartmental collaboration, what really halted this initiative was Agriculture Canada's unwillingness to support it. The department's reluctance was rooted in the changes such an approach would impose on its traditional clients—the food production, processing, and distribution sectors. The ministry was unwilling to entertain the possibility that it had broader responsibilities.

Agriculture Canada did, some years later, adopt a nutrition policy statement in support of Health Canada's work on nutrition, but again one that reflected the primacy of production over nourishment of the population: 'In order to support the Canadian agri-food industry, Agriculture Canada has a major responsibility with respect to nutrient composition and nutritional value of agri-food products' (Agriculture Canada 1989).

Canada's Action Plan for Food Security (CAPFS), adopted on 16 October 1998, was another, ultimately aborted, attempt at developing a national food policy. It was Canada's response to the World Food Summit of 1996, at which Canada's then agriculture minister, Ralph Goodale, was considered a star player. While it identified targets to achieve food security nationally and globally, using a multi-sectoral approach involving all levels of government, civil society organizations, and the private sector, it was a still-birth, quickly forgotten with little public reaction to its implementation failures. CAPFS recognized that food security implied 'access to adequate food and sufficient food supplies and that poverty reduction, social justice and sustainable food systems are essential conditions' (Agriculture and Agri-food Canada 1998: 24). But, it was riddled with tensions and contradictions about social, economic, and environmental priorities, imbued as it was with Canada's long-standing commitment to a productionist agricultural approach (Koç and Bas in press).

Separate from CAPFS, in 2002, the federal, provincial, and territorial governments agreed to a new agricultural policy framework with five 'pillars': business risk management, environmental protection, food safety, innovation, and rural renewal. Although an important attempt to make agricultural policy making more coherent, it failed to address the full range of issues that should make up a national food policy, being particularly weak on health, social, and cultural matters beyond those related to food safety. Renewed in 2008–9,[4] the framework reflects an awareness that significant environmental issues need to be addressed, especially in the face of threats to Canada's international reputation on agri-environmental performance, but the impact of programs implemented to date has only been modest.[5] Moreover, new programs, including investments in ethanol biofuels and genetic engineering, may actually cause more detrimental environmental and economic impacts over the long term. However, to governments' credit, the agreement exists and created many new structures and lines of communication. It provides a potential—though partial—template for a national food policy.

Midway through the first decade of the twenty-first century, Agriculture and Agri-food Canada (AAFC), Health Canada, and the Public Health Agency of Canada (PHAC) resumed discussions of a national food policy framework, but little information is publicly available on their motivation or progress. A 2005 draft document (*National Food Policy Framework: Overview 2005*) indicates that a central theme was policy coordination: the need to create a system-wide approach to link, through collaboration and multidisciplinary thinking and implementation, the domains of agriculture, fisheries, health protection and promotion, and food inspection. However, the supply side of the food story, including food safety matters, appears to have remained the focus (Hedley 2006), and the policy scope remains somewhat narrow, only modestly expanded from earlier food policy iterations. The commentary on the role of consumers focuses mostly on fraud prevention, building consumer confidence, and individual (rather than structural) commitments to healthy living—the historical approaches to consumer-related regulation. Interestingly, the draft refers to CAPFS and its implementation. In fact, virtually all aspects of social development are proposed for implementation through CAPFS. On the surface, this appeared to be a way to revitalize CAPFS, but little has transpired since 2005.

Health Canada's involvement in food policy continues to be limited, its role confined to improving the nutritional quality of the food supply, defined primarily through providing dietary guidelines, monitoring nutrition labelling, and meeting the Food and Drugs Act regulations, many of which define what a food is (e.g., ice cream must contain a minimum specified level of dairy fat), rather than its role in a healthy diet or how its nutritional value might be optimized. The healthy eating guidelines are not mandatory in any sense and they have been only minimally integrated into other policy arenas. Most Canadians have little idea how to implement them in their meals.

Equally problematic, no traditional or current common institutional arrangement links the institutions that share responsibility for regulating consumer choice in food, food products, and production processes. Such issues would need to be managed by at least four federal cabinet committees: social affairs, economic affairs, foreign affairs and defence, and national security. As well, few issues rest within one order of government. While federal–provincial meetings of ministers are common in Canada, they tend to be restricted to similar mandates: health, agriculture, or environment. Joint meetings of health and agriculture ministers, for example, are rare or non-existent. As a result, there are exceedingly limited opportunities for joint action across ministerial mandates and orders of government to deal with the breadth of the food–health–environmental linkages (Hedley 2006: 24).

In the last few years, three federal opposition parties have presented significant food policy platforms, with the New Democratic (Atamanenko 2010) and Liberal (Ignatieff 2010) parties holding consultations. The Canadian Federation of Agriculture has developed a vision of a food strategy, an early iteration of which has been presented to ministers of agriculture. The People's Food Policy Project of Food Secure Canada, building on hearings from the late 1970s, conducted a community-based process to develop a comprehensive national food policy (People's Food Policy Project 2011). The Canadian Agri-food Policy Institute (CAPI 2011) has produced a food strategy report. The Conference Board of Canada is producing numerous reports related to food policy. While encouraging, these are all partial initiatives, lacking in scope or depth, or both.

Policy for the Twenty-First Century

The Challenges of Food Policy Change

According to MacRae (2011), food policy development is a complex issue for policy makers, because

- the intersections between policy systems are historically divided intellectually, constitutionally, and departmentally
- governments lack institutional places from which to work, and the instruments of multi-departmental policy making are immature; there is no 'department of food'
- supporting new approaches means addressing existing and entrenched policy frameworks and traditions
- the externalized costs of the conventional food, health, economic, and social systems must be

addressed, and these costs are only partially understood and quantified
- food must be understood as more than a marketable commodity, which creates problems for certain departments
- it challenges many of the central tenets of current agricultural and economic development, and a curative (rather than preventative) health-care system

Consequently, there are numerous obstacles to be overcome in changing food policy.

Overcoming the Current Paradigm and Goals

Ideally, the food system would be rooted in an ecological and health-oriented paradigm that is consistent with profound ideas of sustainability (see Chapter 20 as well as the discussion below). With increasingly complex problems has come the realization that traditional Canadian government policy goals, institutional arrangements, and instruments are insufficient. Earlier eras of state regulation revolved around a productivist paradigm that worked well when the state had significant capacity and the issue was targeted (Howlett 2005). But in the era of bilateral and multilateral trade arrangements and international institutions based on neo-liberalism, many traditional policy and regulatory tools have been replaced to support these new policy orientations. More dramatically, in response to their trade commitments, some states appear to have given up some of their capacity to determine national priorities (see chapters 1 and 2 in this volume). Governments are searching for new and effective regulatory instruments without unduly straining what limited human and financial resources they are prepared to devote to solutions (Gunningham 2005). Food and agricultural policy themes are acutely affected by this regulatory situation, by the complexities of the changes required, by larger shifts in the loci of the national state's decision making, and by the new prominence of health concerns about food.

Ideally, the goals of the food system would be coherent, joined up (Barling, Lang, and Caraher 2002), transparent, and comprehensive. But the dominant approach is to provide 'an ample supply of safe, high quality food at reasonable prices for all Canadians',[6] often referred to as Canada's 'cheap food policy'.

The Obstacles of Current Governance Structures

Ideally, there would be a set of coordinated structures, rooted in the new dominant paradigm and goals, which would facilitate actions across the multiple actors and jurisdictions of the food system. But the current structures are enormous, dispersed, and varied. 'For food safety alone, it is estimated that there are 90 statutes and 37 agencies across the country whose mandate, in some way, encompasses food.'[7] Beyond the main legislation are numerous regulations, regulatory directives, and protocols; three layers of government carrying out different or overlapping functions in a more or less coordinated fashion;[8] and several agencies involved within each layer (although certain ones tend to be central, e.g., the Canadian Food Inspection Agency [CFIA] federally). Numerous functions are carried out: for example, training and education, pre-market consultations, product approvals and licensing, labelling and advertising, monitoring, inspection, post-market monitoring, recalls, enforcement, policy making, and import controls.[9] These functions target multiple operations within the food chain, such as farms, processing plants, warehouses, retail stores, restaurants, and import businesses and their foreign facilities, and target as well a full range of food and packaged products.[10]

The other significant problem of governance is the limited role of Parliament. Most recent significant federal government decisions in agriculture have not been publicly debated. The recent tendency is to use existing legislation as a foundation from which the appropriate line department and central agencies take action

(usually AAFC or CFIA, the Privy Council Office [PCO] and the Prime Minister's Office [PMO]). Orders-in-council and the departmental Estimates (part of the budget process) are used to create any additional necessary authorities.[11] Two recent high-profile examples, the Agricultural Policy Framework (APF) and GMO (genetically modified organism) regulation, were largely products of the bureaucracy, with some broad oversight from the central agencies and Cabinet. Limited parliamentary discussion of the APF has occurred on 'hot-button' issues (such as farm financial safety nets) usually at the committee level. Similarly, Parliament's participation in GMO regulation has been the result of private member's bills on mandatory GMO labelling of foods. Although public consultations often take place in association with these largely bureaucratic initiatives, these are rarely designed to facilitate a national consensus. Rather, the pattern is to generate numerous ideas from which government officials can choose their preferred approach. This process has produced frustration among stakeholders, who increasingly display much cynicism and annoyance in consultations, further limiting useful discussion.

The Absence of Good Feedback Mechanisms

Ideally, a national food policy would have robust feedback mechanisms sending signals to the main actors about how the food system is functioning and what interventions are working. 'Feedback allows the system to regulate itself by providing information about the outcome of different actions back to the source of the actions' (Mahli et al. 2009: 469).

Canada's policy system is generally weak on feedback mechanisms. Much economic and social data is collected, but environmental, health promotion, and cultural information is limited. Equally important are the failures in sharing useful information. A significant amount of environmental data is private, held by farmers, farm organizations, or private data collection agencies. Public agencies do not have access, for reasons of price or fear of legal action if the private data reveal poor performance. Given the absence of collaborative mechanisms related to jurisdictional divisions (see above), information and analysis does move readily across public agencies. Although the situation has improved recently, public agencies are seldom well connected to the organizations with an interest in food policy, treating many of them with suspicion. Although new forms of regulatory pluralism are emerging (MacRae and Abergel in press), governments and food system actors are not yet particularly skilled at, or committed to, their implementation.

The Limited Set of Subsystem Elements

Ideally, the policy system would be deeply knowledgeable about food system function, and have numerous instruments at its disposal to solve problems. But, at all levels, a limited range of policy tools and instruments are currently used,

based on a lack of knowledge, resources, or paradigmatic opposition. Human resources are limited at all levels of the system, which means that policy actors are in short supply or not properly resourced and equipped. There is a significant lack of capacity to deal with complexity.

The Key Elements of Food Policy Development for the Twenty-First Century

Table 19.1 summarizes the elements that need changing to create better food policy in the twenty-first century. We are unlikely to see dramatic changes in governance and Parliament's role in the short to medium term (MacRae and Abergel in press) to facilitate better food policy development. Therefore, change agents must alter existing mechanisms and elements. A major restructuring of governing units would be desirable, along the lines proposed by MacRae and the TFPC (1999), but this will be feasible only after implementation of some of the changes proposed here.

Table 19.1 Key Policy Elements Requiring Changes

Policy statements	Usually high-level statements, delivered or approved by members of governing parties
Legislation	In recent Canadian tradition, legislation is broad and enabling and is revised infrequently, but change requires new legislation and modification of existing acts.
Regulatory changes	Senior bureaucracies create regulations that interpret legislation and guide its application, For a list of legislation and regulations pertinent to food policy change in Canada, see Annexes 8 and 9 of CAPI (2009).
Regulatory protocols and directives	Since regulations themselves are also relatively vague, agencies must create detailed regulatory protocols and directives to guide day-to-day activities and decision making. These are not always public.
Other instrument choices and changes	Governments often use a range of other instruments, including programs, educational mechanisms, and taxes or tax incentives to support their policy statements, legislation, and/or regulations.
Structural changes	The loci of decision making often significantly affect how changes are made (Hill 1994).

Source: Adapted from MacRae (2011).

Ideally, changes would be inspired and dynamically influenced by a major paradigmatic shift in how we understand the role of the food system in society. Lang and Heasman (2004) have referred to this as the 'ecologically integrated paradigm', which places a premium on health promotion. The following proposals are all based on gradual policy changes consistent with such a paradigmatic change.

Goals (and Policy Statements)

Ideally, a comprehensive food policy would create a food system that reflected the biological and social realities of food (adapted from MacRae 1999, 2011; MacRae and the Toronto Food Policy Council 1999), where:

1. Everyone has the resources to obtain the quality and quantity of food they need to be healthy and the knowledge to optimize nutritional health.
2. Food production, processing, and consumption are suited to the environmental, economic, technological, and cultural needs, potentials, and limits of the distinct regions of Canada. Food supply and quality are dependable. They are not threatened by social, political, economic, and environmental changes.
3. The food system provides an essential public service, and is linked to other public services such as health care and education. Ownership of food system resources is widely and often publicly held.
4. Food is safe both for people who produce, work with, and eat it, and for the environment.
5. Resources (energy, water, soil, genetic resources, forests, fish, wildlife) are used efficiently with no ecological waste.
6. The resources of the food system are distributed in a way that ensures that those who provide the most essential tasks have a decent income. In particular, people in rural communities have enough work and income to maintain or improve their lifestyle and to care for the rural environment.
7. Everyone who wants to be involved in determining how the food system works has a chance to participate.
8. Opportunities are available for creative and fulfilling work.
9. Food creates positive personal and cultural identity, and social interaction.
10. Our food system functions in a way that allows other countries to develop food systems with similar purposes and values, and we prioritize trade with those countries.

Key Principles on Which to Build Food Policy Frameworks

To implement such goals requires adherence to a different set of principles than those that currently dominate the system (adapted from MacRae 1999, 2011; MacRae and the Toronto Food Policy Council 1999):

1. Integrated responsibilities and activities: Systems reflect the interconnectedness of activities in agriculture, food, health, culture, and social and economic development. Professionals have expertise across these domains and work collaboratively with others.
2. An emphasis on macro-policy: The policy-making process starts with global questions and options, and then, as appropriate, develops more specific policy tools and interventions consistent with the macro-policy. Policy making is about identifying what is societally desirable.
3. Trans-disciplinary policy development:

   - Because food is a multidimensional endeavour, policy units must include professionals with a diverse range of training, only one of which is economics. In this system, economics and science are tools to help society achieve identified goals.

- Policy makers are well linked to the diverse groups affected by problems.
- A more diverse group of people is involved in policy work, and community development principles are employed.

4. Food systems policy: Policy makers apply systems thinking to the analysis of problems and design of solutions. The framework of Malhi et al. (2009) is useful in this regard, as it includes the paradigm of the system, its goals, the system structures (including governance), the feedback mechanisms that help inform system activities and performance, and the subsystem elements (in a policy sense, this includes the actors and the policy tools). To be effective, all these layers are interconnected.

5. **Demand–supply coordination**: The presumption has been that the food marketplace efficiently allocates resources with minimal state intervention to ensure equitable and efficient distribution. However, as many chapters in this volume describe, this is not actually happening. Demand and supply must be coordinated beyond market functions.

Structures, Feedback Loops, and Subsector Elements

Describing the structures, feedback loops, and subsector elements to implement all the required changes is beyond the scope of this chapter, so Table 19.2 sets out in broad terms what portfolios

Table 19.2 Key Portfolios Requiring Changes

Goal	Portfolios to be Changed to Meet the Goal
1. Everyone has the resources to obtain the quality and quantity of food they need to be healthy and the knowledge to optimize nutritional health.	Employment and economic development strategies in and beyond the food system Income support and security architecture, policies, and programs Community growing spaces Fisheries management Aboriginal hunting and fishing rights and access to traditional foods, Aboriginal housing, food mail program, Aboriginal economic development and housing (on-reserve and off-reserve), pollution reduction, food production in Aboriginal communities Equitable access to the food distribution system, retail, and alternative projects Consumer food information systems Breastfeeding promotion
2. Food production, processing, and consumption are suited to the environmental, economic, technological, and cultural needs, potentials, and limits of the distinct regions of Canada. Food supply and quality are dependable. They are not threatened by social, political, economic, and environmental changes.	Regional optimal consumption planning Agricultural planning Fisheries planning
3. The food system provides an essential public service, and is linked to other public services such as health care and education. Ownership of food system resources is widely and often publicly held.	Health promotion planning Integrating food into educational processes Reducing corporate concentration and broadening ownership of food system assets
4. Food is safe both for people who produce, work with, and eat it, and for the environment.	Food safety Food quality

Goal	Portfolios to be Changed to Meet the Goal
5. Resources (energy, water, soil, genetic resources, forests, fish, wildlife) are used efficiently with no ecological waste.	Sustainable food and aquaculture production, processing, and consumption Agricultural land protection Energy efficiency in the food system Protecting genetic resources Municipal organic waste and sewage sludge management
6. The resources of the food system are distributed in a way that ensures that those who provide the most essential tasks have a decent income. In particular, people in rural communities have enough work and income to maintain or improve their lifestyle and to care for the rural environment.	Farm market income Business risk management programs Support to small and medium-sized enterprise processing in rural communities Seasonal worker programs Minimum wages for farm, restaurant, and food-service workers
7. Everyone who wants to be involved in determining how the food system works has a chance to participate.	Food system governance Food citizenship
8. Opportunities are available for creative and fulfilling work.	Intergenerational farm transfer and new farmer programs Rural development
9. Food creates positive personal and cultural identity, and social interaction.	Work–life balance Food and culture Food and body image
10. Our food system functions in a way that allows other countries to develop food systems with similar purposes and values, and we prioritize trade with those countries.	Trade agreements (both bilateral and multilateral) Food export mandates, supports, and programs Food aid policy

need to be changed, organized according to the goals listed above. Most nations in the industrialized world have to address similar kinds of issues to create their own national food policies. Some of the portfolios described above do not currently exist, as they cross existing lines of responsibility or include unaddressed policy arenas. Most portfolios would require alterations to legislation, regulation, and programs at all three levels of government.

Conclusion

Clearly, complex and multifaceted changes are required, based on a **joined-up food policy** approach (Barling, Lang, and Caraher 2002). Canada faces challenges similar to those in other jurisdictions in the industrial world, making this a long-term agenda. Despite the imperative for change, the forces favouring the status quo are powerful, as many chapters of this volume describe. Multiple jurisdictions, enormous complexity, hundreds of thousands of actors, and global forces all mean that minimizing state functions and letting market forces run free is not the best course of action.

Completely re-writing the Canadian Constitution to better align food system function with appropriate jurisdictions and to limit jurisdictional disputes is not a viable option in the near term. As well, as food and agriculture files do not usually generate parliamentary debate unless they represent a 'hot-button' issue, it is unlikely that a complex, multidimensional, and multi-departmental food policy issue would undergo substantive parliamentary discussion.[12] Such policy is unlikely to be a PMO priority and Cabinet participation in policy making has been eroded, so that agriculture or health ministers are not likely to bring forward significant food and agriculture legislation without PMO approval (Savoie 1999). This has effectively removed many traditional advocacy levers for civil society organizations. Potential shifts, however, in approaches to regulatory pluralism and government present short-term opportunities to widen the set of actors in policy development (MacRae and Abergel in press). But with more significant structural change possible only in the longer term (MacRae and TFPC 1999), many changes proposed here will rely on existing architecture.

Financing food policy change will also be challenging. Given current budget contractions in most industrial countries, one of the first steps is to generate savings from first order changes to pay for second order ones. Three areas are strategically promising here: shifting production and export subsidies to operations that generate multiple benefits (ecological, social, and financial), often referred to as multi-functionality; supporting the farm transition to low-input systems that reduce demands on government-funded financial safety nets; and investments in health promotion programs that reduce demands on acute care and government budgets in countries with state-funded health insurance, such as Canada. Setting up mechanisms to identify and capture the savings will be part of this challenge.

Discussion Questions

1. What explains the failure of most Western countries to have sustainable and health promoting food systems?

2. Which level of government is most responsible for creating food policy?

3. What roles can non-governmental organizations play in creating and implementing a joined-up food policy?

4. Which goals will be most challenging to implement?

Further Reading

1. Baker, L., P. Campsie, and K. Rabinowicz. 2010. *Menu 2020: Ten Good Food Ideas for Ontario*. Toronto: Metcalf Foundation. http://metcalffoundation.com/wp-content/uploads/2011/05/menu-2020.pdf.

   Reviews 10 key initiatives for creating a more sustainable and health-promoting food system for Ontario that enhance the economic viability of small to medium-sized farms.

2. Epp, S. 2009. *Provincial Approaches to Food Security: A Scan of Food Security Related Policies in Canada*. Winnipeg: Manitoba Food Charter. http://bitsandbytes.ca/sites/bitsandbytes.ca/files/provincial%20policy%20scan.pdf.

   A scan of policies and initiatives to create food security at the provincial and municipal levels.

3. Hutchison, L., ed. 2006. *What Are We Eating?: Towards a Canadian Food Policy*. Named issue of *Canadian Issues* (Winter).

   Selected papers from a conference on food policy development entitled 'What's to Eat in Canada?' held in Montreal and sponsored by the McGill Institute for the Studies of Canada.

4. *Food Systems and Public Health: Linkages to Achieve Healthier Diets and Healthier Communities. Journal of Hunger and Environmental Nutrition* Special Issue 4(3/4, 2009).

   A special issue of the journal with a range of papers from a conference on linking food policy and health promotion.

5. Lang, T., D. Barling, and M. Caraher. 2009. *Food Policy: Integrating Health, Environment and Society*. Oxford, UK: Oxford University Press.

   This book provides a concise, accessible, and comprehensive review of issues surrounding the production, distribution, and consumption of food, largely from the UK perspective of the authors. They share their thinking on the multiple layers and levels of public and private action required to improve food policy.

6. Rideout, K., G. Riches, A. Ostry, D. Buckingham, and R. MacRae. 2007. 'Bringing Home the Right to Food in Canada: Challenges and Possibilities for Achieving Food Security'. *Public Health Nutrition* 10: 566–73.

   Using a right to food framework, this paper explores Canada's failure to implement right to food, despite its international commitments and the need to advance food security to solve multiple food–related problems.

Notes

1. Portions of this chapter are reproduced with the permission of Canada's International Development Research Centre (www.idrc.ca).
2. These problems were revealed in particular by the Food Prices Review Board which functioned in the mid 1970s.
3. Only one ever was.
4. With a second five-year version, Growing Forward, in the process of being implemented
5. In truth, very few Canadian agri-environmental programs have been properly evaluated.
6. According to Hedley (2006), this or similar wording can be found in AAFC policy statements dating back to the 1960s.
7. National Food Policy Framework (2005: 8). The main relevant federal ones are: Food and Drugs Act, Canadian Food Inspection Agency Act (Bill C-60), Canadian Agricultural Products Act, Feeds Act, Fish Inspection Act, Seeds Act, Consumer Packaging and Labelling Act, Plant Protection Act, Plant Breeders Act, Health of Animals Act, Meat Inspection Act, Hazardous Products Act, and the Pest Control Products Act. The provinces and territories also have food safety legislation that covers food products that are not registered in the federal system, and provides for oversight of food-related facilities that are not generally involved in interprovincial trade (e.g., slaughtering plants not involved in interprovincial or international trade) or that serve local markets (e.g., restaurants, food retail stores). However, increasingly the provinces are amending their slaughtering rules to conform with federal ones, even for provincial plants that do not sell meat across borders.
8. A new federal–provincial–territorial framework for working on food safety was put in place in 1996, and new programs have been introduced since the Agricultural Policy Framework was adopted in 2003.
9. For an overview, see the CFIA website, www.inspection.gc.ca.

10. For a summary overview of responsibilities, commodities covered, and pertinent pieces of legislation see Exhibit 25.1 of the *2000 Report of the Auditor General of Canada* (www.oag-bvg.gc.ca/internet/English/att_0025xe01_e_10976.html).

11. This is not unique to agriculture (see Savoie 1999), but appears to play a significant role in agricultural governance.

12. Note that more limited and highly politically charged issues, such as the fate of the Canadian Wheat Board, are still occasionally part of parliamentary debate.

References

Agriculture and Agri-food Canada (AAFC). 1998. *Canada's Action Plan on Food Security*. Ottawa: Agriculture and Agri-food Canada. Available at www.agr.gc.ca/misb/fsec-seca/pdf/action_e.pdf.

Agriculture Canada. 1989. 'Nutrition Policy Statement'. *Rapport* (Newsletter of the National Institute of Nutrition) 4(1): 7.

Atamanenko, A. 2010. *Food for Thought: Towards a National Food Strategy*. Ottawa: New Democratic Party of Canada.

Barling, D., T. Lang, and M. Caraher. 2002. 'Joined up Food Policy? The Trials of Governance, Public Policy and the Food System'. *Social Policy & Administration* 36(6): 556–74.

Canadian Agri-food Policy Institute (CAPI). 2009. *Regulatory Reform in Canada's Agri-food System*. Ottawa: CAPI. Available at www.capi-icpa.ca/pdfs/CAPI_Regulatory%20Framework%20March%204%202009_.pdf.

———. 2011. *Canada's Agri-food Destination: A New Strategic Approach*. Ottawa: CAPI.

Forbes, J.D. 1985. *Institutions and Influence Groups in Canadian Farm and Food Policy*. Monographs on Canadian Public Administration #6, Institute of Public Administration #10. Toronto: Institute of Public Administration of Canada.

Fowke, V.C. 1946. *Canadian Agricultural Policy*. Toronto: University of Toronto Press.

Gunningham, N. 2005. 'Reconfiguring Environmental Regulation'. In *Designing Government: From Instruments to Governance*, ed. P. Eliadis, M.M. Hill, and M. Howlett. Montreal and Kingston: McGill-Queen's University Press, 333–52.

Health Canada. 1976. *Report of the Committee on Diet and Cardiovascular Disease*. Ottawa: Health Canada.

Hedley, D.D. 2006. 'Why Is There No Canadian Food Policy In Place?' *Canadian Issues* (Winter): 20–7.

Hill, M. 1994. 'The Choice of Mode for Regulation: A Case Study of the Federal Pesticide Registration Review, 1988–1992'. PhD dissertation. Ottawa: Carleton University.

Howlett, M. 2005. 'What Is a Policy Instrument? Policy Tools, Policy Mixes and Policy Styles'. In *Designing Government: From Instruments to Governance*, ed. P. Eliadis, M.M. Hill, and M. Howlett. Montreal and Kingston: McGill-Queen's University Press, 31–50.

Ignatieff, M. 2010. *Rural Canada Matters: Highlights of the Liberal Plan for Canada's First National Food Policy*. Ottawa: Liberal Party of Canada.

Interdepartmental Steering Group on Food Policy. 1978. *Recent Developments in Food Strategy*. 13 December. Ottawa: Government of Canada.

Koç, M., and J. Bas. In press. 'Canada's Action Plan on Food Security: The Interactions between Civil Society and the State to Advance Food Security in Canada'. In *Advancing Sustainability and Health in the Canadian Food System: New Opportunities for Civil Society to Influence Policy Development and Implementation*, ed. R. MacRae and E. Abergel. Vancouver: University of British Columbia Press.

Lalonde, M. 1974. *A New Perspective on the Health of Canadians*. Ottawa: Ministry of Supply and Services Canada.

Lang, T., and M. Heasman. 2004. *Food Wars: The Global Battle for Mouths, Minds and Markets*. London: Earthscan.

McCarrison, R. 1943. *Nutrition and Natural Health*. London: Faber and Faber.

MacDougall, H. 1990. *Activists and Advocates: Toronto's Health Department 1883–1983*. Toronto: Dundurn Press.

MacRae, R.J. 1999. 'This Thing Called Food: Policy Failure in the Canadian Food and Agriculture System'. In *For Hunger-proof Cities: Sustainable Urban Food Systems*, ed. M. Koç, R.J. MacRae, L. Meugeot, and J. Welsh. Ottawa: International Development Research Centre and the Ryerson Centre for Studies in Food Security, 182–94.

MacRae, R.J. 2011. 'A Joined-Up Food Policy for Canada'. *Journal of Hunger and Environmental Nutrition* 6: 424–57.

MacRae, R.J., and the Toronto Food Policy Council (TFPC). 1999. 'Not Just What, But How: Creating Agricultural Sustainability and Food Security by Changing Canada's Agricultural Policy Making Process'. *Agriculture and Human Values* 16: 187–201.

MacRae, R.J., and E. Abergel, eds. In press. *Advancing Sustainability and Health in the Canadian Food System: New Opportunities for Civil Society to Influence Policy Development and Implementation*. Vancouver: University of British Columbia Press.

Mahli, L., O. Karanfil, T. Merth, M. Archeson, A. Palmer, and D.T. Finegood. 2009. 'Places to Intervene to Make Complex Food Systems More Healthy, Green, Fair, and Affordable'. *Journal of Hunger and Environmental Nutrition* 4: 466–76.

Mill, John Stuart. 1965. *Principles of Political Economy with Some of Their Applications to Social Philosophy: The Collected Works of John Stuart Mill*, VIII. Toronto: University of Toronto Press.

National Food Policy Framework: Overview. 2005. Draft— Work in Progress, 21 November 2005. (The document appears to be directed to a federal–provincial–territorial committee.)

Norwegian Ministry of Agriculture. 1975. *On Norwegian Nutrition and Food Policy* (Report #32 to the Storting). Oslo: Norwegian Ministry of Agriculture.

Ostry, A. 2006. *Nutrition Policy in Canada, 1870–1939*. Vancouver: University of British Columbia Press.

People's Food Policy Project. 2011. *Setting the Table: A People's Food Policy for Canada*. Ottawa: People's Food Policy Project.

Picton, L.J. 1946. *Thoughts on Feeding*. London: Faber and Faber.

Sabry, Z.I. 1975. 'The Cost of Malnutrition in Canada'. *Canadian Journal of Public Health* 66: 291–3.

Savoie, D.J. 1999. *Government from the Centre: The Concentration of Power in Canadian Politics*. Toronto: University of Toronto Press.

Skogstad, G. 1987. *The Politics of Agricultural Policy-Making in Canada*. Toronto: University of Toronto Press.

PART V

Food for the Future

interconnected system. Rather, it stresses a linear configuration, thus demonstrating the thermodynamic problem of converting natural cycles into one-way flows of waste to overloaded environmental sinks (see Rees 2004).

In contrast, Hay (2000) defines a system as a group of elements organized such that each element is in some way interdependent (either directly or indirectly) with every other element. We can use aspects of these two explanations to define a food system as *an interdependent web of activities that include the production, processing, distribution, consumption, and disposal of food.* This interdependent web can be very local, as in the self-provisioning of small, isolated groups, or huge, as in the global corporate food system. Regardless of scale, food systems are dynamic entities built by people to satisfy their needs and desires. In this way, food systems are relational—they embody relations among humans and between humans and the environment. And since food has always been about power and money (Friedmann 1993), these relations are seldom positive. Nowhere is this more evident than in the global corporate food system.

The Global Corporate Food System

Following the definition of a food system, the global corporate food system can be understood as an interdependent web of corporate-controlled activities at the global scale that include the production, processing, distribution, consumption, and disposal of food. Several authors in this volume have critically analyzed the global corporate food system (see, for example, chapters 2, 6, 12, and 17). In his book *Stuffed and Starved*, Patel (2007: 15) describes the global corporate food system as 'a battlefield', maintaining that it is impossible to think about such a food system without attending to the corporations that have controlled it for centuries, and who crack the supply chain like a whip:

Today, transnational agricultural corporations control 40 per cent of world trade in food, with twenty companies controlling the world coffee trade, six controlling 70 per cent of wheat trade, and one controlling 98 per cent of packaged tea. (Patel 2007: 99–100)

The drive for control of the food system is corroborated by Goodall (2005) who claims that 10 multinational corporations control over half the world's food supply. And in the United States, 95 per cent of the food Americans eat is a corporate product (McMichael 2000).

This growing control has long been facilitated by government policy (see Chapter 19 in this volume). According to Patel (2007: 108), 'food system corporations lobby, threaten, plead and demand political favour'; thus, political expediency and gain enable the consolidation of control of the food system. In this way, 'although the food system is largely in the hands of the private sector, the markets in which they operate are allowed, and shaped by, societies and governments' (Patel 2007: 111).

Patel's observation helps us to understand that markets are neither natural nor God-given but socially constructed. As such, they can be, and have been, re-constructed. The social construction of markets is evident in Karl Polanyi's (2001) seminal work, *The Great Transformation*. Polanyi defines a market as 'a meeting place for the purpose of barter or buying and selling' (Polanyi 2001: 59) and describes how early markets emerged from trade and were *embedded within social relations*. Over time, various forms of trade developed and introduced enormous changes, but the economic system was still 'submerged in general social relations' with these embedded markets merely 'accessories of economic life' (Polanyi 2001: 70–1).

In the 'great transformation', disembedded markets emerged with the development of a market economy during the Industrial Revolution. According to Polanyi (2001: 71), 'a market economy is an economic system controlled, regulated and directed by market prices; order in the production and distribution of goods is entrusted to this self-regulating mechanism.' Uniquely derived from the principle of gain, such a 'self-regulating' market requires the deliberate commodification of labour, land, and money, and 'demands nothing less than the institutional separation of society into an economic and a political sphere' (Polanyi 2001: 74). In effect, a 'market economy involves a society the institutions of which are subordinated to the requirements of the market mechanism' (Polanyi 2001: 187). Such subordination, in turn, creates the eloquently described 'perils to society' (Polanyi 2001: 75). Throughout his book, he argues forcefully that the 'market economy if left to evolve according to its own laws would create great and permanent evils' (Polanyi 2001: 136).

The 'great and permanent evils' of a deliberately unregulated market economy are clearly evident in today's global corporate food system. Rosset (2006 in Albritton 2009: 200) sums up these evils when he asks:

> Why must we put up with a global food system that ruins rural economies worldwide, drives family and peasant farmers off the land in droves, and into slums, ghettos and international migrant streams? . . . That imposes a kind of agriculture that destroys the soil, contaminates ground water, eliminates trees from rural areas, creates pests that are resistant to pesticides, and puts the future productivity of agriculture in doubt? . . . Food that is laden with sugar, salt, fat, starch, carcinogenic colours and preservatives, pesticide residues and genetically modified organisms, and that may well be driving global epidemics of obesity for some (and hunger for others), heart disease, diabetes and cancer? A food system that bloats the coffers of unaccountable corporations, corrupts governments and kills farmers and consumers while wrecking the environment?

While these debilitating effects are becoming increasingly apparent, cracks were beginning to form in the fortress of the global corporate food system as far back as the early 1990s:

> Those with common sense are becoming aware of the fragility of a food system that creates so much distance, both socially and geographically, between an unprecedentedly urban world of consumers and a global farm, linked by the perpetual motion of an oil-fueled transportation network and a shaky international monetary framework. (Friedmann 1993: 213–14)

As these cracks have widened, spaces have opened up for constructing more sustainable alternatives—alternatives that are re-embedded within, and serve, society. Such alternatives begin with the meaning of sustainability itself.

Sustainability

Over a quarter of a century ago, Hill (1984: 1) lamented that 'there is something seriously wrong with a society that requires one to argue for sustainability.' And yet, since *sustainability* was coined in 1972, it has been a subject of controversy (Sumner 2005). The watershed in the sustainability debates was undoubtedly the Report of the World Commission on Environment and Development (WCED 1987), commonly known as the Brundtland Report. Published as *Our Common Future*, the report defined sustainable development as that which meets the needs of the present without compromising the ability of future generations to meet their own. Even though the report brought *sustainability* to international attention and made it a household word, the vagueness of its definition ensured that no drastic changes were needed in the ways people treated the environment or each other. Non-renewable resource extraction and human exploitation could proceed without interruption.

Over the next two decades, people began to grapple with the meaning of sustainability.

The original research and thinking on the concept derived primarily from worries over the destruction of natural systems and their regenerative capacity, along with a concern for the loss of Indigenous and traditional culture (Dahlberg 1993). This concern, however, gradually spread to other areas to the extent that meanings of sustainability now fill a spectrum of understanding from the maintenance of profitable investments on Wall Street through the Dow Jones Sustainability Index to the deep ecology of the inherent rights of nature (Sumner 2005). All in all, *sustainability* can be a confusing term that no one opposes but few can explain. Instead, many people have warm, fuzzy feelings about what it means, and they project those feelings onto the term. But without a clear definition of *sustainability*, it is difficult to know whether our food system is actually becoming more or less sustainable. In addition, the aim of a sustainable food system is a more sustainable society, one that is socially responsible, economically fair, and environmentally viable. On what basis can we work toward such a society?

One way to understand sustainability is through the idea of the civil commons. According to McMurtry (1999), this term describes a long-standing way of doing things. The civil commons is 'any co-operative human construction that protects and/or enables the universal access to life goods' (McMurtry 1999: 1). This means that the civil commons is based on co-operation, not competition. It does not occur naturally, but is constructed by people, and thus centres on human agency. It protects through rules and regulations, and it enables through opening up possibilities and opportunities. The civil commons involves universal access, not access only for those who can afford it. And it provides life-goods such as clean air, unadulterated food, potable water, education, and health care, not destructive goods like junk food, violent entertainment, and weapons. Examples of the civil commons are all around us: public education, the Canadian health-care system, old-age pensions, libraries, the Charter of Rights and Freedoms, parks, and the Montreal Protocol on Substances That Deplete the Ozone Layer. In essence, the civil commons is:

> *society's organized and community-funded capacity of universally accessible resources to provide for the life preservation and growth of society's members and their environmental life-host.* The civil commons is, in other words, what people ensure together as a society to protect and further life, as distinct from money aggregates. (McMurtry 1998: 24)

From this foundation, we can define sustainability as *a set of structures and processes that build the civil commons* (Sumner 2005: 93). The structures can be either formal or informal, as long as they build the civil commons. Formal structures can include governments, non-governmental organizations such as Greenpeace, clubs, associations such as the Greenbelt Association, co-operatives such as Organic Meadow, non-profit organizations such as FoodShare, and corporations such as Newman's Own. Informal structures cover traditions and customs such as co-operation, sharing, and neighbourliness. The processes include developmental activities such as teaching, learning, researching, writing, collaborating, and decision making, as long as they build the civil commons. If oriented toward sustainability, these structures and processes can work dynamically together to build co-operative human constructions that protect and/or enable universal access to life-goods.

The concept of sustainability has been applied to many areas, including, for example, sustainable development, **sustainable livelihoods** and sustainable rural communities. But what does the concept mean in terms of food systems?

Sustainable Food Systems

As the mother concept of sustainability evolved, it inevitably spread as it was combined with other words. Shearman (1990) argues that using *sustainability* as a modifier in compound terms such as *sustainable development* changes the way we come to understand the second half of those terms. In this way, *sustainable* is used not only as an adjective, but also as a contradiction. For Shearman, *sustainability* as a modifier implies that the status quo is inconsistent with the facts. If not, then terms like *sustainable development* would be redundant, because development would already be sustainable. The same logic applies to sustainable food systems.

The concept of sustainability was first applied to food systems in a prescient article by Stuart Hill (1984), 'Redesigning the Food System for Sustainability'. He proposed that

> It is obvious that our food producing systems must be operated in a sustainable way, for to do otherwise would be to practice delayed genocide on our descendants. (Hill 1984: 1)

Hill (1984: 1) then describes 'some characteristics of a sustainable food system' and outlines the goals of any food system: nourishment for everyone, fulfillment, justice, flexibility, evolution, and sustainability.

In spite of this promising beginning, it took many years for academics to adopt the idea. Some authors mentioned sustainable food systems in passing (Power 1999; Friedmann 2007), but did not define them. Others have dealt with the concept head-on. For example, Feenstra (2002) proposes that sustainable food systems be characterized as more environmentally sound; more economically viable for a larger percentage of community members; and more socially, culturally, and spiritually healthful. She writes that

> They tend to be more decentralized, and invite the democratic participation of community residents in their food systems. They encourage more direct and authentic connections between all parties in the food system, particularly between farmers and those who enjoy the fruits of

their labor—consumers or eaters. They attempt to recognize, respect, and more adequately compensate the laborers we often take for granted—farmworkers, food service workers, and laborers in food processing facilities, for example. And they tend to be place-based, drawing on the unique attributes of a particular bioregion and its population to define and support themselves. (Feenstra 2002: 100)

Many of Feenstra's characteristics of a sustainable food system resonate with the civil commons: democratic participation, two-way communication, liveable wages, food sovereignty, and especially her primary goal of a community food system—'improved access by all community members to an adequate, nutritious diet' (Feenstra 2002: 100). In this way, we can understand the vital role of the civil commons in sustainable food systems. If we understand sustainability as building the civil commons, we can apply the meaning of sustainability to the definition of a food system formulated above: *A sustainable food system involves an interdependent web of activities that build the civil commons with respect to the production, processing, distribution, consumption, and disposal of food.* In other words, to qualify as sustainable, the activities within a food system would have to contribute to co-operative human constructs that protect and/or enable universal access to the life-good of food.

This definition not only incorporates Shearman's (1990) argument that using *sustainability* as a modifier implies that the status quo is inconsistent with the facts—that is, food systems are not automatically sustainable. It also takes his argument one step further. A new understanding of sustainability as building the civil commons means that in compound terms, the adjective *sustainable* not only implies a contradiction, but also indicates a way out of the problem. The idea of the civil commons that underpins the meaning of sustainability allows fresh insights to emerge about sustainable food systems.

Right away it becomes clear that a food system dominated by transnational corporations would preclude sustainability by definition. The fiduciary responsibility of corporations to maximize private shareholder return fundamentally conflicts with and even violates the public interest of ensuring that citizens are fed. This incompatibility is emphasized by Michele Simon (2006), a public-health attorney, who argues that 'under our current economic system it's not a corporation's job to protect public health'. Since a corporation's purview does not include public health, she observes:

> Like water (and unlike most other commodities such as toys or electronics), food is indispensable and a basic human right. Why have we turned its production over to private interests? Shouldn't at least some aspects of society remain off-limits to corporate control? (Simon 2006: 318)

In other words, a sustainable food system must be anchored within the public domain. This stance reflects the experience of participants in the People's Food Policy Project, many of whom suggested that

> food should be a public good, that a just system would make healthy food accessible, affordable and universal by bringing more of it into the public sphere, for example, through universal baby-bonus-style healthy-food dollars, school programs, community gardening and non-profit community markets. . . . It was agreed that citizens should control a system that serves the needs of eaters first and protects producers who serve the consumers. (Webb 2011: 28)

In addition to being anchored within the public domain, a sustainable food system would follow natural cycles and close loops as tightly as possible, so that positive synergies could be achieved. Overall, the nodes in a sustainable food system would be governed by civil-commons regulation geared toward ensuring that everyone is fed, within the ecological limits of the planet.

Components of a Sustainable Food System

As in any food system, in a sustainable food system a number of components would make up its interdependent web of activities. Kaufman's (2004) components of a food system listed at the beginning of this chapter provide some initial thoughts about the parameters of a sustainable food system: production, processing, distribution, consumption, and disposal.

Production

In a sustainable food system, those who did not own land but wanted to farm would be given access to land and mentored in the production process. A current example can be found in Cuba, where people have the right to use land as long as they grow food, and are given seeds, tools, and other extension services by the government. In Canada, FarmStart is a not-for-profit organization that encourages young and new farmers to take up farming. Its mission is to facilitate, support, and encourage a new generation of farmers drawn from four different demographic groups: young people from farm backgrounds, young people who are new to farming, second-career farmers, and new-Canadian farmers (FarmStart 2011). One of the programs it offers is the New Farmers Incubator Program, which

> supports new farm enterprises by offering access to land, equipment and infrastructure at reasonable rates, along with business planning support, technical training, mentorship and experience with ecological and emerging farming methods. (FarmStart 2011)

In a sustainable food system, producers would also join co-operatives or collectives to support each other and sell the food they have grown or raised on their farms. A current example can be found in Venezuela, where farmers' co-operatives control production, with the government providing assistance for managing co-operatives and for establishing processing plants, so that farmers are no longer victim to prices set by processors and distributors (Broughton 2011). In Canada, examples include Organic Meadow, a dairy farmers' co-operative based in southwestern Ontario; the Falls Brook Centre in New Brunswick; and Farmer Direct, a co-op of 70 certified organic farms in Saskatchewan that is the first business in North America to receive domestic fair-trade certification.

Producers in a sustainable food system would be certified for a range of sustainability parameters, along the lines of Local Food Plus (see chapter 2), and fairly compensated for their work. Food that needs to be imported into the system, such as coffee, tea, and out-of-season fruits and vegetables, would be sourced from a worldwide network of organic fair-trade co-operatives, non-profits, or other social-economy organizations in other countries. Any surplus produced in the system would be exported through these same networks.

Processing

In a sustainable food system, processors would be organized into producers' or workers' co-operatives, non-profits, and other social-economy organizations that specialize in canning, drying, curing, freezing, preserving, slaughtering, etc. The processing would be small- or medium-scale at the local or regional level, to provide employment where the food grows and minimize food miles. Current examples include the Haida Gwaii Local Food Processing Co-op. The aim of this co-op is to 'create local employment and ensure that wild food resources are harvested sustainably with local benefits' (Haida Gwaii Local Food Processing Co-op 2011).

Distribution

In a sustainable food system, a web of primary, secondary, and tertiary distribution hubs would be set up in order to receive food from farmers and send it to other distribution centres or consumer outlets. A current example is the Ontario Natural Food Co-op (ONFC), which distributes natural, organic, and local food to member co-ops throughout Eastern Canada. Its mission is to support a sustainable food system 'by providing, with integrity, quality service in the distribution of organic and natural foods and products within a socially responsible, co-operative network' (ONFC 2010). For the ONFC, the development of a sustainable food system includes support of the local economy, organic farmers, buying clubs, and community-based co-ops.

In a sustainable food system, retailing would look different than it does today. Currently, food retailers dedicate an average of 31 per cent of their shelf space to pseudo-foods—laden with salt, sugar, and oil—because these items generate high profit margins (Winson 2004). In a sustainable food system, such 'edible food-like substances' (Pollan 2008: 1) would be taxed like cigarettes, hidden from public view, and carry health warnings. Retail options would include a combination of civil commons–oriented structures, such as farmers' markets, neighbourhood shops, consumer and worker co-ops, '100-mile' stores, and mobile outlets. Current examples include the Moss Street Market in Victoria and Fiesta Farms in Toronto; workers' co-ops like Planet Bean in Guelph, Ontario, and Just Us! Coffee Roasters Co-op in Nova Scotia; and the 100 Mile Market in Meaford, Ontario, and Creemore 100 Mile Store in Creemore, Ontario. As far as possible, retail options would be located within communities and neighbourhoods, and on public transportation routes, to facilitate physical access.

Consumption

In a sustainable food system, consumption would include the acquisition of basic, low-cost, healthy foodstuffs. This 'cheap food policy' would not depend on the exploitation of farmers, processors, distributors, retailers, or the environment, but would be subsidized by the state through taxation on junk food and a realignment of agriculture and food policies and subsidies. A current example is the city of Belo Horizonte, Brazil, which declared food to be a right and developed dozens of innovations to ensure that everyone could exercise that right—including offering farmers choice public spaces from which to sell to urban consumers, setting up low-priced food markets on city property, and opening People's Restaurants that serve meals for the equivalent of less than 50 cents (Lappé 2009). In addition, Belo Horizonte has subsidized farmers' markets in low-income areas, ensured that free meals made from unsold produce are available to participants in neighbourhood clubs serving low-income residents, developed special food packages for pregnant women—all featuring safe and nutritious food in dignified and convenient settings—and set up a department of supply and services to deal directly with making healthy food readily accessible to everyone (Roberts 2011). The example of Belo Horizonte is being taken up in a number of other places. For instance, in Toronto, FoodShare has set up Good Food Markets to sell subsidized fresh local fruits and vegetables in low-income neighbourhoods (Sumner, McMurtry, and Classens 2011). The Stop offers an array of services and initiatives, including community gardens and kitchens, after-school cooking and gardening programs, a farmers' market, community advocacy training, a nutrition and support program for new and expectant mothers, and a sustainable-food-systems education centre (Saul 2011).

Disposal

In a sustainable food system, food would move as short a distance as possible from its place of origin, providing the opportunity for full-circle recycling, thus healing the 'metabolic rift' set up by the global corporate food system. Each household and business would either compost all of its food waste for its own use or contribute it to neighbourhood composting programs for community gardens or local farm use. A current example is the growth of municipal composting programs in Canada.

Implementing a Sustainable Food System

The components outlined above open up spaces for imagining and setting up a sustainable food system by providing working examples that we can learn from and emulate. As the examples show, a sustainable food system is compatible with a variety of economic realities: it would not eliminate family farms, private enterprise, transnational corporations, or global trade. But it would assume a growing primacy, turning the focus of the food system from promoting trade to providing nourishing food for everyone, within the ecological limits of the planet.

The implementation of a sustainable food system would involve both top-down and bottom-up approaches at multiple scales. The top-down approaches would introduce various forms of civil-commons legislation and initiatives at the municipal, provincial, national, and international scales. At the municipal level, the work of Belo Horizonte, Brazil, and the Toronto Food Policy Council offers templates for implementation. At the provincial level, the creation of the Greenbelt around Toronto prevents farmland from being paved over and thus permanently lost to other uses, including agriculture. This establishes a common-pool resource that we can collectively manage into the future. At the national level, the development of a national food policy would complement other civil-commons programs of care such as the national health care system. And at the international scale, organizations like the Fairtrade Labelling Organizations International and the International Federation of Organic Agriculture Movements provide guidelines for moving international trade within sustainability parameters.

The bottom-up approaches would entail grassroots projects and initiatives at both the local and the global scales. At the local level, for example, Thompson et al. (2011) describe how the Nisichawayasihk First Nation's Country Food Program in northern Manitoba is providing Nelson House First Nation residents with healthy foods, while building community and creating jobs that honour Aboriginal values. Based on 'Cree principles of caring and promoting traditional and healthy ways of life', the hunted and gathered food is distributed for free to as many as 1500 of the community's 2500 residents, with priority given to elders, the sick, and low-income, single-parent families (Thompson et al. 2011: 13). And in Nova Scotia, Beaton (2011) explains how fishers in the Bay of Fundy have teamed up with the province's oldest environmental organization—the Ecology Action Centre—to launch Atlantic Canada's first community-supported fishery called Off the Hook. Modelled on community-supported agriculture (see chapter 2), Off the Hook 'hopes to showcase a sustainable fishing enterprise that nurtures the connections between communities, economies and the environment' (Beaton 2011: 14). At the international level, social movements focused on food act locally and network globally. The food sovereignty, organic, slow food, and fair trade movements all set the tone for a global food system based on such values as the human right to food, local control, environmentalism, protection of heritage species, co-operation, and fair trade.

While examples abound, however, Deumling et al. (2003) remind us that making them a reality depends on overcoming special interests, providing recognition and financial support, and restructuring the current incentive system that subsidizes and encourages unsustainable behaviour. But making them a reality is worth the effort because

> The beauty of a sustainable food system is its ability to generate benefits in numerous areas: health, biodiversity, ecological restoration, energy savings, aesthetic values, and economic justice. None of these benefits alone may outweigh the apparent short-term gains of the current destructive system. But the sum of these benefits will make society far better off and help to avoid the trap of increasing production at the expense of people and the planet. (Deumling et al. 2003: 9)

In this way, a sustainable food system can create benefits far beyond the field of food itself. Moreover, the implementation of a sustainable food system 'provides an opportunity to generate the operating manual for a sustainable world, while uniting the basic need and pleasure of food with ecological and social responsibility' (Deumling et al. 2003).

Conclusion

As fossil fuels deplete, food prices fluctuate, the climate destabilizes, and hunger continues to grow, the idea of a sustainable food system becomes more attractive—part of the social safety net of a civilized society. In the best of all possible worlds, a sustainable food system would form one aspect of a larger collective system of public care that provides a variety of life-goods, including health care, energy, transportation, daycare, education, shelter, and water. As Dahlberg (1993) reminds us, sustainable food systems need to be understood both as part of many larger systems and as made up of many smaller systems. And while individualized, charitable responses to the provision of life-goods can have some small, positive effects, only an organized, holistic, systemic public response can address the range and scale of issues we will face in an uncertain future. In other words, we need 'a more sustainable, life-giving food system for all' (Feenstra 2002: 105).

Currently, our food system is in the hands of the private sector, whose values and practices are not geared for sustainability, but for 'profit-maximization, growth and accumulation' (Wallis 2010: 35). Such a system is not organized to feed the world, but to fatten the bank accounts of shareholders and top-level management. In our current system, 'basic human needs are not met' (Allen 2008: 157). Indeed, food is almost incidental to this system—it just happens to be the chosen vehicle for private enrichment. For this reason, our current food system is not remotely capable of protecting us all against hunger, especially in an era of looming economic, social, and environmental uncertainties.

In the shadow of real hunger now and more crises to come, only publicly funded systems have the equity, resilience, power, and reach to address problems in a humane fashion. To avoid the kind of social breakdown that occurred in the aftermath of the flooding of New Orleans, we need solid public infrastructure paid for through taxation and ready to act for the public good, not the private profit opportunities of 'disaster capitalism' (Klein 2007). A sustainable food system would be part of this infrastructure, built into our modes of thinking, parameters of practice, and ways of life.

Discussion Questions

1. How has the global corporate food system become so powerful?

2. Define the civil commons and describe its role in sustainability.

3. What is a sustainable food system and why is it necessary?

4. Why are pseudo-foods not part of a sustainable food system?

5. How is it possible to have more than 1 billion hungry people and more than 1 billion obese people in the world at the same time?

Further Reading

1. American Planning Association. 2007. *Policy Guide on Community and Regional Food Planning.* Available at www.planning.org/policy/guides/adopted/food.htm.

   A practical handbook for considering the issues associated with planning a sustainable food system.

2. Friedmann, Harriet. 1993. 'After Midas's Feast: Alternative Food Regimes for the Future'. In *Food for the Future: Conditions and Contradictions of Sustainability*, ed. Patricia Allen. New York: John Wiley and Sons, 213–33.

   A seminal work that uses the myth of King Midas to illustrate how history decisively changed when the magical powers of money became deeply rooted in the real relations among people. Describes both sustainable and unsustainable alternatives to the present food economy.

3. Hill, Stuart. 1984. 'Redesigning the Food System for Sustainability'. Ecological Agriculture Projects, McGill University. http://eap.mcgill.ca/publications/eap23.htm.

   A classic paper that asks serious questions about food and sustainability.

4. McMichael. Phillip. 2000. 'The Power of Food'. *Agriculture and Human Values* 17: 21–33.

   A timeless article on the power of food to both dominate and liberate people, while examining the role of development in making this happen.

References

Albritton, Robert. 2009. *Let Them Eat Junk: How Capitalism Creates Hunger and Obesity.* Winnipeg: Arbeiter Ring Publishing.

Allen, Patricia. 2008. 'Mining for Justice in the Food System: Perceptions, Practices and Possibilities'. *Agriculture and Human Values* 25: 157–61.

Beaton, Sadie. 2011. 'Angling for Change'. *Alternatives Journal* 37(2): 14.

Broughton, Alan. 2011. 'Venezuela's Chocolate Solution'. *Alternatives Journal* 37: 2, 20.

Dahlberg, Kenneth A. 1993. 'Regenerative Food Systems: Broadening the Scope and Agenda of Sustainability'. In

Patricia Allen (ed.), *Food for the Future: Conditions and Contradictions of Sustainability*. New York: John Wiley and Sons, 75–102.

Deumling, Diana, Mathis Wackernagel, and Chad Monfreda. 2003. 'Eating Up the Earth: How Sustainable Food Systems Shrink Our Ecological Footprint'. Agricultural Footprint Brief, Redefining Progress. Available at www.RedefiningProgress.org.

FarmStart. 2011. New Farms Incubator Program. Available at www.farmstart.ca/programs/new-farms-incubator-program.

Feenstra, Gail. 2002. 'Creating Space for Sustainable Food Systems: Lessons from the Field'. *Agriculture and Human Values* 19: 99–106.

Friedmann, Harriet. 1993. 'After Midas's Feast: Alternative Food Regimes for the Future'. In Patricia Allen (ed.), *Food for the Future: Conditions and Contradictions of Sustainability*. New York: John Wiley and Sons, 213–233.

———. 2007. 'Scaling Up: Bringing Public Institutions and Food Service Corporations into the Project for a Local, Sustainable Food System in Ontario'. *Agriculture and Human Values* 24: 389–98.

Goodall, Jane. 2005. *Harvest for Hope: A Guide to Mindful Eating*. New York: Warner Books.

Haida Gwaii Local Food Processing Co-op. Accessed 27 January 2011 at www.haidagwaiifutures.ca/success-stories/haida-gwaii-local-food-processing-coop/.

Hay, Alan. 2000. 'System'. In R.J. Johnston, Derek Gregory, Geraldine Pratt, and Michael Watts (eds.), *The Dictionary of Human Geography*, 4th edn. Malden, Mass: Blackwell, 818–19.

Hill, Stuart. 1984. 'Redesigning the Food System for Sustainability'. Ecological Agriculture Projects, McGill University. Accessed 27 August 2010 at http://eap.mcgill.ca/publications/eap23.htm.

Kaufman, Jerome L. 2004. 'Introduction'. *Journal of Planning Education and Research* 23(4): 335–40.

Klein, Naomi. 2007. *The Shock Doctrine: The Rise of Disaster Capitalism*. Toronto: Alfred A. Knopf.

Lappé, Francis Moore. 2009. 'A Visit to Belo Horizonte: The City that Ended Hunger'. Accessed 24 March 2009 at www.counterpunch.org/lappe03182009.html.

McMichael, Phillip. 2000. 'The Power of Food'. *Agriculture and Human Values* 17: 21–33.

McMurtry, John. 1998. *Unequal Freedoms: The Global Market as an Ethical System*. Toronto: Garamond.

———. 1999. 'The Lifeground, the Civil Commons and Global Development'. Paper presented at the annual meeting of the Canadian Association for Studies in International Development, Congress of the Social Sciences and Humanities, Sherbrooke, Quebec, 7 June.

ONFC. 2010. Mission Statement. Ontario Natural Food Co-op. Accessed 5 September 2010 at www.onfc.ca/amission.php.

Patel, Raj. 2007. *Stuffed and Starved: Markets, Power and the Hidden Battle for the World's Food System*. Toronto: HarperCollins.

Polanyi, K. (2001). *The Great Transformation: The Political and Economic Origins of Our Time*. Boston: Beacon Press.

Pollan, Michael. 2008. *In Defence of Food*. New York: Penguin Press.

Power, Elaine M. 1999. 'Combining Social Justice and Sustainability for Food Security'. In Mustafa Koç, Rod MacRae, Luc J.A. Mougeot, and Jennifer Welsh, *For Hunger-Proof Cities: Sustainable Urban Food Systems*. Ottawa: International Development Research Centre, 30–7.

Rees, William E. 2004. 'The Eco-Footprint of Agriculture: A Far-from-(Thermodynamic)-Equilibrium Interpretation'. In Allan Eaglesham, Alan Wildeman, and Ralph W.F. Hardy (eds.), *Agricultural Biotechnology: Finding Common International Goals*. Ithaca, New York: National Agricultural Biotechnology Council, 87–109.

Roberts, Wayne. 2011. 'Taking It All In'. *Alternatives Journal* 37(2): 8–10.

Saul, Nick. 2011. 'No Stopping The Stop'. *Alternatives Journal* 37(2): 11.

Shearman, Richard. 1990. 'The Meaning and Ethics of Sustainability'. *Environmental Management* 14(1): 1–8.

Simon, Michele. 2006. *Appetite for Profit: How the Food Industry Undermines Our Health and How to Fight Back*. New York: Nation Books.

Sumner, Jennifer. 2005. *Sustainability and the Civil Commons: Rural Communities in the Age of Globalization*. Toronto: University of Toronto Press.

———. 'From Land to Table: Rural Planning and Development for Sustainable Food Systems'. In David Douglas (ed.), *Rural Planning and Development in Canada*. Toronto: Nelson Education, 179–224.

Sumner, Jennifer, J.J. McMurtry, and Michael Classens. 2011. 'Community Development, the Social Economy and FoodShare's Good Food Markets: Background and Preliminary Findings'. Paper presented at the annual meeting of the Canadian Association for Food Studies, Congress of the Humanities and Social Sciences, University of New Brunswick, Fredericton, New Brunswick, 30 May.

Thompson, Shirly, Asfia Gulrukh, and Aruna Murthy. 2011. 'Back to Traditional Aboriginal Food'. *Alternatives Journal* 37(2): 13.

Wallis, Victor. 2010. 'Beyond "Green Capitalism"'. *Monthly Review* 61(9): 32–48.

WCED (World Commission on Environment and Development). 1987. *Our Common Future*. New York: Oxford University Press.

Webb, Margaret. 2011. 'Fire in Their Bellies'. *Alternatives Journal* 37(2): 27–8.

Winson, Anthony. 2004. 'Bringing Political Economy into the Debate on the Obesity Epidemic'. *Agriculture and Human Values* 21: 299–312.

Ziegler, Jean. 2004. 'The Right to Food'. Report of the Special Rapporteur of the United Nations Commission on Human Rights, submitted to the General Assembly, New York.

Quantifying Food Systems
Assessing Sustainability in the Canadian Context
Alison Blay-Palmer, Jonathan Turner, and Shannon Kornelsen

Learning Objectives

Through this chapter, you can:

1. Follow the links between food systems and research and thinking about sustainability
2. Understand the interconnections within sustainable food systems (SFSs)
3. See the value and limitations of indicators as a tool for assessment and understanding

---

Introduction

This chapter makes the case for using indicators—measures of economic and social well-being—to understand more about the linkages and interconnections within sustainable food systems, by including ecological, community, and economic factors in assessing these systems. This approach is consistent with international research projects that, for example, broaden the conversation about well-being beyond economic indicators such as gross domestic product (GDP) to include measures of social well-being (e.g., Stiglitz et al. 2009). A Canadian 'report card', Food Counts, shows how, by spelling out different dimensions of a food system, we can begin to understand where to intervene as we move toward increasingly resilient and transformative food systems.

Benefits of a Sustainable Food System (SFS) Report Card

As the world grows more complex, it is worth considering ways to clarify how we understand key facets of our society. Increasingly it is recognized that many essential elements are linked in some way to food sustainability—human health, community well-being, economic viability, and environmental resilience are intimately connected to food systems. For example, the food we eat impacts our health, and some food choices are linked to diseases such as diabetes and cancer; community gardens provide food and build more vibrant, safer communities; buying local food helps keep dollars in the community; and eating from our **foodshed** helps reduce 'food miles' and cut greenhouse-gas emissions (Blay-Palmer 2010; Marsden 2008).

Given the central role of food in society, there are several benefits to developing a clearer understanding about sustainable food systems (SFSs). It is important that the connections within an SFS be made explicit; thus it is worth unpacking the relevant dimensions of SFSs. It is also useful to link these dimensions to indicators to determine how a food system is functioning (Marsden 2010; Morgan and Sonnino 2010; Blay-Palmer and Koç 2010; and chapters in this volume).

The rationale for creating SFSs is the desire to facilitate regenerative and transformative food system pathways (Dahlberg 1993) rather than 'palliative' systems (Marsden et al. 2010). A palliative system is characterized by structural weaknesses that precipitate food crises through mechanisms including corporate concentration and consolidation throughout the food chain, the food system's increasing vulnerability to contamination and the related heightened risk management and consumer preoccupation with food safety, the increasing scientification of food, intensified market liberalization, and speculative investors entering food commodity markets (Marsden et al. 2010; Blay-Palmer and Koç 2010; Clapp and Cohen 2009; Friedmann 2009; McMichael 2009). It is in the context of these weaknesses that people have turned to principles of sustainability as one way to achieve an alternative food system.

An SFS incorporates the well-known interconnected pillars of economy, environment, and society (World Commission on Environment and Development 1986). Each of these spaces can be considered from the perspective of guiding principles, best practices, and institutions (Figure 21.1) (Blay-Palmer and Koç 2010). In the intersection of policy with economic, socio-communal, and economic spaces, SFSs favour regulation and governance that privilege principles of food democracy. Food security, food sovereignty, and a public ethic of care are foundational to SFS policy (Hamm and Bellows 2003, IPC Food Sovereignty 2009, Morgan and Sonnino

2008). On the process side, multifunctionality offers a space where the multiple dividends associated with SFSs can be recognized (Friedmann 2005). The concept of multifunctionality was introduced at the 1992 Rio Summit. Although controversial when implemented, the idea is that agriculture provides more than food production for rural communities (UN 1992). For example, agriculture promotes good-quality drinking water through effective riparian management. Subsidiarity is the principle that 'decisions are taken as closely as possible to the citizen and that constant checks are made to verify that action at Union level is justified in light of the possibilities available at national, regional or local level' (Europa Glossary n.d.) Subsidiarity is also critical to ensuring that food systems are developed and implemented by communities as close to the ground as feasible.

Socio-communal spaces in SFSs are guided by principles of social justice, equity, and responsibility. Putting this concept into practice means paying attention to food citizenship and literacy so that community members are informed about food (Wilkins 2004). It also highlights the need for extensive communication within 'food webs' through supportive relationships and face-to-face interaction (Friedmann 2007). Food also needs to be appropriate and accessible in keeping with food security goals (Hamm and Bellows 2003). Community is essential and can be enhanced by embedding agriculture within the community, as in the case of Lyson's civic agriculture, or through adhering to ideals of commensality (Lyson 2008). Drawing on the work of Waddell (2005), Friedmann encapsulates this connectivity and dynamism in describing the Toronto community of 'food practice':

> . . . more than their skillful access to
> institutional resources . . . organizations
> have provided strategic resources, as well
> as opportunities to experiment and learn
> from others' experiments, to the diverse
> individuals who move through them,
> usually leaving behind new projects

and ideas. These institutions are unique in linking a wide range of top-down and bottom-up initiatives that emerge and evolve within and across a range of 'sectors'—public, voluntary (NGO), and market. (Friedmann 2007: 395)

Economic spaces are guided by the desire to achieve economic viability. Practically, this notion translates into multiple supports such as

making food and the land that grows it affordable, promoting food-based local economic development such as institutional buying of local sustainable food, branding sustainable products as such, establishing appropriately scaled infrastructure including food processing and distribution, creating supportive mechanisms for entrepreneurial activity, and enabling a detailed understanding of the supply chain (Morgan and Sonnino 2008; St Jacques 2010;

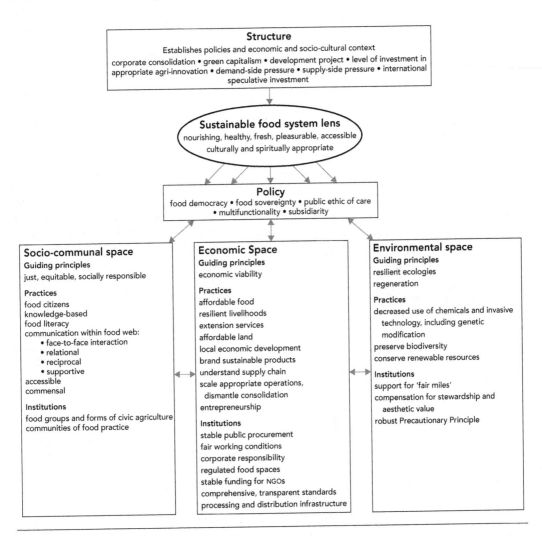

Figure 21.1 Sustainable Food Systems Spaces

Source: Reprinted by permission of the Publishers from 'Imagining sustainable food systems: the path to regenerative food systems', in Imagining Sustainable Food Systems ed. Alison Blay-Palmer (Farnham: Ashgate, 2010), pp. 223–47. Copyright © 2010.

Desjardins 2010; Donald 2008). It also implies attention to resilient livelihoods where

> A livelihood comprises the capabilities, assets (including both material and social resources) and activities required for a means of living. A *livelihood is sustainable* when it can cope with and recover from stresses and shocks, maintain or enhance its capabilities and assets, while not undermining the natural resource base. (Chambers and Conway 1992 in Scoones 1998: 5 [italics added for emphasis])

In addition to stable procurement and infrastructure, necessary institutional supports include fair working conditions, corporate responsibility, appropriately regulated food spaces, stable funding, and comprehensive, transparent standards (Donald 2008; Levitte 2010).

Environmental spaces for SFSs are characterized by attention to resilient ecologies and principles of regeneration (Dahlberg 1993). The goal is not simply to maintain but to improve ecosystems, which can be achieved in SFSs by decreasing the use of chemicals and invasive technologies, preserving biodiversity, and conserving renewable resources. Also needed are institutions that support **fair miles**, provide compensation for ecological stewardship and aesthetic value, and are dedicated to a robust precautionary principle (e.g., Hinrichs and Lyson 2008, Marsden 2008, Morgan and Sonnino 2008).

We can see, therefore, that an SFS comprises multiple, interconnected dimensions. To grasp the opportunities and challenges in emerging SFSs, then, we need a comprehensive measurement tool—a report card—that takes the pulse of all the facets of an SFS.

The Need to Know

It is within this dynamic and complex context that we consider the benefits of bracketing different dimensions of SFSs. The rationale for creating a metric to reflect different facets of SFSs comes from many different sources.

Many jurisdictions have increasingly used measurements to inform decision making since the introduction of GDP in 1934, but the value of conventional, one-dimensional indicators is being questioned. In the face of huge global income disparities, growing numbers of people living in poverty, rising rates of food insecurity, and declining health, decision makers are beginning to appreciate that there is more to well-being than economic activity and that overall prosperity includes natural, social, and human capital (Costanza et al. 2009, Rifkin 2010). Nearly 15 years ago, Costanza and his colleagues estimated the value of environmental benefits delivered for 'free' by the world's ecosystems to be worth US\$33 trillion (Costanza et al. 1997). Since then, Costanza and his team have been working on metrics such as the Genuine Progress Indicator to include social well-being and natural capital indicators in assessing overall societal health (Figure 21.2) (Costanza et al. 2007, 2009). This thinking nests economy and society within natural systems, and thus challenges neo-classical assumptions about economic activity and competition as the natural and foundational forces. The recognition that there is interaction and iteration among social, human, and ecosystem dimensions is changing the way some policy makers understand their mandates. For example, through its *Commission on the Measurement of Economic Performance and Social Progress*, France is shifting away from GDP-based analysis toward more comprehensive and inclusive measures, using the rationale that

> . . . those attempting to guide the economy and our societies are like pilots trying to steering [sic] a course without a reliable compass. The decisions they (and we as individual citizens) make depend on what we measure, how good our measurements are and how well our measures are understood. We are almost blind when the metrics on which action is based are ill-designed or when they are not well understood. For many purposes, we need better metrics. (Stiglitz et al. 2009: 9)

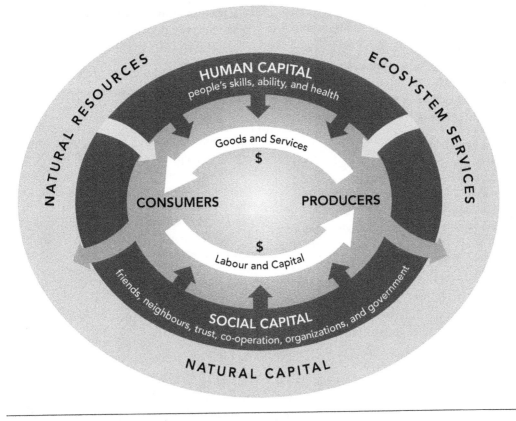

Figure 21.2 View of Economy as Part of a Larger System

Source: Costanza. R, Hart. M, Posner. S and Talberth. J. 2009. Beyond GDP: The Need for New Measures of progress. Boston University, The Frederick S. Pardee Center for the study of the longer-range future. The Pardee Papers, No.4, January 2009. Copyright 2009 M. Hart/Sustainable Measures (www. sustainablemeasures.com). Used with permission.

The need to reach beyond existing parameters is also expressed in the well-being literature that derives from work on developing countries:

> . . . well-being cannot be thought of only as an outcome, but as a state of being that arises from the dynamic interplay of outcomes and processes. This inter-play of outcomes and processes must be understood as firmly located in society and shaped by social, economic, political, cultural and psychological processes. (McGregor 2006: 3–4)

As well, metrics are neither impartial nor neutral. They reflect the classification tools used and the institutions and experts who gather, interpret, and legitimate the information

(Hacking 2007: 296–7). Thus, indicators are the products of the circumstances that create them.

Larner and LeHeron (2002b) describe bench-marking—comparing measured performance to a defined standard—in the context of globalization. While they focus on business practices, economic flows and spaces, and innovation, their work is relevant to sustainability indicators. Most interestingly they link benchmarking to the creation of homogeneous spaces where standards have taken hold, in contrast to the heterogeneous spaces to which standards have not spread. Thus indicators are used to compare performance within and between firms and countries. These standards scale down to a smaller scale to create more reflexive, relational spaces where people can interact and (re)create spaces of food. This perspective offers a chance to understand the ways that sustainability is 'imagined', as indicators can help develop

> . . . explicitly situated project-conscious knowledge that interrogates imaginaries, inventions, and experimentation and the ways in which these are actively reconstituting spaces and subjectivities (Larner and Le Heron, 2002[a]). What flows are prioritised in particular contexts? What are their imaginaries? What is assembled through these flows? What is included and excluded? We might also take up the interrogation of global flows in other ways. (Larner and LeHeron 2002b: 770)

The same thinking is appropriate to SFSs; a metric can complement existing case study and other empirical work. Metrics allow for a more comprehensive understanding of socio-communal, policy, environmental, and economic dimensions. So, for example, the Council of Food Policy Advisors of the UK Department for Environment, Food and Rural Affairs (Defra) lists such benefits of SFSs as a lower impact, healthier diet; an improved environment; more stable local economies; and overall fairer food (2009) and states that 'indicators are part of the evidence base for formulating policy' (Defra 2009: 1). Insightfully, Defra recognizes that the indicators 'embrace [the] whole food chain' (Defra 2009: 1) and that measuring SFSs is an iterative, ongoing process.

While metrics do not reflect every dimension of a food system or capture its interactive dimensions, they can provide a selected snapshot of different points in an SFS's development; they measure one facet of a given system at one point in time. When examined in isolation a single metric gives us very limited information, but when several indicators are viewed at once, they can provide a bigger picture of the state of a system. And while we must remember that indicators reflect biases in many ways, they can be part

of a process to improve a system's well-being. When measured over time, they can show progress—or its lack—toward established goals.

Existing SFSs Metrics

As we consider the merits of creating increasingly sustainable food systems, it is instructive to develop an integrated picture of overall well-being. A more complete picture helps us to identify successes we can build on and indicates where there is room for improvement. Part of this scoping exercise lies in the creation of metrics as guidelines to an SFS's state of affairs.

Defra's approach in its *Food 2030* report (Defra 2010) is to measure the extent of food system sustainability based on six themes:

1. Enabling and encouraging people to eat a healthy, sustainable diet
2. Ensuring a resilient, profitable and competitive food system
3. Increasing food production sustainability
4. Reducing the food system's greenhouse gas emissions
5. Reducing, reusing and reprocessing waste
6. Increasing the impact of skills, knowledge, research and technology (Defra 2010: 73)

Building on these themes, the report identifies existing and proposed indicators and links them to local, regional, national, and global food system well-being.

An earlier project in California led by Feenstra and her colleagues at the University of California identified 22 goals for an SFS through expert and public consultation (Feenstra et al. 2005). These goals were used to select appropriate indicators for the state of California. Subsequently, a set of US indicators was gathered and consolidated through a Kellogg-funded project (Anderson 2009): the *Charting Growth* project provides indicators for environment, health, fairness, and affordability.

From the perspective of social theory and change, the process of developing an SFS may reflect what Marsden and his colleagues call '**social glasnost**' (Marsden et al. 2010). This 'wind of social change'—toward greater openness and forthrightness in dealings between public and private institutions—began to challenge the existing ethos of authority and submission in transactions between the executive state and the client public (Marsden et al. 2010: 16).

In the European Union, this shift from government to governance took place through the 1990s and into the 2000s with a move from paternalistic regulation to increasing levels of accountability. This shift included increasing levels of participatory democracy (Marsden et al. 2010).

The United Kingdom in particular can serve as an example for Canada. While the United Kingdom is moving into a third, hybrid phase of food governance, many of Canada's current challenges parallel the earlier barriers faced in the UK food system in the 1980s. Most notably, the Canadian food system is dominated by corporate interests that privilege profit over other considerations such as human, community, and ecological well-being. As a result, we face a diabetes and obesity health-care crisis, we experience degraded environments from food production stresses, and farmers are unable to make a consistently profitable living from food production.

The report card Food Counts, presented in the balance of this chapter, is an attempt to help us understand relevant factors at the national, provincial, and community level so we can make better-informed decisions about food systems. As in the UK, our period of social glasnost is being born of social crises as well as food system failures.

The Food Counts Project

A set of indicators can help policy makers and community stakeholders make more informed decisions and can support or point to opportunities for SFSs. For example,

quantifying the institutional demand for food can help determine whether a more locally focused food system is feasible. A more resilient food system can be facilitated through government procurement that also supports a healthy, sustainable food system. For example, as part of a local-food-to-hospital project, it was determined that in Ontario over 32 million hospital meals are served every year, pointing to the huge potential for public procurement of local, sustainably produced food (Padanyi and Varangu 2010). Making this number explicit can produce multiple dividends: by deliberately building an SFS we can improve patient health; create more resilient rural economies; increase the profits of farmers, who would then have the latitude to be better stewards of their land; lower food miles; and improve awareness about eating healthy food. These benefits are the rationale that led to the creation of Food Counts—a pilot project to develop an SFS report card for Canada. Generally, a report card can help in three ways. First, it allows us to benchmark our current situation, giving us baseline measurements for comparison. The benchmarks permit communities to identify what they are doing right (and thus what to celebrate and share) and where they can improve and learn from the best practices of other communities. Second, it points to information gaps, helping us to build better tools for the future. Third, it points to areas where case studies can elaborate on successes.

Given the importance of indicators in developing an SFS, it is essential to consider the parameters for these indicators. Drawing from the literature, criteria for the Food Counts indicators require that indicators as far as possible be measurable, available, affordable, reliable and credible, easy to understand, usable and scale relevant, and sensitive (Feenstra et al. 2005; Anderson 2009). As Defra explains about its own attempts to develop and use SFS indicators, although meeting these criteria is a formidable challenge and a continuous process of fine-tuning and adjusting, it is a task worth beginning.

That said, it is difficult to reach agreement on the metrics around sustainability, particularly in light of all the elements involved (water, carbon, other greenhouse gases, etc.). With the various methods of (and different inputs used in) agricultural production and processing, it is also difficult to test the metrics and reach agreement on the best technique for doing so. However, this difficulty should not prevent the work being done, and where there is evidence, it should be used as the foundation for taking the work forward (Defra 2009: 8).

Food Counts is a new tool to measure the sustainability of food systems in Canada and its communities. The project includes two phases: Phase One uses a top-down data reporting strategy (through national and then regional/community level statistics), while Phase Two uses a bottom-up approach (through case studies of unique community projects) to paint an evolving picture of community-based food system sustainability in Canada. This chapter reports on aspects of Phase One.

Funded by the Canadian Social Sciences and Humanities Research Council, the indicators identified in Phase One include measurements of environmental, economic, and socio-communal well-being for Canada, the provinces of Ontario and Prince Edward Island (PEI), and the Region of Waterloo, comprising the cities of Waterloo, Kitchener, and Cambridge, and their surrounding rural areas, in Ontario. These case study sites were selected as they offer a range of community sizes, degrees of legislative autonomy, and regional distinctiveness. For example, the entire permanent population of PEI is just over 138,000. This island province offers an interesting case study with respect to alternative governance strategies. For example, PEI recently considered declaring itself a GMO-free zone. As well, PEI farmers, municipal governments, and the provincial government have expressed the need to understand more about sustainable food systems, opportunities for food re-localization, and agri-tourism in the face of global pressures. And given its traditional emphasis on

industrial-scale potato farming, the Island makes an especially interesting case study. Finally, PEI is unique as it offers a window into municipal, regional, provincial, and federal scales simultaneously. Waterloo Region is an interesting example of a medium-sized urban centre. With a population approaching 500,000 it leads the way on urban food policy through its regional public health unit. As well, there are pressing land-use conflicts as urban spread continually threatens to pave over some of the best agricultural land in Canada. While steps to protect food production are apparent in Ontario programs such as Places to Grow, there is a need to study the effects of these initiatives in the context of the entire food system. As well, the large local Mennonite farming community brings interesting socio-cultural and production practices to the project. Accordingly, it is expected that the Waterloo Region case study will provide insights into socially embedded facets of sustainable food systems while the PEI study will highlight tensions in policy and governance.

The data are drawn from a number of reliable sources including Statistics Canada; Canadian Federation of Municipalities; Farmers Markets Ontario Member Market Profiles; Ontario Ministry of Agriculture, Food and Rural Affairs; Food Banks Canada; Agriculture and Agri-Food Canada; Canadian Organic Growers Association; Forest Products Association of Canada; National Forestry Database; Canadian Council of Forest Ministers; Industry Canada; and Natural Resources Canada. While the Food Counts project has undertaken only minimal original data collection, it brings together a range of previously disconnected indicators to paint a picture of SFSs in Canada. We cast a wide net in seeking out indicators to describe as many facets of the food system as possible. Categories (and subcategories) include: population characteristics (Aboriginal/immigrant populations, dependency ratio, urban/rural population); environmental indicators (land and water use, waste management, ecological health); social indicators (food access, food security);

health (disease/illness, food choices, public support, education); and economic indicators (producer indicators, industry classifications, socio-economic dimensions). At this time over 60 indicators make up the Food Counts report card. While the bulk of the indicators are available at the national level, scaling them down to the provincial and community level was often challenging.

As it is beyond the scope of this chapter to elaborate on all of the indicators, in the remainder of the chapter we present groupings of indicators that illustrate the benefits and challenges of Food Counts as a tool for assessing sustainability.

Socio-communal Dimensions

To set the national-, provincial-, and community-scale contexts, basic population data was accessed based on known risk groups for food access and low income. We know from research that off-reserve Aboriginal people, recent immigrants, lone-parent families, and unattached individuals aged 45 to 64 years are the groups most represented in the after-tax low-income cut-off (LICO) category (Figure 21.3). Given the links between income and food, changes in the numbers of people in these groups could impact food access at the community level. This work helps to frame the demographic information we extracted from available data sets (Table 21.1). A comparison of 2001 and 2006 census data shows that Canada, Ontario, Waterloo Region, and PEI all experienced substantial increases (ranging from 20.1 per cent to 44.0 per cent) in Aboriginal populations. There were also increases in all study areas in the number of lone-parent families, with increases ranging from 0.5 per cent in PEI to 13 per cent in Waterloo Region. Overall population also grew by a small increment of 0.4 per cent in PEI to a 9 per cent increase in Waterloo Region. While population

Low-Income Rates among Various Groups, 2007

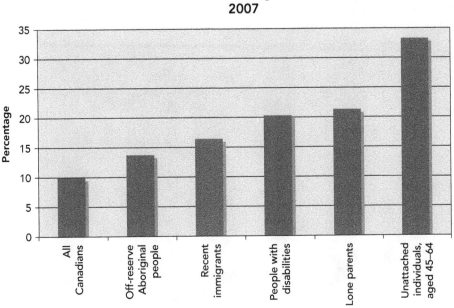

Figure 21.3 After–Tax Low Income Cut-Offs (LICOs)

Source: Statistics Canada, 2009 Indicators of well-being in Canada. LICOs data. Income Trends in Canada 1976 to 2007. Catalogue no. 13F0022X1E. Table 202-0802.

density and the number of recent immigrants are both important pieces of information, this data was available only for the 2006 census, so changes in these figures are unknown.

The social dimensions explored through Food Counts include indicators of food access

and human health and well-being. For food insecurity, we see an uneven pattern between the three study areas (Figure 21.4). At the national scale, the average percentage of moderate and severe food insecurity for people over 12 years old is 7.1 per cent (6.1 per cent for males

Table 21.1 Demographic Data for Canada, Ontario, Region of Waterloo, and Prince Edward Island, with Percentage Changes from 2001 to 2006

	Canada		Ontario		Region of Waterloo		Prince Edward Island	
	2006	% change	2006	% change	2006	% change	2006	% change
Population	31,012,897	3.4	12,160,282	6.6	478,121	9.0	135,851	0.4
Lone-parent families	1,414,065	7.8	540,715	11.2	19,340	13.0	6,400	0.5
Aboriginal population	1,172,785	20.1	242,490	28.8	4,810	44.0	1,730	28.6
Recent immigrants (2001–6)	1,109,980	N/A	580,740	N/A	17,020	N/A	855	N/A
Population density (people/km²)	3.5	N/A	13.4	N/A	349.3	N/A	23.9	N/A

Source: Adapted from Statistics Canada 2006 Census, www12.statcan.gc.ca/cehsus-recensement/2006/as-sa/97-553/table/t4-eng.cfm; www40.statcan.gc.ca/l01/cst01/demo24a-eng.htm; www.statcan.gc.ca/bsolc/olc-cel/olc-cel?catno=92-596-XWE&lang=eng; www.statcan.gc.ca/bsolc/olc-cel/olc-cel?catno=97-558-XWE2006002&lang=eng&lang=eng.

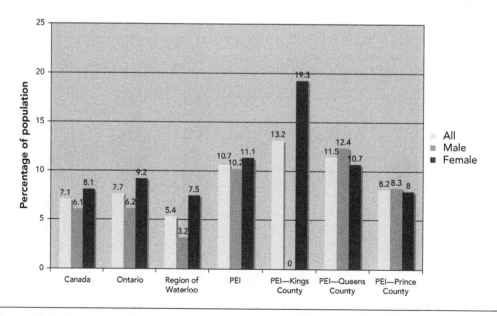

Figure 21.4 Percentage of the Population Reporting Moderate or Severe Food Insecurity in 2007, for Canada, Prince Edward Island and Its Counties, Ontario, and Region of Waterloo
Source: CCHS (2010).

and 8.1 per cent for females). In Ontario, the provincial average is 7.7 per cent (6.2 per cent for males and 9.2 per cent for females). In Waterloo Region, the rate is statistically significantly lower compared to both the national and provincial averages: 5.4 per cent (3.2 per cent for males and 7.5 per cent for females). Several points are worth highlighting. First, females generally tend to be more food insecure than males. Interestingly, this trend is reversed in PEI, where females are relatively more food secure than males. It is also noteworthy that Waterloo Region has the overall lowest rates of food insecurity with 5.4 per cent versus 7.7 per cent and 10.7 per cent for Ontario and PEI, respectively, and a national rate of 7.1 per cent.

With respect to personal and community health we consider five variables that reflect different aspects of the Canadian food system. With the exception of Waterloo Region, the percentage of people eating more than five fruits and vegetables a day increased between 2003 and 2009 (in Canada from 41.4 to 45.6; in Ontario from 41.9 to 44.1; in Waterloo Region from 45.1 to 41.1; and in PEI from 31.6 to 38.9) (Statistics Canada 2010). In all cases a lower percentage of males than females consume the recommended daily number of fruits and vegetables. A similar pattern is evident in measuring the percentage of those of both sexes who have a 'sense of community belonging', as there are increases for Canada (from 63.9 to 65.4), Ontario (from 64.4 to 67.1), and PEI (from 73.7 to 74.7) and a decrease for Waterloo Region (from 67.1 to

59.0, with a notable decline for men between 2007 and 2009 from 71.2 to 59.0) (Statistics Canada 2010).

Increasingly, food is recognized as being related to certain conditions and diseases, especially obesity and diabetes. Table 21.2 confirms much reported and disturbing news about the health of Canadians. At least 44.1 per cent (i.e., females in Waterloo Region) and up to 68.3 per cent (i.e., males in PEI) of the adult population are overweight or obese. While in PEI there have been slight shifts about the 60 per cent mark in the general population since 2003, all the other study groups have shown small increases since 2003. In all cases, men are more often overweight or obese than women.

While the percentage of Canadians with diabetes is low compared to that of overweight or obese people, the increases are worrisome. In several groupings, significant increases were identified. Between 2003 and 2009 the percentage of Canadians with diabetes increased: a 30 per cent increase for the general population (34.7 per cent for men and 23.3 per cent for women). In Waterloo Region, females were more likely to have diabetes than men. This case is striking, as the percentage of women with diabetes nearly tripled between 2003 and 2009. In the general Canadian population and in Ontario and PEI, men were more likely to have diabetes than women (CCHS 2010).

The final social dimension reported here relating to overall well-being is Canadians'

Table 21.2 Percentage of Overweight and Obese People, 18 Years and Over, for Canada, Ontario, Region of Waterloo, and Prince Edward Island, 2003–09

	Canada			Ontario			Region of Waterloo			Prince Edward Island		
	All	Males	Females	All	Males	Females	All	Males	Females	All	Males	Females
2003	49.4	57.3	41.3	49.4	56.2	41.6	50.1	59.0	41.0	59.7	69.8	49.4
2005	50.0	58.1	41.8	49.8	57.8	41.6	49.8	55.9	43.3	60.6	65.9	55.3
2007	50.8	58.8	42.9	51.6	59.6	43.6	56.9	65.6	47.5	60.0	69.4	50.8
2009	51.6	59.2	43.9	51.4	58.7	44.1	53.5	61.8	44.7	59.0	68.3	50.5

Source : Adapted from Statistics Canada CANSIM Database www5.statcan.gc.ca/cansim/a01?lang=eng, Table 105-0501.

level of activity (Table 21.3). Overall, more than half of Canadians are moderately active or active. In 2009, women in Canada (48.7 per cent) and Ontario (46.7 per cent) and men in Waterloo Region (49.4 per cent) are the exceptions. The most active group is Canadian males (56.4 per cent).

Economic Dimensions

While economic dimensions are not the sole consideration, they do factor strongly into Food Counts reporting. For present purposes we will consider three different indicators of food system economic well-being: (1) the amount of **redundant food trade**, i.e., imported food that could be produced locally (Maan Miedema 2006); (2) farmer income; and (3) the average cost of a food basket across communities. These three indicators point in turn to the market potential for local food; producers' income stability, and hence their viability and resilience; and the affordability of healthy food.

Redundant food trade is an important consideration for SFSs, as reducing redundant food imports and exports can reduce food transportation and related greenhouse gas (GHG) emissions. It also keeps more money in the local economy. For example, a California study found that marketing food in the global, conventional food system keeps about US$0.09 of each dollar

in the local economy, while farmers engaged in direct marketing retain US$0.80–0.90 (International Society for Ecology and Culture 2004 in Maan Miedema 2006: 3). For our study, the value of raw and processed food that is imported but could be produced locally was extracted from the North American Industrial Classification System codes (Figures 21.5 and 21.6). It is important to qualify these calculations by emphasizing that market conditions such as seasonal and varietal availability are not considered in this assessment (Maan Miedema 2006).[1] For example, while these numbers assume that all apples purchased could be grown in Ontario, some varieties (e.g., 'Pink Ladies') do not grow well in the province and must be imported. It was assumed that if the product could be grown locally but was imported, then a direct sale by a farmer or processor was foregone. It is also important to note that no attempt was made to determine if there were exports of the particular products over this period. As it is difficult to tease out these finer differences it is acknowledged that these numbers are rough estimates of the increasing potential for food localization. As such, they suggest that market opportunities could be exploited but are not intended to point to precise opportunities.

Food imports increased nationally and in Ontario, but declined in the Atlantic region. In Canada, the amount of redundant trade increased

Table 21.3 Physical Activity during Leisure Time (moderately active or active), 12 Years and Over, for Canada, Ontario, Region of Waterloo, and Prince Edward Island

	Canada			Ontario			Region of Waterloo			Prince Edward Island		
	All	Males	Females	All	Males	Females	All	Males	Females	All	Males	Females
2003	51.8	55.1	48.6	51.4	54.9	48.0	53.2	58.9	47.8	44.9	47.0	42.9
2005	52.2	54.8	49.7*	52.9*	56.2	49.6*	53.3	56.0	50.5	44.1	45.1	43.1
2007	50.4†	53.4†	47.6†	50.0†	53.4†	46.7†	46.5†	53.9	39.1†	48.4*	49.3	47.6
2009	52.5*	56.4*	48.7*	50.7	54.8	46.7	50.3	49.4	51.1	52.4	54.4	50.7

† a significant decrease from the previous reporting period
* a significant increase from the previous reporting period

Source: Adapted from Statistics Canada CANSIM Database www5.statcan.gc.ca/cansim/a01?lang=eng, Table 105-0501.

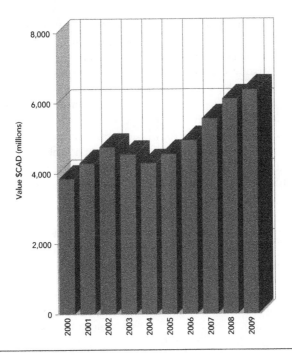

Figure 21.5 Canadian Food Imports, Redundant Trade for 82 Selected NAICS Codes Excluding Milk and Powdered Milk, 2000–09

Source: Industry Canada - Trade data online 2010, Figure 228-001, www.ic.gc.ca/sc_mrkti/tdst/tdo/tdo.php#tag. Reproduced with the permission of the Minister of Public Works and Government Services Canada, 2012.

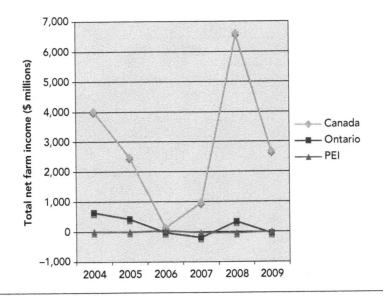

Figure 21.6 Total Net Farm Income for Canada, Ontario, and Prince Edward Island, 2004–2009

Source: Statistics Canada CANSIM database http://cansim2.statcan.gc.ca, Table 002–0009, date of extraction.

from $3.8 billion in 2000 to $6.4 billion in 2009 (Figure 21.5). In Ontario, it rose from $2.2 billion in 2000 to $4.1 billion in 2009. The pattern is reversed in Atlantic Canada, where imports fell from slightly over $102 million in 2000 to under $75 million in 2009.

When we look at farm income over time we find huge variation in Canada (Figure 21.6). In 2006, total net farm income was close to zero while in 2008, during the world food crisis, net income spiked to over $6.5 billion. Provincially, the numbers are less erratic; however, in both Ontario and PEI they hover near zero. In Ontario the number dipped into negative territory in 2007, while in PEI numbers were consistently at or below zero. These data confirm the existence of the farm income crisis; the National Farmers Union points out that recent farm income levels are near the levels during the 1930s Depression (National Farmers Union 2007).

Food costs have also risen[2] (Figure 21.7). The cost of purchasing a nutritious food basket in Ontario rose from $122.50 in 2003 to $139.26 in 2008—a 12 per cent increase over five years. The same trend is evident in Waterloo Region, where the cost increased 20.3 per cent over the same period. While the cost of a nutritious food basket has been tracked only for Ontario, it is reasonable to extrapolate that the Ontario increases would be paralleled across the country. Based on a Diabetes Canada national food-cost survey, we expect that the cost of the food basket would be higher in many parts of the country, as some Ontario cities surveyed frequently have lower food costs for such items as apples, potatoes, whole wheat pasta, brown rice, 1-per-cent milk, cheddar cheese, lean ground beef, and peanut butter (HSFC 2009). As comparable data is not available for PEI or federally, we cannot comment on these trends.

Linked to rising food costs is the affordability of healthy food such as fruits and vegetables, which are more expensive than processed food (HSFC 2009). This problem is compounded by

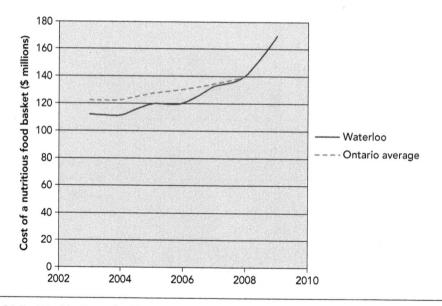

Figure 21.7 Weekly Cost of a Nutritious Food Basket for a Family of Four, for Ontario (average) and Region of Waterloo

Source: Stewart (2009); Region of Waterloo Public Health (2009).

the decreasing household spending capacity that accompanies increasing unemployment rates (Figure 21.8). As we can see, unemployment spiked upward in 2009, and although it trended downward in 2010, it is nowhere near the rates earlier in the decade. In PEI we see chronically higher levels of unemployment. In Waterloo Region, thought to be 'recession-proof' due to its high-tech economy, unemployment spiked higher than the Ontario and Canadian rates as a result of the 2008 economic recession.

While the LICOs numbers are not available for 2009 and 2010, we can assume that they did not fall below the levels earlier in the decade. Given that many groups identified through LICOs are more vulnerable than others to economic stresses (Figure 21.3) it is reasonable to infer that these groups would have increasing difficulty in obtaining healthy food in recent years. This inference is indirectly confirmed by the increasing number of people who accessed

food banks in 2009 (Table 21.4). Across Canada and in Ontario, fewer people used food banks between 2004 and 2008, but in 2009 food bank use returned to rates comparable with those of 1999. While PEI numbers increased in the middle of the decade, they are now close to 1999 levels.

Ecological Dimensions

This section reports selected data related to overall ecological health. Indicators include protected areas, general data about the number of farms and whether they are rented or owned, agricultural inputs and their associated greenhouse gas emissions, and the amount of irrigated land. These indicators reflect the relative (in)attention to sustainability through the level of mindfulness to biodiversity, capacity for stewardship, and the impact of food production on land, air, and water.

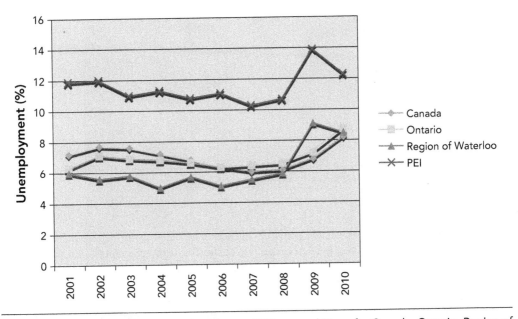

Figure 21.8 Unemployment Rates for Persons 15 Years and Over, for Canada, Ontario, Region of Waterloo, and Prince Edward Island, 2001–10

Source: Statistics Canada (2010).

Table 21.4 Number of Individuals Assisted by Food Banks, March of Each Year, 1999–2009

	Canada	Ontario	Prince Edward Island
1999	718,292	277,207	2,602
2000	726,902	283,110	3,541
2001	708,334	278,543	2,657
2002	737,665	295,228	2,800
2003	776,783	308,452	3,118
2004	803,335	322,911	3,150
2005	786,968	338,563	3,208
2006	744,055	330,491	3,260
2007	703,051	318,540	2,811
2008	675,735	314,258	2,892
2009	794,738	374,230	2,706

Source: Adapted from Statistics Canada CANSIM Database www5.statcan.gc.ca/cansim/a01?lang=eng, Table 105-0501.

Table 21.5 Total Size and Percentage of Federal and Provincial Government-Protected Areas for Canada, Ontario, and Prince Edward Island, as of 30 July 2010

	Terrestrial	Marine
Canada		
total area protected (ha)	97,452,078	4,393,509
% protected	9.64%	0.78%
Ontario		
total area protected (ha)	10,646,531	
% of protected	9.89%	
Prince Edward Island		
total area protected (ha)	15,862	726
% of protected	2.80%	N/A

Source: Canadian Council on Ecological Areas. 2010. Carts Reports: www.ccea.org/en_cartsreports.html.

In the three study areas, national and provincial indicators show that up to nearly 10 per cent of the land or water is protected (Table 21.5), with much more land than marine areas being conserved.

On the food production front, the number of farms either remained the same or decreased between 2001 and 2006. At the same time the amount of land being farmed also declined. This decrease could be interpreted as a positive sign that more land was being returned to a natural state. It could, however, be interpreted as signalling that more land fell into development. The amount of land rented for agricultural production increased in all of the study areas. This could be a problem, as a farmer renting land

Table 21.6 GHG Emissions from Agriculture by Production System for Canada for Selected Years[1]

Production System	GHG Emissions (megatonnes CO_2 equivalent)						
	1990	1996	2001	2005	2006	2007	2008
Agriculture (Total)	48.0	56.0	58.0	62.0	61.0	61.0	62.0
Livestock	30.0	36.0	40.0	42.0	41.0	41.0	40.0
Dairy Cows	5.2	4.9	4.6	4.5	4.4	4.3	4.5
Beef Cattle	21.0	27.0	30.0	32.0	31.0	31.0	30.0
Swine	2.4	2.6	3.2	3.5	3.4	3.3	2.9
Other Livestock[2]	1.5	1.7	2.2	2.2	2.2	2.2	2.2
Crop	18.0	19.0	18.0	19.0	19.0	21.0	23.0
Synthetic Nitrogen Fertilizers	9.2	11.0	12.0	11.0	11.0	13.0	13.0
Crop Residue Decomposition	7.1	6.8	5.6	7.6	7.9	7.6	9.1
Other Management Practices[3]	1.8	1.5	0.86	0.54	0.45	0.35	0.17

1. Totals may not add up due to rounding.
2. Other livestock includes sheep, lamb, goat, horse, bison, poultry, llama, and alpacas.
3. Other management practices include summer fallow, conservation tillage practices, irrigation, and cultivation of organic soils.

Source: National Inventory Report: 1990-2008, Part , page 59, Table 2-9, Environment Canada, 2010. Reproduced with the permission of the Minister of Public Works and Government Services Canada, 2012.

may be less committed to environmental stewardship than an owner would be, because of either financial constraints or lack of a long-term bond with the land.

The amount of land where herbicides are applied decreased across the study areas from 2000 to 2005, except for Waterloo Region, where application increased by 6.8 per cent. In Canada, insecticide, fungicide, and commercial fertilizer applications rose 7.6 per cent, 11.2 per cent, and 5.6 per cent respectively. Ontario witnessed huge increases in the number of hectares being sprayed with insecticides and fungicides—41.3 per cent and 36.3 per cent—with a modest increase in commercial fertilizer applications of 8.2 per cent (Statistics Canada n.d. 2001, 2006 Census of Agriculture).

Agriculture is both a source of and a sink for GHG (a GHG sink takes the gases out of the atmosphere). While no data is currently available at the regional or provincial scale, nationally agriculture produced 8.5 per cent of GHG emissions in 2008,

up by 29 per cent since 1990 (Environment Canada 2010: 59) (Table 21.6). Increasingly agriculture is also a GHG sink, through soil management practices such as no-tillage. In 2008, arable land in Canada provided 4,400 kt CO_2 equivalent in sink capacity (ibid.).

Water usage for agricultural irrigation increased between 2000 and 2005 across the study areas. Waterloo Region, while still using very little water, more than tripled its use of water for irrigation (Statistics Canada n.d., 2006 Census of Agriculture).

Conclusion

Phase One of the Food Counts project as reported in this chapter points to several possible areas for improvement in the food system. Given the linkages between decreased access to healthy food, declining incomes related to increased unemployment, and more people in the LICO groups, areas for intervention become more clearly focused. Generally, males are more food insecure than women; this tendency points to another space for improvement. Overall, fruit and vegetable consumption, sense of community belonging, and physical activity levels are moving in a positive direction, although numbers need to continue to improve across the board. Obesity and diabetes are growing problems and require urgent attention in all jurisdictions. The economic analysis points to opportunities for increased consumption of locally produced and processed food. This is good news and offers hope for farmers facing chronic income crises. For consumers, food costs have risen—especially for healthy food. Given the data on family incomes, food bank use, and unemployment, this trend is of particular concern. On the ecological front, there are mixed results. Land under conservation is increasing, although historical data are not available. On-farm data also show mixed results. Herbicide use is generally lower from 2000 to 2005, but use of insecticide, fungicide, and commercial fertilizers is on the rise, with an increase in one case of nearly 150 per cent. The number of farms is declining while land rental is increasing. This trend points to increasing mechanization as farms get larger. It also signals fewer opportunities for environmental stewardship. Finally, data on increasing rates of food imports indicates increased food miles as more food comes into Canada that could be produced locally.

One of the next challenges for the Food Counts project is to determine how to present the data in a report card format so that overall trends can be indicated. There is a danger in taking so much information and boiling it down into palatable sound bites. Several models from the United Kingdom and the United States are being considered for the report card, including work by Defra.

As made clear earlier in the chapter, data is not neutral (Hacking 2007; Larner and LeHeron 2002b). The data presented in this chapter is

no exception. First, the indicators reported highlight weaknesses in data availability. For example the food security data in Figure 21.4 is an excellent example of the micro-level data that is critical for relevant intervention. In Figure 21.4 the county-level data for PEI points to food-insecure males in Queen and Prince counties who would be overlooked if only provincial data were used to develop intervention programs. This emphasizes the need for access to more refined levels of data and more comprehensive data collection. While Canada has been considered a world leader in data collection, current policy directions that threaten to reduce the reliability of data need to be carefully scrutinized.

Caution is also needed in drawing boundaries around categories such as economics and environment, as there is so much overlap. For example, is food insecurity an indicator of social or of economic challenges? Its immediate cause is families lacking the money to feed themselves properly, but the roots of food insecurity are buried deeply in matters of social justice and equity.

The Food Counts project, as do similar initiatives, tends to raise more questions than it answers. For example, Food Counts points to interesting differences between communities at multiple scales and provokes questions about community-based urban–rural and gender issues related to food security. These are questions that we can dig into through more targeted research. This is one goal of Phase 2, when we will supplement existing sources with our own data collection, gathering information about, for example, the number of community gardens, rooftop gardens, and community-supported agriculture projects. Phase Two will add to existing work on best practices and models. While the Food Counts project does not provide answers, it does point to areas for future research. Equally importantly, it makes the point that SFSs are incredibly complex and need to be considered from a multidisciplinary and multisectoral perspective for progress to occur.

Discussion Questions

1. How can indicators make an important contribution to our understanding of SFSs?

2. Do the indicators in this chapter capture key dimensions of an SFS? What indicators would you add to make this analysis more comprehensive?

3. Are Canada, PEI, and Waterloo Region making progress or falling behind as reflected by the indicators for socio-communal, economic, and ecological well-being?

4. Do indicators contribute to broader conversations about sustainability?

Further Reading

1. Friedmann, H. 2007. 'Scaling Up: Bringing Public Institutions and Food Service Corporations into the Project for a Local, Sustainable Food System in Ontario'. *Agriculture and Human Values* 34(2): 389–98.

   This paper provides an excellent case study of scaling up local food system capacity through the activation of institutional procurement that is embedded in a locale with a track record of food-related health and social justice initiatives.

2. Marsden, T., Lee, R. Flynn, A., and Thankappan, S. 2010. *The New Regulation and Governance of Food: Beyond the Food Crisis?* Routledge: London.

   This book provides excellent insights into the regulatory challenges that have shaped the current food system in the United Kingdom. It provides valuable insights for other jurisdictions building towards more sustainable food systems.

3. Morgan, K., Marsden, T., and Murdoch, J. 2008. *Worlds of Food: Place, Power and Provenance in the Food Chain.* Oxford University Press: London.

   From farm to fork, the conventional food chain is under enormous pressure to respond to a whole series of new challenges—food scares in rich countries, food security concerns in poor countries, and a burgeoning problem of obesity in all countries. As more and more people demand to know where their food comes from and how it is produced, issues of place, power, and provenance assume increasing significance for producers, consumers, and regulators, challenging the corporate forces that shape the 'placeless foodscape'.

4. Morgan, K., and Sonnino, R. 2008. *The School Food Revolution: Public Food and the Challenge of Sustainable Development.* Earthscan: London.

   School food suddenly finds itself at the forefront of contemporary debates about healthy eating, social inclusion, ecological sustainability, and local economic development. All around the world it is becoming clear—to experts, parents, educators, practitioners and policy makers—that the school food service can deliver multiple dividends that would significantly advance the sustainable development agenda at global, national, and local levels.

5. Roberts, W. 2008. *The No Nonsense Guide to World Food.* Between the Lines: Toronto.

   Roberts connects the dots in the often disjointed realm of food security. Through engaging anecdotes and examples, this book takes you on a whirlwind journey connecting health, institutions, fast food, organics, and community well-being to bring the critical issues related to food security into sharp focus.

Notes

1. Thanks to the excellent graduate student research support from Mike Nagy and Paula Bryk. We also acknowledge the support from the community, especially the Region of Waterloo Food Systems Roundtable, and individuals who worked on the Toronto Food Strategy. This project is funded by the Canadian Social Sciences and Humanities Research Council (SSHRC). Thank you also to Mustafa Koç, Jennifer Sumner, and Anthony Winson for making this volume possible.
2. Thank you to Dr MacRae for clarifying important market, breeding, and consumer preferences constraints in considering this variable.
3. The cost of the 2009 Nutritious Food Basket is 10.8 per cent higher; using the new Protocol (2008) it is $169.41, compared to $152.94 using the former Protocol (1998). Using the former Protocol (1998), the cost of the Nutritious Food Basket for the Region of Waterloo increased by 8.3 per cent compared to 2008, and by 26.6 per cent from 2007 to 2009 (Region of Waterloo Public Health 2009).

References

Anderson, M. 2009. *Charting Growth: Developing Indicators and Measures of Good Food.* Wallace Center. Accessed 9 January 2011 at www.wallacecenter.org/our-work/current-initiatives/sustainable-food-indicators/sustainable-indicators-report/CHARTING%20GROWTH%20BOOK%20final%20with%20charts.pdf.

Blay-Palmer, A. (ed). 2010. *Imagining Sustainable Food Systems: Theory and Practice.* Aldershot, UK: Ashgate.

Blay-Palmer, A., and M. Koç. 2010. 'Imagining Sustainable Food Systems: The Path to Regenerative Food Systems'. In Blay-Palmer, *Imagining Sustainable Food Systems*, 223–47.

Canadian Community Health Survey (CCHS). 2010. Statistics Canada. Accessed 9 January 2011 at www.statcan.gc.ca/cgi-bin/imdb/p2SV.pl?Function=getSurvey&SDDS=3226&lang=en&db=imdb&adm=8&dis=2.

Canadian Council on Ecological Areas. 2010. Carts Reports. Accessed 9 January 2011 at www.ccea.org/en_cartsreports.html.

Chambers, R., and G. Conway. 1992. *Sustainable Rural Livelihoods: Practical Concepts for the 21st Century.* IDS Discussion Paper 296. Brighton, UK: IDS.

Chi, K., MacGregor, J., and R. King. 2009. 'Big Ideas in Development. Fair Miles: Recharting the Food Miles Map'. IIED and Oxfam. Accessed 9 January 2011 at http://pubs.iied.org/pdfs/15516IIED.pdf.

Clapp, J., and M. Cohen (eds). 2009. *The Global Food Crisis: Governance Challenges and Opportunities.* Waterloo, ON: Wilfrid Laurier University Press.

Costanza, R., R. d'Arge et al. 1997. 'The Value of the World's Ecosystem Services and Natural Capital'. *Nature* 387: 253–60.

Costanza, R., B. Fisher et al. 2007. 'Quality of Life: An Approach Integrating Opportunities, Human Needs, and Subjective Well-being'. *Ecological Economics* 61: 267–76.

Costanza, R., M. Hart, S. Posner, and J. Talberth. 2009. *Beyond GDP: The Need for New Measures of Progress.* Boston University, The Frederick S. Pardee Center for the Study of the Longer-Range Future. *The Pardee Papers*, No. 4, January 2009. Accessed 26 June 2010 at www.oecd.org/dataoecd/29/6/42613423.pdf.

Dahlberg, K. 1993. 'Regenerative Food Systems: Broadening the Scope and Agenda of Sustainability'. In *Food for the Future: Conditions and Contradictions of Sustainability*, ed. P. Allen. New York: Wiley & Sons, 75–102.

Defra (Department for Environment, Food and Rural Affairs). 2009. *First Report from the Council of Food Policy Advisors.* Accessed 9 January 2011 at www.defra.gov.uk/foodfarm/food/policy/council/pdf/cfpa-rpt-090914.pdf.

———. 2010. *Food 2030.* Report prepared for HM Government. Accessed 5 August 2010 at http://archive.defra.gov.uk/foodfarm/food/pdf/food2030strategy.pdf.

Desjardins, E. 2010. 'The Urban Food Desert: Spatial Inequality or Opportunity for Change'. In Blay-Palmer, *Imagining Sustainable Food Systems*, 87–114.

Donald, B. 2008. 'Food Systems Planning and Sustainable Cities and Regions: The Role of the Firm in Sustainable Food Capitalism'. *Regional Studies* 42(9): 1251–62.

Environment Canada. 2010. *National Inventory Report: 1990–2008. Part 1, Greenhouse Gas Sources and Sinks in Canada.* Accessed 14 August 2010 at www.ec.gc.ca/publications/492D914C-2EAB-47AB-A045-C62B2CDACC29/NationalInventoryReport19902008GreenhouseGasSourcesAndSinksInCanada.pdf.

Europa Glossary. N.d. Available at http://europa.eu/legislation_summaries/glossary/index_en.htm.

Feenstra, G., C. Jaramillo, S. McGrath, and A. Grunnell. 2005. *Proposed Indicators for Sustainable Food Systems.* Ecotrust—Vivid Picture Project.

Food Banks Canada. 2010. *HungerCount—Selected Information from 1999–2009.* Accessed 13 August 2010 at http://foodbankscanada.ca/main2.cfm?id=107185CB-B6A7–8AA0–6FE6B5477106193A.

Friedmann, H. 2005. 'Feeding the Empire: The Pathologies of Globalized Agriculture'. In *The Empire Reloaded: Socialist Register 2005*, ed. L. Panitch and C. Leys. London: Merlin Press, 124–43.

Friedmann, H. 2007. 'Scaling Up: Bringing Public Institutions and Food Service Corporations into the Project for a Local, Sustainable Food System in Ontario'. *Agriculture and Human Values* 34(2): 389–98.

———. 2009. 'Discussion: Moving Food Regimes Forward: Reflections on Symposium Essays'. *Agriculture and Human Values* 26: 335–44.

Getz, A. 1991. 'Urban Foodsheds'. *The Permaculture Activist* 24: 26–7.

Hacking, I. 2007. 'Kinds of People: Moving Targets'. *Proceedings of the British Academy* 151: 285–318.

Hamm, M., and A. Bellows. 2003. 'Community Food Security and Nutrition Educators'. *Journal of Nutrition Education Behavior* 35: 37–43.

Heart and Stroke Foundation of Canada (HSFC) 2009. *What's in Store for Canada's Heart Health?* Accessed 12 August 2010 at www.newswire.ca/en/releases/archive/February2009/09/c6632.html.

Hinrichs, C., and T. Lyson. (eds). 2008. *Remaking the North American Food System*. Lincoln, NB: University of Nebraska Press.

IPC Food Sovereignty. 2009. 'Food Sovereignty'. Available at www.foodsovereignty.org/new/.

Larner, W., and R. LeHeron. 2002a. 'From Economic Globalisation to Globalising Economic Processes: Towards Post-Structuralist Political Economies'. *Geoforum* 33: 415–19.

———. 2002b. 'The Spaces and Subjects of a Globalizing Economy: A Situated Exploration of Method'. *Environment and Planning D: Society and Space* 20: 753–74.

Levitte, Y. 2010. Thinking about Labour in Alternative Food Systems. In Blay-Palmer, *Imagining Sustainable Food Systems*, 71–86.

Lyson, T. 2008. Civic Agriculture and the North American Food System. In C. Hinrichs and T. Lyson (eds.). *Remaking the North American Food System*. Lincoln, NB: University of Nebraska Press, 19–32.

Maan Miedema, J. 2006. *Neighbourhood Markets Initiative*. Report prepared for the Region of Waterloo Public Health.

McGregor, A. 2006. *Researching Wellbeing: From Concepts to Methodology*. WeD Working Paper 20. ESRC Research Group on Wellbeing in Developing Countries. Accessed 26 June 2010 at www.welldev.org.uk/research/workingpaperpdf/wed20.pdf.

McMichael, P. 2009. 'A Food Regime Analysis of the "World Food Crisis"'. *Agriculture and Human Values* 26: 281–95.

Marsden, T. (ed.). 2008. *Sustainable Communities: New Spaces for Planning, Participation and Engagement*. London: Elsevier.

———. 2010. 'Mobilising the Region Eco-economy: Evolving Webs of Agri-food and Rural Development in the UK'. *Cambridge Journal of Regions, Economy and Society* 3: 225–44.

Marsden, T., R. Lee, A. Flynn, and S. Thankappan. 2010. *The New Regulation and Governance of Food: Beyond the Food Crisis?* London: Routledge.

Morgan, K., T. Marsden, and J. Murdoch. 2008. *Worlds of Food: Place, Power and Provenance in the Food Chain*. London: Oxford University Press.

Morgan, K., and R. Sonnino. 2008. *The School Food Revolution: Public Food and the Challenge of Sustainable Development*. London: Earthscan.

——— and ———. 2010. 'The Urban Foodscape: World Cities and the New Food Equation'. *Cambridge Journal of Regions, Economy and Society* 3: 209–24.

National Farmers Union. 2007. *Farm Income Crisis and the Next Generation Agricultural Policy Framework*. Presented to the House of Commons Standing Committee on Agriculture and Agri-Food. Accessed 4 September 2010 at www.nfu.ca/briefs/2007/Ontario_Farm_Income_brief_to_Parliamentary_Ag_Committee.pdf.

Padanyi, P., and L. Varangu. 2010. 'Hospital Food Systems: Assessing the Capacity to Go Local'. Presentation at *Future of Food in Healthcare* conference, Ottawa, 15 October.

Region of Waterloo Public Health. 2009. *Nutritious Food Basket in Waterloo Region 2009*. NFB Factsheet Sept 09 Waterloo Region, Document #668283, v.3. Accessed 11 August 2010 at http://chd.region.waterloo.on.ca/web/health.nsf/vwSiteMap/649B410D689BEA2E8525713B0069B429/$file/Nutritious%20Food%20Basket_09.pdf?openelement.

Region of Waterloo. 2010. *LICOS RWPH: From RW VitalSigns*. Available at www.wrvitalsigns.ca/thegap#median.

Rifkin, J. 2010. *The Empathic Civilization*. Cambridge: Polity Press.

Roberts, W. 2008. *The No Nonsense Guide to World Food*. Toronto: Between the Lines.

St Jacques, H. 2010. 'The Nexus between Alternative Food Systems and Entrepreneurism: Three Local Stories'. In Blay-Palmer, *Imagining Sustainable Food Systems*, 135–56.

Scoones, I. 1998. *Sustainable Rural Livelihoods: A Framework for Analysis*. IDS Working paper 72. Accessed 15 August 2010 at www.ids.ac.uk/download.cfm?file=wp72.pdf.

Statistics Canada. n.d. 2001 Census of Agriculture. Accessed 9 January 2012 at www.statcan.gc.ca/ca-ra2001/index-eng.htm.

———. n.d. 2006 Census of Agriculture. Accessed 9 January 2012 at http://statcan.gc.ca/ca-ra2006/.

———. n.d. Food import Data, NAICS codes, 'Merchandise imports and exports, by major groups and principal trading areas for all countries, monthly (dollars) (592 series)'. CANSIM Table 228-0001. Available at www5.statcan.gc.ca/cansim/a05?lang=eng&rid=2280001.

———. n.d. 'Health indicator profile, annual estimates, by age group and sex, Canada, provinces, territories, health regions (2007 boundaries) and peer groups, occasional (1382400 series)'. CANSIM Table 105–0501. Available at www5.statcan.gc.ca/cansim/a05?lang=eng&rid=1050501

———. n.d. 'Household food insecurity measures, by living arrangement, Canada, provinces and territories, occasional (number unless otherwise noted)'. CANSIM Table 105–0545. Available at www5.statcan.gc.ca/cansim/a05?lang=eng&rid=1050545.

———. n.d. 'Income Trends in Canada 1976 to 2007'. Catalogue no. 13F0022XIE. Table 202–0802. Available at www.statcan.gc.ca/pub/13f0022x/13f0022x2007000-eng.htm.

———. n.d. 'Unemployment rate, Canada, provinces, health regions and peer groups, annual (percent) (328 series)'. CANSIM Table 109–5304. Available at www5.statcan.gc.ca/cansim/a05?lang=eng&rid=1095304.

———. 2006. 'Major Withdrawal Uses of Water. Total Intake'. Catalogue no. 16–201-X.

———. 2009. 'Financial Security—Low Income Incidence'. (LICOs provincial data). Indicators of Well-being in Canada. Accessed 13 August 2010 at www4.hrsdc.gc.ca/.3ndic.1t.4r@-eng.jsp?iid=23.

———. 2010. 2006 Census Data Products. Accessed 13 August 2010 at www12.statcan.gc.ca/census-recensement/2006/dp-pd/index-eng.cfm.

Stewart, L. 2009. 'Nutritious Food Basket Survey—Update February 2009'. Report prepared for Association of Local Public Health Agencies (alPHa). Accessed 12 August 2010 at www.alphaweb.org/files/NFB%20Summary%20Report_2009apr.pdf.

Stiglitz, J., Sen. A., and J.P. Fitoussi. 2009. *Report by the Commission on the Measurement of Economic Performance and Social Progress*. France. Accessed 9 January 2011 at www.stiglitz-sen-fitoussi.fr/documents/rapport_anglais.pdf.

United Nations. 1992. *The Rio Declaration, Agenda 21, Chapter 14*. Accessed 9 January 2012 at www.unep.org/Documents.Multilingual/Default.Print.asp?DocumentID=52&ArticleID=62.

Waddell, S. 2005. *Societal Learning and Change*. Sheffield, UK: Greenleaf Publishing.

Wilkins, J. 2004. Eating Right Here: Moving from Consumer to Food Citizen. 2004 Presidential Address to the Agriculture, Food and Human Values Society, Hyde Park, New York, 11 June. *Agriculture, Food and Human Values* 22(3): 269–73.

World Commission on Environment and Development (WCED). 1986. *Our Common Future*. Report of the World Commission on Environment and Development (Brundtland Commission). Accessed 9 January 2011 at www.un-documents.net/wced-ocf.htm.

Building Food Sovereignty
A Radical Framework for Alternative Food Systems
Annette Aurélie Desmarais

Learning Objectives

Through this chapter, you can:

1. Appreciate the limitations of the idea and practice of food security
2. Understand the importance of a radical alternative like food sovereignty
3. Raise awareness of the key elements of food sovereignty

Introduction

When the 2007–8 food crisis triggered food riots and hit the national headlines in many countries, the official **food security** response was 'more of the same' (Claeys 2009: 2)—that is, an emphasis on increasing global production, productivity, and liberalized trade, and pursuing another green revolution through the greater use of genetically modified organisms (GMOs) in agricultural production (*The Economist* 2008a, 2008b, and 2009). Vía Campesina, on the other hand, argued that the food crisis—now linked to the economic and environmental crisis—is the direct result of decades of destructive policies that spurred the globalization of a **neo-liberal** industrial and corporate-led model of agriculture and that 'the time for **food sovereignty** has come' (Vía Campesina, 2008a: 7).

Vía Campesina is an international **peasant** movement bringing together 148 organizations based in 69 countries in the Americas, Europe, Asia, and Africa. Many now consider it to be the world's most politically significant 'transnational agrarian movement' (Borras et al. 2008: 172), in large part because of its radical resistance to the globalization of a neo-liberal model of agriculture and the way in which it is working to expand, further define, and disseminate the idea and practice of food sovereignty (Desmarais 2007, Borras and Franco 2010, Martínez-Torres and Rosset 2010).

Food sovereignty is also being discussed in Canada.[1] Farm organizations like the National Farmers Union and the Union Paysanne in Quebec, both members of Vía Campesina, increasingly use the food sovereignty framework to define and argue for more sustainable farm policies and socially just rural development programs in Canada and elsewhere. And, in a session of the government of Canada's Standing Committee on Agriculture and Agri-Food Canada held on 27 February 2007,[2] after having heard the testimony of seven witnesses well versed with the issues facing rural Canada, André Bellavance, a Member of Parliament from Quebec, commented:

> It has to be said, there is a crisis in agriculture. It's an income crisis. Immediately following the 2006 elections, thousands of agricultural producers came to Parliament Hill. I was there, along with agricultural producers from my riding. . . . I have the feeling that we are at a crossroads. There's a political choice to be made. What kind of agriculture do we want? Do we still want family farming? Do we believe in it? And if that is what we want, then we need to take the necessary steps to ensure that this type of agriculture lasts. [Or,] do we prefer an industrial agriculture? (quoted in Standing Committee on Agriculture and Agri-Food 2007)

These are precisely the questions that many Canadians, along with millions of people around the world, are posing: Do citizens want a globalized industrial model of agriculture that is increasingly dominated by corporate interests? Or, do we want a model of agriculture that is based on food sovereignty, a model that, among other things, keeps people on the land and able to make their livelihoods from farming, and provides nutritious and safe food? These questions reflect two visions of agriculture and food and point to a very real political struggle over two competing—and in many ways diametrically opposed—models of social and economic development.

While others in this book have critiqued the Canadian food system (see, for example, chapters 7, 12, and 20), this chapter explores the roots, meanings, challenges, and potential of food sovereignty as a radical alternative to the corporate-led, neo-liberal, industrial model of agriculture.

Going beyond Sustainability and Food Security—Food Sovereignty

Food sovereignty did not surface in a vacuum. A brief examination of the political, social,

and economic context in which it emerged sheds light on the specific content of the food sovereignty alternative.

Concepts, however revolutionary, are often misinterpreted, misused, and usurped by those in positions of power. Consider, for example, the concept of 'sustainable agriculture'. Originally embracing a conscious move away from capital-intensive, high-input, monoculture agriculture, the idea and practice of sustainable agriculture reflected a profound respect for ecology; it focused on local production for local consumption and required environmentally friendly practices such as, among others, integrated pest management, organic or low-input and small-scale agricultural production, and polyculture. However, over a relatively short time the term acquired new meaning as international institutions— the World Bank, the International Fund for Agricultural Development, the United Nations Commission on Sustainable Development, and the Global Forum on Agricultural Research, and others—and national governments integrated environmental concerns into their policies and programs as a result of the Report of the World Commission on Environment and Development (1987) called *Our Common Future*, commonly known as the Brundtland Commission Report.

In effect, the 'greening' of the rural development discourse occurred within a wholehearted embrace of a free-market ideology. Nowhere is this more evident than in the Brundtland Commission Report's definition of 'sustainable development':

> Humanity has the ability to make development sustainable—to ensure that it meets the needs of the present without compromising the ability of future generations to meet their own needs. The concept of sustainable development does imply limits—not absolute limits but limitations imposed by the present state of technology and social organization on environmental resources and by the ability of the biosphere to absorb the effects of human activities. But technology and social organization can

be both managed and improved to make way for a new era of economic growth. (World Commission on Environment and Development 1987: 16)

Indeed, it was the report's call for worldwide economic growth that governments and major players in international development readily embraced, thus ensuring that sustainable development quickly became synonymous with economic growth, or better yet, *sustained economic growth.*[3] Subsequently, power-holders re-envisioned 'sustainability' in the practice of sustainable agriculture as the successful integration of food and agriculture into a global marketplace.[4]

Tied to this development were important shifts in the meaning and practice of the concept of 'food security'. The World Food Conference of 1974, using the language of food security, sought to resolve the growing world food crisis through state involvement at the national and international levels to, among other things, establish the conditions for adequate production of food and reasonable prices. Thus, the international community understood that state intervention in the market was an important element of global food security (Fairbairn 2010: 22–3). However, over a short time, this state-centric approach to food security was successfully displaced by the market-oriented neo-liberal framework. By the early 1990s, food was considered a commodity and food security was re-conceptualized as 'household food security' with a focus on the individual's purchasing power, a decreased role for national governments, increased power for transnational corporations and international institutions, and the prioritization of market liberalization over social concerns (Fairbairn 2010).

As governments restructured their economies through increased trade liberalization, privatization, deregulation, and public sector reform, rural landscapes everywhere were dramatically altered. In agriculture, this shift meant increasing production for export at the expense of production for domestic consumption, dismantling numerous state-supported mechanisms that had helped to ensure the survival of peasant families and small farmers, and substantially decreasing government budgets for agricultural research and extension services, while introducing legislation that enabled the concentration of agricultural resources and markets into the hands of fewer and larger landowners and agri-business corporations.[5] Perhaps most importantly, with the signing of the Uruguay Round of the GATT in 1994 that created the **World Trade Organization (WTO)**, all agricultural policies now had to comply with regional trade and WTO agreements.

The WTO's **Agreement on Agriculture** reflected the belief that food security could best be reached by increasing agricultural trade accompanied by expanding the power of the WTO in global governance over food, genetic resources, natural resources, and agricultural markets. This fit well with the WTO's view of food security that increasingly emphasized ensuring access to an 'adequate supply of imported food' (Stevens et al. 2000: 3). In the speech to the World Food Summit: Five Years Later held in Rome in June 2002, Miguel Rodriguez Mendoza, Deputy Director-General of the WTO, put it like this:

> History has shown that food security does not equal self-sufficiency of a country. It has more to do with international trade in food products that makes them available at competitive prices and sets the right incentives for those countries where they can be produced most efficiently. Food shortages have to do with poverty rather than with being a net food importer. Food security nowadays lies not only in the local production of food, but in a country's ability to finance imports of food through exports of other goods. (Mendoza 2002: 1)

The current definition of food security, according to the United Nations Food and Agriculture Organization (FAO) is 'a situation that exists when all people, at all times, have physical, social and economic access to sufficient, safe and nutritious food that meets their dietary needs and food preferences for an active and healthy life' (FAO 2003: 28). As laudable as this goal of food security might be, Raj Patel (2010: 187) argues because 'neo-liberal triumphalism' reigned in political decision making, this definition indicates that the international community was no longer prepared to specify what domestic and international political arrangements were necessary to create the conditions for food security to actually be realized. Instead, in Patel's (2010: 188) words,

the terms on which food is, or isn't, made available by the international community have been taken away from institutions [such as the United Nations Food and Agriculture Organization] that might be oriented by concerns of food security and given to the market, which is guided by an altogether different calculus.

The concept of food sovereignty emerged as peasants and small-scale farmers struggled to survive in this much harsher political and economic environment that effectively threatened their very modes of existence. As peasants and farmers were being driven off the land, rural impoverishment was on the rise, and environmental degradation worsened, organizations of peasants from the global South and small- to medium-scale farmers in the North gathered together to form Vía Campesina to work together and develop an alternative model of agriculture.

Vía Campesina discussed food sovereignty at its Second International Conference held on 18–21 April 1996, in Tlaxcala, Mexico. Peasant and farm leaders who gathered there argued that 'food security' did little to change the existing inequitable structures and policies that were destroying livelihoods and environments in the countryside in both North and South. Instead, Vía Campesina (1996a: 21) defined an altogether different approach: food sovereignty—a

framework 'directly linked to democracy and justice', a framework that exposed the power dimensions so central to the ongoing agriculture debate, and put the control of productive resources (land, water, seeds, and natural resources) in the hands of those who produce food. As Nettie Wiebe, former member of the International Coordination Commission of Vía Campesina, recalls:

Food sovereignty . . . was our way of differentiating our agenda from that liberalized agenda and it was also a way to introduce a much more complex set of ideas about what it really meant to be food secure which included political power ideas about who controls resources, who has access to resources and who gets to control their own production and their own consumption. (Quoted in Long 2005: 25)

What Is Food Sovereignty?

In a nutshell, food sovereignty 'is the right of peoples and nations to control their own food and agricultural systems, including their own markets, production modes, food cultures, and environments' (Wittman et al. 2010: 2). This alternative model of rural development is designed to keep small-scale producers on the land and enable them to make a living from growing food. As such, it is a radical alternative to the corporate-led, neo-liberal, industrial model of agriculture. Indeed, in the words of GRAIN (2005), food sovereignty effectively 'turns the global food system upside down'.

Going far beyond the concept of food security, food sovereignty stresses that it is not enough to ensure that a sufficient amount of food is produced nationally and made accessible to everyone. Equally significant are the issues of what food is produced, who grows the food, where and how it is produced, and at what scale. Most importantly, food sovereignty includes farmers' and peasants' 'right to produce our own food in our own territory' and 'the right of consumers to be able to decide what they consume and how and by whom it is produced' (Vía Campesina 2003: 1). In effect, it places those who produce and consume food at the centre of decision making for agriculture and food policies.

The Tlaxcala Conference defined the basic principles of food sovereignty, which were then integrated into Vía Campesina's (1996b) position that was presented to delegates to the NGO Forum on Food Security and the World Food Summit held in Rome in November of 1996. Because the Vía Campesina position reflects the essence of food sovereignty and formed the basis of subsequent international documents, it is worth examining it closely (see Box 22.1).

In a world increasingly dominated by the ideals of liberalized trade governed by undemocratic and distant global institutions, food

---

Box 22.1 La Vía Campesina Position at the World Food Summit

The Right to Produce and Access to Land

Food Sovereignty—A Future without Hunger

We, the Vía Campesina, a growing movement of farm workers, peasant, farm and indigenous peoples' organizations from all the regions of the world know that food security cannot be achieved without taking full account of those who produce food. Any discussion that ignores our contribution will fail to eradicate poverty and hunger.

Food is a basic human right. This right can only be realized in a system where food sovereignty is guaranteed. Food sovereignty is the right of each nation to maintain and develop its own capacity to produce its basic foods respecting cultural and productive diversity. We have the right to produce our own food in our own territory. Food sovereignty is a precondition to genuine food security.

We, the Vía Campesina reject the economic and political conditions which destroy our livelihoods, our communities, our cultures and our natural environment. The liberalization of trade and its economic policies of structural adjustment have globalized poverty and hunger in the world and are destroying local productive capacities and rural societies. This corporate agenda takes no account of food security for people. It is an inequitable system that treats both nature and people as a means to an end with the sole aim of generating profits for a few. Peasants and small farmers are denied access to and control over land, water, seeds and natural resources. Our response to the increasingly hostile environment is to collectively challenge these conditions and develop alternatives.

We are determined to create rural economies that are based on respect for ourselves and the earth, on food sovereignty and fair trade. Women play a central role in household and community food sovereignty. Hence they have an inherent right to resources for food production, land, credit, capital, technology, education and social services, and equal opportunity to develop and employ their skills. We are convinced that the global problem of food insecurity can and must be resolved. Food sovereignty can only be achieved through solidarity and the political will to implement alternatives.

Long-term food security depends on those who produce food and care for the natural environment. As the stewards of food producing resources we hold the following principles as the necessary foundation for achieving food security.

Food—a Basic Human Right

Food is a basic human right. Everyone must have access to safe, nutritious and culturally appropriate food in sufficient quantity and quality to sustain a healthy life with full human dignity. Each nation should declare that access to food is a constitutional right and guarantee the development of the primary sector to ensure the concrete realization of this fundamental right.

Agrarian Reform

[Food sovereignty] demands genuine agrarian reform which gives landless and farming people—especially women—ownership and control of the land they work and returns territories to Indigenous peoples. The right to land must be free of discrimination on the basis of gender, religion, race, social class or ideology; land belongs to those who work it. Peasant families, especially women, must have access to productive land, credit, technology, markets and extension services. Governments must establish and support decentralized rural credit systems that prioritize the production of food for domestic consumption to ensure food sovereignty. Production capacity rather than land should be used as security to guarantee credit. To encourage young people to remain in rural communities as productive citizens, the work of producing food and caring for the land has to be sufficiently valued both economically and socially. Governments must make long-term investments of public resources in the development of socially and ecologically appropriate rural infrastructure.

Protecting Natural Resources

Food sovereignty entails the sustainable care and use of natural resources especially land, water and seeds. We, who work the land, must have the right to practice sustainable management of natural resources and to preserve biological diversity. This can only be done from a sound economic basis with security of tenure, healthy soils and reduced use of agrochemicals. Long-term sustainability demands a shift away from dependence on chemical inputs, on cash-crop monocultures and intensive, industrialized production models. Balanced and diversified natural systems are required. Genetic resources are the result of millennia of evolution and belong to all of humanity. They represent the careful work and knowledge of many generations of rural and indigenous peoples. The patenting and commercialization of genetic resources by private companies must be prohibited. The World Trade Organization's Intellectual Property Rights Agreement is unacceptable. Farming communities have the right to freely use and protect the diverse genetic resources, including seeds, which have been developed by them throughout history.

Reorganizing the Food Trade

Food is first and foremost a source of nutrition and only secondarily an item of trade. National agricultural policies must prioritize production for domestic consumption and food self-sufficiency. Food imports must not displace local production nor depress prices. This means that export dumping or subsidized export must cease. Peasant farmers have the right to produce essential food staples for their countries and to control the marketing of their products. Food prices in domestic and international markets must be regulated and reflect the true cost of producing that food. This would ensure that peasant families have adequate incomes. It is unacceptable that the trade in foodstuffs continues to be based on the economic exploitation of the most vulnerable—the lowest earning producers—and the further degradation of the environment. It is equally unacceptable that trade and production decisions are increasingly dictated by the need for foreign currency to meet high debt loads. These debts place a disproportionate burden on rural peoples. . . . [T]hese debts must be forgiven.

Ending the globalization of hunger

Food sovereignty is undermined by multilateral institutions and by speculative capital. The growing control of multinational corporations over agricultural policies has been facilitated by the economic policies of multilateral organizations such as the WTO, World Bank and the IMF. . . . [T]he regulation and taxation of speculative capital and a strictly enforced Code of Conduct for transnational corporations [is necessary].

Social Peace—a pre-requisite to food sovereignty

Everyone has the right to be free from violence. Food must not be used as a weapon. Increasing levels of poverty and marginalization in the countryside, along with the growing oppression of ethnic minorities and indigenous populations aggravate situations of injustice and hopelessness. The increasing incidence of racism in the countryside, ongoing displacement, forced urbanization and repression of peasants cannot be tolerated.

Democratic control

Peasants and small farmers must have direct input into formulating agricultural policies at all levels. This includes the current FAO World Food Summit from which we have been excluded. The United Nations and related organizations will have to undergo a process of democratization to enable this to become a reality. Everyone has the right to honest, accurate information and open and democratic decision-making. These rights form the basis of good governance, accountability and equal participation in economic, political and social life, free from all forms of discrimination. Rural women, in particular, must be granted direct and active decision-making on food and rural issues.

Source: *Via Campesina Position at the World Food summit*, November 11-17, 1996, Rome Italy www.viacampesina.org.

sovereignty is nothing less than revolutionary. McMichael (2008b: 220) argues that as a mobilizing slogan, food sovereignty 'serves to appropriate and reframe the dominant discourse, and as a political tactic to gain traction in the international political-economy en route to a global moral economy organized around "co-operative advantage"'. He means that food sovereignty subordinates trade relations and transcends the fetishism for agricultural commodities as it reintegrates social, ecological, and co-operative production relations; revalues land, food, and those who work the land; and addresses questions of rights and social reproduction of agrarian cultures and ecological sustainability (McMichael 2006; 2008a; 2008b). In fact, food sovereignty demands the 'right to have rights' (Patel 2010: 186) and in the process it expands our understanding of human rights to include the right to land and natural resources (Claeys 2009).[6] In many ways, food sovereignty is a social justice 'counter-frame to food security': it emphasizes solidarity over individualism, insists food is more than a commodity, rejects 'free' markets, and demands state intervention and market regulation (Fairbairn 2010).

Perhaps most importantly, food sovereignty is fundamentally changing the ways we think about and relate to food, agriculture, and each other because it politicizes the current global food system and agrarian policy (Wittman et al. 2010; Fairbairn 2010; McMichael 2008a; Patel 2010). As such, it is best understood as a radical democratic project that, on the one hand, exposes the power dynamics within the current global food system, and on the other hand, cultivates new spaces for inclusive debate on food and agriculture. And as Patel (2006: 85) argues, it does so in ways that 'the deepest relations of power come to be contested publicly'. Many of these claims are reflected in Table 22.1, which summarizes the specific ways in which food sovereignty directly challenges the corporate-led, neo-liberal, industrial model of agriculture.

Table 22.1 Key Differences between the Corporate-led Neo-liberal Industrial Model of Agriculture and the Food Sovereignty Model of Agriculture

	Neo-liberal Model	Food Sovereignty Model
Trade	'Free' trade in most commodities and services	Food and agriculture exempt from trade agreements Food geared to domestic needs and only the excess is fairly traded in regulated markets
Production priority	Food and agro-products for export and foreign exchange	Food for local markets
Crop prices	'What the market dictates' (leave intact mechanisms that enforce low prices to producers)	Fair prices that cover costs of production and allow farmers and farm workers a life with dignity
Market access	Increase access to foreign markets	Access to local markets End displacement of farmers from their own markets by agribusiness
Subsidies	While prohibited in the global South, many subsidies are allowed in the United States and Europe and paid mainly to the largest farmers	Allow subsidies that do not damage small- and medium-scale farming in other countries, e.g., grants to family farmers for direct marketing, price/income support, soil conservation, conversion to sustainable farming, research, rural education, etc.
Food	Considered primarily a commodity Increasingly involves processed food that contains high levels of fat, sugar, high-fructose corn syrup, and toxic residues	Considered a human right Should be healthy, nutritious, affordable, culturally appropriate, and locally produced
Being able to produce and provide food	An option for the economically 'efficient'	A right of peasants and small-scale family farmers, pastoralists, artisanal fishers, forest dwellers, Indigenous peoples, agricultural and fisheries workers, and migrants involved in food provision
Hunger	A problem caused by high prices and therefore by insufficient supply, production, and productivity	A problem of access and distribution caused by poverty and inequality

	Neo-liberal Model	Food Sovereignty Model
Food security	Achieved by importing food from where it is cheapest	Greatest when food production is in the hands of the hungry or when food is produced locally
Control over factors of production (i.e., land, water, etc.)	Privatized	Local Community-controlled
Access to land	Via the market	Via systemic and state-supported agrarian reform and long-term tenure security
Seeds	A patentable commodity	A common heritage of humanity, held in trust by rural communities and cultures 'No patents on life'
Rural credit and investment	From private banks and corporations	From the public sector Designed to support small- and medium-scale family agriculture
Corporate monopolies	Rarely an issue	A systemic and pathological feature of an industrialized international food system
Overproduction	No such thing, by definition	Drives prices down and pushes farmers into poverty Supply management policies effectively resolve overproduction issues
Small- and medium-scale farmers	Anachronisms The inefficient will disappear	Guardians of culture and crop germplasm Stewards of productive resources Repositories of knowledge Internal market and building block of broad-based, inclusive economic development
Gender	Policies and programs aimed at integrating food and agriculture into the global marketplace with no consideration of the gender division of labour and women's unpaid labour Little consideration of how the policies affect women and men differently	Aims to transform existing unequal gender relations Recognizes and respects the key roles women play in the production, gathering, distribution, preparation, and cultural dimensions of food and agriculture Demands equality and the end of all forms of violence against women
Urban consumers vs. agricultural workers	Since labour is considered a major cost in production, workers paid as little as possible to keep prices down for consumers	Workers need living wages
Research	Focuses on science and innovation Depends largely on new technology aimed at fixing problems caused by previously introducing new technology into the environment	Led and driven by peasants/farmers
Policy development	Developed by mostly urban 'experts' and may involve multi-stakeholder consultations on an already-defined policy agenda	Led and driven by peasants/farmers Participatory Starts from lived realities of farming families

Source: Adapted from Rosset (2003:2) and Patel (2006:84).

Building a Global Movement for Food Sovereignty

Initially, food sovereignty focused on issues of production, reflecting mainly the interests of peasants and small-scale farmers. However, food sovereignty quickly gained momentum as Vía Campesina began to work in alliance with **social movements**, national and international development non-governmental organizations, and community-based organizations that were embracing food sovereignty in efforts to shift agriculture and food policy in different parts of the world (NOUMINREN 2006; International Workshop 2003). In the process, food sovereignty evolved to encompass a much broader agenda to include pastoralists, fishers, and urban dwellers, and to address consumption issues and gender equality.

Throughout the decade since it was first introduced, food sovereignty generated a great deal of debate and action. For example, on 6 November 2001, the Our World Is Not For Sale coalition launched 'Priority to Peoples' Food Sovereignty', a statement which specified concrete mechanisms and structures to ensure food sovereignty.[7] The concept was further elaborated at two international civil society events: the World Forum on Food Sovereignty held in Cuba (Final Declaration 2001) and the 2002 NGO/CSO Forum on Food Sovereignty in Rome, held in conjunction with the World Food Summit: Five Years Later. Meanwhile, several major universities, including Yale University, Wageningen University, Tufts University, and the University of Saskatchewan, to name a few, held workshops and conferences to better understand the viability and practical implementation of food sovereignty. NGOs produced glossy campaign posters featuring food sovereignty, and coalitions like the European Platform for Food Sovereignty and the People's Caravan for Food Sovereignty in Asia were formed to promote the concept.

This flurry of grassroots activity and pressure for an alternative vision of rural development prompted responses from various levels of government and international bodies. Mayors in some parts of Europe endorsed a commitment to local production for local consumption, a key element of food sovereignty. The Green Party in some European countries held meetings to examine how it might help redefine European agricultural policy. And, between 1999 and 2009, food sovereignty was included in the national legislation promulgated by the governments of Venezuela, Mali, Bolivia, Ecuador, Nepal, and Senegal (Beauregard 2009).

Food sovereignty has also been brought to the attention of official international bodies. For example, reports to the United Nations Commission on Human Rights (now called the Human Rights Council) advocate food sovereignty as a means of ensuring the human **right to food** and food security (Ziegler 2003, 2004). More recently, the International Assessment of Agricultural Knowledge, Science and Technology for Development (IAASTD 2009) recognized the potential of food sovereignty to help move us away from the 'business as usual' approach to a more ecologically sustainable and socially just framework for agriculture and food.[8] And, since 2003, the International NGO/CSO Planning Committee for Food Sovereignty (IPC)—bringing together representatives of Indigenous peoples, fishers, farmers/peasants, youth, women, and NGOs from all regions of the world—is the principal civil society interlocutor with the FAO for work on food sovereignty.

To ensure that the concept of food sovereignty did not get distorted in the same way sustainable development did, and to strengthen the food sovereignty movement, the IPC worked with other groups, including Vía Campesina, to organize the International Forum on Food Sovereignty, held in February 2007 in Nyéléni, Mali—an event that represents an important turning point for food sovereignty. The Nyéléni Forum brought together 500 representatives of peasants, farmers, farm workers, fishers, pastoralists, Indigenous peoples, rural women, and non-governmental development organizations from 80 countries to debate and further define food sovereignty. Participants reached consensus on some basic principles of food sovereignty (see Box 22.2), opened the space for consumer associations and urban-based community organizations, and vowed to return to their respective countries to build food sovereignty networks and coalitions.

Box 22.2 Nyéléni 2007 Principles of Food Sovereignty

Food Sovereignty

1. **Focuses on Food for People:** Food sovereignty puts people . . . at the centre of food, agriculture, livestock and fisheries policies, ensuring sufficient, healthy and culturally appropriate food for all individuals, peoples and communities; and rejects the proposition that food is just another commodity or component for international agri-business.

2. **Values Food Providers:** Food sovereignty values and supports the contributions, and respects the rights of women and men, peasants and small-scale family farmers, pastoralists, artisanal fisherfolk, forest dwellers, indigenous peoples and agricultural fisheries workers, including migrants, who cultivate, grow, harvest and process food; and rejects those policies, actions and programmes that undervalue them, threaten their livelihoods and eliminate them.

3. **Localises Food Systems:** Food sovereignty brings food providers and consumers closer together; puts providers and consumers at the centre of decision-making on food issues; protects food providers from the dumping of food and food aid in local markets; protects consumers from poor quality and unhealthy food, inappropriate food aid and food tainted with genetically modified organisms; and resists governance structures, agreements and practices that depend on and promote unsustainable and inequitable international trade and give power to remote and unaccountable corporations.

4. **Puts Control Locally:** Food sovereignty places control over territory, land, grazing, water, seeds, livestock and fish populations on local food providers and respects their rights. They can use and share them in socially and environmentally sustainable ways which conserve diversity; . . . and [food sovereignty] rejects the privatization of natural resources through laws, commercial contracts and intellectual property rights regimes.

5. **Builds Knowledge and Skills:** Food sovereignty builds on the skills and local knowledge of food providers and their local organizations who conserve, develop and manage localized food production and harvesting systems, developing appropriate research systems to support this and passing on this wisdom to future generations; and rejects technologies that undermine, threaten or contaminate these skills and knowledge.

6. **Works with Nature:** Food sovereignty uses the contributions of nature in diverse, low-external-input agro-ecological production and harvesting methods that maximize the contribution of ecosystems and improve resilience and adaptation, especially in the face of climate change; it seeks to heal the planet so that the planet may heal us; and, rejects methods that harm beneficial ecosystem functions, that depend on energy-intensive monocultures and livestock factories, destructive fishing practices and other industrialized production methods, which damage the environment and contribute to global warming.

Source: Nyéléni 2007 Principles of Food Sovereignty. www.nyeleni.org.

In effect, the Nyéléni Forum shifted food sovereignty beyond its rural roots to embrace a wide range of social actors and consolidate a global food sovereignty movement. As Paul Nicholson, former member of the International Coordination Commission of Vía Campesina, recalls,

Food sovereignty was not designed as a concept only for farmers, but for people—that is why we call it peoples' food sovereignty. We see the need for a bottom up process to define alternative practices—an international space or platform for food sovereignty. We're talking about identifying allies, developing alliances with many movements of fisher folk, women, environmentalists and consumer associations, finding cohesion, gaining legitimacy, being aware of co-optation processes, the need to strengthen the urban-rural dialogue, to generate alternative technical models. And above all there is the issue of solidarity. (Quoted in Wittman et al. 2010: 7)

Since Nyéléni the momentum for food sovereignty continues to grow as national and regional coalitions are emerging or existing ones are adopting the food sovereignty framework. For example, in the global North—the heartland of the corporate-led, neo-liberal, industrial model of agriculture—European social movements are consolidating a European Movement for Food Sovereignty to move European agricultural policy away from WTO rules by 're-localizing agricultural production, supporting small producers and facilitating access to land for new farmers and collectives, while challenging the dominance of industry and private interests in the production, transformation and distribution of food for European citizens' (European Coordination Vía Campesina 2010). In the United States in the autumn of 2010 citizens launched the US Food Sovereignty Alliance that promises to be a key social actor in transforming the food system in that country.[9] Many are also involved in building food sovereignty in

Canada. As a follow-up to the Nyéléni Forum, representatives of Canadian non-governmental organizations—the National Farmers Union, Food Secure Canada, and others—established the People's Food Policy Project in 2008 to engage rural and urban Canadians from all walks of life and across the country in debates about what kind of national food and agriculture policy they want. The participatory and inclusive consultation process led to the successful launch in April 2011 of *Resetting the Table: A People's Food Policy for Canada*—a Canadian food policy firmly grounded on food sovereignty principles (Kneen 2011).[10] And communities across the country are working to improve and strengthen important instruments of food sovereignty like orderly marketing and supply management, while others are growing community gardens, strengthening the ties between farmers and urban consumers through community shared agriculture, practising urban agriculture, and supporting farmers' markets (Wittman et al. 2011).

In the global South, from the pampas, highlands, and islands of the Americas and the drylands and river basins of Africa to the busy city streets, lowlands, and fertile valleys of Asia, urban-based social movements, peasant organizations, rural women, and farm workers are actively engaged in building food sovereignty (Wittman et al. 2010; McMichael 2010; Pimbert 2008, 2010; Rosset 2009; Beauregard 2009). These are all promising developments and clearly demonstrate that an alternative model of agriculture is in the works.

Food sovereignty, as we have seen here, goes beyond food and agriculture. It also creates the opportunities and possibilities for us to fundamentally alter social relations, cultures, and politics—the very basis of modern societies (Handy and Fehr 2010). Food sovereignty is ultimately about a different way of being, a different way of relating to nature, a different way of relating with one another—what Hannah Wittman (2010) calls a new '**agrarian citizenship**'. For example, Vía Campesina's recent assertion (2008c: 2) that 'food sovereignty means stopping violence against women' speaks to the enormity of change required. As the Declaration of Maputo (Vía Campesina 2008b: 4) went on to say: 'If we do not eradicate violence towards women within our movement, we will not advance in our struggles, and if we do not create new gender relations, we will not be able to build a new society.'

Conclusion—The Challenges of Food Sovereignty

The challenges to food sovereignty are, of course, enormous and numerous. Given the space limitations I will keep the discussion to what might be the most obvious and significant challenges. The first challenge is the sheer extent and complexity of change required. After all, we are talking about a fundamental transformation of societies—a transformation that involves the redistribution of all kinds of resources, including power. For example, in talking about only one aspect of food sovereignty, land reform, Borras and Franco (2010: 107) point out that 'it is difficult to imagine how any initiative towards food sovereignty can take off when the community pushing for such an alternative vision has no effective control over land resources, and those who have the control (the elite—state and non-state) have visions of development fundamentally opposed to food sovereignty.' These powerful forces—including the political and economic elite, international institutions, transnational corporations, and national governments—who structured and are benefiting from the neo-liberal model of agriculture are precisely what food sovereignty is up against, making the struggle intense, long, and in many cases life-threatening.

Rafael Alegría Moncado, a Honduran peasant leader and former Operational Secretariat of Vía Campesina, in speaking about the ongoing political upheaval in his country says that food sovereignty is not possible unless and until real democracy is established (Alegría 2011). As the Nyéléni Forum (Nyéléni 2007: 5) stated 'in order to be able to apply policies that allow autonomy

in food production it is necessary to have political conditions that exercise autonomy in all the territorial spaces, countries, regions, cities and rural communities. Food sovereignty is only possible if it takes place at the same time as the political sovereignty of peoples.' But this struggle for public engagement and widespread democracy and autonomy is often extremely dangerous. Vía Campesina's (2006) annual report on human rights abuses in the countryside showed how some powerful interests respond to those who advance food sovereignty.[11] Rafael Alegría knows this only too well. He has been imprisoned and has received death threats because of his role in demanding democracy and changes to legislation that would bring about a genuine agrarian reform (Marentes 2009; Telesur 2009).

When the necessary political conditions are created and food sovereignty succeeds in carving democratic spaces for debate on food and agriculture issues, a second challenge emerges. As Patel (2007: 91) puts it, since 'no "peoples" have a single and unifying perspective on food policy' food sovereignty in effect 'calls for new political spaces to be filled with argument'. This brings us to the very real and messy business of building consensus. What mechanisms and processes can those advocating food sovereignty introduce to reconcile class interests and balance power dynamics to ensure that all voices are heard and acted upon? There is no easy answer to this question. The power of food sovereignty lies in its demand that such spaces for arguments be created in the first place and thus allow us to engage in the process of building community. Ultimately, as history tells us, community opposition can be the strongest form of resistance to the forces of global capitalism (Parajuli 1996; Chatterjee 1993).

A third challenge to food sovereignty is the threat of usurpation by powerful interests who can reshape its meaning and thus dilute it of revolutionary potential. It is important to note that one of the reasons Vía Campesina helped organize the Nyéléni Forum was precisely that it sought to preserve and cultivate the authenticity of the framework. Fairbairn (2010) argues that there may be less opportunity for usurpation, because food sovereignty evolved from the marginalized and oppressed, and it seeks to overturn the whole food regime within which it was created while attempting to create an entirely different one. Nevertheless, the global food sovereignty movement will need to be vigilant to ensure that the food sovereignty framework is not misappropriated and drained of its transformatory potential.

In conclusion, there is much potential in the food sovereignty framework. It allows opportunities for a major overhaul of the existing environmentally unsustainable and socially unjust global food system, and in the process it can facilitate revolutionary social and political change. In Patel's (2007: 88) words, food sovereignty calls for

> a mass re-politicization of food politics, through a call for people to figure out for themselves what they want the right to food to mean in their communities. . . .

In this mass engagement, a rights-driven food-system policy is one outcome. More important, though, is the building of a sustainable and widespread process of democracy that can provide political direction to the appropriate level of government required to see implementation through to completion.

The difficulties in establishing the necessary political conditions for food sovereignty to flourish should not be underestimated. The barriers to food sovereignty are everywhere, powerful, and often violent. But there are also significant cracks in the foundation of the corporate-led, neo-liberal, industrial model of agriculture that nature itself is revealing on a daily basis. Food sovereignty allows us to imagine and build an agriculture that can, in the words of Vía Campesina (2010: 1) 'feed the world and cool the planet'—both are absolutely necessary.

Discussion Questions

1. What are some of the major limitations of the idea and practice of food security?

2. Is a radical alternative like food sovereignty necessary? Why?

3. What are the key elements of food sovereignty, and how do these compare with the existing food system?

4. What are some of the key limitations and challenges in implementing food sovereignty?

Further Reading

1. Desmarais, Annette Aurélie. 2007. *La Vía Campesina: Globalization and the Power of Peasants*. Point Black and London: Fernwood Publishing and Pluto Books.

   This book explores the social and political significance of what is now the world's most important transnational agrarian movement, Vía Campesina. It explores the main issues, strategies, and collective actions of the social movement and highlights its contributions to building alternatives to the powerful forces of neo-liberal economic globalization. In doing so, the book demonstrates how food sovereignty was conceptualized to fundamentally transform the idea and practice of rural development and to redefine the role of agriculture in international development.

2. Pimbert, Michel. 2008. Towards Food Sovereignty: Another World Is Possible

for Food and Agriculture. Part I: Chapters 1–3 in *Towards Food Sovereignty: Reclaiming Autonomous Food Systems*. London: International Institute for Environment and Development. Available at http://pubs.iied. org/G02268.html.

This work is the first section of an online publication on food sovereignty that highlights the importance of locally controlled food systems to effectively sustain people and nature. Three chapters are available to date. The first describes some of the key ecological aspects of food and agriculture; the second examines the major social and environmental impact of modern food systems; and the third discusses the policy transformations needed to implement food sovereignty. Throughout the publication there are numerous video and audio clips of peasants, small-scale farmers, Indigenous peoples, and consumers who are working to promote food sovereignty in various parts of the world.

3. Wittman, Hannah, Annette Aurélie Desmarais, and Nettie Wiebe (eds.). 2010. *Food Sovereignty: Reconnecting Food, Nature and Community*. Point Black, Oakland, and Oxford: Fernwood Publishing, Food First Book, and Pambazuka Press.

Around the world, people are resisting the global industrial agricultural system by adopting the radical framework and practice of food sovereignty. Food sovereignty aims to provide for the food needs of all people while respecting the principles of environmental sustainability, local empowerment, and agrarian citizenship. Bringing together internationally recognized experts in the field, this book critically engages contemporary debates concerning food sovereignty while exploring new research directions. The collection examines the historical rise of the industrial agricultural system, outlines the environmental and social consequences of this system, and gives voice to the peasant movements that are planting the seeds of a revolution that could fundamentally alter our relationship with food and with each other.

4. Wittman, Hannah, Annette Aurélie Desmarais, and Nettie Wiebe. 2011. *Food Sovereignty in Canada*. Pt. Black, Nova Scotia: Fernwood Publishing.

A food sovereignty framework offers Canadian citizens, researchers, and policymakers the opportunity to build alternative agriculture and food models that are less environmentally damaging and keep farmers on the land while ensuring that those living in cities have access to healthy and safe food. Bringing together a diverse set of perspectives, this book explores how communities in various parts of Canada are actively engaged in implementing food sovereignty. By analyzing Indigenous food sovereignty, experiences with orderly marketing, community gardens, the political engagement of nutritionists, forays into urban agriculture, and links between the rural and urban, the book clearly demonstrates that the urgent work of building food sovereignty in Canada is well under way. It also highlights policy directions and the challenges to building agriculture and food systems that are ecologically sustainable, socially just, and based on community.

Notes

1. *Farm Women and Canadian Agricultural Policy* (Roppel, Desmarais, and Martz 2006) was one of the first in-depth studies to propose food sovereignty to Canadian policy makers. Available at www.foodstudies.ca/Documents/Farm_Women_ and_the_APF.pdf.

2. The Standing Committee on Agriculture and Agri-Food was holding meetings to investigate

the extent of the farm crisis and views on the 'Next Generation' Agricultural Policy Framework. The Committee's final report, entitled 'Fact-Finding Mission on Canada's New Agriculture and Agri-food Policy' is available at www2.parl.gc.ca/HousePublications/Publication.aspx?DocId=3066010&Language=E&Mode=1&Parl=39&Ses=1&File=18#part3.

3. The UN Declarations of the World Conference on Environment and Development held in 1992 in Rio de Janeiro and Johannesburg both specify the importance of economic growth for sustainable development. The World Bank's *World Development Reports* consistently present the view that sustained economic growth is critical for sustainable development. In 2006 the World Bank created the Commission on Growth and Development to look at issues and policies designed to ensure sustained economic growth for development.

4. This view is reflected in a number of international publications and national govern-ment policies. See for example, the International Fund for Agricultural Development's *Rural Poverty Report 2001: The Challenge of Ending Rural Poverty*, the World Bank's *World Development Report 2008: Agriculture for Development*, Agriculture Canada's 'Growing Together: A Vision for Canada's Agri-Food Industry' (1989) and Agriculture and Agri-Food Canada's national policy documents called the Agricultural Policy Framework (2003) and Growing Forward Policy Framework (2008).

5. See, for example, the FAO (2000) study that examines the changes in 14 developing countries following the implementation of the WTO's Agreement on Agriculture. UNCTAD's (2006) study of the agricultural input industry provides evidence of the extent of corporate concentration in that sector.

6. In 2004 Vía Campesina (2004) petitioned the United Nations Human Rights Commission for a declaration of peasant rights. The declaration is available at www.viacampesina.org.

7. The statement was released just prior to the Fourth Ministerial Meeting of the WTO held in Doha, Qatar. It was developed by Vía Campesina; COASAD; Collectif Stratégies Alimentaires; ETC Group; Focus on the Global South; Foodfirst/Institute for Food and Development Policy; Friends of the Earth Latin America and Caribbean; Friends of the Earth England, Wales and Northern Ireland; GRAIN; Institute for Agriculture and Trade Policy; IBON Foundation, and Public Citizen's Energy and Environment Program. After its release numerous movements signed on to the statement.

8. See especially the Latin America and Caribbean (LAC) Report of the IAASTD, available at www.agassessment-watch.org.

9. See www.usfoodsovereigntyalliance.org.

10. See http://peoplesfoodpolicy.ca/ for informa-tion on the People's Food Policy Project and Wittman et al. (2011) for a discussion of various food sovereignty initiatives in Canada.

11. See also Terra de Direitos, Vía Campesina, and MST's 2008 'The case of Syngenta' and a number of other documents on human rights violations available at www.viacampesina.org.

References

Agriculture and Agri-Food Canada. 2003. Agriculture Policy Framework. Available at www4.agr.gc.ca/AAFC-AAC/display afficher.do?id=1183127394087&lang=eng.

———. 2008. Growing Forward Policy Framework. Available at www4.agr.gc.ca/AAFC-AAC/display-afficher.do?id=1238606407452&lang=eng.

Agriculture Canada. 1989. Growing Together: A Vision for Canada's Agri-Food Industry. Available at www.archive.org/details/growingtogetherv00cana.

Alegría Moncado, Rafael. 2011. Interview conducted by author. Tegucigalpa, Honduras, 11 February.

Beauregard, S. 2009. 'Food Policy for People: Incorporating Food Sovereignty Principles into State Governance'. Senior Comprehensive Report, Urban and Environmental Policy Institute, Occidental College, Los Angeles. April. Available at departments.oxy.edu/uepi/uep/index.htm.

Borras, Saturnino M. Jr., Marc Edelman, and Cristóbal Kay. 2008. 'Transnational Agrarian Movements: Origins and

Politics, Campaigns and Impact'. *Journal of Agrarian Change* 8(2/3): 1–36.

Borras, Saturnino M. Jr., and Jennifer Franco. 2010. 'Food Sovereignty and Redistributive Land Policies: Exploring Linkages, Identifying Challenges'. In Wittman et al. *Food Sovereignty*, 106–19.

Chatterjee, Partha. 1993. *The Nation and Its Fragments: Colonial and Postcolonial Histories*. Princeton, NJ: Princeton University Press.

Claeys, Priscilla. 2009. 'The Right to Food and Food Sovereignty: Complementary or Contradictory Discourses on the Global Food Crisis?' Paper presented at the Conference on the World Food Crisis, Zacatecas, Mexico, 13–15 August.

Desmarais, A. 2007. *La Vía Campesina: Globalization and The Power of Peasants*. Halifax: Fernwood Books.

European Coordination Vía Campesina. 2010. 'Call to Nyéléni Europe Forum and Camp'. Common Ground. Newsletter #8, September. Available at www.eurovia.org/spip.php?article359&lang=fr.

Fairbairn, Madeleine. 2010. 'Framing Resistance: International Food Regimes and the Roots of Food Sovereignty'. In Wittman et al. *Food Sovereignty*, 15–32.

FAO. 2000. 'Agriculture, Trade and Food Security: Issues and Options in the WTO Negotiations from the Perspective of Developing Countries'. Volume II, Country Case Studies, Commodities and Trade Division of the FAO: Rome. Accessed 14 January 2003 at www.fao.org/DOCREP/033/x8731e/x8931e01a.htm.

———. 2003. 'Trade Reforms and Food Security: Conceptualising the Linkages'. Rome: Commodity Policy and Projections Service, Commodities and Trade Division.

Final Declaration of the World Forum on Food Sovereignty. 2001. Havana, Cuba, 7 September. Available at ukabc.org/havanadeclaration.pdf.

GRAIN. 2005. 'Food Sovereignty: Turning the Global Food System Upside Down'. *Seedling*. April. Available at www.grain.org/seedling/?id=329.

Handy, Jim, and Carla Fehr. 2010. ' 'Drawing Forth the Force that Slumbered in Peasants' Arms': the Economist, High Agriculture and Selling Capitalism'. In Wittman et al., *Food Sovereignty*, 45–61.

IAASTD. 2009. *Agriculture at a Crossroads: Global Report*. Washington, DC: Island Press.

International Fund for Agricultural Development. 2001. *Rural Poverty Report 2001: The Challenge of Ending Rural Poverty*. Oxford: Oxford University Press.

International Workshop on the Review of the Agreement on Agriculture. 2003. 'Towards Food Sovereignty; Constructing an Alternative to the World Trade Organization's Agreement on Agriculture'. Geneva, February.

Kneen, Cathleen. 2011. 'Food Secure Canada: Where Agriculture, Environment, Health, Food and Justice Intersect'. In Wittman et al., *Food Sovereignty in Canada*.

Long, Clara. 2005. 'Food Sovereignty and the Vía Campesina: The Evolution of a Counter-hegemonic Discourse'. Unpublished MSc Dissertation. Department of Geography and Environment, London School of Economics and Political Science.

McMichael, Philip. 2006. 'Peasant Prospects in the Neoliberal Age'. *New Political Economy* 11(3): 407–18.

———. 2008a. 'Food Sovereignty, Social Reproduction and the Agrarian Question'. In *Peasants and Globalization: Political Economy, Rural Transformation and the Agrarian Question*, ed. A.H. Adram-Lodhi and Cristóbal Kay. Routledge ISS Studies in Rural Livelihoods Series. New York: Routledge, 288–312.

———. 2008b. 'Peasants Make Their Own History, But Not Just as They Please . . .'. *Journal of Agrarian Change* 8(2–3): 205–28.

Marentes, Carlos. 2009. 'Broaden and Maintain the International Solidarity to Stop the Repression against Honduran People'. Available at www.viacampesina.org.

Martínez-Torres, Maria Elena, and Peter Rosset. 2010. 'La Vía Campesina: The Birth and Evolution of a Transnational Social Movement'. *Journal of Peasant Studies* 37(1): 149–76.

Mendoza, Miguel Rodriguez. 2002. 'Trade Liberalisation and Food Security'. Speech of the Deputy Director General of the WTO to the World Food Summit. Rome, 11 June. Available at www.wto.org/English/news_e/news02_e/speech_rodriguez_mendoza_11june02_e.htm.

NGO/CSO Forum for Food Sovereignty. 2002. 'Food Sovereignty: A Right for All'. Political Statement of the NGO/CSO Forum for Food Sovereignty. Rome, 13 June. Available at 222.croceviaterra.it/FORUM/DOCUMENTI520DEL%20FORUM/political%20statement.pdf.

NOUMINREN. 2006. 'Draft Declaration of Food Sovereignty for the Japanese Farmers and Consumers'. Position paper presented at Nyéléni 2007 by the Japanese National Coalition of Workers, Farmers and Consumers for Safe Food and Health. Selingué, Mali, 23–7 February.

Nyéléni. 2007. Proceedings of the Forum for Food Sovereignty. Selingué, Mali, 23–7 February.

Parajuli, Pramod. 1996. 'Ecological Ethnicity in the Making: Developmentalist Hegemonies and Emergent Identities in India'. *Identities* 3(1–2): 15–59.

Patel, Rajeev. 2005. 'Global Fascism, Revolutionary Humanism and the Ethics of Food Sovereignty'. *Development* 48(2): 79–83.

———. 2006. 'International Agrarian Restructuring and the Practical Ethics of Peasant Movement Solidarity'. *Journal of Asian and African Studies* 41: 71–93.

———. 2007. 'Transgressing Rights: La Vía Campesina's Call for Food Sovereignty'. *Feminist Economics* 13(1): 87–116.

———. 2010. 'What Does Food Sovereignty Look Like?' In Wittman et al., *Food Sovereignty*, 186–96.

People's Food Sovereignty Network. 2001. Peoples' Food Sovereignty Statement. Accessed 5 July 2007 at www.peoplesfoodsovereignty.org.

Pimbert, Michel. 2008. 'Towards Food Sovereignty: Reclaiming Autonomous Food Systems'. London: International Institute for Environment and Development. Available at http://pubs.iied.org/G02268.html.

———. 2010. *Democratising Agricultural Research for Food Sovereignty in West Africa*. Co-published by International Institute for Environment and Development, Coordination Nationale des Organisations Paysannes du Mali (CNOP), Centre Djoliba, the Institut de Recherche et de Promotion des Alternatives en Développement (IRPAD), Kene Conseils, and the Union des Radios et Télévisions libres du Mali (URTEL). Available at www.iied.org/natural-resources/media/world-food-day-marked-call-democratise-agricultural-research-and-ensure-food.

Roppel, Carla, Annette Aurélie Desmarais, and Diane Martz. 2006. *Farm Women and Canadian Agricultural Policy*. Ottawa: Status of Women Canada. Available at food-studies.ca/Documents/Farm_Women_and_the_APF.pdf.

Rosset, Peter. 2003. 'Food Sovereignty: Global Rallying Cry of Farmer Movements'. Institute for Food and Development Policy. *Backgrounder* 9(4). Available at www.foodfirst.org/node/47.

———. 2009. 'Food Sovereignty in Latin America: Confronting the "New" Crisis'. *NACLA Report on the Americas* 42(3): 16–21.

Standing Committee on Agriculture and Agri-Food. 2007. 39th Parliament, 1st Session, Draft transcript of evidence. 22 February. Available at www.parl.gc.ca/HousePublications/Publication.aspx?DocId=2737536&Language=E&Mode=1&Parl=39&Ses=1.

Telesur. 2009. 'Rafael Alegría Has Been Released'. 25 July. Available at www.telesurtv.net/noticias/secciones/nota/54707-NN/rafael-alegria-es-liberado-y-continua-en-la-lucha-por-la-democracia/.

The Economist. 2008a. 'The Silent Tsunami: The Food Crisis and How to Solve it'. 387(8576): 13.

———. 2008b. 'The New Face of Hunger'. 387(8576): 32–4.

———. 2009. 'Whatever Happened to the Food Crisis?: World Food Prices'. 392(8638): 57.

UNCTAD. 2006. 'Tracking the Trend Towards Market Concentration: The Case of the Agricultural Input Industry'. Report prepared by the United Nations Conference on Trade and Development. Available at www.unctad.org/en/docs/ditccom200516_en.pdf.

Vía Campesina. 1996a. 'Proceedings of the II International Conference of the Vía Campesina'. Tlaxcala, Mexico, 18–21 April. Brussels: NCOS Publications.

———. 1996b. 'The Right to Produce and Access to Land'. Position of the Vía Campesina on Food Sovereignty presented at the World Food Summit. Rome, 13–17 November.

———. 2003. 'What Is Food Sovereignty?' Jakarta: Operational Secretariat of Vía Campesina.

———. 2004. 'Vía Campesina in Geneva at Session of the Human Rights commission of the UN'. Geneva, 4 April.

———. 2006. 'Violations of Peasants' Human Rights: A Report on Cases and Patterns of Violence'. Jakarta. Available at www.viacampesina.org/main_en/images/sotries/annual-report-HR-2006.pdf.

———. 2008a. 'An Answer to the Global Food Crisis: Peasants and Small Farmers Can Feed the World!'. Jakarta, 1 May. Available at viacampesina.org.

———. 2008b. 'Declaration of Maputo: V Internacional Conference of La Vía Campesina. Maputo, Mozambique, 19–22 October.

———. 2008c. 'Declaration of the III Women's Assembly of La Vía Campesina'. Maputo, Mozambique, 22–3 October.

———. 2009. 'Massiva protesta en defensa de la verdadera democracia en Honduras'. Press release. Available at http://viacampesina.org/sp/index.php?option=com_content&view=articl e&rid=762:massiva-protesta-en-defensa-de-la-democracia-en-honduras&catid=15:noticias-de-las-regiones&Itemid=29.

———. 2010. 'The people create thousands of solutions to confront climate change!'. 1 September. Available at www.viacampesina.org/en/index.php?option=com_content&view=article&rid=941:the-people-create-thousands-of-solutions-to-confront-climate-change&catid=48:-climate-change-and-agrofuels&Itemid=75.

Wittman, Hannah. 2010. 'Reconnecting Agriculture and the Environment: Food Sovereignty and the Agrarian Basis of Ecological Citizenship'. In Wittman et al. *Food Sovereignty*, 91–105.

Wittman, Hannah, Annette Aurélie Desmarais, and Nettie Wiebe (eds). 2010. *Food Sovereignty: Reconnecting Food, Nature and Community*. Black Point, NS, Oakland, CA, and London: Fernwood Publishing, Food First Books, and Pambazuka Press.

———, ———, and ——— (eds). 2011. *Food Sovereignty in Canada*. Black Point, NS: Fernwood Publishing.

World Bank. 2007. *World Development Report 2007: Agriculture for Development*. Washington, DC: World Bank.

World Bank. 2008. *World Development Report 2008: Agriculture for Development*. Washington, DC: World Bank.

World Commission on Environment and Development. 1987. *Our Common Future*. Oxford: Oxford University Press. Available at www.un-documents.net/ocf-ov.htm.

Ziegler, Jean. 2003. 'Report by the Special Rapporteur on the Right to Food: Mission to Brazil'. United Nations Commission on Human Rights, 59th session. 3 January.

———. 2004. 'Report Submitted by the Special Rapporteur on the Right to Food'. United Nations Commission on Human Rights, 60th session. 9 February.

Conclusion

In Canada, as in other countries, food studies is still in its infancy. This book aims to contribute to the development of the field both at home and abroad. It has provided an overview of the emergence of food studies from a critical perspective, with a Canadian point of view. In this way, it is unique—the beginning of what we hope will be a dynamic tradition to support, reflect, and inform the burgeoning teaching, research, and scholarship focused on the study of food.

The book has examined theoretical development as well as practical issues such as governance and definitions of basic terms. It has also addressed current crises and challenges, and looked ahead to more sustainable and just food systems in the future. The topics in this volume cover some of the broad debates and segments of the field. However, we know that a complete list is practically impossible, given that food touches every aspect of human interaction and interactions between humans and nature. In this inaugural volume, contributors presented some of the key issues of concern and theoretical insights developed through food studies scholarship. We hope that future work will also focus on a synthesis of the original analytical and methodological contributions of this field.

As a young area of inquiry, food studies exhibits the strengths and weaknesses of a new field. Interdisciplinarity is one obvious strength—unlike the disciplines from which food studies emerged, its boundaries are not yet set. Its ability to move 'outside the lines' allows food studies to encompass a wide range of subject areas, from art and culture, through history and current events, and to politics and economics, and is open to the crosscutting issues of gender, class, race, and ethnicity. Recognizing the interconnections between complex processes and relations involved in different aspects of production, distribution, consumption, and waste management, food studies encourages a systemic approach to food. The field's youthful energy and enthusiasm represent another strength—food studies is not content with the status quo, but questions authority, crosses boundaries, makes new alliances, and discovers new identities.

But the strengths of food studies can also hide its weaknesses. Like any interdisciplinary endeavour, it could turn out to be a mile wide and an inch deep, without the focus and depth that builds knowledge within a discipline. This book, and the many other books, chapters, and articles that deal with food, will help to mitigate this problem. Likewise, the energy and enthusiasm swirling around food studies can obscure the need for seasoned wisdom, solid scholarship, and careful research. Indeed, there is a particular need for a broad range of in-depth empirical research to counter the considerable speculative conjecture that characterizes some of the literature to date.

In spite of these potential problems, food studies in Canada has come a long way in a few short years. The Canadian Association for Food Studies (CAFS), founded in 2006, is leading the field and holds annual meetings at the Congress of the Humanities and Social Sciences. Journals dedicated to the study of food are being published or planned, including McGill University's *Cuizine* and a journal of its own that CAFS is planning to develop. Courses in food are springing up across the country in disciplines such as sociology, geography, and adult education. Centres for the study of particular food issues have been developed in a number of universities, such as Ryerson's Centre for Studies in Food Security and Lakehead

University's Food Security Research Network. National and regional research partnerships have also formed around food studies, which bring together researchers from academic institutions, community organizations, government departments, NGOs, and the private sector.

Gaps remain, however. Primarily, there is no Department of Food Studies in any Canadian university, nor any dedicated food studies program. While interdisciplinary partnerships are emerging, mainstream disciplines that have played a key role in the development of the modern agri-food system such as food science, agricultural economics, and nutrition and dietetics (with some notable exceptions) still remain outside of the food studies networks. We also lack a leading scholarly journal dedicated to the analytical and methodological development of food studies as a scholarly field of expertise in Canada.

Despite these limitations, the development of food studies has both mirrored and encouraged interest outside of academia by helping to move food from the periphery toward the centre of public consciousness. Food is now on the agenda of many school boards, with new curriculum about food, increased attention to school lunches, and the establishment of school gardens. Provincial governments are finally paying attention to local food issues, and some have very substantially revised the guidelines around what can and cannot be served in school food environments. The role of food in community development is also gaining some attention from government, while three of the four federal political parties have food policy in their platforms. Towns and cities are creating or bolstering farmers' markets in reaction to public demand for fresh, local food. Food policy councils and food security roundtables are being established in a number of communities across the country. And the media show a healthy interest in food, expressed by a growing number of books, films, newspaper stories, and magazine spreads devoted to the subject.

The future for food studies seems without limit, and this book reflects some of that boundless potential. We hope it has given you a taste for more—more ideas, more learning, more curiosity, and more interest in the field of food studies. And we encourage you to join the food studies movement and contribute to the development of this new field of inquiry.

Glossary

actor-network theory An approach that tracks relations as they are created by actors and that are natural and physical as well as social; especially useful in food studies, and most especially in understanding food system change.

agrarian citizenship A concept that links agricultural practice to environmental sustainability and social justice, thus defining new ways of being and interacting with nature and one another.

Agreement on Agriculture One of the World Trade Organization's trade agreements that deals specifically with food and agriculture. The key pillars of the Agreement on Agriculture are improving market access by reducing tariffs and imposing an import food requirement of national consumption, increasing export competition by reducing export subsidies, and reducing direct and indirect domestic government support.

agrofuel Any agricultural crop converted into fuel to run engines.

alternative hedonism Coined by philosopher Kate Soper, the idea that alternative forms of consumption are motivated not only by altruistic concerns and a desire for 'a better world'—they can be motivated also by the self-interested pleasures of consuming differently.

aquaculture Specifically with regard to fish and seafood, a range of practices including the centuries-old carp farming in small ponds across China, the conversion of rice fields into shrimp farms across south and southeast Asia, the highly controlled marine fish farms for salmon in Canada, and the marine pens in the Mediterranean where juvenile bluefin tuna captured in the wild are held and fattened for export to the Japanese market.

banking model of education A practice of education that assumes the teacher is the all-knowing expert who defines the content and process of learning, depositing knowledge into the head of the student, who is assumed to be ignorant. The concept was developed by Brazilian educator Paulo Freire to contrast with his proposed 'problem-posing' model of **popular education**.

biodiversity The range of plant and animal species in a given area, and their complex interactions.

biophysical overrides External inputs such as fertilizers and pesticides used to compensate for the biological and physical problems caused by industrial agriculture.

biotechnology Both an industry that uses and develops products using materials from living processes, and a set of engineering technologies and molecular techniques that manipulate the genetic material of organisms in order to make them express desired characteristics. *Biotechnology, genetic engineering* (GE) and **genetic modification** (GM) are all commonly used terms to describe the artificial insertion of genes from one organism into another to generate a **transgenic** or **genetically modified organism** (GMO) using **recombinant** DNA technology.

body Used in sociological and cultural studies to conceptualize the social, cultural, metaphoric, and symbolic aspects of the physical body, including the construction of identity.

Canada's Aboriginal peoples Indigenous populations within Canada that include diverse First Nations, Inuit, and Métis collectives.

Canadian Wheat Board (CWB) A marketing agency that exports wheat and barley grown by western Canadian farmers, pooling prices and returning all profits from sales, minus marketing costs, to farmers.

canon In a textual context, a group of significant works that together represent a particular period or kind of writing.

capitalism An economic system in which privately owned and controlled autonomous units of production hire wage workers to produce commodities for the sake of maximizing profits in competitive markets.

certification Confirmation by a recognized body of certain characteristics or qualities of a person, organization, or commodity.

circuits of capital/turnover time The movement of capital: original money, to investment, to final profit is one turnover of the circuit. Other things being equal, the faster the turnover of capital, the greater the profit.

civil commons Any co-operative human construction that protects and/or enables universal access to life goods.

civil society The segment of society outside of the state and the market. In everyday language, civil society organizations are community-based organizations or non-governmental organizations (NGOs) such as faith groups, unions, associations, and social movements.

class A concept for differentiating between groups of people based on property relations, as when masters own slaves, lords own the land, and capitalists own the means of production. See also **stratification**.

class relations Social relations entered into by people who share similar relations to means of production.

climate change adaptation The mix of planning, policy, technological, and infrastructural responses for coping with unfolding and projected climate changes.

climate change mitigation The need to reduce GHG emissions (carbon dioxide, methane, and nitrous oxide) and enhance sequestration capacity (removing existing GHGs from the atmosphere). Some argue that massive-scale geo-engineering (technological interventions) must be part of this discussion; others insist that this could entail untold risks.

colonization The historical and continued undermining of Indigenous peoples' beliefs, values, and traditions in favour of non-Indigenous beliefs, values, and traditions.

co-management A resource management strategy by government and resource users that involves shared rights and responsibilities, access to information, and decision making.

commodity chains (or systems) All stages of specific production, distribution, and consumption of commodities such as wheat, beef, tomatoes, and fish. These focus on economy, sometimes emphasizing specific aspects such as power or culture.

commodity fetishism Implies, in essence, that in a capitalist economy consumers encounter a vast range of commodities in markets which are measured by price (or their 'exchange value'), while the range of social and biophysical relations involved in their production (including unmeasured or undervalued costs) are hidden and largely incomprehensible.

commodity futures contract A tradable contract that promises future delivery of a commodity at a given price.

commodity index funds (CIFS) Financial products sold by banks that are based on commodity price indices.

commodity speculation The trade in commodity futures investment products for the sole purpose of profiting financially from commodity price changes.

common property resources Natural resources owned and managed collectively by communities or societies rather than by individuals; can include water bodies, pastures, fisheries, forests, or clean air.

community arts A wide range of practices and traditions that engage people in representing their collective identities, histories, and aspirations in multiple forms of cultural expression.

communities of food practice Networks of individuals and organizations—public, private, and non-profit—engaged in creating a regional, networked, inclusive agri-food economy.

community-supported agriculture (CSA) An innovation that came of age in the 1990s, in which customers buy a farmer's crops in advance of the season and receive produce throughout the season.

community-supported fishery A strategy to share resources of the sea by the local fishing community and fishers. Similar to community-supported agriculture, it may involve contractual agreements between fishers and the local community for accessing harvested food.

confined animal feeding operation (CAFO) Animals confined and force-fed in small areas. Most beef, pork, chicken, dairy products, and eggs are produced in such operations containing thousands of animals.

connotation The implied meaning of a word, in contrast to *denotation*, which is a word's direct meaning. For example, *white* denotes a particular colour, but often connotes innocence or goodness. Similarly, *food* can connote meaning, in the way that *turkey*, for example, denotes a type of fowl but also connotes or suggests a celebratory meal in contemporary North America. In this way, food has an inherent 'narrativity', such that a meal can tell a nuanced story in the language of food.

consumer culture   A description of late-industrial capitalist societies where consumerism reigns supreme. While other cultures give symbolic weight to material objects, consumer culture is characterized by extensive capitalist commodification and the ubiquity of consumer imperatives in everyday life.

consumerism   The ideological dimension of consumer culture—a culture where commodity acquisition is a primary and perpetual source of meaning and purpose. Consumerism is commonly critiqued for diverting public attention from other important social and public issues, and for enabling unsustainable capitalist expansion. Consumerism is distinct from the more neutral term *consumption*, which refers to the process of using up goods and services.

co-opting   Tendency of elites to assimilate resistance and use it to their advantage; in industrial societies, the tendency of the industrial model to assimilate any resistance to it and commercialize the resistance for its own profit.

corporate concentration   In contrast to the claim of orthodox economics that our economy is characterized by competitive firms, many sectors of the food economy outside of farming are concentrated in the hands of a very few powerful corporate organizations. Most processing in such sectors as red meat, poultry, and grain handling is largely controlled by four or fewer firms, while at the retail level in Canada, supermarket chain-store operations, which control most of the retail sales of food, are dominated by three or fewer corporations, depending on the city or region. This high degree of corporate concentration confers on these firms tremendous market power to determine prices and influence what foods people buy, via costly advertising programs and the saturation of product via **spatial colonization**.

cost–price squeeze   The small or negative margins farmers realize when the costs of producing food—capital investment, agricultural inputs, and labour—are larger than the income generated from the sale of that food.

counter-hegemony   The withdrawal of spontaneous consent by the large percentage of the population ruled by the dominant hegemonic bloc.

critical dietetics   An initiative to counter the dominant approach in dietetics that values food only for its nutritional content (see **nutritionism**). Critical dietetics embraces new ways of conceptualizing and conducting dietetic research, education, and practice to help the dietetic profession become more effective in promoting a broad form of health; to address complex social issues related to food, such as hunger; and to promote social justice in all its professional activities.

critical obesity studies   A field of social science scholarship that examines the flaws and inherent contradictions in obesity science and medical practice, and demonstrates how moralism and negative stereotypes about obesity undermine rigorous scientific practice.

culinary historian   A scholar who identifies key moments of change in food history—for example, the invention of a recipe or food production technique. There is a key distinction between the culinary historian and the cultural or social historian interested in food studies: the latter looks at the meanings and practices associated with food as indicators of cultural and social change more broadly, with food being only one possible lens of approach.

dead zone   An ocean area where the growth of algae or other plants due to excess nitrogen in water causes the oxygen levels of the water to drop to a level that will not support most forms of life other than algae.

decolonization   An amalgam of several different processes: acknowledging the history of colonialism; working to undo the effects of colonialism; striving to unlearn habits, attitudes, and behaviours that perpetuate colonialism; and challenging and transforming institutional manifestations of colonialism.

demand–supply coordination   A situation where demand for food is optimized for population health and food supply is planned and coordinated to meet that optimal demand.

differential profits   The concept that some commodities in a capitalist economy attract higher profits than average. Evidence indicates that **pseudo-foods** return a higher profit to producers and retailers than many other edible commodities—a differential profit—and this explains their growing prominence in a host of food environments.

discourse Ways of understanding a phenomenon or an issue that circulates through a society and is enacted through everyday practices.

distancing (in the food system) The separation between consumers and the sources of their food typical of the industrial food system (introduced by Brewster Kneen in *From Land to Mouth: Understanding the Food System*, 2nd ed. [Toronto: NC Press, 1993], 11).

Doha Round International trade negotiations launched in 2001, in Doha, Qatar, on a new international trade agreement under the World Trade Organization, including a revision to the Agreement on Agriculture.

eco-labelling See **certification**.

economies of scale The need to increase output per worker in order to reduce the relative cost of labour in production. The pursuit of economies of scale is ultimately driven by the need to be competitive and has been associated with tremendous technological innovation; less recognized is the pivotal role of fossil energy.

ecosystem approach An approach to fisheries management which moves away from the modelling of individual stocks to recognize the interdependence of marine flora and fauna, as well as their sensitivity to multiple factors, from destructive fishing gear to land-based pollution.

ecosystem services A term generally associated with attempts to quantify and attach monetary values to the role that ecosystems play in human economies; can be approached at different scales up to the global level (e.g., the role of rain forests in the carbon cycle). The economic valuation of the natural world is a central feature in the sub-disciplines of environmental and ecological economics, in response to normative accounting logic which assigns neither value to the health of the environment nor costs to its degradation. Critics, however, argue that attempting to assign such values and costs is ultimately an impossible task, and can dangerously reinforce the prevailing tendency to turn everything into commodities and the dominant role of markets in determining value.

embodied Describes one's experiences of one's particular physical body with respect to socially constructed positions and roles (e.g., gender, racialization, sexuality, age), relationships (e.g., motherhood), thoughts, and emotions.

ethical foodscape A food environment that prioritizes ethical and moral principles in food provisioning.

ethnicity Affiliation of a group of people who share a common national, cultural, or racial heritage.

eutrophication A process in which excess nutrients deposited into freshwater ecosystems and oceans around coastal riverheads produce algae blooms that deplete oxygen and can devastate aquatic life. This is a major 'downstream' environmental problem associated with industrial agriculture, particularly with the run off of nutrients from fertilizers and from the waste of concentrated animal populations.

exclusive economic zone (EEZ) A zone of 200 miles from its coast over which a coastal state has sovereignty, codified in the UN Convention on the Law of the Sea (UNCLOS), which came into effect in 1982. Ninety percent of the world's fishing grounds are contained by the EEZs of coastal states, which are therefore responsible for their conservation.

exploitation In a capitalist society, the difference between the value that a working class produces and the value that it receives as wage or salary.

export restrictions Policies imposed by a government to restrict the export of a particular product, such as food.

extensive aquaculture Marine farming carried out by creating artificial environments for marine animals (fish, shrimp, etc.) to be produced and harvested by using more labour-intensive sustainable practices. Contrast with **intensive aquaculture**.

externalities Social, environmental, and economic costs or benefits that are not reflected in the market prices of products.

fair miles A modification of the concept of **food miles**, which seeks to limit the distance food travels between farm to table. Consideration of fair miles demands that reducing food miles should not threaten the livelihoods of small farmers in the developing world.

family farm A farming operation in which the labour, management, and ownership investment is primarily supplied by family members, resulting in smaller-scale farming units.

FAO Code of Conduct for Responsible Fisheries An international agreement adopted in 1995 by 124 nations to stop destructive fishing practices, which pays attention to relevant biological, technological, economic, social, environmental, and commercial aspects of fishing and fisheries management.

fat studies A new interdisciplinary field of scholarship that critiques implicit and explicit negative stereotypes, assumptions, and stigma associated with fatness and fat bodies.

feminism An academic field of study and a political movement concerned with understanding and changing the systematic marginalization of all women, but especially those who are further marginalized by racism, class, sexual orientation, (dis)ability, age, and other axes of inequity.

fishing down the marine food web Practices that are likely to result in mass extinctions of marine species; a concept originally developed by Daniel Pauly et al. in 'Fishing Down Marine Food Webs', *Science* 279(5352): 860–3.

food bank A non-profit, charitable organization that solicits private donations of food, money, and services in kind. The organization distributes mainly food to smaller emergency food programs in the region or directly to households in need.

food charters Public endorsements that identify guiding principles, values, and goals for the operation of the food system in a given locality such as a municipality or a province.

food choices Decisions made by an individual about food sourcing, selection, and preparation. Contrast *food choices* with **foodways**, which more broadly refers to the systems through which food is sourced, prepared, served, and consumed. Foodways are inevitably dynamic, changing with each shift in food choice and the entrance and exit of each actor in the system.

food deserts Geographic areas with insufficient numbers of stores and other food-related facilities that provide access to fresh and healthy foods; usually found in low-income or minority communities but also present in some rural communities, in some institutional domains (e.g., schools, universities, bus stations) and characteristic of food environments along many major highways, turnpikes, etc., in North America and elsewhere.

food environments Institutional spheres where food is displayed for sale and/or consumed.

food justice movement A growing movement of food activists who emphasize production that is not only environmentally sustainable but also socially just, taking into account workers in all sectors of the food system, and bringing an anti-oppression analysis to food system transformation, linking anti-racism, feminism, and Indigenous rights movements to the food movement.

food labels Mandatory or voluntary messages on food packaging that serve as a communicative tool between manufacturers and consumers.

food miles An increasingly popular term that describes the distance that food travels from 'land to mouth' or 'field to fork'. The increasing recognition of the oil and carbon emissions embedded in food miles has had an important role in local food movements.

food policy The guiding principles and sets of rules that direct the actions of public or private actors involved in various aspects of food provisioning (production, trade, processing and manufacturing, consumption, safety, waste management, etc.)

food policy councils Groups of citizens, politicians, and businesspeople who meet to develop municipal food policies to overcome such food-related problems as hunger, food deserts, and food insecurity.

food price volatility Sharp fluctuations in food prices—both upward and downward—over a period of time.

food regimes A global and historical approach to food systems. Food regime analysis combines the 'bottom-up' approach of commodity studies with the 'top-down' approach of world-systems theory, and focuses on cycles of stability and transition, both lasting several decades.

foodscape The food environment; the range of places where food can be purchased and consumed.

food security According to the United Nations Food and Agriculture Organization, 'a situation that exists when all people, at all times, have physical, social and economic access to sufficient, safe and nutritious food that meets their dietary needs and food preferences for an active and healthy life' (FAO, 'Trade Reforms and Food Security: Conceptualising the Linkages' [Rome: Commodity Policy and Projections Service, Commodities and Trade Division, 2003]).

foodshed An area or a region into and out of which food flows.

food sovereignty A political framework developed by La Vía Campesina that focuses on the right of peoples and governments to determine their own agriculture systems, food markets, environments, and modes of production. Food sovereignty is a radical alternative to corporate-led, neo-liberal, industrial agriculture.

food system An interdependent web of activities that include the production, processing, distribution, retailing, consumption, and disposal of food.

food system governance The systems and institutions by which the food system is directed.

foodways The systems through which food is sourced, prepared, served, and consumed. See also **food choices**.

foodwork The efforts involved in food production, procurement, preparation, service, and clean-up. It may be paid (as employment) or unpaid (in the household). Unpaid foodwork is generally performed by women in the context of caring for members of their families and kinship networks. Paid foodwork is performed by men and women; however, women tend to occupy insecure, part-time positions that are less prestigious and receive less pay.

gender Socially prescribed understandings of appropriate ways of being a man or woman.

gender division of household labour The way in which paid and unpaid work roles have been allocated to men and women based on prevailing notions of masculinity and femininity.

genetic drift There are two definitions. The scientific definition describes the natural processes by which the gene frequencies of particular species randomly change over time. The more common definition describes how pollen and seed from genetically modified varieties drift from one farm to another.

genetic enhancement In conventional terms, the yield gains made by crossing varieties *within* the same species of plant and livestock breeds. This practice was instrumental to the rising productivity gains in the second half of the twentieth century.

genetic modification (GM) Genetic modification is any process using **recombinant DNA** techniques by which genetic material is transferred, removed, or modified. Genetic modification is the human manipulation of genes or genetic material, distinct from traditional plant-breeding techniques. Also known as *genetically engineered (GE)*.

genetically modified organism (GMO) In this context, an organism transformed via the deliberate insertion of one of more new pieces of new genetic material or DNA into its genome. GMOs are organisms developed through biotechnology.

genetically modified (GM) seeds Seeds that are engineered to express desired traits by inserting into them genes from unrelated species.

genre A kind of text; for example, cookbooks and corporate cookbooklets (short pamphlet-like publications that promote a particular product) can be understood as two distinct genres of cookery literature.

global corporate food system An interdependent web of corporate-controlled activities at the global scale that include the production, processing, distribution, wholesaling, retailing, consumption, and disposal of food.

governance A broadening of the understanding of **government** to refer to a process of decision-making that may or may not be more transparent and participatory, involving not only the formal institutions of the state ('government') but equally those in civil society or the market.

government The exercise of authority over a political jurisdiction by the 'state' (whether it is a municipality, a region, or country).

habitus   A concept used by the sociologist Pierre Bourdieu to refer to the idea of 'embodied history' or to a 'way of being' that predisposes each individual to certain practices and perceptions. The habitus is shaped by structural forces (e.g., early socialization experiences in the family, the class system), but also involves an element of individual agency, shaping cultural tastes and preferences that are individually articulated.

healthism   An ideology that sees health as a metaphor for all that is good in life, and that holds the individual responsible for health.

healthy eating   Foods and ways of eating that are defined as enhancing well-being, particularly physical health.

herbicide tolerant (HT) crops   Crops developed to survive application of particular herbicides through the insertion of genes that enable plants to break down the active chemical ingredients contained in the herbicides.

holistic education   A learning process that teaches people about themselves, relationships, emotional and social development, resilience, and beauty; it advocates multi-sensory and interdisciplinary learning, countering the fragmentation of formal schooling.

Holocene   The short period (in a geological time scale) of relative climatic stability in which agriculture and human civilization arose; roughly the past 10,000 years. Scientists are now suggesting that with climate change, the earth may be moving out of the Holocene.

human appropriation of the net primary production (of photosynthesis) (HANPP)   A concept developed by biologists to conceptualize the scale of human impact on the biosphere, quantified in terms of the control of annual biomass production.

iconic foods   Foods that epitomize or represent particular people, places, or events (e.g., Montreal smoked meat, maple syrup).

identity   A person's perception of self; 'who I am'. It is simultaneously social and individual.

ideology   A system of beliefs, values, and ideas that shape how individuals and groups interact with and view the world.

illegal, unregulated, and unreported (IUU) fishing   Irresponsible fishing activities that hinder the sustainability of the fishery.

Indigenous peoples   People with an ancestral and ongoing connection to a particular geographic area.

industrial food system   A food system characterized by mass production of standardized food items, driven by motives of profit and efficiency often at the cost of human health and of environmental and social justice.

industrial grain–oilseed–livestock complex   Describes how agricultural systems across much of the temperate world are dominated by a small number of grain and oilseed monocultures and a small number of livestock species reared in high-density factory farms and feedlots, with large volumes of grains and oilseeds cycled through livestock.

intellectual property rights   The legal rights associated with inventions, artistic expressions, and other products of the imagination (e.g., patent, copyright, and trademark law) (from Royal Society of Canada's Expert Panel Report on the Future of Food Biotechnology in Canada, *Elements of Precaution: Recommendations for the Regulation of Food Biotechnology* [Ottawa, 2001, 235]). Also includes legal protection of new technologies and new organisms (such as plant varieties created through genetic modification). In Canada, however, patents are not granted on higher life forms such as plants, although such patents are recognized in some other jurisdictions, including the United States.

intensive aquaculture   Marine farming by creating artificial environments for marine animals (fish, shrimp, etc.) to be produced and harvested by using more capital-intensive industrial practices. Contrast with **extensive aquaculture**.

intensive livestock operations   Large-scale operations where animals are confined and raised with industrial management techniques to maximize growth rates and ensure uniform product. Also known as 'factory farms'.

intercropping   The close cultivation of two or more crops in order to achieve complementary biological interactions (e.g., reducing the impacts of pests) and enhance the efficiency of resource use (i.e., using crops that don't compete with each other for physical space, nutrients, water, or light). The goal is to maximize production on a given land area.

interdisciplinary Describing a field of study that combines two or more disciplines into a single discipline.

joined-up food policy Integration and coordination of policies across all the domains, departments, and jurisdictional levels that affect or are affected by food policy.

land grab The recent tendency of corporations and governments to purchase large areas of farmland in poor countries for the production of export crops.

land-use planning The process of deciding how land is used or 'developed' in urban, peri-urban, and rural areas.

liability Responsibility for damage or harm. 'Civil liability law' refers to the responsibility of private entities (individuals or corporations) for damage suffered by another private entity, where claims can be brought before a court.

livestock revolution Global expansion of production and consumption of livestock in recent years that makes meat and dairy products more accessible for wider segments of the human population while creating ethical and environmental concerns.

local food movement A social movement that emerged in response to a global industrialized food system that distances producers from consumers, which promotes local food production and self-sufficiency; the 'local' need not exclude the import of produce that can't be grown locally, but imports should be produced in a sustainable and just manner.

market foods Foods that are purchased through the monetary economy.

market fundamentals Supply and demand forces in a market for a particular good such as food.

mass advertising and product differentiation A phenomenon of the recent industrial era, pioneered by such food-processing behemoths as Kellogg's and Coca-Cola. Its purpose, whether in the early twentieth century or today, is to create an enduring resonance in the minds of the consuming public that a product is superior and more desirable than its competitors and worth the higher price it would typically attract. Successful product differentiation via mass advertising results in an enduring brand.

maximum sustainable yield (MSY) The largest average catch or yield that can continuously be taken from a stock under existing environmental conditions without impairing the stock's ability to reproduce itself and generate the same level of catch in subsequent years.

monoculture The biological simplification of a farm or landscape to focus on the production of a single crop, which also typically entails a reduction in genetic diversity within that given crop type.

multidisciplinary Describing a collaborative research strategy where researchers remain loyal to their own disciplinary methodologies and assumptions.

neo-liberalism A political ideology and practice that emphasizes the withdrawal of government from services that promote the health and well-being of communities of citizens; these needs would be met through individual responsibility and for-profit, commercial services.

nutrition transition A change in the nutrition status of a population characterized by increasing rates of obesity, cardiovascular disease, and various cancers.

nutritionism A paradigm that reduces the value and benefits of food to its nutrients, assuming that we eat only to promote physical health.

participatory action research A form of critical, libratory research in which groups identify the issues to be studied, participate in the data gathering and analysis, take action, and reflect on that action. It has been critiqued by postcolonial, feminist, and critical development scholars for potentially perpetuating colonial relations, but has been taken up by Indigenous researchers for its relational qualities and emancipatory methods.

patent A legal convention that grants exclusive use of an invention to an individual or corporation for a limited period of time.

peak oil The increasingly recognized term that describes the fact that human economies are at, are near, or have just passed the halfway point in the consumption of all global oil reserves. It implies that all of the world's most accessible and lowest-cost oilfields have already been discovered; low-cost oilfields are in marked decline; the extraction of the remaining reserves will become ever more difficult, costly, and energy intensive; and the second half of the world's oil supply will be consumed a lot faster than the first half was. Peak oil poses enormous challenges for all sectors of modern industrial economies, none more so than agriculture.

peasants   Rural inhabitants who make their living from the land, employ their own and their family's labour in production, produce for subsistence and the market, and are not driven primarily by market considerations in determining the use and/or sale of the land.

pesticides   Natural or artificial ingredients used for preventing, destroying, repelling, or mitigating pest infestation.

pesticide treadmill   The cycle of dependence in which monocultures exacerbate pest problems, more or new pesticides are needed as natural predators and controls are eliminated, pest and disease resistance develops over time, and localized ecological knowledge and the ability to use non-chemical responses are lost.

place-based environmental education   A practice that grounds learning in a particular ecological context, unearthing its social and environmental histories, and nurturing a reciprocal notion of human–non-human relations.

policy   The set of rules, spoken or unspoken, that determines how things are run.

political ecology   A growing field of research on human–environment relations, environmental change, and development, combining attention to political economy, environmental science, and human ecology. There is no one methodological blueprint, however, and research in the field of political ecology is located in a range of disciplines, such as geography, sociology, anthropology, political science, and environmental studies.

popular education   A practice developed largely in Latin America that uncovers and challenges power relations inherent in education by drawing upon and revaluing the experiences and perceptions of learners, thus making the learner–teacher relationship reciprocal; links collective analysis to action for social change.

post-modernism, post-structuralism   Closely associated perspectives critical of modernist frameworks and Enlightenment thinking. They question the modernist emphases on discovering 'truth' through objectivity, progress, and scientific approaches and studying culture through structures.

precautionary principle   The position that the formulation of environmental policy and regulations should be heavily influenced by the negative outcomes and worst-case scenarios that may result. This position entails a large burden of proof that a given decision will have a benign long-term impact.

prescriptive and descriptive practice   *Prescriptive practice* refers to what people are told to do, while *descriptive practice* refers to what they actually do. Always present is the danger of confusing the two. Advertisements are a good example of prescriptive practice, while candid photographs of every food item consumed by an individual during the day might be an excellent record of descriptive practice. In food studies, examples of prescriptive practice (e.g., cookbooks or instruction manuals) are more readily available than reliable records of descriptive practice; the latter rely largely on self-reporting, and individuals have an understandable tendency to filter the information they provide.

profit   Most simply, the difference between a capitalist's costs to produce a commodity and its selling price.

pseudo-foods   Nutrient-poor edible products which are typically high in fat, sugar, and salt, and other than the excess calories they contain are notably low in nutrients essential for health such as proteins, minerals, and vitamins. A more inclusive category than 'junk foods', pseudo-foods also refers to a variety of nutrient-poor edible products not traditionally thought of as 'junk foods', which are found in supermarkets and elsewhere among, for example, juice, dairy, and breakfast food products.

public sphere and private sphere   Two halves of a socially constructed dichotomy. The public sphere encompasses the spaces and activities that occur outside of the domestic home (e.g., paid employment) and is more highly valued than the private sphere, which is associated with the spaces and activities that occur within the boundaries of the home and family life (e.g., unpaid foodwork).

recombinant DNA (r DNA) DNA molecule created by splicing together two or more different pieces of DNA.

redundant food trade Food that can be grown locally but that is being imported.

right to food The UN International Covenant on Economic, Social and Cultural Rights (ICESCR) recognizes 'the right of everyone to an adequate standard of living for himself and his family, including adequate food, clothing and housing, and to the continuous improvement of living conditions. The States Parties will take appropriate steps to ensure the realization of this right . . .' (Office of the United Nations High Commissioner for Human Rights, 'International Covenant on Economic, Social and Cultural Rights', Article 11, available at www2. ohchr.org/english/law/cescr.htm). The UN also recognizes the right to food in the Declaration on Human Rights, the Convention on the Rights of the Child, the Convention on the Elimination of All Forms of Discrimination against Women (CEDAW), and the Optional Protocol to CEDAW.

salinization A process in which salt that was dissolved in water remains after evapotranspiration (water evaporating from the land or transpiring from plants) and builds up in soils over time. Beyond a certain point, salinization can severely limit plants' moisture uptake and crop yield, and land rehabilitation becomes very difficult and costly.

scientific reductionism The school of thought that proposes that complex phenomena can be understood through science by being broken down into simple processes/interactions, which can be then studied individually. While necessary for much of scientific study, reductionism runs the risk of oversimplifying phenomena.

social glasnost A spirit of openness within society, especially in communication and forms of social organization.

soil mining Rapid depletion of soil nutrients due to persistent monocrop agriculture.

social movement Groups of people with common interests and purposes who work together and engage in collective action in efforts to effect social change. As a key component of civil society, a social movement represents a collective, organized, and sustained challenge to the status quo.

spatial colonization The process whereby food corporations secure the *physical visibility and availability* of a products within a particular food environment, and thus the power of food processors to place products *in the most visible and effective selling spaces*. Processors and retailers have aggressively promoted the spatial colonization of **pseudo-foods** because of their high rates of return on investment (see **differential profits**).

stratification Any differences among people that give rise to a hierarchy of distinct strata. A looser term than **class**.

supply management Legislated limits on the amount of production in the poultry, egg, and dairy sectors to match domestic requirements, while ensuring costs of production are met by the established pricing.

sustainability The ability to meet present needs without compromising the ability of future generations to meet their own needs; the outcome of structures and processes that build the civil commons.

sustainable food system An interdependent web of activities generated by structures and processes that build the civil commons with respect to the production, processing, distribution, retailing, consumption, and disposal of food.

sustainable livelihood A sufficient income earned while attempting to balance present economic, social, and environmental priorities that will secure the ability of future human societies to sustain themselves.

total allowable catch (TAC) A catch limit set for a particular fishery, generally for a year or a fishing season, calculated as a proportion of the MSY for that species.

traditional foods Plants and animals for food procured through Indigenous practices.

transgene A gene that has been incorporated into the genome of another organism which may be unrelated. Often refers to a gene that has been introduced into a multi-cellular organism (adapted from A. Zaid et al., 'Glossary of Biotechnology and Genetic Engineering' [Rome: FAO, 1999], available at ftp://ftp.fao.org/docrep/fao/003/X3910E/X3910E00.pdf). *Transgenesis* refers to the insertion or transfer of unrelated genetic material into from one organism into the genome of another. An example of a transgenic organism is a plant containing bacterial genetic material that expresses a toxin gene.

transgenic   An organism which has had a foreign gene (a transgene) incorporated into its genome. The transgene is inherited in subsequent generations.

turnover time   See **circuits of capital**.

UN **Convention on the Law of the Sea (UNCLOS)** See **exclusive economic zone (EEZ)**.

UN **Fish Stocks Agreement**   International agreement (Straddling Fish Stocks Agreement) initiated by the United Nations in 1982 for enhancing the co-operative management of fisheries resources and dealing with economic and environmental issues related to fisheries in a number of nations.

urban food policy   Food system decisions and actions that fall within the jurisdiction of urban municipal governments, through zoning, by-laws, or other forms of land-use regulation, or through partnerships with other levels of government.

urban food system   A food system specific to the urban area in which it is located, but also nested within regional, provincial/state, national, and international food systems.

validity   Accuracy or relevancy of measuring what one intends to measure.

world-systems theory   A global and historical approach to capitalism, which dates its origins to the creation of a world market through colonial expansion roughly 500 years ago. Key to the theory is its recognition that for the first time in history the market became bigger than any national territory; that the system of nation-states arose at about the same time; and that the power hierarchy among states shapes the market and is shaped by it.

World Trade Organization (WTO)   An unelected supra-national organization established in 1995 that re-regulates trade and investment among nations so transnational corporations have freedom from protections in such realms as agriculture, food, and the environment.

Index

Note: Page numbers in bold refer to key terms.